Brief Contents

Introduction: Using TEST When You Read and Write   1

Unit 1 Reading to Write ⓔ 9

1 Understanding the Active Reading Process   11
2 Building Vocabulary for Reading and Writing   35
3 Understanding the Writing Process   60
4 Understanding Introductions, Body Paragraphs, and Conclusions   104
5 Thinking, Reading, and Writing Critically   123
6 Reading and Writing about Different Kinds of Texts   155

Unit 2 Reading and Writing Essays 189

7 Reading and Writing Exemplification Essays   191
8 Reading and Writing Narrative Essays   206
9 Reading and Writing Cause-and-Effect Essays   223
10 Reading and Writing Comparison-and-Contrast Essays   239
11 Reading and Writing Argument Essays   256
12 Additional Options for Organizing Essays   276

Unit 3 Research 329

13 Working with Sources   331

Unit 4 Basic Grammar Guide ⓔ 363

14 Understanding Verbs   365
15 Understanding Nouns and Pronouns   380
16 Understanding Adjectives and Adverbs   403
17 Writing Simple, Compound, and Complex Sentences   413
18 Writing Varied Sentences   436
19 Using Parallelism   450
20 Using Words Effectively   457
21 Run-Ons   474
22 Fragments   487
23 Subject-Verb Agreement   503
24 Illogical Shifts   515
25 Misplaced and Dangling Modifiers   523
26 Using Commas   530
27 Using Apostrophes   544
28 Understanding Mechanics   551

Unit 5 Reading Essays 567

29 Readings for Writers   569

ⓔ **LearningCurve** activities and additional multiple-choice grammar exercises are available for the topics in this unit. Visit **bedfordstmartins.com/forw**.

Focus on Reading and Writing

Essays

Focus on Reading and Writing

Essays

Laurie G. Kirszner

University of the Sciences, Emeritus

Stephen R. Mandell

Drexel University

in collaboration with reading specialists

Dr. Lana Myers

Lone Star College

Dr. Michelle Francis

West Valley College

Bedford/St. Martin's

Boston ◆ New York

For Bedford/St. Martin's

Publisher for College Success and Developmental Studies: Edwin Hill
Developmental Editor: Karrin M. Varucene
Senior Production Editor: Peter Jacoby
Senior Production Supervisor: Jennifer Peterson
Marketing Manager: Christina Shea
Editorial Assistant: Jonathan Douglas
Copy Editor: Virginia Perrin
Indexer: Kirsten Kite
Photo Researcher: Julie Tesser
Text Design: Jerilyn Bockorick
Cover Design: Donna Lee Dennison
Cover Art: © Fotofeeling/Westend61/Corbis
Composition: Cenveo Publisher Services
Printing and Binding: RR Donnelley and Sons

Manufactured in the United States of America.

9 8 7 6 5 4
f e d c b a

For information, write: Bedford/St. Martin's, 75 Arlington Street, Boston, MA 02116 (617-399-4000)

ISBN 978-1-4576-6502-8 (Student Edition)
ISBN 978-1-4576-8613-9 (Loose-Leaf Edition)
ISBN 978-1-4576-8157-8 (Instructor's Annotated Edition)

Preface

Our goal with this first edition of *Focus on Reading and Writing: Essays* was to create an engaging, integrated text that motivates students to improve their reading and writing skills and that gives them the tools to do so. TEST, our unique assessment tool, is designed specifically for this purpose. The letters T-E-S-T stand for Thesis statement, Evidence, Summary statement, and Transitions, the key elements found in effective essays. Thus, TEST helps students to keep in mind the four key elements to look for as they **read** and enables them to make sure all these elements are also present in the essays they **write**.

In addition to this important student-tested assessment tool, *Focus on Reading and Writing* reflects our core pedagogical belief—that students learn best by practicing a new skill or concept in the context of their own work. Accordingly, throughout Units 1 and 2, chapters begin by prompting students to consider their prior knowledge of a subject; then, they are encouraged to expand their knowledge of this theme as they learn and practice active reading strategies; and finally, they are asked to apply these new skills in their own writing.

With a complete grammar guide, online grammar practice, and twenty-one professional reading selections, this comprehensive text gets students reading, writing, and thinking critically in preparation for academic, career, and life success. Arresting images and contemporary design appeals to today's ever-more-visual learners, as do the graphic organizers we have included as chapter review exercises in Unit 1 and as exercises for understanding essay organization in Unit 2.

And with LaunchPad Solo for *Focus on Reading and Writing*, we bring the book's instruction into an online, interactive space, where students can continue their practice of key concepts such as critical reading, vocabulary, grammar, and mechanics. Also included in the LaunchPad Solo is a full model student APA research paper, which illustrates the APA documentation guidelines discussed in Chapter 13. LaunchPad Solo is available to package with this book. See the inside back cover for more information.

With the help of two reading specialists, we have built a book with a truly integrated approach to reading and writing instruction. We are confident in the book's pedagogy, flexibility, and accessibility; it is our hope that this first edition of *Focus on Reading and Writing* will motivate and empower students to become critical readers and confident writers.

Organization

Focus on Reading and Writing has a flexible organization that permits instructors to teach various topics in the order that works best for them and for their students. The book is divided into three sections, which are color-coded to help students and instructors more easily navigate the book:

- **Units 1–3**, Chapters 1–13, offer a comprehensive discussion of the reading and writing processes. Included in these units are nine full-length professional essays, several excerpts from professional writing, and numerous student writing examples.

- **Unit 4**, Chapters 14–28, is a thorough yet accessible review of sentence skills, grammar, punctuation, and mechanics.

- **Unit 5**, Chapter 29, offers a thematically organized selection of twelve additional professional essays. Each essay is preceded by a brief headnote and a "Before you read" prompt and followed by critical reading, thinking, and discussion questions as well as by two writing prompts.

Features

Integration of Reading and Writing

TEST—A unique tool that inspires student confidence and independence: This simple and unique assessment tool helps students to remember the key elements to look for as they read and as they revise their own writing. Thus, TEST lays the groundwork for student reading and writing: it prepares them to work independently to analyze their reading and empowers them to revise their own writing with confidence.

> **T** ▪ **Thesis Statement**—Does the essay include a thesis statement that presents the main idea—the idea that will be developed in the essay?
>
> **E** ▪ **Evidence**—Does the essay include evidence—examples and details—that supports the thesis statement?
>
> **S** ▪ **Summary Statement**—Does the essay's conclusion include a summary statement that reinforces the thesis and sums up the main idea?
>
> **T** ▪ **Transitions**—Does the essay include transitional words and phrases that show readers how ideas are related?

Focus on Reading and Writing prompts: These prompts introduce a connected strand of activities, a hallmark of the Kirszner/Mandell approach, that prompts students to activate their prior knowledge on the topic of a chapter's central reading, sends them back to the reading as they practice active reading strategies, and prompts them to apply the new skills they are learning in their own writing.

Reading, Writing, and Integrated icons: Each section within the patterns chapters (7–12) is marked with a colored honeycomb icon, which serves as a visual cue for the connection of reading and writing skills.

Reading Tips: Featured in the grammar chapters, these marginal tips appear next to connected discourse practice exercises and essay-length editing exercises, encouraging students to practice active and critical reading skills as they master important writing skills.

Graphic organizers: Used as chapter review exercises in Unit 1 and as exercises for understanding essay organization in Unit 2, these graphic organizers visually aid students in understanding the reading and writing processes.

Additional Features

Word Power boxes: Marginal Word Power boxes help students build their vocabulary by defining unfamiliar words that appear in the text's explanations and reading selections.

FYI boxes: Throughout the book, these boxes highlight useful information and explain difficult concepts.

LaunchPad Solo for *Focus on Reading and Writing*: Throughout this textbook you will see an icon in the margins indicating when additional online content is available through our LaunchPad Solo platform.

- LearningCurve, innovative adaptive online quizzes, let students learn at their own pace, with a game-like interface that keeps them engaged. Quizzes are keyed to grammar instruction in the book. Instructors can also check in on each student's activity in an online gradebook.

- Additional multiple-choice grammar exercises offer students even more practice with their most challenging grammar concepts. The exercises are auto-gradable and report directly to the instructor's grade book.

- Also included in the LaunchPad Solo is a full model student APA research paper, which illustrates the APA documentation guidelines discussed in Chapter 13.

Please see the inside back cover for more information on LaunchPad Solo.

7a Reading Exemplification Essays

When you **read** an exemplification essay, use TEST to help you identify its key elements. Be sure to follow the reading process outlined in Chapter 1.

7b Writing Exemplification Essays

When you **write** an exemplification essay, you follow the process outlined in Chapter 3. The essay you write will include the same elements you have learned to recognize in the exemplification essays you read. When you finish your draft, you can use TEST to make sure it includes all the elements of an exemplification essay.

7c Integrating Reading and Writing

Now, it is time to practice what you have learned and put your reading and writing skills together. The following essay, "Around the World, Women Are On the Move," by Richard Rodriguez, supports its thesis with examples. **Read** the essay, following the active reading process outlined in Chapter 1, and then answer the questions on pages 202–203. When you have finished, you will **write** an exemplification essay in response to Rodriguez's ideas.

14a Regular Verbs

Regular verbs form the past tense by adding either *-ed* or *-d* to the **base form** of the verb (the present tense form of the verb that is used with *I*).

We registered for classes yesterday.
Walt Disney produced short cartoons in 1928.

bedfordstmartins.com /forw LearningCurve > Verbs; Additional Grammar Exercises > Regular Verbs

Support for Instructors and Students

Focus on Reading and Writing is accompanied by comprehensive teaching and learning support.

📖 = Print   🖥 = Online   💿 = CD-ROM

Student Resources

Free with a New Print Text

🖥 **LaunchPad Solo for *Focus on Reading and Writing*,** at **bedfordstmartins.com/forw**, provides students with interactive and adaptive grammar exercises and an annotated APA-style student essay. Please see the inside back cover for more information on LaunchPad Solo. **Free** when packaged with the print text. Package ISBN: 978-1-319-00572-6.

🖥 ***Re:Writing 2*,** at **bedfordstmartins.com/rewriting**, gives students even more ways to think, watch, practice, and learn about writing concepts. This fully online resource includes an interactive online game, *Peer Factor*; videos of professional writers; tutorials on numerous relevant topics; logic games that allow students to practice their reasoning skills; accurate citation examples in all of the major styles; and more.

📖 ***The Bedford/St. Martin's Planner*** includes everything that students need to plan and use their time effectively, with advice on preparing schedules and to-do lists plus blank schedules and calendars (monthly and weekly). The planner fits easily into a backpack or purse, so students can take it everywhere. **Free** when packaged with the print text. Package ISBN: 978-1-4576-9916-0

📖 ***From Practice to Mastery*** (study guide for the Florida Basic Skills Exit Tests) gives students all the resources they need to practice for— and pass—the Florida tests in reading and writing. It includes pre- and post-tests, abundant practices, many examples, and clear instruction in all the skills covered on the exams. **Free** when packaged with the print text. Package ISBN: 978-1-4576-9917-7

Premium

🖥 ***SkillsClass*** provides students with a dynamic, interactive online course space preloaded with LearningCurve quizzes, exercises, diagnostics, video tutorials, writing and commenting tools, plus guidance and practice in reading and study skills. *SkillsClass* helps students stay focused and lets instructors see how they are progressing. It is available at a significant discount when packaged with the print text. To learn more about *SkillsClass*, visit **yourskillsclass.com**. For access card: ISBN: 978-1-4576-2346-2

WritingClass provides students with a dynamic, interactive online course space preloaded with exercises, diagnostics, video tutorials, writing and commenting tools, and more. *WritingClass* helps students stay focused and lets instructors see how they are progressing. It is available at a significant discount when packaged with the print text. To learn more about *WritingClass*, visit **yourwritingclass.com**. For access card: ISBN: 978-0-312-57385-0

The Bedford/St. Martin's Textbook Reader, **Second Edition,** by Ellen Kuhl Repetto, gives students practice in reading college textbooks across the curriculum. This brief collection of chapters from market-leading introductory college textbooks can be packaged inexpensively with *Focus on Reading and Writing*. Beginning with a chapter on college success, *The Bedford/St. Martin's Textbook Reader* also includes chapters from current texts on composition, mass communication, history, psychology, and environmental science. Comprehension questions and tips for reading success guide students in reading college-level materials efficiently and effectively. Package ISBN: 978-1-319-00398-2

Free Instructor Resources

The Instructor's Annotated Edition of *Focus on Reading and Writing* contains answers to all grammar practice exercises as well as many of the exercises throughout the reading and writing instructional chapters, in addition to numerous teaching ideas, reminders, and cross-references useful to teachers at all levels of experience. ISBN: 978-1-4576-8157-8

Classroom Resources and Instructor's Guide for Focus on Reading and Writing offers advice for teaching developmental reading and developmental writing as well as general teaching suggestions for important aspects of the course, including structure, diagnostics, conferencing, and syllabi. Additionally, this instructor's manual includes chapter-by-chapter pointers for using *Focus on Reading and Writing* in the classroom; answers to all of the book's practice exercises; and suggested responses to the critical reading, thinking, and discussion questions that follow each of the professional essays. To download, go to **bedfordstmartins.com/forw/catalog**.

Testing Tool Kit: Writing and Grammar Test Bank CD-ROM allows instructors to create secure, customized tests and quizzes from a pool of nearly 2,000 questions covering 47 topics. It also includes 10 prebuilt diagnostic tests. ISBN: 978-0-312-43032-0

Teaching Central at **bedfordstmartins.com/teachingcentral** offers the entire list of Bedford/St. Martin's print and online professional resources in one place. You will find landmark reference works, sourcebooks on pedagogical issues, award-winning collections, and practical advice for the classroom.

⬛ **Bedford *Bits*** is our award-winning blog where, every week, a host of Bedford authors, including Andrea Lunsford, Emily Isaacs, Susan Naomi Bernstein, and Elizabeth Wardle, bring you new ideas for the classroom. Join the conversation at **bedfordbits.com**.

e-Book Options

The e-Book for *Focus on Reading and Writing*, value priced, can be purchased in formats for use with computers, tablets, and e-readers. Visit **bedfordstmartins.com/ebooks** for more information.

Ordering Information

To order any of the ancillaries for *Focus on Reading and Writing*, contact your local Bedford/St. Martin's sales representative, e-mail **sales_support @bfwpub.com**, or visit our website at **bedfordstmartins.com**.

Acknowledgments

In our work on *Focus on Reading and Writing*, we have benefited from the help of a great many people.

We are grateful to our reading consultants, Michelle Francis of West Valley College and Lana Myers of Lone Star College, for their expert advice and guidance. Additionally, we thank Randee Falk, who made important contributions to the research chapter, and Jessica Carroll, who made valuable contributions to exercises and writing activities.

Instructors throughout the country have contributed suggestions and encouragement at various stages of the book's development. For their collegial support, we thank Joe Antinarella, Tidewater Community College; Elizabeth Baldridge, Illinois Central College; Andrea Berta, University of Texas at El Paso; Donna Beverly, Montgomery Community College; Marilyn Black, Middlesex Community College; Reed Breneman, Wake Technical Community College; Robyn Browder, Tidewater Community College; Marta Brown, Community College of Denver; Elizabeth Buchanan, Porterville College; Susan Buchler, Montgomery Community College; Gricelle Cano, Houston Community College; Patti Casey, Tyler Junior College; Annette Cole, Tarrant County College; Cathy Colton, College of Lake County; Lori Conrad, University of Arkansas; Linda Crawford, McLennan Community College; Patricia Davis, Houston Community College; Cynthia DeLauder, Spokane Falls Community

College; Lynn Dornink, Northeastern University; Mary Dubbé, Thomas Nelson Community College; Maryann Errico, Georgia Perimeter College; Richard Farias, Alamo Colleges–San Antonio; Jennifer Ferguson, Cazenovia College; Judith Gallagher, Tarrant County College; Kris Giere, Ivy Tech Community College of Indiana; Virginia Gleason, Tarrant County College; Priscilla Hall, Wytheville Community College; Beth Hashemzadeh, Bluefield State College; Sharon Hayes, Community College of Baltimore; Thomasa Henry, Tarrant County College; Ferdinand Hunter, Gateway Community College; Janis Innis, Houston Community College; Tamara Kuzmenkov, Tacoma Community College; Mimi Leonard, Wytheville Community College; Beverly Mason, Paul D. Camp Community College; Margaret McClain, Arkansas State University; Robbi Muckenfuss, Durham Technical Community College; Alexis Nelson, Spokane Falls Community College; Nicole Oechslin, Piedmont Virginia Community College; Sandra Padilla, El Paso Community College; Catherine Parra, Northern Virginia Community College; Elaine Pascale, Suffolk University; Pam Price, Greenville Technical College; Rhonda Pruitt, John Tyler Community College; Mary Reed, Lord Fairfax Community College; Jennifer Riske, Northeast Lakeview College; Linda Robinett, Oklahoma City Community College; David Roloff, University of Wisconsin–Stevens Point; Becky Rudd, Citrus College; Stacey Said, Northern Virginia Community College; Charis Sawyer, Johnson County Community College; Pattie See, University of Wisconsin–Eau Claire; Vanessa Sekinger, Germanna Community College; Gail Shearer, Madison Area Technical College; Kitty Spires, Midlands Technical College; Catherine Swift, University of Central Arkansas; Kerry Thomas, Rufus King International School; Jason Todd, Xavier University of Louisiana; Patricia Tymon, Virginia Highlands Community College; Beverly Van Citters, Citrus College; Nancy Warren, Paul D. Camp Community College; Jeanine Williams, Community College of Baltimore; Lisa Wilmot, Tacoma Community College; Kenneth Wilson, Cuyahoga Community College.

At Bedford/St. Martin's, we thank founder and former president Charles Christensen, former president Joan Feinberg, and former editor in chief Nancy Perry, who believed in this project and gave us support and encouragement from the outset. We thank vice president of editorial Denise Wydra, and Karen Henry, Alexis Walker, and Edwin Hill for overseeing this edition. We are also grateful to Shuli Traub, Jennifer Peterson, Jessica Gould, and Peter Jacoby, for guiding the book ably through production, and to Lucy Krikorian, for once again overseeing the book's design. Many thanks also go to Christina Shea, senior marketing manager, and Vivian Garcia, market development manager. And finally, we thank our fantastic editor, Karrin Varucene, for all her hard work on this project. Her energy, insight, and intelligence are truly impressive.

It almost goes without saying that *Focus on Reading and Writing* could not exist without our students, whose work inspired the sample sentences, paragraphs, and essays in this book. We thank all of them, past and present, who allowed us to use their work.

We are grateful in addition for the continued support of our families. Finally, we are grateful for the survival and growth of the writing partnership we entered into when we were graduate students. We had no idea then of the wonderful places our collaborative efforts would take us. Now, we know.

Laurie G. Kirszner

Stephen R. Mandell

Contents

Preface   vii

Introduction: Using TEST When You Read and Write   1

TESTing Essays   2

   TESTing for a Thesis Statement   2   ▪   *TESTing for Evidence*   3   ▪   *TESTing for a Summary Statement*   4   ▪   *TESTing for Transitions*   4   ▪   *Putting It Together*   6

TESTing Body Paragraphs   8

Unit 1   Reading to Write   9

1 Understanding the Active Reading Process   🄴   11

1a   Before You Read   12

   Creating a Reading Schedule   12   ▪   *Assessing Prior Knowledge*   13   ▪   *Understanding Your Purpose*   14   ▪   *Previewing*   15

1b   As You Read   18

   Highlighting   18   ▪   *Annotating*   21

1c   After You Read   24

   Outlining   24   ▪   *Summarizing*   26   ▪   *Reviewing and Self-Quizzing*   27

1d   Writing a Response Paragraph   28

   Chapter Review   30

2 Building Vocabulary for Reading and Writing   🄴   35

2a   Understanding Your Vocabularies   36

2b   "Knowing" Words   37

   Achieving Full Knowledge   37   ▪   *Activating Your Schemata*   37   ▪   *Understanding Denotations, Connotations, Synonyms, and Antonyms*   40

🄴 **LearningCurve** activities are available for the topics in this chapter. Visit **bedfordstmartins.com/forw**.

XV

2c   Acquiring New Words   43

Learning from Reference Tools   43 ▪ *Learning from Context Clues   45* ▪ *Learning from Your Coursework   47* ▪ *Learning from Roots, Prefixes, and Suffixes   50* ▪ *Learning from Your Reading   53*

2d   Using New Words in Your Writing   54

Chapter Review   57

3 Understanding the Writing Process   60

Step 1: Planning   61

3a   Understanding Essay Structure   61

3b   Moving from Assignment to Topic   67

3c   Finding Ideas to Write About   69

Freewriting   69 ▪ *Brainstorming   70* ▪ *Keeping a Journal   72* ▪ *Clustering   73*

3d   Stating Your Thesis   74

Step 2: Organizing   80

3e   Choosing Supporting Points   80

3f   Making an Outline   81

Step 3: Drafting   84

3g   Drafting Your Essay   84

Step 4: TESTing and Revising   86

3h   TESTing Your Essay   87

3i   Revising Your Essay   88

Step 5: Editing and Proofreading   93

3j   Editing Your Essay   93

3k   Proofreading Your Essay   94

Chapter Review   99

4 Understanding Introductions, Body Paragraphs, and Conclusions   e   104

4a   Introductions   105

4b   Body Paragraphs   110

4c   Conclusions   116

Chapter Review   119

5 Thinking, Reading, and Writing Critically 🄴 123

5a Identifying Audience, Purpose, and Tone   124

5b Identifying Connotations and Figurative Language   130

5c Identifying the Main Idea   132

5d Identifying Major and Minor Supporting Points   134

5e Evaluating the Writer's Ideas   136

Distinguishing between Fact and Opinion   136 ▪ *Making Inferences   139* ▪ *Identifying Bias   142*

5f Reading and Writing Critically   144

Summarizing   144 ▪ *Analyzing   146* ▪ *Synthesizing   148* ▪ *Evaluating   149*

Chapter Review   153

6 Reading and Writing about Different Kinds of Texts 155

6a Reading Written Texts   156

Textbooks   156 ▪ *News Articles   157* ▪ *Business Documents   161* ▪ *Web Pages   162* ▪ *Blogs   164*

6b Reading Visuals   167

Previewing   167 ▪ *Highlighting and Annotating   172*

6c Types of Visuals   173

Charts, Graphs, and Tables   173 ▪ *Maps   175* ▪ *Diagrams   177* ▪ *Photographs   178* ▪ *Editorial Cartoons   180* ▪ *Advertisements   182*

Chapter Review   185

Unit 2 Reading and Writing Essays 189

7 Reading and Writing Exemplification Essays 191

7a Reading Exemplification Essays   192

7b Writing Exemplification Essays   197

7c Integrating Reading and Writing   200

Richard Rodriguez ▪ *Around the World, Women Are On the Move*   200

Chapter Review   204

🄴 **LearningCurve** activities are available for the topics in this chapter. Visit **bedfordstmartins.com/forw**.

8 Reading and Writing Narrative Essays 206

8a Reading Narrative Essays 207
8b Writing Narrative Essays 212
8c Integrating Reading and Writing 215

Lynda Barry ▪ *The Sanctuary of School* 216

Chapter Review 221

9 Reading and Writing Cause-and-Effect Essays 223

9a Reading Cause-and-Effect Essays 224
9b Writing Cause-and-Effect Essays 229
9c Integrating Reading and Writing 233

Julia Angwin ▪ *How Facebook Is Making Friending Obsolete* 233

Chapter Review 237

10 Reading and Writing Comparison-and-Contrast Essays 239

10a Reading Comparison-and-Contrast Essays 240
10b Writing Comparison-and-Contrast Essays 246
10c Integrating Reading and Writing 250

Steven Conn ▪ *The Twin Revolutions of Lincoln and Darwin* 250

Chapter Review 254

11 Reading and Writing Argument Essays 256

11a Reading Argument Essays 257
11b Writing Argument Essays 265
11c Integrating Reading and Writing 269

Mary Sherry ▪ *In Praise of the F Word* 269

Chapter Review 274

12 Additional Options for Organizing Essays 276

12a Description   276

Rachel Carson ▪ *A Fable for Tomorrow*   284

12b Process   288

Amy Ma ▪ *My Grandmother's Dumpling*   296

12c Classification   303

Scott Russell Sanders ▪ *The Men We Carry in Our Minds*   311

12d Definition   316

Julia Alvarez ▪ *What Is a* Quinceañera?   324

Unit 3 Research   329

13 Working with Sources   331

13a Finding and Evaluating Sources   331

Finding Information in the Library   331 ▪ *Evaluating Library Sources   332* ▪ *Finding Information on the Internet   332* ▪ *Evaluating Internet Sources   333*

13b Using Sources in Your Writing   334

Paraphrasing   335 ▪ *Summarizing   336* ▪ *Quoting   337* ▪ *Working Sources into Your Writing   337* ▪ *Synthesizing   338*

13c Avoiding Plagiarism   339

13d Documenting Sources   342

MLA Documentation Style   342 ▪ *The Works-Cited List   344* ▪ *Sample MLA-Style Student Paper   347* ▪ *APA Documentation Style   352* ▪ *The Reference List   353*

Chapter Review   357

Unit 4 Basic Grammar Guide   363

14 Understanding Verbs 🄴 365

14a Regular Verbs   365

14b Irregular Verbs   366

🄴 **LearningCurve** activities and additional multiple-choice grammar exercises are available for the topics in this chapter. Visit **bedfordstmartins.com/forw**.

14c Problem Verbs: *Be* 368

14d Problem Verbs: *Can/Could* and *Will/Would* 369

14e Regular Past Participles 371

14f Irregular Past Participles 372

14g The Present Perfect Tense 375

14h The Past Perfect Tense 376

  Chapter Review 378

15 Understanding Nouns and Pronouns e 380

15a Identifying Nouns 380

15b Forming Plural Nouns 380

15c Identifying Pronouns 383

15d Pronoun-Antecedent Agreement 385

15e Special Problems with Agreement 387

  Compound Antecedents 387 ■ Indefinite Pronoun Antecedents 388 ■ Collective Noun Antecedents 390

15f Vague and Unnecessary Pronouns 391

  Vague Pronouns 391 ■ Unnecessary Pronouns 392

15g Pronoun Case 393

  Subjective Case 393 ■ Objective Case 393 ■ Possessive Case 393

15h Special Problems with Pronoun Case 394

  Pronouns in Compounds 394 ■ Pronouns in Comparisons 396 ■ Who and Whom, Whoever *and* Whomever *397*

15i Reflexive and Intensive Pronouns 399

  Reflexive Pronouns 399 ■ Intensive Pronouns 399

  Chapter Review 401

16 Understanding Adjectives and Adverbs e 403

16a Identifying Adjectives and Adverbs 403

16b Comparatives and Superlatives 406

e **LearningCurve** activities and additional multiple-choice grammar exercises are available for the topics in this chapter. Visit **bedfordstmartins.com/forw**.

Forming Comparatives and Superlatives 406 ▪ *Solving Special Problems with Comparatives and Superlatives 407*

Chapter Review 411

17 Writing Simple, Compound, and Complex Sentences ⓔ 413

Simple Sentences 413

17a   Identifying Subjects in Simple Sentences 413

17b   Identifying Prepositional Phrases in Simple Sentences 414

17c   Identifying Verbs in Simple Sentences 416

Action Verbs 416 ▪ *Linking Verbs 417* ▪ *Helping Verbs 418*

Compound Sentences 420

17d   Forming Compound Sentences with Coordinating Conjunctions 420

17e   Forming Compound Sentences with Semicolons 423

17f   Forming Compound Sentences with Transitional Words and Phrases 425

Complex Sentences 427

17g   Forming Complex Sentences with Subordinating Conjunctions 428

17h   Forming Complex Sentences with Relative Pronouns 430

Chapter Review 433

18 Writing Varied Sentences ⓔ 436

18a   Varying Sentence Types 436

18b   Varying Sentence Openings 437

Beginning with Adverbs 437 ▪ *Beginning with Prepositional Phrases 438*

18c   Combining Sentences 440

Using -ing Modifiers 440 ▪ *Using -ed Modifiers 441* ▪ *Using a Series of Words 442* ▪ *Using Appositives 444*

18d   Mixing Long and Short Sentences 445

Chapter Review 448

ⓔ **LearningCurve** activities and additional multiple-choice grammar exercises are available for the topics in this chapter. Visit **bedfordstmartins.com/forw**.

19 Using Parallelism e 450

19a Recognizing Parallel Structure 450
19b Using Parallel Structure 451

Paired Items 451 ▪ Items in a Series 452 ▪ Items in a List or in an Outline 452

Chapter Review 454

20 Using Words Effectively e 457

20a Using Specific Words 457
20b Using Concise Language 459
20c Using Similes and Metaphors 461
20d Avoiding Slang 462
20e Avoiding Clichés 463
20f Avoiding Sexist Language 465
20g Identifying Commonly Confused Words 466

Chapter Review 472

21 Run-Ons e 474

21a Recognizing Run-Ons 474
21b Correcting Run-Ons 475

Chapter Review 484

22 Fragments e 487

22a Recognizing Fragments 487
22b Missing-Subject Fragments 489
22c Phrase Fragments 491

Appositive Fragments 491 ▪ Prepositional Phrase Fragments 491 ▪ Infinitive Fragments 492

22d *-ing* Fragments 494

22e Dependent-Clause Fragments 495

Chapter Review 501

23 Subject-Verb Agreement [e] 503

23a Understanding Subject-Verb Agreement 503

23b Compound Subjects 504

23c *Be*, *Have*, and *Do* 505

23d Words between Subject and Verb 507

23e Collective Noun Subjects 508

23f Indefinite Pronoun Subjects 509

23g Verbs before Subjects 511

Chapter Review 513

24 Illogical Shifts [e] 515

24a Shifts in Tense 515

24b Shifts in Person 516

24c Shifts in Voice 518

Chapter Review 521

25 Misplaced and Dangling Modifiers [e] 523

25a Correcting Misplaced Modifiers 523

25b Correcting Dangling Modifiers 525

Chapter Review 528

26 Using Commas [e] 530

26a Commas in a Series 530

[e] **LearningCurve** activities and additional multiple-choice grammar exercises are available for the topics in this chapter. Visit **bedfordstmartins.com/forw**.

26b Commas with Introductory Phrases and Transitional Words and Phrases 532

Introductory Phrases 532 ◾ *Transitional Words and Phrases 533*

26c Commas with Appositives 534

26d Commas with Nonrestrictive Clauses 535

26e Commas in Dates and Addresses 538

Dates 538 ◾ *Addresses 538*

26f Unnecessary Commas 539

Chapter Review 542

27 Using Apostrophes 🅔 544

27a Apostrophes in Contractions 544

27b Apostrophes in Possessives 545

Singular Nouns and Indefinite Pronouns 545 ◾ *Plural Nouns 546*

27c Incorrect Use of Apostrophes 547

Chapter Review 549

28 Understanding Mechanics 🅔 551

28a Capitalizing Proper Nouns 551

28b Punctuating Direct Quotations 554

Identifying Tag at the Beginning 555 ◾ *Identifying Tag at the End 555* ◾ *Identifying Tag in the Middle 555* ◾ *Identifying Tag between Two Sentences 556*

28c Setting Off Titles 557

28d Using Hyphens 559

28e Using Abbreviations 560

28f Using Numbers 560

28g Using Semicolons, Colons, Dashes, and Parentheses 561

Semicolons 561 ◾ *Colons 561* ◾ *Dashes 562* ◾ *Parentheses 562*

Chapter Review 564

Unit 5 Reading Essays 567

29 Readings for Writers 569

Reading and Writing 570

Amy Tan ■ *Mother Tongue* 570

Richard Lederer ■ *The Case for Short Words* 577

Richard Wright ■ *The Library Card* 581

Teaching and Learning 590

Joshuah Bearman ■ *My Half-Baked Bubble* 590

Adam Goodheart ■ *How to Mummify a Pharaoh* 594

Carolyn Foster Segal ■ *The Dog Ate My Flash Drive, and Other Tales of Woe* 597

Gender 601

John Gray ■ *Men Are from Mars, Women Are from Venus* 601

Judy Brady ■ *I Want a Wife* 606

D. B. Grady ■ *Why Women Soldiers Don't Belong on the Front Lines* 609

Current Issues 613

John Edgar Wideman ■ *The Seat Not Taken* 613

Bob Herbert ■ *Tweet Less, Kiss More* 616

Adam Winkler ■ *The Guns of Academe* 619

Acknowledgments 625

Index 627

Introduction: Using TEST When You Read and Write

Throughout college, you will read and write essays for many of your classes. An **essay** is a group of paragraphs that develops an idea about a subject.

- An essay's first paragraph—the **introduction**—begins with opening remarks that create interest and ends with a **thesis statement**. This thesis statement presents the main idea that the rest of the essay will develop.
- The **body** of the essay contains the paragraphs that support, explain, and develop the thesis. Each body paragraph focuses on one point in support of the thesis statement. Because the body paragraphs carry the weight of the discussion, they are the most important part of the essay.
- The last paragraph—the **conclusion**—ends the essay. It reinforces the essay's main idea and brings the essay to a close.

Essay Structure

The **introduction** begins with opening remarks that introduce the subject of the essay. The **thesis statement** states the essay's main idea.

The first **body paragraph** discusses point 1 in support of the thesis statement.

The second **body paragraph** discusses point 2 in support of the thesis statement.

The third **body paragraph** discusses point 3 in support of the thesis statement.

The fourth **body paragraph** discusses point 4 in support of the thesis statement.

The **conclusion** reinforces the main idea of the essay.

TESTing Essays

As you **read** and **write** essays, you should look for the elements that make them effective. You do this by asking the following four TEST questions.

T ▪ **Thesis Statement**—Does the essay include a thesis statement that presents the main idea—the idea that will be developed in the essay?

E ▪ **Evidence**—Does the essay include evidence—examples and details—that supports the thesis statement?

S ▪ **Summary Statement**—Does the essay's conclusion include a summary statement that reinforces the thesis and sums up the main idea?

T ▪ **Transitions**—Does the essay include transitional words and phrases that show readers how ideas are related?

The processes of reading and writing are so closely linked that it is sometimes difficult to tell where one process ends and the other begins. For example, as you *read* an essay, you can TEST it to identify its key elements. When you *write* an essay, you can TEST it as you begin revising it to make sure that it includes all the necessary elements.

Teaching Tip
Tell students that their thesis statements will most likely change as they write their essays. As they revise, they should check periodically to make sure that their thesis statement actually communicates the main idea of the essay. If it does not, it will require revision.

TESTing for a Thesis Statement

The first thing you do when you TEST an essay is to make sure it has a clear **thesis statement (T)** that identifies the essay's main idea. By stating the main idea, the thesis statement helps to unify the essay.

The following introduction is from an essay written by a student, Amber Ransom, on the dangers of social networking. Notice that Amber states her thesis in the last sentence of her introduction, where readers expect to see it.

INTRODUCTION

Social-networking sites have many advantages. These sites, such as Facebook and MySpace, enable people to create profiles and to personalize them with pictures. "Friends" can browse these profiles and post comments that can then be viewed by anyone who has access to the profile. Many people meet online and then go on to form close friendships in real life. Some schools even set up social-networking sites for students so they can keep in touch, get advice, ask questions about schoolwork, and get feedback on assignments. Despite their many benefits, however, social-networking sites can create serious problems that people should be aware of.

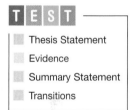

T E S T

- Thesis Statement
- Evidence
- Summary Statement
- Transitions

TESTing for Evidence

The next thing you do when you **TEST** an essay is to check the **evidence (E)** to make sure that the body of the essay includes enough examples and details to support the thesis. Remember that without evidence, an essay is really only a series of unsupported general statements. A well-developed essay includes enough evidence to explain, illustrate, and clarify the points the writer is making.

The following body paragraphs are from Amber's essay on the dangers of social networking. Notice that Amber's body paragraphs present the evidence she needs to develop and support the points she makes in her essay. In addition, the first sentence of each body paragraph—the **topic sentence**—connects the paragraph to the essay's thesis.

BODY PARAGRAPHS

One problem with social-networking sites is the amount of time people devote to them. Some users spend hours every day just checking in with their "friends." This can be an especially serious problem for some students, who can become more interested in socializing online than in learning. Because they can access social-networking sites with their smartphones and laptops, students often spend more time in class communicating with their friends than listening to their instructors. These problems are not limited to students. In fact, some people have been fired from their jobs because of their excessive involvement with social-networking sites. For example, a waitress was fired because she couldn't resist posting pictures of herself at the beach on a day when she was supposed to be at home sick, and a medical technician was fired because of negative comments he made online about his supervisor.

Another problem with social-networking sites is that they can reveal a lot of personal information. Some people include so much personal information in their profiles that they risk identity theft, identity fraud, or even worse. Even though sites like Facebook have privacy settings, users often ignore them and post personal information such as birthdays, schools they attended, dates of graduation, email addresses, job titles, and even phone numbers. Dishonest people can access this information, allowing them to establish false identities, get credit cards, and gain access to checking accounts. An even more serious problem occurs with sexual predators, who routinely surf

T E S T

- Thesis Statement
- Evidence
- Summary Statement
- Transitions

social-networking sites to search for victims. Children are especially vulnerable to these predators because they are often unaware of the danger.

One of the most serious problems with social-networking sites is that they make cyberbullying—the use of computers (as well as cell phones and other devices) to embarrass, annoy, or even threaten others—easier. Cyberbullies spread vicious rumors in online social spaces. Sometimes they set up false profiles on networking sites, using people's real names, pictures, and email addresses. As a result, victims are flooded with anonymous email messages that harass and threaten them. In one famous case, Megan Meier, a fourteen-year-old girl, committed suicide after being cyberbullied by the jealous mother of a former friend. The mother set up a false MySpace account and pretended to be a boy, taunting Megan so much that she eventually committed suicide.

TESTing for a Summary Statement

The third thing you do when you TEST an essay is to look at the conclusion and make sure that it includes a **summary statement (S)**. Often, a conclusion will begin with this statement, which reinforces the essay's thesis. By reinforcing the thesis, this summary statement helps to unify the essay.

The following conclusion is from Amber's essay on the dangers of social networking. Notice that it begins with a summary statement and ends with some general concluding remarks.

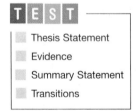

T E S T
- Thesis Statement
- Evidence
- Summary Statement
- Transitions

CONCLUSION

Despite their benefits, social-networking sites have created many problems. The amount of time that people spend on these sites, the lack of privacy, and the use of sites by cyberbullies are concerns for everyone. Unfortunately, many people underestimate the potential danger of social-networking sites. As a result, they post personal information and make it easy for someone to target them. Once users know the risks, however, they can take steps to keep themselves and their families safe. The basic rule for everyone who uses these sites is not to post information about yourself that you do not want everyone to know.

TESTing for Transitions

The last thing you do when you TEST an essay is to make sure that it includes **transitions (T)**—words and phrases that connect ideas and tell readers how one sentence (or paragraph) is related to another. Transitions make an essay coherent, connecting its sentences in a clear, logical sequence that helps readers understand the essay's ideas.

By linking sentences and paragraphs, transitions emphasize the relationship between ideas and help readers understand an essay's logic. By reminding readers of what has come before, transitions prepare readers for new information and help them understand how it fits into the discussion. In this sense, transitions are the glue that holds the ideas in an essay together. For a full list of transitions, see 4b.

Here are the thesis statement and the body paragraphs from Amber's essay on the dangers of social networking. Notice how the highlighted transitions link the sentences and the paragraphs of the essay.

THESIS + BODY PARAGRAPHS

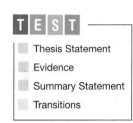

	Thesis Statement
	Evidence
	Summary Statement
	Transitions

Despite their many benefits, however, social-networking sites can create serious problems that people should be aware of.

One problem with social-networking sites is the amount of time people devote to them. Some users spend hours every day just checking in with their "friends." This can be an especially serious problem for some students, who can become more interested in socializing online than in learning. Because they can access social-networking sites with their smartphones and laptops, students often spend more time in class communicating with their friends than listening to their instructors. These problems are not limited to students. In fact, some people have been fired from their jobs because of their excessive involvement with social-networking sites. For example, a waitress was fired because she couldn't resist posting pictures of herself at the beach on a day when she was supposed to be at home sick, and a medical technician was fired because of negative comments he made online about his supervisor.

Another problem with social-networking sites is that they can reveal a lot of personal information. Some people include so much personal information in their profiles that they risk identity theft, identity fraud, or even worse. Even though sites like Facebook have privacy settings, users often ignore them and post personal information such as birthdays, schools they attended, dates of graduation, email addresses, job titles, and even phone numbers. Dishonest people can access this information, allowing them to establish false identities, get credit cards, and gain access to checking accounts. An even more serious problem occurs with sexual predators, who routinely surf social-networking sites to search for victims. Children are especially vulnerable to these predators because they are often unaware of the danger.

Teaching Tip
You may want to point out to students how Amber's topic sentences help to unify her essay by repeating the word *problem*, which echoes the wording of her thesis statement.

One of the most serious problems with social-networking sites is that they make cyberbullying—the use of computers (as well as cell phones and other devices) to embarrass, annoy, or even threaten others—easier. Cyberbullies spread vicious rumors in online social spaces. Sometimes they set up false profiles on networking sites, using people's real names, pictures, and email addresses. As a result, victims are flooded with anonymous email messages that harass and threaten them. In one famous case, Megan Meier, a fourteen-year-old girl, committed suicide after being cyberbullied by the jealous mother of a former friend. The mother set up a false MySpace account and pretended to be a boy, taunting Megan so much that she eventually committed suicide.

Putting It Together

Here is Amber's completed essay, which includes a title and the heading required by her instructor.

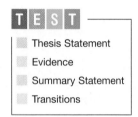

Thesis Statement
Evidence
Summary Statement
Transitions

Amber Ransom
Professor Fallows
Composition 101
5 Mar. 2014

The Dangers of Social Networking

Introduction

Social-networking sites have many advantages. These sites, such as Facebook and MySpace, enable people to create profiles and to personalize them with pictures. "Friends" can browse these profiles and post comments that can then be viewed by anyone who has access to the profile. Many people meet online and then go on to form close friendships in real life. Some schools even set up social-networking sites for students so they can keep in touch, get advice, ask questions about schoolwork, and get feedback on assignments. Despite their many benefits, however, social-networking sites can create serious problems that people should be aware of.

Topic sentence (states first point in support of thesis)

One problem with social-networking sites is the amount of time people devote to them. Some users spend hours every day just checking in with their "friends." This can be an especially serious problem for some students, who can become more interested in socializing online than in learning. Because they can access social-networking sites with their smartphones and laptops, students often spend more time in class communicating with their friends than listening to their instructors. These problems are not limited to students.

Examples and details

In fact, some people have been fired from their jobs because of their excessive involvement with social-networking sites. For example, a waitress was fired because she couldn't resist posting pictures of herself at the beach on a day when she was supposed to be at home sick, and a medical technician was fired because of negative comments he made online about his supervisor. Instead of getting better, this situation seems to be getting more and more serious.

Another problem with social-networking sites is that they can reveal a lot of personal information. Some people include so much personal information in their profiles that they risk identity theft, identity fraud, or even worse. Even though sites like Facebook have privacy settings, users often ignore them and post personal information such as birthdays, schools they attended, dates of graduation, email addresses, job titles, and even phone numbers. Dishonest people can access this information, allowing them to establish false identities, get credit cards, and gain access to checking accounts. An even more serious problem occurs with sexual predators, who routinely surf social-networking sites to search for victims. Children are especially vulnerable to these predators because they are often unaware of the danger.

One of the most serious problems with social-networking sites is that they make cyberbullying—the use of computers (as well as cell phones and other devices) to embarrass, annoy, or even threaten others—easier. Cyberbullies spread vicious rumors in online social spaces. Sometimes they set up false profiles on networking sites, using people's real names, pictures, and email addresses. As a result, victims are flooded with anonymous email messages that harass and threaten them. In one famous case, Megan Meier, a fourteen-year-old girl, committed suicide after being cyberbullied by the jealous mother of a former friend. The mother set up a false MySpace account and pretended to be a boy, taunting Megan so much that she eventually committed suicide.

Despite their benefits, social-networking sites have created many problems. The amount of time that people spend on these sites, the lack of privacy, and the use of sites by cyberbullies are concerns for everyone. Unfortunately, many people underestimate the potential danger of social-networking sites. As a result, they post personal information and make it easy for someone to target them. Once users know the risks, however, they can take steps to keep themselves and their families safe. The basic rule for everyone who uses these sites is not to post information about yourself that you do not want everyone to know.

Topic sentence (states second point in support of thesis)

— **Body paragraphs**

Examples and details

Topic sentence (states third point in support of thesis)

Examples and details

Conclusion

TESTing Body Paragraphs

Just as you TEST an essay, you can also TEST an essay's body paragraphs to determine whether they include all the elements they need to be effective. (Note that when it applies to a paragraph, the T in TEST stands for the **topic sentence**, the sentence that unifies the paragraph and tells readers what the focus of the paragraph will be.)

- **T** **Topic Sentence**—Does the body paragraph have a topic sentence that states its main idea—the idea that will be developed in the paragraph?
- **E** **Evidence**—Does the body paragraph include the examples and details needed to support the topic sentence?
- **S** **Summary Statement**—Does the body paragraph end with a statement that reinforces the main idea?
- **T** **Transitions**—Does the body paragraph include transitional words and phrases that show readers how ideas are related?

If you TEST the following body paragraph, you will see that it contains all four elements of an effective paragraph.

TEST

- Topic Sentence
- Evidence
- Summary Statement
- Transitions

One problem with social-networking sites is the amount of time people devote to them. Some users spend hours every day just checking in with their "friends." This can be an especially serious problem for some students, who can become more interested in socializing online than in learning. Because they can access social-networking sites with their smartphones and laptops, students often spend more time in class communicating with their friends than listening to their instructors. These problems are not limited to students. In fact, some people have been fired from their jobs because of their excessive involvement with social-networking sites. For example, a waitress was fired because she couldn't resist posting pictures of herself at the beach on a day when she was supposed to be home sick, and a medical technician was fired because of negative comments he made online about his supervisor. Instead of getting better, this situation seems to be getting more and more serious.

TESTing as you read the work of others can help you identify the key information you need to understand the text. TESTing your own work as you begin revising will enable you to make sure that your essays, and the body paragraphs that make up your essays, have the elements that they need to be clear and effective.

Reading to Write

1 **Understanding the Active Reading Process** 11

2 **Building Vocabulary for Reading and Writing** 35

3 **Understanding the Writing Process** 60

4 **Understanding Introductions, Body Paragraphs, and Conclusions** 104

5 **Thinking, Reading, and Writing Critically** 123

6 **Reading and Writing about Different Kinds of Texts** 155

1 Understanding the Active Reading Process

focus on reading and writing

Think about what you already know about how to manage your time. Later in this chapter, you will read and write about a passage on this topic.

In this chapter, you will learn to

- use active reading strategies before you read (1a)
- use active reading strategies as you read (1b)
- use active reading strategies after you read (1c)
- write a response paragraph (1d)

Most of the writing you do in college will be in response to reading. For example, you might be asked to read an essay and write an informal response to its ideas or to write a research paper that incorporates information from several sources and blends them with your own ideas. For this reason, reading is an important preliminary step in the writing process.

Instead of thinking in terms of being "good" or "bad" at reading, it makes more sense to see reading as a process that you control. Since reading is essential in all of your college courses, you need to get the most out of it, and this means that you should approach the books, articles, and web pages you read systematically, as an active reader.

Being an **active reader** means participating in the reading process: approaching a reading assignment with a clear understanding of the strategies you can use *before* you read, *while* you read, and *after* you read.

1a Before You Read

Before you even begin reading a text, you should be aware of the active reading strategies that will help you when you read. These strategies include *creating a reading schedule, assessing prior knowledge, understanding your purpose,* and *previewing.*

Creating a Reading Schedule

As a college student, you have a lot to do, so planning your reading and study time is very important. One useful time-management strategy is creating a **reading schedule** that maps out how many pages you will read and when you will read them.

For example, if you are assigned to read thirty-six pages in your biology textbook, and the time you have available is between 3 p.m. Monday and 11 a.m. Wednesday, you could map out a reading schedule like the following one.

Teaching Tip
Refer students to the reading on pages 16–17 for more on time-management strategies.

> *36 pages/3 days = 12 pages per day*
>
> *Monday: Read pages 1–12 (7:30–8:45 p.m.)*
>
> *Tuesday: Read pages 13–24 (3:15–4:30 p.m.)*
>
> *Wednesday: Read pages 25–36 (7:30–8:45 a.m.)*
>
> *TOTAL PAGES = 36*

When creating your reading schedule, be sure to specify exact times for your reading. If you know you have blocked out specific times, you will be less likely to procrastinate. Also, be realistic about the number of pages you will read each time, and give yourself more time than you think you will need.

PRACTICE
1-1

In the box below, practice creating a reading schedule for an assignment in another class.

Answers will vary.

> _____ (number of pages)/_____ (number of days) = _____ (total pages per day)
>
> Day 1: _____ (pages) _____ (time)
>
> Day 2: _____ (pages) _____ (time)
>
> Day 3: _____ (pages) _____ (time)

Assessing Prior Knowledge

Another strategy that you can engage in before reading a text is **assessing prior knowledge**—that is, asking yourself what you already know about a subject and what you still need (or want) to know about it. Assessing your prior knowledge will help you to decide how much time you will need to read and what specific reading strategies to use. For example, if you already know a good deal about animal and plant cells, reading a chapter about them may not be very difficult for you. However, if you have no idea how animal and plant cells are different, you will probably have to spend more time reading the chapter.

To assess your prior knowledge, start by asking the following questions.

WORD POWER

assessing measuring; determining the value, extent, or significance

prior preceding in time or order

Questions for Assessing Prior Knowledge

- Can you predict what the text will be about?
- What do you already know about the subject of the text?
- How is the text similar to (or different from) other texts you have read?
- Is there anything in your background that helps you relate to or understand the text?
- How interested are you in this subject?
- What do you hope to learn from your reading?

Understanding Your Purpose

Before you begin to read, you should make sure you have a clear understanding of your **purpose** for reading. For example, are you reading for pleasure? For information? To complete an assignment? Understanding your purpose, like assessing your prior knowledge, can help you to decide how much time you will need and what reading strategies you will use. For example, if you are reading to prepare for an informal discussion with your study group, you will not need to read as carefully as you might if you were studying for an exam. You can start by considering the following questions.

Questions for Understanding Your Purpose

- Why are you reading?
- Will you be expected to discuss what you are reading? If so, will you discuss it in class? In a conference with your instructor?
- Will you have to write about what you are reading? If so, will you be expected to write an informal response (for example, a journal entry) or a more formal one (for example, an essay)?
- Will you be tested on the material?

FYI

Adjusting Reading Strategies

You may need to adjust your reading strategy based on your purpose or on the type of text you are reading. For example, if you are reading an essay about something you have little or no knowledge about, and you will be tested on it, you might need to use more than one active reading strategy; if you will be discussing a reading in class, you may need to construct an outline of the important points. As you practice reading actively, you will begin to know which strategies are best for which purposes.

Previewing

Now that you have set up a reading schedule, assessed your prior knowledge, and established your purpose for reading, you can begin to **preview**, focusing on *skimming* the text.

Skimming

When you **skim** a text, you read it quickly, just to get a sense of the writer's main idea and key supporting points. This strategy is particularly useful when you need to read many pages in a short amount of time. (Skimming can also help you determine if a text will be useful to you.) When you skim, you look at the text's **visual signals**: the title, the author's name, the first paragraph (which often contains a thesis statement or overview), and the last paragraph (which often contains a summary of the writer's points). You might also look at each paragraph's first sentence, which is often the topic sentence. As you skim a text, you should also look for clues to content and emphasis in other visual signals, such as headings, boxed text, and images. (Later on, as you read, you will look at **verbal signals**—the words and phrases the writer uses to indicate which points are emphasized and how ideas are arranged.)

> ### Guidelines for Skimming
>
> When skimming a text, look at the visual signals.
>
> - The title
> - The author's name
> - The opening paragraph, searching for the sentence that best expresses the main idea
> - The closing paragraph, searching for a summary of the writer's ideas
> - Each paragraph's first sentence
> - Headings and subheadings
> - *Italicized* and **boldfaced** words
> - Numbered lists
> - Bulleted lists (like this one)
> - Graphs, charts, tables, diagrams, photographs, and other visuals
> - Any information that is boxed
> - Any information that is in color

Scanning

Sometimes, depending on your purpose for reading, you may also want to *scan* a text. **Scanning** is a purposeful, focused look at a text to locate specific information—often to enable you to answer specific questions

Teaching Tip
Explain to students that previewing a textbook chapter is different from previewing an essay because a textbook chapter is generally longer and has certain elements (headings, bulleted lists, boxed information, and so on) that don't often appear in other kinds of writing.

Teaching Tip
Refer students to pages 19–20 for a list of verbal signals.

Teaching Tip
Remind students that looking at each paragraph's first sentence might not always work for a long textbook chapter. It might be better to focus on headings and visuals.

about the material. For example, if you need to prepare for a quiz or answer questions on a worksheet, you would scan the text looking only for specific words and phrases that might answer the questions.

Guidelines for Scanning

When scanning a text, look for the following elements.

WORD POWER

enumerate to name one by one

- Bulleted or numbered lists that might enumerate the writer's key points
- **Bold-faced** or *italicized* words
- Organizational words such as *first*, *second*, *third*, *next*, and *finally*
- Proper nouns (capitalized)
- Numbers
- Words set in quotation marks
- Specific words or ideas related to information you are looking for

When you have finished previewing, you should have a general sense of what the writer wants to communicate.

focus on reading and writing

Below is a discussion of time management from a first-year college textbook. In preparation for class discussion and for other activities that will be assigned throughout this chapter, **skim** the textbook passage. As you skim, try to identify the writer's main idea and key supporting points, and then write them on the lines that follow the passage on page 17.

TIME-MANAGEMENT STRATEGIES

Learning to manage your time is very important for success in college. Here are some strategies you can adopt to make this task easier.

1. ***Use an organizer.*** New electronic tools are constantly being developed to help you stay organized. For example, Schoolbinder, a free online organizer, can help you manage your time and create a study schedule. If you have trouble blocking out distractions when you are studying, a site like StudyRails can be helpful. For a small monthly fee, this site will help you plan a study schedule and alert you to when it's time to focus on schoolwork. It can also be programmed to block your go-to recreational sites during hours when you should be studying.

You can use the calendar function on your smartphone or tablet to keep track of deadlines and appointments (see the example on page 11). At the beginning of the semester, enter key pieces of information from each course syllabus—for example, the date of every quiz and exam and the due date of every paper. As the semester progresses, continue to add assignments and deadlines. In addition, enter information such as days when a class will be canceled or will meet in the computer lab or in the library, reminders to bring a particular book or piece of equipment to class, and appointments with instructors or other college personnel. (If you like, you can also note reminders and schedule appointments that are not related to school—for example, changes in your work hours, a dental appointment, or lunch with a friend.) Some students also like to keep a separate month-by-month "to do" list. Deleting completed items can give you a feeling of accomplishment—and make the road ahead look shorter.

   Note: If you are most comfortable with paper and pencil, purchase a "week-on-two-pages" academic year organizer—one that begins in September, not January; this format gives you more writing room for Monday through Friday than for the weekend, and it also lets you view an entire week at once.

2. *Use a calendar.* Buy a large wall calendar, and post it where you will see it every morning—on your desk, on the refrigerator, or wherever you keep your phone, your keys, and your ID. At the beginning of the semester, fill in important dates such as school holidays, work commitments, exam dates, and due dates for papers and projects. When you return from classes each day, update the calendar with any new information you have entered into your organizer.

3. *Plan ahead.* If you think you will need help from a writing center tutor to revise a paper that is due in two weeks, don't wait until day thirteen to make an appointment; all the tutoring slots may be filled by then. To be safe, make an appointment about a week in advance.

4. *Learn to enjoy downtime.* When you have a free minute, take time for yourself—and don't feel guilty about it.

Writer's main idea

   Effective time management is important for college success.

Key supporting points

   1. Using an organizer can help you keep important information in one place.

   2. Using a calender can help you keep track of important dates.

   3. Planning ahead will help you make sure you have time to get the help you need.

   4. Don't forget to take time for yourself.

Teaching Tip
Ask students to evaluate the previewing strategies they used. Did skimming help them to find the information they needed? If so, how? If not, why not? Ask them how they could change their previewing process to make it more useful.

focus on reading and writing

Look once again at "Time-Management Strategies." This time, **scan** the passage to look for the following details, and write down where you found each piece of information.

- Examples of electronic tools that can help you stay organized
  Section 1, "Use an organizer"

- Suggestions for the best places to put a calendar
  Section 2, "Use a calendar"

- How far in advance you should make an appointment with a writing center tutor *Section 3, "Plan ahead"*

1b   As You Read

e bedfordstmartins.com
/forw LearningCurve >
Topics and Main Ideas

Once you have finished previewing a text, it is time to begin reading. Two active reading strategies—*highlighting* and *annotating*—can aid your comprehension as you read a text.

FYI

Using TEST

As you learned in the Introduction to this text, TEST is both a reading and a writing strategy: you can use it to make sure the essays you write include all the necessary elements, and you can also use it as you read, to help you identify these elements in various texts. Using TEST to survey a text as you read will help you to get a general idea of what you are reading.

Highlighting

Highlighting means using underlining and symbols to identify key ideas. This active reading strategy will help you understand the writer's ideas and make connections among them when you reread. Be selective as you highlight. You will eventually be rereading every highlighted word, phrase, and sentence—so highlight only the most important information.

Using Highlighting Symbols

- <u>Underline</u> key ideas—for example, topic sentences.
- Box or circle words or phrases you want to remember.
- Place a check mark (✓) or star (✳) next to an important idea.
- Place a double check mark (✓✓) or double star (✳✳) next to an especially significant idea.
- Draw lines or arrows to connect related ideas.
- Put a question mark (?) beside a word or idea that you need to look up.
- Number the writer's key supporting points or examples.

FYI

Knowing What to Highlight

You want to highlight what is important—but how do you *know* what is important?

- *Look for visual signals.* As a general rule, you should look for the same **visual signals** you looked for when you did your previewing. Many of the ideas you will need to highlight will probably be found in material that is visually set off from the rest of the text—opening and closing paragraphs, lists, and so on.
- *Look for verbal signals.* At this stage, you should also look for **verbal signals**—words and phrases that often introduce key points. (See the list below.)

Together, these visual and verbal signals will give you clues to the writer's meaning and emphasis.

Verbal Signals

- Repeated words and phrases
- Phrases that signal emphasis ("The *primary* reason"; "The *most important* idea")
- Words that signal addition (*also, in addition, furthermore*)
- Words that signal time sequence (*first, after, then, next, finally*)

(continued)

Teaching Tip

Highlighting is a particularly helpful strategy for students who are visual learners.

(continued from previous page)

- Words that identify causes and effects (*because, as a result, for this reason*)
- Words that introduce examples (*for example, for instance*)
- Words that signal comparison (*likewise, similarly*)
- Words that signal contrast (*unlike, although, in contrast*)
- Words that signal contradiction (*however, on the contrary*)
- Words that signal a narrowing of the writer's focus (*in fact, specifically, in other words*)
- Words that signal summaries or conclusions (*to sum up, in conclusion*)

Here is how one student highlighted an excerpt from a newspaper column, "Barbie at Thirty-Five" by Anna Quindlen.

But consider the recent study at the University of Arizona investigating the attitudes of white and black teenage girls toward body image. The attitudes of the white girls were a nightmare. Ninety percent expressed dissatisfaction with their own bodies, and many said they saw dieting as a kind of all-purpose panacea. "I think the reason I would diet would be to gain self-confidence," said one. "I'd feel like it was a way of getting control," said another. And they were curiously united in their description of the perfect girl. She's 5 feet 7 inches, weighs just over 100 pounds, has long legs and flowing hair. The researchers concluded, "The ideal girl was a living manifestation of the Barbie doll."

While white girls described an impossible ideal, black teenagers talked about appearance in terms of style, attitude, pride, and personality. White respondents talked "thin," black ones "shapely." Seventy percent of the black teenagers said they were satisfied with their weight, and there was little emphasis on dieting. "We're all brought up and taught to be realistic about life," said one, "and we don't look at things the way you want them to be. You look at them the way they are."

The student who highlighted the passage above was preparing to write an essay about eating disorders. Because the passage included no visual signals apart from the paragraph divisions, she looked carefully for verbal signals.

The student began her highlighting by underlining and starring the writer's main idea. She then boxed the names of the two key groups the passage compares—*white girls* and *black teenagers*—and underlined two phrases that illustrate how the attitudes of the two groups differ (*dissatisfaction with their own bodies* and *satisfied with their weight*). Check marks in the margin remind the student of the importance of these two phrases, and arrows connect each phrase to the appropriate group of girls.

The student also circled three related terms that characterize white girls' attitudes—*perfect girl*, *Barbie doll*, and *impossible ideal*—drawing lines to connect them. Finally, she circled the unfamiliar word *panacea* and put a question mark above it to remind herself to look up the word's meaning.

PRACTICE

1-2 Review the highlighted passage on page 20. How would your own highlighting of this passage be similar to or different from the sample student highlighting? How does the purpose of your reading affect how you might highlight?

---

focus on reading and writing

Reread "Time-Management Strategies" (pp. 16–17). As you reread, highlight the passage by underlining and starring the main idea, boxing and circling key words, checkmarking important points, and drawing lines and arrows to connect related ideas. Be sure to circle each unfamiliar word and put a question mark above it so that you will remember to look it up later.

FYI

Using Context Clues

Before you turn to a dictionary to determine the meaning of an unfamiliar word, see if you can figure out the meaning from **context clues** in the text. (See 2c for information on how to use context clues to expand your vocabulary.)

Annotating

Once you have highlighted a passage, your next step is to *annotate* it. **Annotating** a passage means reading critically and making notes—of questions, reactions, reminders, and ideas for writing or discussion—in the margins or between the lines. (If you run out of room on the page, you can use sticky notes.) Keeping an informal record of ideas as they occur to you will prepare you for class discussion and for writing.

As you read, keeping the following questions in mind will help you make useful annotations.

Teaching Tip
Refer students to 5a for more on purpose and audience.

Teaching Tip
As they read, students may find it helpful to consider how ideas are arranged in a text. For example, seeing that an essay is comparing two subjects or explaining a process will help them understand the writer's ideas and see how they are related. (Refer students to Unit 2 for more on patterns of essay development.)

Questions for Annotating

- What is the writer saying? What do you think the writer is suggesting or implying? What makes you think so?
- What is the writer's purpose (his or her reason for writing)?
- What kind of audience is the writer addressing?
- Is the writer responding to another writer's ideas?
- What is the writer's main idea?
- How does the writer support his or her points? Does the writer use facts? Opinions? Both?
- What kind of supporting details and examples does the writer use?
- Does the writer include enough supporting details and examples?
- What pattern of development does the writer use to arrange his or her ideas? Is this pattern the best choice?
- Does the writer seem well informed? Reasonable? Fair?
- Do you understand the writer's vocabulary?
- Do you understand the writer's ideas?
- Do you agree with the points the writer is making?
- How are the ideas presented in this reading selection like (or unlike) those presented in other selections you have read?

FYI

Making Useful Annotations

As you annotate, remember that you should not write too much or too little; good annotations fit in the margins or on a small sticky note. You should *not* write your annotations on a separate sheet of paper. If you do, you will be tempted to write too much, and you can easily lose track of where a particular note belongs or what point it comments on. (Moreover, if you lose the sheet of paper, you will also lose all your notes and thoughts.) Think of annotations as a study aid that you can consult when you return to the text a few days later. Brief, useful annotations will help you follow the writer's ideas and remember what is most important in the text.

The following passage, which reproduces the student's highlighting from page 20, also includes her annotations.

But consider the recent study at the University of Arizona investigating

✳ the <u>attitudes of white and black teenage girls toward body image</u>. The

attitudes of the |white girls| were a nightmare. Ninety percent expressed

✓ <u>dissatisfaction with their own bodies</u>, and many said they saw dieting

as a kind of all-purpose (panacea.) "I think the reason I would diet would   = cure-all

be to gain self-confidence," said one. "I'd feel like it was a way of getting

control," said another. And they were curiously united in their description   Need for control,
                                                                                  perfection. Why?
of the (perfect girl.) She's 5 feet 7 inches, weighs just over 100 pounds, has   Media? Parents?

long legs and flowing ~~hair~~. The researchers concluded, "The ideal girl

was a living manifestation of the (Barbie doll.")   Barbie doll
                                                                                  = plastic, unreal
While white girls described an (impossible ideal,) |black teenagers|

talked about appearance in terms of style, attitude, pride, and personality.

White respondents talked "thin," black ones "shapely." Seventy percent   "Thin" vs. "shapely"

✓ of the black teenagers said they were <u>satisfied with their weight</u>, and   Only 30% dissatisfied–
                                                                                  but 90% of white girls
there was little emphasis on dieting. "We're all brought up and taught to

be realistic about life," said one, "and we don't look at things the way you

want them to be. You look at them the way they are."
                                              overgeneralization?
vs. Barbie doll (= unrealistic)

In her annotations, this student wrote down the meaning of the word *panacea*, put the study's conclusions and the contrasting statistics into her own words, and recorded questions she intended to explore further.

focus on reading and writing

Reread "Time-Management Strategies" (pp. 16–17). This time, refer to the Questions for Annotating (p. 22) and use them to guide you as you write down your own thoughts and questions in the margins of the passage. Note where you agree or disagree with the writer, and briefly explain why. Quickly summarize any points you think are particularly important. Take time to look up any unfamiliar words you have circled and to write brief definitions. Think of these annotations as your preparation for discussing the passage in class—and, eventually, for writing about it.

focus on reading and writing

Exchange books with another student, and read his or her highlighting and annotating of "Time-Management Strategies." How are your written responses similar to the other student's? How are they different? Do your classmate's responses help you see anything new about the passage? Looking again at your own annotations, consider how you might use them to write a response to the suggestions in "Time-Management Strategies."

1c   After You Read

After you finish reading a text, some additional active reading strategies—*outlining, summarizing, reviewing,* and *self-quizzing*—will enable you to better retain and use the information you acquired when you read. Once you have a good command of the material, you will be prepared to express your reactions by writing a *response paragraph.*

Outlining

Teaching Tip
Tell students that formal outlines can help them keep track of ideas in long essays or research papers. Refer them to 3f for an example of a formal outline.

Outlining a text you have read is an active reading strategy that you can use to help you understand it. Unlike a **formal outline**, which follows strict conventions, an **informal outline** is just a list of a passage's key ideas and supporting points in the order in which they are presented. After you have made an informal outline of a passage, you should be able to see the writer's emphasis (which ideas are more important than others) as well as how the ideas are related.

FYI

Constructing an Informal Outline

To construct an informal outline, follow these guidelines.

1. Write or type the passage's main idea at the top of a sheet of paper. (This will remind you of the writer's focus and help keep your outline on track.)
2. At the left margin, write down the most important idea of the first body paragraph or first part of the passage.
3. Indent the next line a few spaces, and list the examples or details that support this idea. (You can use your computer's Tab key to help you set up your outline.)
4. As ideas become more specific, indent further. (Ideas that have the same degree of importance are indented the same distance from the left margin.)

Repeat the process with each body paragraph or part of the passage.

The student who highlighted and annotated the excerpt from Anna Quindlen's "Barbie at Thirty-Five" (pp. 20 and 23) made the following informal outline to help her understand the writer's ideas.

Main idea: Black and white teenage girls have very different attitudes about their body images.

White girls dissatisfied
    90% dissatisfied with appearance
    Dieting = cure-all
      –self-confidence
      –control
    Ideal = unrealistic
      –tall and thin
      –Barbie doll

Black girls satisfied
    70% satisfied with weight
    Dieting not important
    Ideal = realistic
      –shapely
      –not thin

focus on reading and writing

Make an informal outline of "Time-Management Strategies" (pp. 16–17). Refer to your highlighting and annotations as you construct your outline. When you have finished, check to make certain your outline accurately represents the writer's emphasis and the relationships among his or her ideas.

Summarizing

Teaching Tip
Refer students to 5f for more on how to write a summary.

Once you have highlighted, annotated, and outlined a passage, you may want to *summarize* it to help you understand it better. A **summary** is a brief restatement, *in your own words*, of a passage's main idea. A summary does not include supporting examples and details, and it does not include your own ideas or opinions. For this reason, a summary is always much shorter than the original passage—usually no longer than a few sentences.

> **Guidelines for Writing a Summary**
> 1. Review your outline.
> 2. Consulting your outline, restate the passage's main idea *in your own words*.
> 3. Reread the original passage to make sure you have accurately summarized the main idea and that you have not included any unrelated or unnecessary material.

To avoid accidentally using the exact language of the original, do not look at the passage while you are writing your summary. If you decide to use a distinctive word or phrase from the original passage, be sure to put it in quotation marks.

The student who highlighted, annotated, and outlined the excerpt from "Barbie at Thirty-Five" (pp. 20, 23, and 25) wrote the following summary.

> As Anna Quindlen reports in "Barbie at Thirty-Five," a University of Arizona study found that African-American and white teenage girls have very different attitudes about their body images. Almost all white girls said they were dissatisfied with their appearance; African-American girls in the study, however, were generally happy with their weight.

focus on reading and writing

Write a summary of "Time-Management Strategies" (pp. 16–17).
Use your informal outline to guide you, and keep your summary
brief—no more than three sentences long.

Reviewing and Self-Quizzing

In order to remember the information you have read, you will need to
review it carefully and perhaps quiz yourself after you read.

When you **review**, you repeat information so that you can remember
and use it—just as you might keep repeating the items you need to buy
until you get to the grocery store. Typically, this review strategy works
best when you have only five to seven items (or concepts) to remember.
For example, if you need to remember the sequence of key U.S. immigration laws, the relative distance of planets from the sun, or the muscles in
the shoulder, you can just list these items and study them until you have
memorized them. This strategy will help to prepare you for class discussion or for writing an exam answer.

Self-quizzing helps you make connections to the information so you
can truly learn it. If you want to remember information for a long time—
and understand it—you will find this strategy helpful. Self-quizzing not
only helps you identify important information, but it also helps you
apply information to a specific situation—for example, to a final exam.

Self-quizzing involves creating thoughtful questions from the information in a text. You can create three kinds of questions.

Teaching Tip
You can point students to
questions of each type
that accompany the read-
ings in Chapter 29.

1. **Literal questions** test your comprehension of factual material.
   If you scan the text, you will find the answers to these questions.
   For example, to answer the question, "What percent of African-
   American teenagers in the study said they were satisfied with their
   weight?" you can point to the answer—"70 percent"—in the second
   paragraph of the passage from Anna Quindlen's article.

2. **Inferential questions** are those that go beyond facts; they ask you
   to look at the ideas in the text and **infer** (figure out) what the writer
   means. For example, if you asked, "What does the writer think
   about the attitudes of white girls toward body image?" you would
   have to review your highlighting to see what the text suggests about
   Quindlen's personal opinion.

Teaching Tip
Refer students to 5e
for more on making
inferences.

3. **Evaluative questions** force you to go beyond the literal meaning
   of the text and make a judgment or generate an opinion about the

material. For example, if you asked, "Do you believe that girls have poor body images? What in your experience has led you to believe that your answer is correct?" you would have to think about your own experiences and observations in light of what you have read.

Once you create your questions, you can use them as you study and interact with the text. Keep in mind that different kinds of questions serve different purposes. For example, if you were taking a multiple-choice quiz, you might want to focus on creating literal study questions, but if you were preparing for class discussion or taking an essay exam, it might be helpful to practice answering inferential and evaluative questions.

PRACTICE

1-3 To practice self-quizzing, work with another student to create one literal question, one inferential question, and one evaluative question for one of the model student essays in Unit 2 of this book. Write your questions, without the answers, on a sheet of paper. Then, trade questions with another group, and answer their questions while they answer yours.

1d Writing a Response Paragraph

After you have highlighted and annotated a reading selection, you are ready to write about it—perhaps in a **response paragraph** in which you record your informal reactions to the writer's ideas.

Because a response paragraph is informal, no special guidelines or rules govern its format or structure. As in any paragraph, however, you should include a topic sentence, support the topic sentence with specific evidence (examples and details), use complete sentences, and link sentences with appropriate transitions. In a response paragraph, informal style and personal opinions are acceptable.

The student who highlighted, annotated, outlined, and summarized "Barbie at Thirty-Five" wrote the following response paragraph.

Teaching Tip
Remind students that contractions are acceptable here only because this is an informal paragraph.

Why are white and African-American girls' body images so different? Why do African-American girls think it's okay to be "shapely" while white girls want to be thin? Maybe it's because music videos and movies and fashion magazines show so many more white models, all half-starved, with perfect hair and legs. Or maybe white girls get different messages from their parents or from the people they date. Do white and black girls' attitudes about their bodies stay the same when they get older? And what about <u>male</u> teenagers' self-images? Do white and black <u>guys</u> have different body images, too?

The process of writing this paragraph was very helpful to the student. The questions she asked suggested some interesting ideas that she could explore in class discussion or in a more fully developed piece of writing.

focus on reading and writing

Now that you have practiced the complete active reading process with the textbook excerpt on pages 16–17, write a response paragraph that explains your thoughts about the time-management strategies presented in the excerpt. In your paragraph, you can discuss why these strategies would (or would not) be useful to you, or you can write about strategies you already use to manage your time. When you have finished, TEST what you have written.

REVIEW ACTIVITY

Graphic Organizer: *Active Reading Strategies*

Drawing on the information you learned in Chapter 1, use the graphic organizer on page 31 to map the various strategies that can be applied before, during, and after reading. Also include a brief explanation of how you plan to use each reading strategy this semester.

Before Reading Strategies

Strategy 1: _Creating a reading schedule_

I will apply strategy 1 by
Reading at least 15 pages of each textbook on Mon. – Thurs. between 7:00–9:00 p.m.

Strategy 2: _Assessing prior knowledge_

I will apply strategy 2 by
Answers will vary.

Strategy 3: _Understanding your purpose_

I will apply strategy 3 by
Answers will vary.

Strategy 4: _Previewing_

I will apply strategy 4 by
Answers will vary.

During Reading Strategies

Strategy 1: _Highlighting_

I will apply strategy 1 by
Suggested Answer: Underlining key ideas in my textbook and drawing arrows to connect related ideas.

Strategy 2: _Annotating_

I will apply strategy 2 by
Answers will vary.

After Reading Strategies

Strategy 1: _Outlining_

I will apply strategy 1 by
Suggested Answer: Listing key ideas and supporting points after I read an important chapter or essay.

Strategy 2: _Summarizing_

I will apply strategy 2 by
Answers will vary.

Strategy 3: _Reviewing_

I will apply strategy 3 by
Answers will vary.

Strategy 4: _Self-Quizzing_

I will apply strategy 4 by
Answers will vary.

COLLABORATIVE ACTIVITY

Fill in the crossword puzzle on page 33 with the help of the clues listed below. Answers to clues that fall under the heading "Across" will appear only in the boxes ordered from left to right in the puzzle. Answers to clues that fall under the heading "Down" will appear only in boxes ordered from top to bottom in the puzzle. The answers are drawn from the key terms in Chapter 1 (which are set in boldface), and page numbers are provided to guide you back to the proper place in the chapter.

Hint: Five of the answers consist of two-word terms.

Example (1 across):

The words and phrases the writer uses to indicate which points are emphasized and how ideas are arranged: VERBAL SIGNALS

ACROSS

1. the words and phrases the writer uses to indicate which points are emphasized and how ideas are arranged [p. 15]
8. a plan that maps out how many pages you will read and when you will read them [p. 12]
9. clues to content and emphasis, such as headings, boxed text, and images [p. 15]
12. taking a purposeful, focused look at a text to locate specific information [p. 15]
13. tools to help you manage your time [p. 16]

DOWN

2. a process involving strategies that include creating a reading schedule, assessing prior knowledge, understanding your purpose, and previewing [p. 12]
3. using underlining and symbols to identify key ideas [p. 18]
4. a technique to help you understand the structure of a reading assignment as well as the ideas it communicates [p. 24]
5. what you already know about a subject and what you still need (or want) to know about it [p. 13]
6. your reason for reading, such as for pleasure, for information, or to complete an assignment [p. 14]
7. writing a brief restatement, in your own words, of a passage's main idea [p. 26]
10. reading critically and making notes—of questions, reactions, reminders, and ideas for writing or discussion—in the margins or between the lines [p. 21]
11. reading a text quickly and trying to get a sense of the writer's main idea and key supporting points [p. 15]
14. repeating information so that you can remember and use it [p. 27]

Across:
1. VERBAL SIGNALS
8. READING SCHEDULE
9. VISUAL SIGNALS
12. SCANNING
13. ORGANIZERS

Down:
2. ACTIVE READER
3. HIGHLIGHTING
4. OUTLINING
5. PRIOR KNOWLEDGE
6. PURPOSE
7. SUMMARIZING
10. ANNOTATING
11. SKIMMING
14. REVIEWING

review checklist

☐ Being an active reader involves using strategies before, during, and after you read to help you retain and use the information in the text.

☐ Before you read, you should assess your prior knowledge, set a purpose for your reading, and preview the text. (See 1a.)

☐ As you read, highlight and annotate to help you identify the writer's key ideas. (See 1b.)

☐ After you read, outlining, summarizing, reviewing, and self-quizzing can help you remember what you have read. (See 1c.)

☐ Once you have highlighted and annotated a text, you can write a response paragraph to record your reactions to the writer's ideas. (See 1d.)

2 Building Vocabulary for Reading and Writing

focus on reading and writing

List some things that you already know about taking standardized tests.
Later in this chapter, you will read and write about a passage on this topic.

In this chapter, you will learn to

- understand your vocabularies (2a)
- "know" words (2b)
- acquire new words (2c)
- use new words in your writing (2d)

Words are everywhere. Between the time you entered kindergarten and the time you entered the college classroom, you learned thousands of words. However, there are still many words left to learn. Learning these new words—and using those that you already know correctly and effectively—are important keys to becoming a better reader and writer.

In order to build a stronger vocabulary, you need to be aware of the different vocabularies you use, understand what it means to "know" a word, learn how to acquire new words, and practice using new words in your writing.

2a Understanding Your Vocabularies

When people refer to "vocabulary," they are actually talking about four separate vocabularies: a *listening vocabulary*, a *reading vocabulary*, a *speaking vocabulary*, and a *writing vocabulary*. If you want to be a better reader, writer, and learner, you need to work on improving all four of these vocabularies.

1. Your **listening vocabulary** consists of the words you hear daily—in conversation, on television, or in song lyrics. This is the first vocabulary that you develop as a child. Your listening vocabulary is part of your *receptive vocabulary*—the words you generally understand but may not know well enough to use.

2. Your **reading vocabulary**, which is also part of your receptive vocabulary, consists of the words you recognize when you read. It develops as you begin to learn to read, usually early in elementary school. This vocabulary is generally your largest; many words in your reading vocabulary are not part of your speaking or writing vocabularies. This is especially true of discipline-specific words such as *jurisprudence, tort, acidification, arbitrage, antigen, meniscus, conditioning, titration,* and *algorithm.*

3. Your **speaking vocabulary** consists of the words you use in conversation. It comes from interacting with people around you as you communicate orally. Your speaking vocabulary is part of your

expressive vocabulary—the words that you know well enough to use when you speak and write. (Your expressive vocabulary is generally smaller than your receptive vocabulary.)

4. Your **writing vocabulary** is also part of your expressive vocabulary. It consists of the words you use when you write, and it is the last vocabulary to develop. For most people, it is their most limited vocabulary because it is much more difficult to use a word effectively in writing than to recognize it when listening or reading. Many words in your speaking vocabulary are part of your writing vocabulary, but academic words—such as *simile*, *deduce*, *empirical*, *aesthetic*, and *paradigm*—are much more common in your writing vocabulary.

2b   "Knowing" Words

Achieving Full Knowledge

When you learn a new word, your ultimate goal is to be able to use it in all four of your vocabularies. In other words, you want to achieve **full knowledge** of the word—to recognize it in conversation, use it correctly when you speak, understand its meaning when you come across the word in your reading, and use it accurately in your writing.

Activating Your Schemata

People come to college with different degrees of knowledge. According to one theory, the knowledge you have is organized into individual units, each of which is called a **schema**. These *schemata* (plural of schema), or units of existing knowledge, help you understand new material, and they expand as you acquire this new information. In other words, as you read, you gain information from the text as well as from what you already know about the subject of the text. As you read further, the information that you have just acquired helps you understand and interpret new information. When you gain new knowledge, you create new schemata or expand (or revise) existing ones.

This concept holds true when you learn new words. When you first encounter a word, you create a schema for that word and expand it as you learn more about the word. Every time you encounter this word, you access the schema associated with it. As you see the word in different contexts, you add to your knowledge about how the word is used.

For example, when you look at the title of the following passage by Amy Tan, you might have some idea what the writer means by the words *mother tongue*. If so, you have automatically activated your prior knowledge—or schema—for that phrase as soon as you read it.

focus on reading and writing

The passage that follows is excerpted from "Mother Tongue," an essay by Amy Tan. (The full essay is included in Chapter 29, pp. 570–575.) In preparation for class discussion and writing that will be assigned later in this chapter, read the passage. Then, choose one of the following terms from the essay—a term that you already know—to use in Practice 2-1.

Terms: *sociologists, immigrant families, IQ tests, SAT, math*

FROM "MOTHER TONGUE"

Amy Tan

1   I think my mother's English almost had an effect on limiting my possibilities in life as well. Sociologists and linguists probably will tell you that a person's developing language skills are more influenced by peers. But I do think that the language spoken in the family, especially in immigrant families which are more insular, plays a large role in shaping the language of the child. And I believe that it affected my results on achievement tests, I.Q. tests, and the SAT. While my English skills were never judged as poor, compared to math, English could not be considered my strong suit. In grade school I did moderately well, getting perhaps B's, sometimes B-pluses, in English and scoring perhaps in the sixtieth or seventieth percentile on achievement tests. But those scores were not good enough to override the opinion that my true abilities lay in math and science, because in those areas I achieved A's and scored in the ninetieth percentile or higher.

2   This was understandable. Math is precise; there is only one correct answer. Whereas, for me at least, the answers on English tests were always a judgment call, a matter of opinion and personal experience. Those tests were constructed around items like fill-in-the-blank sentence completion, such as, "Even though Tom was _____, Mary thought he was _____." And the correct answer always seemed to be the most bland combinations of thoughts, for example, "Even though Tom was shy, Mary thought he was charming," with the grammatical structure "even though" limiting the correct answer to some sort of semantic opposites, so you wouldn't get answers like, "Even though Tom was foolish, Mary thought he was ridiculous." Well, according to my mother, there were very few limitations as to what Tom could have been and what Mary might have thought of him. So I never did well on tests like that.

The same was true with word analogies, pairs of words in 3
which you were supposed to find some sort of logical, semantic
relationship—for example, "*Sunset* is to *nightfall* as _____ is
to _____." And here you would be presented with a list of four
possible pairs, one of which showed the same kind of relationship:
red is to *stoplight*, *bus* is to *arrival*, *chill* is to *fever*, *yawn* is to *boring*:
Well, I could never think that way. I knew what the tests were ask-
ing, but I could not block out of my mind the images already created
by the first pair, "*sunset* is to *nightfall*"—and I would see a burst of
colors against a darkening sky, the moon rising, the lowering of a
curtain of stars. And all the other pairs of words—red, bus, stoplight, boring—just threw up a mass of confusing images, making it
impossible for me to sort out something as logical as saying: "A sunset precedes nightfall" is the same as "a chill precedes a fever." The
only way I would have gotten that answer right would have been to
imagine an associative situation, for example, my being disobedient
and staying out past sunset, catching a chill at night, which turns
into feverish pneumonia as punishment, which indeed did happen
to me.

PRACTICE

2-1   Activate your schemata for the term you chose from the Tan
passage. Write the term in the circle, and then list five pieces
of information you already know about this term.   *Answers will vary.*

1. _____
   _____
   _____

2. _____
   _____
   _____

3. _____
   _____
   _____

4. _____
   _____
   _____

5. _____
   _____
   _____

PRACTICE

2-2 Working with another student, read each other's lists and add information you know about both terms. Together, you will be building your schemata by adding to each other's knowledge of the word.

Understanding Denotations, Connotations, Synonyms, and Antonyms

To achieve full knowledge of a word—that is, to learn what a word means and how to use it—you need to understand the word's *denotations*, *connotations*, *synonyms*, and *antonyms*.

Denotations

The **denotation** of a word is its literal meaning—the definition of the word that you find in a dictionary. This **formal definition** has a three-part structure.

1. The word being defined
2. The general class to which the word belongs
3. The qualities or characteristics that distinguish the word from the other words in the class

TERM	CLASS	DIFFERENTIATION
A graphic novel	is a work of fiction	that tells its story through a series of pictures.
Democracy	is a form of government	in which supreme power rests with the people.
Geology	is a science	that deals with the study of the earth.

PRACTICE

2-3 Create your own formal definitions by filling in the following templates.

Answers will vary.

A disaster movie is _____ that _____

_____.

Happiness is _____ that _____

_____.

Teaching Tip
Because some students are visual learners, you might ask the class to create graphic templates for the definitions in Practice 2.3, using geometric shapes and lines and then copying the words and their definitions into their templates.

A tablet is ————————————— that ———————————

————————————————————————————————.

Connotations

The **connotations** of a word are its shared emotional associations or underlying meanings. For example, *angry* has the same denotation as *furious* and *livid*, but the words have different connotations, depending on who is speaking and why. Would you be angry, furious, or livid if someone wrecked your car? (It might depend on how old your car was.) Connotations can be positive or negative (*sunshine*, *peace*, and *rainbow* have positive connotations for most people), more or less forceful (*furious* is more forceful than *angry*), and sometimes neutral, depending on context.

Whenever you are in doubt about the connotation of a word, look up the word's definition in a dictionary. (It never hurts to double-check your understanding of a word's precise meaning.) Sometimes a word's connotation is quite different from its denotation. For example, even though the words *aggressive* and *assertive* have the same general denotations, their connotations are quite different: *aggressive* suggests that a person is pushy or hostile while *assertive* implies confidence and assurance.

PRACTICE

2-4   Look up each of the following word pairs in a dictionary. Then, working in small groups, consider how their connotations differ.

demonstration/riot

handicap/disability

illegal alien/undocumented worker

smile/smirk

thrifty/frugal

Synonyms and Antonyms

Another important aspect of learning words is becoming familiar with their synonyms and antonyms. **Synonyms** are words that have the same or similar meaning (*happy* and *euphoric*, for example). **Antonyms** are words that have opposite meanings (for example, *happy* and *distraught*).

Even though two words are synonyms, they may not have the same connotations. You may be happy, but not necessarily euphoric.

Teaching Tip
See if students can determine the meaning of the word *euphoric* based on the information they're given in the examples here.

Teaching Tip
Go online and show students all the vocabulary websites that are out there (www.dictionary.com, www.vocabsushi.com, and www.merriam-webster.com are just a few). Using a word from one of their lists, show students how to look up words in both an online dictionary and a thesaurus. Point out that many websites also have a pronunciation key that will allow them to hear the word pronounced correctly.

PRACTICE
2-5 Look at the following list of words and think of as many synonyms and antonyms as you can for each word. Next, working in pairs, decide if each synonym and antonym has generally positive or negative connotations. The first item has been filled in for you.

1. **Smart**
   a. Synonyms: _clever; intelligent_
      Connotations: _positive_
   b. Antonyms: _stupid; uninformed_
      Connotations: _negative_

2. **Slim**
   a. Synonyms: _skinny; slender_
      Connotations: _negative; positive_
   b. Antonyms: _fat; wide_
      Connotations: _negative_

3. **Enthusiastic**
   a. Synonyms: _eager; excited_
      Connotations: _positive_
   b. Antonyms: _apathetic; indifferent_
      Connotations: _negative_

4. **Fake**
   a. Synonyms: _artificial; unauthentic_
      Connotations: _negative_
   b. Antonyms: _genuine; real_
      Connotations: _positive_

5. **Young**
   a. Synonyms: _youthful; immature_
      Connotations: _positive/neutral; negative_
   b. Antonyms: _old; mature_
      Connotations: _neutral/negative; neutral/positive_

focus on reading and writing

What words in the Amy Tan passage on pages 38–39 are not familiar to you? List those words on the lines below. Then, look up the words, and supply some synonyms and antonyms for each. Do the synonyms have the same connotations as the original words? If not, how are they different?

2c Acquiring New Words

Now that you understand what it means to "know" a word, you will want to learn how to achieve full knowledge of the words you come across in your college classes and textbooks. We acquire new vocabulary words from five sources: *reference tools*; *context clues*; *coursework*; *roots, prefixes, and suffixes*; and *reading*.

> **WORD POWER**
>
> **acquire** to gain through experience

Learning from Reference Tools

Many people believe that looking up words in a dictionary is the easiest way to learn new words, but other reference tools—such as a thesaurus and the Internet—can also help you acquire new vocabulary words.

Using a Dictionary

A **dictionary** is often the first resource for defining new words. Using a print dictionary is helpful, as long as you know how to spell the word. Many online dictionaries, however, have a spell-check feature that enables you to find a word even if you don't know its exact spelling.

Although some dictionaries list the oldest definition first (often preceded by the word *archaic*), many list the most common usage first. Some dictionaries also tell you whether a word's usage is slang or formal. Be sure to read all the listed definitions so that you can identify the definition that best fits the **context** in which you found the word.

The **boldfaced** words after the definition tell you the other parts of speech that can be formed from the word. These are useful because they show you how to change the word from a verb to a noun or from an adjective to an adverb. (The parts of speech are abbreviated: *v.* for verb, *n.* for noun, *adj.* for adjective, and *adv.* for adverb.)

Now, suppose you encountered the unfamiliar word *portage* in the following sentence.

As they stood on the shore, they thought the *portage* looked daunting, but it had to be completed before the journey could continue.

The online version of Merriam-Webster's Collegiate Dictionary, at merriamwebster.com, lists the following definitions of *portage*.[1]

por·tage   noun

1 : the labor of carrying or transporting
2 *archaic* : the cost of carrying : porterage
3 *a* : the carrying of boats or goods overland from one body of water to another or around an obstacle (as a rapids)
  b : the route followed in making such a transfer

Which definition of *portage* best corresponds to how the word is used in the example sentence? Write the sentence on the lines below.

_____

_____

Keep in mind that a dictionary records the meanings that occur most often in speech and writing. If a word is new or is in the process of acquiring new meanings, it may not be listed.

Using a Thesaurus

A **thesaurus** lists words in groups of **synonyms** (words that have the same meanings) and sometimes also **antonyms** (words that have opposite meanings). By consulting a thesaurus, you can vary your vocabulary and make your writing more interesting. Remember that words that seem to mean the same thing will often have subtle differences in meanings, so you should not automatically assume you can substitute one word you find in a thesaurus for another.

For example, if you wanted to find a synonym for the word *daunting*, which appears in the example sentence above, you could consult an online thesaurus, where you might find the following suggested synonyms.

Synonyms: intimidating, discouraging, disheartening, dismaying

Teaching Tip
Remind students about denotation and connotation. Have them review the different words that could be used in place of *daunting* and discuss how each substitution might change the meaning of the sentence.

[1]From Merriam-Webster's Collegiate Dictionary, 11th Edition, © 2013 by Merriam-Webster, Inc.

Which of the synonyms for *daunting* do you think would work best in the sentence at the top of page 44? On the lines below, recopy the sentence, replacing the word *daunting* with the synonym you chose.

_____

_____

Using the Internet

Many websites and cell-phone applications can help you acquire words (www.google.com; www.dictionary.com; www.vocabsushi.com). If you download one of the free phone apps, such as the Merriam-Webster Dictionary app, you will always have a dictionary and a thesaurus at your fingertips. One thing to keep in mind, however, is that you will not be able to use websites or smartphone apps during exams; therefore, you should buy a college-level dictionary and a thesaurus for these occasions.

Learning from Context Clues

bedfordstmartins.com /forw LearningCurve > Vocabulary

You can often figure out the meaning of a word by looking at its **context**—the words around it. **Context clues** are hints in the text that can help you figure out the meaning of unfamiliar words that you encounter as you read. If you learn the different types of context clues, you will be able to determine the meanings of words without having to constantly stop to look them up. Learning to use context clues is especially important for reading textbooks, which contain many subject-specific words.

There are four types of context clues: *definition/synonym clues*, *example clues*, *general information clues*, and *contrast clues*.

Definition/Synonym Clues

Definition/synonym clues signal a definition of a word. These types of clues are common in nonfiction writing, such as textbooks or journal articles. Definition/synonym clues can often be identified by their use of certain words (*or*, *means*, *such as*) or by parentheses or pairs of commas or dashes.

> #### Example
>
> The Gates Foundation's *philanthropy*—charitable donations to numerous educational institutions and AIDS research—is impressive.

Based on this definition/synonym context clue, what do you think *philanthropy* means?

Example Clues

Example clues state the word or concept and then list examples of that word or concept. These clues can often be identified by their use of a colon or by their use of certain expressions (*including*, *such as*, *for example*).

Example

> Many once deadly *maladies*, such as polio, diphtheria, and tetanus, have been wiped out in the United States by vaccination programs.

Based on this example context clue, what do you think *maladies* means?

General Information Clues

General information clues provide readers with the ideas surrounding a specific word or concept; readers must piece the ideas together to determine the word or concept's definition. These are the hardest clues to use and understand. You will likely have to read some sentences that come before or after the word or concept in order to understand the definition.

Example

> One of my coworkers is a *sycophant*. She constantly flatters our supervisor. When he looks tired, she tells him that he looks great. When she comes back from lunch, she brings him his favorite latte. Once, she even left work early to pick up office supplies for him. She thinks she's helping her career, but most of us think that our supervisor is simply taking advantage of her.

Based on these *general information* context clues, what do you think *sycophant* means?

Contrast Clues

Contrast clues help readers figure out the meaning of an unfamiliar word by using a word that has the opposite meaning. Contrast clues are sometimes called **antonym clues** because they are often the word's antonym. Words and phrases such as *however, in contrast, unlike,* and *but* can indicate that another word has the opposite meaning of the unknown word.

Example

> For years, coaches praised his athletic skills, but more recently they have begun to *disparage* him.

Based on this *contrast* context clue, what do you think *disparage* means?

Teaching Tip
You might ask students to choose a textbook excerpt from another class and identify how the excerpt uses context clues.

PRACTICE

2-6   Read the following excerpts from two professional essays included in this book, and use context clues to help you determine the definitions of the boldfaced words. Then, identify the type of context clues you used for each word.

1. The women smirked at the **acrid** words—she had been equally harsh to all of them when they first joined the family. Grandmother had taken her lumps too: After she married my grandfather, her mother-in-law had harassed her on the ways of making a proper dumpling. Now Grandmother reigned over her kitchen; it was a classroom and **crucible.**— from "My Grandmother's Dumpling" by Amy Ma (pp. 298–304)

   Definition: *deeply bitter*

   Context clue type: *Definition/Symptom Clue*

   Definition: *a place that forces people to change or make difficult decisions*

   Context clue type: *General Information Clue*

2. The early stages of the process can be a bit **malodorous**, so it's recommended that you follow the ancient custom of relocating to a well-ventilated tent. (You'll have trouble breathing anyway, since tradition also prescribes that you wear a jackal-head mask in honor of Anubis, god of the dead.)—from "How to Mummify a Pharaoh" by Adam Goodheart (pp. 596–597)

   Definition: *having a bad smell*

   Context clue type: *General Information Clue*

Learning from Your Coursework

You spend a good deal of time in college listening to lectures and reading textbooks, so it makes sense that you learn new words from these hours of listening, reading, and taking notes. In order to learn about a given **discipline** or field of study, you must be able to understand **discipline-specific words**—the key words experts use in discussing the discipline.

For example, in a communications course, you will learn the term *rhetoric* and what that means in the context of persuasion. You might hear this word initially in a lecture, and then come across it in a chapter of the textbook. After these encounters with the word, you should realize that you need to learn its meaning in order to understand and write about the course's subject matter.

To learn the meaning of discipline-specific words, you can use three different strategies: *concept cards*, *mnemonics*, and *visual cues*.

Using Concept Cards

Concept cards can be 3- by 5-inch index cards or online flash cards that you create with a smartphone or tablet. On the front of each card, you write the word you want to learn, its part of speech, and its source (the sentence in which you found the word); on the back you record the definition,

Teaching Tip
Show students the sites that they can use to make their own concept cards (e.g., quizlet.com, dictionary.com, and flashcardmachine .com). Show them how to register for the sites and how to access and construct the cards.

synonym, antonym, and an image to help you remember the definition of the word. Studying concept cards can help you master the words you want to know.

Concept cards are useful because they are portable. You can study them on a bus, in a doctor's office waiting room, or whenever you have a few spare moments.

Example

Front of card   *Back of card*

	Part of Speech
WORD	
Source	

Definition: (find this in the dictionary)
Synonyms: (find these in the thesaurus)
Antonyms: (you can often find these in a thesaurus or by using online search tools)
Image: (you can either draw this or find it on the Internet)

Teaching Tip
Allow students time in class to fill in the rest of this card. If they work in pairs, you can ask each pair to share with the class what they wrote.

PRACTICE
2-7   Use the information you have learned in this section of the chapter to fill in the back of the concept card below for the word *cohesion*.

Front of card   *Back of card*

	noun
cohesion	
"Units will not see an improvement in physical readiness, nor will cohesion improve." (p. 613, from "Why Women Soldiers Don't Belong on the Front Lines")	

Definition: a condition in which people or things are closely united
Synonyms: unity, coherence
Antonyms: incoherence
Image:

Using Mnemonics

Mnemonics are strategies such as short rhymes, memorable phrases, or acronyms (new words created from the first letters of other words) that help you remember information. They do this by tying new information to images or concepts that you can easily remember. The acronym *FANBOYS*, for example, is a mnemonic designed to help you remember the coordinating conjunctions *for, and, nor, but, or, yet,* and *so.* Another mnemonic is the familiar rhyme, "*I* before *E* except after *C.*" You can invent your own mnemonics to help you remember words. For example, to learn the word *ingot* (a block of metal), you could remember "*I got* a metal block."

PRACTICE

2-8 Working in pairs, try to create mnemonics to help you remember the meanings of two new words from this chapter.

Teaching Tip
Have each pair share their mnemonics with the class.

Using Visual Clues

Visual clues are pictures or images that help you to remember a word's definition. By representing the word with a picture, you are more easily able to fix the word in your mind and remember it. For example, if you want to remember the definition of the word *amphibian* ("a cold-blooded class of animals, such as frogs or toads") you could associate it with a picture of a frog.

Don Farral/Getty Images

You can draw a picture on the back of a 3- by 5-inch note card or cut and paste an image from a website to the back of an electronic flash card.

FYI

You can often find useful images by entering the word you want to remember in the Google search box and then clicking on the Images tab at the top of the search results page.

PRACTICE

2-9 Look up the meaning of each word below in a dictionary, and then think of a visual clue that will help you remember it. Then, find or draw your own visual clue for each word. Finally, make a concept card for each word, including your visual clues.

pyrotechnics

ego

sequence

vocational

referendum

introspection

bedfordstmartins.com
/forw LearningCurve >
Vocabulary

Learning from Roots, Prefixes, and Suffixes

English has taken many of its words from other languages, such as Latin and French. An important (and effective) strategy for learning new words is learning word parts: **roots**, **prefixes**, and **suffixes**. When you come across an unknown word, you can attempt to determine the meaning of the word by identifying its parts. By learning common roots, prefixes, and suffixes, you can often figure out the meanings of words simply by using these word-part clues.

Teaching Tip
You might ask students to memorize the common roots, prefixes, and suffixes listed in this section for homework, and then quiz them in class.

Using Roots

Many English words are formed by taking the basic part of a word—called a **root**—and adding prefixes and suffixes to it. The chart below lists some of the most common roots, their meanings, and examples of words that include those roots.

ROOT	DEFINITION	EXAMPLE
aqua	water	aquarium
auto	self	automatic
bene	good	benefit
bio	life	biology
chrono	time	chronology
graph	writing	graphic
hydr	water	hydration
jud	judge	judicial
man	hand	manual
nym	name	antonym
pater	father	paternal
phon	sound	telephone
port	to carry	portable
psych	mind	psychology
spect	to look	inspect
struct	to build	construct
tele	far off	television
vac	empty	vacuum

Because roots of English words come from many different languages, it is sometimes helpful when you encounter a new word to think of other words that have the same root and that you already know the meaning of. For example, if you know that *vacuum* has the root *vac*, which means "empty," you can figure out that when you *vacate* an apartment, you leave it "empty of occupants."

PRACTICE

2-10 Working in pairs, find the roots in the list on page 50. Then, try to determine the meaning of each word, and write that meaning on the lines. Finally, look up the word in a dictionary, and see how close you came to the actual definition.

Answers will vary.

1. **benevolent:** —————————————————————————————————

2. **chronic:** ——————————————————————————————————

3. **evacuate:** —————————————————————————————————

4. **export:** ———————————————————————————————————

5. **biography:** ————————————————————————————————

Using Prefixes

Prefixes are letters or groups of letters that have a specific meaning and are added before a root (as in *pre-*, which means "before") to change its meaning. For example, the prefix *contra-* means "against." If you see this prefix in front of the root *dict*, which means "speak," then you can figure out the meaning of the word *contradict*: "to speak against, or in opposition to." By learning the meanings of some common prefixes, you can determine the meanings of many unfamiliar words. The chart below lists the most common prefixes, their meanings, and examples of words that include those prefixes.

PREFIX	DEFINITION	EXAMPLE
anti	against	antibiotic
bi	two	bimonthly
con	together	congregation
contra	against	contradict
ex	out	exhale
inter	between	international
intra	within	intramural
mal	bad, wrong	malware
mini	small	miniature
multi	many	multiplex
non	not	nonpartisan
pent	five	pentagon
post	after	postgame
pre	before	prehistoric
semi	half	semicircle
super	above	superior
trans	across	transmit
uni	one	unity

PRACTICE

2-11   Choose five prefixes from the list on page 51. Then, list as many words as you can that contain each of the prefixes. If you don't know the exact meaning of a word, look it up in a dictionary.

Using Suffixes

Suffixes are groups of letters that are added to the end of a word, often changing its part of speech. When the part of speech changes, the word's meaning changes as well. For example, *educate* is a verb meaning "to give moral or social instruction to." If you add the suffix *-tion* to the verb *educate*, it becomes the noun *education*, meaning "the process of giving or receiving instruction." (Like prefixes, suffixes cannot stand alone as words.) English has very few suffixes that form verbs and adverbs; a large number of suffixes, however, form nouns and adjectives. The chart below lists some common suffixes, their meanings, and examples of words that include those suffixes.

VERB SUFFIX	DEFINITION	EXAMPLE
-en	to cause or become	cheapen
-ate	cause to be	activate
-ify, -fy	to make or cause	magnify
-ize	to make, to give	memorize

ADVERB SUFFIX

The only regular adverb suffix is *–ly*, as in *quickly* or *wisely*.

ADJECTIVE SUFFIX	DEFINITION	EXAMPLE
-al	capable	comical
-ic	pertaining to	democratic
-ly	at specific intervals	hourly
-ous	full of	porous
-less	lack of	toothless
-ish	having the qualities of	ticklish

NOUN SUFFIX	DEFINITION	EXAMPLE
-ance, -ence	the quality of	competence
-arium	place for	aquarium
-ary	place for	dictionary
-ics	the science or art of	economics
-ism	quality or doctrine of	capitalism
-ology	the study of	biology

PRACTICE

2-12 Consult the chart on page 52 to help you determine what part of speech each suffix below creates. Then, think of an example (other than the one listed in the chart) of a word that uses that suffix.

1. *-ism*

   Part of speech: *noun*_____ Example word: *Answers will vary.*_____

2. *-ly*

   Part of speech: *adverb*_____ Example word: *Answers will vary.*_____

3. *-ish*

   Part of speech: *adjective*_____ Example word: *Answers will vary.*_____

4. *-ic*

   Part of speech: *adjective*_____ Example word: *Answers will vary.*_____

5. *-ize*

   Part of speech: *verb*_____ Example word: *Answers will vary.*_____

Learning from Your Reading

All the strategies previously discussed are effective, but the single best way to improve your vocabulary is by reading as much as possible. Finding time for reading becomes challenging when you have large amounts of work for each course as well as other responsibilities, such as working or raising a family. However, you can improve your vocabulary by setting realistic reading goals. Try reading one magazine article a day, subscribing to an online newspaper, or regularly reading a respected blog.

Keep in mind that reading passively will not improve your vocabulary. You need to look up and study any new words—and, ideally, use them in conversation and in writing. As you read, keep a list of the words you don't know. Create your own dictionary that lists each word, its definition, and the sentence in which the word appeared.

Here is an example of an entry you might make in your dictionary.

Word	Sentence	Definition
malodorous	The early stages of the process can be a bit malodorous, so it's recommended that you follow the ancient custom of relocating to a well-ventilated tent.	foul smelling

You can keep your dictionary in a computer file or in the front of your binder, and you can add to it each time you come across a word you do not know, either in your reading or during a class.

FYI

Tips for Building Your Vocabulary

Keep the following points in mind as you go about learning new words.

- It takes time to learn new words.
- In order to truly know a word, you have to be able to use it in your reading, writing, and speaking.
- It is all right to know only the most commonly used definition of a word; you don't have to know all of its meanings and usages.
- If you encounter an unfamiliar word while reading, you don't always have to stop and look it up; you can use the word's context to help you. However, if it is a word in a textbook for a class, you should be sure you know exactly what it means because it may be key to your understanding of the subject matter.

2d   Using New Words in Your Writing

As you study new words and their meanings and start to feel comfortable with your new vocabulary, you may find yourself using some of these words in conversation or in writing. This is exactly what you should be doing. Remember, the ultimate goal of your vocabulary-building process is **full knowledge** of a word: not just the ability to understand a word when you hear it, use it correctly in conversation, and figure out its meaning when you read it, but also to use it correctly—and with confidence—in your writing.

Full Knowledge

"I can use this word in my speaking, reading, and writing vocabularies."

↑

Meaning Knowledge

"I understand the connotations, synonyms, and antonyms of this word."

↑

Denotation Knowledge

"I can tell someone else the definition of this word."

↑

Some Knowledge

"I have seen it or heard it, but I can't define it."

↑

No Knowledge

"I have never seen it or heard it."

PRACTICE

2-13   Below are six words you have read in this chapter's discussions of vocabulary building. Use the context in which each word appears to help you understand its meaning. Then, use each word in a new sentence.

standardized (p. 35)	context (p. 43)
ultimate (p. 37)	discipline (p. 47)
reference (p. 43)	mnemonic (p. 48)

focus on reading and writing

Reread the list you made at the start of this chapter (about things you know about taking standardized tests) and also reread the passage from Amy Tan's essay "Mother Tongue" (pp. 38–39). Then, **write** a response paragraph discussing your experiences with taking standardized tests. How are your experiences like and unlike Tan's? Did your family's language play a role in your performance on these tests? If so, how? Try to use two or three of the new words you have learned in this chapter in your paragraph. When you have finished, TEST what you have written.

REVIEW ACTIVITY

Graphic Organizer: *Building Vocabulary*

Chapter 2 identified the different types of vocabularies and explained how to build your vocabulary for reading and writing. Using the graphic organizer on page 58, fill in the main concepts presented in the chapter, and provide examples as required.

COLLABORATIVE ACTIVITY

Create (or find) a visual for each unfamiliar word you identified in the box on page 43. (For example, for the word *percentile*, you might draw a percent sign.) Then, trade your pictures with another student, and have your classmate try to guess which words you are representing.

Teaching Tip
You can also have students work in pairs and then assign each pair a word. Have them do the collaborative activity and then post their drawings on the board. Number the drawings and have the other pairs guess which word each drawing represents.

The four types of vocabularies

1. Listening

2. Reading

3. Speaking

4. Writing

These vocabularies all influence my: *ability to communicate effectively and to understand the verbal and written words of others.*

I can improve my vocabularies by: *expanding my schemata; understanding denotation and connotation; accessing synonyms and antonyms; and acquiring new words.*

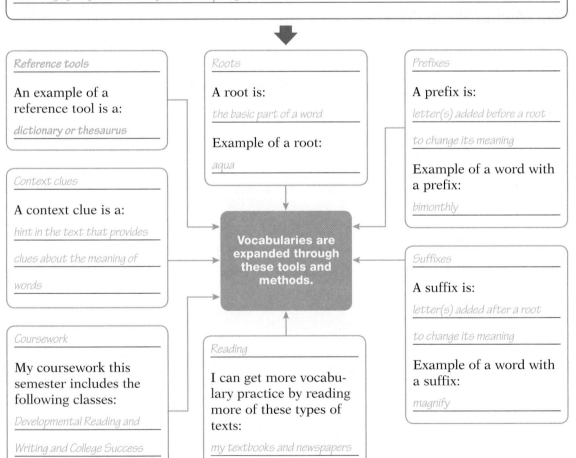

Reference tools

An example of a reference tool is a:

dictionary or thesaurus

Context clues

A context clue is a:

hint in the text that provides

clues about the meaning of

words

Coursework

My coursework this semester includes the following classes:

Developmental Reading and

Writing and College Success

Strategies

Roots

A root is:

the basic part of a word

Example of a root:

aqua

Reading

I can get more vocabulary practice by reading more of these types of texts:

my textbooks and newspapers

Vocabularies are expanded through these tools and methods.

Prefixes

A prefix is:

letter(s) added before a root

to change its meaning

Example of a word with a prefix:

bimonthly

Suffixes

A suffix is:

letter(s) added after a root

to change its meaning

Example of a word with a suffix:

magnify

review checklist

☐ You have listening, reading, speaking, and writing vocabularies, and you must work on each one if you want to improve your overall vocabulary. (See 2a.)

☐ "Knowing" a word means you are able to use that word in your listening, reading, speaking, and writing vocabularies. (See 2b.)

☐ You acquire new words through reference tools; context clues; coursework; roots, prefixes, and suffixes; and reading. (See 2c.)

☐ As you build your vocabulary, it is important for you to practice using new words correctly in your writing. (See 2d.)

3 Understanding the Writing Process

focus on reading and writing

Think about the different jobs you've had and the challenges you faced in them. Then, list a few ideas about each job. Later in this chapter, you will **read** an essay about a challenging job and **write** an essay about the most difficult job you've ever had.

In this chapter, you will learn to

- understand essay structure (3a)
- move from assignment to topic (3b)
- find ideas to write about (3c)
- state your thesis (3d)
- choose supporting points (3e)
- make an outline (3f)
- draft your essay (3g)
- TEST and revise your essay (3h–3i)
- edit and proofread your essay (3j–3k)

Writing is not something that you do just in school; writing is a life skill. If you can write clearly, you can express your ideas convincingly to others—in school, on the job, and in your community.

- In college, you often write in response to reading—for example, in essays, on exams, or in research papers.
- At work, you might write a memo, a letter, a proposal, or a report.
- As a member of your community, you might write a letter or email to a government agency or to the editor of your local newspaper.
- In your personal life, you might respond to emails, post on social-networking sites and blogs, and text friends.

As you can see, writing is an important activity. If you can write, you can communicate; if you can communicate effectively, you have a good chance of succeeding in school and beyond.

When you write an essay, you begin by planning what you will write about and then move on to organizing your ideas, drafting, TESTing and revising, and editing and proofreading. In this chapter, you will learn strategies that you can use as you move through the writing process.

Step 1: Planning

3a Understanding Essay Structure

In your college courses, you are frequently asked to write an **essay**—a group of paragraphs on a single subject.

- The essay's first paragraph—the **introduction**—begins with opening remarks that create interest and closes with a **thesis statement** that presents the essay's main idea. (For more on introductions, see 4a.)

- The **body** of the essay consists of several **body paragraphs** that support the thesis statement. Each body paragraph begins with a **topic sentence** that states the main idea of the paragraph. The other sentences in the paragraph support the topic sentence with **evidence**—details and examples. (For more on body paragraphs, see 4b.)

- **Transitional words and phrases** lead readers from sentence to sentence and from paragraph to paragraph. (For a list of transitions, see 4b.)

- The last paragraph—the **conclusion**—ends the essay. The conclusion often includes a **summary statement** that reinforces the thesis. (For more on conclusions, see 4c.)

Teaching Tip
Refer students to the introduction of this book for more on TESTing essays.

FYI

The first letters of these four key elements—Thesis statement, Evidence, Summary statement, and Transitions—spell **TEST**. As you begin the revision process, you can **TEST** the essays you write to see whether they include all the elements of an effective essay.

Teaching Tip
Take this opportunity to explain thesis-and-support structure to students.

Teaching Tip
Be sure students understand that an essay can have more than three body paragraphs.

Essay

Introduction
> **Opening remarks** introduce the subject being discussed in the essay. The **thesis statement** presents the essay's main idea.

First body paragraph
> The **topic sentence** states the essay's first point.
> **Evidence** supports the topic sentence.
> **Transitional words and phrases** connect the examples and details and show how they are related.

Second body paragraph
> The **topic sentence** states the essay's second point.
> **Evidence** supports the topic sentence.
> **Transitional words and phrases** connect the examples and details and show how they are related.

The **topic sentence** states the essay's third point.
Evidence supports the topic sentence.
Transitional words and phrases connect the examples and details and show how they are related.

Third body paragraph

The **summary statement** reinforces the thesis, summarizing the essay's main idea. **Concluding remarks** present the writer's final thoughts on the subject.

Conclusion

Teaching Tip
You might want to tell students that although the model student essays in this book show the summary statement as the first sentence of the conclusion, it can also appear elsewhere in the conclusion.

The following essay by Jennifer Chu illustrates the structure of an essay. (Note that transitional words and phrases are shaded.)

Becoming Chinese American

Although I was born in Hong Kong, I have spent most of my life in the United States. However, my parents have always made sure that I did not forget my roots. They always tell stories of what it was like to live in Hong Kong. To make sure my brothers and sisters and I know what is happening in China, my parents subscribe to Chinese cable TV. When we were growing up, we would watch the celebration of the Chinese New Year, the news from Asia, and Chinese movies and music videos. As a result, even though I am an American, I value many parts of traditional Chinese culture.

Introduction

Thesis statement

The Chinese language is an important part of my life as a Chinese American. Unlike some of my Chinese friends, I do not think the Chinese language is unimportant or embarrassing. First, I feel that it is my duty as a Chinese American to learn Chinese so that I can pass it on to my children. In addition, knowing Chinese enables me to communicate with my relatives. Because my parents and grandparents do not speak English well, Chinese is our main form of communication. Finally, Chinese helps me identify with my culture. When I speak Chinese, I feel connected to a culture that is over five thousand years old. Without the Chinese language, I would not be who I am.

Topic sentence (states essay's first point)

First body paragraph

Evidence (supports topic sentence)

Chinese food is another important part of my life as a Chinese American. One reason for this is that everything we Chinese people eat has a history and a meaning. At a birthday meal, for example, we serve long noodles and buns in the shape of peaches. This is because we believe that long noodles represent long life and that peaches are served in heaven. Another reason is that to

Topic sentence (states essay's second point)

Second body paragraph

Evidence (supports topic sentence)

Chinese people, food is a way of reinforcing ties between family and friends. For instance, during a traditional Chinese wedding ceremony, the bride and the groom eat nine of everything. This is because the number nine stands for the Chinese words "together forever." By taking part in this ritual, the bride and groom start their marriage by making Chinese customs a part of their life together.

Topic sentence (states essay's third point)

Third body paragraph

Religion is the most important part of my life as a Chinese American. At various times during the year, Chinese religious festivals bring together the people I care about the most. During Chinese New Year, my whole family goes to the temple, where we say prayers and welcome others with traditional New Year's greetings. After leaving the temple, we all go to Chinatown and eat dim sum until the lion dance starts. As the colorful lion dances its way down the street, people beat drums and throw firecrackers to drive off any evil spirits that may be around. Later that night, parents give children gifts of money in red envelopes that symbolize joy and happiness in the coming year.

Evidence (supports topic sentence)

Summary statement (reinforces essay's thesis)

Conclusion

My family has taught me how important it is to hold on to my Chinese culture. When I was six, my parents sent me to a Chinese-American grade school. My teachers thrilled me with stories of Fa Mulan, the Shang Dynasty, and the Moon God. I will never forget how happy I was when I realized how special it is to be Chinese. This is how I want my own children to feel. I want them to be proud of who they are and to pass their language, history, and culture on to the next generation.

PRACTICE

3-1 Following is an essay written by Aimee Groth for *Business Insider* about her experience working at Starbucks. Read the essay, and then answer the questions that follow it.

WHY WORKING AT STARBUCKS FOR THREE WEEKS WAS THE TOUGHEST JOB I'VE EVER HAD

Aimee Groth

A few months ago, I had the opportunity to work for Starbucks as a barista. I had recently moved to New York City, and I was freelancing at the time. But I had to get a part-time job in order to pay next month's rent. So one afternoon, I printed off a stack of resumes, and hand-delivered them to nearly 30 Starbucks in Lower Manhattan and one in Brooklyn. Only one manager called me back: the one from Brooklyn, just a few blocks from my apartment—and the last store I visited. She offered me the job at $10/hour; and if I worked part-time for three months, I'd be eligible for health insurance. I'd later find out that the store is located next to the busiest transit hub in Brooklyn, which makes it the busiest Starbucks outside of Manhattan. My initial idea of working a leisurely part-time job was completely false. This was going to be hard work—and a lot of it.

My first day was deceptively easy—watching videos of Starbucks CEO Howard Schultz on the store's laptop with my fellow three trainees, and taste-testing coffee and tea. We had some pamphlets that explained the drinks, and our task was to memorize all of them—including some several dozen variations of shots, sizes and flavors. We tried making a few of these with our trainers at the bar, but it wasn't easy. There was usually a steady stream of 20-some people waiting in line, and there simply wasn't the space or environment to train properly. It was always chaotic, with several people on the floor, calling orders, shifting from station to station, and asking you to get out of the way. Not to mention 10 customers waiting at the end of the bar for their drinks.

My first real 7:30 a.m. shift was jarring. The intensity of what goes on behind the counter is simply not visible from the customer's point of view. During the peak morning hours, we'd work through around 110 people every half hour with seven employees on the floor. Since there was no chance my new colleagues—or "partners," as Starbucks calls its employees—and I would ever memorize all the drinks, we handled everything else: brewing and changing coffees (staying on top of which ones are decaf, light and bold roasts, while rotating them via Starbucks' "coffee cadence" using 2-minute timers and grinding the beans, having them all prepared to brew—and never leaving one pot sitting longer than 30 minutes without dumping, since it's no longer "fresh"), marking drinks (there's a complicated shorthand that you've got to memorize, while translating what a customer is saying into "Starbucks speak" and calling it properly), rotating pastries, the food case, and tossing hot items into the oven—all while managing the register. Just as I was tempted to remind my coworkers that they were new once, too, I wanted to tell customers that I was way over-qualified for this job, and hoped they'd see me on the street in normal clothes, not in khakis, a black T-shirt, bright-green apron and baseball cap.

On my third day, my boss handed my fellow trainee—who would later disappear after a 10-minute break never to return—and me a mop and supplies to clean the bathroom, because the toilet was broken. It turned out not to be so horrible, but again, I quickly learned to swallow my pride.

We got two 10-minute breaks and one unpaid 30-minute break for every 8 hours on the floor. There we'd have to decide between running next door to use the restroom (because ours always had a line of customers in front of it), quickly eating a bag lunch (there was never time to stand in line and buy something from the store), or making a cell phone call. If you're lucky, you got to sit down on the one chair in the break room, or on the ladder, because there were never any open seats in the store.

Some of my coworkers were more demanding than others. Most were nice and welcoming. And there were office politics. On more than one occasion I walked into the break room to see someone crying, or talking about other coworkers. I mostly avoided this, until what would be my last week on the job. I told my boss that I got a new, full-time job, and could work until I started at *Business Insider*. But the next day my name disappeared from the schedule.

For many people, service industry jobs are not a supplementary income or short-term solution. And hats off to them—especially those who do it without even complaining.

1. Underline the essay's thesis statement.

2. Underline the topic sentence of each body paragraph.

3. What point does the first body paragraph make? What evidence supports this point?

4. What point does the second body paragraph make? What evidence supports this point?

5. What point does the third body paragraph make? What evidence supports this point?

6. What point does the fourth body paragraph make? What evidence supports this point?

7. What point does the fifth body paragraph make? What evidence supports this point?

8. What transitions does the essay include? How do they connect the essay's ideas?

9. Does this essay have a clear summary statement? If so, what is it? If not, write one on the lines below.

Answers will vary.

3b   Moving from Assignment to Topic

Many essays you write in college begin as **assignments** given to you by your instructors. Before you focus on any assignment, however, you should take time to think about your **purpose** (what you want to accomplish by writing your essay) and your **audience** (the people who will read your essay). Once you have considered these issues, you are ready to move on to thinking about the specifics of your assignment.

Teaching Tip
Refer students to 5a for more on audience and purpose.

The following assignments are typical of those you might be given in a composition class.

- Discuss some things you would change about your school.
- What can college students do to improve the environment?
- Discuss an important decision you made during the past few years.

Because these assignments are so general, you need to narrow them before you can start to write. What specific things would you change? Exactly what could you do to improve the environment? Answering these questions will help you narrow these assignments into **topics** that you can write about.

ASSIGNMENT	TOPIC
Discuss some things you would change about your school.	Three things I would change to improve the quality of life on campus
What can college students do to improve the environment?	The campus recycling project

Jared White, a student in a first-year composition course, was given the following assignment.

ASSIGNMENT

Discuss an important decision you made during the past few years.

Jared narrowed this assignment to the following topic.

TOPIC

Deciding to go back to school

In the rest of this chapter, you will be following Jared's writing process.

PRACTICE

3-2 Decide whether the following topics are narrow enough for an essay of five or six paragraphs. If a topic is suitable, write *OK* in the blank. If it is not, write in the blank a revised version of the same topic that is narrow enough for a brief essay.

Examples

Successful strategies for quitting smoking _____*OK*_____

Horror movies _____*1950s Japanese monster movies*_____

1. Violence in American public schools _____*Answers will vary.*_____

 Example: the need for metal detectors in a local high school

2. Ways to improve your study skills _____*OK*_____

_____

3. Using pets as therapy for nursing-home patients _____*OK*_____

_____

4. Teachers _____*Answers will vary.*_____

 Example: qualities of an effective teacher

5. Safe ways to lose weight _____*OK*_____

_____

decide on a topic

Look back at the Focus on Reading and Writing prompt on page 60. To find a topic you can write about, you need to decide which job to focus on. Begin by reviewing your list of ideas about the different jobs you've had.

FYI

Visit the Study Guides and Strategies website (studygs.net /writing/prewriting.htm) to learn how to use one of the graphic organizers or to find other information about the writing process.

3c   Finding Ideas to Write About

Before you start writing about a topic, you need to find out what you have to say about it. Sometimes ideas may come to you easily. More often, you will have to use specific strategies—such as *freewriting, brainstorming, keeping a journal,* or *clustering*—to help you come up with ideas.

Teaching Tip
Tell students that they do not have to use all of these strategies every time they write.

Freewriting

When you **freewrite**, you write for a set period of time—perhaps five minutes—without stopping, and you keep freewriting even if what you are writing doesn't seem to have a point or a direction. Your goal is to relax and let ideas flow without worrying whether or not they are related—or even if they make sense. Sometimes you can freewrite without a topic in mind, but at other times, you can focus on a specific topic. This is called **focused freewriting**.

When you finish freewriting, read what you have written. Then, underline any ideas that you think you might be able to use. If you find an idea that you want to explore further, freewrite again, using that idea as a starting point.

The following focused freewriting was written by Jared White on the topic "deciding to go back to school."

Deciding to go back to school. When I graduated high school, I swore I'd never go back to school. Hated it. Couldn't wait to get out. What was I thinking? How was I supposed to support myself? My dad's friend needed help. He taught me how to paint houses. I made good money, but it was boring. I couldn't picture myself doing it forever. Even though I knew I was going to have to go back to school, I kept putting off the decision. Maybe I was lazy. Maybe I was scared—probably both. I had this fear of being turned down. How could someone who had bad grades all through high school go to college? Also, I'd been out of school for six years. And even if I did get in (a miracle!), how would I pay for it? How would I live? Well, here I am—the first one in my family to go to college.

Jared's freewriting

PRACTICE

3-3   Reread Jared White's freewriting. If you were advising Jared, which ideas would you tell him to explore further? Why?

freewrite

Choose two of the jobs you have been thinking about, and freewrite about each of them. Then, choose the job you think was the most challenging. Circle the ideas about this job that you would like to explore further in an essay.

Brainstorming

Unlike freewriting, **brainstorming** is sometimes written in list form and sometimes scattered all over a page. You don't have to use complete sentences; single words or phrases are fine. After you have recorded as much information as you can, you can look over your brainstorming and decide which ideas are useful and which ones are not, underlining, starring, or boxing important ideas. You can also ask questions, draw arrows to connect important ideas, and even draw pictures or diagrams.

Usually you brainstorm on your own, but at times you may find it useful to do **collaborative brainstorming**, working with other students to find ideas. Sometimes your instructor may ask you and other students to brainstorm together. At times the class may even brainstorm as a group while your instructor writes down the ideas you think of. Whenever you brainstorm, however, your goal is the same: to come up with as much material about your topic as you can.

Here are Jared's brainstorming notes about his decision to go back to school.

Deciding to Go Back to School

Money a problem

Other students a lot younger

Paying tuition—how?

No one in family went to college

Friends not in college

Couldn't see myself in college

Considered going to trade school

Computer programmer?

Grades bad in high school

Time for me to grow up

Wondered if I would get in

Found out about community college

Admission requirements not bad

Afraid—too old, looking silly

Took time to get used to routine

Found other students like me

Liked studying

Jared's brainstorming

PRACTICE
3-4
Which ideas in Jared's brainstorming notes would you advise him to explore further? Why?

brainstorm

Review your freewriting. Then, brainstorm about the job you plan to write about. What ideas about this job did you get from brainstorming that you did not get from freewriting?

Keeping a Journal

A journal is a notebook or computer file in which you keep an informal record of your thoughts or ideas. In your journal, you can reflect, question, summarize, or even complain. Your journal is also a place where you record ideas about your assignments and note possible ideas to write about. Here you can try to resolve a problem, restart a stalled project, argue with yourself about your topic, or comment on a draft. You can also try out different versions of sentences, list details or examples, or keep a record of things you read, see, or hear.

Journal writing works best when you write regularly, preferably at the same time each day, so that it becomes a habit. Once you have started making regular entries in your journal, take the time every week or so to go back and read over what you have written. You may find ideas that you want to explore in further journal entries or to use in an essay.

Following is an entry in Jared's journal that he eventually used in his essay about returning to school.

> When I was working as a house painter, I had a conversation that helped convince me to go to college. One day, I started talking to the guy whose house I was painting. I told him that I was painting houses until I figured out what I was going to do with the rest of my life. He asked me if I had considered going to college. I told him that I hadn't done well in high school, so I didn't think college was for me. He told me that I could probably get into the local community college. That night I looked at the community college's website to see if going to college might be a good idea.

Jared's journal entry

write journal entries

Write at least two journal entries for the topic you have been exploring for this chapter: the most difficult job you've ever had. Which of your entries do you want to explore further? What material could you use in your essay?

Clustering

Clustering, sometimes called *mapping*, is another strategy that you can use to find ideas to write about. When you cluster, you begin by writing your topic in the center of a sheet of paper. Then, you branch out, writing relevant ideas on the page in groups, or clusters, around the topic. As you add new ideas, you circle them and draw lines to connect the ideas to one another and to the topic at the center. (These lines will look like a spiderweb or the spokes of a wheel.) As you move from the center out to the corners of the page, your ideas will be more and more specific.

Sometimes one branch of your cluster diagram will give you all the material you need. At other times, you may decide to write about the ideas from several branches or to choose one or two ideas from each branch. If you find you need additional material after you finish your first cluster diagram, you can repeat the process on a new sheet of paper, this time beginning with a topic from one of the branches.

Jared's cluster diagram on the topic of deciding to go back to school appears below.

Jared's cluster diagram

Draw a cluster diagram

Draw a cluster diagram for your essay on your most difficult job.
Was this method of finding ideas useful? Why or why not?

PRACTICE

3-5 Look at Jared's cluster diagram on deciding to go back to
school. How is it similar to his brainstorming on the same
subject (p. 71)? How is it different? If you were advising Jared, which
branches of the cluster diagram would you suggest that he develop
further? Why? Would you add any branches? Be prepared to discuss
your suggestions with the class or in a small group.

3d Stating Your Thesis

After you have gathered information about your topic, you need to
decide on a thesis for your essay. You do this by reviewing the ideas from
your brainstorming, freewriting, journal entries, or cluster diagrams
and then asking, "What is the main point I want to make about my
topic?" The answer to this question is the **thesis** of your essay. You
express this point in a **thesis statement**: a single sentence that clearly
expresses the main idea that you will discuss in the rest of your essay.

Keep in mind that each essay has just *one* thesis statement. The
details and examples in the body of the essay all support (add to, discuss,
or explain) this thesis statement.

TOPIC	THESIS STATEMENT
Three things I would change to improve the quality of life on campus	If I could change three things to improve the quality of life on campus, I would expand the food choices, decrease class size in first-year courses, and ship some of my classmates to the North Pole.
The campus recycling project	The recycling project recently begun on our campus should be promoted more actively.

Like a topic sentence in a paragraph, a thesis statement in an essay tells readers what to expect. An effective thesis statement has two important characteristics.

Teaching Tip
You may want to remind students not to state the thesis in their essay's first sentence.

1. *An effective thesis statement makes a point about a topic, expressing the writer's opinion or unique view of the topic. For this reason, it must do more than state a fact or announce what you plan to write about.*

   STATEMENT OF FACT   Many older students are returning to school.

   ANNOUNCEMENT   In this essay, I will discuss older students going back to school.

A statement of fact is not an effective thesis statement because it gives you nothing to develop in your essay. After all, how much can you say about the *fact* that many older students are returning to school? Likewise, an announcement of what you plan to discuss gives readers no indication of the position you will take on your topic. Remember, an effective thesis statement makes a point.

2. *An effective thesis statement is clearly worded and specific.*

   VAGUE THESIS STATEMENT   Returning to school is difficult for older students.

The vague thesis statement above gives readers no sense of the ideas the essay will discuss. It does not say, for example, *why* returning to school is difficult for older students. Remember, an effective thesis statement is specific.

Teaching Tip
Tell students that at this stage of the process, their thesis statements are tentative. They will probably change this tentative thesis statement as they write and revise their essays.

FYI

Evaluating Your Thesis Statement

Once you have a thesis statement, you need to evaluate it to determine if it is effective. Asking the following questions will help you decide.

- Is your thesis statement a complete sentence?
- Does your thesis statement clearly express the main idea you will discuss in your essay?
- Is your thesis statement specific and focused? Does it make a point that you can cover within your time and page limits?
- Does your thesis statement make a point about your topic—not just state a fact or announce what you plan to write about?
- Does your thesis statement avoid vague language?
- Does your thesis statement avoid statements like "I think" or "In my opinion"?

After freewriting, brainstorming, and reviewing his journal entries and cluster diagram, Jared decided on a topic and wrote the following effective thesis statement for his essay.

EFFECTIVE THESIS STATEMENT   Although I realized it would be difficult in some ways, I decided that if I really wanted to attend college full-time, I could.

Jared knew that his thesis statement had to be a complete sentence that made a point about his topic and that it should be both clearly worded and specific. When he reviewed his thesis statement, he felt sure that it satisfied these criteria and expressed an idea he could develop in his essay.

PRACTICE

3-6

In the space provided, indicate whether each of the following items is a statement of fact (*F*), an announcement (*A*), a vague statement (*VS*), or an effective thesis (*ET*).

Examples

My drive to school takes more than an hour. _____F_____

I hate my commute between home and school. _____VS_____

1. Students who must commute a long distance to school are at a disadvantage compared to students who live close by. _____ET_____

2. In this paper, I will discuss cheating. _____A_____

3. Schools should establish specific policies to discourage students from cheating. _____ET_____

4. Cheating is a problem. _____VS_____

5. Television commercials are designed to sell products. _____F_____

6. I would like to explain why some television commercials are funny. _____A_____

7. Single parents have a rough time. _____VS_____

8. Young people are starting to abuse alcohol and drugs at earlier ages than in the past. _____F_____

9. Alcohol and drug abuse are both major problems in our society. _____VS_____

10. Families can do several things to help children avoid alcohol and drugs. ___ET___

PRACTICE
3-7 Label each of the following thesis statements *F* if it is a statement of fact, *A* if it is an announcement, *VS* if it is a vague statement, or *ET* if it is an effective thesis. Revise those that are not effective thesis statements. *Answers to rewrites will vary.*

Examples

The World Health Organization has warned that people can get sick from drinking unclean water. ___F___

Possible rewrite: The World Health Organization should make access to clean

water its first priority in disease prevention.

A few simple changes could make the dining halls safer for students with food allergies. ___ET___

1. The TV show *Heroes* was on the air for four seasons before being canceled in 2010. ___F___

2. To survive in Los Angeles, a new restaurant needs a good location and a unique menu. ___ET___

3. My essay will show that Johnny Depp is a better actor than Brad Pitt. ___A___

4. Highway speed limits are ineffective. ___VS___

5. In this essay, I will discuss the pros and cons of choosing tap water over bottled water. ___A___

6. Studying abroad enables college students to gain independence and self-confidence. ___ET___

7. The National Weather Service predicts this will be an average year for hurricanes. _____F_____

8. By teaching me critical problem-solving skills, the Army prepared me well for a career in engineering. _____ET_____

9. Sugary soda is high in calories and low in nutritional value. _____F_____

10. People have their own definitions of justice. _____VS_____

PRACTICE

3-8 Rewrite the following vague thesis statements to make them effective.

Example

My relatives are funny.

Rewrite: _My relatives think they are funny, but sometimes their humor_
can be offensive.

Answers will vary.

1. Online courses have advantages.

2. Airport security is more trouble than it is worth.

3. Athletes are paid too much.

4. Many people get their identities from their cars.

5. Cheating in college is out of control.

PRACTICE

Teaching Tip
Have students read their thesis statements aloud, and let the class discuss whether they are effective or not.

3-9 A list of broad topics for essays follows. Select five of these topics, narrow them, and generate a thesis statement for each.

Answers will vary.

1. Careers	6. Required courses
2. Reality television	7. Computer games
3. U.S. immigration policies	8. Disciplining children
4. Music	9. Street sense
5. Texting in class	10. The cost of gasoline

PRACTICE

3-10 Read the following groups of statements. Then, write a thesis statement that could express the main point of each group.

Answers will vary.

1. Thesis statement _Suggested answer: Taking a year off between high school and_

   college can benefit students in several ways.

   - *Gap year* is a term that refers to a year that students take off before they go to college.
   - Many college students spend most of their time studying and socializing with their peers.
   - Studies show that high school students who take a year off before they go to college get better grades.
   - Many students take community-service jobs in order to broaden their interests and to increase their social awareness.

2. Thesis statement _Suggested answer: Social networking sites can pose such_

   dangers as addictive behavior, privacy issues, vulnerability to child predators, and

   breaches of employment confidentiality.

   - Some people post too much personal information on social-networking sites.
   - Child predators frequently use social-networking sites to find their victims.
   - Some experts believe that people can become addicted to social-networking sites.
   - Employers have fired employees because of information they have seen on their employees' social-networking sites.

3. Thesis statement _Suggested answer: Allowing students the freedom to design_

   their own majors can be attractive to students, universities, and employers.

   - A student at Indiana University at Bloomington was able to create her own major in environmental ethics.
   - Drexel University has begun recruiting students who would design their own majors.
   - Some students get bored with traditional majors that force them to choose from a rigid list of courses.
   - Many employers are impressed with students who design their own majors.

4. Thesis statement _Suggested answer: Students can find assistance for paying_

   college costs in several ways.

ESL Tip
Nonnative speakers may be reluctant to read their work aloud in front of the class. In pairs or small groups, have students exchange their work and read each other's thesis statements. Make sure you assign native speakers and nonnative speakers to work together.

- One way to pay for college is to get a job.
- The majority of students supplement their college tuition with loans or grants.
- According to the College Board, only 22 percent of all federal aid for college tuition goes to scholarships.
- Some students enlist in the armed forces and become eligible for tuition assistance programs.

5. Thesis statement *Suggested answer: People can save time in the kitchen by* *employing several simple strategies.*

- You can save time in the kitchen by washing and putting away items as you cook.
- Keep your kitchen well stocked so that you will not have to run to the store to get an ingredient.
- Keep your countertops free of clutter so you don't have to put things away before you cook.
- Shred things like cheese in advance and store them in plastic bags.

state your thesis

Review your freewriting, brainstorming, journal entries, and cluster diagram. Then, write a thesis statement for your essay about the most difficult job you've ever had.

Step 2: Organizing

3e　Choosing Supporting Points

Teaching Tip
You may want to remind students that they do not have to use this many prewriting strategies every time they write.

Once you have decided on a thesis statement, it is time to look over your freewriting, brainstorming, journal entries, and cluster diagram again to identify the **evidence** (details and examples) that best supports your thesis.

When Jared looked over the notes he had accumulated, he saw that his brainstorming had given him so much to work with that he didn't need to use the material he'd come up with through clustering and journal writing. At this point, he reviewed his brainstorming notes, crossing out several points that he thought would not support his thesis.

Deciding to Go Back to School: Pros and Cons

Money a problem

Other students a lot younger

Paying tuition—how?

No one in family went to college

Friends not in college

Couldn't see myself in college

~~Considered going to trade school~~

~~Computer programmer?~~

Grades bad in high school

Wondered if I would get in

Found out about community college

Admission requirements not bad

Afraid—too old, looking dumb

~~Took time to get used to routine~~

Found other students like me

Liked studying

Jared's list of supporting points

PRACTICE

3-11   Review Jared's list of supporting points above. Do you see any points he crossed out that you think he should have kept? Do you see any other points he should have crossed out?

3f   Making an Outline

After you have selected the points you think will best support your thesis, you should make an informal outline. Begin by arranging your supporting points into groups. Then, arrange them in the order in which you will discuss them (for example, from general to specific, or from least to most important). Arrange the supporting points for each group in the same way. (As you construct your outline, you will think of additional ideas.) This informal outline can guide you as you write.

When Jared looked over his list of supporting points, he saw that they fell into three groups of excuses for not going back to school: not being able to pay tuition, not being a good student in high school, and not being able to picture himself in college. He arranged his points under these three headings to create the following informal outline.

Excuse 1: Not being able to pay tuition

    Needed to work to live

    Didn't have much money saved

    Found out about community college (low tuition)

    Found out about grants, loans

Excuse 2: Not being a good student in high school

    Got bad grades in high school: wasn't motivated and didn't work

    Looked into admission requirements at community college—doable!

    Made a commitment to improve study habits

Excuse 3: Not being able to picture myself in college

    No college graduates in family

    Friends not in college

    Afraid of being too old, looking dumb

    Found other students like me

    Found out I liked studying

Jared's informal outline

PRACTICE

3-12 Look over Jared's informal outline above. Do you think his arrangement is effective? Can you suggest any other ways he might have arranged his points?

FYI

Preparing a Formal Outline

An informal outline like the one that Jared prepared is usually all you need to plan a short essay. However, some writers—especially when they are planning a longer, more detailed essay—prefer to use formal outlines.

Formal outlines use a combination of numbered and lettered headings to show the relationships among ideas. For example, the most important (and most general) ideas are assigned a Roman numeral; the next most important ideas are assigned capital letters. Each level develops the idea above it, and each new level is indented.

Here is a formal outline of the points that Jared planned to discuss in his essay.

Thesis statement: Although I realized it would be difficult in some ways, I decided that if I really wanted to attend college full-time, I could.

    I.   Difficulty: Money
        A. Needed to work to live
        B. Didn't have much money saved
        C. Found out about community college (low tuition)
        D. Found out about grants/loans
   II.   Difficulty: Academic record
        A. Got bad grades in high school
            1. Didn't care
            2. Didn't work
        B. Found out about reasonable admission requirements at community college
        C. Committed to improving study habits
  III.   Difficulty: Imagining myself as a student
        A. Had no college graduates in family
        B. Had no friends who went to college
        C. Felt anxious
            1. Too old
            2. Out of practice at school
        D. Found other students like me
        E. Discovered I like studying

Teaching Tip

Tell students that each level of an outline must include at least two points—two Roman numerals, two capital letters, two numbers, and so on.

Teaching Tip

Take this opportunity to explain to students that all headings in a formal outline are stated in parallel terms. You might want to refer students to Chapter 19, Using Parallelism.

make an informal outline

Review your freewriting, brainstorming, journal entries, and cluster diagram. Then, list the points you plan to use to support your thesis statement. Cross out any points that do not support your thesis statement. Finally, group the remaining points into an informal outline that will guide you as you write.

Step 3: Drafting

3g   Drafting Your Essay

Teaching Tip
Refer students to
Chapter 4 for a
discussion of
introductions and
conclusions.

After you have decided on a thesis for your essay and have arranged your supporting points in the order in which you will discuss them, you are ready to draft your essay.

FYI

Using Patterns of Essay Development

Writers have a variety of options for developing ideas in an essay. These options, which are discussed and illustrated in Unit 2 of this text, include *exemplification, narration, description, process, cause and effect, comparison and contrast, classification, definition,* and *argument.* Sometimes an essay combines several of these **patterns of development**; often, however, a single pattern dominates. Recognizing a pattern or patterns that emerge as you draft can help you arrange ideas in your essays.

At this stage of the writing process, you should not worry about spelling or grammar or about composing a perfect introduction or conclusion. Your main goal is to get your ideas down so that you can react to them. Remember that the draft you are writing will be revised, so leave extra space between lines as you type. Follow your outline, but don't hesitate to depart from it if you think of new points.

Teaching Tip
Refer students to Chapter 4
for a discussion of titles.

As you draft your essay, be sure that it has a **thesis-and-support** structure—that it states a thesis and supports it with evidence. Include a **working title**, a temporary title that you will revise later so that it accurately reflects the content of your completed essay. This working title will help you focus your ideas.

Following is the first draft of Jared's essay.

Going Back to School

I was out of school for six years after I graduated from high school. The decision to return to school was one I had a lot of difficulty making. I had been around enough to know that without more education, I'd never get anywhere in life, but I always found reasons for not taking the plunge. However, after a lot of thinking, I realized that my reasons for not going to college were just excuses. Although I realized it would be difficult in some ways, I decided that if I really wanted to attend college full-time, I could.

My first excuse for not going to college was that I couldn't afford to go to school full-time. I had worked since I finished high school, but I hadn't put much money away. I kept wondering how I would pay for books and tuition. I needed to support myself and pay for rent, food, and car expenses. I was working as a house painter, and a house I was painting belonged to a college instructor. Painting wasn't hard work, but it was boring. I'd start in the morning and work without a break until lunch. We began talking. When I told him about my situation, he told me I should look at our local community college. He also told me about some loans and grants I'd probably be able to apply for. I went online and looked at the college's website. I found out that tuition was one hundred dollars a credit, less than I thought it would be. If I got just one of the grants he mentioned, I might be able to make it.

Now that I had taken care of my first excuse, I had to deal with my second—that I hadn't been a good student in high school. When I was a teenager, I didn't care much about school. School bored me to death. Probably as a result, I got bad grades. Now that I was considering going back to school, though, I wondered what price I would have to pay for my laziness and immaturity. The answer to this question was not as bad as I thought it would be. According to the community college's website, all I needed to be admitted was a high school diploma and county residence. I would have to take some placement tests, but I would be judged on my ability, not my high school grades. I knew I could do better if I made a real effort to study harder and smarter. The website was easy to navigate, and I had no problem finding information.

I had a hard time picturing myself in college. No one in my family had ever gone to college. My friends were just like me; they all went to work right after high school. I had no role model or mentor who could give me advice. I thought I was just too old for college. After all, I was probably at least

(continued)

ESL Tip

Have students copy this essay, one paragraph at a time, reading each sentence aloud as they write.

Teaching Tip

Tell your students that Jared's paper is an exemplification essay, since it primarily uses the pattern of exemplification to explain why he decided to go back to school.

(continued from previous page)

six years older than most of the students. How would I be able to keep up with the younger students in the class? I hadn't opened a textbook for years, and I'd never really learned how to study. Most of my fears disappeared during my first few weeks of classes. I saw a lot of students who were as old as I was, and some were even older. Studying didn't seem to be a problem either. I actually enjoyed learning. History, which had put me to sleep in high school, suddenly became interesting. So did math and English. It soon became clear to me that I was going to like being in college.

Going to college as a full-time student has changed my life, both personally and financially. I am no longer the same person I was in high school. I allowed laziness and insecurity to hold me back. Now, I have options that I didn't have before. When I graduate from community college, I plan to transfer to the state university and get a four-year degree.

Jared's first draft

PRACTICE

3-13 What changes would you suggest Jared make to his draft? What might he add? What might he delete? Which of his supporting details and examples do you find most effective? Why?

draft your essay

Draft an essay about your most difficult job. When you finish your draft, give your essay a working title.

Step 4: TESTing and Revising

When you revise your essay, you do not simply correct errors; instead, you resee, rethink, reevaluate, and rewrite your work. Some of the changes you make—such as adding, deleting, or rearranging sentences or even whole paragraphs—will be major. Others will be small—for example, adding or deleting words or phrases.

Before you begin revising, put your essay aside for a while. This "cooling-off" period allows you to see your draft more objectively when you return to it. When you are ready to revise, keep in mind that the revision process is usually not a neat one. It is a good idea, therefore, to revise on hard copy and not on the computer screen. On hard copy, you arc able to see a full page—or even two or three pages next to each other—as you revise. Revising on hard copy also gives you more options in terms of how you interact with your draft: you can draw arrows, underline, cross out, and write above lines and in the margins. When you have finished, you can type your changes into your document. Be careful, though, not to delete sentences or paragraphs until you are certain you do not need them. Instead, move unwanted material to the end of your draft—or save multiple, dated drafts.

3h   TESTing Your Essay

When you revise the first draft of your essay, you should begin by **TEST**-ing it to make sure it contains the four elements that make it clear and effective.

T hesis Statement
E vidence
S ummary Statement
T ransitions

If your essay includes all four **TEST** elements, you can continue re-vising. If it does not, you should supply whatever is missing.

When Jared reread the draft of his essay, he **TEST**ed it to see if it was complete.

- He decided that his **thesis statement** clearly stated his main idea.
- He thought he could add some more **evidence** in his body para-graphs and delete some irrelevant details.
- He thought his **summary statement** summed up the idea expressed in his thesis statement.
- He realized he needed to add more **transitions** to connect ideas.

TEST your essay

TEST your draft to make sure it includes all the elements of an effective essay. If any elements are missing, add them now.

3i Revising Your Essay

Once you have completed the first revision step—TESTing your essay—there are a number of additional strategies you can use to help you revise your essay. The following chart lists these revision strategies and explains the advantages of each.

Teaching Tip
Direct students to the FYI box on page 89 for tips on getting the most out of a conference.

Teaching Tip
Using your school's course management system, you can have students post their essays to an online class discussion board and respond to one another, or you can have pairs of students exchange essay drafts by email.

STRATEGIES FOR REVISING	
STRATEGY	**ADVANTAGES**
FACE-TO-FACE CONFERENCE WITH INSTRUCTOR	▪ Provides one-to-one feedback that can't be obtained in the classroom ▪ Builds a student-teacher relationship ▪ Enables students to collaborate with their instructors ▪ Allows students to ask questions that they might not ask in a classroom setting
WRITING CENTER	▪ Offers students a less formal, less stressful environment than an instructor conference ▪ Enables students to get help from trained tutors (both students and professionals) ▪ Provides a perspective other than the instructor's ▪ Offers specialized help to students whose first language is not English
PEER REVIEW	▪ Enables students working on the same assignment to share insights with one another ▪ Gives students the experience of writing for a real audience ▪ Gives students several different readers' reactions to their work ▪ Enables students to benefit from the ideas of their classmates

STRATEGY	ADVANTAGES
ELECTRONIC COMMUNICATION WITH INSTRUCTOR	<ul><li>Enables students to submit email questions before a draft is due</li><li>Gives students quick answers to their questions</li><li>Enables instructors to give feedback by annotating drafts electronically</li><li>Enables students to react to their instructor's responses when they have time</li><li>Eliminates time spent traveling to instructor's office</li></ul>
REVISION CHECKLIST	<ul><li>Gives students a tool that enables them to revise in an orderly way</li><li>Enables students to learn to revise independently</li><li>Enables students to focus on specific aspects of their writing</li></ul>

Teaching Tip
Students can see examples of revision and editing checklists on pages 90 and 93–94.

FYI

Getting the Most Out of a Conference

If you need help at any point in the writing process, you can get it from your instructor or from a tutor in your school's writing center. Following the guidelines below will help you get the most out of your conferences.

- Make an appointment in advance, either by phone or by email.
- Arrive on time; instructors and tutors often schedule several appointments in a row, and if you are late, you may miss your appointment entirely.
- Bring a copy of your assignment.
- Bring all drafts and prewriting notes for the assignment you are working on.

(continued)

(continued from previous page)

- Bring a list of specific questions you would like the instructor or tutor to answer.
- Pay attention, ask your questions, and be sure you understand the answers.
- Write the instructor's or tutor's suggestions directly on your latest draft.
- Schedule a follow-up appointment if necessary.

Remember, your instructor or tutor will answer questions and make recommendations, but he or she will *not* revise or edit your work for you. That is your job.

self-assessment checklist

Revising Your Essay

- [ ] Does your essay have an introduction, a body, and a conclusion?
- [ ] Does your introduction include a clearly worded thesis statement that states your essay's main idea?
- [ ] Does each body paragraph have a topic sentence?
- [ ] Does each topic sentence introduce a point that supports the thesis?
- [ ] Does each body paragraph include enough examples and details to support the topic sentence?
- [ ] Are the body paragraphs unified, well developed, and coherent?
- [ ] Does your conclusion include a concluding statement that restates your thesis or sums up your main idea?

When Jared finished **TEST**ing his essay, he decided to arrange a conference with his instructor to discuss how to further revise and polish it. He made sure to follow the guidelines in the FYI box on page 89 in order to get the most out of the conference. After the conference, Jared continued revising his essay. He used the Self-Assessment Checklist above to guide him through his final revisions.

Jared's first draft, with his handwritten revisions—including those he made after he **TEST**ed the draft—appears on the following pages. Notice that when Jared typed his draft, he left extra space so he could write more easily between the lines and in the margins.

~~Going Back to School~~ Starting Over

I was out of school for six years after I graduated from high school. The decision to return to school was one I had a lot of difficulty making. I had been around enough to know that without more education, I'd never get anywhere in life, but I always found reasons for not taking the plunge. However, after a lot of thinking, I realized that my reasons for not going to college were just excuses. Although I realized it would be difficult in some ways, I decided that if I really wanted to attend college full-time, I could.

The other day, my sociology instructor mentioned that half the students enrolled in college programs across the country are twenty-five or older. His remark caught my attention because I am one of those students.

My first excuse for not going to college was that I couldn't afford to go to school full-time. I had worked since I finished high school, but I hadn't put much money away. I kept wondering how I would pay for books and tuition. The solution to my problem came unexpectedly. I also needed to support myself and pay for rent, food, and car expenses. I was working as a house painter, and a house I was painting belonged to a college instructor. ~~Painting wasn't hard work, but it was boring. I'd start in the morning and work without a break until lunch.~~ During my lunch break, we We began talking. When I told him about my situation, he told me I should look at our local community college. He also told me about some loans and grants I'd probably be able to apply for. Later, I went online and looked at the college's website. I found out that tuition was one hundred dollars a credit, less than I thought it would be. If I got just one of the grants he mentioned, I might be able to make it!

The money I'd saved, along with what I could make painting houses on the weekends, could get me through.

Now that I had taken care of my first excuse, I had to deal with my second—that I hadn't been a good student in high school. When I was a teenager, I didn't care much about school. In fact, school ~~School~~ bored me ~~to death.~~ Probably as a result, I got bad grades. Now that I was considering going back to school, though, I wondered what price I would have to pay for my laziness and immaturity. The answer to this question was not as bad as I

In class, I would stare out the window or watch the second hand on the clock move slowly around. I never bothered with homework. School just didn't interest me.

thought it would be. According to the community college's website, all I

needed to be admitted was a high school diploma and county residence. I

would have to take some placement tests, but I would be judged on my

ability, not my high school grades. I knew I could do better if I made a real

effort to study harder and smarter. ~~The website was easy to navigate, and I~~

~~had no problem finding information.~~

My biggest problem still bothered me:

I had a hard time picturing myself in college. No one in my family

had ever gone to college. My friends were just like me; they all went to

work right after high school. I had no role model or mentor who could

Besides,

give me advice. I thought I was just too old for college. After all, I was

probably at least six years older than most of the students. How would I

be able to keep up with the younger students in the class? I hadn't

opened a textbook for years, and I'd never really learned how to study.

However, most

~~Most~~ of my fears disappeared during my first few weeks of classes. I saw a

lot of students who were as old as I was, and some were even older.

Studying didn't seem to be a problem either. I actually enjoyed learning.

History, which had put me to sleep in high school, suddenly became

interesting. So did math and English. It soon became clear to me that I

was going to like being in college.

Going to college as a full-time student has changed my life, both

personally and financially. I am no longer the same person I was in high

In the past,

school. I allowed laziness and insecurity to hold me back. Now, I have options

that I didn't have before. When I graduate from community college, I plan to

transfer to the state university and get a four-year degree. The other day,
one of my instructors asked me if I had ever considered becoming a
teacher. The truth is, I never had, but now I might. I'd like to be able to
give kids like me the tough, realistic advice I wish someone had given me.

PRACTICE

3-14 Working in a group of three or four students, answer the following questions.

- What kind of material did Jared add to his draft?
- What did he delete?
- Why do you think he made these changes?
- Do you agree with the changes he made?

Be prepared to discuss your reactions to these changes with the class.

---

revise your essay

Choose one or two of the additional revision strategies from the chart on pages 88–89, and continue revising your essay.

Step 5: Editing and Proofreading

3j Editing Your Essay

When you **edit** your essay, you check grammar and sentence structure. Then, you look at punctuation, mechanics, and spelling. As you edit, think carefully about the questions in the Self-Assessment Checklist below.

Teaching Tip
You might create a class wiki at wikispaces.com and encourage or require students to use that space for group work in writing and editing an essay online.

self-assessment checklist

Editing Your Essay

EDITING FOR COMMON SENTENCE PROBLEMS

☐ Have you avoided run-ons? (See Chapter 21.)

☐ Have you avoided sentence fragments? (See Chapter 22.)

☐ Do your subjects and verbs agree? (See Chapter 23.)

(continued)

(continued from previous page)

☐ Have you avoided illogical shifts? (See Chapter 24.)

☐ Have you avoided dangling and misplaced modifiers?
(See Chapter 25.)

EDITING FOR GRAMMAR

☐ Are your verb forms and verb tenses correct? (See Chapter 14.)

☐ Have you used nouns and pronouns correctly? (See Chapter 15.)

☐ Have you used adjectives and adverbs correctly? (See Chapter 16.)

EDITING FOR PUNCTUATION AND MECHANICS

☐ Have you used commas correctly? (See Chapter 26.)

☐ Have you used apostrophes correctly? (See Chapter 27.)

☐ Have you used capital letters where they are required?
(See 28a.)

☐ Have you used quotation marks correctly where they are needed?
(See 28b.)

3k Proofreading Your Essay

When you proofread, you look for typos, check your formatting, and double-check for anything you might have missed while you were editing. Remember that Spell Check and Grammar Check tools are helpful starting points in the editing process, but they can also introduce errors, so as you proofread, double-check any words whose spelling you are not sure of. It is also a good idea to print your essay and proofread on hard copy because it is easy to miss typos and other small errors on a computer screen.

Now, look at your essay's format. The **format** of an essay is the way it looks on a page—for example, the size of the margins, the placement of page numbers, and the amount of space between lines. Most instructors expect you to follow a certain format when you type an essay. The model essay format illustrated on the following page is commonly used in composition classes. Before you hand in an essay, you should make sure that it follows this model (or the guidelines your instructor gives you).

Essay Format: Sample First Page

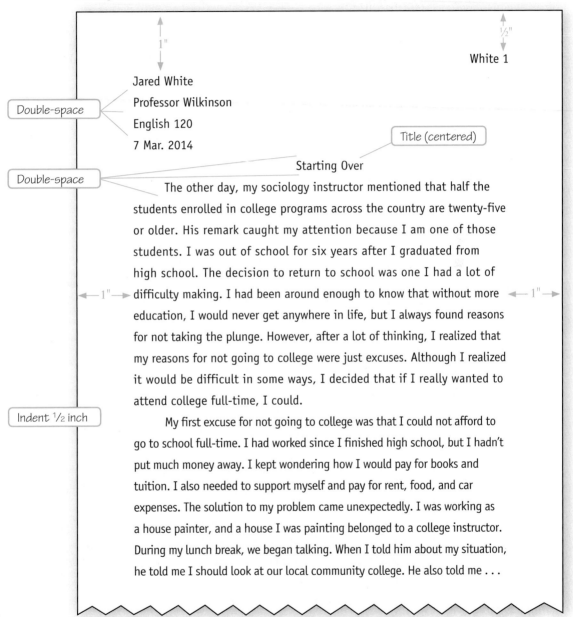

White 1

Jared White

Professor Wilkinson

English 120

7 Mar. 2014

Double-space

Double-space

Title (centered)

Starting Over

    The other day, my sociology instructor mentioned that half the students enrolled in college programs across the country are twenty-five or older. His remark caught my attention because I am one of those students. I was out of school for six years after I graduated from high school. The decision to return to school was one I had a lot of difficulty making. I had been around enough to know that without more education, I would never get anywhere in life, but I always found reasons for not taking the plunge. However, after a lot of thinking, I realized that my reasons for not going to college were just excuses. Although I realized it would be difficult in some ways, I decided that if I really wanted to attend college full-time, I could.

    My first excuse for not going to college was that I could not afford to go to school full-time. I had worked since I finished high school, but I hadn't put much money away. I kept wondering how I would pay for books and tuition. I also needed to support myself and pay for rent, food, and car expenses. The solution to my problem came unexpectedly. I was working as a house painter, and a house I was painting belonged to a college instructor. During my lunch break, we began talking. When I told him about my situation, he told me I should look at our local community college. He also told me . . .

Indent ½ inch

1″

Note: The bottom margin of each page should be one inch.

When his revisions were complete, Jared edited and proofread his essay, deleting all the contractions, which he thought made his essay seem too informal. The final version of his essay appears on pages 96–97. (Marginal annotations have been added to highlight key features.) Note that the final draft includes all the elements Jared looked for when he TESTed his essay.

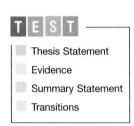

T E S T

- ▢ Thesis Statement
- ▢ Evidence
- ▢ Summary Statement
- ▢ Transitions

Jared White

Professor Wilkinson

English 120

7 Mar. 2014

Starting Over

Introduction

The other day, my sociology instructor mentioned that half the students enrolled in college programs across the country are twenty-five or older. His remark caught my attention because I am one of those students. I was out of school for six years after I graduated from high school. The decision to return to school was one I had a lot of difficulty making. I had been around enough to know that without more education, I would never get anywhere in life, but I always found reasons for not taking the plunge. However, after a lot of thinking, I realized that my reasons for not going to college were just excuses. Although I realized it would be difficult in some ways, I decided that if I really wanted to attend college full-time, I could.

Topic sentence (first point)

Examples and details

My first excuse for not going to college was that I could not afford to go to school full-time. I had worked since I finished high school, but I hadn't put much money away. I kept wondering how I would pay for books and tuition. I also needed to support myself and pay for rent, food, and car expenses. The solution to my problem came unexpectedly. I was working as a house painter, and a house I was painting belonged to a college instructor. During my lunch break, we began talking. When I told him about my situation, he told me I should look at our local community college. He also told me about some loans and grants I would probably be able to apply for. Later, I went online and looked at the college's website. I found out that tuition was one hundred dollars a credit, less than I thought it would be. If I got just one of the grants he mentioned, I might be able to make it. The money I had saved, along with what I could make painting houses on the weekends, could get me through.

Body paragraphs

Topic sentence (second point)

Now that I had taken care of my first excuse, I had to deal with my second—that I had not been a good student in high school. When I was a teenager, I didn't care much about school. In fact, school bored me. In class, I would stare out the window or watch the second hand on the clock move slowly around. I never bothered with homework. School just didn't interest me. Probably as a result, I got bad grades. Now that I was considering going back to school, though, I wondered what price I would have to pay for my laziness and immaturity. The answer to this question was not as bad as I thought it would be. According to the community college's website, all I needed to be admitted was a high school diploma and county residence. I would have to take some placement tests, but I would be judged on my ability, not my high school grades. I knew I could do better if I made a real effort to study harder and smarter.

Examples and details

My biggest problem still bothered me: I had a hard time picturing myself in college. No one in my family had ever gone to college. My friends were just like me; they all went to work right after high school. I had no role model or mentor who could give me advice. Besides, I thought I was just too old for college. After all, I was probably at least six years older than most of the students. How would I be able to keep up with the younger students in the class? I had not opened a textbook for years, and I had never really learned how to study. However, most of my fears disappeared during my first few weeks of classes. I saw a lot of students who were as old as I was, and some were even older. Studying didn't seem to be a problem either. I actually enjoyed learning. For example, history, which had put me to sleep in high school, suddenly became interesting. So did math and English. It soon became clear to me that I was going to like being in college.

Topic sentence (third point)

Examples and details

Body paragraphs

Going to college as a full-time student has changed my life, both personally and financially. I am no longer the same person I was in high school. In the past, I allowed laziness and insecurity to hold me back. Now, I have options that I didn't have before. When I graduate from community college, I plan to transfer to the state university and get a four-year degree. The other day, one of my instructors asked me if I had ever considered becoming a teacher. The truth is, I never had, but now I might. I would like to be able to give kids like me the tough, realistic advice I wish someone had given me.

Conclusion

PRACTICE

3-15   Reread the final draft of Jared White's essay. Working in a group of three or four students, answer these questions.

■ Do you think this draft is better than his first draft (shown on pages 85–86)?

■ What other changes could Jared have made?

Be prepared to discuss your group's answers with the class.

edit and proofread your essay

Edit your draft, using the Self-Assessment Checklist on page 93 to guide you. Then, proofread your essay for typos and other errors. Finally, make sure that your essay's format follows your instructor's guidelines.

REVIEW ACTIVITY

1. The following student essay is missing its thesis statement and topic sentences and has no summary statement. First, write an appropriate thesis statement on the lines provided. (Make sure your thesis statement clearly communicates the essay's main idea.) Then, fill in the topic sentences for the second, third, and fourth paragraphs. Finally, add a summary statement in the conclusion.

Preparing for a Job Interview

A lot of books and many websites give advice on how to do well on a job interview. Some recommend practicing your handshake, and others suggest making eye contact. This advice is useful, but not many books tell how to get mentally prepared for an interview. [Thesis statement:] *Answers will vary.*

_____

_____

_____

[Topic sentence for the second paragraph:] *Answers will vary.*

_____

_____

_____

Feeling good about how you look is important, so you should probably wear a dress or skirt (or, for males, a jacket and tie) to an interview. Even if you will not be dressing this formally on the job, try to make a good first impression. For this reason, you should never come to an interview dressed in jeans or shorts. Still, you should be careful not to overdress. For example, wearing a suit or a dressy dress to an interview at a fast-food restaurant might make you feel good, but it could also make you look as if you do not really want to work there.

[Topic sentence for the third paragraph:] *Answers will vary.*

_____

_____

Going on an interview is a little like getting ready to compete in a sporting event. You have to go in with the right attitude. If you think you are not going to be successful, chances are that you will not be. So, before you go on any interview, spend some time building your confidence. Tell yourself that you can do the job and that you will do well in the interview. By the time you get to the interview, you will have convinced yourself that you are the right person for the job.

[Topic sentence for the fourth paragraph:]   *Answers will vary.*

_____

_____

Most people go to an interview knowing little or nothing about the job. They expect the interviewer to tell them what they will have to do. Most interviewers, however, are impressed by someone who has taken the time to do his or her homework. For this reason, you should always do some research before you go on an interview—even for a part-time job. Most of the time, your research can be nothing more than a quick look at the company's website, but this kind of research really pays off. Being able to talk about the job can give you a real advantage over other candidates. Sometimes the interviewer will be so impressed that he or she will offer you a job on the spot.

[Summary statement:]   *Answers will vary.*

_____

_____

Of course, following these suggestions will not guarantee that you get a job. You still have to do well at the interview itself. Even so, getting mentally prepared for the interview will give you an advantage over people who do almost nothing before they walk in the door.

2. Now, using the topic sentence below, write another body paragraph that you could add to the essay above. (This new paragraph will go right before the essay's conclusion.)

Another way to prepare yourself mentally is to anticipate and answer some

typical questions interviewers ask.

Answers will vary.

_____

_____

_____

_____

COLLABORATIVE ACTIVITY

Graphic Organizer: *Finding Ideas to Write About*

This chapter identified six strategies for finding ideas to write about. Fill in these six strategies in the graphic organizer on page 102, and then write a brief description of each strategy.

Strategy:
Freewriting

Description: Writing continuously without a specific topic in mind

Strategy:
Focused Freewriting

Description: Writing continuously with a specific topic in mind

Strategy:
Brainstorming

Description: Writing single words or phrases to express ideas

Strategy:
Collaborative Brainstorming

Description: In a group, writing single words or phrases to express ideas

Finding Ideas to Write About

Strategy:
Keeping a Journal

Description: Recording thoughts and ideas in a notebook or file

Strategy:
Clustering

Description: Writing a topic in the center of a sheet of paper and then writing relevant ideas in clusters

review checklist

Writing an Essay

☐ Most essays have a thesis-and-support structure. The thesis statement presents the main idea, and the body paragraphs support the thesis. (See 3a.)

☐ Begin by focusing on your assignment, purpose, and audience to help you find a topic. (See 3b.)

☐ Find ideas to write about. (See 3c.)

☐ Identify your main idea, and develop an effective thesis statement. (See 3d.)

☐ List the points that best support your thesis, and arrange them in the order in which you plan to discuss them, creating an informal outline of your essay. (See 3e and 3f.)

☐ Write your first draft, making sure your essay has a thesis-and-support structure. (See 3g.)

☐ TEST and revise your essay. (See 3h and 3i.)

☐ Edit and proofread your essay. (See 3j and 3k.)

4 Understanding Introductions, Body Paragraphs, and Conclusions

© Jeff Greenberg 3 of 6/Alamy

focus on reading and writing

Reread the essay you wrote in Chapter 3. You will continue working with your essay throughout this chapter.

In this chapter, you will learn to
- write an introduction (4a)
- write body paragraphs (4b)
- write a conclusion (4c)

A well-constructed thesis-and-support essay is more than a collection of paragraphs. It begins with an **introduction** that includes a **thesis statement**—the sentence that states the main idea that the essay will develop. The next part of the essay—the **body**—includes several paragraphs that develop, support, or explain the essay's thesis. The essay's **conclusion** reinforces the thesis and ideally brings the essay to an effective and memorable close.

As you read the essays in this book, you should evaluate their introductions, body paragraphs, and conclusions to see how different writers achieve their goals. This kind of focused reading can make you a stronger writer. The student and professional essays in Chapters 7–12 and the readings in Chapter 29 can all serve as good models for your own writing. In addition, the specific guidelines for understanding introductions, body paragraphs, and conclusions discussed in this chapter can help you as you write and revise.

4a Introductions

An **introduction** is the first thing people see when they read your essay. If your introduction is interesting, it will make readers want to read further. If it is not, readers may get bored and stop reading.

Your introduction should be a full paragraph that moves from general to specific ideas. It should begin with some general **opening remarks** that will draw readers into your essay. The **thesis statement**, a specific sentence that presents the main idea of your essay, usually comes at the end of the introduction. The following diagram illustrates the shape of an introduction.

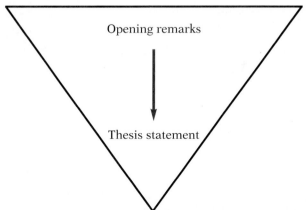

Teaching Tip
Advise students to draft their body paragraphs before they spend much time writing introductions or conclusions. After they have developed the body of their essay, they can revise their introduction and conclusion so those paragraphs are consistent with the direction that their essay has taken.

Teaching Tip
Explain to students that the inverted triangle refers to the movement of ideas from general to specific in the introductory paragraph.

105

Here are some options you can experiment with when you write your introductions. (In each of the sample introductory paragraphs that follow, the thesis statement is underlined and labeled.)

Beginning with a Narrative

Teaching Tip
Find two introductory paragraphs (one that is catchy and one that is dull), and read each one to the class. After you read each introduction, ask students whether they would like to hear the rest of the essay—and why or why not.

You can begin an essay with a narrative drawn from your own experience or from a current news event.

> On the first day my sister and I attended school in America, our parents walked us directly to the entrance of our new classroom. Even though she barely spoke any English, Mom tried earnestly to teach us how to ask for permission to use the bathroom: "Can I go to the bathroom?" Like parrots, she had us repeat this question over and over. At the time, neither of us realized that the proper way of asking for permission is "May I go to the bathroom?" This grammar slip did not matter, though, because we forgot the question as soon as our parents left. Reluctantly, we entered the classroom, more timid than two mice trying not to awaken a sleeping cat. <u>We didn't know yet that going to school where English was the only language spoken would prove to be very difficult.</u>

Thesis statement

—Hilda Alvarado (student)

Beginning with a Question (or a Series of Questions)

Teaching Tip
Remind students that general questions should be used only in an essay's introductory paragraph. Overusing questions in an essay may show that the writer does not know what he or she wants to say.

Asking one or more questions at the beginning of your essay is an effective strategy. Because readers expect you to answer the questions, they will want to read further.

> Is it worth giving up a chance to go to college to make a respectable salary today? "For me it was," says Mario Sarno, general manager of Arby's store #219. At nineteen years of age, Mario looks like a salesman. He is of medium height and build and has an outgoing personality that makes him stand out. As general manager, Mario's major tasks are to maintain the fast-food environment and to ensure that customers are happy. At the age of seventeen, Mario was noticed by an Arby's corporate supervisor and was promoted to manager. <u>Mario's positive experience suggests that students should consider the advantages of going directly into the job market.</u>

Thesis statement

—Lucus J. Anemone (student)

Beginning with a Definition

A definition at the beginning of your essay can give readers important information. As the following introduction shows, a definition can help explain a complicated idea or a confusing concept.

Teaching Tip
Encourage students to avoid introducing a definition with a tired opening phrase such as "According to *Webster's* . . ." or "*The American Heritage Dictionary* defines . . ."

> "Getting inked" is how many people refer to the act of getting a tattoo. Although some people may see it as a form of torture, tattooing is an art form that dates back over hundreds of years. The craft has been more formally defined as the practice of permanently marking the skin through punctures or incisions, which receive various dyes or pigments. Although Polynesian in origin, tattooing has a rich history in the United States.
>
> —Kristen L. McCormack (student)

Thesis statement

Beginning with a Quotation

An appropriate saying or some interesting dialogue can draw readers into your essay.

Teaching Tip
Send students to an online source such as bartleby.com to find appropriate quotations for both introductions and conclusions.

Teaching Tip
Remind students that when they quote or paraphrase, they must document their sources. Refer them to 13b-d.

> According to the comedian Jerry Seinfeld, "When you're single, you are the dictator of your own life. . . . When you're married, you are part of a vast decision-making body." In other words, before you can do anything when you are married, you have to talk it over with someone else. These words kept going through my mind as I thought about asking my girlfriend to marry me. The more I thought about Seinfeld's words, the more I put off asking. I never thought about the huge price that I would pay for this delay.
>
> —Dan Brody (student)

Thesis statement

Beginning with a Surprising Statement

You can begin your essay with a surprising or unexpected statement. Because your statement takes readers by surprise, it catches their attention.

> Some of the smartest people I know never went to college. In fact, some of them never finished high school. They still know how to save 20 percent on the price of a dinner, fix their own faucets when they leak, get discounted prescriptions, get free rides on a bus to Atlantic City, use

public transportation to get anywhere in the city, and live on about twenty-two dollars a day. Some people would call them old and poor, but I would call them survivors who have learned to make it through life on nothing but a Social Security check. <u>These survivors are my grandparents' friends, and they have taught me many things I cannot learn in school.</u>

Thesis statement

—Sean Ragas (student)

FYI

What to Avoid in Introductions

When writing an introduction, avoid the following.

- Beginning your essay by announcing what you plan to write about.

  PHRASES TO AVOID

  This essay is about . . .

  In my essay, I will discuss . . .

- Apologizing for your ideas.

  PHRASES TO AVOID

  Although I don't know much about this subject . . .

  I might not be an expert, but . . .

FYI

Choosing a Title

Every essay should have a **title** that suggests the subject of the essay and makes people want to read it. Here are a few tips for properly formatting your title.

- Capitalize all words except for articles (*a, an, the*), prepositions (*at, to, of, around,* and so on), and coordinating conjunctions (*and, but,* and so on), unless they are the first or last word of the title.
- Do not underline or italicize your title or enclose it in quotation marks. Do not type your title in all capital letters.
- Center the title at the top of the first page. Double-space between the title and the first line of your essay.

As you consider a title for your paper, think about the following options.

- ■ *A title can highlight a key word or term that appears in the essay.*
  In Praise of the F Word

  The Sanctuary of School
- ■ *A title can be a straightforward announcement.*
  The Case for Short Words

  How to Mummify a Pharaoh
- ■ *A title can express a point of view or state a position.*
  Why Women Soldiers Don't Belong on the Front Lines

  Tweet Less, Kiss More
- ■ *A title can be a familiar saying or a quotation from the essay itself.*
  Men Are from Mars, Women Are from Venus

  I Want a Wife

PRACTICE

4-1   Look through the student essays in Chapters 7–12, and find one introduction you think is particularly effective. Be prepared to explain the strengths of the introduction you chose.

PRACTICE

4-2   Using the different options for creating titles discussed in the FYI box above, write two titles for each of the essays described below.   *Answers will vary.*

1. A student writes an essay about three people who disappeared mysteriously: Amelia Earhart, aviator; Ambrose Bierce, writer; and Jimmy Hoffa, union leader. In the body paragraphs, the student describes the circumstances surrounding their disappearances.

   _____

   _____

ESL Tip

ESL students may need help understanding the cultural context of this exercise. You may want to offer an alternative exercise or spend extra time on giving instructions.

2. A student writes an essay arguing against doctors' letting people select the gender of their babies. In the body paragraphs, she presents reasons why she thinks it is unethical.

   _____

   _____

3. A student writes an essay explaining why America should elect a woman president. In the body paragraphs, he gives his reasons.

_____

_____

focus on reading and writing

Reread the essay that you wrote in Chapter 3 about the most difficult job you've ever had. Evaluate your introduction. Then, choose one of the strategies discussed in 4a and write a new introduction. Which introduction—the old one or the new one—do you think is more effective? Why?

4b Body Paragraphs

e bedfordstmartins.com
/forw LearningCurve >
Topic Sentences and
Supporting Details

The middle part of your essay is the **body**—the paragraphs that develop and support your thesis statement. Each body paragraph begins with a **topic sentence** that indicates the main idea the paragraph will discuss, and it goes on to support that idea with **evidence**—examples and details. **Transitional words and phrases** help readers follow the discussion. Often, the paragraph ends with a **summary statement** that reinforces the main idea.

Body Paragraphs

> The **topic sentence** states the main idea of the paragraph.
> **Evidence** supports the main idea.
> **Transitional words and phrases** show the connections among ideas.
> A **summary statement** often ends the paragraph.

Every body paragraph should support your essay's thesis. If your thesis states that there are four reasons for high unemployment, then each of your body paragraphs should discuss one of these reasons. The topic sentence should identify the reason, and the rest of the paragraph should develop this point with examples and details.

Introduction

. . . Despite optimistic predictions to the contrary, unemployment will remain high for four reasons.

First body paragraph

The first reason unemployment will remain high is . . .

Second body paragraph

The second reason unemployment will remain high is . . .

Third body paragraph

The third reason unemployment will remain high is . . .

Fourth body paragraph

The fourth reason unemployment will remain high is . . .

Conclusion

Even though some experts believe that the economy is improving, the truth is that unemployment will continue to be high. . . .

Teaching Tip
Tell students that they can use TEST to help them determine if their paragraphs include all the necessary elements to make them unified (topic sentence, summary statement), coherent (transitions), and well developed (evidence).

Because the body paragraphs of your essay carry the weight of the discussion, they are the most important (and longest) part of your essay. To be effective, each body paragraph should not only clearly support the essay's thesis but also be *unified, coherent,* and *well developed.*

- **Body paragraphs should be unified.** A body paragraph is **unified** when all its sentences support the main idea stated in the **topic sentence**. Just as a thesis statement presents the essay's main idea, the topic sentence in a paragraph presents the paragraph's main idea. If the sentences in a body paragraph wander from the main idea stated in the topic sentence, the paragraph lacks unity.

Consider the following body paragraph from a student essay. (Note that the topic sentence is underlined.)

> Another effect of the weak economy is that it has caused young people to move out of rural communities. Over the years, farmland has become more and more expensive. A decade ago, a family could afford to buy each of its children twenty-five or thirty acres on which they could start farming. Today, the price of land is so high that the average farmer cannot afford to buy this amount of land, and those who cannot farm have few alternatives. Young people cannot find good jobs anymore. The prolonged economic downturn has caused many factories to move out of the area, and they have taken with them the jobs that many young people used to get after high school. As a result, many eighteen-year-olds have no choice but to move away to find employment.

Notice that each sentence in the paragraph above develops the main idea in the topic sentence. For this reason, the paragraph is unified.

Constructing Effective Topic Sentences

The first step in writing effective body paragraphs is to construct effective topic sentences. As you write, keep the following guidelines in mind.

- **A topic sentence should be a complete sentence.** Like any sentence, a topic sentence should have a subject and a verb and express a complete thought.
- **A topic sentence should make a point about the idea you plan to discuss.** For this reason, it should be more than just an announcement of what you plan to write about.

ANNOUNCEMENT	TOPIC SENTENCE
Now I am going to discuss another characteristic of a hero.	Another characteristic of heroes is that they take action instead of waiting for others to act.

- **A topic sentence should present an idea that you can discuss in a single paragraph.** If your topic sentence is too broad, you will not be able to develop it in a single paragraph. If it is too narrow, you will not be able to say much about it.

  TOPIC SENTENCE TOO BROAD

  Students with jobs have additional challenges.

  TOPIC SENTENCE TOO NARROW

  The tutoring center closes at 5 p.m.

  EFFECTIVE TOPIC SENTENCE

  The tutoring center's limited hours present another problem.

- **Body paragraphs should be coherent.** A body paragraph is **coherent** if its sentences are arranged in a clear, logical order. You can create coherence by using **transitional words and phrases** that emphasize the logical connections among ideas. You can also create coherence by repeating **key words** from one sentence to another. Finally, you can use **pronouns** that point to nouns in preceding sentences. These three strategies enable readers to see how your ideas are related within your body paragraphs.

  The following body paragraph, from Amy Chua's *Battle Hymn of the Tiger Mother*, uses transitional words and phrases, repeated key words, and pronouns to create coherence. (Note that the transitions are shaded.)

  What Chinese parents understand is that nothing is fun until you're good at it. To get good at anything, you have to work, and children on their own never want to work, which is why it is crucial to override their preferences. This often requires fortitude on the part of their parents because the child will resist; things are always the hardest at the beginning, which is where Western parents tend to give up. But if done properly, the Chinese strategy produces a virtuous circle. Tenacious practice, practice, practice is crucial for excellence; rote repetition is underrated in America. Once a child starts to excel at something—whether it's math, piano, pitching, or ballet—he or she gets praise, admiration, and satisfaction. This builds confidence and makes the once not-so-fun activity fun. This in turn makes it easier for the parent to get the child to work even more.

WORD POWER

fortitude strength, determination

tenacious determined or stubborn

Transitions

Sequence or Addition

again	first, . . . second, . . . third	next
also	furthermore	one . . . another
and	in addition	still
besides	last	too
finally	moreover	

Time

afterward	finally	simultaneously
as soon as	immediately	since
at first	in the meantime	soon
at the same time	later	subsequently
before	meanwhile	then
earlier	next	until
eventually	now	

Comparison

also	likewise
in comparison	similarly
in the same way	

Contrast

although	in contrast	on the one hand . . .
but	instead	on the other hand . . .
conversely	nevertheless	still
despite	nonetheless	whereas
even though	on the contrary	yet
however		

Examples

for example	specifically
for instance	that is
in fact	thus
namely	

Conclusions or Summaries

as a result	in summary
in conclusion	therefore
in short	thus

Causes or Effects

as a result	so
because	then
consequently	therefore
since	

- **Body paragraphs should be well developed.** A body paragraph is **well developed** when it includes enough **evidence**—examples and details—to support the main idea stated in the topic sentence. If your paragraph contains only general statements, it will not provide the information readers need to understand (and accept) its point.

The following body paragraph from a student essay uses examples and details to support its main idea.

> Hearing people also have some mistaken ideas about the deaf community. First, some hearing people think that all deaf people consider themselves disabled and would do anything not to be "handicapped." Hearing people do not realize that deaf people are proud to be part of a community that has its own language, customs, and culture. Second, many hearing people think that all deaf people read lips, so there is no need to learn sign language to communicate with them. However, lip reading—or speech reading, as deaf people call the practice—is extremely difficult. Not all hearing people say words the same way, and facial expressions can also change the meaning of words. If hearing people make more of an attempt to understand the deaf culture, communication between deaf people and hearing people will certainly improve.

Evidence (examples and details)

PRACTICE

4-3 Choose two body paragraphs from one of the essays in Chapter 29, "Readings for Writers." Using the criteria discussed in 4b, decide whether the paragraphs are unified, coherent, and well developed. Be prepared to discuss your decisions with the class.

focus on reading and writing

Reread the essay that you wrote in Chapter 3 about the most difficult job you've ever had. Check to make sure that all your body paragraphs support your essay's thesis. Then, evaluate your body paragraphs, and revise and edit them as necessary to make them unified, coherent, and well developed.

4c   Conclusions

Because your conclusion is the last thing readers see, they often judge your entire essay by its effectiveness. For this reason, conclusions should be planned, drafted, and revised carefully.

Like an introduction, a **conclusion** should be a full paragraph. It should begin with a **summary statement** that reinforces the essay's main idea, and it should end with some general **concluding remarks**. The following diagram illustrates the shape of a conclusion.

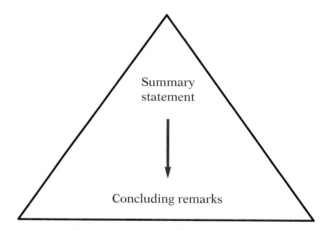

Here are some options you can experiment with when you write your conclusions. (In each of the sample concluding paragraphs that follow, the summary statement is underlined and labeled.)

Concluding with a Narrative

A narrative conclusion can bring an event discussed in the essay to a logical, satisfying close.

I went to Philadelphia with my boys to share the thing my father and I had shared—a love for history. Unfortunately, they were more interested in horse-and-buggy rides, overpriced knickknacks, the tall buildings, and parades. As we walked into Independence Hall, though, I noticed that the boys became quiet. They felt it. They felt the thick historical air around us. I watched them look around as the guide painted a vivid picture of the times and spoke of the marches down Broad Street and the clashing of ideas as our forefathers debated and even fought for freedom. I felt my husband behind me and took my eyes off of my boys to turn to the left; I could almost see my father. I almost whispered out loud to him, "We were here."

Summary statement

—Shannon Lewis (student)

Concluding with a Recommendation

Once you think you have convinced readers that a problem exists, you can make recommendations in your conclusion about how the problem should be solved.

Solutions for the binge-drinking problem on college campuses are not easy, but both schools and students need to acknowledge the problem and to try to solve it. Schools that have an alcohol-free policy should aggressively enforce it, and schools that do not have such a policy should implement one. In addition, students should take responsibility for their actions and resolve to drink responsibly. No one should get hurt or die from drinking too much, but if something does not change soon, many more students will.

Summary statement

—April Moen (student)

Concluding with a Quotation

A well-chosen quotation—even a brief one—can be an effective concluding strategy. In the following paragraph, the quotation reinforces the main idea of the essay.

I'll never forget the day I caught the ball on a penalty kick, winning the game for my team. My opponent's foot made contact with the ball, and everything around me fell silent. The ball came at me, hurtling over my head toward the top right of the goal. As I dived to catch it, I closed my eyes. The ball smacked into my hands so hard I thought it must have split my gloves. When I opened my eyes, I realized that I had caught the ball and saved the game for our team. The crowd cheered wildly, and my team surrounded me as I got to my feet. As the celebration died down, my coach walked up to me and, as I handed him the game-winning ball, he said, "To the playoffs we go!"

Summary statement

—Jacob Kinley (student)

Concluding with a Prediction

This type of conclusion not only sums up the thesis but also looks to the future.

Summary statement

<u>Whether people like it or not, texting is not going to go away anytime soon.</u> This generation and future generations are going to use "text speak" and become even more comfortable with communicating via text messages. Texting has already had a large impact on today's world. In fact, texting has helped put the written word back into our lives, making people more comfortable with the skill of writing. & it's a fast, EZ way 2 communic8.

—Courtney Anttila (student)

FYI

What to Avoid in Conclusions

When writing a conclusion, avoid the following.

- Introducing new ideas. Your conclusion should sum up the ideas you discuss in your essay, not open up new lines of thought.
- Apologizing for your opinions, ideas, or conclusions. Apologies will undercut your readers' confidence in you.

PHRASES TO AVOID

At least that is my opinion . . .

I could be wrong, but . . .

- Using unnecessary phrases to announce your essay is coming to a close.

PHRASES TO AVOID

In summary, . . .

In conclusion, . . .

Teaching Tip
Explain that in essay exams, when time is limited, a one-sentence restatement of the thesis is often enough for a conclusion. Likewise, an essay exam may require just a one- or two-sentence introduction.

PRACTICE

4-4   Choose a conclusion from one of the essays in Chapter 29 that you think is particularly effective. Be prepared to explain the strengths of the conclusion you chose.

focus on reading and writing

Reread the essay that you wrote in Chapter 3 about the most difficult job you've ever had. Evaluate your conclusion. Then, choose one of the strategies discussed in 4c, and write a new conclusion. Which conclusion—the old one or the new one—do you think is more effective? Why?

REVIEW ACTIVITY

The following student essay has an undeveloped introduction and conclusion. Decide what introductory and concluding strategies would be best for the essay. Then, rewrite both the introduction and the conclusion. Then, suggest an interesting title for the essay.   *Answers will vary.*

The Most Dangerous Jobs

This essay is about three of the most dangerous jobs. They are piloting small planes, logging, and fishing.

Flying a small plane can be dangerous. For example, pilots who fly tiny planes that spray pesticides on farmers' fields do not have to comply with the safety rules for large airplanes. They also have to fly very low in order to spray the right fields. This leaves little room for error. Also, pilots of air-taxis and small commuter planes die in much greater numbers than airline pilots do. In some places, like parts of Alaska, there are long distances and few roads, so many small planes are needed. Their pilots are four times more likely to die than other pilots because of bad weather and poor visibility. In general, flying a small plane can be very risky.

Another dangerous job is logging. Loggers always are at risk of having parts of trees or heavy machinery fall on them. Tree trunks often have odd shapes, so they are hard to control while they are being transported. As a result, they often break loose from equipment that is supposed to move them. In addition, weather conditions, like snow or rain, can cause dangers. Icy or wet conditions increase the risk to loggers, who can fall from trees or slip when they are sawing a tree. Because loggers often work in remote places, it is very hard to get prompt medical aid. For this reason, a wound that could easily be treated in a hospital may be fatal to a logger.

Perhaps the most dangerous occupation is working in the fishing industry. Like loggers, professional fishermen work in unsafe conditions. They use heavy machinery to pull up nets and to move large amounts of fish. The combination

119

of icy or slippery boat decks and large nets and cages makes the job unsafe. The weather is often very bad, so fishermen are at risk of falling overboard during a storm and drowning. In fact, drowning is the most common cause of death in this industry. Also, like logging, fishing is done far from medical help, so even minor injuries can be very serious.

In conclusion, piloting, logging, and fishing are three of the most dangerous occupations.

Now, evaluate the body paragraphs of the essay above. Choose one body paragraph, and strengthen it by adding some examples and details.

COLLABORATIVE ACTIVITY

Graphic Organizer: *Introductions, Body Paragraphs, and Conclusions*

The components of introductions, body paragraphs, and conclusions are presented in the graphic organizer on page 121. Work with another student to fill in the organizer with any information that is missing.

Introductions

The introduction _____ begins the essay and presents the thesis statement.

> A thesis statement is:
>
> _A sentence that states the main point of the essay._
>
> Write a thesis statement for the following essay topic: "Rising college tuition and fees"
>
> _(Answers will vary) Example: The rising cost of college tuition and fees negatively impacts_
>
> _college students._
>
> Write a thesis statement for the following essay topic: "Reducing childhood obesity"
>
> _(Answers will vary) Example: Childhood obesity can be reduced through various_
>
> _school programs._

Body Paragraphs

Body paragraphs _____ should be unified, coherent, and well developed.

> A body paragraph is unified when it includes _a topic sentence and a summary statement_.
>
> A body paragraph is coherent when it includes _transitions_.
>
> A body paragraph is well developed when it includes _evidence (examples and details)_.

Conclusion

The conclusion _____ brings the essay to an effective close.

> The conclusion should include _a summary statement_ and _concluding remarks_.

review checklist

Introductions and Conclusions

☐ The introduction of your essay should include opening remarks and a thesis statement. (See 4a.) You can begin an essay with any of the following options.

A narrative   A quotation
A question   A surprising statement
A definition

☐ Your title should suggest the subject of your essay and make people want to read further. (See 4a.)

☐ Your body paragraphs should be unified, coherent, and well developed. They should also clearly support the essay's thesis. (See 4b.)

☐ The conclusion of your essay should include a summary statement and some general concluding remarks. (See 4c.) You can conclude an essay with any of the following options.

A narrative   A quotation
A recommendation   A prediction

5 Thinking, Reading, and Writing Critically

The Parnassus, detail of Venus and Mars (oil on canvas), Mantegna, Andrea (1431–1506)/Louvre, Paris, France/Giraudon/
The Bridgeman Art Library

focus on reading and writing

Brainstorm to discover what you already know about the differences between
how men and women behave. Then, preview the essay "Men Are from Mars,
Women Are from Venus," by John Gray (p. 601).

In this chapter, you will learn to

- identify audience, purpose, and tone (5a)
- identify connotations and figurative language (5b)
- identify the main idea (5c)
- identify major and minor supporting points (5d)
- evaluate the writer's ideas (5e)
- read and write critically (5f)

Teaching Tip
Although this discussion focuses on reading, remind students that the "E" in TEST applies to both reading and writing. They should identify and evaluate evidence when they read critically and when they TEST what they have written.

In Chapter 1, you learned about the active reading process, a series of activities that enable you to identify key information and to determine the meaning of a text. In this chapter, we will take this process a step further and discuss some strategies that will help you to think critically about the texts you read—and, eventually, to write about them. Keep in mind that thinking critically about a text does *not* mean challenging every idea you encounter. What **thinking critically** *does* mean is considering a writer's motives, weighing evidence, evaluating both the strengths and weaknesses of a text, keeping an open mind, and seeing connections between your own ideas and those in the text.

5a Identifying Audience, Purpose, and Tone

Teaching Tip
Remind students that some features of the text are obvious, such as the introduction, conclusion, and so on, but there are also less-obvious features that convey the writer's message. By understanding both, readers can determine the main idea and critically engage with the text.

As you begin to think critically about a text, you should consider its intended *audience*, its *purpose*, and its *tone*.

The Writer's Audience

The writer's **intended audience** is the group of readers the writer wants to address. The publication in which a piece of writing appears often provides clues about its intended audience. For example, an article about childhood obesity in a popular magazine such as *Discover* or the digital edition of *Newsweek* would be written for an intended audience that has only a general knowledge of the subject. However, an article in a scholarly journal, such as *Nature* or the *New England Journal of Medicine*, would be aimed at an intended audience that knows a great deal about the subject—for example, researchers or medical doctors. Identifying the intended audience of a piece of writing is helpful because it enables you to consider how the writer's view of his or her audience has determined the text's level and content. For example, has the writer included definitions of key terms and explanations of basic concepts, or are readers expected to know them?

e bedfordstmartins.com
/forw LearningCurve >
Critical Reading

Identifying the Writer's Intended Audience

To help identify the intended audience of a piece of writing, ask the following questions.

- **Age**   Does anything in the text—for example, slang or cultural references—indicate that it is aimed at a particular age group?
- **Education level**   How much education does the writer assume readers have? Does the text's vocabulary reveal the writer's assumptions?
- **Biases**   Does the writer expect readers to have preconceived ideas about the subject?
- **Knowledge**   Does the writer expect readers to know a lot (or a little) about the subject? How much space does the writer devote to defining terms, explaining concepts, and providing background information?

Teaching Tip
Direct students to 5e for a discussion of bias.

focus on reading and writing

Now that you have previewed John Gray's essay about the differences between men and women, go back and read it, highlighting and annotating it. Who do you think is the intended audience for this essay? What led you to your conclusion?

The Writer's Purpose

In general, a writer has one of three main purposes.

- To **inform** readers about something
- To **explain** something to readers
- To **persuade** readers to do something or to act certain way

In addition to one **primary purpose**, a writer often has one or more **secondary purposes**. For example, in a blog posting, a writer's main purpose might be to inform readers about the dangers of performance-enhancing drugs. His secondary purpose might be to persuade readers not to take them.

Keep in mind that there is a difference between *informing, explaining*, and *persuading*. When writers **inform**, they present information and let readers draw their own conclusions. When writers **explain**, they interpret information, adding their own insights and judgments. When writers **persuade**, they try to change readers' minds—in other words, they try to convince readers that one side of an issue is preferable to another. Sometimes they even try to move readers to action.

Determining the Writer's Purpose

To determine the writer's purpose, consider the following.

- **Statements**   Writers frequently make statements that reveal their primary purpose. For example, does a writer say that he or she wants to *inform* readers about the advantages of recycling or that he or she wants to *convince* them to recycle? (You can often discover a writer's purpose by looking at an essay's thesis statement.)

- **Knowledge about the writer**   The more you know about a writer, the more accurately you can determine his or her purpose. For example, if you know that a writer is a scientist, you might assume that his or her purpose is to inform. If the writer is an environmental activist, however, you might assume that his or her purpose is to further that cause. Keep in mind, however, that you can't just assume that one writer is always out to inform and another is always out to persuade. You should base your conclusion about the writer's purpose on what he or she says, not on your preconceptions.

- **Knowledge about the publication**   The type of publication in which an article appears can provide clues about a writer's purpose. For example, an article in *National Geographic* might present information about the damage caused by the *Exxon Valdez* oil spill in a straightforward way. An article in a publication sponsored by Exxon, however, might have a different purpose—for example, to publicize the company's support for its environmental efforts.

focus on reading and writing

Referring to "Men Are from Mars, Women Are from Venus" by John Gray (p. 601), which you have now highlighted and annotated, consider why Gray wrote this essay. What was his purpose? How can you tell?

The Writer's Tone

The **tone** of a piece of writing indicates a writer's attitude toward readers or toward his or her subject. Just as people use various tones when speaking, written texts can also have different tones. Unlike speakers, who can create tone by changing their emphasis, timing, or volume, writers create tone largely through their choice of words.

A writer's purpose usually determines tone. For example, textbooks call for an *objective* tone, with an emphasis on facts and clear explanations and the use of relatively formal language. Creative literature and personal essays, however, often use a *subjective* tone, relying on informal language and words that communicate feelings and opinions. Other types of writing can convey different types of tone—for example, an email to a friend can be intimate, a letter to a customer can be polite, and an editorial in a newspaper can be critical.

Because a writer's tone can affect how you respond to a piece of writing, you should be aware of it when you read (as you are aware of your own tone when you write). For example, an angry or sarcastic tone might indicate that a writer is biased; a conciliatory tone might suggest that a writer is fair and will consider opposing points of view.

Teaching Tip
Ask students if they can determine the meaning of the word *conciliatory*, based on the skills and strategies they learned in Chapter 2.

Describing Tone

You can use any of the words below to describe a writer's tone. Keep in mind that this is just a sampling of the words that can be used to characterize tone.

aloof	emotional	sad
ambivalent	friendly	sarcastic
angry	happy	sentimental
apathetic	hostile	serious
appreciative	insincere	sincere
authoritative	ironic	subjective
bitter	objective	sympathetic
critical	playful	tender
distant	respectful	

Determining a Writer's Tone

The following questions can help you identify a writer's tone.

- How does the writer communicate his or her attitude to readers? Which word in the box above best describes this attitude?
- How does the writer use adverbs and adjectives in descriptions (see 16a)?
- What connotations do the writer's words have (see 2b and 5b)?

PRACTICE

5-1   Read the following short passages. Choose the word from the box on page 127 that best describes the author's tone.

1. My summer job at a fast-food restaurant was my all-time worst job because of the endless stream of rude customers, the many boring and repetitive tasks I had to perform, and my manager's insensitive treatment of employees. —Sarah Herman, student

   What is the passage's tone? *Possible answers: bitter, critical*

   What words helped you determine the tone? *"all-time worst,"*

   "endless stream," "boring and repetitive," "insensitive treatment"

2. Sam wears a Mexican poncho to school every Friday. Like a number of things about our middle child, the "why" of it is a mystery. When he started wearing it about two years ago, I guessed that he was perhaps reinterpreting the idea of casual Friday for high school. Or he might have just thought, "I will wear a poncho to school on Friday. See what happens." —John Schwartz, "The Poncho Bearer"

   What is the passage's tone? *Possible answers: humorous, admiring*

   What words helped you determine the tone? *"like a number of*

   things about our middle child," "reinterpreting the idea"

3. So, while politicians debate the finer points of immigration reform, the Department of Homeland Security is already carrying out its own. Unfortunately, these actions can not only plunge families into financial decline, but also sever them forever. —Edwidge Danticat, "Impounded Fathers"

   What is the passage's tone? *Possible answers: serious, emotional*

   What words helped you determine the tone? *"unfortunately,"*

   "plunge," "sever them forever"

focus on reading and writing

Review "Men Are from Mars, Women Are from Venus," by John Gray (p. 601), as well as your highlighting and annotations. How would you describe Gray's tone in this essay? What words and phrases led you to your conclusion?

PRACTICE
5-2
Graphic Organizer: *Audience, Purpose, and Tone*

In the following graphic organizer, fill in the details about audience, purpose, and tone. Be sure to provide examples where required.

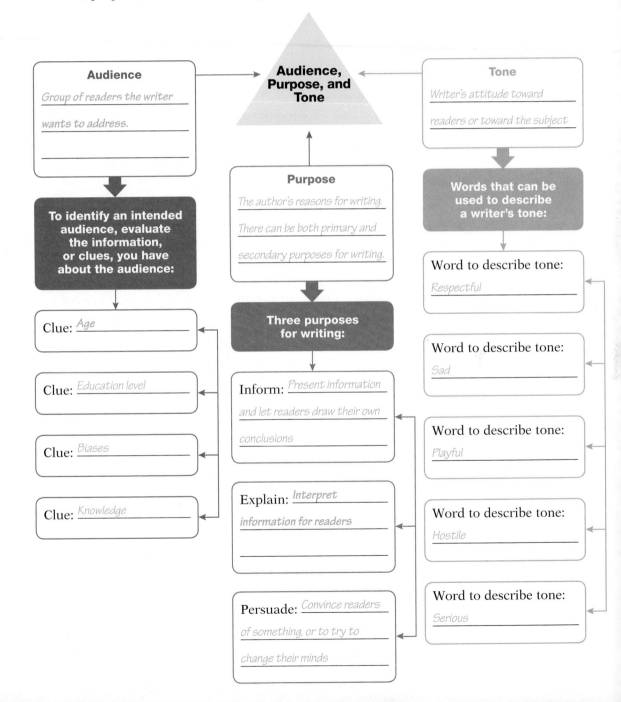

Audience

Group of readers the writer

wants to address.

Audience, Purpose, and Tone

Tone

Writer's attitude toward

readers or toward the subject

To identify an intended audience, evaluate the information, or clues, you have about the audience:

Purpose

The author's reasons for writing.

There can be both primary and

secondary purposes for writing.

Words that can be used to describe a writer's tone:

Clue: Age

Clue: Education level

Clue: Biases

Clue: Knowledge

Three purposes for writing:

Inform: Present information

and let readers draw their own

conclusions

Explain: Interpret

information for readers

Persuade: Convince readers

of something, or to try to

change their minds

Word to describe tone:

Respectful

Word to describe tone:

Sad

Word to describe tone:

Playful

Word to describe tone:

Hostile

Word to describe tone:

Serious

5b Identifying Connotations and Figurative Language

Teaching Tip
Direct students to 2b for more on connotations.

Connotations

As you think critically about a text, your goal is to interpret what the writer is saying. Learning connotations of words can help you to accomplish this goal.

A word's **connotations** are its emotional or cultural associations—apart from its literal (or **denotative**) meanings. Consider the following sentences.

■ If the economy weren't so horrible, I wouldn't have to live in this miserable apartment. (In this sentence, the words *horrible* and *miserable* have negative connotations.)

■ This apartment may be tiny and dark, but because it is my first, it will always have a special place in my heart. (In this sentence, the words *tiny* and *dark* have negative connotations, but the phrase "will always have a special place in my heart" has positive connotations.)

■ The apartment had two rooms, and all its windows faced an airshaft. (In this sentence, the words are neutral. None of them has any emotional associations apart from its literal or denotative meaning.)

Because no two words have exactly the same meaning, when you read and write, you should be sensitive to the different shades of meaning that various words have. Don't say *cheap* when you mean *inexpensive*, or *vagrant* when you mean *homeless person*. Although these words may have similar meanings, they have decidedly different connotations.

PRACTICE

5-3   Consider the different connotations of the three words in each group listed below. Which words have positive connotations? Which have negative connotations? Which are neutral? (Not every group includes all three categories.)

1. house/home/cabin

2. talkative/chatty/mouthy

3. arrogant/snobbish/proud

4. nutritious/edible/delicious

5. car/automobile/lemon

focus on reading and writing

Throughout "Men Are from Mars, Women Are from Venus," John Gray uses pairs of words to express the differences between men and women. For example, in paragraph 2, he says that while a woman thinks that she is *nurturing* a man, he thinks that she is being *controlling*. Find four or five of these word pairs in Gray's essay, and be prepared to explain how the connotations of the two words in each pair differ.

Figurative Language

When you read a text, keep in mind that not everything a writer says should be taken literally. Sometimes writers use **figurative language**, describing something by comparing it to something else. For example, when a writer describes a neighborhood as a "food desert" or an athlete as moving "as fast as a cheetah on the Serengeti," he or she is using figurative language.

Figurative language allows writers to expand language beyond the literal meaning of words. It enables them to surprise readers with unexpected—and sometimes memorable—comparisons, suggesting that a neighborhood without stores can be like a desert and that an athlete can be as thrilling to watch as a cheetah running across a wide African plain. Remember, though, that figurative language only makes sense if you understand that the comparison the writer is making is not to be taken literally. (The neighborhood is not really a "desert," and the runner is not really "as fast as a cheetah.")

There are three basic types of figurative language—*simile*, *metaphor*, and *personification*.

- A **simile** uses the words *like* or *as* to compare two unlike things.

    Her smile was like sunshine.

- A **metaphor** compares two unlike things without using the words *like* or *as*.

    Her smile was a light that brightened the room.

- **Personification** suggests a comparison between a nonliving thing and a person by giving the nonliving thing human traits.

    The sun smiled down on the crowd.

PRACTICE

5-4   Label each of the following as a simile (*s*), a metaphor (*m*), or a personification (*p*).

1. Life is a fashion show. _____*m*_____

2. The sunlight seemed to dance across the water. _____*p*_____

3. Her laugh hung in the air like a song. _____*s*_____

4. Love is a battlefield. _____*m*_____

5. Time stood still. _____*p*_____

6. The air smelled as clean as freshly cut wood. _____*s*_____

7. Life without love is like a tree without fruit or blossoms. _____*s*_____

   (Kahlil Gibran)

8. The ocean sparkled like diamonds. _____*s*_____

9. America is a melting pot. _____*m*_____

10. The leaves skipped in the wind. _____*p*_____

focus on reading and writing

Review "Men Are from Mars, Women Are from Venus," by John Gray (p. 601). In what sense is the title of this essay an example of figurative language? Where in the essay does Gray use similes and metaphors?

5c   Identifying the Main Idea

**bedfordstmartins.com
/forw** LearningCurve >
Topics and Main Ideas

One of the first things you do when you think critically about a text is look for the writer's main idea—the key point the text is making. As you have already learned, writers frequently express this main idea in a **thesis statement** that often—but not always—appears in the introduction.

For example, in "The Case for Short Words" (p. 577), Richard Lederer expresses his main idea in a thesis statement at the end of his essay's introductory paragraph. This strategy enables him to communicate the main idea to readers before he goes on to support it with examples in the rest of his essay.

When you speak and write, there is no law that says you have to use big words. Short words are as good as long ones, and short, old words—like *sun* and *grass* and *home*—are best of all. <u>A lot of</u> <u>small words, more than you might think, can meet your needs with</u> <u>a strength, grace, and charm that large words do not have.</u>

Sometimes, however, a writer may decide to state the main idea later in an essay. This is a good strategy when a writer is dealing with a controversial topic and wants to prepare readers for a main idea that may disturb or even shock them. Alternatively, a writer may choose to *imply* the main idea instead of stating it. This is often the case in narrative or process essays, where a thesis statement might seem forced or artificial.

To locate a text's main idea, follow the active reading process outlined in Chapter 1, identifying verbal and visual signals that point to important information and marking the text as you read to highlight the writer's key points. If a text has an **implied main idea**, identifying the main idea can be a challenge, but it is an important part of the critical reading process. In this case, you will need to review your highlighting and annotations especially carefully to see what key sentences and passages reveal about the writer's purpose and meaning.

Teaching Tip
Refer students to the Introduction of this book and to Chapter 4 for more on placement of thesis statements and topic sentences.

Teaching Tip
Encourage students to write a text's main idea in the margin as they make their annotations.

FYI

Stating Your Main Idea

Although professional writers may not always include an explicitly stated main idea at the beginning of an essay or paragraph, it is a good idea for you to do so. This strategy will help keep you on track as you write and help readers follow your discussion as they read.

PRACTICE

5-5 Choose one professional essay from the readings in Chapters 7–12 or Chapter 29, and answer these questions.

- If the main idea is explicitly stated, why did the writer choose to state it instead of implying it? Where is it stated? Why did the writer decide to locate this statement here instead of elsewhere in the essay?
- If the main idea is implied, why did the writer decide not to state the main idea directly?

focus on reading and writing

Look again at the essay "Men Are from Mars, Women Are from Venus" by John Gray (p. 601). Does Gray state his main idea directly, or does he imply it? Do you think this was the right choice?

5d Identifying Major and Minor Supporting Points

bedfordstmartins.com
/forw LearningCurve >
Topic Sentences and
Supporting Details

In addition to identifying the main idea of a passage, you should also be able to identify its major and minor supporting points.

The **major supporting points** are the points that provide important information about the main idea. They relate directly to the main idea and establish the structure of the discussion. **Minor supporting points** provide additional information about the major supporting points. They supply the **evidence** (examples and details) that develops the major points and enables readers to understand exactly what a writer is saying. By evaluating the strength of a writer's major and minor supporting points, readers can determine whether they accept the main idea.

The following diagram illustrates the relationship between the main idea and the major and minor supporting points.

Teaching Tip
Remind students to read actively—for example, to highlight the writer's major points. Refer them to 1b.

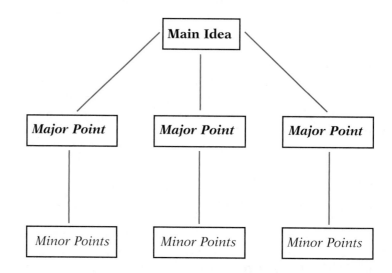

Teaching Tip
Tell students that they can also use an informal or formal outline to identify the major and minor points of something they read (or write). An informal outline of Jared White's essay appears on page 82. A formal outline appears on page 83.

You can use this diagram to help you evaluate the essay "Starting Over" by Jared White on page 96. The following diagram shows how the major and minor supporting points of Jared's essay support his essay's main idea.

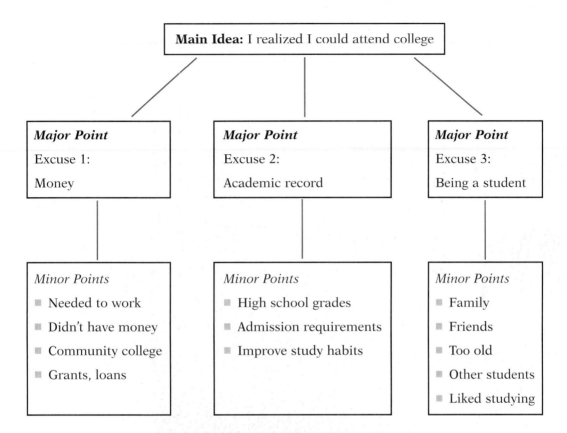

The diagram above illustrates the relationship between Jared's major supporting points—the three excuses he had for not attending college—and his minor supporting points, which present the examples and details that illustrate how he faced and overcame his difficulties. (You can also use this strategy to identify and evaluate the major and minor points in your own essays.)

PRACTICE

5-6 Diagram an essay that you have written for this course (or for another course). Then, decide whether you included enough major supporting points as well as sufficient minor supporting points.

focus on reading and writing

Reread "Men Are from Mars, Women Are from Venus," by John Gray (p. 601). Construct a diagram that shows the relationship between the essay's main idea and its major and minor supporting points.

5e   Evaluating the Writer's Ideas

When you think critically about a text, you should not simply accept the writer's ideas. You should carefully evaluate these ideas as well as the **evidence** that the writer uses to support them. To do this, you need to understand the difference between fact and opinion, and you need to learn to make inferences from what you read as well as to identify bias in a text.

Distinguishing between Fact and Opinion

bedfordstmartins.com
/forw LearningCurve >
Critical Reading

A **fact** is a statement that is either generally accepted or proven to be true. Facts are usually established through experience and observation. An **opinion** is a belief or an expression of values. It can never be fully established and, for that reason, is debatable. In other words, a fact is a statement that can be verified, but an opinion is a statement that can never be proven. Consider the following statements.

> **Fact:** Football is a game played by two teams with eleven players on each side and an oval ball.

> **Opinion:** Because football players have a high incidence of concussions, steps should be taken to make the game less dangerous.

WORD POWER

substantiated
supported with proof
or evidence

Because the first statement can be substantiated, it is a fact. The second statement, however, expresses a personal belief and, for this reason, is an opinion. No amount of evidence can demonstrate beyond a doubt that the second statement is true. The best you can do is to convince people that the position has merit and is therefore worth considering. As you read, be on the alert for words, such as *should* in the sentence above, that may introduce personal opinions, not facts.

Words That Indicate an Opinion	
assume	right/wrong
believe	opinion
best/worst	ought
good/bad	seems
great	should

When you identify an opinion in your reading, you need to determine if it is *supported* or *unsupported*. An **unsupported** opinion is not backed up by facts, examples, or **expert opinion**—the testimony of someone with expertise in the particular subject under discussion. A **supported opinion** includes facts, examples, and expert opinion to back it up. Consider the following examples.

Unsupported Opinion: It is important to save the wilderness from development.

Supported Opinion: It is important to save the wilderness from development. According to the Wilderness Society website, only 110 million acres of true wilderness remain in the United States. Experts warn that oil and natural gas drilling and logging as well as commercial development are threatening this national legacy (Baden and Stroup). As environmentalist John Griffith points out, it is time to enact legislation that will protect the wilderness for future generations (37).

The unsupported opinion above is simply an expression of the writer's personal beliefs. The supported opinion, however, is backed up by material from the Wilderness Society website as well as from two environmental experts. For this reason, it is much more convincing than the unsupported opinion.

As you read, keep in mind that even if a writer supports an opinion, you still can question it or disagree with it. Support—even a great deal of support—does not turn an opinion into a fact, although it can make a statement more convincing.

Teaching Tip
At this point, you may want to introduce the concept of documentation. Explain to students that if they use sources in their writing, they have to supply proper documentation. Refer them to 13d.

Evaluating Support

As you read, evaluate how effectively the writer supports his or her opinions. The more convincing the support, the more willing you should be to accept the writer's ideas. To be effective, support should be *accurate*, *relevant*, *representative*, *sufficient*, and *reliable*.

- **Accurate** support is truthful.
- **Relevant** support applies directly to the issue being discussed.
- **Representative** support gives a balanced picture of the issue.
- **Sufficient** support contains enough evidence to back up the statement.
- **Reliable** support is drawn from trustworthy sources.

PRACTICE
5-7   Read the following statements and decide whether each is Fact (*F*); Unsupported Opinion (*UO*); or Supported Opinion (*SO*).

1. The Treaty of Versailles ended World War I on June 28, 1919.

   _____ *F* _____

2. The Treaty of Versailles, which ended World War I, was a misguided attempt to penalize Germany for the war. _____ *UO* _____

3. According to the economist John Maynard Keynes, the Treaty of Versailles did almost nothing to stabilize Europe. _____SO_____

4. Rachel Carson's book *Silent Spring* was published in 1962. _____F_____

5. Rachel Carson's book *Silent Spring* helped start the modern American environmental movement. _____UO_____

6. Salsa now outsells ketchup in the United States. _____F_____

7. A recent study revealed that many people believe professional athletes are overpaid. _____F_____

8. In 2013, Joe Flacco, quarterback for the Baltimore Ravens, signed a contract for $120.6 million. _____F_____

9. According to Mothers Against Drunk Driving (MADD), we must do more to eliminate drunk driving. _____UO_____

10. According to the Mothers Against Drunk Driving (MADD) website, drunk drivers killed almost ten thousand people in 2011. _____F_____

PRACTICE

5-8   Read the following paragraph about American poet Walt Whitman. As you read, decide whether each sentence is a statement of fact (*F*) or an opinion (*O*). The first sentence has been answered for you.

(1) I believe Walt Whitman was not only one of the most influential American poets but also one of the most considerate. _O_ (2) In 1862, when he learned that his younger brother George had been injured fighting with the Union army in the American Civil War, he trekked south from New York to Virginia just to visit him. _F_ (3) George had only suffered a minor cut to the face. _F_ (4) Nevertheless, Whitman could see that other soldiers, both Union and Confederate, desperately needed his help. _F_ (5) What Whitman did for the wounded, I would argue, was just as important as what he did for American literature. _O_ (6) At overcrowded army hospitals in Virginia and Washington DC, Whitman visited the sick and dying, running errands for them, helping them to write letters home, and even bringing them small gifts, such as ice cream. _F_ (7) Throughout his time as a volunteer, Whitman kept a number of journals. _F_ (8) In fact, his best poetry comes from this period of his life. _O_ (9) In poems like "The Wound-Dresser" and "A March in the Ranks Hard-Prest, and the Road-Unknown," my personal favorites, he shows how modern war is not grand and heroic,

but horrific. __O__ (10) He also manages to show his remarkable compassion, precisely what made him such a great poet. __O__

---

focus on reading and writing

Look once again at "Men Are from Mars, Women Are from Venus," by John Gray (p. 601). Underline three facts, and then underline three opinions. Are the opinions supported or unsupported? Explain.

Making Inferences

When you make an **inference**, you arrive at a conclusion by examining specific pieces of evidence. For example, when you see a car on the side of the road with its hood up and a white cloth tied to its antenna, you infer that the driver needs help. You make this assumption by examining bits of information and drawing a conclusion from that information. When people make inferences, they use what they already know to reach conclusions about what they don't know. For example, because you have seen drivers who needed help before, you know that a stalled car, a raised hood, and a white cloth indicate trouble. As a result, you are able to infer that the driver of the car you are now seeing is in need of help. Because inferences are basic to the way we think, they are part of everyday life. Consider the following examples.

WORD POWER

infer conclude from evidence

- A doctor will infer the cause of a patient's illness by looking at his or her symptoms.
- A jury will infer a person's guilt or innocence by considering statements by the defendant, witness testimony, and photographs of the crime scene.
- An automobile mechanic will infer the cause of an engine problem by consulting a computer analysis of engine functions.

Writers do not always tell readers everything they need to know to understand a text. They expect readers to consider what the text suggests, not just what it literally states. In other words, writers expect you to "read between the lines" and determine what they are implying, not just what they are stating outright.

Keep in mind that an inference is not just a guess. It is an **educated guess**, a conclusion based on evidence in the text. In fact, the more evidence you can find, the stronger your inference will be. Still, as you read, you need to make sure that the inferences that you are making can be supported by the text. If not, reexamine the text and form more solid conclusions.

Teaching Tip
This may be a good time to introduce the concepts of inductive and deductive reasoning. You can tell students that inductive reasoning moves from specific observations to a general conclusion while deductive reasoning moves from general premises to a specific conclusion.

Making Inferences

The following questions will help you go beyond the literal level of a text and make inferences.

- What do you already know about the subject being discussed?
- What facts can you identify in the text?
- What inferences can you make from the information in the text?
- Is there enough evidence to support your inference? If not, do you need to change your thinking?

PRACTICE

5-9 Look at the public-service advertisement on page 141, from the Humane Society of the United States. After examining the image and the words, fill in the inference diagram below. Be prepared to discuss and explain the items in your list.

Inference Diagram

Describe the images

_____

_____

_____

Summarize the text

_____

_____

_____

Summarize what you already know

_____

_____

_____

Inference

_____

_____

_____

_____

_____

I'VE NEVER UNDERSTOOD WHY MY HUMAN WON'T LEAVE THE HOUSE WITHOUT HER LEASH. I THINK SHE'S AFRAID OF GETTING LOST. BUT IT'S OK, I KIND OF LIKE SHOWING HER AROUND.

–HARPER
adopted 08-18-09

A PERSON IS THE BEST THING TO HAPPEN TO A SHELTER PET

adopt

theshelterpetproject.org

The Humane Society of the United States, Maddie's Fund and the Advertising Council

PRACTICE

5-10   In the following passage from the essay "The Guns of Academe" (page 619), Adam Winkler takes a position on the issue of allowing guns on college campuses. Read the passage, and then answer the questions that follow it.

> Even if a student with a gun can use it to defend against a mass murderer, it's hardly clear that anyone, including the armed student, is made safer. Policemen or other students with guns might

WORD POWER

academe an academic environment

not be able to differentiate among gunmen, putting the person defending herself at risk of being shot by mistake. Even well-trained gun owners suffer enormous mental stress in a shootout, making hitting a target extremely difficult.

1. What do you already know about the subject Winkler is discussing?

2. What point is Winkler making about guns on campus?

3. Based on the information in this passage, what inference can you make about Winkler's opinion of gun advocates? What evidence in the passage leads you to your conclusion?

4. What is Winkler likely to think of proposals to make college campuses gun-free zones? How do you know?

focus on reading and writing

Look once again at the essay "Men Are from Mars, Women Are from Venus," by John Gray (p. 601). Based on your reading of this essay, what can you infer about Gray's attitude toward women? About his attitude toward men? Be prepared to explain your conclusions.

Identifying Bias

Teaching Tip
Ask students to use the skills and strategies they learned in Chapter 2 to determine the meaning of the word *preconceived*.

Bias is a tendency to base conclusions on preconceived ideas rather than on evidence. For example, some people vote for one candidate over another simply because he or she is a Democrat or a Republican. Other people think that one television news program is fairer than another, and still others are convinced that one brand of gasoline is superior to all others. Without evidence, there is no way to support these assumptions.

Keep in mind, however, that there is a difference between *bias* and *point of view*. A **point of view** is a position on a particular issue; any time you voice an opinion, you are expressing a point of view. For example, if someone states that the death penalty is wrong, his or her point of view is clear. When the person goes on to support this position with **evidence**, this point of view may seem reasonable, even persuasive. If, on the other hand, the person provides no supporting evidence and does not consider opposing arguments, you can assume that bias has gotten in the way of his or her ability to think clearly.

Of course, writers do not usually announce that they are biased; often, you have to infer bias. For example, if in an essay on gun violence a writer states that he or she cannot understand why anyone would want to own a gun, you should be prepared for a one-sided discussion of the issue. A writer also demonstrates bias if he or she includes information that only supports his or her position and leaves out (or ignores) information that does not. And, of course, a writer who makes overtly disparaging remarks about a particular group of people is clearly expressing bias.

You would also suspect bias if a writer uses language that expresses a value judgment. Consider the following statements.

> The United States entered into the Iraq War in response to the World Trade Center attack.

> The United States foolishly entered into the Iraq War in response to the World Trade Center attack.

> The United States courageously entered into the Iraq War in response to the World Trade Center attack.

The first sentence is a statement of fact, while the second and third sentences use words that express the biases of the individuals who wrote them. Even if you agree with these sentiments, noting the writers' biases should alert you to the likelihood that you are getting a one-sided, and possibly distorted, picture.

To one degree or another, everyone is biased. When you read, you have to determine if the extent of the writer's bias makes it impossible for him or her to discuss a subject fairly or logically.

Identifying the Writer's Bias

The following questions can help you identify a writer's bias.

- Does the writer promote a particular point of view without supplying evidence for his or her opinions?
- Does the writer consider opposing points of view?
- Does the writer make offensive statements?
- Does the writer use language that expresses a value judgment?

focus on reading and writing

Look back at the essay "Men Are from Mars, Women Are from Venus," by John Gray (p. 601). Do you detect any bias? If so, where and what kind of bias? How does this bias affect your response to Gray's essay?

5f Reading and Writing Critically

There are times when you read just to find information—for example, when you read a textbook. Other kinds of reading—for example, editorials and opinion essays, journal articles, and works of fiction—require you to read critically. When you **read critically**, you go beyond reading for facts. As a critical reader, you engage in a systematic process that enables you to determine how a text does what it does, how successful it is in achieving its purpose, and how your interaction with the text changes your view of a subject.

Teaching Tip
Remind students that the reading they do in college is often done in preparation for writing.

Steps in the Critical Reading Process

When you read a text critically, follow these steps.

1. **Summarize**   Identify the main idea of the text, and state it in your own words.
2. **Analyze**   Break the text into its parts, and consider how the parts relate to one another.
3. **Synthesize**   Integrate your own ideas with the ideas of the text.
4. **Evaluate**   Determine how successful the writer is in presenting his or her ideas.

Summarizing

Teaching Tip
Refer students to 1b for more on highlighting and annotating.

When you **summarize** a text, you briefly restate its main idea in your own words. Because a summary forces you to condense a text's ideas, it helps you to understand its meaning. Keep in mind, though, that a summary should focus on the ideas of the text, not on your own interpretations or opinions, and it should use your own original wording, not the language of the text. (If you include a distinctive word or phrase from the original, be sure to put it in quotation marks.)

Summarizing a Text

Follow these steps to summarize a text.

1. Reread the text, reviewing your highlighting and annotations, until you are sure that you understand it.
2. Identify the writer's main idea.
3. Using your own words, summarize the text in a sentence or two.
4. Reread your summary to make sure that you have not used the writer's words or included your own interpretations or opinions.

Read the following paragraph from the essay "In Praise of the F Word," by Mary Sherry (p. 271).

> Flunking as a regular policy has just as much merit today as it did two generations ago. We must review the threat of flunking and see it as it really is—a positive teaching tool. It is an expression of confidence by both teachers and parents that the students have the ability to learn the material presented to them. However, making it work again would take a dedicated, caring conspiracy between teachers and parents. It would mean facing the tough reality that passing kids who haven't learned the material—while it might save them grief for the short term—dooms them to long-term illiteracy. It would mean that teachers would have to follow through on their threats, and parents would have to stand behind them, knowing their children's best interests are indeed at stake. This means no more doing Scott's assignments for him because he might fail. No more passing Jodi because she's such a nice kid.

Now, read the following summary of this paragraph.

> Because the possibility of failure motivates students to work hard, both teachers and parents should understand that failure is part of both the teaching and learning processes.

This one-sentence summary is an accurate and objective restatement of the paragraph's main idea. It uses no distinctive words from the original paragraph and includes no opinions about the paragraph's ideas.

PRACTICE

5-11 Write your own one-sentence summary of the following paragraph from "Around the World, Women Are On the Move," by Richard Rodriguez (p. 202). Make sure your summary includes just the ideas in the text and not your own ideas or opinions, and be careful not to use any distinctive language from the original.

> Even so, at U.S. colleges, female students are signing up for study-abroad programs by a 2-to-1 ratio over males. Indeed, female students, many the daughters and granddaughters of women who did not assume college in their lives, now outnumber male students on American campuses.

Suggested answer: More female students than male students attend college and

study in other countries.

focus on reading and writing

Reread the essay "Men Are from Mars, Women Are from Venus," by John Gray (p. 601). Then, write a one- or two-sentence summary of the essay on the lines below.

Suggested answer: Men and women are fundamentally different in a number

of ways.

Analyzing

After you summarize a text, you **analyze** it, dividing it into its parts to help you better understand it. When you analyze a text, you focus not only on what the text says but also on *how* it says it, and you focus on the text itself, not on your reaction to the text or what it means to you. In a sense, analyzing a text is like putting it under a microscope: you look at its structure, its main idea, its support for this idea, its conclusion, and its use of words, and its purpose. You can also examine the writer's purpose and audience and the context or situation that created the need for the text.

By analyzing a text, you see how the parts of the text work together, and as a result, you gain an understanding of what the writer is trying to say. This is true whether you are reading an essay or letter, a work of fiction, an article in a magazine, or a discussion in an online journal.

Teaching Tip
If you discussed inductive and deductive reasoning when you covered inferences (5e), you can reinforce these concepts here. If not, this section might be a good place to discuss some basic principles of formal logic.

Analyzing a Text

Consider these questions when you analyze a text.

- **Who is the writer's audience?**   Is the writer targeting general readers or a particular group?
- **Who is the writer?**   Is the writer an expert or a person with limited knowledge of the subject? Does the writer try to identify with readers, or does he or she remain aloof?
- **What are the key characteristics of the text?**   How is the text organized? What strategies does the writer use to make his or her point? What kind of language does the writer use? What types of evidence does the writer use? How effective is this evidence? How effective is the overall presentation or argument?
- **What is the context for the text?**   What are the historical, political, economic, or social forces that shaped the text?
- **What motivated the writer?**   What events led the writer to compose the text? In the case of an argument, what issue (or issues) caused the writer to begin thinking about the topic? Does the writer hold a set of values or beliefs that motivated him or her?

Notice how the following excerpt from a student's analysis of Martin Luther King Jr.'s "Letter from Birmingham Jail" addresses some of these questions.

Martin Luther King Jr.'s most compelling argument in favor of nonviolent protest occurs in his 1963 "Letter from Birmingham Jail." At the time he wrote the letter, King, who was the leader of the Southern Christian Leadership Conference, was in prison after being arrested during a march against segregation in Birmingham, Alabama. The letter is addressed to moderate white clergymen, who considered King an outside agitator. It is also aimed at other readers who King assumes are sympathetic to his cause. Overall, the letter is organized as an argument. King begins his argument by

Teaching Tip
At this point, you may want to introduce the concept of documentation. Explain to students that if they use sources in their writing, they have to supply proper documentation. Refer them to 13d.

stating his thesis—that he is in Birmingham, Alabama, "because injustice is here" (3). King then addresses the charge that his actions are extreme and untimely. If anything, says King, his actions are not timely enough—after all, African Americans have waited hundreds of years for their "constitutional and God-given rights" (14). He addresses the charge that he is breaking the law and draws the distinction between just and unjust laws. Because he considers laws upholding racial segregation to be unjust, he believes that he has a moral obligation to disobey them. King then makes the point that white moderates should follow his example and peacefully protest racial segregation in the South. King ends his letter by reinforcing his solidarity with the church and with the white clergy. Eventually, "Letter from Birmingham Jail" became an important document in the struggle for civil rights.

The student who wrote this paragraph examines some of the strategies King uses to construct his argument. In the rest of the analysis, the student goes on to discuss the specific evidence that King uses to support his points as well as the stylistic techniques he employs to make his argument more persuasive.

focus on reading and writing

Choose two or three paragraphs from "Men Are from Mars, Women Are from Venus," by John Gray (p. 601). Then, write a one- or two-paragraph analysis of these paragraphs. Be sure to consult the box on page 147 as you plan your analysis.

Synthesizing

After you analyze a text, your next step is to **synthesize** material, to see how ideas from the text relate to your own ideas. As you synthesize, you think of new ideas and arrive at new insights, piecing the parts of a text together in new ways and seeing ideas (or even the entire text) differently. In a sense, synthesizing ideas is like putting the pieces of a puzzle together so that you can see the complete picture.

Synthesizing is part of a critical reading strategy that enables you to build on prior knowledge to develop new opinions, new insights, and possibly new interpretations. When you read, you gain information, and you keep this information in mind as you read further. Throughout the process, you consider material in the text as well as information you already know; eventually, you draw conclusions.

For example, as you read an essay on green campuses, you gain factual information. This information enables you to understand more of the essay as you read further. Eventually, you consider the information in the essay alongside what you already know about green campuses—for example, that your own school is installing solar cells and sustainable heating and cooling units on campus—and you realize that although the process is desirable, it is also expensive. As you read further, you might conclude that although the initial cost of a green campus is high, it is offset by reduced energy costs and reduced environmental damage. Of course, depending on your previous knowledge of the subject, you could draw the opposite conclusion—that despite its advantages, achieving a green campus may not be worth the money.

Not only can you synthesize information from a single text with what you already know, but you can also synthesize ideas from more than one text. For example, you might read two articles about online instruction. One article might support it, and the other might be critical of it. You would begin by summarizing each article and then analyzing them to identify their major points. Then, you would compare the ideas in the two articles and measure them against what you already know about online instruction—for example, what you have learned from taking two online courses. Finally, you might conclude that although online instruction may not be for every student, it could be beneficial for some. Thus, synthesizing information from different sources can enable you to expand your view of the topic, to generate ideas that you didn't have before, and to form your own ideas about a subject.

$$\boxed{\text{PRIOR INFORMATION}} \rightarrow \boxed{\text{NEW INFORMATION}} \rightarrow \boxed{\text{SYNTHESIS}}$$

focus on reading and writing

Look back once more at the essay "Men Are from Mars, Women Are from Venus," by John Gray (p. 601), and try to synthesize the information in the essay with your own ideas. Then, write several sentences explaining how reading this essay has changed your thinking about the differences between men and women.

Evaluating

So far, we have focused on understanding the ideas in a text. However, like everything else you encounter in life, texts vary in quality, and for this reason, you need to evaluate them. When you **evaluate** a text, you put it into perspective, assessing its strengths and weaknesses and discussing how successful it is in achieving its purpose. In other words, you form your own judgments about the text and its value as a source of information.

For example, if you were evaluating a newspaper opinion piece about the practicality of electric cars, you would begin by asking questions. For instance, what is the writer's thesis? What is the writer's tone, and is this tone appropriate? Does the writer appear to be biased? What part of the writer's essay is particularly effective (or ineffective)? These kinds of questions will lead you toward a fair and critical evaluation of a text.

On the following pages you can see how Andrew Bishop, an environmental science major, evaluated an opinion piece on electric cars from the *Wall Street Journal*. Below is the article along with Andrew's annotations.

Green Cars Have a Dirty Little Secret

Bjorn Lomborg

?chic = stylish; sophisticated

? harbinger = something that shows what's coming

? pipe dream = dream that's impossible to achieve

Tone seems sarcastic

slang term contributes to mocking tone

Thesis: electric cars aren't truly green

Evidence: production of electric cars = a lot of CO₂

Evidence: production of gas-powered cars = a lot less CO₂

Evidence: charging electric cars takes electricity—uses fossil fuels = bad

Electric cars are promoted as the chic harbinger of an environmentally benign future. Ads assure us of "zero emissions," and President Obama has promised a million on the road by 2015. With sales for 2012 coming in at about 50,000, that million-car figure is a pipe dream. Consumers remain wary of the cars' limited range, higher price and the logistics of battery-charging. But for those who do own an electric car, at least there is the consolation that it's truly green, right? Not really.

For proponents such as the actor and activist Leonardo DiCaprio, the main argument is that their electric cars—whether it's a $100,000 Fisker Karma (Mr. DiCaprio's ride) or a $28,000 Nissan Leaf—don't contribute to global warming. And, sure, electric cars don't emit carbon-dioxide on the road. But the energy used for their manufacture and continual battery charges certainly does—far more than most people realize.

A 2012 comprehensive life-cycle analysis in Journal of Industrial Ecology shows that almost half the lifetime carbon-dioxide emissions from an electric car come from the energy used to produce the car, especially the battery. The mining of lithium, for instance, is a less than green activity. By contrast, the manufacture of a gas-powered car accounts for 17% of its lifetime carbon-dioxide emissions. When an electric car rolls off the production line, it has already been responsible for 30,000 pounds of carbon-dioxide emission. The amount for making a conventional car: 14,000 pounds.

While electric-car owners may cruise around feeling virtuous, they still recharge using electricity overwhelmingly produced with fossil fuels. Thus, the life-cycle analysis shows that for every mile driven, the average electric car indirectly emits about six ounces of carbon-dioxide. This is still a lot better than a similar-size conventional car, which emits about 12 ounces per mile. But remember, the production of the electric car has already resulted in sizeable emissions—the equivalent of 80,000 miles of travel in the vehicle.

So unless the electric car is driven *a lot*, it will never get ahead environmentally. And that turns out to be a challenge. Consider the Nissan Leaf. It has only a 73-mile range per charge. Drivers attempting long road trips, as in one BBC test drive, have reported that recharging takes so long that the average speed is close to six miles per hour—a bit faster than your average jogger.   *again, sarcastic tone*

To make matters worse, the batteries in electric cars fade with time, just as they do in a cellphone. Nissan estimates that after five years, the less effective batteries in a typical Leaf bring the range down to 55 miles. As the MIT Technology Review cautioned last year: "Don't Drive Your Nissan Leaf Too Much."

If a typical electric car is driven 50,000 miles over its lifetime, the huge initial emissions from its manufacture means the car will actually have put more carbon-dioxide in the atmosphere than a similar-size gasoline-powered car driven the same number of miles. Similarly, if the energy used to recharge the electric car comes mostly from coal-fired power plants, it will be responsible for the emission of almost 15 ounces of carbon-dioxide for every one of the 50,000 miles it is driven—three ounces more than a similar gas-powered car.   *assumes electricity will come from coal-powered plants—is this a fair assumption?*

Even if the electric car is driven for 90,000 miles and the owner stays away from coal-powered electricity, the car will cause just 24% less carbon-dioxide emission than its gas-powered cousin. This is a far cry from "zero emissions." Over its entire lifetime, the electric car will be responsible for 8.7 tons of carbon-dioxide less than the average conventional car.

Those 8.7 tons may sound like a considerable amount, but it's not. The current best estimate of the global warming damage of an extra ton of carbon-dioxide is about $5. This means an optimistic assessment of the avoided carbon-dioxide associated with an electric car will allow the owner to spare the world about $44 in climate damage. On the European emissions market, credit for 8.7 tons of carbon-dioxide costs $48.

Yet the U.S. federal government essentially subsidizes electric-car buyers with up to $7,500. In addition, more than $5.5 billion in federal grants and loans go directly to battery and electric-car manufacturers like California-based Fisker Automotive and Tesla Motors. This is a very poor deal for taxpayers.

The electric car might be great in a couple of decades but as a way to tackle global warming now it does virtually nothing. The real challenge is to get green energy that is cheaper than fossil fuels. That requires heavy investment in green research and development. Spending instead on subsidizing electric cars is putting the cart before the horse, and an inconvenient and expensive cart at that.   *acknowledges opposing argument*

After reading and annotating Lomborg's opinion piece on electric cars, Andrew wrote the following evaluation.

In "Green Cars Have a Dirty Little Secret," Bjorn Lomborg provides too little evidence and sounds too angry to be convincing. He does make an important point: electric cars may not be quite as green as we like to think. They are, as he notes throughout the essay, expensive to make and to recharge. However, Lomborg relies on only one source to support his point—a study published in the *Journal of Industrial Ecology*. If he had provided more evidence, his essay would be more persuasive. He could also use a less sarcastic tone. Lomborg makes fun of people like Leonardo DiCaprio, but celebrities are not the typical buyers of electric cars. Many middle-class people buy green cars not to save the world but to save money because they cannot afford to keep paying such high gas prices. Lomborg, however, seems to assume that all electric car owners are rich and stupid. He also fails to consider one major opposing argument: if it is true, as he says, that "the electric car might be great in a couple of decades," should our government not spend *more* money investing in it? Lomborg's essay does encourage me to think more critically about electric cars. Right now, they may be imperfect. To convince me, however, that they are such a poor alternative to gas-powered vehicles, Lomborg would need to include more evidence, from a variety of sources, and present the evidence in a more reasonable and less biased way.

Even though you might disagree with a writer, you should acknowledge the strengths as well as the weaknesses of the text. Remember that an effective evaluation relies on information in the text, not just on your own ideas or opinions. Unsupported opinions and preconceived ideas about an issue should not form the basis of your evaluation.

focus on reading and writing

Look back at "Men Are from Mars, Women Are from Venus," by John Gray (p. 601), and write a one-paragraph evaluation of the essay.

TEST · revise · edit

Review your evaluation of Gray's essay. **TEST** what you have written, and then revise, edit, and proofread your work.

REVIEW ACTIVITY

Read the passage below, from Deborah Tannen's 1994 *New York Times* article "The Triumph of the Yell," following the critical reading process outlined in this chapter. Then, write an essay in which you evaluate the passage. Briefly summarize and analyze the passage, synthesizing its ideas with what you already know. When you have finished, TEST and revise what you have written. Then, edit and proofread your work.

FROM "THE TRIUMPH OF THE YELL"

Deborah Tannen

In many university classrooms, "critical thinking" means reading someone's life work, then ripping it to shreds. Though critique is surely one form of critical thinking, so are integrating ideas from disparate fields and examining the context out of which they grew. Opposition does not lead to truth when we ask only "What's wrong with this argument?" and never "What can we use from this in building a new theory and a new understanding?"

Several years ago I was on a television talk show with a representative of the men's movement. I didn't foresee any problem, since there is nothing in my work that is anti-male. But in the room where guests gather before the show I found a man wearing a shirt and tie and a floor-length skirt, with waist-length red hair. He politely introduced himself and told me he liked my book. Then he added: "When I get out there, I'm going to attack you. But don't take it personally. That's why they invite me on, so that's what I'm going to do."

When the show began, I spoke only a sentence or two before this man nearly jumped out of his chair, threw his arms before him in gestures of anger and began shrieking—first attacking me, but soon moving on to rail against women. The most disturbing thing about his hysterical ranting was what it sparked in the studio audience: they too became vicious, attacking not me (I hadn't had a chance to say anything) and not him (who wants to tangle with someone who will scream at you?) but the other guests: unsuspecting women who had agreed to come on the show to talk about their problems communicating with their spouses.

This is the most dangerous aspect of modeling intellectual interchange as a fight: it contributes to an atmosphere of animosity that spreads like a fever. In a society where people express their anger by shooting, the result of demonizing those with whom we disagree can be truly demonic.

153

COLLABORATIVE ACTIVITY

Working in a group of three or four students, select an image of a piece of fine art from the options provided by your instructor, or find one using an online resource such as Art Resource, Bridgeman Art Library, or Google Art Project. Challenge yourselves by choosing a piece of art that is not open to easy interpretation. Discuss as a group what you see, and then share your observations with the rest of the class. Select one group member to record your group's observations, listing all the observations on one side and all the inferences on the other side of the board. As a class, discuss the differences between the two lists.

review checklist

- ■ Identify a writer's audience, purpose, and tone. (See 5a.)

- ■ Distinguish between the denotations and connotations of words. (See 5b.)

- ■ Identify a text's main idea—often expressed in a thesis statement. (See 5c.)

- ■ Identify major and minor supporting points. (See 5d.)

- ■ Evaluate the writer's ideas, distinguishing between fact and opinion, making inferences, and identifying bias. (See 5e.)

- ■ When you *read and write critically*, you go beyond reading for facts. You summarize, analyze, synthesize, and evaluate. (See 5f.)

6 Reading and Writing about Different Kinds of Texts

focus on reading and writing

The images above come from a chapter opener of a psychology textbook. Brainstorm to discover what you already know about what makes a good textbook. In this chapter you will learn strategies for reading and writing about textbooks and a variety of other texts.

6a Reading Written Texts

A **written text** is composed of printed words. (**Visual texts**, such as those discussed in **6b**, are composed largely of images.) Although the active reading process you were introduced to in Chapter 1 can generally be applied to almost all texts, some kinds of texts require slightly different strategies during the previewing stage. One reason for this is that different texts often have different purposes—for example, to present information or to persuade. Another reason is that the various texts you read (including visuals) are aimed at different audiences, who often require different content and emphasis. For these reasons, when you **preview** different kinds of texts, you need to look for their characteristic features. Keep in mind that you will often read texts in order to write about them. Reading a text carefully—and with a critical eye—will help you write about it accurately and convincingly.

Teaching Tip
Refer students to 5a for a discussion of audience.

Textbooks

Much of the reading you do in college is in textbooks (like this one). The purpose of a textbook is to present information, and when you read a textbook, your goal is to locate, understand, and remember that information. To do this, you need to determine which ideas are most important as well as which points support those key ideas and which examples illustrate them.

Before you look at individual sections or pages of a textbook, you should skim the preface to see what the authors' purpose and emphasis is, and you should also look through the table of contents, which shows how the text is organized. In addition, you should consult any end-of-chapter study questions and perhaps look at the book's glossary, which defines key terms. Familiarizing yourself with these features will help you get oriented to your textbook so you can use it more easily to find the information you need.

checklist

Reading Textbooks

Look for the following features as you preview.

- [ ] Chapter titles

- [ ] Section headings and subheadings

- [ ] **Boldfaced** and *italicized* words, which can indicate terms to be defined

- [ ] Boxed checklists or summaries, which may appear at the ends of sections or chapters

- [ ] Bulleted or numbered lists, which may list key reasons or examples or summarize important material

- [ ] Diagrams, charts, tables, graphs, photographs, and other visuals that illustrate the writer's points

- [ ] Marginal quotations and definitions

- [ ] Marginal cross-references

- [ ] Web links

Look at the textbook excerpt on the next page, which was taken from Hockenbury and Hockenbury's *Psychology*, Sixth Edition. It has been annotated to show some of the features you should look for when previewing a textbook reading.

PRACTICE

6-1 Using the checklist above as a guide, preview a page from one of your textbooks. Then, following the reading process outlined in Chapter 1, highlight and annotate the page, writing your comments on small sticky notes. Finally, make an informal outline of the information presented on the page.

Section heading

Subheading

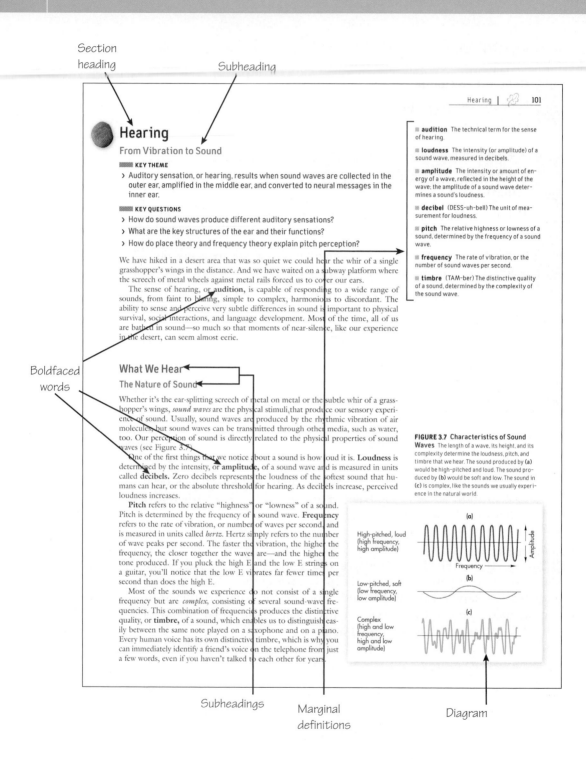

Hearing | 101

Hearing

From Vibration to Sound

▓▓ **KEY THEME**

› Auditory sensation, or hearing, results when sound waves are collected in the outer ear, amplified in the middle ear, and converted to neural messages in the inner ear.

▓▓ **KEY QUESTIONS**

› How do sound waves produce different auditory sensations?
› What are the key structures of the ear and their functions?
› How do place theory and frequency theory explain pitch perception?

We have hiked in a desert area that was so quiet we could hear the whir of a single grasshopper's wings in the distance. And we have waited on a subway platform where the screech of metal wheels against metal rails forced us to cover our ears.

The sense of hearing, or **audition,** is capable of responding to a wide range of sounds, from faint to blaring, simple to complex, harmonious to discordant. The ability to sense and perceive very subtle differences in sound is important to physical survival, social interactions, and language development. Most of the time, all of us are bathed in sound—so much so that moments of near-silence, like our experience in the desert, can seem almost eerie.

What We Hear

The Nature of Sound

Whether it's the ear-splitting screech of metal on metal or the subtle whir of a grasshopper's wings, *sound waves* are the physical stimuli that produce our sensory experience of sound. Usually, sound waves are produced by the rhythmic vibration of air molecules, but sound waves can be transmitted through other media, such as water, too. Our perception of sound is directly related to the physical properties of sound waves (see Figure 3.7).

One of the first things that we notice about a sound is how loud it is. **Loudness** is determined by the intensity, or **amplitude,** of a sound wave and is measured in units called **decibels.** Zero decibels represents the loudness of the softest sound that humans can hear, or the absolute threshold for hearing. As decibels increase, perceived loudness increases.

Pitch refers to the relative "highness" or "lowness" of a sound. Pitch is determined by the frequency of a sound wave. **Frequency** refers to the rate of vibration, or number of waves per second, and is measured in units called *hertz*. Hertz simply refers to the number of wave peaks per second. The faster the vibration, the higher the frequency, the closer together the waves are—and the higher the tone produced. If you pluck the high E and the low E strings on a guitar, you'll notice that the low E vibrates far fewer times per second than does the high E.

Most of the sounds we experience do not consist of a single frequency but are *complex,* consisting of several sound-wave frequencies. This combination of frequencies produces the distinctive quality, or **timbre,** of a sound, which enables us to distinguish easily between the same note played on a saxophone and on a piano. Every human voice has its own distinctive timbre, which is why you can immediately identify a friend's voice on the telephone from just a few words, even if you haven't talked to each other for years.

▪ **audition** The technical term for the sense of hearing.

▪ **loudness** The intensity (or amplitude) of a sound wave, measured in decibels.

▪ **amplitude** The intensity or amount of energy of a wave, reflected in the height of the wave; the amplitude of a sound wave determines a sound's loudness.

▪ **decibel** (DESS-uh-bell) The unit of measurement for loudness.

▪ **pitch** The relative highness or lowness of a sound, determined by the frequency of a sound wave.

▪ **frequency** The rate of vibration, or the number of sound waves per second.

▪ **timbre** (TAM-ber) The distinctive quality of a sound, determined by the complexity of the sound wave.

FIGURE 3.7 Characteristics of Sound Waves The length of a wave, its height, and its complexity determine the loudness, pitch, and timbre that we hear. The sound produced by **(a)** would be high-pitched and loud. The sound produced by **(b)** would be soft and low. The sound in **(c)** is complex, like the sounds we usually experience in the natural world.

(a)
High-pitched, loud (high frequency, high amplitude)
Amplitude
Frequency →

(b)
Low-pitched, soft (low frequency, low amplitude)

(c)
Complex (high and low frequency, high and low amplitude)

Boldfaced words

Subheadings   Marginal definitions   Diagram

News Articles

As a student, as an employee, and as a citizen, you read school, community, local, and national newspapers in print and online. Like textbooks, news articles communicate information. In addition, newspapers also publish editorials (which aim to persuade) as well as feature articles (which may entertain as well as inform).

Many people read news articles online rather than in print form. If this is what you usually do, keep in mind that newspaper web pages are often very busy and crowded, so you may have difficulty distinguishing important information from not-so-important material. For example, a news article that you read online may be surrounded by advertising and include links to irrelevant (and potentially distracting) material—such as commercial sites or Facebook pages. For this reason, it is very important to read online material carefully and methodically.

Teaching Tip
Refer students to 3f for information on how to construct an informal outline.

checklist

Reading News Articles

Look for the following features as you preview.

- [ ] Headlines

- [ ] **Boldfaced** headings within articles

- [ ] Labels like *editorial*, *commentary*, or *opinion*, which indicate that an article communicates the writer's own views

- [ ] Brief biographical information at the end of an opinion piece

- [ ] Phrases or sentences in **boldface** (to emphasize key points)

- [ ] The article's first sentence, which often answers the questions *who*, *what*, *why*, *where*, *when*, and *how*

- [ ] The **dateline**, which tells you the date and the city the writer is reporting from

- [ ] Photographs, charts, graphs, and other visuals

- [ ] In *print news articles*, related articles that appear on the same page—for example, boxed information and **sidebars**, short related articles that provide additional background on people and places mentioned in the article

- [ ] In *online news articles*, links to related articles, reader comments, and other useful material

Teaching Tip
Tell students that an *op-ed piece* expresses the opinion of an individual writer who may not be associated with the publication's full-time staff, and that "op-ed" stands for *opposite editorial*, because of its traditional position opposite the editorial page in the newspaper.

The following online newspaper article from the *Wall Street Journal*, has been annotated to show some of the features you should look for when previewing a newspaper article.

Dateline →

Headline →

Who, what, where, why →

Photo →

PRACTICE

6-2 Print out a news article from the web. Using the checklist on page 159 as a guide, preview the article, and then highlight and annotate it, following the reading process outlined in Chapter 1. Finally, write a response paragraph commenting on the article's ideas.

Teaching Tip
Refer students to 1d for information on how to write a response paragraph.

Business Documents

In your workplace, you will read memos, letters, emails, and reports. These documents, which may be designed to convey information as well as persuade, are often addressed to a group rather than to a single person. (Note that the most important information often comes *first*—in a subject line or in the first paragraph.)

checklist

Reading Business Documents

Look for the following features as you preview.

☐ Numbered or bulleted lists of tasks or problems (numbers indicate the order of the items' importance)

☐ In an email, links to the web

☐ In a memo or an email, the person or persons addressed, as well as their titles

☐ In a memo or an email, the subject line

☐ In a memo or a report, headings that might highlight key topics or points

☐ In a memo or report, the **executive summary** and the Conclusions and Recommendations sections

☐ In a letter or an email, the first and last paragraphs and the first sentence of each body paragraph, which often contain key information

☐ **Boldfaced**, underlined, or *italicized* words

The following professional email has been annotated to show some of the features you should look for when previewing a business document.

Persons
addressed

Subject line

Key
information

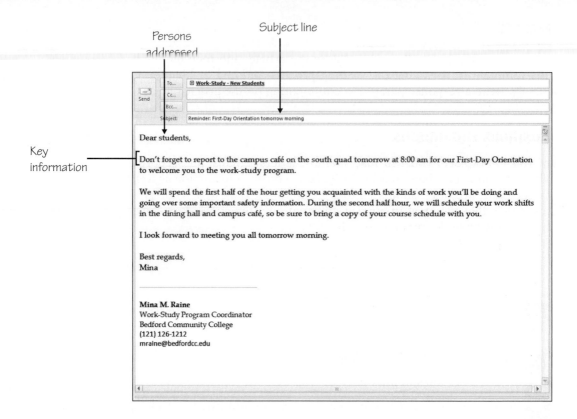

```
                    To...    ⊞ Work-Study - New Students
  ⌷                 Cc...
 Send               Bcc...
                    Subject:  Reminder: First-Day Orientation tomorrow morning

  Dear students,

  Don't forget to report to the campus café on the south quad tomorrow at 8:00 am for our First-Day Orientation
  to welcome you to the work-study program.

  We will spend the first half of the hour getting you acquainted with the kinds of work you'll be doing and
  going over some important safety information. During the second half hour, we will schedule your work shifts
  in the dining hall and campus café, so be sure to bring a copy of your course schedule with you.

  I look forward to meeting you all tomorrow morning.

  Best regards,
  Mina


  Mina M. Raine
  Work-Study Program Coordinator
  Bedford Community College
  (121) 126-1212
  mraine@bedfordcc.edu
```

PRACTICE

6-3 Ask your employer or an office worker at your school to share a memo with you. Using the checklist on page 161 as a guide, preview the memo. Following the reading process outlined in Chapter 1, highlight and annotate the memo, and then write a one-sentence summary that conveys its main idea.

Teaching Tip
Refer students to 5f for information on how to write a summary.

Web Pages

Web pages can be written to provide information (as in a page from the website of a charity or a government office), to provoke a response (as in a commercial site advertising a product or a political site advocating a position or course of action), or simply to entertain or amuse.

Web pages are generally not *linear*—that is, they are not laid out neatly on the page in lines or columns (as is the case for textbooks, newspaper articles, and business documents). For this reason, web pages are not likely to be read from left to right, one line at a time. Instead, your eyes wander around the page; sometimes you read a line or two from left to right and then move down vertically or diagonally to read boxed text or look at an advertisement or a visual. Often, you interrupt your reading of a page to follow a link. For this reason, you do not usually read web pages word for word. Instead, you **scan** pages, looking for individual words, sentences, and headings.

It is also important to note that web pages may include irrelevant material—for example, links to articles only tangentially related to the site's topic, advertising, solicitations for donations, and links to free trial offers. One of the most important strategies for reading web pages is learning to recognize—and skip over—irrelevant material.

Teaching Tip

Ask students if they can determine the meaning of *tangentially*, using the skills they learned in Chapter 2.

checklist

Reading Web Pages

Look for the following features as you preview.

- ☐ Use of color to highlight important information
- ☐ Tabs for drop-down menus
- ☐ "Read more" links that expand summaries or excerpts
- ☐ Search box to help you narrow your focus
- ☐ Boxed information, with box titles in large type
- ☐ **Boldfaced**, <u>underlined</u>, or *italicized* words
- ☐ Bulleted lists (like this one)
- ☐ Images and their captions
- ☐ Links to podcasts, press releases, videos, slideshows, and related articles and reports

Following is the home page of the American Museum of Natural History, in New York City. It has been annotated to show some of the features you should look for when previewing a web page.

American Museum of Natural History

Search box
Tabs for drop-down menus

Image with caption

Boxed information

Color highlights important information.

Links to press releases

Teaching Tip
Refer students to 5f for information on how to write an evaluation.

PRACTICE

6-4 Print out a web page. Using the checklist on page 163 as a guide, preview the page, and then highlight and annotate it, following the reading process outlined in Chapter 1. Finally, write an evaluation of the page assessing the usefulness of its information.

Blogs

Blogs are websites on which bloggers (professional or amateur writers) post information (including visuals) to encourage comments and discussion. Blog posts, which can range in length from single sentences or paragraphs to pages of text, appear in chronological order, with the most recent post first. An individual or an organization can blog about virtually any topic—sports, politics, education, fashion, or music, for example—and a blog can stand alone or be part of a larger website.

The focus of a blog can be quite narrow—for example, the issues facing kindergarten parents in a particular town or neighborhood. Blogs can also have a wider focus, as is the case with blogs run by elected officials to discuss important issues or by newspapers and magazines to engage their readers. Some of the most popular blogs focus on entertainment gossip, political issues, and business advice. As with web pages, be careful not to be distracted by advertising or by irrelevant links.

checklist

Reading Blogs

Look for the following features as you preview.

- [ ] Title of post
- [ ] The first comment (to bring the conversation up to date)
- [ ] The furthest-back comment available (to see where the responses to a post began)
- [ ] Links to related blogs or articles
- [ ] "Read more" links that expand summaries or excerpts
- [ ] The search box, which enables you to search all blog posts
- [ ] Sidebars (Home, About, FAQs, and so on)
- [ ] Monthly archives
- [ ] Photos and other images (some submitted by the author, others by those commenting on the original post)

Look at page 166, which shows a post on the geology of Antelope Canyon in Arizona, written by geology instructor Garry Hayes. It has been annotated to show some of the features you should look for when previewing a blog.

PRACTICE

6-5   Find a blog that interests you on tumblr.com, and print out one post from the blog along with a few of the related comments. Using the checklist above as a guide, preview the blog post. Then, highlight and annotate it, following the reading process outlined in Chapter 1. Finally, write your own comment on the writers' ideas.

Search box

Sidebar includes information about the writer.

Title of post

Monthly archives

The first comment

Photo submitted by the writer

Garry Hayes

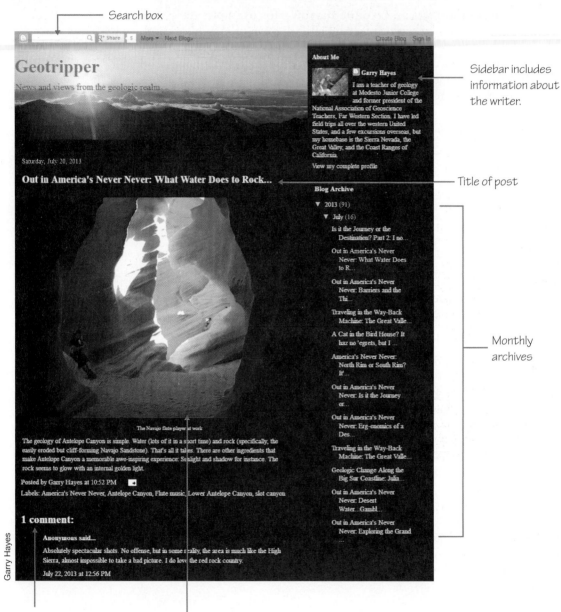

focus on reading and writing

What different kinds of reading do you do in a typical week? Do you read for pleasure? To get information? In response to assignments? When—and where—do you generally do your reading? How carefully, and with how much interest, do you read each kind of text? Write a paragraph or two explaining why, when, where, and how you read.

6b   Reading Visuals

The written texts you read often include **visuals**—graphs, charts, maps, diagrams, photographs, cartoons, or advertisements—to enhance the appeal of the text and convey the writer's ideas. For example, a photograph of an overcrowded prison can make a news article about the inmates' plight more vivid; a diagram of the heart can supplement a biology text's explanation of the circulatory system; and a map can help readers understand a historical novel's discussion of seventeenth-century explorers' conquests. Sometimes, too, a visual will stand alone, communicating its own message instead of enhancing the message of a written text. For example, an editorial cartoon or advertisement can persuade readers to support a cause, take some kind of social action, buy a product, or vote in a particular way.

> **WORD POWER**
>
> **plight** a difficult or unfortunate situation

When you "read" a visual—particularly one that will be the subject of class discussion or writing—you should do so with a critical eye. Your primary goal is to understand the point that the creator of the visual is trying to make, but you also need to understand how the information or message is conveyed as well as how it is intended to affect you. The strategies that will help you achieve these goals are similar to the active reading strategies you were introduced to in Chapter 1.

Previewing

When you approach a visual, you should look for clues to its main idea, or message. Some visuals, particularly advertising images, include written text that conveys the main idea. Apart from words, however, the images themselves can help you understand the visual's purpose, its intended audience, and the argument (if any) that it is making.

When you preview a visual, considering the following questions will help you understand its content, purpose, and message.

■ Who is the visual's target audience?

■ What individual images appear in the visual?

■ How close together (or far apart) are these images?

■ How large is each image? Why are some larger than others?

■ How is each image visually connected to the background?

■ How is empty space used?

■ How are color and shading (for example, contrast between light and dark) used?

■ Are any design elements or words repeated?

■ Does the visual include any special effects, such as blurring or nonrealistic images?

■ Does the visual include people?

■ If so, what do people's activities, gestures, facial expressions, positions, body language, dress, and the like tell you about the visual's purpose?

■ Does the visual include any written text? If so, what purpose does it serve? Is it necessary?

■ Are any two images juxtaposed to suggest an association between them—for example, a Prius and a meadow?

WORD POWER

juxtaposed placed side by side for comparison or contrast

When you have considered the items listed in the box above, you should have a sense of why a visual was created and what message it was designed to communicate. Look, for example, at the following visual.

The editorial cartoon on page 168 by Nick Anderson was published in the *Houston Chronicle* on May 3, 2013, in response to a shocking industrial accident in Bangladesh: over 1,100 workers were killed and some 2,500 injured, many seriously, in the collapse of a building that housed a clothing factory. This factory was located on the eight-story building's upper floors, which were not strong enough to bear the weight of the factory's heavy machinery. Cracks had been discovered in the building the day before the collapse, but it had been deemed safe and the factory supervisor had ordered employees to return to work. Because the factory manufactured clothing for a number of American companies, the creator of the cartoon could assume that its subject matter would be of interest to American consumers.

The cartoon has three main visual elements: the message in the upper left-hand corner directed to employers, the central scene of devastation, and the "factory death toll" sign in the lower right-hand corner. These three elements work together to convey the cartoon's message: when clothing is produced under substandard conditions, workers pay a terrible price.

The first element sends an ironic (but supposedly positive) message to manufacturers; its bold black-on-white capital letters and even rectangular shape stand in contrast to the random destruction shown in the central scene. The second element, the scene itself, conveys a highly negative message, showing a collapsed building surrounded by rubble and stretcher bearers carrying bodies away. (Additional bodies can be seen lined up in rows in the lower left-hand corner of the image.) Juxtaposed with the seemingly positive message at the upper left is the sign in the lower right-hand corner. Unlike the optimistic invitation to employers, this sign conveys the ugly truth in very straightforward language. Set beside the terrible central image of the collapsed building and the dead bodies, this sign makes the ironic point of the cartoon clear: manufacturing clothing under unsafe, potentially deadly, conditions can exact a heavy price.

PRACTICE

6-6   Look at the following three visuals and apply the Questions for Previewing (p. 168) to each one. What do you conclude about each visual's purpose and intended message?

Photograph of New York City retired firefighter Jerry Collins and his wife, Suzanne, at the 9/11 Memorial in New York City

Editorial cartoon by award-winning political cartoonist Stuart Carlson

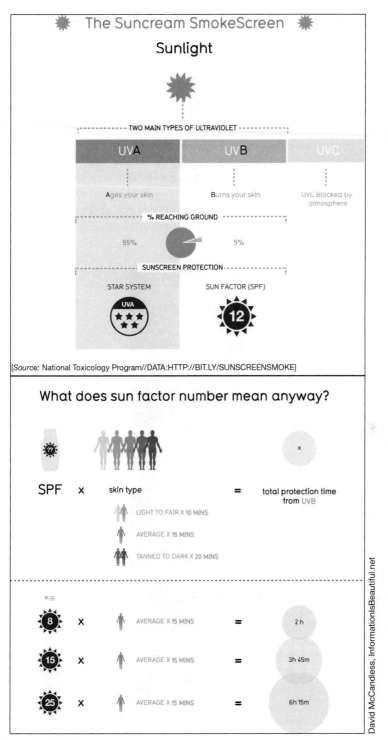

Infographic by David McCandless, an independent data journalist and information designer

Highlighting and Annotating

Once you have previewed a visual, you should **highlight** and **annotate** it. Unlike highlighting and annotating a written text, marking a visual text involves focusing your attention on images as well as words.

Begin by marking key images—by starring, boxing, or circling them—and perhaps drawing lines or arrows to connect related images. Then, go on to make annotations directly on the visual (or on sticky notes), commenting on the effectiveness of its individual images in communicating the message of the whole. As in the case of a written text, your annotations can be in the form of comments or questions.

The following visual, an ad for Discover The Forest, a public service advertising campaign aimed at reconnecting children and their families with nature, includes highlighting and annotations.

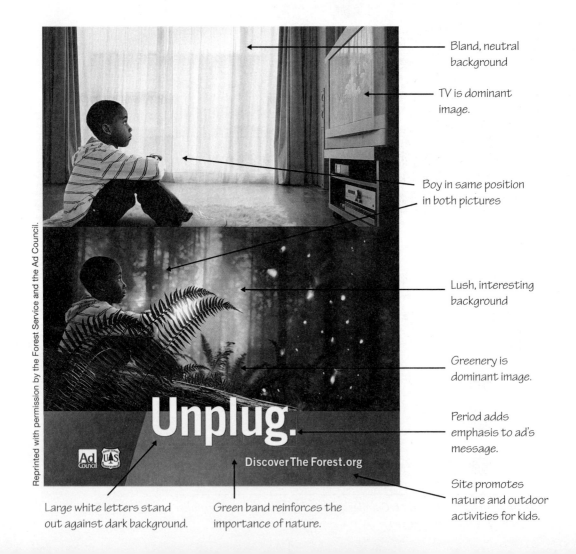

Bland, neutral background

TV is dominant image.

Boy in same position in both pictures

Lush, interesting background

Greenery is dominant image.

Period adds emphasis to ad's message.

Site promotes nature and outdoor activities for kids.

Large white letters stand out against dark background.

Green band reinforces the importance of nature.

Reprinted with permission by the Forest Service and the Ad Council.

PRACTICE

6-7   Look at the following visual, and then highlight and annotate it to identify its most important images and their relationship to one another. When you have finished, think about how the images work together to communicate information or a central message. What ideas does the visual convey to the audience?

Tyler Hicks/The New York Times/Redux

Photograph of some of the devastation caused in central Philippines by Typhoon Haiyan.

6c   Types of Visuals

Different kinds of visuals call for different kinds of approaches. When you examine visual texts, particularly those you plan to write about, consider the special characteristics of each type of visual.

Charts, Graphs, and Tables

Charts, graphs, and tables often appear in textbooks, newspapers, magazines, business reports, and articles on websites. They can be used to present information, to provide support for a position, or to correct misconceptions. Charts, graphs, and tables enable readers to visualize complicated information; it is often easier to understand numerical data when they are presented and organized visually than when the same information is presented in a dense paragraph of description or explanation. (Visuals called **infographics**, or information graphics, like the one seen on page 171, are especially effective at conveying complex information.)

A **chart**—for example, a pie chart—is a visual representation of statistics or data that illustrates ideas and concepts in a written text. For example, in a discussion of green energy, a chart might show the number of people in a given city who use hybrid, low-gas-mileage, and electric cars. A **graph**—for example, a line graph or a bar graph—also presents data, but it shows the data over time or compares individual bits of data. For example, an economics report could include a graph showing a supply-and-demand curve, a communications text could include a graph showing the increase in Twitter use since 2005, and a graph in a government document could show shifts in population in various congressional districts. **Tables** are often used to compare and contrast ideas that are explained in a text, identifying key points so readers can understand concepts more easily. For example, a table in an article from a psychology journal could compare academic performance of well-rested and sleep-deprived students.

Teaching Tip

Tell students that skimming charts, graphs, and tables before they read can help them focus on important concepts in the written text.

checklist

Reading Charts, Graphs, and Tables

Look for the following features as you preview.

- [ ] Captions
- [ ] Labels
- [ ] **Boldfaced** information
- [ ] Use of color
- [ ] Use of headings

The following graph shows how much a $15,000 student loan will actually cost a student over a period of ten years, depending on the type of loan and the interest rate. It has been labeled to show you the key features to look for as you preview a graph, a chart, or a table.

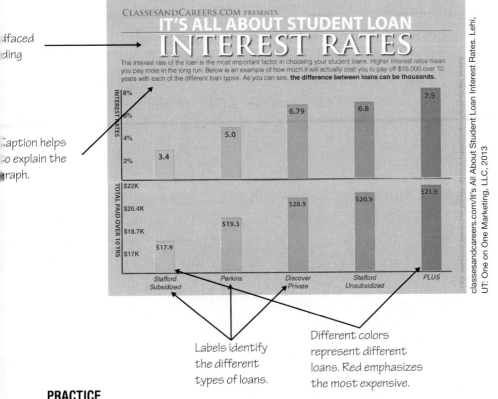

dfaced
ding →

Caption helps
to explain the
graph.

Labels identify
the different
types of loans.

Different colors
represent different
loans. Red emphasizes
the most expensive.

PRACTICE

6-8 Find a chart, graph, or table on the web or in one of your textbooks. Preview it to identify its key features; then, highlight and annotate it. Finally, write a one- or two-sentence summary of the information it presents.

Teaching Tip
Refer students to 5f for information on how to write a summary.

Maps

Maps often appear in textbooks and in newspaper and magazine articles, where they can provide supplementary information or illustrate a discussion. They are visual representations of continents, regions, countries, states, cities, or towns (and can also identify smaller features, such as parks or museums). By indicating boundaries, geographical and topographical features, and structures such as roads and bridges, maps provide a geographical context for anything from a discussion of drought conditions in sub-Saharan Africa to the path of explorers on the Silk Road to the relative size of the five Great Lakes. Maps can also supplement a discussion of historical, political, or scientific developments by providing comparative information—for example, a pair of maps can show Poland's boundaries before and after World War II, and a series of maps can show changes in the size of the polar ice caps over time.

checklist

Reading Maps

Look for the following features as you preview.

- [ ] Names of countries and cities indicated by different type sizes
- [ ] Shaded or colored areas that distinguish different parts of a region
- [ ] Legend (often boxed) that explains the map's scale and the meaning of various symbols (such as dots or stars to indicate capital cities)

The following map of Africa has been labeled to show you the key features to look for as you preview a map.

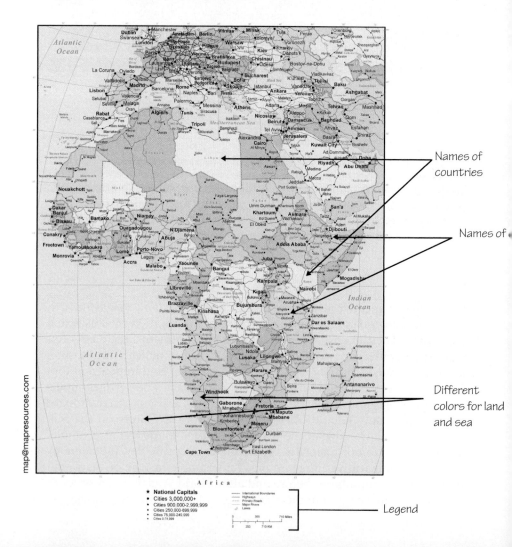

Names of countries

Names of

Different colors for land and sea

Legend

map@mapresources.com

PRACTICE

6-9   Find a map on the web or in one of your textbooks. Preview it to identify its key features; then highlight and annotate it. Finally, write a sentence that summarizes the information it presents.

Diagrams

Diagrams are often used in textbooks as well as in scientific, engineering, or business reports, where they can supplement a description or explain a process in visual terms. A diagram can represent a structure, mechanism, or piece of equipment, or it can illustrate a process. (A **flowchart** is a diagram used to visually represent a process.) In a biology textbook, a step-by-step process such as mitosis or photosynthesis can be represented as a diagram, with arrows indicating the direction of the process. In a business report, a flowchart can show how management and union officials negotiate a contract. Finally, in an engineering report, a diagram of a building could show areas of structural weakness or damage.

Teaching Tip
Tell students that they can use a diagram as a study aid by photocopying the diagram and then filling in labels to identify individual parts or steps.

checklist

Reading Diagrams

Look for the following features as you preview.

☐ Title or caption that identifies the subject of the diagram

☐ Labels that identify individual steps in a process or parts of a piece of equipment

The following diagram, from the textbook *Life, The Science of Biology*, by David Sadava, H. Craig Heller, Gordon H. Orians, William K. Purves, and David M. Hillis, shows the process by which living organisms gain energy. It has been labeled to show you the key features to look for as you preview a diagram.

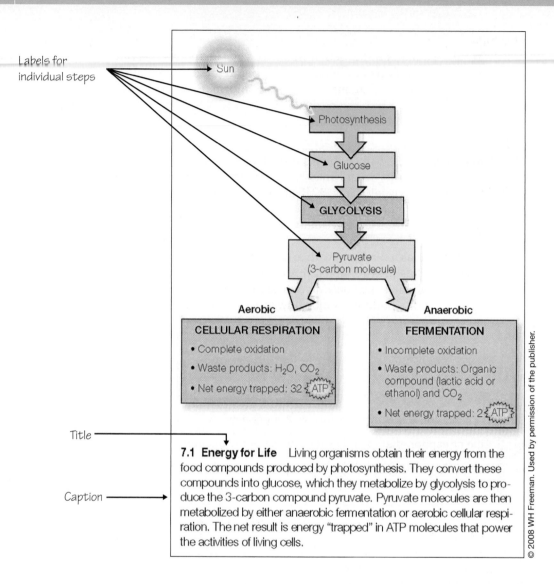

Labels for individual steps

Sun

Photosynthesis

Glucose

GLYCOLYSIS

Pyruvate (3-carbon molecule)

Aerobic

Anaerobic

CELLULAR RESPIRATION
- Complete oxidation
- Waste products: H_2O, CO_2
- Net energy trapped: 32 ATP

FERMENTATION
- Incomplete oxidation
- Waste products: Organic compound (lactic acid or ethanol) and CO_2
- Net energy trapped: 2 ATP

Title

Caption

7.1 Energy for Life Living organisms obtain their energy from the food compounds produced by photosynthesis. They convert these compounds into glucose, which they metabolize by glycolysis to produce the 3-carbon compound pyruvate. Pyruvate molecules are then metabolized by either anaerobic fermentation or aerobic cellular respiration. The net result is energy "trapped" in ATP molecules that power the activities of living cells.

PRACTICE

6-10 Find a diagram on the web or in one of your textbooks. Preview the diagram to identify its key features; then, highlight and annotate it. Finally, write a paragraph describing the object pictured or explaining the process the diagram illustrates.

Photographs

Photographs are found in textbooks as well as in magazines and newspapers and on websites, where they can make a discussion more accessible and add visual appeal by breaking up large blocks of text. Photographs are also frequently used to convey information. For example, a textbook description of pre–*Brown v. Board of Education* "separate but equal" schools in the American South can be enriched by side-by-side photos of white-only and black-only schools. In the same way, a photo of an animal, machine, or landscape can clarify technical discussions in biology, engineering, or earth science, respectively. Photos can also be persuasive, conveying emotion or eliciting sympathy or even shock—as in photos of Appalachia in the 1930s, crowded refugee camps, or victims of violence. Finally, a photo can also be used to advocate a position on a social or political issue. Thus, photos of grieving families of gun-violence victims might be used to make a plea for gun-safety regulation.

Teaching Tip

Tell students that if they examine a text's photographs before they start to read, they can often get an idea of the text's content and the writer's purpose.

checklist

Reading Photographs

Consider the following features as you preview.

- [ ] Composition—the relative sizes of images and the relationship of individual images to one another and to the background

- [ ] Use of color

- [ ] Use of shadow

- [ ] Use of light

The photograph on the following page shows all five living U.S. presidents together at the George W. Bush Presidential Library in Dallas, Texas. It has been labeled to show you the key features to look for as you preview a photograph.

The smiling presidents in the foreground are set in contrast to the stern-faced marine in the background.

Military band emphasizes importance of occasion.

Large capital letters identify place.

AP Photo/Charles Dharapak

Line of shadows, beginning with President Obama's, visually connect the five presidents.

Former President George H. W. Bush's bright-colored socks contrast with the other presidents' dark suits.

PRACTICE

6-11 Find a photograph in a newspaper or magazine or on the web. Preview the photograph to identify its key features; then, highlight and annotate it. Finally, write a response paragraph expressing your reaction to the photograph.

Teaching Tip
Refer students to 1d for more on writing a response paragraph.

Editorial Cartoons

Cartoons can appear in newspapers and magazines, on websites, and even in college textbooks and business reports. Many cartoons are designed solely to entertain or amuse. Thus, a *Dilbert* cartoon might lighten the tone of a business report, and a psychology textbook might use a cartoon to illustrate complicated family dynamics in an amusing way.

An **editorial cartoon**, however, is designed to persuade. It takes a position on a controversial issue and conveys that position through an image (often accompanied by a few words of text). Images of people are typically presented as **caricatures**, which exaggerate their most prominent physical features, often for negative effect. Editorial cartoons have a sharp satirical edge, and they are often highly critical of a social or political situation or event, designed to provoke discomfort, anger, and even shock. These cartoons, created for newspapers, are often reprinted in other kinds of texts, where they can provide commentary on an issue. For example, a classic editorial cartoon showing a power struggle between Republicans and Democrats that is reprinted in a political science textbook can shed light on today's national political climate.

checklist

Reading Editorial Cartoons

Consider the following features as you preview.

☐ Presence or absence of written text (in the form of a caption or heading or in dialogue)

☐ How the people depicted are portrayed (sympathetically or negatively)

☐ Facial expressions and body language

☐ Prominent physical features exaggerated for comic or satirical effect

☐ Images that serve as symbols

The following editorial cartoon makes a statement about the issue of professional athletes using steroids. It has been labeled to show you the key features to look for as you preview an editorial cartoon.

Facial expression (raised eyebrows and tight mouth) shows that the reporter is skeptical.

Facial expression shows that the player is nervous.

Negative image of a baseball player

Text poses question easily answered by dominant image.

Upper-body size exaggerated for comic effect

Teaching Tip
Refer students to 5f for information on analyzing a text.

PRACTICE

6-12   Find an editorial cartoon in a print or online newspaper. Preview it to identify its key features, then, highlight and annotate it. Finally, write a paragraph analyzing its message.

Advertisements

Advertisements appear in newspapers and magazines and on websites and are sometimes reprinted in textbooks to illustrate persuasion techniques. A *public service advertisement*, created by a nonprofit social-action organization such as Mothers Against Drunk Driving, is likely to be informative—for example, citing the decline in highway deaths as a result of the "designated driver" campaign—as well as persuasive, presenting grim pictures of alcohol-related accidents. The purpose of *commercial advertisements* is always persuasive; these ads want consumers to purchase the products they advertise—anything from designer dresses to dog food—and the ads are designed to make the product appealing (even irresistible) to consumers. Ads created by special-interest groups can get their message across with anything from images that make a simple emotional appeal to shocking images—such as photographs of dead baby seals to protest the annual seal hunt in Alaska.

checklist

Reading Advertisements

Consider the following features as you preview.

- [ ] Size and placement of the central image (and its relationship to other images)

- [ ] The message—such as "Just Do It" or "Friends Don't Let Friends Drive Drunk" (usually appears as a slogan or tagline)

- [ ] Clues to the ad's intended audience and purpose

- [ ] Relationship of text and images—How do they work together to convey the ad's central message?

The following Partners for Healthy Pets advertisement has been labeled to show you the key features to look for as you preview an advertisement.

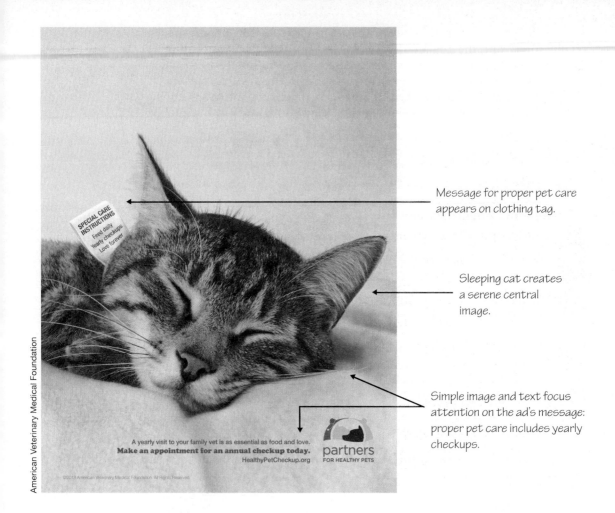

American Veterinary Medical Foundation

Message for proper pet care appears on clothing tag.

Sleeping cat creates a serene central image.

Simple image and text focus attention on the ad's message: proper pet care includes yearly checkups.

SPECIAL CARE INSTRUCTIONS
Feed daily
Yearly checkups
Love forever

A yearly visit to your family vet is as essential as food and love.
Make an appointment for an annual checkup today.
HealthyPetCheckup.org

partners
FOR HEALTHY PETS

©2013 American Veterinary Medical Foundation. All Rights Reserved.

Teaching Tip
Refer students to 5f for information on analyzing a text.

PRACTICE

6-13 Find an advertisement in a magazine or newspaper or on the web. Preview the ad to identify its key features; then, highlight and annotate it. Finally, write a paragraph analyzing its purpose, intended audience, and message.

focus on reading and writing

Look through your textbooks, and focus your attention on a chapter that is attractively designed and includes visuals as well as written text. Then, write an essay in which you evaluate how the chapter gets its information across. Be sure to consult the Reading Textbooks Checklist on page 157 as well as the relevant checklists for any types of visuals that appear in your textbook chapter.

REVIEW ACTIVITY

Graphic Organizer: *Strategies for Previewing Different Kinds of Texts*

Chapter 6 addresses different kinds of texts, both written and visual. In the graphic organizer on pp. 186-87, list in the purple box the features you should look for when previewing a written text and in the pink box the features you should look for when previewing a visual text.

COLLABORATIVE ACTIVITY

Read the following passage from Betty Smith's 1943 novel *A Tree Grows in Brooklyn*. Then, as a group, develop a visual—an ad, cartoon, or diagram, for example—that expresses the passage's main idea.

FROM *A TREE GROWS IN BROOKLYN*

Betty Smith

The library was a little old shabby place. Francie thought it was 1 beautiful. The feeling she had about it was as good as the feeling she had about church. She pushed open the door and went in. She liked the combined smell of worn leather bindings, library paste and freshly-inked stamping pads better than she liked the smell of burning incense at high mass.

Francie thought that all the books in the world were in that library 2 and she had a plan about reading all the books in the world. She was reading a book a day in alphabetical order and not skipping the dry ones. She remembered that the first author had been Abbott. She had been reading a book a day for a long time now and she was still in the B's. Already she had read about bees and buffaloes, Bermuda vacations and Byzantine architecture. For all of her enthusiasm, she had to admit that some of the B's had been hard going. But Francie was a reader. She read everything she could find: trash, classics, time tables and the grocer's price list. Some of the reading had been wonderful; the Louisa Alcott books for example. She planned to read all the books over again when she had finished with the Z's.

Saturdays were different. She treated herself by reading a book not 3 in the alphabetical sequence. On that day she asked the librarian to recommend a book.

Written Texts

Chapter titles

Section headings and subheadings

Boldfaced and italicized words

Boxed checklists or summaries

Bulleted or numbered lists

Visuals—diagrams, charts, tables, graphs, photographs

Marginal quotations, definitions, and cross-references

Web links

Headlines

Labels like editorial, commentary, or opinion

Brief biographical information at the end of an opinion piece

The dateline

Related articles that appear on the same page, or links to related articles and reader comments

The person(s) addressed and subject line headings that might highlight key topics or points

The first and last paragraph and the first sentence of each body paragraph

Use of color to highlight important information

Tabs for drop-down menus

"Read more" links that expand summaries or excerpts

Search box to help you narrow your focus

The furthest back and most recent comments

Sidebars (Home, About, FAQs, etc.)

Monthly archives

Visuals

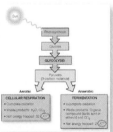

Captions and labels

Use of color and headings

Shaded or colored areas—to distinguish different parts of a region

Legend (usually boxed)

Title or caption that identifies subject

Labels that identify individual parts or steps in a process

Composition

Use of color, shadow, and light

Presence or absence of written text

How the people depicted are portrayed

Facial expressions and body language

Prominent physical features exaggerated for comic effect

Images that serve as symbols

Size and placement of the central image

The message

Clues to the intended audience and purpose

Relationship between text and images

review checklist

Reading and Writing about Different Kinds of Texts

☐ Use active reading strategies to help you understand and write about information in textbooks, news articles, business documents, web pages, and blogs. (See 6a.)

☐ Use active reading strategies to help you interpret and write about information in charts, graphs, and tables; maps; diagrams; photographs; editorial cartoons; and advertisements. (See 6b and 6c.)

unit

2 Reading and Writing Essays

7 Reading and Writing Exemplification Essays 191

8 Reading and Writing Narrative Essays 206

9 Reading and Writing Cause-and-Effect Essays 223

10 Reading and Writing Comparison-and-Contrast Essays 239

11 Reading and Writing Argument Essays 256

12 Additional Options for Organizing Essays 276

7 Reading and Writing Exemplification Essays

AP Photo/Marcio Jose Sanchez

focus on reading and writing

Look at this photo of Marissa Mayer, a previous executive and spokesperson for Google and current president and CEO of Yahoo!, and then brainstorm to discover what you already know about the progress women have made in American society and around the world. Later in this chapter, you will **read** an essay on this topic and then have an opportunity to **write** about it.

In this chapter, you will learn to

• read exemplification essays (7a)
• write exemplification essays (7b)
• connect reading and writing (7c)

What do we mean when we tell a friend that an instructor is *good* or that a football team is *bad*? What do we mean when we say that a movie is *boring* or that a particular war was *wrong*? To clarify general statements like these, we use **exemplification**—that is, we give **examples** to illustrate a general idea. In daily conversation and in your college courses, you use specific examples to help explain your ideas.

GENERAL STATEMENT	SPECIFIC EXAMPLES
Today is going to be a hard day.	Today is going to be a hard day because I have a math test in the morning, a lab quiz in the afternoon, and work in the evening.

GENERAL STATEMENT	SPECIFIC EXAMPLES
My car is giving me problems.	My car is burning oil and won't start on cold mornings. In addition, I need a new set of tires.

Exemplification illustrates a general idea with one or more specific examples. An **exemplification essay** uses specific examples to support a thesis.

7a Reading Exemplification Essays

When you **read** an exemplification essay, use TEST to help you identify its key elements. Be sure to follow the reading process outlined in Chapter 1.

T ▪ **Thesis Statement**—The introduction of an exemplification essay includes a clear **thesis statement** that identifies the essay's main idea—the idea the examples will support.

E ▪ **Evidence**—The body paragraphs present **evidence**, fully developed examples that support the thesis. Each body paragraph is introduced by a topic sentence that identifies the example or group of related examples that the paragraph will discuss.

S ▪ **Summary Statement**—The conclusion of an exemplification essay often includes a **summary statement** that reinforces the essay's thesis.

T ▪ **Transitions**—An exemplification essay uses appropriate **transitional words and phrases** to connect examples within paragraphs and between one paragraph and another.

In an exemplification essay, each body paragraph can develop a single example or discuss several related examples. The topic sentence introduces the example (or a group of related examples) that the paragraph will discuss. Each example supports the essay's thesis. The examples used to support the essay's thesis should be **relevant** (directly related to the main idea) and **distinct** (different from other points used as support).

Supporting examples are arranged in **logical order**—for example, from least to most important or from general to specific. The number of examples included depends on the scope of the essay's main idea: a complicated or controversial thesis might require many supporting examples, while a straightforward idea might require just a few.

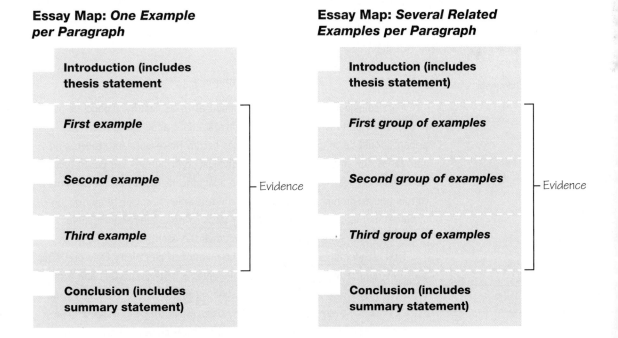

Essay Map: *One Example per Paragraph*

| **Introduction (includes thesis statement** |
| **First example** |
| **Second example** |
| **Third example** |
| **Conclusion (includes summary statement)** |

Evidence

Essay Map: *Several Related Examples per Paragraph*

| **Introduction (includes thesis statement)** |
| **First group of examples** |
| **Second group of examples** |
| **Third group of examples** |
| **Conclusion (includes summary statement)** |

Evidence

Reading a Model Student Essay: Exemplification

The following exemplification essay was written by Alison Perry in response to this assignment in a composition class:

> Take a walk around campus, carefully observing people and places. Then, write an exemplification essay that answers the question, "What steps can individual students take to make our campus a better place?"

Read Alison's essay, following the active reading process outlined in Chapter 1, and then fill in the essay map in Practice 7-1 on page 196. (Note that the TEST elements in the essay have been highlighted and color-coded.)

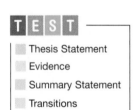

T E S T

- Thesis Statement
- Evidence
- Summary Statement
- Transitions

Making a Difference

1   Most college students want their campuses to be healthy, productive places to live, work, and learn. Usually, they have opinions about what university leaders should do to make their campuses better. However, many students do not realize how important their own individual contributions can be. In reality, students' attitudes and choices can have a significant impact on the campus culture and environment. This is especially true when it comes to conserving resources and reducing waste. By taking steps to make their schools more energy efficient, students can help to improve the quality of life on campus.

2   First, students can cut down on the amount of electricity they use. This does not require big sacrifices; it just involves a little awareness and a few small changes. Turning off the lights when no one is in the room is a good place to start. However, there are many other ways to avoid waste and save money. For example, students can shut down their computers and electronics

rather than putting them in sleep mode. They can also switch off power strips and unplug chargers when they are finished using them. Additionally, students can help their campuses save energy by turning down the thermostat in dorms, offices, and classrooms. Ultimately, by using only the electricity they need, students can make a real contribution to preserving their environment.

3   The second way students can help create a more energy-efficient campus is by walking, biking, carpooling, or taking public transportation instead of driving back and forth to school alone. Though these alternatives may require a little more effort (and are not always possible), students can start small. By commuting in one of these ways just once or twice a week, everyone can make a difference and experience the rewards. In addition to reducing their fuel consumption, students who walk or bike to campus get exercise and fresh air, and those who carpool get time to rest or talk with friends. Those who take a bus, subway, or light rail have additional time to study. All of these alternatives are less expensive, and often less stressful, than driving alone and paying for parking. Moreover, campuses with fewer cars have less traffic and therefore less pollution. They also have less need to put money and resources toward new parking lots and garages. All in all, the payoffs in campus health and happiness make these changes well worth the effort.

4   Finally, students can make a difference by talking to other students about energy-saving choices. For instance, students can let others know why they recycle their used paper rather than throw it in the trash where it cannot be reused. They can explain how filling up water bottles at the tap is less wasteful than buying water in disposable bottles. Furthermore, students can speak up when they see unnecessary energy use, and they can help others come up with creative solutions. For example, if they see an outdoor light left on all night in a campus building, they can talk with someone in charge about using motion-activated lights. If they notice people using Styrofoam takeout containers at the snack bar, they might let diners know that they are allowed to bring their own reusable containers. Often, people are simply not aware that there is another option, and they may be willing to change if they know there is a reasonable, less expensive way. Sharing knowledge and offering new ideas help to create a more thoughtful, more cooperative, and less wasteful community.

5   Though campus-wide projects like constructing new energy-efficient buildings or replacing outdated equipment are important, every student can commit to making small but valuable contributions to energy conservation on his or her own campus. These little changes may seem insignificant. However, when added together, all of the energy-saving choices can strengthen social bonds, encourage cooperation, help students stay fit, and

reduce expenses. Students should not underestimate the positive effects of choosing to walk, unplug, turn off, refill, share, and change.

PRACTICE

7-1   Now that you have read Alison's essay, fill in the essay map below to help you understand how she organized her essay. Then, decide whether her organization is effective.

Introduction _Answers will vary._
_____
_____

First group of examples _Answers will vary._
_____
_____

Second group of examples _Answers will vary._
_____
_____

Third group of examples _Answers will vary._
_____
_____

Conclusion _Answers will vary._
_____
_____

PRACTICE

7-2   1. Does the thesis statement indicate that Alison will use exemplification to structure her essay? How?

2. Does she need more examples in any of her body paragraphs? Can you suggest some examples that she could have added?

3. Should any examples be deleted because they are not relevant to the topic or because they are not distinct from other examples?

4. Does the order in which the examples are discussed make sense, or should they be arranged in a different order?

5. What is the essay's greatest strength? What is its greatest weakness?

● 7b Writing Exemplification Essays

When you **write** an exemplification essay, you follow the process out-lined in Chapter 3. The essay you write will include the same elements you have learned to recognize in the exemplification essays you read. When you finish your draft, you can use TEST to make sure it includes all the elements of an exemplification essay.

When you are given a writing assignment, the wording of your assign-ment may suggest that you write an exemplification essay. For example, you may be asked to *illustrate* or to *give examples*. Once you decide that your assignment calls for exemplification, you need to develop a thesis that reflects this purpose.

ASSIGNMENT	THESIS STATEMENT
Education Should children be taught only in their native languages or in English as well? Support your answer with examples of specific students' experiences.	The success of students in a bilingual third-grade class suggests the value of teaching elementary school students in English as well as in their native languages.
Literature Does William Shakespeare's *Othello* have to end tragically? Illustrate your position with references to specific characters.	Each of the three major characters in *Othello* contributes to the play's tragic ending.
Composition Discuss the worst job you ever had, including plenty of specific examples to support your thesis.	My summer job at a fast-food restaurant was my worst job because of the endless stream of rude customers, the many boring tasks I had to perform, and my manager's insensitivity.

Teaching Tip
Tell students that many everyday writing tasks call for exemplification. For example, a parent committee's report for a day-care center might present examples of possible environmental hazards in the school building.

Case Study: A Student Writes an Exemplification Essay

Kyle Sims, a student in a first-year writing course, was asked to write an essay about a popular hobby or interest. He decided to use his knowledge by writing about extreme sports.

Once he had settled on a topic, Kyle did some **freewriting** on his laptop. When he read over his freewriting, he saw that he had come up with three kinds of information: ideas about the dangers of extreme sports, about the challenges they present, and about the equipment they require. He then wrote a **thesis statement** that identified the three points he wanted to make. After **brainstorming** about each of these points, he had enough material for a first draft.

As he wrote his **first draft**, Kyle devoted one paragraph to each point, using examples to develop his body paragraphs. When he finished his draft, he TESTed it. He was satisfied with his thesis, which told readers what points he was going to make about extreme sports and also conveyed the idea that they were not like ordinary sports. His summary statement seemed logical and appropriate. However, realizing that his readers might not know much about extreme sports, Kyle added more examples to illustrate a range of different kinds of extreme sports and more transitions to lead readers from one example to the next.

When Kyle **revised** his draft, he rewrote his topic sentences so they clearly identified the three points he wanted to make about extreme sports. After he finished his revision, he **edited** and **proofread** carefully and made sure his essay met his instructor's **format** requirements.

The following final draft includes all the elements Kyle looked for when he TESTed his essay. Read Kyle's essay, and then answer the questions in Practice 7-3 on page 199.

Going to Extremes

1   For years, sports like football, baseball, and basketball have been popular in cities, suburbs, and small rural towns. For some young people, however, these sports no longer seem exciting, especially when compared to "extreme sports," such as snowboarding and BMX racing. Extreme sports are different from more familiar sports because they are dangerous, they are physically challenging, and they require specialized equipment.

2   First, extreme sports are dangerous. For example, snowboarders take chances with snowy hills and unpredictable bumps. They zoom down mountains at high speeds, which is typical of extreme sports. In addition, snowboarders and skateboarders risk painful falls as they do their tricks. Also, many extreme sports, like rock climbing, bungee jumping, and skydiving, are performed at very high altitudes. Moreover, the bungee jumper has to jump from a very high place, and there is always a danger of getting tangled with the bungee cord. People who participate in extreme sports accept—and even enjoy—these dangers.

3   In addition, extreme sports are very difficult. For instance, surfers have to learn to balance surfboards while dealing with wind and waves. Bungee jumpers may have to learn how to do difficult stunts while jumping off a high bridge or a dam. Another example of the physical challenge of extreme sports can be found in BMX racing. BMX racers have to learn to steer a lightweight bike on a dirt track that has jumps and banked corners. These

extreme sports require skills that most people do not naturally have. These special skills have to be learned, and participants in extreme sports enjoy this challenge.

4   Finally, almost all extreme sports require specialized equipment. For example, surfers need surfboards that are light but strong. They can choose epoxy boards, which are stronger, or fiberglass boards, which are lighter. They can choose shortboards, which are shorter than seven feet and are easier to maneuver, or they can use longboards, which are harder and slower to turn in the water but are easier to learn on. Also, surfers have to get special wax for their boards to keep from slipping as they are paddling out into the water. For surfing in cold water, they need wetsuits that trap their own body heat. Other extreme sports require different kinds of specialized equipment, but those who participate in them are willing to buy whatever they need.

5   Clearly, extreme sports are very different from other sports. Maybe it is because they are so different that they have become so popular in recent years. Already, snowboarding, BMX racing, and other extreme sports are featured in the Olympics. The Summer and Winter X Games are televised on ESPN and ABC, and sports like BMX racing, snowboarding, surfing, and snowmobiling get national attention on these programs. With all this publicity, extreme sports are likely to become even more popular—despite their challenges.

PRACTICE
7-3

1. Underline Kyle's thesis statement; then, restate it in your own words.

2. What evidence does Kyle present to support his thesis? For instance, what examples of extreme sports does he give in paragraph 1? What examples of dangers does he give in paragraph 2?

3. Circle some of the transitional words and phrases Kyle uses to move from one example to another.

4. Underline Kyle's summary statement. Then, restate it in your own words.

5. Use TEST to evaluate Kyle's essay. What revisions would you suggest he make? Why?

grammar in context

Exemplification

When you write an exemplification essay, you may introduce your examples with transitional words and phrases like *First* or *In addition*. If you do, be sure to use a comma after the transitional word or phrase.

> First, extreme sports are dangerous.
>
> In addition, extreme sports are very difficult.
>
> Finally, almost all extreme sports require specialized equipment.

For information on using commas with introductory and transitional words and phrases, see 26b.

 For practice with comma usage, complete the LearningCurve Commas activity at **bedfordstmartins.com/forw.**

7c Integrating Reading and Writing

Now, it is time to practice what you have learned and put your reading and writing skills together. The following essay, "Around the World, Women Are On the Move," by Richard Rodriguez, supports its thesis with examples. **Read** the essay, following the active reading process outlined in Chapter 1, and then answer the questions on pages 202–203. When you have finished, you will **write** an exemplification essay in response to Rodriguez's ideas.

AROUND THE WORLD, WOMEN ARE ON THE MOVE

Richard Rodriguez

Richard Rodriguez, a Mexican-American writer whose work explores the issues of class, race, and ethnicity, is best known for his autobiographical trilogy, which includes *Hunger of Memory* (1982), *Days of Obligation: An Argument with My Mexican Father* (1992), and *Brown: The Last Discovery of America* (2002). In 1997, Rodriguez won a Peabody Award, one of television's highest honors, for the essays on American life that he contributes regularly to PBS's *NewsHour*, where "Around the World, Women Are On the Move" first aired in 2009.

Before you read, think about the "women on the move" in your own life.

In 1996, President Bill Clinton appointed Madeleine Albright as Secretary of State. Because of Madeleine Albright, because of Condoleezza Rice who came soon after, because of Hillary Clinton, we scarcely mark the gender revolution that has taken place in just over a decade. Today, the diplomatic face of America is a woman's face.

All over the world, women and girls are on the move. In Pakistani and Afghan villages, girls make their way to school, sometimes furtively, wary of boys or men who might splash them with acid for daring to learn to read and to write. In the last half-century, hundreds of thousands of Mexican women have left their villages to find jobs in America or to work in Mexican border town assembly plants. In Ciudad Juárez, hundreds of women who ventured into the world alone have been murdered. The world remains a dangerous place for women.

> **WORD POWER**
> **furtively** cautiously and secretly

Even so, at U.S. colleges, female students are signing up for study-abroad programs by a 2-to-1 ratio over males. Indeed, female students, many the daughters and granddaughters of women who did not assume college in their lives, now outnumber male students on American campuses.

In American legend, as in so many of the world's myths, it is the young man who leaves home to find gold or slay the dragon. Lewis and Clark are paradigmatic American explorers, blazing a trail from St. Louis to the Pacific Coast. But as it happened, they were led up the Missouri River and across the Rockies by a Shoshone Indian. Her name was Sacagawea.

> **WORD POWER**
> **paradigmatic** typical; serving as a model

In the Americas, there were other stories like hers, native women who became go-betweens, translators, even lovers of the foreign. In colonial Virginia, Pocahontas left her tribe to marry an Englishman, and she traveled with him to London to become a figure in history. In Mexico, male history still reviles Doña Marina, La Malinche, as a sexual traitor. She was an Indian woman who became the lover of the Spaniard Cortés. Marina conspired with Cortés against the Aztecs who had imprisoned her own tribe.

What are we to make of these stories of women moving among cultures and conflict? Today we have the story of Kansas-born Ann Dunham, an anthropologist, whose son is now president of the United States. In interviews, Barack Obama describes his mother as searching but also reckless. Her life was a series of journeys. In Hawaii, white Ann Dunham married a black Kenyan. When their marriage failed, he returned to Africa, which for him was the known world. She ventured outward to Muslim Indonesia.

In American homes when marriages fail, it is usually the husband who disappears. Women become the head of the family, responsible for instilling in sons as well as daughters the meaning of adulthood.

Professional athletes, movie stars, convicts, presidents all testify to the importance of single mothers. At last summer's Olympics, the world saw Michael Phelps emerge from the pool after each event to search the crowd for his mother.

The news this evening is of failing male oligarchies on Wall Street.   8
The news this evening is of tribal chieftains at war with modernity. The news is of religious leaders who forbid the ordination of women, even as they stumble from one diplomatic gaffe to another.

Throughout history, the world has been largely governed by men.   9
When the male order falters and fails—as it seems now—we would make a mistake if we assumed the world was collapsing. All over the world, millions of women are valiantly venturing far from custom, little girls are walking across the desert to school.

WORD POWER

oligarchies organizations led by small groups of people
ordination the giving of ministerial or priestly authority
gaffe a noticeable mistake

Focus on Reading

1. Look back at the work you did when you previewed, highlighted, and annotated this essay. Did you number Rodriguez's key examples? If not, do so now.

2. Now, put a check mark beside the example that you think most convincingly supports the essay's thesis.

Focus on Meaning

1. What failures does Rodriguez suggest men have been responsible for? What specific criticisms does he have of male world leaders, financiers, and religious leaders? Do you agree with these criticisms?

2. How does Rodriguez expect women to solve the problems men have created? Do you think he is right to expect this?

Focus on Strategy

1. At the end of paragraph 1, Rodriguez says, "Today, the diplomatic face of America is a woman's face." Is this sentence his essay's thesis? Explain.

2. In paragraph 6, Rodriguez notes that Barack Obama "describes his mother as searching but also reckless." How does this paragraph support Rodriguez's thesis?

Focus on Language and Style

1. What different meanings could the expression "on the move" have? Which meaning do you think Rodriguez has in mind? What makes you think so?

2. What words are repeated in the three sentences in paragraph 8? Why?

Focus on the Pattern

1. In paragraph 2, Rodriguez says that despite their advances, the "world remains a dangerous place for women." What examples does he give to support this statement? Can you give additional examples?

2. How are the examples that Rodriguez gives in paragraph 2, paragraph 3, and paragraphs 4–5 different? Why are these different kinds of examples grouped as they are?

Focus on Critical Thinking

1. Do you think Rodriguez was right to include the material about single mothers in paragraph 7? Does this paragraph support his thesis? Why or why not?

2. Do you agree with Rodriguez that the world is still a "dangerous place for women" (2)? Do you agree with him that women are "on the move"? Explain.

focus on reading and writing

Now that you have read Richard Rodriguez's essay, write your own exemplification essay in response to one of the following prompts. (If you prefer, you can write on one of the additional topics listed in the box below.) Be sure to follow the writing process outlined in Chapter 3.

1. Write an exemplification essay called "In My Family, Women Are On the Move." Support your thesis with specific examples of achievements by the women in your family. You may focus on one example in each body paragraph, or you can combine several related examples in some of your paragraphs.

2. In paragraph 3, Rodriguez presents some information about the progress made by college women. Write an exemplification essay in which you develop this idea further, illustrating the advances and achievements of female students at your school.

additional topics

Exemplification

Reasons to start (or not start) college right after high school

The three best products ever invented

Athletes who really are role models

National or world news events that gave you hope

READING AND WRITING ACTIVITY

Reread the draft of your essay, and then revise it. Begin by answering the questions in the TEST checklist below. When you have finished revising, edit and proofread your essay.

TESTing your exemplification essay

Thesis Statement Unifies Your Essay

☐ Does your introduction include a **thesis statement** that clearly states your essay's main idea?

Evidence Supports Your Essay's Thesis Statement

☐ Do you have enough **evidence**—fully developed examples—to support your thesis?

☐ Do all your examples support your thesis, or should some be deleted?

Summary Statement Reinforces Your Essay's Main Idea

☐ Does your conclusion include a **summary statement** that reinforces your essay's thesis?

Transitions Connect Examples

☐ Do you include **transitions** that move readers from one example to the next?

COLLABORATIVE ACTIVITY

Work with another student to consider the strengths and weaknesses of both of your exemplification essays. Do you think one of your essays is more effective than the other one? If so, why? Based on your reactions to the essays you and your classmate wrote, write a few sentences explaining what an exemplification essay should accomplish.

review checklist

Reading and Writing Exemplification Essays

☐ When you *read* an exemplification essay, follow the reading process outlined in Chapter 1, and use TEST to help you identify the essay's key elements. (See 7a.)

☐ When you *write* an exemplification essay, follow the writing process outlined in Chapter 3, and use TEST to make sure you have included all the necessary elements. (See 7b.)

☐ Keep in mind that in college courses, you often write in response to reading. (See 7c.)

8 Reading and Writing Narrative Essays

focus on reading and writing

Look at the image above, which shows four panels from *One! Hundred! Demons!*, a graphic memoir by Lynda Barry about her childhood. Brainstorm to discover what you already know about your own elementary-school experiences. Later in this chapter, you will **read** an essay on this topic and then have an opportunity to **write** about it.

In this chapter, you will learn to
- read narrative essays (8a)
- write narrative essays (8b)
- connect reading and writing (8c)

Narration is writing that tells a personal or fictional story or traces a series of events. For example, a narrative could tell how you were changed by an experience you had as a child, how the life of Martin Luther King Jr. helped him to develop as a civil rights leader, or how the Battle of Gettysburg became the turning point in the Civil War.

A narrative usually presents events in chronological (time) order, moving from beginning to end. Sometimes, however, to add interest to a narrative, a writer may decide to start at the end of a story and then move back to the beginning to trace the events that led to this outcome.

> **WORD POWER**
>
> **memoir** a collection of memories about a writer's life

8a Reading Narrative Essays

When you **read** a narrative essay, use **TEST** to help you identify its key elements. Be sure to follow the active reading process outlined in Chapter 1.

T ■ **Thesis Statement**—The introduction of a narrative essay includes a **thesis statement** that communicates the main idea—the point the story is making.

E ■ **Evidence**—The body paragraphs tell the story, one event at a time, with each event providing **evidence**—examples and details—to support the thesis. Events are usually presented in chronological (time) order.

S ■ **Summary Statement**—The conclusion of a narrative essay often includes a **summary statement** that reinforces the essay's main idea.

T ■ **Transitions**—Throughout a narrative essay, **transitional words and phrases** connect events in time, showing how one event leads to the next.

In a narrative essay, each body paragraph can discuss one event or several events. The topic sentence of the first body paragraph introduces the first event (or first group of events) that the paragraph will discuss. The events and details presented in the body paragraphs support the essay's thesis, and events are generally arranged in chronological order.

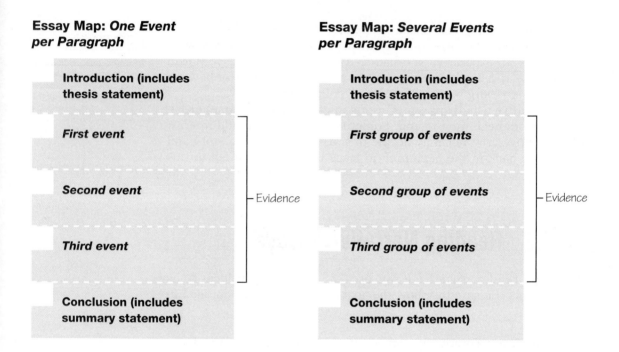

Essay Map: *One Event per Paragraph*

Introduction (includes thesis statement)

First event

Second event

Third event

Conclusion (includes summary statement)

Evidence

Essay Map: *Several Events per Paragraph*

Introduction (includes thesis statement)

First group of events

Second group of events

Third group of events

Conclusion (includes summary statement)

Evidence

Some Transitional Words and Phrases for Narration

Transitional words and phrases help readers follow a narrative by indicating the order in which events occurred.

after	eventually	next
as	finally	now
as soon as	first . . . second . . .	soon
at first	third	then
at the same time	immediately	two hours (days,
before	later	months, years)
by this time	later on	later
earlier	meanwhile	when

Reading a Model Student Essay: Narration

The following narrative essay was written by Erica Sarno in response to this assignment in a first year writing course.

> Write a literacy narrative, a personal account that traces your development as a reader or writer during a particular period of your life.

Read Erica's essay, following the active reading process outlined in Chapter 1, and then fill in the essay map in Practice 8-1 on page 210. (Note that the TEST elements in the essay have been highlighted and color-coded.)

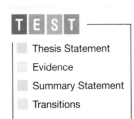

T E S T

- Thesis Statement
- Evidence
- Summary Statement
- Transitions

Becoming a Writer

1   I used to think that writing was just about filling pages. Composing an essay for school meant getting the job done and checking it off my to-do list. During my last two years of high school, however, my attitude started to change. Several experiences helped me understand that writing is not a skill that some people are born with and others are not. If I wanted to write, all I needed was a desire to express myself to others and a willing audience. Realizing that there was someone on the other side of the page, eager to listen, helped me develop into a more active reader and more effective writer.

2   My first real lesson in my development as a writer took place in Mrs. Strickland's Junior English class. Mrs. Strickland was hard to approach. She dressed as if she expected to be giving a press conference at the White House. She wore tan suits and silk scarves and had a helmet of dyed blonde hair. We seemed to disappoint her just because we were high school students. Maybe I saw her lack of interest in us and our work as a challenge because, one day, I took a risk and wrote a very personal essay about losing my aunt to cancer. When I got the paper back, Mrs. Strickland had written only, "Did you read the instructions?" I could not believe it. For the first time, I had actually written about what was important to me rather than just filling the pages with words, and she had not even read past the introduction! Still, I knew then that I had something to say. I just needed someone to listen.

3   The next year, I had Dr. Kelleher for Senior English. My year with Dr. K profoundly changed the way I see myself as a writer (and as a reader). Finally, a teacher was paying attention to what I had written. His only rule for writing was "Don't be boring!" I re-wrote sentences, hoping for an exclamation point or one of Dr. K's other special marks in the margin. Dr. K had a whole list of codes and abbreviations, like "BTH" ("Better than

Hemingway") or "the knife" (when the writer slayed the opponent in an argument). I also relied on Dr. K to tell me when I was falling into my old habit of just filling the page. He would write a funny comment like, "Come back! Log out of Facebook!" Then, he would give me a chance to try again. Trusting him to be a generous reader and an honest critic helped me develop my voice and my confidence as a writer.

4   Meanwhile, I started to become a better reader, too. I could tell when a writer was writing to me, wanting me to understand. I could also tell when a writer was writing to just get the job done. Instead of just skimming the assigned reading, I got in the habit of writing in the margins and making notes about what I thought. I underlined ideas that spoke to me, and I wrote "Really??" next to ideas that seemed silly. Instead of assuming a reading would be boring, I gave every assignment a chance. Whether I liked the book or not, I felt that I could explain my reasons. I was finally seeing for myself that writing is just another way for people to talk to each other.

5   Eventually, in the spring of my senior year, I experienced what it feels like to connect with a broader audience. I suggested a column about "senioritis" to the school paper, and even though I had never written for the public before, the editor loved my idea. I knew what I wanted to say, and I knew I could collect plenty of stories to help me illustrate my ideas. What I did not predict was how much I would learn from the experience of writing those six columns. Knowing that hundreds of people would be reading my pieces, I revised them over and over again. When Dr. K read one of my last columns aloud to our class, I got to see how my work affected people. Watching the expressions on my classmates' faces and hearing them laugh at the funny parts helped me understand what good writing is. In that moment, I truly connected with my audience.

6   Although I still have a lot to learn, I now understand how important the relationship between the writer and the reader is. When I write, I am writing to be heard. When I read, I am reading to understand. The communication may not be perfect, but I know I am not alone in my task. And, even though I am not in Dr. K's class anymore, I still sometimes imagine that he will be reading what I have written. Thinking about him reminds me that someone cares about what I have to say.

PRACTICE

8-1   Now that you have read Erica's essay, fill in the following essay map to help you understand how she organized her essay. Then, decide whether her organization is effective.

Introduction *Answers will vary.*
_____
_____

First event *Answers will vary.*
_____
_____

Second event *Answers will vary.*
_____
_____

Third event *Answers will vary.*
_____
_____

Fourth event *Answers will vary.*
_____
_____

Conclusion *Answers will vary.*
_____
_____

PRACTICE

8-2

1. Does Erica's thesis statement suggest that she will use narration to structure her essay?

2. List the key events in this narrative.

3. Does any body paragraph need additional examples or details? If so, where should additional evidence be added?

4. Does the order in which events are discussed make sense? Could the events have been arranged in any other way?

5. What is the essay's greatest strength? What is its greatest weakness?

● 8b   Writing Narrative Essays

When you **write** a narrative essay, you follow the process outlined in Chapter 3. The essay you write will include the same elements you have learned to recognize in the narrative essays you read. When you finish your draft, you can use TEST to make sure it includes all the elements of a narrative essay.

When you are given a writing assignment, the wording of your assignment may suggest that you write a narrative essay. For example, you may be asked to *tell*, *trace*, *summarize events*, or *recount*. Once you decide that your assignment calls for narration, you need to develop a thesis statement that reflects this purpose.

Teaching Tip
Tell students that many everyday writing tasks call for narration. For example, a job-application letter might summarize previous work experience.

ASSIGNMENT	THESIS STATEMENT
Composition Tell about a time when you had to show courage even though you were afraid.	In extraordinary circumstances, a person can exhibit great courage and overcome fear.
American history Summarize the events that occurred during President Franklin Delano Roosevelt's first one hundred days in office.	Although many thought they were extreme, the measures enacted by Roosevelt during his first one hundred days in office were necessary to fight the economic depression.
Political science Trace the development of the Mississippi Freedom Democratic Party.	As the Mississippi Freedom Democratic Party developed, it found a voice that spoke for equality and justice.

Case Study: A Student Writes a Narrative Essay

WORD POWER

milestone an important event; a turning point

Elaina Corrato, a returning student who was older than most of her classmates, wasn't sure how to proceed when her writing instructor gave the class an assignment to write about a milestone in their lives. The first topic that came to mind was her recent thirtieth birthday, but she was reluctant to reveal her age to her classmates. However, when she learned that no one except her instructor would read her essay, she decided to write about this topic.

Elaina began by rereading entries she had made in her **journal** in the days before and after her birthday as well as on the day itself.

Even before she began to write, she saw that her essay would be a narrative that traced her reactions to the events she experienced on that day.

As she **drafted** her essay, Elaina was careful to discuss events in the order in which they occurred and to include transitional words and phrases to move her discussion smoothly from one event to the next. Because she knew what she wanted to say, she found it easy to write a well-developed first draft that included plenty of information. When she **TEST**ed her essay, however, Elaina saw at once that she had not stated a thesis or included a summary statement to reinforce her main idea.

At this point, Elaina emailed her draft to her instructor and asked him for suggestions. (Her instructor offered this option to students whose off-campus work or family commitments made it difficult for them to schedule face-to-face conferences.) He explained that her thesis should not be just a general overview of the day's events; instead, it should make a point about how those events affected her. With this advice, Elaina found it was not difficult to write a thesis that expressed how she felt about turning thirty. Once she had a **thesis statement**, she was able to add a summary statement that reinforced her main idea, ending her essay on an optimistic note. With all the required elements in place, she continued **revising** and went on to **edit** and **proofread** her essay.

Read Elaina's essay, and then answer the questions in Practice 8-3 on page 215.

Reflections

1   Turning thirty did not bother me at all. My list of "Things to Do before I Die" was far from complete, but I knew I had plenty of time to do them. In fact, turning thirty seemed like no big deal to me. If anything, it was a milestone I was happy to be approaching. Unfortunately, other people had different ideas about this milestone, and eventually their ideas made me rethink my own.

2   As the big day approached, my family kept teasing me about it. My sister kept asking me if I felt any different. She couldn't believe I wasn't upset, but I didn't pay any attention to her. I was looking forward to a new chapter in my life. I liked my job, I was making good progress toward my college degree, and I was healthy and happy. Why should turning thirty be a problem? So, I made no special plans for my birthday, and I decided to treat it as just another day.

3   My birthday fell on a Saturday, and I enjoyed the chance to sleep in. After I got up and had breakfast, I did my laundry and then set out for the

supermarket. I rarely put on makeup or fixed my hair on Saturdays. After all, I didn't have to go to work or to school. I was only running errands in the neighborhood. Later on, though, as I waited in line at the deli counter, I caught sight of my reflection in the mirrored meat case. At first, I thought it wasn't really me. The woman staring back at me looked so old! She had bags under her eyes, and she even had a few gray hairs. I was so upset by my reflection that on my way home I stopped and bought a mud mask— guaranteed to make me look younger.

4   As I walked up the street toward my house, I saw something attached to the front railing. When I got closer, I realized that it was a bunch of black balloons. There was also a big sign that said "Over the Hill" in big black letters. I'd been trying to think about my birthday in positive terms, but my family seemed to have other ideas. Obviously, it was time for the mud mask.

5   After quickly unloading my groceries, I ran upstairs to apply the mask. The box promised a "rejuvenating look," and that was exactly what I wanted. I spread the sticky brown mixture on my face, and it hardened instantly. As I sat on my bed, waiting for the mask to work its magic, I heard the doorbell ring. Then, I heard familiar voices and my husband calling me to come down, saying that I had company. I couldn't answer him. I couldn't talk (or even smile) without cracking the mask. At this point, I retreated to the bathroom to make myself presentable for my friends and family. This task was not easy.

6   When I managed to scrub off the mud mask, my face was covered with little red pimples. Apparently, my sensitive skin couldn't take the harsh chemicals. At first, I didn't think the promise of "rejuvenated" skin was what I got. I had to admit, though, that my skin did look a lot younger. In fact, when I finally went downstairs to celebrate my birthday, I looked as young as a teenager—a teenager with acne.

7   Despite other people's grim warnings, I discovered that although turning thirty was a milestone, it wasn't a game-changer. I learned a lot that day, and I learned even more in the days that followed. What I finally realized was that I couldn't ignore turning thirty, but having a thirtieth birthday didn't have to mean that my life was over.

PRACTICE

8-3   1. Underline the thesis statement of "Reflections"; then, re-write it in your own words.

2. What specific events and details support Elaina's thesis? List as many pieces of evidence as you can.

3. Circle some of the transitional words and phrases Elaina uses to move readers from one event to the next.

4. Underline Elaina's summary statement. Do you think her summary statement effectively reinforces her essay's main idea?

5. Use **TEST** to evaluate Elaina's essay. What revisions would you recommend? Why?

grammar in context

Narration

When you write a narrative essay, you tell a story. When you get caught up in your story, you might sometimes find yourself stringing details together without proper punctuation, creating a **run-on**.

> **INCORRECT**   As the big day approached, my family kept teasing me about it, my sister kept asking me if I felt any different.

> **CORRECT**   As the big day approached, my family kept teasing me about it. My sister kept asking me if I felt any different.

For information on how to identify and correct run-ons, see Chapter 21.

 For practice with run-ons, complete the LearningCurve Run-Ons activity at **bedfordstmartins.com/forw.**

Teaching Tip
Before your students write narrative essays, you might want to explain how to identify and correct run-ons (Chapter 21) and have them do Practices 21-1 and 21-7.

ESL Tip
Your ESL students may need to review verb tenses before writing a narrative essay. Refer them to Chapter 14.

8c   Integrating Reading and Writing

Now, it is time to practice what you have learned and put your reading and writing skills together. The following essay, "The Sanctuary of School," by Lynda Barry, is a narrative about the writer's childhood. **Read** the essay, following the active reading process outlined in Chapter 1, and then answer the questions on pages 218–219. When you have finished, you will **write** a narrative essay of your own in response to Barry's ideas.

THE SANCTUARY OF SCHOOL

Lynda Barry

In her many illustrated works—including graphic novels, comic books, and a weekly cartoon strip, *Ernie Pook's Comeek*, which appears in a number of newspapers and magazines—Lynda Barry looks at the world through the eyes of children. Her characters remind adult readers of the complicated world of young people and of the clarity with which they see social situations. In "The Sanctuary of School," first published in the *Baltimore Sun* in 1992, Barry tells a story from her own childhood.

Before you read, think about the strategies you used to cope with difficult periods in your own childhood.

1   I was 7 years old the first time I snuck out of the house in the dark. It was winter and my parents had been fighting all night. They were short on money and long on relatives who kept "temporarily" moving into our house because they had nowhere else to go.

2   My brother and I were used to giving up our bedroom. We slept on the couch, something we actually liked because it put us that much closer to the light of our lives, our television.

3   At night when everyone was asleep, we lay on our pillows watching it with the sound off. We watched Steve Allen's mouth moving. We watched Johnny Carson's mouth moving.[1] We watched movies filled with gangsters shooting machine guns into packed rooms, dying soldiers hurling a last grenade and beautiful women crying at windows. Then the sign-off finally came and we tried to sleep.

4   The morning I snuck out, I woke up filled with a panic about needing to get to school. The sun wasn't quite up yet but my anxiety was so fierce that I just got dressed, walked quietly across the kitchen and let myself out the back door.

5   It was quiet outside. Stars were still out. Nothing moved and no one was in the street. It was as if someone had turned the sound off on the world.

6   I walked the alley, breaking thin ice over the puddles with my shoes. I didn't know why I was walking to school in the dark. I didn't think about it. All I knew was a feeling of panic, like the panic that strikes kids when they realize they are lost.

7   That feeling eased the moment I turned the corner and saw the dark outline of my school at the top of the hill. My school was made up of about 15 nondescript portable classrooms set down on a fenced concrete lot in a rundown Seattle neighborhood, but it had the most beautiful view of the Cascade Mountains. You could see them from

WORD POWER

nondescript lacking
distinctive qualities;
uninteresting

1. Steve Allen and Johnny Carson were late-night television hosts.

anywhere on the playfield and you could see them from the windows of my classroom—Room 2.

I walked over to the monkey bars and hooked my arms around the 8 cold metal. I stood for a long time just looking across Rainier Valley. The sky was beginning to whiten and I could hear a few birds.

In a perfect world my absence at home would not have gone un- 9 noticed. I would have had two parents in a panic to locate me, instead of two parents in a panic to locate an answer to the hard question of survival during a deep financial and emotional crisis.

But in an overcrowded and unhappy home, it's incredibly easy for 10 any child to slip away. The high levels of frustration, depression and anger in my house made my brother and me invisible. We were children with the sound turned off. And for us, as for the steadily increasing number of neglected children in this country, the only place where we could count on being noticed was at school.

"Hey there, young lady. Did you forget to go home last night?" It was 11 Mr. Gunderson, our janitor, whom we all loved. He was nice and he was funny and he was old with white hair, thick glasses and an unbelievable number of keys. I could hear them jingling as he walked across the play-field. I felt incredibly happy to see him.

He let me push his wheeled garbage can between the different por- 12 tables as he unlocked each room. He let me turn on the lights and raise the window shades and I saw my school slowly come to life. I saw Mrs. Holman, our school secretary, walk into the office without her orange lipstick on yet. She waved.

I saw the fifth-grade teacher Mr. Cunningham, walking under the 13 breezeway eating a hard roll. He waved.

And I saw my teacher, Mrs. Claire LeSane, walking toward us in a 14 red coat and calling my name in a very happy and surprised way, and suddenly my throat got tight and my eyes stung and I ran toward her crying. It was something that surprised us both.

It's only thinking about it now, 28 years later, that I realize I was cry- 15 ing from relief. I was with my teacher, and in a while I was going to sit at my desk, with my crayons and pencils and books and classmates all around me, and for the next six hours I was going to enjoy a thoroughly secure, warm and stable world. It was a world I absolutely relied on. Without it, I don't know where I would have gone that morning.

Mrs. LeSane asked me what was wrong and when I said "Nothing," 16 she seemingly left it at that. But she asked me if I would carry her purse for her, an honor above all honors, and she asked if I wanted to come into Room 2 early and paint.

She believed in the natural healing power of painting and drawing 17 for troubled children. In the back of her room there was always a draw-ing table and an easel with plenty of supplies, and sometimes during the day she would come up to you for what seemed like no good reason and quietly ask if you wanted to go to the back table and "make some pictures for Mrs. LeSane." We all had a chance at it—to sit apart from the class for a while to paint, draw and silently work out impossible problems on 11 × 17 sheets of newsprint.

Drawing came to mean everything to me. At the back table in 18 Room 2, I learned to build myself a life preserver that I could carry into my home.

We all know that a good education system saves lives, but the people 19 of this country are still told that cutting the budget for public schools is necessary, that poor salaries for teachers are all we can manage and that art, music and all creative activities must be the first to go when times are lean.

Before- and after-school programs are cut and we are told that pub- 20 lic schools are not made for baby-sitting children. If parents are neglectful temporarily or permanently, for whatever reason, it's certainly sad, but their unlucky children must fend for themselves. Or slip through the cracks. Or wander in a dark night alone.

We are told in a thousand ways that not only are public schools not 21 important, but that the children who attend them, the children who need them most, are not important either. We leave them to learn from the blind eye of a television, or to the mercy of "a thousand points of light"[2] that can be as far away as stars.

I was lucky. I had Mrs. LeSane. I had Mr. Gunderson. I had an abun- 22 dance of art supplies. And I had a particular brand of neglect in my home that allowed me to slip away and get to them. But what about the rest of the kids who weren't as lucky? What happened to them?

By the time the bell rang that morning I had finished my drawing and 23 Mrs. LeSane pinned it up on the special bulletin board she reserved for drawings from the back table. It was the same picture I always drew—a sun in the corner of a blue sky over a nice house with flowers all around it.

Mrs. LeSane asked us to please stand, face the flag, place our right 24 hands over our hearts and say the Pledge of Allegiance. Children across the country do it faithfully. I wonder now when the country will face its children and say a pledge right back.

WORD POWER

fend to manage

Focus on Reading

1. Look back at the work you did when you previewed, highlighted, and annotated this essay. What do you think the word *sanctuary* means? Look through the essay for **context clues** that can help you understand this word, and write a brief definition in the margin. (Write a question mark beside your definition to remind yourself to look the word up later on.)

2. Circle the names of the key people featured in this essay. In the margin beside each name, write a few words to identify each person.

2. Phrase used by former president George Herbert Walker Bush to promote volunteerism.

Focus on Meaning

1. In paragraph 10, Barry characterizes herself and her brother as "children with the sound turned off." What do you think she means?

2. How are Barry's home and school worlds different? Identify specific negative features of her home life and specific positive features of her school life.

3. A number of adults came to Barry's rescue during her childhood. Who were these adults? What did each one contribute?

Teaching Tip
You may have students work collaboratively to answer some of these questions.

Focus on Strategy

1. What point is Barry making in paragraph 10? In paragraphs 20–21? In her conclusion? To whom does she seem to be addressing her comments? Explain.

2. What is the main idea of Barry's essay—the idea she wants to convince readers to accept? Is this idea actually stated in her essay? If so, where? If not, do you think it should be?

ESL Tip
Have native- and nonnative-speaking students work in groups or in pairs to discuss the exercises before they write their answers.

Focus on Language and Style

1. Look up the word *sanctuary* in several different dictionaries. Which of the definitions do you think comes closest to Barry's meaning? Why?

2. Now, look up the word *sanctuary* in a thesaurus. What synonyms are listed? Would any other word be a better choice in Barry's title? Explain.

Teaching Tip
Remind students to answer all questions in complete sentences.

Focus on the Pattern

1. Paragraphs 9–10 and 19–22 interrupt Barry's narrative. What purpose do these paragraphs serve? Do you think the essay would be more effective if paragraphs 9 and 10 came earlier? If paragraphs 19–22 came after paragraph 24? Explain.

2. What transitional words and phrases does Barry use in her narrative to move readers from one event to the next? Do you think her essay needs more transitions? If so, where should they be added?

Focus on Critical Thinking

1. Do you see Barry's narrative primarily as a story of her childhood or as a persuasive essay with a message about needed social change? Why? Specifically, what do you think she expected her essay to accomplish?

2. This essay was first published in the *Baltimore Sun*, a newspaper with a wide general audience. Which sections of the essay do you think would have the strongest impact on this audience? What different reactions would you expect readers to have? Why?

focus on reading and writing

Now that you have read Lynda Barry's essay, write your own narrative essay in response to one of the following prompts. (If you prefer, you can write on one of the additional topics listed in the box below.) Be sure to follow the writing process outlined in Chapter 3.

1. Did you see elementary school as a "sanctuary" or as something quite different? Write a narrative essay that conveys to readers what school meant to you when you were a child.

2. In addition to school, television was a sanctuary for Barry and her brother. Did television watching (or some other activity) serve this function for you when you were younger? Is there some activity that fills this role now? In a narrative essay, write about your own "sanctuary."

additional topics

Narration

A perfect day

A day on which everything went wrong

A story from your family's history

A biography of your pet

READING AND WRITING ACTIVITY

Reread the draft of your essay, and then revise it. Begin by answering the questions in the TEST checklist below. When you have finished revising, edit and proofread your essay.

TESTing your narrative essay

T hesis Statement Unifies Your Essay

☐ Does your introduction include a **thesis statement** that clearly states your essay's main idea?

E vidence Supports Your Essay's Thesis Statement

☐ Does all your **evidence**—events and details—support your thesis, or should some be deleted?

☐ Do you include enough specific details to make your narrative interesting?

☐ Are the events you discuss arranged in clear chronological (time) order?

S ummary Statement Reinforces Your Essay's Main Idea

☐ Does your conclusion include a **summary statement** that reinforces your essay's thesis?

T ransitions Connect Events

☐ Do you include enough **transitions** to make the sequence of events clear to your reader?

COLLABORATIVE ACTIVITY

Work with another student to consider the strengths and weaknesses of both of your narrative essays. Do you think one of your essays is more effective than the other one? If so, why? Based on your assessment of the essays you and your classmate wrote, write a few sentences explaining what a narrative essay should accomplish.

review checklist

Reading and Writing Narrative Essays

☐ A narrative essay tells a story by presenting a series of events, usually in chronological order.

☐ When you *read* a narrative essay, follow the active reading process outlined in Chapter 1, and use TEST to help you identify the essay's key elements. (See 8a.)

☐ When you *write* a narrative essay, follow the writing process outlined in Chapter 3, and use TEST to make sure you have included all the necessary elements. (See 8b.)

☐ Keep in mind that in college courses, you often write in response to reading. (See 8c.)

9 Reading and Writing Cause-and-Effect Essays

Keith Morris/Alamy

focus on reading and writing

The student in the photo above is updating her Facebook profile. Brainstorm to discover what you already know about Facebook and other social-networking sites. Later in this chapter, you will **read** an essay on this topic and then have an opportunity to **write** about it.

In this chapter, you will learn to

- read cause-and-effect essays (9a)
- write cause-and-effect essays (9b)
- connect reading and writing (9c)

Why is the cost of college so high in the United States? How does smoking affect a person's health? What would happen if the city increased its sales tax? How dangerous is the flu? All these questions have one thing in common: they try to determine the causes or effects of an action, event, or situation.

A **cause** is something or someone that makes something happen. An **effect** is a result of a particular cause or event.

CAUSE	EFFECT
Increased airport security ⟶	Long lines at airports
Weight gain ⟶	Health problems
Seat belt laws passed ⟶	Traffic deaths reduced

Cause-and-effect essays can identify or analyze causes, and they can also examine or predict effects; sometimes, they do both. Cause-and-effect essays help readers understand why something happened or show how one thing influences another.

● 9a Reading Cause-and-Effect Essays

When you **read** a cause-and-effect essay, use TEST to help you identify its key elements. Be sure to follow the active reading process outlined in Chapter 1.

T ▪ **Thesis Statement**—The introduction of a cause-and-effect essay includes a **thesis statement** that communicates the essay's main idea and indicates whether it will focus on causes or on effects.

E ▪ **Evidence**—The body paragraphs include **evidence**—examples and details—to illustrate and explain the causes or effects you examine. The topic sentence of each paragraph identifies the causes or effects the paragraph will discuss.

S ▪ **Summary Statement**—The conclusion of a cause-and-effect essay usually includes a **summary statement** that reinforces the essay's thesis.

T ■ **Transitions**—A cause-and-effect essay includes **transitional words and phrases** that make clear which causes lead to which effects.

In a cause-and-effect essay, a full paragraph is usually devoted to each cause or effect. Alternatively, several related causes (or effects) can be grouped together in each body paragraph.

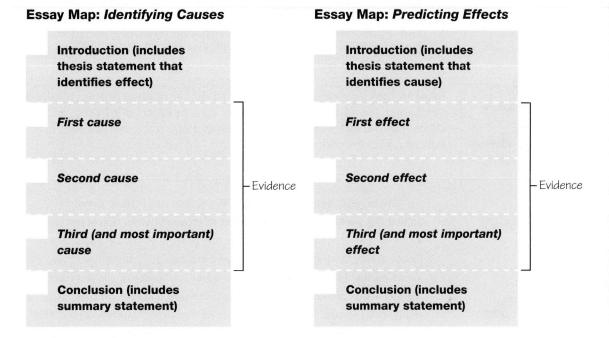

Essay Map: _Identifying Causes_

Introduction (includes thesis statement that identifies effect)

First cause

Second cause

Third (and most important) cause

⎤
│ —Evidence
⎦

Conclusion (includes summary statement)

Essay Map: _Predicting Effects_

Introduction (includes thesis statement that identifies cause)

First effect

Second effect

Third (and most important) effect

⎤
│ —Evidence
⎦

Conclusion (includes summary statement)

Some Transitional Words and Phrases for Cause and Effect

Transitions are important in cause-and-effect essays because they establish causal connections, telling readers that A caused B and not the other way around.

accordingly	for this reason	the most important
another cause	since	cause
another effect	so	the most important
another reason	the first (second,	effect
as a result	third) cause	the most important
because	the first (second,	reason
consequently	third) effect	therefore
for	the first (second,	

Reading a Model Student Essay: Cause and Effect

The following cause-and-effect essay was written for a history exam by Mehul Shah. Here is the exam question:

> In the textbook *Ways of the World: A Brief Global History*, author Robert Strayer identifies the years 500–1500 as a time of increasing global connections. Choose one trade network (Silk Roads, Sea Roads, or Sand Roads) that experienced growth during this period, and consider what caused it to expand. What events led to this expansion? In addition, briefly discuss the effects of this growth. What changes did it bring about?

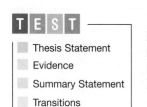

TEST

■ Thesis Statement
■ Evidence
■ Summary Statement
■ Transitions

Read Mehul's exam answer, following the active reading process outlined in Chapter 1, and then fill in the essay map in Practice 9-1 on page 228. (Note that the TEST elements in the essay exam answer have been high-lighted and color-coded.)

Expanding Connections across the Indian Ocean

1   In the years between 500 and 1500, several major trade networks around the world exploded in size. One of those networks connected people as far east as China and as far west as the coast of Africa by way of sea routes across the Indian Ocean. Centered around India, these routes are known as the Sea Roads. Like the land-based Silk Roads of the same era, the Sea Roads brought together people from very different cultures; as a result, those groups of people experienced significant transformations. This increase in sea-based commerce and the resulting changes did not happen without cause, though. Three central factors caused the growth of the Sea Roads between 500–1500.

2   The first reason for the expansion of these sea routes was the development of new knowledge and technology. Understanding the weather patterns in the Indian Ocean was key. Once merchants had this information, merchants could plan their voyages to take advantage of the best wind currents. Another important factor was the invention of the magnetic compass. Developed by the Chinese in the 11th century, the magnetic compass gave sailors a more accurate and reliable way to tell direction. As a result, they could travel more safely and more quickly across longer distances. At the same time, several societies in the region learned how to build ships that could accommodate bigger, heavier loads. Because they now had these larger ships, merchants could transport more goods to more people. Soon, increased exposure to a diversity of goods led to increased

demand for those goods. Together, these developments enabled sea-based commerce in the Indian Ocean to thrive.

3   The second reason the Sea Roads grew and flourished during this time period was the emergence of a stronger Chinese state. After years of instability, China was experiencing economic and political recovery. From the early 7th century to the late 13th century, the country was unified under powerful dynasties. These governments actively supported commerce, particularly sea trade. Under their rule, Chinese merchants delivered iron, silk, porcelain, and other Chinese products to ports all across the Indian Ocean. China also became a valuable market for imports from other regions served by the Sea Roads. Thus, the entire trade network benefited from China's new strength.

4   The third and most important reason the Sea Roads grew was the rapid rise of Islam. Founded in the 7th century, the religion spread quickly and led to the emergence of a powerful Arab Empire. By the 16th century, this empire reached beyond the Middle East to Europe, Africa, India, and Southeast Asia. Across the Indian Ocean basin, Arab political rule united diverse groups of people and encouraged greater connections between them. These connections were not just religious, however. Unlike many other religions, Islam was very supportive of commerce, and during this period Muslim traders dominated the Sea Roads. Because Muslims were so prosperous, many more people were attracted to the religion, and this further strengthened the trade networks. The most powerful civilization in the world during this millennium, Islam was a key factor in the expansion of the Sea Roads.

5   As a result of this growth in Indian Ocean trade, countless changes took place. People were in contact with each other more than ever before. With more interactions came cultural exchange, political change, and religious conversion. New merchant classes developed. People were introduced to new products, new technology, and new languages. A number of cities gained power as a result of their geographical advantages. For example, the kingdom of Srivijaya in Southeast Asia arose because of its valuable position between China and India and its profitable commercial resources. In addition, cities on the East African coast grew as they became important go-betweens for foreign traders and African producers. The Sea Roads had a lasting impact on religious traditions as well. Although Islam gained the most new followers during this period, Buddhism and Hinduism also widened their influence. Ultimately, the cultural effects of this expanded trade network were immense.

6   The growth in trade across the Indian Ocean, and the changes that followed, resulted from three specific features of the millennium (500–1500). Without the spread of Islam, the powerful Chinese government, and a few

well-timed innovations, the Sea Roads would not have developed as they did. Without the Sea Roads, many significant interactions would never have occurred, and the people of this millennium and the following centuries would have led very different lives. Therefore, learning about the causes and effects of this growth is essential to understanding global history.

PRACTICE

9-1   Now that you have read Mehul's essay, fill in the essay map below to help you understand how he organized his essay. Then, decide whether his organization is effective.

Introduction _Answers will vary._
_____
_____

First cause _Answers will vary._
_____
_____

Second cause _Answers will vary._
_____
_____

Third cause _Answers will vary._
_____
_____

Conclusion _Answers will vary._
_____
_____

PRACTICE

9-2   1. Reread the exam question on page 226. What words signal that students are to write a cause-and-effect essay?

2. Does the thesis statement make it clear that Mehul will use cause and effect to structure his exam answer?

3. What do you think is the most important cause the essay identifies? What seems to be the most important effect?

4. Do you think the essay's last sentence is necessary? Why or why not?

5. What is the essay's greatest strength? What is its greatest weakness?

9b Writing Cause-and-Effect Essays

When you **write** a cause-and-effect essay, you follow the process out-lined in Chapter 3. The essay you write will include the same elements you have learned to recognize in the cause-and-effect essays you read. When you finish your draft, you can use TEST to make sure it includes all the elements of a cause-and-effect essay.

When you are given a writing assignment, the wording of your assign-ment may suggest that you write a cause-and-effect essay. For example, the assignment may ask you to *explain why*, *predict the outcome*, *list con-tributing factors*, *discuss the consequences*, or tell what *caused* something else or how something is *affected* by something else. Once you decide that your assignment calls for cause and effect, you need to develop a thesis statement that reflects this purpose.

ASSIGNMENT	THESIS STATEMENT
Women's studies What factors contributed to the rise of the women's movement in the 1970s?	The women's movement of the 1970s had its origins in the peace and civil rights movements of the 1960s.
Public health Discuss the possible long-term effects of smoking.	In addition to its well-known negative effects on smokers themselves, smoking also causes significant problems for those exposed to secondhand smoke.
Media and society How has the Internet affected the lives of those who have grown up with it?	The Internet has created a generation of people who learn differently from those in previous generations.

Teaching Tip
Tell students that many everyday writing tasks involve discussing causes and effects. For example, a letter to a community's zoning board might discuss possible con-sequences of building a road, mall, or multiplex.

A cause-and-effect essay can focus on causes or on effects. When you write about causes, be sure to examine *all* relevant causes. You should emphasize the cause you consider the most important, but do not forget to consider other causes that may be significant. Similarly, when you write about effects, consider *all* significant effects of a particular cause, not just the first few that you think of.

If your focus is on finding causes, as it is in the first assignment on page 229, your introductory paragraph should identify the effect (the women's movement). If your focus is on predicting effects, as it is in the second and third assignments, you should begin by identifying the cause (smoking, the Internet).

Case Study: A Student Writes a Cause-and-Effect Essay

In an orientation course for first-year education majors, Andrea DeMarco was asked to write a personal essay about an event that changed her life. She decided immediately to write about her parents' brief separation, an event that occurred when she was eight years old.

Before she wrote her first draft, Andrea talked to her older sister and brother to see what they remembered about the separation. As they spoke, Andrea **took notes** so she wouldn't forget any details. Armed with her siblings' and her own memories, Andrea **drafted** her essay.

The wording of her assignment—to write about an event that changed her life—told Andrea that her essay would have a cause-and-effect structure. In her draft, she included a **thesis statement**—"My parents' separation made everything different"—that echoed the wording of the assignment. As she wrote, she was careful to include transitional words and phrases like *because* and *as a result* to make the cause-and-effect emphasis clear and to distinguish between the cause (the separation) and its effects. Her summary statement also reinforced the cause-and-effect emphasis of her essay.

When Andrea **TEST**ed her draft, she saw that it included all the required elements—thesis statement, evidence, summary statement, and transitions—so she continued **revising** her draft. When she finished her revisions, she **edited** and **proofread** her essay.

Read Andrea's essay, and then answer the questions in Practice 9-3 on page 232.

Read Andrea's essay, and then answer the questions in Practice 9-3 on page 232.

Teaching Tip

Because the student is telling the story in her own voice, the essay includes many contractions. Remind students that contractions are generally not acceptable in college writing.

How My Parents' Separation Changed My Life

1   Until I was eight, I lived the perfect all-American life with my perfect all-American family. I lived in a suburb of Albany, New York, with my parents, my sister and brother, and our dog, Daisy. We had a Ping-Pong table in the basement, a barbecue in the backyard, and two cars in the garage. My dad and mom were high school teachers, and every summer we took a family vacation. Then, it all changed. My parents' separation made everything different.

2   One day, just before Halloween, when my sister was twelve and my brother was fourteen (Daisy was seven), our parents called us into the

kitchen for a family conference. We didn't think anything was wrong at first; they were always calling these annoying meetings. We figured it was time for us to plan a vacation, talk about household chores, or be nagged to clean our rooms. As soon as we sat down, though, we knew this was different. We could tell Mom had been crying, and Dad's voice cracked when he told us the news. They were separating—they called it a "trial separation"—and Dad was moving out of our house.

3   After that day, everything seemed to change. Every Halloween we always had a big jack-o'-lantern on our front porch. Dad used to spend hours at the kitchen table cutting out the eyes, nose, and mouth and hollowing out the insides. That Halloween, because he didn't live with us, things were different. Mom bought a pumpkin, and I guess she was planning to carve it up. But she never did, and we never mentioned it. It sat on the kitchen counter for a couple of weeks, getting soft and wrinkled, and then it just disappeared.

4   Other holidays were also different because Mom and Dad were not living together. Our first Thanksgiving without Dad was pathetic. Christmas was different, too. We spent Christmas Eve with Dad and our relatives on his side and Christmas Day with Mom and her family. Of course, we got twice as many presents as usual. I realize now that both our parents were trying to make up for the pain of the separation. The worst part came when I opened my big present from Mom: Barbie's Dream House. This was something I had always wanted. Even at eight, I knew how hard it must have been for Mom to afford it. The trouble was, I had gotten the same thing from Dad the night before.

5   The separation affected each of us in different ways. The worst effect of my parents' separation was not the big events but the disruption in our everyday lives. Dinner used to be a family time, a chance to talk about our day and make plans. But after Dad left, Mom seemed to stop eating. Sometimes she would just have coffee while we ate, and sometimes she wouldn't eat at all. She would microwave some frozen thing for us or heat up soup or cook some hot dogs. We didn't care—after all, now she let us watch TV while we ate—but we did notice.

6   Other parts of our routine changed, too. Because Dad didn't live with us anymore, we had to spend every Saturday and every Wednesday night at his apartment, no matter what else we had planned. Usually, he would take us to dinner at McDonald's on Wednesdays, and then we would go back to his place and do our homework or watch TV. That wasn't too bad. Saturdays were a lot worse. We really wanted to be home, hanging out with our friends in our own rooms in our own house. Instead, we had to do some planned activity with Dad, like go to a movie or a hockey game.

7　　As a result of what happened in my own family, it is hard for me to believe any relationship is forever. By the end of the school year, my parents had somehow worked things out, and Dad was back home again. That June, at a family conference around the kitchen table, we made our summer vacation plans. We decided on Williamsburg, Virginia, the all-American vacation destination. So, things were back to normal, but I wasn't, and I'm still not. Now, ten years later, my mother and father are all right, but I still worry they'll split up again. And I worry about my own future husband and how I will ever be sure he's the one I'll stay married to.

PRACTICE

9-3　1. Underline Andrea's thesis statement. Does this statement identify a cause or an effect?

2. List the specific effects of her parents' separation that Andrea identifies.

3. Review the transitional words and phrases Andrea uses to make causal connections clear to her readers. Do you think she needs to add more transitions? If so, where?

4. Is Andrea's concluding paragraph effective? Why or why not? Do you think it should be shortened or divided into two paragraphs? If so, would you revise or relocate Andrea's summary statement?

5. Is Andrea's straightforward title effective, or should she have chosen a more creative or eye-catching title? Can you suggest an alternative?

6. Use **TEST** to evaluate Andrea's essay. What revisions would you recommend she make? Why?

grammar in context

Cause and Effect

When you write a cause-and-effect essay, you may have trouble remembering the difference between *affect* and *effect*.

　　　　　　　　effect
The worst ~~affect~~ of my parents' separation was not the big
　　　　　　　^

events but the disruption in our everyday lives. (*effect* is a noun)

　　　　　　　　　　　affected
The separation ~~effected~~ each of us in different ways.
　　　　　　　　　　　^

(*affect* is a verb)

Teaching Tip
Before your students write cause-and-effect essays, you might want to review the use of *affect* and *effect*, pointing them to the examples in 20g.

9c Integrating Reading and Writing

Now, it is time to practice what you have learned and put your reading and writing skills together. The following essay, "How Facebook Is Making Friending Obsolete," by Julia Angwin, examines Facebook's effect on friendship. **Read** the essay, following the active reading process outlined in Chapter 1, and then answer the questions on pages 235–236. When you have finished, you will **write** a cause-and-effect essay in response to Angwin's ideas.

HOW FACEBOOK IS MAKING FRIENDING OBSOLETE

Julia Angwin

Before taking up her current post as a reporter for the independent news organization ProPublica, Julia Angwin covered technology at the *San Francisco Chronicle* and the *Wall Street Journal.* In 2009, she published the book *Stealing MySpace*, which examines the cultural phenomenon of MySpace and other social-networking sites. In "How Facebook Is Making Friending Obsolete," first published in the *Wall Street Journal*, Angwin comments on the potential consequences of Facebook's efforts to make it harder to keep profiles private.

Before you read, think about your own feelings about Facebook and privacy.

"Friending" wasn't used as a verb until about five years ago, when 1 social networks such as Friendster, MySpace and Facebook burst onto the scene.

Suddenly, our friends were something even better—an audience. If 2 blogging felt like shouting into the void, posting updates on a social network felt more like an intimate conversation among friends at a pub.

Inevitably, as our list of friends grew to encompass acquaintances, 3 friends of friends and the girl who sat behind us in seventh-grade homeroom, online friendships became devalued.

Suddenly, we knew as much about the lives of our distant acquaintances as we did about the lives of our intimates—what they'd had for dinner, how they felt about Tiger Woods and so on.

Enter Twitter with a solution: no friends, just followers. These one-5 way relationships were easier to manage—no more annoying decisions about whether to give your ex-boyfriend access to your photos, no more fussing over who could see your employment and contact information.

Twitter's updates were also easily searchable on the Web, forcing users 6 to be somewhat thoughtful about their posts. The intimate conversation

WORD POWER

void empty space; emptiness

WORD POWER

prowess ability; skill

became a talent show, a challenge to prove your intellectual prowess in 140 characters or less.

7   This fall, Twitter turned its popularity into dollars, inking lucrative deals to allow its users' tweets to be broadcast via search algorithms on Google and Bing.

8   Soon, Facebook followed suit with deals to distribute certain real-time data to Google and Bing. (Recall that despite being the fifth-most-popular Web site in the world, Facebook is barely profitable.) Facebook spokesman Barry Schnitt says no money changed hands in the deals but says there was "probably an exchange of value."

9   Just one catch: Facebook had just "exchanged" to Google and Microsoft something that didn't exist.

10   The vast majority of Facebook users restrict updates to their friends, and do not expect those updates to appear in public search results. (In fact, many people restrict their Facebook profile from appearing at all in search results.)

11   So Facebook had little content to provide to Google's and Bing's real-time search results. When Google's real-time search launched earlier this month, its results were primarily filled with Twitter updates.

12   Coincidentally, Facebook presented its 350 million members with a new default privacy setting last week. For most people, the new suggested settings would open their Facebook updates and information to the entire world. Mr. Schnitt says the new privacy suggestions are an acknowledgement of "the way we think the world is going."

13   Facebook Chief Executive Mark Zuckerberg led by example, opening up his previously closed profile, including goofy photos of himself curled up with a teddy bear.

14   Facebook also made public formerly private info such as profile pictures, gender, current city and the friends list. (Mr. Schnitt suggests that users are free to lie about their hometown or take down their profile picture to protect their privacy; in response to users' complaints, the friends list can now be restricted to be viewed only by friends.)

15   Of course, many people will reject the default settings on Facebook and keep on chatting with only their Facebook friends. (Mr. Schnitt said more than 50% of its users had rejected the defaults at last tally.)

16   But those who want a private experience on Facebook will have to work harder at it: if you inadvertently post a comment on a friend's profile page that has been opened to the public, your comment will be public too.

17   Just as Facebook turned friends into a commodity, it has likewise gathered our personal data—our updates, our baby photos, our endless chirping birthday notes—and readied it to be bundled and sold.

18   So I give up. Rather than fighting to keep my Facebook profile private, I plan to open it up to the public—removing the fiction of intimacy and friendship.

But I will also remove the vestiges of my private life from Facebook 19 and make sure I never post anything that I wouldn't want my parents, employer, next-door neighbor or future employer to see. You'd be smart to do the same.

We'll need to treat this increasingly public version of Facebook with 20 the same hard-headedness that we treat Twitter: as a place to broadcast, but not a place for vulnerability. A place to carefully calibrate, sanitize and bowdlerize our words for every possible audience, now and forever. Not a place for intimacy with friends.

> **WORD POWER**
> **calibrate** to adjust precisely for a particular function
> **bowdlerize** edit by removing or changing parts that might be considered offensive

Focus on Reading

1. Look back at the work you did when you previewed, highlighted, and annotated this essay. Now, circle the **verbal signals** that suggest that this essay has a cause-and-effect structure.

2. In the margin beside paragraph 4, list a few additional examples of things people can learn about their "distant acquaintances" on social-networking sites.

Focus on Meaning

1. Angwin claims that online friendships have been "devalued" (paragraph 3). What does she mean? Do you agree with her? Why or why not?

2. How, according to Angwin, is Facebook "making friending obsolete"?

> **Teaching Tip**
> You may have students work collaboratively to answer some of these questions.

Focus on Strategy

1. In paragraph 19, Angwin explains that she is removing private information from her Facebook page and advises, "You'd be smart to do the same." What kind of audience does she seem to be addressing here—and in her essay as a whole? How can you tell?

2. Angwin is critical of Facebook and its effect on friendship, but she does not call for users to abandon it. What is she actually recommending? Summarize her position in a one-sentence thesis statement.

> **ESL Tip**
> Have native- and nonnative-speaking students work in groups or in pairs to discuss the exercises before they write their answers.

Focus on Language and Style

1. Write a one-sentence definition of the verb *to friend*.

2. In paragraph 18, Angwin says, "Rather than fighting to keep my Facebook profile private, I plan to open it up to the public. . . ." What do the words *private* and *public* mean in this context?

> **Teaching Tip**
> Remind students to answer all questions in complete sentences.

Focus on the Pattern

1. As Angwin points out, Facebook has taken a number of steps to make its information more public. What does she say caused these actions? What has been the result of these actions?

2. Is this essay's emphasis on causes, on effects, or on both causes and effects? Explain.

Focus on Critical Thinking

1. In paragraph 4, Angwin mentions a few things people can learn about their "distant acquaintances" on social-networking sites. Generally speaking, do you think this kind of knowledge is a good thing or a bad thing? Explain.

2. Angwin believes Facebook has "turned friends into a commodity" (17) and reduced them to "an audience" (2). Do you agree that Facebook has changed the nature of friendship? If so, how? If not, why not?

focus on reading and writing

Now that you have read Julia Angwin's essay, write your own cause-and-effect essay in response to one of the following prompts. (If you prefer, you can write on one of the additional topics listed in the box below.) Be sure to follow the writing process outlined in Chapter 3.

1. Angwin plans to open her Facebook profile to the public. Would you do—or have you already done—the same? Why or why not? Write a cause-and-effect essay in which you give your reasons for making your profile public—or your reasons for keeping it private.

2. How would your life change if you lost access to social networking? Write an essay explaining the possible results of this loss of access.

additional topics

Cause and Effect

A teacher's positive (or negative) effect on you

How your life would be different if you dropped out of school (or quit your job)

How a particular invention has changed (or might change) your life

How a particular event made you grow up

READING AND WRITING ACTIVITY

Reread the draft of your essay, and then revise it. Begin by answering the questions in the TEST checklist below. When you have finished revising, edit and proofread your essay.

TESTing your cause-and-effect essay

Thesis Statement Unifies Your Essay

☐ Does your introduction include a **thesis statement** that indicates your main idea and makes clear whether your essay will focus on causes or effects?

Evidence Supports Your Essay's Thesis Statement

☐ Does all your **evidence**—examples and details—support your thesis, or should some of it be deleted?

☐ Do you identify and explain all causes or effects relevant to your topic, or do you need to add any?

☐ Do you arrange causes and effects to indicate which are more important than others?

☐ Does each body paragraph identify and explain one particular cause or effect (or several closely related causes or effects)?

Summary Statement Reinforces Your Essay's Main Idea

☐ Does your conclusion include a **summary statement** that reinforces your essay's thesis?

Transitions Connect Causes and Effects

☐ Do you include **transitions** that introduce each of your causes or effects and make your essay's cause-and-effect connections clear?

COLLABORATIVE ACTIVITY

Work with another student to consider the strengths and weaknesses of both of your cause-and-effect essays. Do you think one of your essays is more effective than the other one? If so, why? Based on your reactions to the essays you and your classmates wrote, write a few sentences explaining what a cause-and-effect essay should accomplish.

review checklist

Reading and Writing Cause-and-Effect Essays

☐ Cause and effect considers what made something happen or what the result was (or will be). Cause-and-effect essays examine causes or effects; sometimes they do both.

☐ When you *read* a cause-and-effect essay, follow the active reading process outlined in Chapter 1, and use **TEST** to help you identify the essay's key elements. (See 9a.)

☐ When you *write* a cause-and-effect essay, follow the writing process outlined in Chapter 3, and use **TEST** to make sure you have included all the necessary elements. (See 9b.)

☐ Keep in mind that in college courses you often write in response to reading. (See 9c.)

10 Reading and Writing Comparison-and-Contrast Essays

North Wind Picture Archives/Alamy | Prisma Archivo/Alamy

focus on reading and writing

Look at these portraits of Charles Darwin and Abraham Lincoln. Brainstorm to discover what you already know about some historical figures who have changed the world or some important historical events that have changed your life. Later in this chapter, you will **read** an essay about Lincoln and Darwin and then have the opportunity to **write** a comparison-and-contrast essay about some of the people and events you identified in your brainstorming.

In this chapter, you will learn to

- read comparison and contrast essays (10a)
- write comparison-and-contrast essays (10b)
- connect reading and writing (10c)

When you buy something—for example, a smartphone, a tablet, or a hair dryer—you often comparison shop, looking at various models to determine how they are alike and how they are different. In other words, you *compare and contrast*. When you **compare**, you consider how things are similar. When you **contrast**, you consider how things are different. A **comparison-and-contrast** essay can examine just similarities, just differences, or both similarities and differences.

In order to compare and contrast two things, you need a clear **basis of comparison**. In other words, the two things must have enough in common to justify the comparison. You can, for example, compare and contrast a play and a short story—both are literary works, with characters, dialogue, plots, and settings. You would have a difficult time, however, comparing a television to a car. The two things simply do not have enough in common to justify the comparison.

● 10a Reading Comparison-and-Contrast Essays

When you **read** a comparison-and-contrast essay, use **TEST** to help you identify its key elements. Make sure that you follow the active reading process outlined in Chapter 1.

T ■ **Thesis Statement**—The introduction of a comparison-and-contrast essay includes a **thesis statement** that communicates the essay's main idea, telling readers what two items are going to be compared or contrasted and whether the essay will emphasize similarities or differences.

E ■ **Evidence**—The body paragraphs include **evidence**—examples and details—that supports the thesis statement. The topic sentence of each paragraph identifies the similarity or difference the paragraph will examine, and the examples and details explain the similarity or difference.

S ■ **Summary Statement**—The conclusion of a comparison-and-contrast essay often includes a **summary statement** that reinforces the essay's thesis.

T ■ **Transitions**—A comparison-and-contrast essay includes **transitional words and phrases** to help readers move from point to point and from subject to subject.

A comparison-and-contrast essay can be organized as either a *point-by-point* comparison or a *subject-by-subject* comparison. A **point-by-point** comparison alternates between the two subjects that are being compared or contrasted, first discussing one point about the first subject and then discussing the same (or a similar) point for the second subject. A **subject-by-subject** comparison discusses one subject at a time. The first part of the essay discusses all the points about one subject, and the second part discusses the same (or similar) points for the second subject.

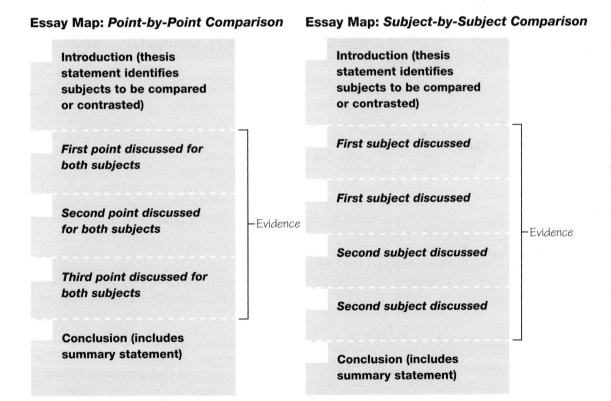

Essay Map: *Point-by-Point Comparison*

Introduction (thesis statement identifies subjects to be compared or contrasted)

First point discussed for both subjects

Second point discussed for both subjects   ⌐Evidence

Third point discussed for both subjects

Conclusion (includes summary statement)

Essay Map: *Subject-by-Subject Comparison*

Introduction (thesis statement identifies subjects to be compared or contrasted)

First subject discussed

First subject discussed

Second subject discussed   ⌐Evidence

Second subject discussed

Conclusion (includes summary statement)

> ### Some Transitional Words and Phrases for Comparison and Contrast
>
> The transitional words and phrases used in a comparison-and-contrast essay tell readers whether an essay is focusing on similarities or on differences and also help move readers through an essay from one subject to the other and from one point of comparison or contrast to the next.
>
> | | |
> |---|---|
> | although | likewise |
> | but | nevertheless |
> | even though | one . . . another |
> | however | on the contrary |
> | in comparison | on the one hand . . . on the other hand |
> | in contrast | similarly |
> | instead | unlike |
> | like | whereas |

Reading a Model Student Essay: Comparison and Contrast

The following comparison-and-contrast essay was written by Colin Volpatti, a criminal justice major, in response to this assignment in his composition class:

> Find two websites that interest you. (They could relate to your major, a hobby, your community, or anything else that appeals to you.) Compare and contrast the two sites, taking care to discuss the same or similar points for both. Before you write, decide whether you will organize your essay as a point-by-point or subject-by-subject comparison.

T E S T

- Thesis Statement
- Evidence
- Summary Statement
- Transitions

Read Colin's essay, following the active reading process discussed in Chapter 1, and then fill in the essay map in Practice 10-1 on page 245. (Note that the TEST elements in the essay have been highlighted and color-coded.)

Two Very Different Resources

1   The amount of information a person can get from a simple web search can be overwhelming. For example, searching the key words "wrongful conviction" results in thousands of hits. The biggest challenge facing a person carrying out such a search is evaluating the trustworthiness of the information on these sites. A comparison and contrast of two websites that

resulted from this search reveals some very interesting differences. The first site, for the People's Law Office, is clearly commercial, while the second site, for the Innocence Project, has a broader purpose. Although both websites claim to help people who have been wrongfully convicted of crimes, they differ significantly in content, purpose, and intended audience.

2   The People's Law Office website presents information about what its lawyers can do for clients. The website is appealing and easy to read; the pages are white and gray with bars of purple and green. The law office's name, logo, and contact information are highlighted at the top of each page. On the site's home page is a bright green bar that contains the main menu. Each of the menu's six tabs takes readers to information about the law office's successes. A tab titled "Victories" leads to a list of cases won. Another page describes the office's "long and illustrious history" of protecting people's civil rights. Under "Areas of Practice" is the office's "remarkable track record" and a discussion of its "decades of experience." Under "News and Commentary," the People's Law Office emphasizes its achievements and includes articles written by its lawyers. Below these tabs is a slide show that displays photos of clients who were freed by the efforts of the firm's lawyers. Throughout these pages, the content emphasizes the dedication and the effectiveness of the firm.

3   The content of the People's Law Office website indicates that its purpose is commercial and that its audience is people who need the services of the firm's lawyers. The website attempts to attract potential clients by appealing to both logic and emotion. By emphasizing its successes, the firm establishes its credibility and tries to convince people that People's Law Office lawyers usually win their cases. The People's Law Office website also appeals to readers' emotions with a slide show of photos. In one image, a police officer is shown mistreating an unnamed protester. In another, a joyful man, with his smiling lawyers, is pictured leaving a courthouse. The accompanying copy addresses the audience as *you* and declares, "If your constitutional rights have been violated, we can help. . . ." This content makes clear that the purpose of the People's Law Office site is to sell the firm's legal services to people who believe that they have been victimized by the legal system.

4   Although the Innocence Project also presents facts about itself, it offers more extensive and varied content than the People's Law Office. Like the commercial People's Law Office, the nonprofit Innocence Project has mostly white and gray pages accented with bars of color; it also has a slide show on its home page. However, there are many notable differences

between the two sites. One difference is that the Innocence Project slide show contains pictures of people who were declared innocent after they had been convicted. Instead of having its address and phone number at the top of each page, the People's Law Office has a search tab and a sign-up button for the organization's email. Another difference is the main menu bar, which has two sides. The slightly larger, rust-colored left side has three tabs: "Know the Cases," "Understand the Causes," and "Fix the System." Each of these tabs directs the reader to an extensive menu of sub-topics. The smaller, mustard-colored right side has four tabs: "Home," "About," "Donate," and "News and Resources." These tabs lead readers to information about the organization as well as to a list of related links. This design is not flashy, but it enables visitors to easily navigate the site.

5   Unlike People's Law Office, the Innocence Project has several purposes and, therefore, multiple audiences. First, the detailed information, including the labeled slide show, indicates that the site's main purpose is to educate. This material is aimed at anyone who is interested in knowing more about wrongful conviction or in reading about individual cases. Second, the organization wants to encourage people to take action. By suggesting numerous ways of getting involved, the site addresses people who already support the organization's cause and want to do more. Finally, the nonprofit Innocence Project wants to offer legal services to people who think they have been wrongly convicted. Unlike People's Law Office, the Innocence Project does not address the reader as *you*. Because this organization is not trying to solicit business, it uses a more straightforward, informative tone.

6   Ultimately, the purpose of the People's Law Office commercial website is to sell services to a specific audience, while the goal of the nonprofit Innocence Project site is to provide free resources to its target audiences. The two organizations share a desire to free innocent people who have been wrongly convicted. They also have clear agendas. On the one hand, the Innocence Project is interested in addressing and remedying problems with the legal system. On the other hand, People's Law Office is interested in soliciting business for its lawyers. Comparing and contrasting these two sites allows readers to see the objectives of each more clearly and thus to choose a source that meets their needs.

Works Cited

Innocence Project. *Innocence Project*. Web. 26 Jul. 2014.
People's Law Office. *People's Law Office*. Web. 26 Jul. 2014.

PRACTICE

10-1   Now that you have read Colin's essay, fill in the essay map below to help you understand how he organized his essay. Then, decide whether his organization is effective.

Introduction _Answers will vary._ _____
_____
_____

First subject discussed _Answers will vary._ _____
_____
_____

First subject discussed _Answers will vary._ _____
_____
_____

Second subject discussed _Answers will vary._ ____
_____
_____

Second subject discussed _Answers will vary._ ____
_____
_____

Conclusion _Answers will vary._ _____
_____
_____

PRACTICE

10-2   1. Does the thesis statement indicate that the essay is a comparison-and-contrast essay?

2. What specific points about the two websites does Colin compare and contrast?

3. Does Colin organize his essay as a point-by-point or a subject-by-subject comparison? Do you think he made the right choice?

4. Reread the topic sentences of Colin's body paragraphs. How do they indicate the differences between the two sites?

5. What is the essay's greatest strength? What is its greatest weakness?

⬢10b Writing Comparison-and-Contrast Essays

When you **write** a comparison-and-contrast essay, you follow the process outlined in Chapter 3. The essay you write will include the same elements you have learned to recognize in the comparison-and-contrast essays you read. When you finish your draft, you can use TEST to make sure it includes all the elements of a comparison-and-contrast essay.

When you are given a writing assignment, the wording of your assignment may suggest that you write a comparison-and-contrast essay—for example, by asking you to *compare*, *contrast*, *discuss similarities*, or *identify differences*. Once you decide that your assignment calls for comparison and contrast, you need to develop a thesis statement that reflects this purpose.

Teaching Tip
Tell students that many everyday writing tasks call for comparison and contrast. For example, a report to a supervisor at work might compare the merits of two procedures or two suppliers.

ASSIGNMENT	THESIS STATEMENT
Philosophy What basic similarities do you find in the beliefs of Henry David Thoreau and Martin Luther King Jr.?	Although King was more politically active, both he and Thoreau strongly supported the idea of civil disobedience.
Nutrition How do the diets of native Japanese and Japanese Americans differ?	As they become more and more assimilated, Japanese Americans consume more fats than native Japanese do.
Literature Contrast the two sisters in Alice Walker's short story "Everyday Use."	Unlike Maggie, Dee—her more successful, better-educated sister—has rejected her family's heritage.

Case Study: A Student Writes a Comparison-and-Contrast Essay

Nisha Jani, a student in a first-year writing course, was given the following assignment.

Some people claim that males and females are so different that at times they seem to belong to two different species. Do you agree, or do you think males and females are more alike than different? Write an essay that supports your position.

When Nisha read this assignment, the key words *different* and *alike* told her that the assignment called for a comparison-and-contrast essay. After **brainstorming**, she decided to write about the differences between boys and girls—specifically, middle school boys and girls. Based on her own experiences and those of her younger brother and sister, Nisha thought that the differences between seventh-grade boys and girls would be more interesting (and more obvious) than the similarities. So, when she drafted a **thesis statement** for her essay, she made sure that it focused on differences: "The typical boy and girl live very different lives."

Once Nisha had a thesis statement, she **listed** some of the most obvious differences between male and female seventh-graders. When she reviewed the ideas on her list, she decided to follow her two subjects (Johnny and Jane) through a typical school day, and this decision led her to structure her essay as a point-by-point comparison that would contrast boys' and girls' behavior at different points of their day.

When Nisha thought she had enough material to write about, she **wrote a draft** of her essay. Then, she TESTed her draft to see if it included a thesis statement, supporting evidence, a summary statement, and transitional words and phrases. Although her TEST showed her that she had included all the required elements, she thought she still needed to **revise** to strengthen her draft. After a **conference** with her instructor, she revised her thesis statement to make it a bit more specific, added more examples and details, sharpened her summary statement so it reinforced her essay's main idea, and added more transitions to make the contrast between her two subjects clearer. After she finished these revisions, she **edited** and **proofread** her essay. Read Nisha's essay, and then answer the questions in Practice 10-3 on page 249.

Another Ordinary Day

1   "Boys are from Jupiter and get stupider / Girls are from Mars and become movie stars / Boys take a bath and smell like trash / Girls take a shower and smell like a flower." As simple playground songs like this one suggest, the two sexes are very different. As adults, men and women have similar goals, values, and occupations, but as children and teenagers, boys and girls often seem to belong to two different species. In fact, from the first moment of the day to the last, the typical boy and girl live very different lives.

2   The sun rises, and the alarm clock signals the beginning of another day for Johnny and Jane, two seventh-grade classmates. Johnny, an average thirteen-year-old boy, wakes up late and has to hurry. He throws on his favorite jeans, a baggy T-shirt, and a baseball cap. Then, he has a hearty high-cholesterol breakfast and runs out of the house to school, usually forgetting some vital book or homework assignment. Jane, unlike Johnny,

wakes up early and takes her time. She takes a long shower and then blow-dries her hair. For Jane, getting dressed can be a very difficult process, one that often includes taking everything out of her closet and calling friends for advice. After she makes her decision, she helps herself to some food (probably low- or no-fat) and goes off to school, making sure she has with her everything she needs.

3　　School is a totally different experience for Johnny and Jane. Johnny will probably sit in the back of the classroom with a couple of other guys, throwing paper airplanes and spitballs. These will be directed at the males they do not like and the females they think are kind of cute. (However, if their male friends ever ask the boys about these girls, they will say girls are just losers and deny that they like any of them.) On the opposite side of the classroom, however, Jane is focused on a very different kind of activity. At first, it looks as if she is carefully copying the algebra notes that the teacher is putting on the board, but her notes have absolutely nothing to do with algebra. Instead, she is writing about boys, clothes, and other topics that are much more important to her than the square root of one hundred twenty-one. She proceeds to fold the note into a box or other creative shape, which can often put origami to shame. As soon as the teacher turns her back, the note is passed and the process begins all over again.

4　　Lunch, a vital part of the school day, is also very different for Johnny and Jane. On the one hand, for Johnny and his friends, it is a time to compare baseball cards, exchange sports facts, and of course tell jokes about every bodily function imaginable. In front of them on the table, their trays are filled with pizza, soda, fries, and chips, and this food is their main focus. For Jane, on the other hand, lunch is not about eating; it is a chance to exchange the latest gossip about who is going out with whom. The girls look around to see what people are wearing, what they should do with their hair, and so on. Jane's meal is quite a bit smaller than Johnny's: it consists of a small low-fat yogurt and half a bagel (if she feels like splurging, she will spread some cream cheese on the bagel).

5　　After school, Johnny and Jane head in different directions. Johnny rushes home to get his bike and meets up with his friends to run around and play typical "guy games," like pick-up basketball or touch football. Johnny and his friends play with every boy who shows up, whether they know him or not. They may get into physical fights and arguments, but they always plan to meet up again the next day. In contrast to the boys, Jane and her friends are very selective. Their circle is a small one, and they do everything together. Some days, they go to the mall (they will not necessarily buy anything there, but they will consider the outing productive anyway

WORD POWER

origami the Japanese art of folding paper into shapes representing flowers or animals

because they will have spent time together). Most days, though, they just talk, with the discussion ranging from school to guys to lipstick colors. When Jane gets home, she will most likely run to the phone and talk for hours to the same three or four girls.

6   At the age of twelve or thirteen, boys and girls do not seem to have very much in common. Given this situation, it is amazing that boys and girls grow up to become men and women who interact as neighbors, friends, and coworkers. What is even more amazing is that so many grow up to share lives and raise families together, treating each other with love and respect.

PRACTICE
10-3

1. Underline Nisha's thesis statement; then, rewrite it in your own words.

2. Does Nisha's introduction identify the two subjects she will discuss? Does it tell whether she will focus on similarities or on differences?

3. Nisha's essay is a point-by-point comparison. What four points does she discuss for each of her two subjects?

4. Circle some of the transitional words and phrases Nisha uses to move from one example to another.

5. Underline Nisha's summary statement. Then, rewrite it in your own words.

6. Use TEST to evaluate Nisha's essay. What revisions would you suggest she make? Why?

grammar in context

Comparison and Contrast

When you write a comparison-and-contrast essay, be sure to present the points you are comparing or contrasting in **parallel** terms to highlight their similarities or differences.

┌─PARALLEL─┐

Johnny, an average thirteen-year-old boy, wakes up late and has to hurry.

┌───PARALLEL───┐

Jane, unlike Johnny, wakes up early and takes her time.

For information on revising to make ideas parallel, see Chapter 19.

ⓔ For practice with parallelism, complete the LearningCurve Parallelism activity at **bedfordstmartins.com/forw.**

Teaching Tip
Before your students write comparison-and-contrast essays, you might want to explain the concept of parallelism (Chapter 19) and have them do Practices 19-1 and 19-2.

10c Integrating Reading and Writing

Now, it is time to practice what you have learned and put your reading and writing skills together. In the following essay, "The Twin Revolutions of Lincoln and Darwin," Steven Conn compares two men who had a profound effect on the times in which they lived. **Read** the essay, following the active reading process outlined in Chapter 1, and then answer the questions on pages 252–253. When you have finished, you will **write** a comparison-and-contrast essay focusing on some of the historical figures or events you identified at the start of this chapter.

THE TWIN REVOLUTIONS OF LINCOLN AND DARWIN

Steven Conn

Steven Conn is a professor of American cultural and intellectual history and director of the Public History Program at Ohio State University. He is the author of several books, most recently *Americans Against the City: Anti-Urbanism in the Twentieth Century* (2014). In "The Twin Revolutions of Lincoln and Darwin," which first appeared in the *Philadelphia Inquirer* in 2009, Conn compares the lives of two seemingly unrelated historical figures—Abraham Lincoln and Charles Darwin.

Before you read, think about what you already know about Lincoln and Darwin.

Abraham Lincoln, the Great Emancipator, has been much on our minds 1 recently. Today, exactly 200 years after Lincoln's birth, Barack Obama's presidency is one fulfillment of the work Lincoln started.

Lincoln shares his birthday with Charles Darwin, the other Great 2 Emancipator of the 19th century. In different ways, each liberated us from tradition.

Charles Darwin and Abraham Lincoln were exact contemporaries. 3 Both were born on Feb. 12, 1809—Darwin into a comfortable family in Shropshire, England; Lincoln into humble circumstances on the American frontier.

They also came to international attention at virtually the same mo- 4 ment. Darwin published his epochal book, *On the Origin of Species*, in 1859. The following year, Lincoln became the 16th president of the United States. Also in 1860, Harvard botanist Asa Gray wrote the first review of Darwin's book to appear in this country.

Lincoln and Darwin initiated twin revolutions. One brought the 5 Civil War and the emancipation of roughly four million slaves; the other, a new explanation of the natural world. Lincoln's war transformed the

WORD POWER

epochal extremely important, significant, or influential

social, political and racial landscape in ways that continue to play out. Darwin transformed our understanding of biology, paving the way for countless advances in science, especially medicine.

With his powerful scientific explanation of the origins of species, 6 Darwin dispensed with the pseudoscientific assertions of African American inferiority. In this way, Darwin provided the scientific legitimacy for Lincoln's political and moral actions.

The two revolutions shared a commitment to one proposition: that 7 all human beings are fundamentally equal. In this sense, both Lincoln and Darwin deserve credit for emancipating us from the political and intellectual rationales for slavery.

For Lincoln, this was a political principle and a moral imperative. 8 He was deeply ambivalent about the institution of slavery. As the war began, he believed that saving the Union, not abolishing slavery, was the cause worth fighting for. But as the war ground gruesomely on, he began to see that ending slavery was the only way to save the Union without making a mockery of the nation's founding ideals.

This is what Lincoln meant when he promised, in the 1863 Gettys- 9 burg Address, that the war would bring "a new birth of freedom." He was even more emphatic about it in his second inaugural address, in 1865. Slavery could not be permitted to exist in a nation founded on the belief that we are all created equal.

Darwin, for his part, was a deeply committed abolitionist from a 10 family of deeply committed abolitionists. Exposed to slavery during his travels in South America, Darwin wrote, "It makes one's blood boil." He called abolishing slavery his "sacred cause." In some of his first notes about evolution, he railed against the idea that slaves were somehow less than human.

For Darwin, our shared humanity was a simple biological fact. What- 11 ever variations exist among the human species—what we call *races*—are simply the natural variations that occur within all species. Like it or not, in a Darwinian world we are all members of one human family. This truth lay at the center of Darwin's science and his abolitionism.

That understanding of human equality—arrived at from different 12 directions and for different reasons—helps explain the opposition to the revolutions unleashed by Lincoln and Darwin. It's also why many Americans—virtually alone in the developed world—continue to deny Darwinian science.

Many white Southerners never accepted Lincoln's basic proposition 13 about the political equality of black Americans. In the years after the Civil War and Reconstruction, they set up the brutal structures and rituals of segregation. All of the elaborate laws, customs and violence of the segregated South served to deny the basic truth that all Americans are created equal. Most Northerners, meanwhile, didn't care much about the "Southern problem."

WORD POWER

imperative an obligation or duty
ambivalent having mixed feelings

WORD POWER

emphatic forceful and insistent

WORD POWER

abolitionist a person who supported ending slavery in the United States

No wonder, then, that many Americans simply rejected Darwin's in- 14 sights out of hand. Slavery and segregation rested on the assumption that black Americans were not fully human. Darwinian science put the lie to all that.

Lincoln insisted on equality as a political fact. Darwin demonstrated 15 it as a biological fact. In their shared commitment to human equality, each in his own realm, these two Great Emancipators helped us break free from the shackles of the past.

Focus on Reading

1. Look back at the work you did when you previewed, highlighted, and annotated this essay. Did you underline the same points about both Lincoln and Darwin?

2. Circle any ideas or references with which you are not familiar. Look them up on the Internet, and add marginal annotations to explain them.

Teaching Tip
You may have students work collaboratively to answer these questions.

Focus on Meaning

1. How are Lincoln and Darwin alike? What are their "twin revolutions"? How are these revolutions similar?

2. How are Lincoln and Darwin different? In Conn's view, is it their similarities or their differences that are most significant?

3. Why, according to Conn, were so many people opposed to both Lincoln's and Darwin's ideas?

ESL Tip
Have native- and nonnative-speaking students work in groups or in pairs to discuss the exercises before they write their answers.

Focus on Strategy

1. What is Conn's thesis? Where does he state it? Write a sentence that states the essay's main idea in your own words.

2. Why does Conn compare Lincoln and Darwin? What is the basis for his comparison?

Focus on Language and Style

1. What does the word *emancipator* mean? What associations does this word have for you?

2. What exactly does Conn mean when he calls Lincoln and Darwin "these two Great Emancipators" (paragraph 15)?

3. What does Conn mean by "the shackles of the past" (paragraph 15)? What connotations does the word *shackles* have for you?

Focus on the Pattern

1. Is this a point-by-point or a subject-by-subject comparison? How can you tell?

2. Does Conn make the same points about Lincoln and Darwin, or does he discuss some points for one man and not for the other? If the points he makes do not match exactly, does this weaken the effect of his comparison? Why or why not?

Focus on Critical Thinking

1. Do you think it makes sense to compare Lincoln and Darwin, or do you think they have too little in common to be compared?

2. Who do you see as the more important historical figure, Lincoln or Darwin? Whose legacy is more significant? Why?

focus on reading and writing

Now that you have read Steven Conn's essay, write your own comparison-and-contrast essay in response to one of the following prompts. (If you prefer, you can write on one of the additional topics listed in the box below.) Be sure to follow the writing process outlined in Chapter 3.

1. Write a comparison-and-contrast essay in which you compare two historical figures. In your thesis statement, be sure to communicate the significance of your comparison.

2. Write a comparison-and-contrast essay in which you compare your life before and after an important personal or historical event. What changed for you, and what remained the same?

additional topics

Comparison and Contrast

Men's and women's body images

Two fictional characters

Two ways of studying for an exam

Country and city living (or, compare suburban living with either)

READING AND WRITING ACTIVITY

Reread the draft of your essay, and then revise it. Begin by answering the questions in the TEST checklist below. When you have finished revising, edit and proofread your essay.

TESTing your comparison-and-contrast essay

Thesis Statement Unifies Your Essay

☐ Does your introduction include a **thesis statement** that expresses your main idea, identifying the two subjects you will compare and indicating whether your essay will examine similarities or differences?

Evidence Supports Your Essay's Thesis Statement

☐ Do you discuss all significant points of comparison or contrast that apply to your two subjects, explaining each similarity or difference using specific examples and details?

☐ Does all your **evidence**—examples and details—support your thesis, or should some be deleted?

☐ Have you treated similar points for both of your subjects?

☐ Is your essay's organization consistent with either a point-by-point comparison or a subject-by-subject comparison?

Summary Statement Reinforces Your Essay's Main Idea

☐ Does your conclusion include a **summary statement** that reinforces your essay's thesis, reminding readers what your two subjects are and how they are alike or different?

Transitions Connect Your Essay's Points

☐ Do you include **transitions** that introduce details and move readers smoothly from one aspect of your subject to another?

COLLABORATIVE ACTIVITY

Work with another student to consider the strengths and weaknesses of each of your comparison-and-contrast essays. Do you think that one of your comparison-and-contrast essays is more effective than the other? Explain. Based on your reactions to the essays that you and your classmate wrote, what do you think an effective comparison-and-contrast essay should accomplish? Write a few sentences in which you explain what a comparison-and-contrast essay should do.

review checklist

Reading and Writing Comparison-and-Contrast Essays

- [ ] A comparison-and-contrast essay can examine just similarities, just differences, or both similarities and differences.

- [ ] When you *read* a comparison-and-contrast essay, follow the active reading process outlined in Chapter 1, and use **TEST** to help you identify the essay's key elements. (See 10a.)

- [ ] When you *write* a comparison-and-contrast essay, follow the writing process outlined in Chapter 3, and use **TEST** to make sure that you have included all the necessary elements. (See 10b.)

- [ ] Keep in mind that in your college courses you often write in response to reading. (See 10c.)

11 Reading and Writing Argument Essays

Grade Distribution Over Time, Nationwide

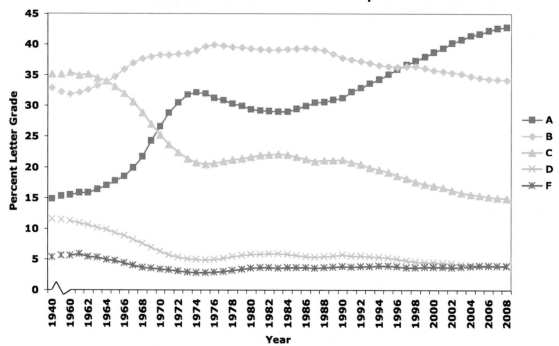

Stuart Rojstaczer, gradeinflation.com

focus on reading and writing

Look at the chart above, which shows the inflation in letter-grade distribution on four-year-college campuses nationwide between 1940 and 2008. Brainstorm to discover what you already know about how instructors grade students and what you think students should do to earn a passing grade. Later in the chapter, you will **read** an essay on a related topic and then have an opportunity to **write** about it.

In this chapter, you will learn to

- read argument essays (11a)
- write argument essays (11b)
- connect reading and writing (11c)

When most people hear the word *argument*, they think of personal conflicts or the heated exchanges they see on television interview programs. These discussions, however, are more like shouting matches than arguments. True **argument** involves taking a stand on a **debatable issue**—an issue that has at least two sides (and can therefore be debated).

Suitable Topics for Argument

Should terrorists be tried in civilian courts?

Is the death penalty "cruel and unusual" punishment?

Should online education replace classroom instruction?

Should the legal drinking age be lowered?

Should guns be more strictly controlled?

Should the federal government do more to control illegal immigration?

In an **argument essay**, the writer attempts to convince readers that his or her position has merit by presenting **evidence**—facts and examples (and sometimes expert opinion).

● 11a Reading Argument Essays

When you **read** an argument essay, use TEST to help you identify its key elements. Make sure that you follow the active reading process outlined in Chapter 1.

T ■ **Thesis Statement**—The introduction of an argument essay includes a **thesis statement** that expresses the essay's main idea: the position the writer takes on the issue. Words like *should* and *should not* in the thesis statement help make the writer's position clear to readers.

E ▪ **Evidence**—The body paragraphs include **evidence**—facts, examples, and expert opinion—to support the thesis statement convincingly. The topic sentence of each body paragraph identifies one point of support for the thesis.

S ▪ **Summary Statement**—The conclusion of an argument essay includes a strong **summary statement** that reinforces the essay's thesis.

T ▪ **Transitions**—An argument essay includes **transitional words and phrases** to show how points are logically related and to move readers through the argument.

An argument essay can be organized *inductively* or *deductively*.

An **inductive argument** moves from specific to general. That is, it begins with a series of specific observations (or examples) that lead to a general conclusion based on these observations. For example, an essay that takes the position that your school should do more to address the needs of physically challenged students could be structured as an inductive argument. After discussing the specific hardships that physically challenged students face on campus every day, the essay could lead to the conclusion that in spite of the steps the school has already taken, it should do more to accommodate students with physical disabilities.

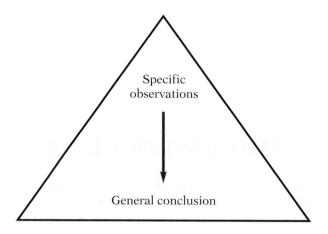

A **deductive argument** moves from general to specific. That is, it begins with a **major premise** (a general statement that the writer believes to be true or believes that readers will accept) and then moves to a **minor premise** (a specific instance of the major premise). It ends with a **conclusion** that logically follows from the two premises. For example, an essay that supports an increase in the federal minimum wage could be structured as a deductive argument. It could begin with the major premise that all workers are entitled to a living wage. It could then go on to state the minor premise that minimum-wage workers are just like other workers. (It could also present facts, examples, and the opinions of experts to make the point that many of these workers live close to the poverty line and, for this reason, are not earning a living wage.) The essay could conclude by saying that minimum-wage workers are, therefore, entitled to an increase in pay.

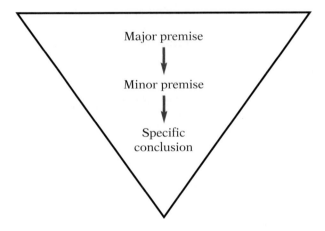

Major premise

↓

Minor premise

↓

Specific
conclusion

In an argument essay, each body paragraph begins with a **topic sentence** that clearly states a point in support of the thesis. Throughout the essay, **evidence**—facts and examples—makes the argument convincing. In addition to taking a position, an argument essay often identifies opposing arguments and then **refutes** them—that is, argues against them by identifying factual errors, errors in logic, and inconsistencies. If an opposing argument is particularly strong, the writer may **concede** (acknowledge) its strengths—and then go on to point out some weaknesses.

Essay Map: *Inductive Argument*   **Essay Map:** *Deductive Argument*

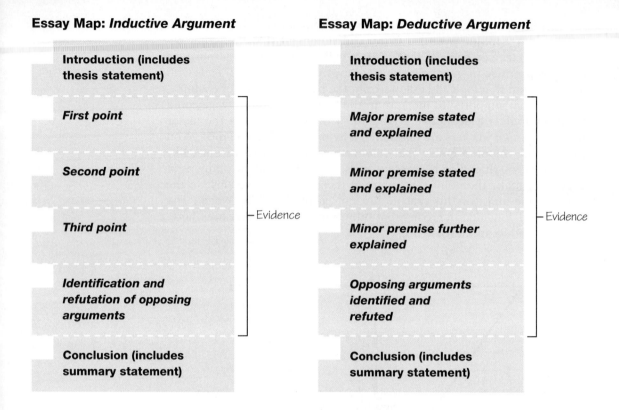

| Introduction (includes thesis statement) | Introduction (includes thesis statement) |

First point | Major premise stated and explained

Second point | Minor premise stated and explained

⎤ Evidence

Third point | Minor premise further explained

Identification and refutation of opposing arguments | Opposing arguments identified and refuted

⎤ Evidence

Conclusion (includes summary statement) | Conclusion (includes summary statement)

Some Transitional Words and Phrases for Argument

Transitions are extremely important in argument essays because they not only signal the movement from one part of the argument to another but also relate specific points to one another and to the thesis statement.

accordingly	granted	of course
admittedly	however	on the one
although	in addition	hand . . . on the
because	in conclusion	other hand
but	indeed	since
certainly	in fact	so
consequently	in summary	therefore
despite	meanwhile	thus
even so	moreover	to be sure
even though	nevertheless	truly
finally	nonetheless	
first, second . . .	now	

Reading a Model Student Essay: Argument

The following argument essay was written by Jessica Mar in response to this assignment in her political science class.

> Should the government play a major role in most (or even all) aspects of our lives, or should we be free to make our own rules when it comes to lifestyle choices, such as what we eat or what safety procedures we follow? Choose one issue and explain why government should (or should not) regulate it.

Read Jessica's essay, following the active reading process discussed in Chapter 1, and then fill in the essay map in Practice 11-1 on pages 263–264. (Note that the **TEST** elements in the essay have been highlighted and color-coded.) As you read, notice that Jessica supported some of her points with information from online sources, which she enumerates in a works-cited list. For a discussion about working with sources, see Chapter 13.

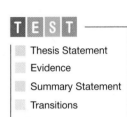

T E S T

- Thesis Statement
- Evidence
- Summary Statement
- Transitions

Stop the Regulators, Empower the Consumers

1   One of the primary functions of government is to keep its citizens safe. Elected officials try to fulfill this duty by making and enforcing laws. However, governments can take this obligation too far—particularly when they overregulate personal behavior—and when they do, citizens often object. Although outlawing people's access to dangerous substances, such as drugs and hazardous chemicals, makes sense, restricting people's personal food choices does not. For this reason, the government should treat people like responsible adults and not tell them what they can eat and drink.

2   First, no government agency can accurately determine what is healthy for everyone. Different people have different health needs, different calorie requirements, and different abilities to tolerate certain foods. Therefore, any standard that the government adopts is bound to favor some people and penalize others. For example, low-income citizens are at a disadvantage because often they cannot find or afford what the government has decided is "healthy." Organic produce, whole grains, and lean meats are more expensive than processed or fast foods. For this reason, by restricting access to "unhealthy" products, the government makes it difficult for many people to get adequate nourishment. In addition, meeting arbitrary government requirements costs stores and restaurants more money, and this cost is passed on to consumers. As one supermarket owner said in response to proposed regulations, "When you incur a significant cost, there is no way that that doesn't get passed on to the customer in some form" (qtd. in

Bream). Government regulation often makes food more expensive, but it does not necessarily result in more nutritious eating.

3   Second, instead of legislating, the government should encourage people to make informed decisions. Good eating habits need to be learned, not imposed. In other words, governments should help educate people but should not make choices for them. At least one state, Mississippi, is trying to uphold its citizens' rights to make their own decisions about what to eat and drink. Recently, Mississippi passed a law that prohibits state regulation of products sold in its restaurants, supermarkets, and convenience stores. The senator who wrote the law explained, "This is about personal responsibility. When I go out to eat with my three daughters they get waters. I don't need the government to tell me to do that" (qtd. in Severson). Certainly, no one is denying that there is a high rate of obesity in this country. However, making it illegal to buy a large soda will not solve this problem. Encouraging individuals to make informed choices will do much more than legislation to improve peoples' long-term health.

4   Finally, consumers must insist that companies provide healthier products and informative labels. It stands to reason that companies want to make products that consumers will buy. So, if consumers insist on more options and more information, then companies will provide those things. For example, there is evidence that companies are listening to consumers' requests for nutritious, low-calorie food and drinks. A recent article in *The Economist* reports that "food companies are keen to show that they take the obesity problem seriously," and "virtually every company has a plan of its own to improve nutrition" ("Food Companies"). Consumers need to support companies in these efforts by buying the best quality food their families can afford. They need to educate themselves about the products they consume, and demand calorie counts as well as detailed ingredient lists. Most importantly, they need to take responsibility for what they and their children are eating. They do not need the government to do this work for them.

5   Some people point out that consumers do not always have the knowledge to make healthy choices. They maintain that the government is better equipped to make such decisions. After all, the government regulates other aspects of daily life, such as highway safety, so why shouldn't it regulate nutrition too? However, in the case of driving, unsafe driving is a behavior that endangers the safety of others. In contrast, eating too much fatty, sugary, or salty food does not put others at risk. Moreover, the argument that consumers do not know enough to feed themselves properly is offensive.

Such a claim assumes that people are as helpless as children. In fact, most people are capable of making mature choices for themselves and should be allowed to do so. Insisting that people need the government to tell them how to eat well is an unwarranted expansion of government into the lives of its citizens. In the end, this kind of overprotection produces dependent, insecure, and even resentful citizens.

6   The government needs to stop telling people what they can and cannot eat and drink. People should have the freedom to decide for themselves what to eat, considering whether a particular food or beverage is affordable, if it is healthy, and if the portion size is appropriate. The only legislation that is needed now is a wide-reaching ban, like Mississippi's, on further regulations of food and beverages. Laws that restrict what individuals can eat or drink prevent people from taking responsibility for their own health, insult the public's intelligence, and can result in higher food prices. If government officials genuinely want to improve people's health, they should stop trying to control their citizens' eating habits and provide them the information they need to make informed choices.

Works Cited

Bream, Shannon. "Supermarkets Cry Foul as FDA Proposes New Food Labeling Rule under ObamaCare." *Fox News*. Foxnews.com, 6 Feb. 2013. Web. 29 May 2014.

"Food Companies Play an Ambivalent Part in the Fight against Flab." *The Economist*. The Economist Newspaper Limited, 15 Dec. 2012. Web. 29 May 2014.

Severson, Kim. "'Anti-Bloomberg Bill' in Mississippi Bars Local Restrictions on Food and Drink." *New York Times*. New York Times, 13 Mar. 2013. Web. 29 May 2014.

PRACTICE

11-1   Now that you have read Jessica's essay, fill in the essay map on the following page to help you to understand how she organized her essay. Then, decide whether her organization is effective.

Introduction _Answers will vary._
_____
_____

First point _Answers will vary._
_____
_____

Second point _Answers will vary._
_____
_____

Third point _Answers will vary._
_____
_____

Opposing arguments and refutation
Answers will vary.
_____
_____

Conclusion _Answers will vary._
_____
_____

PRACTICE
11-2

1. Does Jessica's thesis statement indicate the position she will take? Draft another thesis statement that she could have used. Which do you think is more effective?

2. What arguments does Jessica make? What other arguments could she have made?

3. What evidence does Jessica include? Does she include enough evidence? What other types of evidence could she have used?

4. What arguments against her thesis does Jessica address? How effectively does she refute them? What other arguments could she have refuted?

5. What points does Jessica reinforce in her conclusion? Should she have emphasized another point? Why or why not?

6. What is the essay's greatest strength? What is its greatest weakness?

⬡ 11b   Writing Argument Essays

When you **write** an argument essay, you follow the process outlined in Chapter 3. The essay you write will include the same elements you have learned to recognize in the argument essays you read. When you finish your draft, you can TEST it to make sure it includes all the elements of an argument essay.

When you are given a writing assignment, the wording of your assignment may suggest that you write an argument essay. For example, you may be asked to *debate, argue, consider, give your opinion, take a position,* or *take a stand*. Once you decide that your assignment calls for argument, you need to develop a thesis statement that takes a position on the topic you will write about in your essay.

Teaching Tip
Tell students that many everyday writing tasks call for argument. For example, a letter to the editor of a newspaper might take a stand on a political, social, economic, religious, or environmental issue affecting the writer's family or community.

ASSIGNMENT	THESIS STATEMENT
Composition Explain your position on a current social issue.	People should be able to invest some of their Social Security contributions in the stock market.
American history Do you believe that General Lee was responsible for the South's defeat at the Battle of Gettysburg? Why or why not?	Because Lee refused to listen to the advice given to him by General Longstreet, he is largely responsible for the South's defeat at the Battle of Gettysburg.
Ethics Should physician-assisted suicide be legalized?	Although many people think physician-assisted suicide should remain illegal, it should be legal in certain situations.

Case Study: A Student Writes an Argument Essay

Alex Norman, a student in a first-year writing course, was assigned to write an argument essay on a controversial issue of his choice. His instructor suggested that students find a topic by reading their campus and local newspapers, going online to read national news stories and political blogs, and watching public affairs programs on television. One issue that caught Alex's interest was the question of whether the government should do more to subsidize the cost of college for low-income students. Although Alex sympathized with students who needed help paying for school, he also questioned whether taxpayers should have to foot the bill. Because this issue clearly had at least two sides, and because he wasn't sure at the outset which position he could best support, Alex thought it would be a good topic to explore further.

Alex began by **brainstorming**, recording all his ideas on this complex issue. In addition to ideas he thought of as he read, he also included ideas he developed as he spoke to his sister, a recent college graduate, and to his boss at the bank where he worked part-time. When he read over his brainstorming notes, he saw that he had good arguments both for and against increasing government funding for low-income students. At this point, he wasn't sure which position to take in his essay, so he scheduled an appointment for a **conference** with his instructor.

Alex's instructor pointed out that he could make a good case either for or against greater government subsidies; like many controversial issues, this one had no easy answers. She encouraged him to support the position that seemed right to him and to use the information on the opposing side to present (and refute) opposing arguments. She also recommended that Alex email his first draft to her so she could review it.

After he thought about his instructor's comments, Alex decided to argue in favor of increasing government grants to help low-income students pay for college. Before he began to draft his essay, he wrote a **thesis statement** that presented his position on the issue; then, he arranged supporting points from his brainstorming notes into an **outline** that he could follow as he wrote. As he **drafted** his essay, Alex made sure to support his thesis with evidence and to explain his position as clearly and thoroughly as possible. He paid special attention to choosing transitional words and phrases that would indicate how his points were logically connected to one another.

When Alex finished his draft, he **TEST**ed it, taking a quick inventory to make sure he had included all four necessary components of an essay. Then, he emailed the draft to his instructor. Following her suggestions, he continued **revising** his draft, this time focusing on his topic sentences, his presentation (and refutation) of opposing arguments, and his introductory and concluding paragraphs. When he was satisfied with his revisions, he **edited** and **proofread** his essay. Read Alex's essay, and then answer the questions in Practice 11-3 on page 268.

Increase Grant Money for Low-Income College Students

1   The price of college tuition has more than doubled over the last two decades. Today, low-income students are finding it especially difficult (and sometimes impossible) to pay for school. Should the government help these

students more than it does now? If so, what form should that help take? Rather than reducing aid or asking students to borrow more, the government should give larger grants to subsidize tuition for low-income students.

2   If this is a country that is committed to equal opportunity, then college should be affordable for all. To compete in today's high-tech job market, people need a college degree. However, students' access to college is too often determined by their parents' income. This is unfair. Therefore, the government should make it a priority to support students who are being priced out of a college education. Specifically, the government should give larger grants to low-income students. Although some critics see these grants as unnecessary "handouts," such awards are the best way for the government to invest in the future and to maintain our nation's core values. After all, the country's economy benefits when more of its citizens earn college degrees. Even more important, by giving low-income students the same opportunities to succeed as their more affluent peers, the United States keeps its promise to treat all its citizens fairly.

3   Some people argue that the best way to help students who are struggling to pay for college is to offer them more loans at a lower interest rate. However, this solution is inadequate, unfair, and short-sighted. First of all, lowering the interest rate on student loans only reduces the average monthly payments by a few dollars. Second, student loans already unfairly burden low-income students. Why should they have to take on more debt simply because their parents make less money? The government should be trying to reduce the amount these students have to borrow, not increase it. Finally, forcing graduates to start their careers with such a heavy financial burden will hurt the country's economy. Although loans might cost the government less in the short term, in the long term student debt makes it more difficult for Americans to be successful and competitive.

4   The federal government does have a program in place to help students who demonstrate need, but Pell Grant funding needs to be expanded. As Joy Resmovits reports, despite the rising cost of tuition, college students now actually receive proportionally less government grant money than ever before. In fact, Pell Grants are limited to $5,645 per student per year. At most, Pell Grants cover only a third of average college costs. Meanwhile, the education gap between rich and poor is growing. As education policy expert Andrew J. Rotherham observes, while 75 percent of wealthy students earn a four-year degree by age 24, less than 10 percent of low-income students do. To help close this gap, the government should offer more funding to those most in need of financial assistance.

5   Some would argue, however, that the government should do just the opposite. One of the most common criticisms of government subsidies is that they are in some way to blame for the rising cost of college. Critics point out that government grants only make it easier for schools to charge more. This may be true, but, as Andrew J. Rotherham points out, the government could do more to regulate college tuition. For example, the government could offer incentives to schools that keep their costs down or award more generous grants to students who attend affordable schools. Ultimately, withdrawing aid and abandoning students to the free market is irresponsible as well as counterproductive.

6   With the cost of college continuing to rise, now is the time for the government to help the hardest-hit students by offering them more help to pay for their education. Rather than cutting spending on student aid, the government should fund more grants to low-income students. However, it must do so in ways that discourage future increases in tuition. By acting wisely and prudently, the government can improve access to higher education for all and support the country's economic future.

Works Cited

Resmovits, Joy. "Pell Grants for Poor Students Lose $170 Billion in Ryan Budget." *The Huffington Post*. TheHuffingtonPost.com, Inc., 27 Mar. 2012. Web. 19 Apr. 2014.

Rotherham, Andrew J. "How to Fix Pell Grants." *Time*. Time, Inc., 24 May 2012. Web. 19 Apr. 2014.

PRACTICE

11-3

1. Underline Alex's thesis statement. In your own words, restate the position Alex takes in his essay.

2. List the evidence Alex uses to support his thesis. Where does he include facts? Examples? Expert opinion?

3. Circle some of the transitional words and phrases Alex uses to move from one point to another. How do they advance his argument? Where could he have included additional transitions?

4. Underline Alex's summary statement. Then, restate it in your own words.

5. Use **TEST** to evaluate Alex's essay. What revisions would you suggest he make, and why?

grammar in context

Argument

When you write an argument essay, you need to show the relationships between your ideas by combining sentences to create **compound sentences** and **complex sentences**.

> The federal government does have a program in place to help
>
> students who demonstrate need, *, but* Pell Grant funding needs to be
>
> expanded. (compound sentence)
>
> *Although some critics*
> ~~Some critics~~ see these grants as unnecessary "handouts,*,*"
>
> *^such*
> ~~Such~~ awards are the best way for the government to invest in the
>
> future and to maintain our nation's core values. (complex sentence)

For information on how to create compound and complex sentences, see Chapter 17.

Teaching Tip

Before your students write argument essays, you might want to explain the use of subordinating conjunctions and relative pronouns to form complex sentences and have students do Practices 17-2 through 17-5.

 11c   Integrating Reading and Writing

Now, it is time to practice what you have learned and put your reading and writing skills together. In the following argument essay, Mary Sherry takes a stand on a debatable issue, arguing that it is good for students to fail once in a while, and tries to convince readers to accept her position. **Read** the essay, following the active reading process outlined in Chapter 1, and then answer the questions on pages 271–272. When you have finished, you will **write** an argument essay in response to Sherry's ideas.

IN PRAISE OF THE F WORD

Mary Sherry

Mary Sherry is a writer and an adult literacy educator. "In Praise of the F Word," which was first published in the "My Turn" column of *Newsweek* in 1991, argues that it is good for students to fail once in a while because it motivates them to continue to do their best work.

Before you read, consider what you think about failing grades. Do you think they motivate or discourage students?

WORD POWER

semiliterate barely able to read or write

Tens of thousands of 18-year-olds will graduate this year and be handed 1
meaningless diplomas. These diplomas won't look any different from
those awarded their luckier classmates. Their validity will be questioned only when their employers discover that these graduates are
semiliterate.

Eventually a fortunate few will find their way into educational- 2
repair shops—adult-literacy programs, such as the one where I teach
basic grammar and writing. There, high-school graduates and high-school
dropouts pursuing graduate-equivalency certificates will learn the skills
they should have learned in school. They will also discover they have
been cheated by our educational system.

As I teach, I learn a lot about our schools. Early in each session I 3
ask my students to write about an unpleasant experience they had in
school. No writers' block here! "I wish someone would have had made
me stop doing drugs and made me study." "I liked to party and no
one seemed to care." "I was a good kid and didn't cause any trouble,
so they just passed me along even though I didn't read and couldn't
write." And so on.

I am your basic do-gooder, and prior to teaching this class I blamed 4
the poor academic skills our kids have today on drugs, divorce and other
impediments to concentration necessary for doing well in school. But, as
I rediscover each time I walk into the classroom, before a teacher can
expect students to concentrate, he has to get their attention, no matter
what distractions may be at hand. There are many ways to do this, and
they have much to do with teaching style. However, if style alone won't
do it, there is another way to show who holds the winning hand in the
classroom. That is to reveal the trump card of failure.

WORD POWER

trump card a key resource to be used at the right moment

I will never forget a teacher who played that card to get the attention 5
of one of my children. Our youngest, a world-class charmer, did little to
develop his intellectual talents but always got by. Until Mrs. Stifter.

Our son was a high-school senior when he had her for English. "He 6
sits in the back of the room talking to his friends," she told me. "Why
don't you move him to the front row?" I urged, believing the embarrass-
ment would get him to settle down. Mrs. Stifter looked at me steely-eyed
over her glasses. "I don't move seniors," she said. "I flunk them." I was
flustered. Our son's academic life flashed before my eyes. No teacher
had ever threatened him with that before. I regained my composure and
managed to say that I thought she was right. By the time I got home I
was feeling pretty good about this. It was a radical approach for these
times, but, well, why not? "She's going to flunk you," I told my son. I did
not discuss it any further. Suddenly English became a priority in his life.
He finished out the semester with an A.

WORD POWER

flustered in a state of worry or confusion
composure calmness

I know one example doesn't make a case, but at night I see a pa- 7
rade of students who are angry and resentful for having been passed
along until they could no longer even pretend to keep up. Of average

intelligence or better, they eventually quit school, concluding they were too dumb to finish. "I should have been held back," is a comment I hear frequently. Even sadder are those students who are high-school graduates who say to me after a few weeks of class, "I don't know how I ever got a high-school diploma."

Passing students who have not mastered the work cheats them and   8
the employers who expect graduates to have basic skills. We excuse this dishonest behavior by saying kids can't learn if they come from terrible environments. No one seems to stop to think that—no matter what environments they come from—most kids don't put school first on their list unless they perceive something is at stake. They'd rather be sailing.

Many students I see at night could give expert testimony on unem-   9
ployment, chemical dependency, abusive relationships. In spite of these difficulties, they have decided to make education a priority. They are motivated by the desire for a better job or the need to hang on to the one they've got. They have a healthy fear of failure.

People of all ages can rise above their problems, but they need to 10
have a reason to do so. Young people generally don't have the maturity to value education in the same way my adult students value it. But fear of failure, whether economic or academic, can motivate both. Flunking as a regular policy has just as much merit today as it did two genera- tions ago. We must review the threat of flunking and see it as it really is—a positive teaching tool. It is an expression of confidence by both teachers and parents that the students have the ability to learn the ma- terial presented to them. However, making it work again would take a dedicated, caring conspiracy between teachers and parents. It would mean facing the tough reality that passing kids who haven't learned the material—while it might save them grief for the short term—dooms them to long-term illiteracy. It would mean that teachers would have to follow through on their threats, and parents would have to stand be- hind them, knowing their children's best interests are indeed at stake. This means no more doing Scott's assignments for him because he might fail. No more passing Jodi because she's such a nice kid.

This is a policy that worked in the past and can work today. A wise 11
teacher, with the support of his parents, gave our son the opportunity to succeed—or fail. It's time we return this choice to all students.

> **WORD POWER**
>
> **merit** value or worth
> **conspiracy** a joining or acting together

Focus on Reading

1. Look back at the work you did when you previewed, highlighted, and annotated this essay. What key points did you identify?

2. Which of Sherry's key points do you agree with? Which do you dis- agree with? If you have not already done so, indicate your responses with annotations in the margins of the essay.

Focus on Meaning

1. Who or what does Sherry blame for the "meaningless diplomas" (paragraph 1) that are issued each year? What other reasons for this situation can you think of?
2. What does Sherry mean in paragraph 10 when she says, "Flunking as a regular policy has just as much merit today as it did two generations ago"?
3. How does the experience Sherry's son had in high school convince her that the threat of failure is a "positive teaching tool" (10)?

Focus on Strategy

1. Where does Sherry state her thesis? Where else could she have stated it? Would it have been more or less effective there? Why?
2. Throughout her essay, Sherry establishes her credentials as a teacher. Why? If she weren't a teacher, would her argument be as convincing?

Focus on Language and Style

1. In her title, Sherry refers to flunking as the "F Word." What point is she making by doing this?
2. In paragraph 4, Sherry calls herself a "do-gooder." What does this term mean? How does Sherry use it in her essay? What other term could she have used instead?

Focus on the Pattern

1. Sherry organizes her argument inductively. List the evidence that she uses to reach her conclusion. Has she provided enough evidence? Explain. (For a discussion of inductive reasoning, see page 258.)
2. In paragraph 2, Sherry refers to "educational-repair shops." Why does she think that adult literacy classes are "repair shops"?

Focus on Critical Thinking

In paragraphs 9 and 10, Sherry argues that if students do not have a "healthy fear of failure" (9), they will not be motivated to work. What does she mean? Do you have a "healthy fear of failure"? If so, does it motivate you, or does it get in your way? Explain.

focus on reading and writing

Now that you have read Sherry's essay, write your own argument essay in response to one of the following prompts. (If you prefer, you can write on one of the additional topics listed in the box below.) Be sure to follow the writing process outlined in Chapter 3.

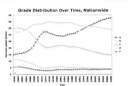

Grade Distribution Over Time, Nationwide

1. Write an argument that supports or opposes the idea of using failure as a teaching tool. Do you, like Sherry, believe that flunking is a policy that "can work today" (paragraph 11)? Or, do you think that there are better ways to motivate students? Try to identify and refute at least two opposing arguments.

2. Write a letter to a teacher who threatened you with failure. Make the case that the teacher's warning either motivated you or did more harm than good. Support your position with specific examples.

3. Do you in any way feel "cheated by our educational system" (paragraph 2)? Write an argument essay in which you answer this question. Use your own experiences as well as ideas from Sherry's essay as evidence.

additional topics

Argument

The federal government should (or should not) forgive all student loans.

Assault-style weapons should (or should not) be banned.

Animals should (or should not) be used in medical research.

READING AND WRITING ACTIVITY

Reread the draft of your essay, and then revise it. Begin by answering the questions in the **TEST** checklist below. When you have finished revising, edit and proofread your essay.

TESTing your argument essay

Thesis Statement Unifies Your Essay

☐ Does your introduction include a **thesis statement** that clearly expresses the stand you take on the issue you will discuss? Is this issue debatable—that is, does it really have two or more sides?

Evidence Supports Your Essay's Thesis Statement

☐ Does all your **evidence**—facts, examples, and expert opinion—support your thesis, or should some be deleted?

☐ Do you have enough evidence to support your points?

☐ Have you considered whether readers are likely to be hostile toward, neutral toward, or in agreement with your position—and have you chosen your points accordingly?

☐ Is your evidence presented in a clear inductive or deductive order?

Summary Statement Reinforces Your Essay's Main Idea

☐ Does your conclusion include a **summary statement** that reinforces your essay's thesis?

Transitions Connect Your Essay's Points

☐ Do you include **transitions** that introduce your points?

☐ Do you include enough transitional words and phrases to help readers follow the logic of your argument?

COLLABORATIVE ACTIVITY

Work with another student to consider the strengths and weaknesses of each of your argument essays. Do you think that one of your argument essays is more convincing than the other? Explain. Based on your reactions to the essays that you and your classmate wrote, what do you think an effective argument essay should accomplish? Write a few sentences in which you explain what an argument essay should do.

review checklist

Reading and Writing Argument Essays

- **Argument** takes a stand on a debatable issue. An **argument essay** attempts to convince readers that the writer's ideas have merit by presenting evidence—facts and examples (and sometimes expert opinion).

- When you *read* an argument essay, follow the reading process outlined in Chapter 1, and use TEST to help you identify the essay's key elements. (See 11a.)

- When you *write* an argument essay, follow the writing process outlined in Chapter 3, and use TEST to make sure that you have included all the necessary elements. (See 11b.)

- Keep in mind that in your college courses you often write in response to reading. (See 11c.)

12 Additional Options for Organizing Essays

As you learned in Chapters 7 through 11, writers have a variety of options—often referred to as *patterns*—for developing ideas within an essay. The patterns explained and illustrated in Chapters 7 through 11 are the ones you are most likely to encounter and to use in your academic career. Four additional ways to organize an essay—*description*, *process*, *classification*, and *definition*—are discussed and illustrated in this chapter.

12a Description

Teaching Tip
See Chapter 12 in the Chapter-by-Chapter guide of the instructor's manual for the Focus on Reading and Writing prompt and additional material for teaching *description*.

Description tells what something looks, sounds, smells, tastes, or feels like. There are two types of description: *objective* and *subjective*.

An **objective** description is primarily factual, omitting the writer's reactions or responses. It relies on precise observations and uses direct and unemotional language. A **subjective** description reflects the writer's thoughts, emotions, and perspective. It uses language that conveys (or suggests) the writer's personal feelings and reactions to what is being described.

OBJECTIVE DESCRIPTION

The columns were ten feet tall and made of white marble.

SUBJECTIVE DESCRIPTION

The columns were tall and powerful looking, and their glistening white marble surfaces reflected the harsh glare of the afternoon sun.

Keep in mind that no description is totally objective or subjective. An objective description often includes language that expresses the writer's mood, and a subjective description can include factual details and neutral language.

FYI

Figures of Speech

Descriptive writing, particularly subjective description, is frequently enriched by **figures of speech**—language that creates special or unusual effects.

- A **simile** uses *like* or *as* to compare two unlike things.

  Her smile was like sunshine.

- A **metaphor** compares two unlike things without using *like* or *as*.

  Her smile was a light that lit up the room.

- **Personification** suggests a comparison between a nonliving thing and a person by giving the nonliving thing human traits.

  The sun smiled down on the crowd.

See 5b for more on figurative language.

Reading Descriptive Essays

When you **read** a descriptive essay, use **TEST** to help you identify its key elements. Be sure to follow the active reading process outlined in Chapter 1.

T ▪ **Thesis Statement**—A descriptive essay includes a **thesis statement** that expresses the essay's main idea.

E ▪ **Evidence**—The body paragraphs include **evidence**, descriptive details that support the thesis. Details are arranged in spatial order—for example, from far to near or from top to bottom.

S ▪ **Summary Statement**—The conclusion of a descriptive essay usually includes a **summary statement** that reinforces the essay's thesis.

T ▪ **Transitions**—A descriptive essay includes **transitional words and phrases** that connect details and show how they are related.

In a descriptive essay, details enable readers to see what the writer sees, hear what the writer hears, and feel what the writer has experienced. Often, the writer's goal is to create a single **dominant impression**, a central theme or idea to which all the details relate—for example, the liveliness of a street scene or the tranquility of a summer night. The dominant impression unifies the description and gives readers an overall sense of what the person, place, object, or scene looks like (and perhaps what it sounds, smells, tastes, or feels like).

The details in a descriptive essay can be arranged in many different ways—for example, from least to most important details, from top to bottom (or from bottom to top), or from near to far (or from far to near). Each of the essay's body paragraphs may focus on one key characteristic of the subject being described or on several related descriptive details.

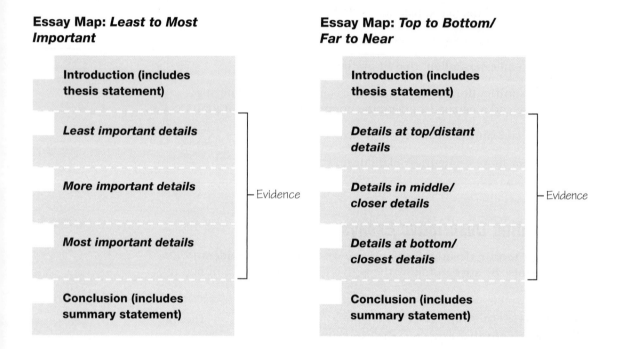

Essay Map: *Least to Most Important*

Introduction (includes thesis statement)

Least important details

More important details — Evidence

Most important details

Conclusion (includes summary statement)

Essay Map: *Top to Bottom/ Far to Near*

Introduction (includes thesis statement)

Details at top/distant details

Details in middle/ closer details — Evidence

Details at bottom/ closest details

Conclusion (includes summary statement)

Some Transitional Words and Phrases for Description

Transitional words and expressions connect details and show how they work together to create a full picture for readers. Many of these useful transitions indicate location or distance.

above	in front of	outside
behind	inside	over
below	nearby	the least important
between	next to	the most important
beyond	on	under
in	on one side . . . on	
in back of	the other side	

Reading a Model Student Essay: Description

The following descriptive essay was written by Rida Sikander in response to this assignment in her composition class.

> Search the Internet to find a work of art that appeals to you. Then, write an essay in which you describe this work of art. Your essay should combine objective and subjective description and should include enough detail so that someone who is not familiar with the work will be able to visualize it.

Read Rida's essay, following the active reading process discussed in Chapter 1, and then fill in the essay map in Practice 12-1 on pages 280–281. (Note that the **TEST** elements in the essay have been highlighted and color-coded.)

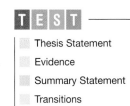

T **E** **S** **T**
Thesis Statement
Evidence
Summary Statement
Transitions

A Message of Peace and Love

1   Many people think that to be an artist, a person has to go to art school and make money selling his or her work. However, there are plenty of artists who do not fit this description. They are known as "outsider artists," and their work is called "outsider art." Outsider artists are self-taught, they often use found or homemade materials, and they rarely get recognition. In spite of these disadvantages, many outsider artists create impressive works with strong messages. Elijah Pierce is one of these artists. An American-African barber, Pierce used his pocketknife to carve pictures in relief on wood; then, he painted the carvings with bright colors. In his woodcarving *"Love" (Martin Luther King, Jr.)*, Pierce shows King protected by an angel. This portrait shows Dr. King embraced by the love and kindness that he embodied when he was alive.

2   At the top of *"Love" (Martin Luther King, Jr.)* is an angel, floating above and behind Dr. King. Although only her upper body is visible, the angel's image fills up most of the top half of the frame. The tips of her paint-spattered wings reach up into the two highest corners of the frame, and her hands spread out to the sides. She looks almost like a protective tree; behind her head, a patch of green is carved to look like leaves. Yet, she seems familiar and human. Her small face is simply drawn, and her expression is calm and kind. Like King, she has brown skin and black hair. Below her face, her open arms stretch her angel's white robe wide. Acting as a background for King's head, the robe resembles a cloud-like pillow. To either side, her open hands reach out to encircle him. In each of these details, the artist shows the angel's mission to love and protect the fallen leader's spirit.

3   Halfway down on the left-hand side of the picture is the word "LOVE." Written on a raised rectangle and surrounded by a turquoise background, the word looks like a large sign posted in the sky. As with the angel, the message here is unmistakable. Love is what King spread, and love is what embraces him now. In addition, the word tells the viewer to love, and it also tells the viewer to see the love in the artist's work. Elijah Pierce created every element of this image by hand. Each of the black letters is roughly carved and hand-painted. The rectangle is decorated with bright splotches of orange and green. The irregular, uneven lines and edges show his use of simple tools. Through these imperfect images, Pierce expresses his love for King and his accomplishments.

4   The dominant image in the picture is Martin Luther King, Jr. sitting on a brown wooden chair. Although the chair is turned sideways, King is facing the viewer. In the center of the frame, his large, gentle face looks a bit too big for his body. Simply carved, his features are out of proportion as well; for instance, his eyes are uneven, and they gaze in slightly different directions. However, these details do not make him look silly or odd. On the contrary, these imperfections, and his very slight smile, make him look human and strangely appealing. Below, he is formally dressed; he wears a dark blue suit, a red tie, and a white shirt. However, he seems at ease. His posture is calm and relaxed, and his hands rest comfortably at his sides. Just below his hands, the picture ends. The artist does not show King's feet or the bottoms of the chair legs, and no ground or horizon is visible. Dr. King seems to float in space, accompanied by the angel and the word "LOVE."

5   In his woodcarving, Pierce surrounds Martin Luther King, Jr. with the love that he exhibited when he was alive. Rather than idealizing its subject, Pierce's simple carving expresses the artist's admiration for the martyred civil rights leader. Although most outsider artists remain unknown, Pierce was recognized when he was alive. Although he was well known in his community, he was not widely appreciated until someone from outside the community noticed his remarkable artwork hanging in his barbershop. As a result, Pierce was "discovered."

PRACTICE

12-1   Now that you have read Rida's essay, fill in the essay map on the following page to better understand how she organized her essay. Then, decide whether her organization is effective.

Introduction *Answers will vary.*
_____
_____
_____

Details at top *Answers will vary.*
_____
_____

Details in middle *Answers will vary.*
_____
_____

Details at bottom *Answers will vary.*
_____
_____
_____

Conclusion *Answers will vary.*
_____
_____

Writing Descriptive Essays

When you **write** a descriptive essay, you follow the process outlined in Chapter 3. The essay you write will include the same elements you have learned to recognize in the descriptive essays you read. When you finish your draft, you can **TEST** it to make sure it includes all the elements of a descriptive essay.

When you are given a writing assignment, the wording of your assignment may suggest that you write a descriptive essay. For example, it may ask you to *describe* or to *tell what an object looks like*. Once you decide that your assignment calls for description, you need to develop a thesis statement that reflects this purpose.

ASSIGNMENT	THESIS STATEMENT
Scientific writing Describe a piece of scientific equipment.	The mass spectrometer is a complex instrument, but every part is ideally suited to its function.
Art history Choose one modern painting and describe its visual elements.	The disturbing images crowded together in Pablo Picasso's *Guernica* suggest the brutality of war.

Teaching Tip
Tell students that many everyday writing tasks call for description. For example, a statement to an insurance company after an automobile accident might describe damage to the car.

The following essay was written by James Greggs in his first-year composition course. Read James's essay, and then answer the questions in Practice 12-2 on pages 283–284.

Building and Learning

1   Throughout the United States, houses reflect not only the lives of the people who live in them but also the diversity of the American population. Some are large and elaborate, others are modest but well maintained, and still others are in need of repair. Unfortunately, most college students know little about homes other than those in their own neighborhood. I too was fairly sheltered until I participated in a service-learning project for my sociology class. For this project, I, along with some classmates, added a deck to a trailer that was the home of three elderly sisters living on Social Security and disability. It was hard work, but my experience convinced me that all college students should be required to do some kind of service-learning project.

2   The trailer we worked on was located at the end of a small dirt road about thirty minutes from campus. Patches of green and brown grass dotted the land around the trailer, and in the far right-hand corner of the property stood three tall poplar trees. Although the bushes in front of the trailer were trimmed, the woods behind the trailer were beginning to overrun the property. (We were told that members of a local church came once a month to trim the hedges and cut back the trees.) Dominating the right front corner of the lawn, a circular concrete basin looked like a large birdbath. The basin housed a white well pipe with a rusted blue cap. About thirty feet to the left of the concrete basin stood a telephone pole and a bright red metal mailbox.

3   Like the property on which it stood, the trailer was well maintained. It was approximately thirty-five feet long and seven feet high; it rested on cinderblocks, which raised it about three feet off the ground. Under the trailer was an overturned white plastic chair. The trailer itself was covered with sheets of white vinyl siding that ran horizontally, except for the bottom panels on the right side, which ran vertically. The vinyl panels closest to the roof were slightly discolored by dirt and green moss.

4   At the left end of the trailer was a small window—about two feet wide and one foot high. Next to the window was a dark red aluminum door that was outlined in green trim. It had one window at eye level divided by metal strips into four small sections. The number "24" in white plastic letters was glued to the door below this window. To the right of the door

was a lightbulb in a black ceramic socket. Next to the light was a large window that was actually two vertical rows of three windows—each the same size as the small window on the left. Further to the right were two smaller windows. Each of these small windows tilted upward and was framed with silver metal strips. On either side of each of these windows was a pair of green metal shutters.

5   The deck we built replaced three wooden steps that had led up to the trailer. A white metal handrail stood on the right side of these steps. It had been newly painted and was connected to the body of the trailer by a heart-shaped piece of metal. In front of the steps, two worn gray wooden boards led to the road.

6   Building the deck was hard work, but the finished deck provided a much better entranceway than the steps did and also gave the trailer a new look. The deck was not very large—ten feet by eight feet—but it extended from the doorway to the area underneath the windows immediately to the right of the door. We built the deck out of pressure-treated lumber so that it wouldn't rot or need painting. We also built three steps that led from the deck to the lawn, and we surrounded the deck with a wooden railing that ran down the right side of the steps. After we finished, we bought two white plastic chairs at a local thrift store and put them on the deck.

7   Now that I look back at the project, I believe that activities like this should be part of every student's college education. Both the residents of the trailer and our class benefited from the service-learning project. The residents of the trailer were happy with the deck because it gave them a place to sit when the weather was nice. They also liked their trailer's new look. Those of us who worked on the project learned that a few days' work could make a real difference in other people's lives.

PRACTICE

12-2   1. Underline James's thesis statement; then, rewrite it in your own words.

2. What details does James provide to describe the property, the trailer, and the deck? What determines the order in which James arranges the details in his description?

3. Circle some of the transitional words and phrases James uses to move from one detail to another. Do you think he includes enough transitions? Could he have added more? Explain.

4. This essay is primarily an objective description. Where does it include some subjective description? What do these subjective details add to the essay?

5. Use TEST to evaluate James's essay. What revisions would you suggest he make? Why?

grammar in context

Description

When you write a descriptive essay, you may use **modifiers**—words and phrases that describe other words in the sentence—to create a picture of your subject. If you place a modifying word or phrase too far from the word it is supposed to describe, you create a potentially confusing **misplaced modifier**.

CONFUSING   Next to the window outlined in green trim was a dark red aluminum door. (Was the window outlined in green trim?)

CLEAR   Next to the window was a dark red aluminum door outlined in green trim.

For information on how to identify and correct misplaced modifiers, see Chapter 25.

Integrating Reading and Writing

Now, it is time to practice what you have learned and put your reading and writing skills together. In the following selection, "A Fable for Tomorrow," Rachel Carson describes a typical small town "in the heart of America." By doing so, she tries to change the way people look at nature and to stimulate a debate about the environment. **Read** the essay, following the active reading process outlined in Chapter 1, and then answer the questions on pages 286–287. When you have finished, you will **write** a descriptive essay in response to Carson's ideas.

A FABLE FOR TOMORROW

Rachel Carson

Rachel Carson (1907–1964) is often credited with starting the modern-day environmental movement. Her book *Silent Spring* (1962) exposed the devastating effects of pesticides on the environment. In the excerpt that follows, part of the introduction to that book, Carson uses specific details to create a powerful picture of the place she describes.

Before you read, consider what reactions today's readers might have to this essay. How would they be different from the reactions of readers in 1962?

There was once a town in the heart of America where all life seemed to live in harmony with its surroundings. The town lay in the midst of a checkerboard of prosperous farms, with fields of grain and hillsides of orchards where, in spring, white clouds of bloom drifted above the green fields. In autumn, oak and maple and birch set up a blaze of color that flamed and flickered across a backdrop of pines. Then foxes barked in the hills and deer silently crossed the fields, half hidden in the mists of the fall mornings.

Along the roads, laurel, viburnum and alder, great ferns and wild- flowers delighted the traveler's eye through much of the year. Even in winter the roadsides were places of beauty, where countless birds came to feed on the berries and on the seed heads of the dried weeds rising above the snow. The countryside was, in fact, famous for the abundance and variety of its bird life, and when the flood of migrants was pouring through in spring and fall people traveled from great distances to observe them. Others came to fish the streams, which flowed clear and cold out of the hills and contained shady pools where trout lay. So it had been from the days many years ago when the first settlers raised their houses, sank their wells, and built their barns.

WORD POWER

viburnum a type of shrub with large, bright flower clusters

Then a strange blight crept over the area and everything began to change. Some evil spell had settled on the community: mysterious maladies swept the flocks of chickens; the cattle and sheep sickened and died. Everywhere was a shadow of death. The farmers spoke of much illness among their families. In the town the doctors had become more and more puzzled by new kinds of sickness appearing among their patients. There had been several sudden and unexplained deaths, not only among adults but even among children, who would be stricken suddenly while at play and die within a few hours.

There was a strange stillness. The birds, for example—where had they gone? Many people spoke of them, puzzled and disturbed. The feeding stations in the backyards were deserted. The few birds seen anywhere were moribund; they trembled violently and could not fly. It was a spring without voices. On the mornings that had once throbbed with the dawn chorus of robins, catbirds, doves, jays, wrens, and scores of other bird voices there was now no sound; only silence lay over the fields and woods and marsh.

WORD POWER

moribund dying

On the farms the hens brooded, but no chicks hatched. The farmers complained that they were unable to raise any pigs—the litters were small and the young survived only a few days. The apple trees were coming into bloom but no bees droned among the blossoms, so there was no pollination and there would be no fruit.

The roadsides, once so attractive, were now lined with browned and 6 withered vegetation as though swept by fire. These, too, were silent, deserted by all living things. Even the streams were now lifeless. Anglers no longer visited them, for all the fish had died.

In the gutters under the eaves and between the shingles of the roofs, 7 a white granular powder still showed a few patches; some weeks before it had fallen like snow upon the roofs and the lawns, the fields and streams.

No witchcraft, no enemy action had silenced the rebirth of new life 8 in this stricken world. The people had done it themselves.

This town does not actually exist, but it might easily have a thou- 9 sand counterparts in America or elsewhere in the world. I know of no community that has experienced all the misfortunes I describe. Yet every one of these disasters has actually happened somewhere, and many real communities have already suffered a substantial number of them. A grim specter has crept upon us almost unnoticed, and this imagined tragedy may easily become a stark reality we all shall know. . . .

Focus on Reading

1. Look back at the work you did when you previewed, highlighted, and annotated this essay. What did you underline? Why?

2. Put a check mark next to words that are particularly descriptive. In the margin, write a synonym for each of the words you selected. In each case, which do you think is more effective, your synonym or Carson's original word?

Teaching Tip
You may have students work collaboratively to answer some of these questions.

Focus on Meaning

1. What is a fable? In what sense was this essay—written for the introduction to Carson's 1962 book *Silent Spring*, which exposed the dangerous effects of pesticides on the environment—a "fable for tomorrow"?

2. What does Carson mean when she says, "The people had done it themselves" (paragraph 8)?

ESL Tip
Have native- and nonnative-speaking students work in groups or in pairs to discuss the exercises before they write their answers.

Focus on Strategy

1. Why do you suppose Carson opened *Silent Spring* with this story? How do you think she expected readers to react? Do you think today's readers would be likely to react differently from those reading in 1962? If so, how? If not, why not?

2. In paragraph 9, Carson admits that the town she has been describing does not exist. Do you think this admission weakens her essay? Why or why not?

Focus on Language and Style

1. This essay is called "A Fable for Tomorrow," but, except for the last paragraph, it is written in past tense. Why do you think Carson uses past tense?

Teaching Tip
Remind students to answer all questions in complete sentences.

2. Throughout this essay, Carson uses strong language, such as "evil spell" (3) and "grim specter" (9), to get her point across. Identify other examples of such language. Do you think these expressions are effective, or do you think Carson goes too far?

Focus on the Pattern

1. How does Carson indicate to readers that she is moving from positive to negative description?

2. Is this a subjective or an objective description? How can you tell?

Focus on Critical Thinking

1. Where might the town "in the heart of America" (1) actually be located? Do you think Carson should have provided more identifying information about this town? Why or why not?

2. Is there a situation affecting our environment today that you see as just as alarming as the one Carson writes about? In what sense do you see this situation as a threat?

focus on reading and writing

Now that you have read Rachel Carson's essay, write your own descriptive essay in response to one of the following prompts. (If you prefer, you can write on one of the additional topics listed in the box on page 288.) Be sure to follow the writing process outlined in Chapter 3.

1. Write your own "fable for tomorrow" describing the likely effects on our environment of the unchecked piling up of nonbiodegradable garbage and trash in our landfills. In your thesis statement, encourage your readers to recycle to avoid the problems you describe.

2. Some people see climate change as a destructive problem of epic proportions—as an even a greater problem than the pesticides that Carson warns against. Write a "fable for tomorrow" in which you describe an extreme scenario that could result from an increase in global warming.

additional topics

Description

An object you cherish

A historical site or monument

The home page of a website you visit often

12b   Process

Teaching Tip
See Chapter 12 in the Chapter-by-Chapter guide of the instructor's manual for the Focus on Reading and Writing prompt and additional material for teaching *process*.

A **process** is a series of chronologically arranged steps that produces a particular result. **Process essays** explain the steps in a procedure, telling how something works or how something is (or was) done—for example, how an optical scanner works, how to hem a pair of jeans, or how to set up an email account on a smartphone. Depending on the writer's purpose, a process essay can be organized as either a *process explanation* (simply telling how something is or was done) or a set of *instructions* (telling readers how to perform the process themselves).

Reading Process Essays

When you **read** a process essay, use **TEST** to help you identify its key elements. Be sure to follow the active reading process outlined in Chapter 1.

T ▪ **Thesis Statement**—A process essay includes a **thesis statement** that expresses the essay's main idea, identifying the process to be explained and telling why it is important or why it is being explained.

E ▪ **Evidence**—The body paragraphs provide **evidence**—examples and details—that explains the steps in the process and supports the essay's thesis. Each paragraph's topic sentence identifies the step (or group of related steps) that the paragraph will explain. Steps are presented in strict chronological (time) order.

S ▪ **Summary Statement**—The conclusion of a process essay includes a **summary statement** that reinforces the essay's thesis.

T ▪ **Transitions**—A process essay includes **transitional words and phrases** that link the steps in the process and show how they are related.

Whether an essay is a process explanation or a set of instructions, it can either devote a full paragraph to each step of the process or group a series of minor steps together in a single paragraph.

Essay Map: *One Step per Paragraph*

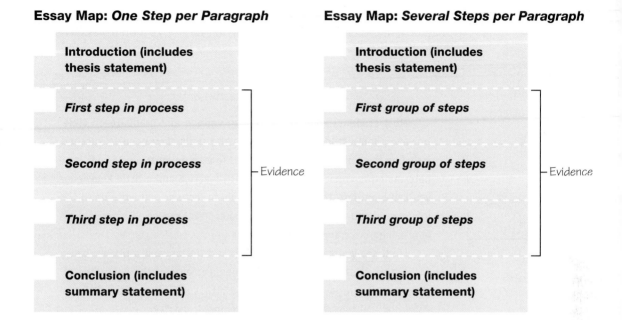

Introduction (includes thesis statement)

First step in process

Second step in process ── Evidence

Third step in process

Conclusion (includes summary statement)

Essay Map: *Several Steps per Paragraph*

Introduction (includes thesis statement)

First group of steps

Second group of steps ── Evidence

Third group of steps

Conclusion (includes summary statement)

Some Transitional Words and Phrases for Process

Transitions in process essays enable readers to follow the sequence of steps in the process and, in the case of instructions, to perform the process themselves.

after that	immediately	the final step
as	later	the first (second,
as soon as	meanwhile	third) step
at the end	next	then
at the same time	now	the next step
before	once	ultimately
finally	soon	when
first	subsequently	while

Reading a Model Student Essay: Process

The following process essay was written by Owen McCann in response to the following assignment in a study skills class.

> Write a set of instructions telling how to perform a process that will help students succeed in college.

Read Owen's essay, following the active reading process outlined in Chapter 1, and then fill in the essay map in Practice 12.3 on pages 291–292. (Note that the TEST elements in the essay have been highlighted and color-coded.)

How to Take Effective Notes

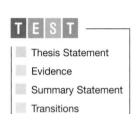

T E S T

- ☐ Thesis Statement
- ☐ Evidence
- ☐ Summary Statement
- ☐ Transitions

1   Most students want to do well in college and graduate on time. However, some students do not have the skills they need to succeed, including the ability to take good notes. To excel in most courses, effective note taking is crucial. Fortunately, with practice and a little knowledge, you can learn how to listen productively in lectures and write down the information you need. Following a few important steps will improve your note-taking skills and help you succeed in your college classes.

2   First, set yourself up for success. Go to class, and arrive on time. Instructors often make important announcements at the beginning of class, so you do not want to miss those first critical minutes. Bring a notebook and two or three different colored pens—or, if you are a fast typist, bring a laptop or tablet. Be sure, however, to close all unrelated applications before coming to class. At the same time, minimize your distractions by silencing your phone and removing it from your desk. Finally, make sure to sit where you can see and hear the instructor. You are more likely to stay focused if you are not sitting at the back of a large, echoey lecture hall. Using these suggestions will prepare you to get the most out of the day's class.

3   Next, get ready to pay attention. Before class, take a couple of minutes to reread your notes from the previous class. Orient yourself to the subject matter, and remind yourself of any questions you may have had after the last lecture. Then, turn to a fresh page, or open a new file, and set up a simple layout. To make your notes easier to reference later, put the date at the top of the page, and include a title for that day's subject, if there is one. To keep your notes organized, try drawing a vertical line down the middle of the page; you can keep your notes on one side and your questions and responses on the other side. Once you have taken these steps, you are ready for the lecture to begin.

4   Now, listen carefully and write down the important ideas. Do not try to write everything down. If you try to record the instructor's every word, you will undoubtedly miss some critical points. Make your note taking efficient by using abbreviations and symbols, and pay close attention to what the instructor emphasizes. Often, he or she will repeat a significant concept or

indicate which material will be on the next test. In your notes, try using different colored pens to underline or highlight these tips, as well as any announcements or reminders. In addition, include examples in your notes whenever possible; examples will help you better remember abstract concepts. For instance, if you are listening to a lecture on nonviolent resistance, write down a few words to remind you of real-world occurrences, such as "Gandhi-Quit India Movement." Meanwhile, throughout class, use the right-hand column of your page to jot down questions you want to ask the instructor. At the end of class, you will have a clear record of issues that need further attention as well as a complete and concise account of the main ideas covered in that class period.

5   Finally, review what you have written. If possible, reread your notes right after class or soon thereafter. At this point, give yourself a chance to fill in gaps, insert examples, and write down additional questions. You are much more likely to understand and absorb the information if you spend a few minutes reviewing what you have written. Be sure to look over your questions while the material is still fresh in your mind. Once you have done all you can on your own, find a classmate or TA to explain any confusing or difficult concepts. You can also see your instructor during office hours or send questions to him or her in an email. All in all, taking the time to clarify and complete your notes will make studying less frustrating and more efficient.

6   Following these steps to establish good note-taking habits will improve your understanding of the course material and help you succeed in college. Take the time to try them out for yourself. Make adjustments to fit your needs and to accommodate the structure of different classes. Share your strategies with others, and learn new methods from them. Ultimately, taking and having reliable notes makes learning easier and more enjoyable, and mastering the note-taking process will make your college experience more productive and satisfying.

PRACTICE

12-3   Now that you have read Owen's essay, fill in the essay map on the following page to help you understand how he organized his essay and to decide whether his organization is effective.

Introduction *Answers will vary.*

_____

_____

First group of steps *Answers will vary.*

_____

_____

Second group of steps *Answers will vary.*

_____

_____

Third group of steps *Answers will vary.*

_____

_____

Fourth group of steps *Answers will vary.*

_____

_____

Conclusion *Answers will vary.*

_____

_____

Writing Process Essays

When you **write** a process essay, you follow the process outlined in Chapter 3. The essay you write will include the same elements you have learned to recognize in the process essays you read. When you finish your draft, you can TEST it to make sure it includes all the elements of a process essay.

When you are given a writing assignment, the wording of your assignment may suggest that you write a process essay. For example, you may be asked to *explain a process, give instructions, give directions,* or *give a step-by-step account.* Once you decide that your assignment calls for process, you need to develop a thesis statement that reflects this purpose.

ASSIGNMENT	THESIS STATEMENT
Pharmacy practice Summarize the procedure for conducting a clinical trial of a new drug.	To ensure that drugs are safe and effective, scientists follow strict procedural guidelines for testing and evaluating the drugs.
Technical writing Write a set of instructions for applying for a student internship in a government agency.	If you want to apply for a government internship, you need to follow several important steps.

Teaching Tip
Tell students that many everyday writing tasks describe a process. For example, a manual for new employees might explain how to operate a piece of equipment or what steps to follow in an emergency.

If your purpose is simply to help readers understand a process, not actually perform it, you will write a process explanation. **Process explanations**, like the first example in the box above, often use present tense verbs ("A scientist first *submits* a funding application") to explain how a procedure is generally carried out. However, when a process explanation describes a procedure that was completed in the past, it uses past tense verbs ("The next thing I *did*").

If your purpose is to enable readers to actually perform the steps in a process, you will write instructions. **Instructions**, like the technical writing example in the box above, always use present tense verbs—in the form of commands—to tell readers what to do ("First, *meet* with your adviser").

Teaching Tip
You might want to tell students that in commands, the second-person subject is implied.

As you write your process essay, discuss each step in the order in which it is performed, making sure your topic sentences clearly identify each step or group of steps. If you are writing instructions, you may also include reminders or warnings that readers might need to keep in mind when performing the process.

The following essay was written by Jen Rossi in her first-year writing course. Read Jen's essay, and then answer the questions in Practice 12-4 on page 295.

For Fun and Profit

1   Selling items at a flea market can be both fun and profitable. In fact, it can lead to a hobby that will be a continuing source of extra income. Your first flea market can take a lot of work, but establishing a routine will make each experience easier and more rewarding than the last one.

2   The first step in the process is to call to reserve a spot at the flea market. If possible, try to get a spot near the entrance, where there is a lot of foot traffic. Once you have your spot, recruit a helper—for example, one of your roommates—and get to work.

3   The next step is sorting through all the items you've managed to accumulate. Your helper will come in handy here, encouraging you to sell ugly or useless things that you may want to hold on to. Make three piles— keep, sell, and trash—and, one by one, place each item in a pile. (Before you decide to sell or discard an item, check with roommates and family members to make sure you aren't accidentally throwing out one of their prized possessions.)

4   Next, price the items for sale. This can actually be the hardest step in the process. It's always difficult to accept the fact that you might have to set a low price for something that has sentimental value for you (a giant-sized stuffed animal, for example). It can be just as hard to set a high price on the ugly lamp or old record album that might turn out to be someone's treasure. In all likelihood, you will return from your first flea market with a lot of unsold items. You will also probably realize, too late, that you sold some items too cheaply. (Don't worry; you won't make these mistakes again.)

5   The next step is packing up items to be sold. You may want to borrow a friend's truck or van for the heavy, bulky items (boxes of books or dishes, for example). The small items (knickknacks, silk flowers, stray teaspoons) can be transported by car.

6   The final steps in your preparation take place on the day before the event. Borrow a couple of card tables. Then, go to the bank and get lots of dollar bills and quarters, and collect piles of newspaper and grocery bags. Now, your planning is complete, and you are ready for the big day.

7   On the day of the flea market, get up early, and (with your trusty helper's assistance) load your vehicle. When you arrive at the site where the event is to be held, have your helper unload the car. Meanwhile, set things up, placing small items (such as plates or DVDs) on the card tables and large items (such as your parents' old lawnmower) on the ground near the tables.

8   Now, the actual selling begins. Before you can even set up your tables, people will start picking through your items, offering you cash for picture frames, pots and pans, and old video games. Don't panic! Try to develop a system: one of you can persuade buyers that that old meat grinder or vase is just what they've been looking for; the other person can negotiate the price with prospective buyers. Then, while one of you wraps small items in the newspapers or bags you brought, the other person can take the money and make change.

9   Finally, at the end of the day, the process will come to an end. Now, count your money. (Don't forget to give a share to your helper.)

Then, load all the unsold items into your vehicle, and bring them back home. The process ends when you store the unsold items in the back of your closet, ready to pack them all up again and follow the same routine for the next flea market.

PRACTICE
12-4

1. Underline Jen's thesis statement; then, rewrite it in your own words.

2. What identifies Jen's essay as a set of instructions rather than a process explanation?

3. Circle some of the transitional words and phrases Jen uses to move from one step in the process to another. Are any other transitions needed? If so, where?

4. Underline Jen's summary statement. Then, rewrite it in your own words.

5. Use **TEST** to evaluate Jen's essay. What, if anything, does she need to revise? Why?

grammar in context

Process

When you write a process essay, you may have problems keeping tense, person, and voice consistent throughout. If you shift from one tense, person, or voice to another without good reason, you will confuse your readers.

> **CONFUSING** Make three piles—keep, sell, and trash—and, one by one, every item should be placed in a pile. (shift from active to passive voice and from present to past tense)

> **CLEAR** Make three piles—keep, sell, and trash—and, one by one, place each item in a pile. (consistent voice and tense)

For information on how to avoid illogical shifts in tense, person, and voice, see Chapter 24.

:e: For practice with shifts in tense and voice, complete the LearningCurve Verbs and Active and Passive Voice activities at **bedfordstmartins.com/forw**.

Teaching Tip
Before your students write process essays, you might want to explain how to avoid illogical shifts (Chapter 24) and have them do Practices 24-1 through 24-3.

Integrating Reading and Writing

Now, it is time to practice what you have learned and put your reading and writing skills together. The following essay, "My Grandmother's Dumpling," by Amy Ma, explains a process. **Read** the essay, following the active reading process outlined in Chapter 1, and then answer the questions on pages 302–303. When you have finished, you will **write** a process essay in response to Ma's ideas.

MY GRANDMOTHER'S DUMPLING

Amy Ma

Amy Ma is a writer who trained as a pastry chef in New York City and now lives in Hong Kong. This article, which first appeared in the *Wall Street Journal* in 2009, provides both information about how to make dumplings and the story of several generations of Ma's family.

Before you read, take some time to think about how cooking and family intersect in your own life.

There was no denying a dumpling error. If the meat tumbled out of a   1
poorly made one as it cooked, Grandmother could always tell who made it because she had personally assigned each of us a specific folding style at the onset of our dumpling-making education. In our house, a woman's folding style identified her as surely as her fingerprints.

"From now on, you and only you will fold it in this way," she in-   2
structed me in our Taipei kitchen in 1994, the year I turned 13. That is when I had reached a skill level worthy of joining the rest of the women—10 in all, from my 80-year-old grandmother, Lu Xiao-fang, to my two middle-aged aunts, my mother and the six children of my generation—in the folding of *jiao zi*, or dumplings, for Chinese New Year. Before then I had been relegated to prep work: mixing the meat filling or cutting the dough and flattening it.

WORD POWER

relegated assigned [to a lower position]

Cousin Mao Mao, the eldest daughter of my grandmother's first son,   3
had been away for four years at college in the U.S. But with casual ease, she fashioned her dumplings in the style of the rat, tucking in the creases and leaving a small tail that pinched together at one end. Two distinct pleats in a fan-shaped dumpling marked the work of Aunt Yee, Mao Mao's mother, who had just become a grandmother herself with the birth of a grandson. A smaller purse-like dumpling with eight folds toward the center was my mother's. Grandmother's dumplings were the simplest of the bunch—flat, crescent-shaped with no creases and a smooth edge. And as I was the youngest in my generation, she'd thought it appropriate to make my signature design a quirky variation of her own, with an added crimping to create a rippling *hua bian*, or flower edge.

"A pretty little edge, for a pretty little girl," she said.   4

While dumplings graced our tables year-round, they were a requisite   5
dish during the Lunar New Year holidays. The Spring Festival, as it is
known in China—*chun jie*—is arguably the most important celebration
of the year: It is a time to be with family, to visit friends and start life
anew—and eat dumplings.

WORD POWER

requisite necessary

The length of observance varies. Today in Taiwan, the national holi-   6
day stretches to nine days—including two weekends—with all businesses and government offices closed. In mainland China, officials
rearrange the working calendar to give the public seven consecutive
days off, while in Hong Kong there are three public holidays and in
Singapore, two. Unofficially, many Chinese people consider the traditional
period of the first 15 days appropriate to welcome the new year.

My family celebrated the first three days of the Spring Festival in   7
a traditional way: Everyone came "home," which meant to my grandfather's house. We were already home—my father, mother, brother and
I lived in Taipei with my father's parents, who had moved from China
in the late 1940s. Most of my father's family lived nearby. On *chu yi*, the
first day of the new year, friends came to our house to extend greetings.
For *chu er*, the second day, married women returned to their parents'
house. The third day, *chu san*, was always celebrated united, as a family.
And on each of those days, dumplings were the main food served during lunch and dinner. There might be other side dishes—leftovers from
New Year's Eve—but no other food was prepared from scratch during
the holiday. It was considered bad luck to do any work during this time;
to ensure a peaceful year ahead, you had to rest and that meant no
cooking.

Though it isn't known exactly when dumplings came into being, au-   8
thor and Chinese food expert Fuchsia Dunlop says *jiao zi* date as far
back as 1,100 years ago. "In the city of Turpan, a tomb was uncovered
that had boiled dumplings from the Tang dynasty (618–907) preserved
in much the same shape with similar fillings as they are today," says
Ms. Dunlop.

Many people believe the practice of eating these dumplings on   9
Chinese New Year became popular in the Yuan and Ming dynasties,
which stretched from 1271 to 1644, when *yuan bao*—gold and silver
ingots—began to take hold as currency in China; the dumplings take the
shape of those coins. During new year celebrations, filling your stomach
with edible replicas of ingots was thought to ensure a year of prosperity
ahead. The packaged bites also celebrated a letting go of the past, since
the word "*jiao*" also means "the end of something."

WORD POWER

ingots solid metal
bars

Traditions have relaxed: Not every family eats only dumplings for   10
three days. They also vary regionally: In the south of China, *nian gao*,
or rice cakes, are often served instead of these dough-swaddled morsels
at Chinese New Year. Still, hefty portions of dumplings undoubtedly
remain a big attraction this time of year in many Chinese households.

WORD POWER

redolent fragrant

Even now, that initial bite of any dumpling transports me back to 11 our Taipei kitchen: the women packed like sardines working on their craft with a Zen-like rhythm, the flour-dusted countertops, the air redolent with the scent of dough, and the faded brown ceramic tiles on the floor polished smooth by countless footsteps over the years.

The great dumpling cook-off commenced each year following 12 Lunar New Year's Eve dinner, a family meal of Grandmother's best dishes—sweet soy-braised pork, *ru yi cai* (10 vegetables tossed together with a soy-sauce vinaigrette), and always steamed fish since its term in Mandarin, *"yu,"* is a homonym for "plenty." By 9 p.m., the plates were cleared and washed, and the women were clustered in the kitchen.

The men, forbidden to enter the cooking area, dispersed to their 13 separate corners to talk politics and play dice or mahjong while awaiting the countdown to midnight. Every room of the house swelled with festivity as the whole family of more than 30 members—four generations—gathered for this night in my grandparents' house.

Amid the bustle, the kitchen alone had an air of serenity and pur- 14 pose as the women worked through the night. Before dawn of the next morning, there would be enough dumplings to cover two large dining room tables and every kitchen countertop.

To start, Grandmother unloaded from the refrigerator the large ball 15 of dough made from flour, cold water and a dash of egg white (her secret ingredient) that she had prepared the day before. Setting it onto the butcher block with her plump and sturdy hands, she ripped off two large balls and rolled each into a log, starting her gentle kneading from the center and stretching out to both sides. The remaining dough she kept covered under a damp towel.

Meanwhile, the rest of the women—my mother and two aunts and 16 my cousins and me—picked over bunches of coriander and peeled off the wilted layers of scallions and cabbages. A liberal douse of salt sprinkled over the cabbage drew out the excess water, and the chopped confetti-like bits were hand-squeezed to prevent a watery dumpling filling. The butcher knife rocked repeatedly back and forth on the ginger and garlic until it was almost a paste. Likewise, the vegetables had to be diced as finely as possible so they would be evenly spread through every bite of the final product.

Ignoring the slew of innovative options for fillings popular in con- 17 temporary restaurants—shrimp and chives, shark's fin and vermicelli—we filled our no-frills dumplings with minced pork. Into the pink ground meat went the chopped speckles of vegetables and herbs along with sesame oil, Shaoxin wine, salt, soy sauce, a pinch of sugar, white pepper, five-spice powder and an egg. Nothing was measured, yet it always tasted the same.

"That's enough mixing," Grandmother cautioned. My mother was 18 using a pair of wooden chopsticks to combine the ingredients in large circular motions. Grandmother insisted on only combing through the filling in one direction—clockwise—so as to not over-mix, which would make it tough.

Then like a carefully orchestrated master plan, a natural assem- 19 bly line formed. First, Grandmother cut off equal-size segments of her log of dough and then passed them to my mother, who used a wooden roller to flatten them into circles, a process called *gan mien*. Two aunts continued to fashion new dough into logs on one end of the kitchen counter, and three cousins lined up on the other end to begin filling and folding dumplings. The positions would alternate periodically, and makers would move up the line over the years as their skills improved. At 5 years old, my job had been the menial task of pressing the just-cut dough segments into flat disks so they would be easier to roll out, but I had since graduated to a dumpling folder. All together, we women stood, each ready to play her part in this culinary theater.

"Every step requires its own *kung fu*," Grandmother instructed in 20 Mandarin. She was short, but her chubby silhouette held the solid stance of a symphony conductor. The process was tedious, but a mere mention of serving a frozen dumpling from a supermarket would be confronted with a gaze that screamed: uncultured, unbelievable, un-*Chinese*. The matriarch in her kitchen was doing more than just cooking; she was training the next generation of wives, daughters and mothers as her mother-in-law had taught her.

"Use your palm to control the roller, not your fingertips," she barked. 21 "Keep a steady rhythm, consistent like your pulse." The dumpling skins weren't flattened in one fell swoop like a pie crust. Each one had to be rolled just around the rim and rotated so that the resulting circle was thinner on the edges than in the center. When folded in half the two sides met; the dumpling skin was uniform in thickness. It was a pains-taking task when repeated over the span of many hours, and my mother once showed me her swollen palms after a night of *gan mien*.

The amount of meat filling had to be just right. Not too much—"too 22 greedy!"—and not too little: "too stingy!"

And dumplings had to be folded with both hands. "It's a superstition," 23 Grandmother told us. "Women who fold dumplings with one hand won't have children. Your right and left hand have to work together to be a good mother." Grandmother demonstrated how she used the fleshy part of the index finger and thumb to press together the dough. Fresh dough, unlike frozen dough, didn't need water to seal the seams. Only a firm pinch.

"Beautifully folded," Grandmother commented on the dumpling of 24 the newest granddaughter-in-law, Mei Fang. "But it took you too long to make. What good is a wife who makes lovely dumplings if there's not enough to feed everyone?" Grandmother asked.

The women smirked at the acrid words—she had been equally 25 harsh to all of them when they first joined the family. Grandmother had taken her lumps, too: After she married grandfather, her mother-in-law had harassed her on the ways of making a proper dumpling. Now,

WORD POWER

acrid sharp

WORD POWER

crucible severe test

Grandmother reigned over her kitchen; it was a classroom and crucible we all endured.

"It's better that I am more strict on you girls now," she sighed. "Lest 26 you get criticized by someone else even worse than me." My mother looked over her shoulder to check on me, her only daughter, and smiled when I gave her an assuring nod.

When no one was looking, Grandmother washed a small coin and 27 hid it in one of the dumplings to be discovered by a lucky winner, who was said to be blessed with extra good fortune for the new year. Despite my best efforts, I never chanced upon it.

Working until the early hours of the next morning in the kitchen 28 brought out the juicier stories, ones laced with family secrets, scandals, gossips and tall tales, all soaked up by my youthful ears.

"Did you hear? Second uncle's daughter got a tattoo." 29

"So-and-so's sister is really her daughter." 30

By the time the echoes of popping firecrackers filled the streets sig- 31 naling the stroke of midnight, hundreds of dumplings, ready for boiling, were lined up on the kitchen sheet pans like tiny soldiers pending a final command.

With only the boiling of the dumplings left to do, the women then 32 took turns cleaning up and bathing, all the while trailing after their children and lulling them to bed. But the majority of the family didn't sleep. The custom of *shou sui*, or staying up all night to symbolize having unlimited energy for the upcoming year, was usually followed.

Around 5 a.m., the tables were set in preparation for the midmorn- 33 ing dumpling brunch. But there was no counting of bowls or chopsticks. "You're not allowed to count anything during the first day of the year," reminded Grandmother. "If you don't count anything today, then the amount of possessions you have will be countless for next year." So we grabbed chopsticks by the handfuls—some wooden, some metal, all mixed in a pile—and laid them on the table alongside stacks of blue and white porcelain bowls and plates.

Before long, the first doorbell rang, and along with it came the bois- 34 terous greetings from guests, friends and neighbors. The words *gong xi fa cai* ("congratulations and be prosperous") were audible even from inside the kitchen, and they drew out the younger girls, who were eager for their *hong bao*, or red packets. These waxy packets stuffed with money were given by elders to children as a gift, and the youngest in the house could often rack up what seemed to them a small fortune. Their flour-covered fingerprints dotted the envelopes as they calculated the year's gains.

At 9 a.m. or when the guest count reached 10—enough to fill a 35 table—we slid the dumplings into the stainless steel pot, careful not to let the boiling water splatter onto our bare toes, peeking out from house slippers. Grandmother insisted on never stirring the pot, and to ensure the dumplings wouldn't stick together, she slid a spatula through the bubbling broth just once in a pushing motion. Thrice the water came to a boil and each time we added more water. By the fourth time, the dumplings bobbed merrily on the surface. They were done.

Grandmother fished out the broken dumplings before turning to 36 Cousin Jia Yin, often the culprit, in half jest. "Ah . . . thanks to you, the dumpling soup will be especially tasty this year since you've flavored it with all the filling that busted out." The casualties were fished out and quickly disposed of; broken dumplings are considered bad luck if served. To save Jia Yin's face, her father, grandmother's second son, often said at the table, "Dumplings are great, but my favorite is still the dumpling soup," ladling up another bowl.

Guests and grandparents ate first and the two large tables in the din- 37 ing room were seated by gender. My grandfather took the head seat at one table with his friends, and my grandmother with hers at the other. After they ate, the tables were reset and the second generation took its turn, with my father and uncles at one table, my mother and aunts at the other. The third and fourth generations had less strict table assignments and took whatever empty chairs opened up—it could be two or three hours before it was our turn to eat.

Steaming plates were heaped high with dumplings still glistening 38 from their hot-water bath. Diners readied themselves with their own taste-tinkering rituals in concocting the perfect dipping sauce—a combination of soy sauce, vinegar, minced garlic and sometimes sesame oil or chili paste. Grandmother's special *la ba* vinegar, marinated with whole garlic cloves, was the most coveted condiment.

Before the first bite, everyone gathered around Grandfather, 39 who made a toast—usually with tea though sometimes he would sneak in some Chinese wine—to ring in the new year. Then, he took the first pick of the dumplings—something of an honor among the women, who held their breath in hopes that his choice of the perfect dumpling would be their own. It would have to have the ideal skin-to-filling ratio, every bite an equal portion of meat and dough, and expert craftsmanship—a balanced and symmetrical shape with firmly sealed seams.

"This one looks good to me," my grandfather decided, gently lifting 40 the plump parcel with the tips of his chopsticks. It was Grandmother's dumpling, and she stood poker-faced next to him, not revealing her triumph.

She remembered a time when her dumplings were the only ones on 41 the platter. As her family grew, so too did the styles of dumplings until the plate resembled an eclectic family tree, and each doughy pouch carried within it the cross-generational memoirs of its maker. The dumpling ritual slowly faded after Grandmother's passing in 1999; Grandfather died soon after and the family scattered. But every Chinese New Year, I still make dumplings in Grandmother's way, repeating her lessons in my head.

"Eat more! Eat more! There's magic in these dumplings," Grand- 42 mother would say. And she meant it truly.

Focus on Reading

1. Look back at the work you did when you previewed, highlighted, and annotated this essay. Now, number the major steps in the process Ma explains. (Begin with paragraph 15.)

2. In the margin beside paragraph 12, write a few words that make a connection between what Ma describes and something in your own life.

Focus on Meaning

1. What different kinds of dumpling "folding style" do the various women have? Why are these differences important?

2. What significance do dumplings have in Chinese culture? What significance do dumplings (and the dumpling-making process) have to Ma?

Focus on Strategy

1. What kind of information does Ma provide in paragraphs 1–11 (before she focuses on the process)? Why do you think she provides all this information?

2. What do paragraphs 5–10 tell you about Ma's purpose in writing this essay? About her intended audience?

Focus on Language and Style

1. At various points, Ma quotes her grandmother. What do these quotations tell you about Ma's grandmother? About Ma herself?

2. In paragraph 19, Ma describes the process of making dumplings as "a carefully orchestrated master plan"; in paragraph 20, she calls the process "tedious." Identify other descriptions of the process in this essay, and then write a single sentence that sums up Ma's view of the process.

Focus on the Pattern

1. How can you tell this is an explanation of a process rather than a set of instructions?

2. Why do you think Ma did not write this essay as a set of instructions? If it were written as instructions, what cautions or reminders might she have had to add?

Focus on Critical Thinking

1. This essay's title is "My Grandmother's Dumpling," but it also discusses other people (and other people's dumplings). Who, or what, do you think is the essay's central focus? What makes you think so? Do you think the essay should have a different title? Explain.

2. In paragraph 41, Ma refers to the dumplings on the plate as "an eclectic family tree" and says that "each doughy pouch carried within it the cross-generational memoirs of its maker." What does she mean? Do you think she is making too much of the significance of the ritual she describes? Why or why not?

focus on reading and writing

Now that you have read Amy Ma's essay, write your own process essay in response to one of the following prompts. (If you prefer, you can write on one of the additional topics listed in the box below.) Be sure to follow the writing process outlined in Chapter 3.

1. Explain the process of preparing a meal or dish that is traditional in your culture or in your family. Begin with several paragraphs of background to help readers understand what the preparation process means to you.

2. Rewrite Ma's process explanation as a set of instructions to be followed by her daughters. Remember to include any necessary cautions and reminders.

additional topics

Process

Applying for a job

A religious ritual or cultural ceremony

Your own writing process

12c Classification

When we **classify**, we sort things (individual people, items, or ideas) into categories or groups. In our daily lives, we classify when we organize bills into those we must pay immediately and those we can pay later, or when we sort clothing in a drawer into socks, T-shirts, and underwear.

Classification essays divide a whole (the subject) into parts and sort various items into categories. Each category must be **distinct**. In other words, none of the items in one category should also fit into another

Teaching Tip
See Chapter 12 in the Chapter-by-Chapter guide of the instructor's manual for the Focus on Reading and Writing prompt and additional material for teaching *classification*.

category. For example, it is not logical to classify novels into the categories *fantasy novels*, *romance novels*, and *ebooks* because fantasy and romance novels can also be ebooks.

Reading Classification Essays

When you **read** a classification essay, use TEST to help you identify its key elements. Be sure to follow the active reading process outlined in Chapter 1.

T ■ **Thesis Statement**—The introduction of a classification essay includes a **thesis statement** that communicates the essay's main idea and indicates what the essay will classify and perhaps the purpose of the classification.

E ■ **Evidence**—The body paragraphs provide **evidence**—examples and details—to support the thesis statement. The topic sentence of each paragraph identifies the category it will discuss, and the examples and details explain the category and indicate how it is different from other categories.

S ■ **Summary Statement**—The conclusion of a classification essay often includes a **summary statement** that reinforces the essay's thesis.

T ■ **Transitions**—A classification essay uses **transitional words and phrases** to show how categories are related to one another and to the thesis.

As a rule, each paragraph of a classification essay examines a separate category—a different part of the whole. For example, a paragraph could focus on one kind of course in the college curriculum, one component of the blood, or one type of student. Within each paragraph, the writer discusses the individual items that have to be put into a particular category—for example, accounting courses, red blood cells, or gifted students. If a writer considers some categories less important than others, he or she may decide to discuss those minor categories together in a single paragraph, devoting full paragraphs only to the most significant categories.

Essay Map: *One Category in Each Paragraph*

Essay Map: *Major Categories in Separate Paragraphs; Minor Categories Grouped Together*

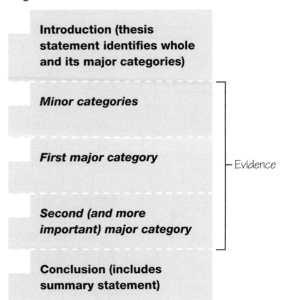

Essay Map: *One Category in Each Paragraph*

Introduction (thesis statement identifies whole and its major categories)

First category

Second category

Third category

Conclusion (includes summary statement)

— Evidence

Essay Map: *Major Categories in Separate Paragraphs; Minor Categories Grouped Together*

Introduction (thesis statement identifies whole and its major categories)

Minor categories

First major category

Second (and more important) major category

Conclusion (includes summary statement)

— Evidence

Some Transitional Words and Phrases for Classification

Transitional words and phrases signal movement from one category to the next and may also tell readers which categories are more (or less) important.

one kind . . .	the first (second,	the most important
another kind	third) category	component
the final type	the last group	the next part

Reading a Model Student Essay: Classification

The following classification essay was written by Jessica Thomas in response to this assignment in her communication course.

> What kinds of videos go viral on YouTube? Classify some of the most popular videos according to criteria such as their purpose, their intended audience, and their content.

Read Jessica's essay, following the active reading process outlined in Chapter 1, and then fill in the essay map in Practice 12 5 on pages 307-308. (Note that the TEST elements in the essay have been highlighted and color-coded.)

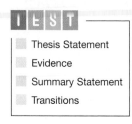

TEST

- Thesis Statement
- Evidence
- Summary Statement
- Transitions

What Kinds of Videos Go Viral?

1   Viral YouTube videos usually appear suddenly and spread quickly. Passed from friend to friend or coworker to coworker, these videos can get millions of hits in just a few months or weeks. Although many people want their videos to go viral, knowing which ones will grab people's attention is difficult. Generally, the most popular YouTube videos show viewers something they have not seen before. They also elicit a strong reaction. Essentially, YouTube videos that go viral fall into three basic categories: outrageous, funny, or inspiring.

2   The first kind of viral video shocks or amazes its viewers. Sometimes the content of these videos is extreme; sometimes, it is just plain bizarre. In any case, people have a hard time looking away. "Felix Baumgartner's Supersonic Freefall" is a good example. Millions of people around the world have viewed this skydiver's record-breaking fall and been amazed by his success. The widely shared "Facebook Parenting: For the Troubled Teen" astonishes for different reasons. This homemade film shows a father getting revenge against his disrespectful teenager by shooting her laptop with a pistol. While some viewers are impressed by this man's action and others are horrified, everyone who sees it reacts strongly. Another example is "Gangnam Style," one of the most-watched YouTube videos of all time. In this music video, Korean pop star Psy sings a catchy song and performs his crazy horse-riding dance moves. This unlikely video has attracted close to two billion viewers. Like the other videos in this category, this video succeeded by making people stare.

3   The second kind of viral video makes people laugh. The humor can come from a variety of sources. Some funny videos are simply clips from comedy shows, such as *Saturday Night Live* or *The Daily Show*. Others are amateur productions showing animals or children doing funny things. For example, in "Dragon Baby," a baby using karate moves fights a stuffed dragon. Even though the filmmaker clearly created the baby's actions

with the help of a computer, the images are hilarious. Other humorous videos use parody or slapstick. The many "Call Me Maybe" spoofs fit into this category. So does Casey Neistat's "Bike Lanes," which shows Neistat on his bike unexpectedly crashing into obstacles left in New York City bike lanes. Although Neistat made the film to protest an unfair ticket he received for not staying in the bike lane, millions of people find the video hilarious.

4   The third kind of viral video spreads because it inspires people. These videos make the audience angry, sad, or sometimes both. The most famous example of this kind of video is "Kony 2012," which reached over 97 million people in just a few months. The short documentary tells about the crimes of African militia leader Joseph Kony and what people are doing to try to stop him. In this case, the filmmaker's goal was to anger his audience and encourage action. Another example of a video that spread by grabbing people's emotions is "Never Ever Give Up: Arthur's Inspirational Transformation." In a sequence of clips, viewers watch a very determined man go from overweight and immobile to healthy and active. Other videos in this category inspire by showing speeches, often by famous people such as Oprah or Steve Jobs, who share the secrets of their success. Like "Kony 2012" and Arthur's story, these videos become immensely popular by reminding people to be grateful or by moving them to take action.

5   Although no one can predict exactly which videos will go viral, the ones that spread the most quickly attract people in three notable ways. They appeal to our curiosity, our need to laugh, or our desire to be inspired. Of course, each individual video is unique, and the next videos to sweep YouTube will surely surprise people in one respect or another. However, viral videos will continue to affect viewers in the same basic ways. And, eager to share their experiences, viewers will continue to share the links with others.

PRACTICE
12-5

Now that you have read Jessica's essay, fill in the essay map on the following page to better understand how she organized her essay. Then, decide whether her organization is effective.

Introduction _Answers will vary._ _____
_____
_____

First category _Answers will vary._ _____
_____
_____

Second category _Answers will vary._ _____
_____
_____

Third category _Answers will vary._ _____
_____
_____

Conclusion _Answers will vary._ _____
_____
_____

Writing Classification Essays

When you **write** a classification essay, you follow the process outlined in Chapter 3. The essay you write will include the same elements you have learned to recognize in the classification essays you read. When you finish your draft, you can TEST it to make sure it includes all the elements of a classification essay.

When you are given a writing assignment, the wording of your assignment may suggest that you write a classification essay. For example, you may be asked to consider *kinds, types, categories, components, segments,* or *parts of a whole.* Once you decide that your assignment calls for classification, you need to develop a thesis statement that reflects this purpose.

Teaching Tip
Tell students that many everyday writing tasks call for classification. For example, the coach of a youth sports team might write a recruitment flyer classifying player requirements by age, grade, and level of experience.

ASSIGNMENT	THESIS STATEMENT
Business What kinds of courses are most useful for students planning to run their own businesses?	Courses dealing with accounting, management, and computer science offer the most useful skills for future business owners.

Biology List the components of blood and explain the function of each.	Red blood cells, white blood cells, platelets, and plasma have distinct functions.

The following essay was written by Rob O'Neal for his first-year writing course. Read Rob's essay, and then answer the questions in Practice 12-6 on page 310.

Selling a Dream

1   The earliest automobiles were often named after the men who manufactured them—Ford, Studebaker, Nash, Olds, Chrysler, Dodge, Chevrolet, and so on. Over the years, however, American car makers began competing to see what kinds of names would sell the most cars. Many car names seem to have been chosen simply for how they sound: Alero, Corvette, Neon, Probe, Caprice. Many others, however, are designed to sell specific dreams to consumers. Americans always seem to want to be, do, and become something different. They want to be tough and brave, to explore new places, to take risks. The names auto manufacturers choose for their cars appeal to Americans' deepest desires.

2   Some American cars are named for places people dream of traveling to. Park Avenue, Malibu, Riviera, Seville, Tahoe, Yukon, Aspen, and Durango are some names that suggest escape—to New York City, California, Europe, the West. Other place names—Sebring, Daytona, and Bonneville, for example—are associated with the danger and excitement of car racing. And then there is the El Dorado, a car named for a fictional paradise: a city of gold.

3   Other car names convey rough and tough, even dangerous, images. Animal names fall into this category, with models like Ram, Bronco, and Mustang suggesting powerful, untamed beasts. The "rough and tough" category also includes car names that suggest the wildness of the Old West: Wrangler and Rodeo, for example. Because the American auto industry was originally centered near Detroit, Michigan, where many cities have Indian names, cars named for the cities where they are manufactured inherited these names. Thus, cars called Cadillac, Pontiac, and Cherokee recall the history of Indian nations, and these too might suggest the excitement of the untamed West.

4   The most interesting car names in terms of the dream they sell, however, were selected to suggest exploration and discovery. Years ago,

some car names honored real explorers, like DeSoto and LaSalle. Now, model names only sell an abstract idea. Still, American car names like Blazer, Explorer, Navigator, Journey, Mountaineer, Expedition, Caravan, and Voyager (as well as the names of foreign cars driven by many Americans, such as Nissan's Pathfinder and Quest and Honda's Passport, Pilot, and Odyssey) have the power to make drivers feel they are blazing new trails and discovering new worlds—when in fact they may simply be carpooling their children to a soccer game or commuting to work.

5   Most people take cars for granted, but manufacturers still try to make consumers believe they are buying more than just transportation. Today, however, the car is just an ordinary piece of machinery, a necessity for many people. Sadly, the automobile is no longer seen as the amazing invention it once was.

PRACTICE

12-6   1. Underline Rob's thesis statement and summary statement; then, rewrite each in your own words.

2. Is Rob's treatment of the three categories of car names similar? Does he present the same kind of information for each kind of car name? Is each category distinct from the others?

3. How do Rob's topic sentences move readers from one category to the next? How do they link the three categories?

4. Circle some of the transitional words and phrases Rob uses to move from one category to another. Are any other transitions needed? If so, where?

5. Use TEST to evaluate Rob's essay. What, if anything, does he need to revise? Why?

grammar in context

Classification

Teaching Tip
Before your students write classification essays, you might want to explain the use of the colon to introduce a list (28g).

When you write a classification essay, you may want to list the categories you are going to discuss or the examples in each category. If you do, use a **colon** to introduce your list, and make sure that a complete sentence comes before the colon.

Many car names seem to have been chosen simply for how they sound: Alero, Corvette, Neon, Probe, Caprice.

For information on how to use a colon to introduce a list, see 28g.

Integrating Reading and Writing

Now, it is time to practice what you have learned and put your reading and writing skills together. The following essay, "The Men We Carry in Our Minds," by Scott Russell Sanders, classifies the workers he has known. **Read** the essay, following the active reading process outlined in Chapter 1, and then answer the questions on pages 314–315. When you have finished, you will **write** a classification essay in response to Sanders's ideas.

THE MEN WE CARRY IN OUR MINDS
Scott Russell Sanders

Scott Russell Sanders is a Distinguished Professor Emeritus at Indiana University, a children's book author, and an essayist. His essays are often personal reflections that include social and philosophical commentary. In the classic essay "The Men We Carry in Our Minds," first published in the *Milkweed Chronicle* in 1984, Sanders reflects on the working lives of the men he knew as a boy and classifies them according to the kind of work they do. His essay discusses not only his boyhood impressions of the men's jobs but also the direction his own professional life has taken.

Before you read, think about the jobs held by men and women you know.

The first men, besides my father, I remember seeing were black convicts and white guards, in the cottonfield across the road from our farm on the outskirts of Memphis. I must have been three or four. The prisoners wore dingy gray-and-black zebra suits, heavy as canvas, sodden with sweat. Hatless, stooped, they chopped weeds in the fierce heat, row after row, breathing the acrid dust of boll-weevil poison. The overseers wore dazzling white shirts and broad shadowy hats. The oiled barrels of their shotguns flashed in the sunlight. Their faces in memory are utterly blank. Of course those men, white and black, have become for me an emblem of racial hatred. But they have also come to stand for the twin poles of my early vision of manhood—the brute toiling animal and the boss.

When I was a boy, the men I knew labored with their bodies. They were marginal farmers, just scraping by, or welders, steelworkers, carpenters; they swept floors, dug ditches, mined coal, or drove trucks, their forearms ropy with muscle; they trained horses, stoked furnaces, built tires, stood on assembly lines wrestling parts onto cars and refrigerators. They got up before light, worked all day long whatever the weather, and when they came home at night they looked as though somebody had been whipping them. In the evenings and on weekends

1

2

WORD POWER

sodden soaked with liquid or moisture

acrid bitter and unpleasant in taste or smell

overseers people who watch over the work of others

WORD POWER

tilling preparing land
for growing crops

they worked on their own places, tilling gardens that were lumpy with clay, fixing broken-down cars, hammering on houses that were always too drafty, too leaky, too small.

The bodies of the men I knew were twisted and maimed in ways 3 visible and invisible. The nails of their hands were black and split, the hands tattooed with scars. Some had lost fingers. Heavy lifting had given many of them finicky backs and guts weak from hernias. Racing against conveyor belts had given them ulcers. Their ankles and knees ached from years of standing on concrete. Anyone who had worked for long around machines was hard of hearing. They squinted, and the skin of their faces was creased like the leather of old work gloves. There were times, studying them, when I dreaded growing up. Most of them coughed, from dust or cigarettes, and most of them drank cheap wine or whiskey, so their eyes looked bloodshot and bruised. The fathers of my friends always seemed older than the mothers. Men wore out sooner. Only women lived into old age.

As a boy I also knew another sort of men, who did not sweat and 4 break down like mules. They were soldiers, and so far as I could tell they scarcely worked at all. During my early school years we lived on a military base, an arsenal in Ohio, and every day I saw GIs in the guard-shacks, on the stoops of barracks, at the wheels of olive drab Chevrolets. The chief fact of their lives was boredom. Long after I left the Arsenal I came to recognize the sour smell the soldiers gave off as that of souls in limbo. They were all waiting—for wars, for transfers, for leaves, for promotions, for the end of their hitch—like so many braves waiting for the hunt to begin. Unlike the warriors of older tribes, however, they would have no say about when the battle would start or how it would be waged. Their waiting was broken only when they practiced for war. They fired guns at targets, drove tanks across the churned-up fields of the military reservation, set off bombs in the wrecks of old fighter planes. I knew this was all play. But I also felt certain that when the hour for killing arrived, they would kill. When the real shooting started, many of them would die. This was what soldiers were *for*, just as a hammer was for driving nails.

Warriors and toilers: those seemed, in my boyhood vision, to be the 5 chief destinies for men. They weren't the only destinies, as I learned from having a few male teachers, from reading books, and from watching television. But the men on television—the politicians, the astronauts, the generals, the savvy lawyers, the philosophical doctors, the bosses who gave orders to both soldiers and laborers—seemed as removed and unreal to me as the figures in tapestries. I could no more imagine growing up to become one of these cool, potent creatures than I could imagine becoming a prince.

A nearer and more hopeful example was that of my father, who had 6 escaped from a red-dirt farm to a tire factory, and from the assembly line to the front office. Eventually he dressed in a white shirt and tie. He carried himself as if he had been born to work with his mind. But his body, remembering the earlier years of slogging work, began to give out on him in his fifties, and it quit on him entirely before he turned sixty-five. Even such a partial escape from man's fate as he had accomplished did not seem possible for most of the boys I knew. They joined the Army, stood in line for jobs in the smoky plants, helped build highways. They were bound to work as their fathers had worked, killing themselves or preparing to kill others.

A scholarship enabled me not only to attend college, a rare enough 7 feat in my circle, but even to study in a university meant for the children of the rich. Here I met for the first time young men who had assumed from birth that they would lead lives of comfort and power. And for the first time I met women who told me that men were guilty of having kept all the joys and privileges of the earth for themselves. I was baffled. What privileges? What joys? I thought about the maimed, dismal lives of most of the men back home. What had they stolen from their wives and daughters? The right to go five days a week, twelve months a year, for thirty or forty years to a steel mill or a coal mine? The right to drop bombs and die in war? The right to feel every leak in the roof, every gap in the fence, every cough in the engine, as a wound they must mend? The right to feel, when the layoff comes or the plant shuts down, not only afraid but ashamed?

I was slow to understand the deep grievances of women. This was 8 because, as a boy, I had envied them. Before college, the only people I had ever known who were interested in art or music or literature, the only ones who read books, the only ones who ever seemed to enjoy a sense of ease and grace were the mothers and daughters. Like the men-folk, they fretted about money, they scrimped and made-do. But, when the pay stopped coming in, they were not the ones who had failed. Nor did they have to go to war, and that seemed to me a blessed fact. By comparison with the narrow, ironclad days of fathers, there was an expansiveness, I thought, in the days of mothers. They went to see neighbors, to shop in town, to run errands at school, at the library, at church. No doubt, had I looked harder at their lives, I would have envied them less. It was not my fate to become a woman, so it was easier for me to see the graces. Few of them held jobs outside the home, and those who did filled thankless roles as clerks and waitresses. I didn't see, then, what a prison a house could be, since houses seemed to me brighter, handsomer places than any factory. I did not realize—because such things were never spoken of—how often women suffered from men's bullying. I did learn about the wretchedness of abandoned wives, single mothers, widows; but I also learned about the wretchedness of lone men. Even then I could see how exhausting it was for a mother to cater all day to the needs of young children. But if I had been asked, as a boy, to choose between tending a baby and tending a machine, I think I would have chosen the baby. (Having now tended both, I know I would choose the baby.)

So I was baffled when the women at college accused me and my 9
sex of having cornered the world's pleasures. I think something like my
bafflement has been felt by other boys (and by girls as well) who grew
up in dirt-poor farm country, in mining country, in black ghettos, in Hispanic barrios, in the shadows of factories, in Third World nations—any
place where the fate of men is as grim and bleak as the fate of women.
Toilers and warriors. I realize now how ancient these identities are, how
deep the tug they exert on men, the undertow of a thousand generations.
The miseries I saw, as a boy, in the lives of nearly all men I continue to
see in the lives of many—the body-breaking toil, the tedium, the call to
be tough, the humiliating powerlessness, the battle for a living and for
territory.

WORD POWER

undertow an under-
lying force or pull

When the women I met at college thought about the joys and privi- 10
leges of men, they did not carry in their minds the sort of men I had
known in my childhood. They thought of their fathers, who were bankers, physicians, architects, stockbrokers, the big wheels of the big cities.
These fathers rode the train to work or drove cars that cost more than
any of my childhood houses. They were attended from morning to night
by female helpers, wives and nurses and secretaries. They were never
laid off, never short of cash at month's end, never lined up for welfare.
These fathers made decisions that mattered. They ran the world.

The daughters of such men wanted to share in this power, this 11
glory. So did I. They yearned for a say over their future, for jobs worthy
of their abilities, for the right to live at peace, unmolested, whole. Yes,
I thought, yes yes. The difference between me and these daughters was
that they saw me, because of my sex, as destined from birth to become
like their fathers, and therefore as an enemy to their desires. But I knew
better. I wasn't an enemy, in fact or in feeling. I was an ally. If I had
known, then, how to tell them so, would they have believed me? Would
they now?

Focus on Reading

1. Look back at the work you did when you previewed, highlighted,
   and annotated this essay. **Scan** paragraphs 1 through 6, looking for
   the specific jobs held by the men Sanders knew when he was young.
   Circle those job titles.

2. Review your highlighting of paragraph 8, revising it if necessary. Now,
   write a one-sentence summary of the paragraph in the margin. Be sure
   to use your own words.

Focus on Meaning

Teaching Tip
You may have students
work collaboratively to
answer some of these
questions.

1. What two types of men did Sanders know when he was young? How
   were they different? What did they have in common?

2. What were the grievances of the women Sanders met at college? Why
   did he have trouble understanding these grievances?

Focus on Strategy

1. Sanders opens his essay with a description of "black convicts and white guards." Why?
2. This essay closes with two questions. Is this an effective closing strategy? Explain.

Focus on Language and Style

1. What connotations do the words *warriors* and *toilers* have?
2. Suggest two or three alternative pairs of names for the categories *warriors* and *toilers*. Do you think your suggestions are better than Sanders's choices? If so, why?

Focus on the Pattern

1. What kinds of men mentioned in this essay do not fit into either of the two categories Sanders identifies in paragraphs 2–4? Why don't they fit?
2. Sanders does not categorize the women he discusses. Can you think of a few categories into which these women could fit?

Focus on Critical Thinking

Who do you believe has an easier life, men or women? Why?

ESL Tip
Have native- and nonnative-speaking students work in groups or in pairs to discuss the exercises before they write their answers.

Teaching Tip
Students may need help defining words. With nonnative-speaking students, consider going over the definitions in class before assigning the reading.

Teaching Tip
Remind students to answer all questions in complete sentences.

---

focus on reading and writing

Now that you have read Scott Russell Sanders's essay, write a classification essay of your own in response to one of the following prompts. (If you prefer, you can write on one of the additional topics listed in the box below.) Be sure to follow the writing process outlined in Chapter 3.

1. Write a classification essay in which you identify and discuss three or four categories of workers (females as well as males) you observed in your community when you were growing up. In your thesis statement, draw a conclusion about the relative status and rewards of these workers' jobs.
2. Write an essay in which you categorize the workers in your current place of employment or on your college campus.

additional topics

Classification

Traits of oldest children, middle children, and youngest children

Types of teachers (or bosses)

Types of reality shows

Teaching Tip
See Chapter 12 in the
Chapter-by-Chapter guide
of the instructor's manual
for the Focus on Reading
and Writing prompt and
additional material for
teaching *definition*.

12d   Definition

During a conversation, you might say that a friend is stubborn, that a stream is polluted, or that a neighborhood is dangerous. In order to make yourself clear, you have to define what you mean by *stubborn*, *polluted*, or *dangerous*. Like conversations, academic assignments also may involve definition. In a history paper, for example, you might have to define *imperialism*; on a biology exam, you might be asked to define *mitosis*.

Definition explains the meaning of a term or concept. When most people think of definitions, they think of the kinds of definitions they see in a dictionary. These **formal definitions** have a three-part structure.

- The term to be defined
- The general class to which the term belongs
- The qualities that make the term different from all other items in the general class to which the term belongs

Teaching Tip
To help students under-
stand the concept of
definition, photocopy a
few pages from a print
dictionary. Ask each
student to choose one
noun from those pages
and to explain to the class
how the word's definition
might be expanded into
a paragraph.

TERM	CLASS	DIFFERENTIATION
Ice hockey	is a game	played on ice by two teams on skates who use curved sticks to try to hit a puck into the opponent's goal.
Spaghetti	is a pasta	made in the shape of long, thin strands.

A single-sentence definition like those above is often not enough to define a specialized term (*point of view* or *premeditation*, for example), an abstract concept (*happiness* or *success*, for example), or a complex subject (*stem-cell research*, for example). In these cases, you may need to move beyond a formal definition to a **definition essay**, which uses various patterns of development to expand a basic dictionary definition.

Reading Definition Essays

When you **read** a definition essay, use TEST to help you identify its key elements. Be sure to follow the active reading process outlined in Chapter 1.

T — **Thesis Statement**—The introduction of a definition essay includes a **thesis statement** that communicates the essay's main idea and identifies the term to be defined.

E ▪ **Evidence**—The body paragraphs include **evidence**—examples and details—that supports the thesis statement and defines the term. Body paragraphs may use different patterns of development.

S ▪ **Summary Statement**—The conclusion of a definition essay often includes a **summary statement** that reinforces the essay's thesis.

T ▪ **Transitions**—A definition essay uses **transitional words and phrases** to move readers from one section of the definition to the next.

Definition essays can be developed in various ways.

- By giving examples (exemplification)
- By telling how something occurred (narration or cause and effect)
- By describing its appearance (description)
- By telling how it is different from something else (comparison and contrast)
- By discussing its parts (classification)

Some definition essays use a single pattern of development; others combine several patterns of development, perhaps using a different pattern in each paragraph.

Essay Map: *Single Pattern of Development*

Essay Map: *Combination of Several Different Patterns of Development*

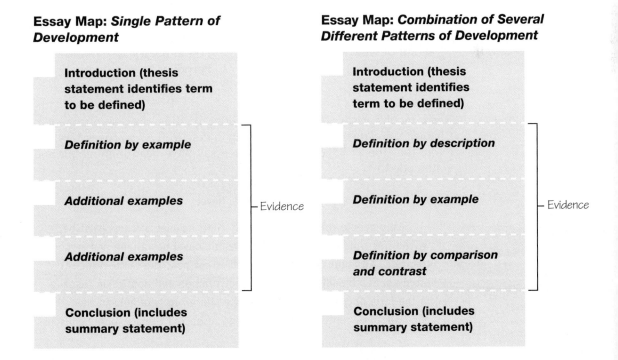

Teaching Tip

Tell students that in addition to the transitional words and expressions listed in the box here, they may also use those appropriate for the particular patterns they use to develop their definition essays. These transitions are listed in boxes throughout Chapters 7–12.

Some Transitional Words and Phrases for Definition

The kinds of transitions used in a definition essay depend on the specific pattern or patterns of development in the essay.

also	like
for example	one characteristic . . . another characteristic
in addition	one way . . . another way
in particular	specifically

Reading a Model Student Essay: Definition

The following definition essay was written by Jacob Miller in response to a question on a take-home Introduction to Literature exam. Here is the exam question.

> Define a literary movement, term, or concept that you learned about in this course. You may select a topic from the list below or a topic of your choice. Assume that your readers are not familiar with the term you are defining.

POSSIBLE TOPICS

Naturalism	The graphic novel
Imagism	The short-short story
Stream of consciousness	The ten-minute play
Point of view	Found poetry
Staging	Parody

Read Jacob's essay, following the active reading process outlined in Chapter 1, and then fill in the essay map in Practice 12-7 on pages 320–321. (Note that the TEST elements in the essay have been highlighted and color-coded.)

The Graphic Novel

1   Many people think that any story that includes pictures must be written for children. However, the graphic novel has a long and respected tradition. Although the concept itself is not new, the term—which is often applied broadly and includes both fiction and nonfiction (usually in the form of graphic memoirs)—only started to take hold in the mid-twentieth century. Now, articles in respected literary journals discuss

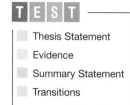

T E S T

☐ Thesis Statement
☐ Evidence
☐ Summary Statement
☐ Transitions

graphic novels, which are also taught in many college literature courses. Today, with bookstores and websites devoting entire sections to graphic novels, more people are discovering these innovative works and enjoying the invitation to participate as active readers. What they are finding is that the graphic novel is a legitimate form of imaginative literature with its own distinctive conventions, using both words and pictures to tell a complex story.

2   The most obvious characteristic of a graphic novel is the use of words and images together on the page. Each page contains panels, generally rectangles made up of individual drawings and handwritten words. However, panels can vary widely in shape, size, and number, making each page look different. Even within one book, an artist frequently varies the layout. By doing so, he is able to convey changes in mood, time, or setting. This shifting appearance of graphics is part of what draws readers in and invites them to participate. Readers not only have to imagine the untold story between each page or panel, but they also have to fill in gaps between the words and the images. Looking at either words or images alone would give the reader only fragments of the story and would fail to appreciate the hybrid nature of this literary genre.

3   Another way to define graphic novels is by recognizing how they are different from and similar to other kinds of illustrated literary works. Graphic novels are not like cartoons or comic books. First of all, graphic novels are not usually written for children; they often have sophisticated subject matter and are created for an adult audience. Second, although cartoons and comics tend to use pictures simply to illustrate their stories, the images in graphic novels are an integral part of the stories. In fact, drawings in graphic novels convey crucial information that is never explained through words; the illustrations are part of the story's narrative framework. The graphic novel is, however, similar to other forms of literature. Like writers of traditional novels, short stories, and memoirs, graphic novelists use literary devices, such as symbols and metaphors, and explore important themes. Rather than telling the reader what a story means, these writers frequently offer visual and written clues; then, they ask the readers to use their imaginations to figure out the meaning for themselves. These features qualify the graphic novel as serious literature.

4   Two recent, well-reviewed graphic novels in particular demonstrate how complex, creative, and interactive this form of literature can be. The first example, Alison Bechdel's graphic memoir *Fun Home: A Family*

Tragicomic, includes clever humor and references to classic literature. Much like writers of traditional memoirs, Bechdel also gives the audience access to her inner thoughts and questions. She treats the reader like an intimate friend and invites the audience into the unique world of her mind and memory. In this world, her drawings and her written thoughts are inseparable. Another remarkable example of the graphic novel is Chris Ware's *Building Stories*. Unique in its design, this graphic novel comes in a large flat box containing fourteen distinct pieces. Through art and writing, each piece tells part of the story. The pieces, however, can be read in any order, so in addition to filling in the gaps, the audience has to physically construct the narrative. Like Bechdel's memoir, Ware's "book" shows how graphic literature, like all great literature, invites readers to become co-inventors.

5   The graphic novel deserves recognition and should be treated not as a novelty but as serious literature. Through rich stories and creative approaches, graphic novels engage audiences. Graphic novelists do not treat their subjects in shallow or trivial ways, and readers of graphic novels are not passively entertained. On the contrary, the artists who create graphic literature frequently examine some of humanity's most difficult themes. In addition, readers of these works are active participants, using their own creativity to make sense of the story. In the years to come, the graphic novel is certain to attract more and more readers with its challenging, entertaining, and multilayered tales.

Teaching Tip
For an example of a graphic novel, refer students to the four panels from Lynda Barry's graphic memoir on page 206.

PRACTICE

12-7 Now that you have read Jacob's essay, fill in the essay map below to help you understand how he organized his essay. Then, decide whether his organization is effective.

Introduction *Answers will vary.* _____

_____

_____

- -

Definition by *Answers will vary.* _____ :

_____

_____

Definition by _Answers will vary._ :

_____

_____

Definition by _Answers will vary._ :

_____

_____

Conclusion _Answers will vary._

_____

_____

Writing Definition Essays

When you **write** a definition essay, you follow the process outlined in Chapter 3. The essay you write will include the same elements you have learned to recognize in the definition essays you read. When you finish your draft, you can **TEST** it to make sure it includes all the elements of a definition essay.

When you are given a writing assignment, the wording of your assignment may suggest that you write a definition essay. For example, you may be asked to _define_ or _explain_ or to answer the question _What is x?_ or _What does x mean?_ Once you decide that your assignment calls for definition, you need to develop a thesis statement that reflects this purpose.

ASSIGNMENT	THESIS STATEMENT
Art Explain the meaning of the term _performance art._	Unlike more conventional forms of art, _performance art_ extends beyond the canvas.
Biology What did Darwin mean by the term _natural selection?_	_Natural selection,_ popularly known as "survival of the fittest," is a good deal more complicated than most people think.

Teaching Tip
Tell students that many everyday writing tasks call for definition. For example, a letter of complaint to a neighborhood business might define terms like _excessive noise_ and _rude behavior._

The following essay was written by Kristin Whitehead in her first-year writing course. Read Kristin's essay, and then answer the questions in Practice 12-8 on page 323.

Street Smart

1   I grew up in a big city, so I was practically born street smart. I learned the hard way how to act and what to do, and so did my friends. To us, being *street smart* meant having common sense. We wanted to be cool, but we needed to be safe, too. Now I go to college in a big city, and I realize that not everyone here grew up the way I did. Many students are from suburbs or rural areas, and they are either terrified of the city or totally ignorant of city life. The few suburban or rural students who are willing to venture downtown are not street smart—but they should be. Being street smart is a vital survival skill, one that everyone should learn.

2   For me, being street smart means knowing how to protect my possessions. Friends of mine who are not used to city life insist on wearing all their jewelry when they go downtown. I think this is asking for trouble, and I know better. I always tuck my chain under my shirt and leave my gold earrings home. Another thing that surprises me is how some of my friends wave their money around. They always seem to be standing on the street, trying to count their change or stuff dollars into their wallets. Street-smart people make sure to put their money safely away in their pockets or purses before they leave a store. A street-smart person will also carry a backpack, a purse strapped across the chest, or no purse at all. A person who is not street smart carries a purse loosely over one shoulder or dangles it by its handle. Again, these people are asking for trouble.

3   Being street smart also means protecting myself. It means being aware of my surroundings at all times and looking alert. A lot of times, I have been downtown with people who kept stopping on the street to talk about where they should go next or walking up and down the same street over and over again. A street-smart person would never do this. It is important that I look as if I know where I am going at all times, even if I don't. Whenever possible, I decide on a destination in advance, and I make sure I know how to get there. Even if I am not completely sure where I am headed, I make sure my body language conveys my confidence in my ability to reach my destination.

4   Finally, being street smart means protecting my life. A street-smart person does not walk alone, especially after dark, in an unfamiliar neighborhood. A street-smart person does not ask random strangers for directions; when lost, he or she asks a shopkeeper for help. A street-smart person takes main streets instead of side streets. When faced with danger or the threat of danger, a street-smart person knows when to run, when to scream, and when to give up money or possessions to avoid violence.

5   Being street smart is vitally important—sometimes even a matter of life and death. Some people think it is a gift, but I think it is something almost anyone can learn. Probably the best way to learn how to be street smart is to hang out with people who know where they are going.

PRACTICE

12-8   1. Underline Kristin's thesis statement; then, rewrite it in your own words.

2. In your own words, define the term *street smart*. Why does this term require more than a one-sentence definition?

3. Where does Kristin use examples to develop her definition? Where does she use comparison and contrast?

4. Kristin's conclusion is somewhat shorter than her other paragraphs. Do you think she should expand this paragraph? If so, what should she add?

5. Use **TEST** to evaluate Kristin's essay. What, if anything, does she need to revise? Why?

grammar in context

Definition

When you write a definition essay, you may begin with a one-sentence definition that you expand in the rest of your essay. When you write your definition sentence, do not use the phrase *is when* or *is where*.

           means knowing
For me, being street smart is~~ is when I know~~ how to protect my
                   ^
possessions.

           means protecting
Being street smart is also ~~where I protect~~ myself.
                 ^

Teaching Tip
Before your students write definition essays, you might want to review the correct structure for a definition sentence, pointing them to the box on page 316. Depending on the particular patterns students use to develop their definitions, you can also refer them to the specific exercises noted in the Grammar in Context boxes in other sections of this chapter.

Integrating Reading and Writing

Now, it is time to practice what you have learned and put your reading and writing skills together. The following essay, "What Is a Quinceañera?" by Julia Alvarez, defines a coming-of-age ritual. **Read** the essay, following the active reading process outlined in Chapter 1, and then answer the questions on pages 326–327. When you have finished, you will **write** a definition essay in response to Alvarez's ideas.

WHAT IS A *QUINCEAÑERA*?

Julia Alvarez

Born in New York City to Dominican parents, Julia Alvarez has published numerous works of fiction and nonfiction, including poetry, children's stories, novels, and essays. One of her most famous books, *In the Time of the Butterflies* (1994), offers a fictionalized account of the tragic story of three sisters who became revolutionary leaders in the Dominican Republic under the dictatorship of Rafael Trujillo. (Alvarez's own family fled this regime in 1960.) This excerpt is from the nonfiction work *Once Upon a Quinceañera: Coming of Age in the USA* (2007).

Before you read, think about a ritual or celebration in your own life and how you might define it.

What exactly is a *quinceañera*? 1

The question might soon be rhetorical in our quickly Latinoizing 2 American culture. Already, there is a *Quinceañera* Barbie; *quinceañera* packages at Disney World and Las Vegas; an award-winning movie, *Quinceañera*; and for tots, *Dora the Explorer* has an episode about her cousin Daisy's *quinceañera*.

A *quinceañera* (the term is used interchangeably for the girl and her 3 party) celebrates a girl's passage into womanhood with an elaborate, ritualized *fiesta* on her fifteenth birthday. (*Quince años*, thus *quinceañera*, pronounced: keen-seah-gnéer-ah.) In the old countries, this was a marker birthday: after she turned fifteen, a girl could attend adult parties; she was allowed to tweeze her eyebrows, use makeup, shave her legs, wear jewelry and heels. In short, she was ready for marriage. (Legal age for marriage in many Caribbean and Latin and Central American countries is, or until recently was, fifteen or younger for females, sixteen or older for males.) Even humble families marked a girl's fifteenth birthday as special, perhaps with a cake, certainly with a gathering of family and friends at which the *quinceañera* could now socialize and dance with young men. Upper-class families, of course, threw more elaborate parties at which girls dressed up in long, formal gowns and danced waltzes with their fathers.

Somewhere along the way these fancier parties became highly ritualized. In one or another of our Latin American countries, the *quinceañera* was crowned with a tiara; her flat shoes were changed by her father to heels; she was accompanied by a court of fourteen *damas* escorted by fourteen *chambelanes*, who represented her first fourteen years; she received a last doll, marking both the end of childhood and her symbolic readiness to bear her own child. And because our countries were at least nominally Catholic, the actual party was often preceded by a Mass or a blessing in church or, at the very least, a priest was invited to give spiritual heft to the *fiesta*. These celebrations were covered in newspapers, lavish spreads of photos I remember poring over as a little girl in the Dominican Republic, reassured by this proof that the desire to be a princess did not have to be shed at the beginning of adulthood, but could in fact be played out happily to the tune of hundreds upon thousands of Papi's *pesos*.

In the late sixties, when many of our poor headed to *el Norte*'s land of opportunity, they brought this tradition along, and with growing economic power, the no-longer-so-poor could emulate the rich back home. The spin-offs grew (*quinceañera* cruises, *quinceañera* resort packages, *quinceañera* videos and photo shoots); stories of where this *quinceañera* custom had come from proliferated (an ancient Aztec tradition, an import from European courts); further elaborations were added (Disney themes, special entrances, staged dance routines à la Broadway musicals); and in our Pan-Hispanic mixing stateside, the U.S. *quinceañera* adopted all the little touches of specific countries to become a much more elaborate (and expensive) ceremony, exported back to our home countries. But rock-bottom, the U.S. *quinceañera* is powered by that age-old immigrant dream of giving the children what their parents had never been able to afford back where they came from.

In fact, the *quince* expression notwithstanding, many of us older first-generation Latinas never had a *quinceañera*. There was no money back when we were fifteen, or we had recently arrived in the United States and didn't want anything that would make us stand out as other than all-American. Or we looked down our noses at such girly-girl fuss and said we didn't want a *quince* because we didn't understand that this was not just about us.

4

5

6

WORD POWER

nominally in name only

heft significance or importance

WORD POWER

emulate try to be like or better than

proliferate to quickly increase in number or amount

These cultural celebrations are also about building community in a   7
new land. Lifted out of the context of our home cultures, traditions like
the *quinceanera* become malleable; they mix with the traditions of other
cultures that we encounter here; they become exquisite performances
of our ethnicities within the larger host culture while at the same time
reaffirming that we are not "them" by connecting us if only in spirit to
our root cultures. In other words, this tradition tells a larger story of our
transformation into Latinos, a Pan-Hispanic group made in the USA,
now being touted as the "new Americans."

WORD POWER

touted promoted

Focus on Reading

1. Look back at the work you did when you previewed, highlighted,
   and annotated this essay. If you have not already done so, underline the formal (dictionary) definition of *quinceañera* that
   Alvarez includes. In the margin, rewrite this definition in your
   own words.

2. Circle all the Spanish words Alvarez uses. If any of them are not
   familiar to you, look them up, and then write a brief definition of
   each word in the margin.

Focus on Meaning

Teaching Tip
You may have students
work collaboratively to
answer some of these
questions.

1. In paragraph 5, Alvarez explains how the *quinceañera* grew and
   changed as Latino families settled in the United States. What is
   her attitude toward these changes? For example, does she seem
   to suggest that they have somehow lessened the meaning of the
   ritual?

2. According to Alvarez, what is the value of the *quinceañera* for Latinas? For the culture of which they are a part?

Focus on Strategy

ESL Tip
Have native- and
nonnative-speaking
students work in groups
or in pairs to discuss the
exercises before they
write their answers.

1. Alvarez opens her essay with a one-sentence paragraph that asks the
   question, "What exactly is a *quinceañera*?" What are the advantages
   and disadvantages of this opening strategy?

2. Do you think Alvarez expects her readers to be familiar with the
   term she is defining? How can you tell? What does your answer tell
   you about her intended audience and purpose?

Focus on Language and Style

Teaching Tip
Remind students to
answer all questions in
complete sentences.

1. Alvarez uses a number of Spanish words other than *quinceañera* in
   this essay, but she does not define them. Do you think she should
   have? Why or why not?

2. In paragraph 4, Alvarez observes that the *quinceañera* has become
   "highly ritualized." What does the word *ritualized* mean in this context? Is it a positive, negative, or neutral term?

Focus on the Pattern

1. Where does Alvarez give information about the origin of the term *quinceañera*?
2. Where does Alvarez develop her definition with examples? Where does she use description? Does she use any other patterns of development?

Focus on Critical Thinking

At different points in her essay, Alvarez sees the *quinceañera* as a "passage into womanhood" (paragraph 3), a traditional religious celebration (4), a way of "building community in a new land" (7), and the realization of an "age-old immigrant dream" (5). Which of these different impressions does her definition communicate most strongly? Explain.

focus on reading and writing

Now that you have read Julia Alvarez's essay, write your own definition essay in response to one of the following prompts. (If you prefer, you can write on one of the additional topics listed in the box below.) Be sure to follow the writing process outlined in Chapter 3.

1. Write an essay defining a coming-of-age ritual that is significant in your own community, culture, or religion. Assume that your readers are not familiar with the ritual you are defining, and develop your definition with **exemplification** and **description**. (You can also use **comparison and contrast** if you think explaining your ritual by showing how it is like a more familiar practice will be helpful to your readers.)
2. Write an essay defining a coming-of-age ritual with which you are familiar. Develop your definition primarily through **narration**— by telling the story of your own introduction to this ritual.

additional topics

Definition

The American Dream

Procrastination

Success

unit
3 Research

13 Working with Sources 331

13 Working with Sources

13a Finding and Evaluating Sources

When you write, you can sometimes use your own ideas and observations to support your points. At many other times, however, you have to move beyond your own experience and support your points with information you find either in the library or on the Internet. In other words, you have to do **research**. Although the idea of research can be intimidating, it shouldn't be. When you carry out research, all you are doing is looking at what other people who have thought long and hard about your subject have to say about it. By doing research, you build on what you already know about a subject as you react to what you read.

When most students do research, they go straight to the Internet and do a Google search. In some cases—for example, for a short, informal essay—this may be fine. If you do this regularly, however—especially for longer assignments—you ignore a valuable resource: your college library. Your library gives you access to many important resources—for example, books, journals, and electronic databases—that are available nowhere else, including on the Internet. For this reason, when you do research, you should use your college library as well as the Internet.

Finding Information in the Library

For the best results, you should do your library research systematically. Once you get a sense of your topic, you should consult the library's **online catalog**—a comprehensive information system that gives you access to the resources housed in the library. The online catalog is not as "open" as the Internet, where anything and everything is posted. Library resources have been screened by librarians (as well as instructors) and, in many cases, are written by experts in a particular field and conform to academic standards of reliability.

You search the online catalog just as you would search the Internet: by carrying out a *keyword search* or a *subject search*. You do a **keyword search** the same way you would search using Google or About.com—by entering your keywords in a search box to retrieve a list of books, periodicals, and other materials that are relevant to your topic. The more specific your keywords, the more focused your search will be. Thus, the keywords *Facebook privacy* will yield more specific (and useful) results than *social networking*.

Teaching Tip
If your college library offers tours, encourage students to take one to familiarize themselves with the library's resources.

You do a **subject search** by entering a subject heading related to your topic. Unlike keywords, subject headings are predetermined and come from a list of subject headings published by the Library of Congress. Many online catalogs provide lists of subject headings that you can use. A subject search is best when you want information about a general topic—for example, *rap music*, *discography*, or *Mark Twain*.

After consulting the online catalog, you should look at the **electronic databases**—such as InfoTrac and ProQuest—that your college library subscribes to. These databases enable you to obtain information from newspapers, magazines, and journals that you often cannot access by doing a web search. Most of the library's electronic databases enable you to retrieve the full text of articles. (You can usually search them remotely, from home or from anywhere on campus.)

Most online catalogs list the databases to which the library subscribes along with descriptions of the type of material the databases contain. For example, a database may contain articles on a wide variety of subjects, or it may focus on a specific subject area.

Evaluating Library Sources

In general, the sources in library databases are more reliable than the sources you access on the Internet. Even so, you should still **evaluate** them—that is, determine their usefulness and reliability—before you use them in your paper. For example, an article in a respected periodical, such as the *New York Times* or the *Wall Street Journal*, is more trustworthy and credible than one in a tabloid, such as the *National Enquirer* or the *Sun*. You should also look at the date of publication to decide if the book or periodical is up-to-date. Finally, consider the author. Is he or she an expert? Does the author have a particular point of view to advance? Your instructor or college librarian can help you select sources that are both appropriate and reliable.

WORD POWER

tabloid a newspaper that emphasizes stories with sensational content

Finding Information on the Internet

Teaching Tip
At the start of the semester, assess your students' levels of computer skills and Internet expertise.

The Internet can give you access to a great deal of information that can help you support your ideas and develop your essay. However, you have to be extremely careful when using the Internet because it is an "open" source; anyone can create a website and upload material. Unlike the resources available in your college library, the resources available on the Internet have not been screened; no one is responsible for checking the accuracy of information or the credentials of people who post on the Internet. For this reason, it is your responsibility (and obligation) to determine the trustworthiness of an Internet source and to decide whether it is credible (believable).

Once you are online, you need to connect to a **search engine**, which helps you find information by sorting through the millions of documents that are available on the Internet. Among the most popular search engines are Google, Yahoo!, and Bing.

There are two ways to use a search engine to access information.

1. *You can do a keyword search.* All search engines let you do a keyword search. You type a term (or terms) into a box, and the search engine looks for documents that contain the term, listing all the hits that it finds.
2. *You can do a subject search.* Search engines such as About.com and Yahoo! let you do a subject search. First, you choose a broad subject from a list: *Humanities, Arts, Entertainment, Business,* and so on. Each of these general subjects then leads you to more specific subjects, until eventually you get to the subtopic that you want.

Evaluating Internet Sources

Just as you would with library sources, you should determine whether information you find on the Internet is credible and useful. With the Internet, however, you have problems that you generally don't have with the sources available in your college library. Because anyone can publish on the Internet, it is often difficult—if not impossible—to determine, let alone judge, the credentials of an author or the accuracy of his or her claims. To make matters worse, sources sometimes have no listed author. Dates can also be missing, so it may be difficult to tell when information was originally posted and when it was updated. Finally, it is often hard to determine if a site has a purpose other than providing information. For example, is the site trying to sell something or advance a political or social agenda? If it is, it may contain information that is biased or even incorrect.

You can evaluate Internet sources by asking some basic questions.

- *Who is the author of the site?* Avoid information from unnamed authors or from authors with questionable credentials.
- *Who is the sponsoring organization?* Be especially careful of using information from websites sponsored by companies selling something or organizations that have a particular agenda.
- *Can you verify information posted on the site?* Make sure you are able to check the source of the information. For example, you should make sure an article on a site includes documentation. Also, cross-check information you find on the site. Does the same information appear in other sources that are reliable?

Teaching Tip
Tell students that it is a good idea to bookmark useful sites by selecting the Bookmark or Favorites option at the top of their Internet browser's screen. Once they bookmark a site, they can easily return to it.

Teaching Tip
Direct students to 5e for tips on identifying bias in a piece of writing.

Teaching Tip
Point out that a URL can give information about the site's purpose. For example, the abbreviation *.edu* indicates that the site is sponsored by an educational institution, *.gov* indicates a government agency, *.org* indicates a nonprofit organization, and *.com* indicates a business.

- *Does the site contain errors?* In addition to factual errors, look out for mistakes in grammar or spelling. Errors such as these should raise a red flag about the accuracy of the information on the site you are visiting.

- *Do the links on the site work?* Make sure that the links on the site are "live." The presence of "dead" links is a good indication that a site is not being properly maintained.

- *Is the information up-to-date?* Make sure the site's information is current. Avoid sites that contain information that is outdated. A reliable site will usually include the date information was posted and the date it was revised.

When in doubt, check with a reference librarian or with your instructor. Unless you can be certain that a site is reliable, do not use it as a source.

FYI

Using Wikipedia as a Source

Most college students regularly consult Wikipedia, the open-source online encyclopedia. The rationale behind Wikipedia is that if a large number of people review information, errors will eventually be discovered and corrected. Because there are no full-time editors, however, Wikipedia articles can (and do) contain inaccurate as well as biased information. In addition, anyone—not just experts—can write and edit entries. Understandably, some instructors distrust—or at least question—the accuracy of Wikipedia entries. Be sure to check the accuracy of the information you find in Wikipedia by comparing it to the information in other sources you are using. (Keep in mind that many instructors do not consider articles from any encyclopedia—print or electronic—acceptable for college research.)

13b Using Sources in Your Writing

Teaching Tip
Point out that students should record full publication information (including page numbers) for all material they photocopy or download. They will need this information when they document their sources.

Once you have gathered the source material you will need, read it carefully, recording any information you think you can use. (You can record your notes either in computer files or on index cards.)

Remember that taking notes involves more than just copying down or downloading information. As you record information, you should put it into a form that you can use when you write your paper. For this reason, you should always *paraphrase*, *summarize*, or *quote* relevant information from your sources.

FYI

Avoiding Plagiarism

When you transfer information from websites into your notes, you may carelessly copy and paste text without recording where the material came from. If you then paste this material into your paper without citing the source, you are committing **plagiarism**—stealing someone else's ideas. Also keep in mind that you must document *all* material that you get from the Internet, just as you document material that you get from print sources. For information on documenting, see 13d. For information on plagiarism, see 13c.

ESL Tip
Spend time showing ESL students examples of plagiarism. They usually have difficulty distinguishing between paraphrased work and plagiarized work.

Paraphrasing

When you **paraphrase**, you use your own words to convey a source's key ideas. You paraphrase when you want to include detailed information from the source but not the author's exact words. Paraphrasing is useful when you want to make a difficult discussion easier to understand while still presenting a comprehensive overview of the original.

Writing a Paraphrase

1. Read the passage until you understand it.
2. Identify the main idea of the passage, and list key supporting points.
3. Draft your paraphrase, beginning with the source's main idea and then presenting the source's most important supporting points.
4. When you revise, check to make sure you have used your own words and phrasing, and not the words or sentence structure of the original. Use quotation marks to identify any unique or memorable phrases that you have borrowed from the source.
5. Document your source.

Here is a passage from the article "Hot Fakes," by Joanie Cox, followed by a student's paraphrase.

ORIGINAL

Always pay close attention to the stitching. On a Kate Spade bag, the logo is stitched perfectly straight; it's not a sticker. Most designers stitch a simple label to the inside of their purses. On Chanel bags,

Teaching Tip
Remind students that they should read a passage several times and then put it aside before trying to paraphrase it. Looking at the material as they write is likely to lead to plagiarism.

Teaching Tip
Explain that Internet sources often do not contain page numbers. For this reason, parenthetical documentation of Internet sources may consist of just the author's last name (or, if no author is given, the shortened title of the article).

however, the interior label is usually stamped and tends to match the color of the exterior. Study the material the bag is made from. A real Chanel Ligne Cambon multipocket bag, for example, is constructed from buttery lambskin leather, not vinyl.

PARAPHRASE

It is often possible to tell a fake designer handbag from a genuine one by looking at the details. For example, items such as logos should not be crooked. You should also look for the distinctive features of a particular brand of handbag. Counterfeiters will not take the time to match colors, and they may use vinyl instead of expensive leather (Cox).

Note that this paraphrase doesn't simply change a word here and there. Instead, the student has taken the time to fully understand the main idea and supporting points of the passage and has restated ideas in her own words.

Summarizing

Teaching Tip
Remind students that in a paraphrase or summary, they present only the source's ideas, not their own ideas or opinions about the source.

Unlike a paraphrase, which presents the key points of a source in detail, a **summary** is a general restatement, in your own words, of just the main idea of a passage. For this reason, a summary is always much shorter than the original.

Writing a Summary

1. Read the passage until you understand it.
2. Identify the main idea of the passage.
3. Draft your summary, making sure you use your own words, not those of your source.
4. When you revise, check to make sure your summary contains only the ideas of the source, not your own opinions or interpretations.
5. Document your source.

Here is a student's summary of the original passage on pages 335–336.

SUMMARY

Buyers who want to identify fake handbags should check details such as the way the label is sewn and the material the item is made from (Cox).

Quoting

When you **quote**, you use the author's exact words as they appear in the source, including all punctuation and capitalization. Enclose all words from your source in quotation marks—*followed by appropriate documentation.* Because quotations can distract readers, use them only when you think that the author's exact words will add something to your discussion.

Teaching Tip
Make sure that you reinforce to students the importance of documenting not just quoted material but also any ideas that they borrow from their sources.

When to Quote

1. Quote when the words of a source are so memorable that to put them into your own words would lessen their impact.

2. Quote when the words of a source are so precise that a paraphrase or summary would change the meaning of the original.

3. Quote when the words of a source add authority to your discussion. The exact words of a recognized expert can help you make your point convincingly.

Here is how a student writer incorporated a quotation from the original passage on pages 335–336 into her notes.

QUOTATION

Someone who wants to buy an authentic designer handbag should look carefully at the material the purse is made from. For example, there is a big difference between vinyl and Chanel's "buttery lambskin leather" (Cox).

Working Sources into Your Writing

When you use material from a source, you don't simply drop it into your paper. To show readers why you are using a source and to help you integrate source material smoothly into your essay, introduce paraphrases, summaries, and quotations with **identifying tags**, phrases that name the source or its author. You can position an identifying tag at various places in a sentence.

As one celebrity fashion columnist points out, "A real Chanel Ligne Cambon multipocket bag, for example, is constructed from buttery lambskin leather, not vinyl" (Cox).

"A real Chanel Ligne Cambon multipocket bag, for example," says one celebrity fashion columnist, "is constructed from buttery lambskin leather, not vinyl" (Cox).

"A real Chanel Ligne Cambon multipocket bag, for example, is constructed from buttery lambskin leather, not vinyl," observes one celebrity fashion columnist (Cox).

FYI

Identifying Sources

Instead of repeating the word *says,* you can use one of the words or phrases below to identify the source of a quotation, paraphrase, or summary.

admits	concludes	points out
believes	explains	remarks
claims	notes	states
comments	observes	suggests

Synthesizing

When you **synthesize**, you combine ideas from two or more sources with your own ideas. The goal of a synthesis is to use sources to develop your own point about a topic. In a synthesis, then, your own ideas, not those of your sources, should dominate the discussion. In a sense, every time you weave together paraphrase, summary, and quotation to support a point, you are writing a synthesis.

Writing a Synthesis

1. Decide on the point you want to develop.
2. Select at least two or three sources to support your point.
3. Read each source carefully, noting of how they are alike, how they are different, and how they relate to your point.
4. Begin drafting your synthesis by clearly stating the point you are going to develop.
5. Use specific examples (paraphrases, summaries, and quotations) from your sources to support your point.
6. When you revise, make sure that you have used appropriate transitions to indicate the movement from one source to another. Also be sure that you have clearly identified each source that you discuss.
7. Document all words and ideas that you take from your sources.

Here is a paragraph from a student's research paper in which she incorporates material from three different sources. (You can read the full paper on pages 348–351.) Notice how she uses source material (underlined) to develop her point that buying counterfeit items is really stealing.

What most people choose to ignore is that buying counterfeit items is stealing. Between 2002 and 2012, 325 percent more counterfeit goods were seized than in the previous decade (O'Donnell 03b). The FBI estimates that in the United States alone, companies lose about $250 billion as a result of counterfeits (Wallace). In addition, buyers of counterfeit items avoid the state and local sales taxes that legitimate companies pay. Thus, New York City alone loses about a billion dollars every year as a result of the sale of counterfeit merchandise ("Counterfeit Goods"). When this happens, everyone loses. After all, a billion dollars would pay for a lot of police officers and teachers, would fill a lot of potholes, and would pave a lot of streets. Even though buyers of counterfeit designer goods do not think of themselves as thieves, that is exactly what they are.

13c   Avoiding Plagiarism

As a rule, you must **document** (give source information for) all words, ideas, or statistics from an outside source. You must also document all visuals—tables, graphs, photographs, and so on—that you do not create yourself. (It is not necessary, however, to document **common knowledge**, factual information widely available in reference works.)

When you present information from another source as if it is your own (whether you do it intentionally or unintentionally), you commit **plagiarism**—and plagiarism is theft. Although most plagiarism is accidental, the penalties can still be severe. You can avoid plagiarism by understanding what you must document and what you do not have to document.

ESL Tip
Ask students whether any culture with which they are familiar defines plagiarism differently. Make sure students understand that in American culture, plagiarism is not acceptable.

FYI

What to Document

You should document

- All quotations from a source
- All summaries and paraphrases of source material
- All ideas—opinions, judgments, and insights—of others
- All tables, graphs, charts, and statistics from a source

You do not need to document

- Your own ideas
- Common knowledge
- Familiar quotations

Teaching Tip
Remind students to keep track of material that they download from the Internet. Caution them not to accidentally commit plagiarism by copying and pasting such information into papers without identifying it as quoted material.

Read the following paragraph from "The Facts on Fakes!," an article by Adele R. Meyer, and the four guidelines that follow it. This material will help you understand the most common causes of plagiarism and show you how to avoid it.

ORIGINAL

Is imitation really the sincerest form of flattery? Counterfeiting deceives the consumer and tarnishes the reputation of the genuine manufacturer. Brand value can be destroyed when a trademark is imposed on counterfeit products of inferior quality—hardly a form of flattery! Therefore, prestigious companies who are the targets of counterfeiters have begun to battle an industry that copies and sells their merchandise. They have filed lawsuits and in some cases have employed private investigators across the nation to combat the counterfeit trade. A quick search of the Internet brings up dozens of press releases from newspapers throughout the country, all reporting instances of law enforcement cracking down on sellers of counterfeit goods by confiscating bogus merchandise and imposing fines.

Teaching Tip
Tell students that the documentation for Adele Meyer's "The Facts on Fakes!" contains no page numbers because Meyer's article appeared on a website that has no page or paragraph numbers. In this case, only the author's name is included.

Guideline 1. Document Ideas from Your Sources

PLAGIARISM

When counterfeits are sold, the original manufacturer does not take it as a compliment.

Even though the student writer does not quote her source directly, she must identify the article as the source of this material because it expresses the article's ideas, not her own.

CORRECT

When counterfeits are sold, the original manufacturer does not take it as a compliment (Meyer).

Guideline 2. Place Borrowed Words in Quotation Marks

PLAGIARISM

It is possible to ruin the worth of a brand by selling counterfeit products of inferior quality—hardly a form of flattery (Meyer).

Although the student writer cites the source, the passage incorrectly uses the source's exact words without quoting them. She must quote the borrowed words.

CORRECT (BORROWED WORDS IN QUOTATION MARKS)

It is possible to ruin the worth of a brand by selling "counterfeit products of inferior quality   hardly a form of flattery" (Meyer).

Guideline 3. Use Your Own Phrasing

PLAGIARISM

Is copying a design a compliment? Not at all. The fake design not only tries to fool the buyer but also harms the original company. It can ruin the worth of a brand. Because counterfeits are usually of poor quality, they pay the original no compliment. As a result, companies whose products are often copied have started to fight back. They have sued the counterfeiters and have even used private detectives to identify phony goods. Throughout the United States, police have fined people who sell counterfeits and have seized their products (Meyer).

Even though the student writer acknowledges Meyer as her source, and even though she does not use the source's exact words, her passage closely follows the order, emphasis, sentence structure, and phrasing of the original.

In the following passage, the student writer uses her own wording, quoting one distinctive phrase from the source.

CORRECT

According to "The Facts on Fakes!," it is not a compliment when an original design is copied by a counterfeiter. The poor quality of most fakes is "hardly a form of flattery." The harm to the image of the original manufacturers has caused them to fight back against the counterfeiters, sometimes using their own detectives. As a result, lawsuits and criminal charges have led to fines and confiscated merchandise (Meyer).

Note: The quotation does not require separate documentation because the identifying tag According to "The Facts on Fakes!" makes it clear that all the borrowed material in the passage is from the same source.

Guideline 4. Distinguish Your Ideas from the Source's Ideas

PLAGIARISM

Counterfeit goods are not harmless. Counterfeiting not only fools the consumer, but it also destroys confidence in the quality of the real thing. Manufacturers know this and have begun to fight back. A number have begun to sue "and in some cases have employed private investigators across the nation to combat the counterfeit trade" (Meyer).

In the passage above, it appears that only the quotation in the last sentence is borrowed from the article by Meyer. In fact, however, the ideas in the second sentence also come from Meyer's article.

In the following passage, the student writer uses an identifying tag to acknowledge the borrowed material in the second sentence.

CORRECT

Counterfeit goods are not harmless. According to the article "The Facts on Fakes!," counterfeiting not only fools the consumer, but it also destroys confidence in the quality of the real thing. Manufacturers know this and have begun to fight back. A number have begun to sue "and in some cases have employed private investigators across the nation to combat the counterfeit trade" (Meyer).

13d Documenting Sources

Whenever you use information from a source, you have to **document** it— that is, you need to indicate to readers where you found it. By doing this, you identify your source and you enable readers to locate the information you use. Because conventions differ from discipline to discipline, there is no single documentation style that you can use in all of your courses. For this reason, you should ask your instructors what formats they require. Two of the most widely used documentation styles are those recommended by the Modern Language Association (MLA), preferred in the humanities, and the American Psychological Association (APA), preferred in the social sciences.

MLA Documentation Style

Parenthetical References in the Text

A parenthetical reference should include enough information to lead readers to a specific entry in your works-cited list. A typical parenthetical reference consists of the author's last name and the page number (Brown 2). Notice that there is no comma and no *p* or *p*. before the page number.

Whenever possible, introduce information from a source with a phrase that includes the author's name. (If you do this, include only the page number in parentheses.) Place documentation so that it does not interrupt the flow of your ideas, preferably at the end of a sentence.

As Jonathan Brown observes in "Demand for Fake Designer Goods Is Soaring," as many as 70 percent of buyers of luxury goods are willing to wear designer brands alongside fakes (2).

FYI

Formatting Quotations

1. **Short quotations**   Quotations of less than four typed lines are inserted into the text of your paper. End punctuation comes after the parenthetical reference (which follows the quotation marks).

   According to Dana Thomas, customers often "pick up knockoffs for one-tenth the legitimate bag's retail cost, then pass them off as real" (A23).

2. **Long quotations**   Quotations of more than four lines are set off from the text of your paper. Begin a long quotation on a new line, indented one inch from the left-hand margin, and do not enclose it in quotation marks. Do not indent the first line of a single paragraph. If a quoted passage has more than one paragraph, indent the first line of each paragraph (including the first) an extra one-quarter inch. Introduce a long quotation with a complete sentence followed by a colon, and place the parenthetical reference one space *after* the end punctuation. Double-space the text throughout.

   The editorial "Terror's Purse Strings" describes a surprise visit to a factory that makes counterfeit purses:

   > On a warm winter afternoon in Guangzhao, I accompanied Chinese police officers on a raid in a decrepit tenement. We found two dozen children, ages 8 to 13, gluing and sewing together fake luxury-brand handbags. The police confiscated everything, arrested the owner and sent the children out. Some punched their timecards, hoping to still get paid. (Thomas A23)

Here are specific guidelines for four special situations.

1. CITING A WORK BY TWO AUTHORS

   Instead of buying nonbranded items of similar quality, many customers are willing to pay extra for the counterfeit designer label (Grossman and Shapiro 79).

2. CITING A WORK WITHOUT PAGE NUMBERS

   A seller of counterfeited goods in California "now faces 10 years in prison and $20,000 in fines" (Cox).

3. CITING A WORK WITHOUT A LISTED AUTHOR OR PAGE NUMBERS

   More counterfeit goods come from China than from any other country ("Counterfeit Goods").

4. CITING A STATEMENT BY ONE AUTHOR THAT IS QUOTED IN A WORK BY ANOTHER AUTHOR

Speaking of consumers' buying habits, designer Miuccia Prada says, "There is a kind of an obsession with bags" (qtd. in Thomas A23).

The Works-Cited List

The works-cited list includes all the works you **cite** (refer to) in your essay. Use the guidelines in the box on page 347 to help you prepare your list.

The following sample works-cited entries cover the situations you will encounter most often.

Periodicals

JOURNALS

When citing an article from a journal, include the journal's volume number and issue number, separating the two numbers by a period, with no space after the period. Then, include the date of publication in parentheses, followed by a colon and the page numbers (if there are any). Give the medium of publication, such as Print or Web. Before the medium, include the italicized name of the online database (such as Academic Search Premier) if you used one to find the source. For all web sources, add the date you accessed the source.

Article in a Print Journal

Gioia, Dana. "Robert Frost and the Modern Narrative." *Virginia Quarterly Review* 89.2 (2013): 185–93. Print.

Article in a Journal Accessed through an Online Database

Wineapple, Brenda. "Ladies Last." *American Scholar* 82.3 (2013): 28–38. *MasterFILEPremier*. Web. 17 Feb. 2014.

MAGAZINES

Include the complete date of publication and page numbers. Frequently, an article in a magazine is not printed on consecutive pages. For example, it may begin on page 40, skip to page 47, and continue on page 49. If this is the case, your citation should include only the first page, followed by a plus sign. Include the medium of publication.

Article in a Print Magazine

Poniewozik, James. "Why I Watch Reality TV with My Kids." *Time* 17 June 2013: 54–55. Print.

Article in a Magazine Accessed through an Online Database

Dobb, Edwin. "The New Oil Landscape." *National Geographic* Mar. 2013: 28–59. *Academic Search Premier*. Web. 7 Aug. 2014.

NEWSPAPERS

List page numbers, section numbers, and any special edition information (such as late ed.) as provided by the source. If the article falls into a
special category, such as an editorial, letter to the editor, or review, add
this label to your entry, after the title.

Article in a Print Newspaper

> Shah, Neil. "More Young Adults Live with Parents." *Wall Street Journal* 28
> Aug. 2013: A2. Print.

Article from a Newspaper Accessed through an Online Database

> Marklein, Mary Beth. "'Caution! Student Loans Must Be Paid Back!'" *USA
> Today* 26 Aug. 2013, sec. A: 04. *National Newspaper Index*. Web.
> 9 Mar. 2014.

Books

Books by One Author

List the author, last name first. Italicize the book's title. Include the city
of publication and a shortened form of the publisher's name—for example, *Bedford* for *Bedford/St. Martin's*. Use the abbreviation *UP* for *University Press*, as in *Princeton UP* and *U of Chicago P*. Include the date of
publication. End with the medium of publication.

> Mantel, Hilary. *Bring up the Bodies*. New York: Holt, 2012. Print.

Teaching Tip
Remind students that an
entry with no listed author
begins with the title. The
remaining parts of the
entry follow in normal
order.

Books by Two or More Authors

For books with more than one author, list second and subsequent
authors with first name first, in the order in which they are listed on the
book's title page.

> Mooney, Chris, and Sheril Kirshenbaum. *Unscientific America: How
> Scientific Illiteracy Threatens Our Future*. New York: Basic, 2009. Print.

For books with more than three authors, you may list only the first
author, followed by the abbreviation *et al*. ("and others").

Two or More Books by the Same Author

List two or more books by the same author in alphabetical order according to title. In each entry after the first, use three unspaced hyphens
(followed by a period) instead of the author's name.

> Eggers, Dave. *The Circle*. New York: Random, 2013. Print.
> ---. *A Hologram for the King*. San Francisco: McSweeney's, 2012. Print.

Teaching Tip
Tell students that when
the abbreviation *ed.*
comes *after* a name, it
means "editor" (*eds.*
means "editors"). When
the abbreviation *Ed.*
comes *before* one or
more names, it means
"edited by."

Edited Book

Austen, Jane. *Persuasion: An Annotated Edition.* Ed. Robert Morrison.
Cambridge: Belknap-Harvard UP, 2011. Print.

Anthology

Adler, Frances P., Debra Busman, and Diana Garcia, eds. *Fire and Ink:
An Anthology of Social Action Writing.* Tucson: U of Arizona P, 2009.
Print.

Essay in an Anthology or Chapter of a Book

Weise, Matthew J. "How the Zombie Changed Videogames." *Zombies Are Us:
Essays on the Humanity of the Walking Dead.* Ed. Christopher M.
Moreman and Cory James Rushton. Jefferson: McFarland, 2011.
151–68. Print.

Internet Sources

Full source information is not always available for Internet sources.
For this reason, when citing Internet sources, include whatever information you can find—ideally, the name of the author (or authors), the
title of the article or other document (in quotation marks), the title of
the site (italicized), the sponsor or publisher, the date of publication
or last update, and the date on which you accessed the source. Include
the medium of publication (Web) between the publication date and the
access date.

It is not necessary to include a web address (URL) when citing an electronic source. However, you should include a URL (in angle brackets) if
your instructor requires it or if you think readers might not be able to locate
the source without it (see the "Personal Site" entry below).

Teaching Tip
Refer students to a
handbook for additional
models.

Article in an Online Periodical

Wilbon, Michael. "The 'One and Done' Song and Dance." *Washington
Post.* The Washington Post Company, 25 June 2009. Web. 1 Sept.
2013.

Document within a Website

Robbins, Michael. "Reimagining Education through Summer Learning
Partnerships." *ED.gov.* U.S. Department of Education, 26 Aug. 2013.
Web. 15 Jan. 2014.

Personal Site

Heffernan, Margaret. Home page. Margaret Heffernan, 7 July 2014. Web.
10 July 2014. <www.mheffernan.com>.

Preparing the Works-Cited List

- Begin the works-cited list on a new page after the last page of your paper.
- Number the works-cited page as the next page of your paper.
- Center the heading Works Cited one inch from the top of the page; do not italicize the heading or place it in quotation marks.
- Double-space the list.
- List entries alphabetically according to the author's last name.
- Alphabetize unsigned articles according to the first major word of the title.
- Begin typing each entry at the left-hand margin.
- Indent second and subsequent lines of each entry one-half inch.
- Separate major divisions of each entry—author, title, and publication information—by a period and one space.

Sample MLA-Style Paper

On the pages that follow is a student's essay on the topic of counterfeit designer goods. The paper uses MLA documentation style and includes a works-cited page. It has been annotated to show you the proper formatting and elements of a research paper.

Compton 1

May Compton
Professor DiSalvo
English 100
29 Apr. 2014

The True Price of Counterfeit Goods

At purse parties in city apartments and suburban homes, customers can buy "designer" handbags at impossibly low prices. On street corners, sidewalk vendors sell name-brand perfumes and sunglasses for much less than their list prices. On the Internet, buyers can buy luxury watches for a fraction of the prices charged by manufacturers. Is this too good to be true? Of course it is. All of these "bargains" are knockoffs—counterfeit copies of the real thing. What the people who buy these items do not know (or prefer not to think about) is that the money they are spending supports organized crime—and, sometimes, terrorism. For this reason, people should not buy counterfeit designer merchandise, no matter how tempted they are to do so.

People who buy counterfeit designer merchandise defend their actions by saying that designer products are expensive. This is certainly true. According to Dana Thomas, the manufacturers of genuine designer merchandise charge more than ten times what it costs to make it (A23). A visitor from Britain, who bought an imitation Gucci purse in New York City for fifty dollars, said, "The real thing is so overpriced. To buy a genuine Gucci purse, I would have to pay over a thousand dollars" (qtd. in "Counterfeit Goods"). Even people who can easily afford to pay the full amount buy fakes. For example, movie stars like Jennifer Lopez openly wear counterfeit goods, and many customers think that if it is all right for celebrities like Lopez to buy fakes, it is all right for them too (Malone). However, as the well-known designer Giorgio Armani points out, counterfeiters create a number of problems for legitimate companies because they use the brand name but do not maintain quality control.

What most people choose to ignore is that buying counterfeit items is stealing. Between 2002 and 2012, 325 percent more counterfeit

---

Annotations:

Include your last name and the page number in the upper-right-hand corner of every page.

Include your name, instructor's name, course title, and date on first page.

Center your title; do not italicize or underline.

Introduction

Thesis statement

Paragraph combines paraphrase, quotation, and May's own ideas.

Compton 2

goods were seized than in the previous decade (O'Donnell 03b). The
FBI estimates that in the United States alone, companies lose about
$250 billion as a result of counterfeits (Wallace). In addition, buyers of
counterfeit items avoid the state and local sales taxes that legitimate
companies pay. Thus, New York City alone loses about a billion dollars every
year as a result of the sale of counterfeit merchandise ("Counterfeit
Goods"). When this happens, everyone loses. After all, a billion dollars
would pay for a lot of police officers and teachers, would fill a lot of
potholes, and would pave a lot of streets. Even though buyers of counterfeit
designer goods do not think of themselves as thieves, that is exactly what
they are.

> Paragraph synthesizes May's own ideas with material from three articles.

Buyers of counterfeit merchandise also do not realize that the sale of
knockoffs is a criminal activity. Most of the profits go to the criminal organization
that either makes or imports the counterfeit goods—not to the person who sells
them. In fact, the biggest manufacturer and distributor of counterfeit items is
organized crime (Nellis). Michael Kessler, who heads a company that investigates
corporate crime, makes this connection clear when he describes the complicated
manufacturing system that is needed to make counterfeit perfume:

> They need a place that makes bottles, a factory with pumps to fill
> the bottles, a printer to make the labels, and a box manufacturer to
> fake the packaging. Then, they need a sophisticated distribution
> network, as well as all the cash to set everything up. (qtd. in
> Malone)

> Long quotation is set off one inch from the left-hand margin. No quotation marks are used.

Kessler concludes that only an organized crime syndicate—not an individual—
has the money to support this illegal activity. For this reason, anyone who
buys counterfeits may also be supporting activities such as prostitution, drug
distribution, smuggling of illegal immigrants, gang warfare, extortion, and
murder (Nellis). In addition, the people who make counterfeits often work in
sweatshops where labor and environmental laws are ignored. As Dana Thomas
points out, a worker in China who makes counterfeits earns only a fraction of
the salary of a worker who makes the real thing (A23).

Compton 3

Paragraph contains May's own ideas as well as a paraphrase and a quotation.

Finally, and perhaps most shocking, is the fact that some of the money earned from the sale of counterfeit designer goods also supports international terrorism. For example, Kim Wallace reports in her *Times Daily* article that during Al-Qaeda training, terrorists are advised to sell fake goods to get money for their operations. According to Interpol, an international police organization, the bombing of the World Trade Center in 1993 was paid for in part by the sale of counterfeit T-shirts. Also, evidence suggests that associates of the 2001 World Trade Center terrorists may have been involved with the production of imitation designer goods (Malone). Finally, the 2004 bombing of commuter trains in Madrid was financed in part by the sale of counterfeits. In fact, an intelligence source states, "It would be more shocking if Al-Qaeda *wasn't* involved in counterfeiting. The sums involved are staggering—it would be inconceivable if money were not being raised for their terrorist activities" (qtd. in Malone).

Conclusion contains May's original ideas, so no documentation is necessary.

Consumers should realize that when they buy counterfeits, they are breaking the law. By doing so, they are making it possible for organized crime syndicates and terrorists to earn money for their illegal activities. Although buyers of counterfeit merchandise justify their actions by saying that the low prices are impossible to resist, they might reconsider if they knew the uses to which their money was going. The truth of the matter is that counterfeit designer products, such as handbags, sunglasses, jewelry, and T-shirts, are luxuries, not necessities. By resisting the temptation to buy knockoffs, consumers could help to eliminate the companies that hurt legitimate manufacturers, exploit workers, and even finance international terrorism.

Compton 4

Works Cited

Armani, Giorgio. "10 Questions for Giorgio Armani." *Time*. Time, 12 Feb. 2009.

Web. 24 Mar. 2014.

"Counterfeit Goods Are Linked to Terror Groups." *International Herald Tribune*.

International Herald Tribune, 12 Feb. 2007. Web. 24 Mar. 2014.

Malone, Andrew. "Revealed: The True Cost of Buying Cheap Fake Goods."

Mail Online. Daily Mail, 29 July 2007. Web. 25 Mar. 2014.

Nellis, Cynthia. "Faking It: Counterfeit Fashion." *About.com: Women's Fashion*.

About.com, 2009. Web. 24 Mar. 2014.

O'Donnell, Jayne. "Counterfeits Are a Growing—and Dangerous—Problem."

USA Today 6 June 2012, sec. Money: 03b. Print.

Thomas, Dana. "Terror's Purse Strings." Editorial. *New York Times* 30 Aug. 2007,

late ed.: A23. *Academic One File*. Web. 25 Mar. 2014.

Wallace, Kim. "A Counter-Productive Trade." *TimesDaily.com*. Times Daily,

28 July 2007. Web. 31 Mar. 2014.

Works-cited list starts a new page.

This Internet source has no listed author.

First lines of entries are set flush left; subsequent lines are indented one-half inch.

APA Documentation Style

Parenthetical References in the Text

Parenthetical references refer readers to sources in the list of references at the end of the paper. In general, parenthetical references include the author's last name and the year of publication (Diamond, 2012). If you are quoting directly from a source, the reference should also include page numbers: (Diamond, 2012, p. 137). If, however, you refer to the author's name in your text, include only the year of publication in parentheses: Diamond asserted . . . (2012). When quoting directly, include the page number as well: Diamond asserted . . . (2012, p. 137).

Once you have cited a source, you can refer to the author again within that same paragraph, without the publication date, so long as it is clear you are referring to the same source: Diamond also found. . . .

Here are some specific guidelines for five special situations.

1. CITING A WORK BY MULTIPLE AUTHORS

   When a work has two authors, cite both names and the year (Reid & Boyer, 2013). Use the word *and* between the author names when you mention the authors in your text, but use an ampersand (&) in the parenthetical reference. For three to five authors, cite all authors in the first reference, along with the year (Jung, Pick, Schluter-Muller, Schmeck, & Goth, 2013). For subsequent references, cite only the first author followed by *et al.* and the year (Jung et al., 2013).

   When a work has six or more authors, use only the first author's name, followed by *et al.* and the year (Malm et al., 2012).

2. CITING A WORK THAT HAS NO PAGE NUMBERS

   Omit page numbers if you are quoting from a source that does not include them, as is the case with many online sources. (Try to find a pdf version of an online source if it is an option; it will usually include page numbers.) If a source shows paragraph numbers, you can use these instead of page numbers, preceded by the abbreviation para. If a source has neither page nor paragraph numbers but has headings, you can cite a shortened version of the heading in quotation marks followed by the number of the paragraph.

3. CITING A WORK THAT HAS NO NAMED AUTHOR

   If no author is identified, use a shortened version of the title of the work ("Mind," 2013).

4. CITING A SOURCE THAT IS QUOTED IN ANOTHER SOURCE

   If you quote a source found in another source, indicate the original author and the source in which you found it.

As Hatzes asserted, "If one analysis produces a planet and another doesn't, that's not robust" (as cited in Cowen, 2013, p. 25).

5. CITING PERSONAL COMMUNICATIONS

Include in-text references to personal communications and interviews that you conducted by providing the person's name, the phrase *personal communication*, and the date (J. Smith, personal communication, February 12, 2014). Do not include these sources in your reference list.

FYI

Formatting Quotations

1. **Short quotations** If a direct quotation is fewer than forty words long, set it within quotation marks without separating it from the rest of the text. The parenthetical reference follows, and if the quotation is at the end of the sentence, the period follows the final parenthesis.

   Scientists use mice in these experiments on smell because "the rodent olfactory system provides a good functional model for at least some aspects of the human system" (Yantis, 2014, p. 438).

2. **Long quotations** When quoting a passage that is forty or more words long, set it off from the rest of your paper. Indent the entire block of quoted text one-half inch from the left margin, begin it on a new line, and do not enclose it in quotation marks. If a quoted passage has more than one paragraph, indent the first line of subsequent paragraphs an extra half-inch. The quoted passage should be double-spaced, like the rest of the paper. Place your parenthetical reference after the final punctuation of the quotation.

   Perceptual organization is critical to vision, as Yantis has noted:

   > Perceptual organization is the visual system's way of dealing with scenes containing multiple overlapping objects—it makes object recognition within complex scenes possible. Without perceptual organization, the visual system would be overwhelmed by the jumbled pattern of brightness and color in the retinal image of most real scenes. (2014, p. 123)

The Reference List

The reference list includes all the works you cite in your essay. Use the guidelines in the box on page 356 to help you prepare your list.

The following sample reference-list entries cover the situations you will encounter most often.

Note: For all sources with authors, give the authors' last name first, followed by a comma and initials. The authors' names are followed by the publication year in parentheses.

Periodicals

Capitalize only the first word of the title and subtitle and any names; do not use quotation marks or italics. Give the title of the publication (journal, magazine, or newspaper) in italics, with all major words capitalized. For journals and magazines, add the volume number, italicized and preceded by a comma, and, if the publication is paginated by issue, follow the volume number with the issue number in parentheses. After a comma, give the page numbers of the article. Use the abbreviation *p.* or *pp.* only for newspaper articles.

Because websites change and disappear without warning, many publishers, particularly journal publishers, have started adding a digital object identifier (DOI) to their articles. A DOI is a unique number that can be retrieved no matter where the article ends up on the web. If an article, electronic or print, has a DOI, include it at the end of your reference-list entry, with no final period.

Article in a Print Journal

Heyns, C., & Srinivasan, S. (2013). Protecting the right to life of journalists: The need for a higher level of engagement. *Human Rights Quarterly, 35,* 304–332. doi: 10.1353/hrq.2013.0030

Article in a Journal Accessed through an Online Database

The name and URL of the database are not required for citations. If the article has a DOI, use the DOI. If no DOI is available, provide the home page URL of the journal or other periodical.

Almeroth, K., & Zhang, H. (2013). Alternatives for monitoring and limiting network access to students in network-connected classrooms. *Journal of Interactive Learning Research, 24,* 237–265. Retrieved from http://www.aace.org/pubs/jilr/

Article in a Print Magazine

Kenny, P. J. (2013, September). The food addiction. *Scientific American, 309*(3), 44–49.

Article in a Print Newspaper

Smith, P. A. (2013, August 27). A quest for even safer drinking water. *The New York Times,* p. D3.

Books

Give book titles in italics, and capitalize only the first word of the title and subtitle and any names. For place of publication, give the city followed by a comma and the two-letter abbreviation for the state. Following a colon, give a shortened form of the publisher's name.

Books by One Author

McCrum, R. (2010). *Globish: How the English language became the world's language.* New York, NY: Norton.

Books by Two to Seven Authors

For works with up to seven authors, give all authors' names, with an ampersand before the last author.

Acemoglu, D., & Robinson, J. (2012). *Why nations fail: The origins of power, prosperity, and poverty.* New York, NY: Crown.

Books by Eight or More Authors

Include the names of the first six authors and then add three ellipsis points and the name of the last author.

Wolfe, J. M., Kluender, K. R., Levi, D. M., Bartoshuk, L. M., Herz, R. S., Klatzky, R. L., . . . Merfeld, D. M. (2012). *Sensation & perception* (3rd ed.). Sunderland, MA: Sinauer.

Edited Book

Sarat, A., Douglas, L., & Umphrey, M. M. (Eds.). (2011). *Law as punishment/ Law as regulation.* Stanford, CA: Stanford University Press.

Essay or Chapter in an Edited Book

Gleiser, M. (2012). We are unique. In J. Brockman (Ed.), *This will make you smarter* (pp. 3–5). New York, NY: Harper.

Internet Sources

Include the information that your readers will need in order to be able to retrieve your sources. As discussed above, when a DOI is not available, provide a URL.

Document within a Website

In your retrieval statement, give the website and its URL.

Roushdy, R., Sieverding, M., & Radwan, H. (2012). *The impact of water supply and sanitation on child health: Evidence from Egypt* (Poverty, Gender, and Youth Working Paper No. 24). Retrieved from Population Council website: http://www.popcouncil.org/

Blog Post or Video Blog Post

In brackets after the title, describe the source type—for example, as *Web log post* or *Video file*.

Siegel, E. (2013, August 30). How would you figure out whether global warming is real? Part 3 [Web log post]. Retrieved from http://scienceblogs .com/startswithabang/2013/08/30/how-would-you-figure-out-whether-global-warming-is-real-part-3/

Preparing the Reference List

- Start your list of references on a separate page at the end of your paper.
- Center the title References at the top of the page.
- Begin each reference flush with the left margin, and indent subsequent lines one-half inch.
- Double-space the list.
- List your references alphabetically by the author's last name (or by the first major word of the title if no author is identified).
- If the list includes references for two sources by the same author, list them in order by the year of publication, starting with the earliest.
- Italicize titles of books and periodicals. Do not italicize article titles or enclose them in quotation marks.
- For titles of books and articles, capitalize only the first word of the title and subtitle as well as any proper nouns. Capitalize words in a periodical title as in the original.

:e bedfordstmartins.com /forw Model Student Papers > APA style.

READING AND WRITING ACTIVITY

Read the paragraph below, from the *New York Times* online article "The New Math on Campus," by Alex Williams. Then, read the three student paragraphs that use this article as a source. In each of these paragraphs, student writers have accidentally committed plagiarism. On the line below each student paragraph, explain the problem. Then, edit the paragraph so that it correctly documents the source and avoids plagiarism.

> North Carolina, with a student body that is nearly 60 percent female, is just one of many large universities that at times feel eerily like women's colleges. Women have represented about 57 percent of enrollments at American colleges since at least 2000, according to a recent report by the American Council on Education. Researchers there cite several reasons: women tend to have higher grades; men tend to drop out in disproportionate numbers; and female enrollment skews higher among older students, low-income students, and black and Hispanic students.

Answers will vary.

About 60% female, the University of North Carolina is an example of large universities with many more women than men. According to a report from the American Council on Education, one reason is that "female enrollment skews higher among older students, low-income students, and black and Hispanic students" (Williams). If this is true, what will this mean for the black and Hispanic communities?

The ideas in the first sentence are taken from the source, but the writer makes it

sound as if only the quotation in the second sentence is from the source.

In recent years, colleges and universities have taken on a very different atmosphere. The reason is clear to anyone who takes a casual look around at just about any college campus. Women now outnumber men, so much so that some colleges at times feel eerily like women's colleges (Williams). This situation seems likely to continue in the years to come.

The writer uses the source's exact words without quoting them.

Why do women outnumber men in today's colleges? Researchers at the American Council on Education mention a few reasons: women often have higher grades, men tend to drop out in larger numbers, and female enrollment is especially high for some groups such as older students, low-income students, and black and Hispanic students (Williams). These reasons may all be true at our school, which certainly has more women than men.

The writer's paraphrase is too close to the words of the source.

COLLABORATIVE ACTIVITY

Working in a group of three or four students, create an MLA works-cited list for a paper that uses the following three sources. Make sure that you arrange the entries in alphabetical order and that you use the correct format for each type of source.

Article in a Journal Accessed through a Library Database

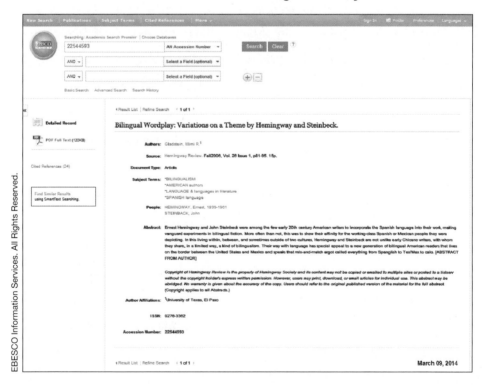

Book (Print)

Library of Congress Cataloging-in-Publication Data

Spanglish / edited by Ilan Stavans.
    p. cm. — (The Ilan Stavans library of Latino civilization, ISSN 1938–615X)
    Includes bibliographical references and index.
    ISBN 978-0-313-34804-4 (alk. paper)
    1. Spanish language—Foreign elements—English. 2. English language—
Influence on Spanish. 3. Languages in contact—America. I. Stavans,
Ilan.
  PC4582.E6S63 2008
  460'.4221—dc22   2008014855

British Library Cataloguing in Publication Data is available.

Copyright © 2008 by Ilan Stavans

All rights reserved. No portion of this book may be reproduced, by any process or technique, without the express written consent of the publisher.

Library of Congress Catalog Card Number: 2008014855
ISBN: 978-0-313-34804-4
ISSN: 1938-615X

First published in 2008

Greenwood Press, 88 Post Road West, Westport, CT 06881
An imprint of Greenwood Publishing Group, Inc.
www.greenwood.com

Printed in the United States of America

The paper used in this book complies with the Permanent Paper Standard issued by the National Information Standards Organization (Z39.48–1984).

10 9 8 7 6 5 4 3 2 1

Every reasonable effort has been made to trace the owners of copyright materials in this book, but in some instances this has proven impossible. The editor and publisher will be glad to receive information leading to a more complete acknowledgments in subsequent printings of the book and in the meantime extend their apologies for any omissions.

iv

Document within a Website

LATISM.org blog post by Elianne Ramos.

Works Cited

Gladstein, Mimi R. "Bilingual Wordplay: Variations on a Theme by Hemingway

and Steinbeck." *Hemingway Review* 26.1 (2006): 81–95. *Academic*

Search Premier. Web. 9 Mar. 2014.

Ramos, Elianne. "#LATISM Party: English, Spanish, Spanglish: Language

and the Latino Future." *#LATISM.* Latinos in Social Media, 26 Aug.

2010. Web. 9 Mar. 2014.

Stavans, Ilan, ed. *Spanglish.* Westport: Greenwood, 2008. Print.

review checklist

☐   When you do research, find and evaluate sources from the library as well as from the Internet. (See 13a.)

☐   Once you locate source information, put it into a form that you can use in your paper—for example, paraphrases, summaries, or quotations from your sources. (See 13b.)

☐   Document all material that you use from outside sources. If you use information from a source and do not document it, you commit **plagiarism**. (See 13c.)

☐   When you document information from your sources, use MLA or APA documentation style, or whatever style your instructor requires. (See 13d.)

Basic Grammar Guide

14 **Understanding Verbs** 365

15 **Understanding Nouns and Pronouns** 380

16 **Understanding Adjectives and Adverbs** 403

17 **Writing Simple, Compound, and Complex Sentences** 413

18 **Writing Varied Sentences** 436

19 **Using Parallelism** 450

20 **Using Words Effectively** 457

21 **Run-Ons** 474

22 **Fragments** 487

23 **Subject-Verb Agreement** 503

24 **Illogical Shifts** 515

25 **Misplaced and Dangling Modifiers** 523

26 **Using Commas** 530

27 **Using Apostrophes** 544

28 **Understanding Mechanics** 551

PARTS OF SPEECH

Bailey (1993–2010)

The English language has eight basic parts of speech: nouns, pronouns, verbs, adjectives, adverbs, prepositions, conjunctions, and interjections.

Nouns   A noun names a person, an animal, a place, an object, or an idea.

Christine brought her dog Bailey to obedience school in Lawndale.
noun   *noun noun*   *noun*   *noun*

Pronouns   A pronoun refers to and takes the place of a noun or another pronoun.

Bailey did very well in her lessons and seemed to enjoy them.
noun   *pronoun noun*   *pronoun*

Verbs   A verb tells what someone or something does, did, or will do.

Sometimes Bailey rolls over, but earlier today she refused.
                    verb   *verb*

Maybe she will change someday.
                    verb

Adjectives   An adjective identifies or describes a noun or a pronoun.

This dog is a small Beagle with a brown and white coat and long ears.
adj noun   *adj   noun*   *adj*   *adj   noun*   *adj noun*

Adverbs   An adverb identifies or describes a verb, an adjective, or another adverb.

Bailey is old, so she moves very slowly and seldom barks.
                              verb   *adverb adverb*   *adverb*   *verb*

Prepositions   A preposition is a word—such as *to*, *on*, or *with*—that introduces a noun or pronoun and connects it to other words in a sentence.

Bailey likes sitting quietly in her box at the foot of the stairs.

Conjunctions   A conjunction is a word that connects parts of a sentence.

People say you can't teach an old dog new tricks, but Bailey might be an exception.

Interjections   An interjection is a word—such as *Oh!* or *Hey!*—that is used to express emotion.

Wow! Bailey finally rolled over!

The eight basic parts of speech can be combined to form sentences, which always include at least one subject and one verb. The subject tells who or what is being talked about, and the verb tells what the subject does, did, or will do.

Bailey graduated from obedience school at the head of her class.
s   *v*

14 Understanding Verbs

Tense is the form a verb takes to show when an action or situation takes place. The **past tense** indicates that an action occurred in the past.

14a Regular Verbs

Regular verbs form the past tense by adding either *-ed* or *-d* to the **base form** of the verb (the present tense form of the verb that is used with *I*).

We register<u>ed</u> for classes yesterday.

Walt Disney produc<u>ed</u> short cartoons in 1928.

Regular verbs that end in *-y* form the past tense by changing the *y* to *i* and adding *-ed*.

tr<u>y</u>	tr<u>ied</u>
appl<u>y</u>	appl<u>ied</u>

PRACTICE
14-1

Change the regular verbs below to the past tense.

Example: Every year, my mother ~~visits~~ her family in Bombay.
visited

(1) My mother always ~~returns~~ from India with henna designs on
returned
her hands and feet. (2) In India, henna artists ~~create~~ these patterns.
created
(3) Henna ~~originates~~ in a plant found in the Middle East, India, Indonesia,
originated
and northern Africa. (4) Many women in these areas ~~use~~ henna to color
used
their hands, nails, and parts of their feet. (5) Men ~~dye~~ their beards as well
dyed
as the manes and hooves of their horses. (6) They also ~~color~~ animal skins
colored
with henna. (7) In India, my mother always ~~celebrates~~ the end of the
celebrated

**bedfordstmartins.com
/forw** LearningCurve >
Verbs; Additional
Grammar Exercises >
Regular Verbs

Teaching Tip
Remind students that not
all verbs ending in *-ed* or
-d are in the past tense.
Some are past participles.
(See 14e.)

ESL Tip
Verb tense is a challenge
for nonnative speakers.
Check everything they
write, and have them
write often.

Teaching Tip
Remind students that all
regular verbs use the
same form for singular
and plural in the past
tense: *I cheered. They
cheered.*

Ramadan religious fast by going to a "henna party." (8) A professional

attended

henna artist attends the party to apply new henna decorations to the women.

^

washed

(9) After a few weeks, the henna designs wash off. (10) In the United States,

attracted

my mother's henna designs attract the attention of many people.

^

14b Irregular Verbs

bedfordstmartins.com /forw Additional Grammar Exercises > Irregular Verbs

Unlike regular verbs, whose past tense forms end in *-ed* or *-d*, **irregular verbs** have irregular forms in the past tense. In fact, their past tense forms may look very different from their present tense forms.

The following chart lists the base form and past tense form of many of the most commonly used irregular verbs.

Irregular Verbs in the Past Tense

BASE FORM	PAST	BASE FORM	PAST
awake	awoke	feel	felt
be	was, were	fight	fought
beat	beat	find	found
become	became	fly	flew
begin	began	forgive	forgave
bet	bet	freeze	froze
bite	bit	get	got
blow	blew	give	gave
break	broke	go (goes)	went
bring	brought	grow	grew
build	built	have	had
buy	bought	hear	heard
catch	caught	hide	hid
choose	chose	hold	held
come	came	hurt	hurt
cost	cost	keep	kept
cut	cut	know	knew
dive	dove (dived)	lay (to place)	laid
do	did	lead	led
draw	drew	leave	left
drink	drank	let	let
drive	drove	lie (to recline)	lay
eat	ate	light	lit
fall	fell	lose	lost
feed	fed	make	made

Teaching Tip
Point out that when students edit their writing, they can use the computer's Search or Find command to locate the irregular verbs that give them the most trouble.

ESL Tip
Ask students to give examples of irregular verbs in their native languages. Write the English equivalents on the board.

ESL Tip
Irregular past tense verb forms are challenging for native speakers and even more so for nonnative speakers. Have students write sentences using some of the verbs in this chart.

BASE FORM	PAST	BASE FORM	PAST
meet	met	spend	spent
pay	paid	spring	sprang
quit	quit	stand	stood
read	read	steal	stole
ride	rode	stick	stuck
ring	rang	sting	stung
rise	rose	swear	swore
run	ran	swim	swam
say	said	take	took
see	saw	teach	taught
sell	sold	tear	tore
send	sent	tell	told
set	set	think	thought
shake	shook	throw	threw
shine	shone (shined)	understand	understood
sing	sang	wake	woke
sit	sat	wear	wore
sleep	slept	win	won
speak	spoke	write	wrote

PRACTICE

14-2   Fill in the correct past tense form of each irregular verb in parentheses, using the chart above to help you. If you cannot find a particular verb on the chart, look it up in a dictionary.

Example: Security on Campus ___*was*___ (be) founded in 1987.

(1) After their daughter, Jeanne, ___*was*___ (be) murdered at Lehigh University, Connie and Howard Cleary ___*began*___ (begin) a movement to improve safety on college campuses. (2) Jeanne ___*thought*___ (think) she was safe. (3) However, her attacker ___*got*___ (get) into her dorm room through three different doors that had all been left unlocked. (4) Shockingly, Jeanne's attacker actually ___*went*___ (go) to Lehigh. (5) Shattered by the loss of their daughter, her parents ___*did*___ (do) not withdraw into their pain. (6) Instead, they ___*felt*___ (feel) that the best memorial to their daughter would be the prevention of similar crimes, so they founded Security on Campus, Inc. (7) SOC ___*made*___ (make) legal

> **READING TIP**
>
> This passage provides evidence (details and examples) that explains the founding of Security on Campus, Inc. What main idea does this evidence support?

information available to victims of crimes on college campuses. (8) Because of the efforts of SOC, Congress _____WROTE_____ (write) a law that forced colleges to disclose their crime statistics.

14c Problem Verbs: *Be*

ⓔ bedfordstmartins.com
/forw Additional
Grammar Exercises >
Problem Verbs: *Be*

Teaching Tip
Point out that *be* is the only verb in English with more than one past tense form. Refer students to 23c for detailed information about subject-verb agreement with *be*.

Teaching Tip
Challenge students to try to identify another verb as irregular as *be*. Explain that *be* is the most irregular verb in the English language.

The irregular verb *be* causes problems because it has two different past tense forms—*was* for singular subjects and *were* for second-person singular subjects as well as for plural subjects. (All other English verbs have just one past tense form.)

Carlo <u>was</u> interested in becoming a city planner. (singular)
They <u>were</u> happy to help out at the school. (plural)

Past Tense Forms of the Verb *Be*

	SINGULAR	PLURAL
First person	I <u>was</u> tired.	We <u>were</u> tired.
Second person	You <u>were</u> tired.	You <u>were</u> tired.
Third person	He <u>was</u> tired.	
	She <u>was</u> tired.	They <u>were</u> tired.
	It <u>was</u> tired.	
	The man <u>was</u> tired.	Frank and Billy <u>were</u> tired.

PRACTICE

14-3 Edit the following passage for errors in the use of the verb *be*. Cross out any underlined verbs that are incorrect, and write the correct forms above them. If a verb form is correct, label it *C*.

ESL Tip
Point out that the verb *be* is irregular in many languages. Ask students to tell the class how *be* is conjugated in their native language. First, make sure they understand the concept of the word *conjugate*, as ESL students may not be familiar with this term.

Example: Before 1990, there ~~was~~ *were* no female Hispanic astronauts in the NASA program.

(1) Although there had never been a Hispanic woman astronaut, it <u>was</u> *C* impossible for NASA to ignore Ellen Ochoa's long career in physics and engineering. (2) When Ochoa <u>was</u> *C* young, her main interests ~~was~~ *were* music, math, and physics. (3) After getting a degree in physics at San Diego State University, she ~~were~~ *was* considering a career in music or business.

(4) However, she was *(C)* convinced by her mother to continue her education. (5) In 1983, Ochoa was *(C)* studying for a doctorate in electrical engineering at Stanford University when the first female astronaut, Sally Ride, flew on the space shuttle. (6) Ochoa were *(was)* inspired by Sally Ride to become an astronaut. (7) More than 2,000 people was *(were)* also inspired to apply for the astronaut program. (8) In 1990, Ochoa was *(C)* picked to fly into space.

14d Problem Verbs: Can/Could and Will/Would

The helping verbs *can/could* and *will/would* present problems because their past tense forms are sometimes confused with their present tense forms.

Can/Could

Can, a present tense verb, means "is able to" or "are able to."

First-year students <u>can</u> apply for financial aid.

Could, the past tense of *can,* means "was able to" or "were able to."

Escape artist Harry Houdini claimed that he <u>could</u> escape from any prison.

Will/Would

Will, a present tense verb, talks about the future from a point in the present.

A solar eclipse <u>will</u> occur in ten months.

Would, the past tense of *will,* talks about the future from a point in the past.

I told him yesterday that I <u>would</u> think about it.

Would is also used to express a possibility or wish.

If we stuck to our budget, we <u>would</u> be better off.
Laurie <u>would</u> like a new stuffed animal.

Teaching Tip
Refer students to 17c for more on helping verbs.

:e bedfordstmartins.com
/forw Additional Grammar Exercises > Problem Verbs: *Can/ Could* and *Will/Would*

FYI

Will and *Would*

Note that *will* is used with *can* and that *would* is used with *could*.

I will feed the cats if I can find their food.

I would feed the cats if I could find their food.

PRACTICE

14-4   Circle the appropriate helping verb from the choices in parentheses.

Example: Anyone who doesn't want to throw things away (can, could) rent a self-storage unit.

(1) Today's self-storage units (can, could) make life easier for people with limited space and many belongings. (2) In the past, warehouse storage (will, would) provide a place to store excess items. (3) However, people (will, would) have to hire moving vans and (can, could) hardly ever have access to their stored items. (4) They (will, would) have to sign an expensive long-term contract. (5) Now, however, they (can, could) take advantage of another option. (6) They (can, could) store possessions in a space as small as a closet or as large as a house. (7) With self-storage, people (can, could) easily move their belongings in and out of the storage unit. (8) When they need more space, they (will, would) be able to get it. (9) In fact, the managers of self-storage facilities (can, could) suggest how much space owners (will, would) need. (10) The only person who (can, could) get into the self-storage unit is the person who has rented it. (11) If people need a hand truck to move their belongings, they (can, could) usually borrow one. (12) All in all, using self-storage (can, could) solve a lot of problems for people with too many possessions.

14e   Regular Past Participles

Every verb has a past participle form. The **past participle** form of a regular verb is identical to its past tense form. Both are formed by adding either *-ed* or *-d* to the **base form** of the verb (the present tense form of the verb that is used with the pronoun *I*).

e bedfordstmartins.com /forw LearningCurve > Verbs; Additional Grammar Exercises > Regular Past Participles

PAST TENSE	PAST PARTICIPLE
He earned a fortune.	He has earned a fortune.

PAST TENSE	PAST PARTICIPLE
He created a work of art.	He has created a work of art.

PRACTICE

14-5   Fill in the correct past participle form of each regular verb in parentheses.

Example: For years, volunteer vacationers have ___visited___ (visit) remote areas to build footpaths, cabins, and shelters.

(1) Recently, vacationers have ___discovered___ (discover) some new opportunities to get away from it all and to do good at the same time. (2) Groups such as Habitat for Humanity, for example, have ___offered___ (offer) volunteers a chance to build homes in low-income areas. (3) Habitat's Global Village trips have ___raised___ (raise) awareness about the lack of affordable housing in many countries. (4) Participants in Sierra Club programs have ___donated___ (donate) thousands of work hours all over the United States. (5) Sometimes these volunteers have ___joined___ (join) forest service workers to help restore wilderness areas. (6) They have ___cleaned___ (clean) up trash at campsites. (7) They have also ___removed___ (remove) nonnative plants. (8) Some volunteer vacationers have ___traveled___ (travel) to countries such as Costa Rica, Russia, and Thailand to help with local projects. (9) Other vacationers have ___served___ (serve) as English teachers. (10) Volunteering vacations have ___helped___ (help) to strengthen cross-cultural understanding.

Teaching Tip
Refer students to 17c for information on helping verbs.

14f Irregular Past Participles

bedfordstmartins.com /forw Additional Grammar Exercises > Irregular Past Participles

Irregular verbs nearly always have irregular past participles. Irregular verbs do not form the past participle by adding *-ed* or *-d* to the base form of the verb.

The following chart lists the base form, the past tense form, and the past participle of the most commonly used irregular verbs.

Irregular Past Participles

BASE FORM	PAST TENSE	PAST PARTICIPLE
awake	awoke	awoken
be (am, are)	was (were)	been
beat	beat	beaten
become	became	become
begin	began	begun
bet	bet	bet
bite	bit	bitten
blow	blew	blown
break	broke	broken
bring	brought	brought
build	built	built
buy	bought	bought
catch	caught	caught
choose	chose	chosen
come	came	come
cost	cost	cost
cut	cut	cut
dive	dove, dived	dived
do	did	done
draw	drew	drawn
drink	drank	drunk
drive	drove	driven
eat	ate	eaten
fall	fell	fallen
feed	fed	fed
feel	felt	felt
fight	fought	fought
find	found	found
fly	flew	flown
forgive	forgave	forgiven
freeze	froze	frozen

BASE FORM	PAST TENSE	PAST PARTICIPLE
get	got	got, gotten
give	gave	given
go	went	gone
grow	grew	grown
have	had	had
hear	heard	heard
hide	hid	hidden
hold	held	held
hurt	hurt	hurt
keep	kept	kept
know	knew	known
lay (to place)	laid	laid
lead	led	led
leave	left	left
let	let	let
lie (to recline)	lay	lain
light	lit	lit
lose	lost	lost
make	made	made
meet	met	met
pay	paid	paid
quit	quit	quit
read	read	read
ride	rode	ridden
ring	rang	rung
rise	rose	risen
run	ran	run
say	said	said
see	saw	seen
sell	sold	sold
send	sent	sent
set	set	set
shake	shook	shaken
shine	shone, shined	shone, shined
sing	sang	sung
sit	sat	sat
sleep	slept	slept
speak	spoke	spoken
spend	spent	spent
spring	sprang	sprung
stand	stood	stood
steal	stole	stolen
stick	stuck	stuck

(continued)

	(continued from previous page)		
	BASE FORM	PAST TENSE	PAST PARTICIPLE
	sting	stung	stung
	swear	swore	sworn
	swim	swam	swum
	take	took	taken
	teach	taught	taught
	tear	tore	torn
	tell	told	told
	think	thought	thought
	throw	threw	thrown
	understand	understood	understood
	wake	woke, waked	woken, waked
	wear	wore	worn
	win	won	won
	write	wrote	written

ESL Tip
After students have completed Practice 14-6, give them a correct version of the exercise. Have them copy the correct paragraph and then compare it with their own version.

Teaching Tip
Point out that some words (such as *not*, *also*, *even*, and *hardly*) can come between the helping verb and the past participle.

PRACTICE

14-6 Edit the following paragraph for errors in irregular past participles. Cross out any underlined past participles that are incorrect, and write in the correct form above them. If the verb form is correct, label it *C*.

Example: In recent years, some people have ~~standed~~ *stood* up against overseas sweatshops.

(1) Buying products from overseas sweatshops has ~~became~~ *become* controversial over the last few decades. (2) American manufacturers have ~~sended~~ *sent* their materials to developing countries where employees work under terrible conditions for very low wages. (3) Violations of basic U.S. labor laws—such as getting extra pay for overtime and being paid on time— have ~~lead~~ *led* to protests. (4) Low-wage workers in developing countries have ~~finded~~ *found* themselves facing dangerous working conditions as well as verbal and sexual abuse. (5) Even well-known retailers—such as Walmart, Nike, Reebok, Tommy Hilfiger, and Target—have gotten *C* in trouble for selling items made in sweatshops. (6) Recently, colleges have ~~be~~ *been* criticized

for using overseas sweatshops to make clothing featuring school names.

spoken   *C*
(7) Students have spoke out against such practices, and schools have had

lost
to respond. (8) While some manufacturers may have losed money by

understood
increasing wages for overseas workers, they have understanded that this

C
is the right thing to do. (9) They have made a promise to their customers

argued
that they will not employ sweatshop labor. (10) Critics have argue, how-

ever, that in developing countries sweatshop jobs are often an improve-

ment over other types of employment.

14g The Present Perfect Tense

The past participle can be combined with the present tense forms of
have to form the **present perfect tense**.

e bedfordstmartins.com
/forw Additional
Grammar Exercises >
Present Perfect and
Past Perfect Tenses

The Present Perfect Tense

(*have* or *has* + past participle)

SINGULAR	PLURAL
I have gained.	We have gained.
You have gained.	You have gained.
He has gained.	They have gained.
She has gained.	
It has gained.	

■ Use the present perfect tense to indicate an action that began in the
past and continues into the present.

    PRESENT PERFECT The nurse has worked at the Welsh Mountain
    clinic for two years. (The working began in
    the past and continues into the present.)

■ Use the present perfect tense to indicate that an action has just
occurred.

    PRESENT PERFECT I have just eaten. (The eating has just occurred.)

Teaching Tip
Tell students that the
words *just*, *now*, *already*,
and *recently* show that an
action has just occurred.

PRACTICE

14-7 Circle the appropriate verb tense (past tense or present perfect) from the choices in parentheses.

Example: When I was in Montreal, I (heard, have heard) both English and French.

(1) When I (visited, have visited) Montreal, I was surprised to find a truly bilingual city. (2) Montreal (kept, has kept) two languages as a result of its history. (3) Until 1763, Montreal (belonged, has belonged) to France. (4) Then, when France (lost, has lost) the Seven Years' War, the city (became, has become) part of England. (5) When I was there last year, most people (spoke, have spoken) both French and English. (6) Although I (knew, have known) no French, I (found, have found) that I was able to get along quite well. (7) For example, all the museums (made, have made) their guided tours available in English. (8) Most restaurants (offered, have offered) bilingual menus. (9) There (were, have been) even English radio and television stations and English newspapers. (10) In Montreal, I (felt, have felt) both at home and in a foreign country.

14h The Past Perfect Tense

bedfordstmartins.com
/forw Additional
Grammar Exercises >
Present Perfect and
Past Perfect Tenses

The past participle can also be used to form the **past perfect tense**, which consists of the past tense of have plus the past participle.

The Past Perfect Tense

(*had* + past participle)

SINGULAR	PLURAL
I had returned.	We had returned.
You had returned.	You had returned.

SINGULAR	PLURAL
He had returned.	They had returned.
She had returned.	
It had returned.	

Use the past perfect tense to show that an action occurred before another past action.

PAST PERFECT TENSE   **PAST TENSE**

Chief Sitting Bull had fought many battles before he defeated General
Custer. (The fighting was done before Sitting Bull defeated Custer.)

PRACTICE

14-8 Underline the appropriate verb tense (present perfect or past perfect) from the choices in parentheses.

Example: Although he (has missed/<u>had missed</u>) his second free throw, the crowd cheered for him anyway.

1. Meera returned to Bangladesh with the money she (has raised/<u>had raised</u>).

2. Her contributors believe that she (<u>has shown</u>/had shown) the ability to spend money wisely.

3. The planner told the commission that she (has found/<u>had found</u>) a solution to the city's traffic problem.

4. It seems clear that traffic cameras (<u>have proven</u>/had proven) successful in towns with similar congestion problems.

5. Emily says she (<u>has saved</u>/had saved) a lot of money by driving a motor scooter instead of a car.

EDITING PRACTICE

Read the following student essay, which includes errors in past tense verb forms and in the use of past participles and perfect tenses. Decide whether each of the underlined verbs or participles is correct. If it is correct, write *C* above it. If it is not, write in the correct verb form. The first error has been corrected for you. *Answers will vary.*

READING TIP

As you read, keep a list of details that support the main idea of this student essay. For example, one supporting detail is the purpose of the first flash mob: to express social commentary.

The Flash Mob Phenomenon

The first flash mob *took* <u>taked</u> place in 2003 when two hundred people *assembled* <u>assemble</u> in Macy's Herald Square store in New York City. Since then, these spontaneous gatherings have popped up in cities around the world and *involved* have <u>involve</u> all kinds of unusual behavior. Occasionally, a group *C* has <u>organized</u> a flash mob for criminal purposes, but in most cases, flash mobs *have* <u>had been</u> harmless acts of group expression.

Organizer Bill Wasik *C* <u>had</u> actually *intended* <u>intend</u> the first flash mob to be a social commentary. Wasik had wanted to make fun of "hipster" New Yorkers who *showed* <u>shown</u> up at events simply because other people did. However, almost no one saw the first flash mob that way. In fact, people mostly *thought* <u>thinked</u> it was cool. As a result, *started* admirers <u>start</u> organizing their own flash mobs.

So far, few flash mobs *have had* <u>had have</u> a political or social purpose. Typically, *have participated* people <u>had participate</u> because these gatherings are fun. For example, dancing to Michael Jackson's "Thriller" is a popular flash mob activity. Having a massive pillow fight is another one. A third example of an enjoyable gathering is the annual "No Pants Subway Ride." In 2013, there *were* <u>was</u> tens of thousands of participants in this silly event. People in sixty countries *rode* <u>rided</u> their usual trains, *C* <u>left</u> their pants at home, and acted as if nothing were different. Part of the fun *was* <u>were</u> not knowing exactly what *would* <u>will</u> happen or how many people *C* <u>would</u> show up.

Although the majority of flash mob organizers have create [*created*] these brief performances to entertain, people have [C] occasionally use [*used*] flash mobs for other purposes. Over the last few years, several groups have robbed [C] stores by entering in large numbers, stealing merchandise, and then separating quickly. Worse, several groups have came [*come*] together to commit violent acts or destroy property. Most of today's flash mobs, however, are peaceful.

Over the last decade, flash mobs have became [*become*] more popular than anyone could have imagined. Although they have not had the social impact that creator Bill Wasik had hoped [C] for, they have given a lot of people a lot of enjoyment. By joining a flash mob, participants could [*can*] be creative, socialize, and have fun. Although a few flash mobs have done [C] harm, most have offer [*offered*] people a way to be a part of something memorable.

review checklist

Verbs

- [ ] The past tense is the form a verb takes to show that an action occurred in the past.

- [ ] Regular verbs form the past tense by adding either *-ed* or *-d* to the base form of the verb. (See 14a.)

- [ ] Irregular verbs have irregular forms in the past tense. (See 14b.)

- [ ] *Be* has two different past tense forms—*was* for singular subjects and *were* for second-person singular subjects as well as for plural subjects. (See 14c.)

- [ ] *Could* is the past tense of *can*. *Would* is the past tense of *will*. (See 14d.)

- [ ] The past participle of regular verbs is formed by adding *-ed* or *-d* to the base form. (See 14e.)

- [ ] Irregular verbs usually have irregular past participles. (See 14f.)

- [ ] The past participle is combined with the present tense forms of *have* to form the present perfect tense. (See 14g.)

- [ ] The past participle is used to form the past perfect tense, which consists of the past tense of *have* plus the past participle. (See 14h.)

e bedfordstmartins.com
/forw LearningCurve > Verbs

Teaching Tip
Have students write a paragraph using a certain number of past tense verbs from the list on pages 372–374.

15 Understanding Nouns and Pronouns

15a Identifying Nouns

 bedfordstmartins.com
/forw LearningCurve >
Nouns and Pronouns

A **noun** is a word that names a person (*singer, Jay-Z*), an animal (*dolphin, Flipper*), a place (*downtown, Houston*), an object (*game, Scrabble*), or an idea (*happiness, Darwinism*).

A **singular noun** names one thing. A **plural noun** names more than one thing.

FYI

When to Capitalize Nouns

Most nouns, called **common nouns**, begin with lowercase letters.

    character   holiday

Some nouns, called **proper nouns**, name particular people, animals, places, objects, or events. A proper noun always begins with a capital letter.

    Homer Simpson   Labor Day

Teaching Tip
Refer students to 28a for information on capitalizing proper nouns.

15b Forming Plural Nouns

Most nouns that end in consonants add -*s* to form plurals. Other nouns add -*es* to form plurals. For example, most nouns that end in -*o* add -*es* to form plurals. Other nouns, whose singular forms end in -*s*, -*ss*, -*sh*, -*ch*, -*x*, or -*z*, also add -*es* to form plurals. (Some nouns that end in -*s* or -*z* double the *s* or *z* before adding -*es*.)

SINGULAR	PLURAL
street	streets
tomato	tomatoes
gas	gases
class	classes
bush	bushes
church	churches
fox	foxes
quiz	quizzes

ESL Tip
Briefly review subject-verb agreement. Remind students that if the subject ends in -*s*, the verb usually does not. Refer students to Chapter 23.

Irregular Noun Plurals

Some nouns form plurals in unusual ways.

- Nouns whose plural forms are the same as their singular forms

SINGULAR	PLURAL
a deer	a few deer
this species	these species
a television series	two television series

ESL Tip
Tell students that they can sometimes tell whether a word is singular or plural by the word that introduces it. For example, *each* always introduces a singular noun, and *many* always introduces a plural noun.

- Nouns ending in -*f* or -*fe*

SINGULAR	PLURAL
each half	both halves
my life	our lives
a lone thief	a gang of thieves
one loaf	two loaves
the third shelf	several shelves

Exceptions: *roof* (plural *roofs*), *proof* (plural *proofs*), *belief* (plural *beliefs*)

- Nouns ending in -*y*

SINGULAR	PLURAL
another baby	more babies
every worry	many worries

Note that when a vowel (*a, e, i, o, u*) comes before the *y*, the noun has a regular plural form: *monkey* (plural *monkeys*), *day* (plural *days*).

(continued)

(continued from previous page)

- Hyphenated compound nouns

SINGULAR	PLURAL
Lucia's sister-in-law	Lucia's two favorite sisters-in-law
a mother-to-be	twin mothers-to-be
the first runner-up	all the runners-up

Note that the plural ending is attached to the compound's first word: *sister, mother, runner.*

- Miscellaneous irregular plurals

SINGULAR	PLURAL
that child	all children
a good man	a few good men
the woman	lots of women
my left foot	both feet
a wisdom tooth	my two front teeth
this bacterium	some bacteria

PRACTICE

15-1

Proofread the underlined nouns in the following paragraph, checking to make sure singular and plural forms are correct. If a correction needs to be made, cross out the noun, and write the correct form above it. If the noun is correct, write *C* above it.

Teaching Tip
Tell students that when a noun has an irregular plural, the dictionary lists its plural form.

Example: Austin's Museum of the Weird displays many delightful
oddities
oddit̲y̲s̲.
^

(1) If America had a contest for the weirdest museum, there would
contestants
be plenty of interesting contestant̲e̲s̲. (2) The United States is full of
C   ^
towns
strange establishments although many are hidden in small town̲n̲e̲s̲ or
C   *histories* ^
down back street̲s̲. (3) Most are dedicated to untold histor̲y̲s̲, unusual
heroes   C   ^
heros̲, or bizarre collection̲s̲ of items. (4) Philadelphia's Mutter Museum
^   *specimens*   *skulls*   C   *bones*   C
offers medical specimen̲, like skull̲z̲, brain̲s̲, bon̲z̲, and organ̲s̲ of peo-
^   *illnesses* ^
ple who suffered from strange illness̲e̲s̲s̲. (5) The Mutter could definitely
^
C
win the prize for the weirdest museum, but other place̲s̲ could easily
runners-up   C
be runner-ups̲. (6) At the Kansas Barbed Wire Museum, visitor̲s̲ can
^

READING TIP

When you read, think about the writer's purpose, which is typically to inform, explain, or persuade. In this paragraph, what is the author's purpose, and how is the purpose made clear to the reader?

see over 2,400 *varieties* of barbed wire. (7) The National Mustard
varietees̲

Museum in Middleton, Wisconsin, has *thousands* of *jars* of mustard
thousandes̲ jarrs̲

from *countries* all over the world. (8) Leila's Hair Museum in Indepen-
countrys̲

dence, Missouri, has hundreds of wreaths̲, necklaces̲, and *brooches* made
                                      C   C   broochs̲

from human hair. (9) All of these weird museums welcome sightseers̲.
                                                                   C

(10) However, *tourists* should know that many of these places do not
touristes̲

have fixed hours and are closed on *holidays*.
                                   holidaies̲

15c Identifying Pronouns

Teaching Tip
Tell students that using
too many pronouns can
make a paragraph boring,
especially when pronouns
begin several sentences in
a row. Encourage them to
vary their sentence open-
ings. Refer them to 18b.

A **pronoun** is a word that refers to and takes the place of a noun or another pronoun. In the following sentence, the pronouns *she* and *her* take
the place of the noun *Michelle*.

> Michelle was really excited because she̲ had finally found a job that
> made her̲ happy. (*She* refers to *Michelle*; *her* refers to *she*.)

Pronouns, like nouns, can be singular or plural.

- Singular pronouns (*I*, *he*, *she*, *it*, *him*, *her*, and so on) always take the
  place of singular nouns or pronouns.

  > Geoff left his jacket at work, so he̲ went back to get it̲ before it̲
  > could be stolen. (*He* refers to *Geoff*; *it* refers to *jacket*.)

- Plural pronouns (*we*, *they*, *our*, *their*, and so on) always take the
  place of plural nouns or pronouns.

  > Jessie and Dan got up early, but they̲ still missed their̲ train.
  > (*They* refers to *Jessie and Dan*; *their* refers to *they*.)

- The pronoun *you* can be either singular or plural.

  > When the volunteers met the mayor, they said, "We really admire
  > you̲." The mayor replied, "I admire you̲, too." (In the first sen-
  > tence, *you* refers to *the mayor*; in the second sentence, *you* refers
  > to *the volunteers*.)

FYI

Demonstrative Pronouns

Demonstrative pronouns—*this, that, these,* and *those*—point to one or more items.

- *This* and *that* point to one item: This is a work of fiction, and that is a nonfiction book.

- *These* and *those* point to more than one item: These are fruits, but those are vegetables.

PRACTICE

15-2 In the following sentences, fill in each blank with an appropriate pronoun.

Example: Ever since _____*I*_____ had my first scuba-diving experience, _____*I*_____ have wanted to search for sunken treasure.

(1) Three friends and _____*I*_____ decided to explore an area off the Florida coast where a shipwreck had occurred almost three hundred years ago. (2) The first step was to buy a boat; _____*we*_____ all agreed on a used rubber boat with a fifteen-horsepower engine. (3) _____*It*_____ had hardly been used and was in very good condition. (4) _____*We*_____ also needed some equipment, including an anchor and metal detectors. (5) If there was treasure on the bottom of the ocean, _____*we*_____ would find it. (6) _____*I*_____ stayed in the boat while my friends made the first dive. (7) At first, _____*they*_____ found only fish and sea worms, but _____*they*_____ didn't give up. (8) Finally, one of the metal detectors started beeping because _____*it*_____ had located a cannon and two cannonballs. (9) Then, it started beeping again; this time, _____*it*_____ had found some pieces of pottery and an old pistol. (10) Although our group didn't find any coins, _____*we*_____ all enjoyed our search for sunken treasure.

15d Pronoun-Antecedent Agreement

The word that a pronoun refers to is called the pronoun's **antecedent**. In the following sentence, the noun *leaf* is the antecedent of the pronoun *it*.

The leaf turned yellow, but it did not fall.

A pronoun must always agree with its antecedent. If an antecedent is singular, as it is in the sentence above, the pronoun must be singular. If the antecedent is plural, as it is in the sentence below, the pronoun must also be plural.

The leaves turned yellow, but they did not fall.

If an antecedent is feminine, the pronoun that refers to it must also be feminine.

Melissa passed her driver's exam with flying colors.

If an antecedent is masculine, the pronoun that refers to it must also be masculine.

Matt wondered what courses he should take.

If an antecedent is **neuter** (neither masculine nor feminine), the pronoun that refers to it must also be neuter.

The car broke down, but they refused to fix it again.

PRACTICE

15-3 In the following sentences, circle the antecedent of each underlined pronoun. Then, draw an arrow from the pronoun to the antecedent it refers to.

Example: College students today often fear they will be the victims of crime on campus.

(1) Few campuses are as safe as they should be, experts say. (2) However, crime on most campuses is probably no worse than it is in any other community. (3) Still, students have a right to know how safe their campuses are. (4) My friend Joyce never walks on campus without her

Teaching Tip
Try to assign both practices in 15d. Pronoun-antecedent agreement errors are very common in student writing.

e bedfordstmartins.com
/forw Additional
Grammar Exercises >
Identifying Antecedents

can of Mace. (5) Joyce believes she must be prepared for the worst. (6) Her boyfriend took a self-defense course that he said was very helpful. (7) My friends do not let fear of crime keep them from enjoying the college experience. (8) We know that our school is doing all it can to make the campus safe.

PRACTICE
15-4

Fill in each blank in the following passage with an appropriate pronoun.

Example: Americans celebrate July 4 because ____*it*____ is Independence Day.

(1) For some Germans, November 9 is a day to celebrate positive change; for others, ____*it*____ recalls the human potential for violence and destruction. (2) November 9, designated "World Freedom Day," is important because ____*it*____ is the day the Berlin Wall fell. (3) On that day in 1989, residents of East and West Germany were allowed to cross the barrier that had separated ____*them*____ since the end of World War II. (4) However, Germans have mixed feelings about this date because November 9 also reminds ____*them*____ of a dark moment in their history. (5) On the night of November 9, 1938, Nazis took sledgehammers and axes to as many Jewish businesses, synagogues, and homes as ____*they*____ could find. (6) In German, this violent event is called *Kristallnacht*; in English, ____*it*____ is known as "the Night of Broken Glass." (7) Because November 9 has been so important in German history, journalists sometimes refer to ____*it*____ as Germany's "day of fate." (8) Coincidentally, Albert Einstein, a German Jew, received the Nobel Prize on November 9, 1921; the theories ____*he*____ described have changed how scientists think. (9) Thus, November 9 in Germany is a day of opposites; like so many dates in human history, ____*it*____ marks both triumph and tragedy.

15e Special Problems with Agreement

Certain kinds of antecedents can cause problems for writers because they cannot easily be identified as singular or plural.

Compound Antecedents

A **compound antecedent** consists of two or more words connected by *and* or *or*.

- Compound antecedents connected by *and* are plural, and they are used with plural pronouns.

  During World War II, Belgium and France tried to protect their borders.

- Compound antecedents connected by *or* may take a singular or a plural pronoun. The pronoun always agrees with the word that is closer to it.

  Is it possible that European nations or Russia may send its [not *their*] troops?

  Is it possible that Russia or European nations may send their [not *its*] troops?

PRACTICE

15-5 In each of the following sentences, underline the compound antecedent, and circle the connecting word (*and* or *or*). Then, circle the appropriate pronoun in parentheses.

Example: Marge (and) Homer Simpson love (his or her/(their)) children very much in spite of the problems they cause.

1. Either *24* (or) *Lost* had the highest ratings for any television show in ((its)/their) final episode.

2. In *South Park*, Geek 1 (and) Geek 2 help create a time machine out of (his/(their)) friend Timmy's wheelchair.

3. Both Netflix (and) Blockbuster offer (its/(their)) movie rentals online.

4. Either cable stations (or) the networks hire the most attractive anchors to host (its/(their)) prime-time shows.

bedfordstmartins.com /forw Additional Grammar Exercises > Pronoun-Antecedent Agreement

Teaching Tip
Refer students to 23b for information on subject-verb agreement with compound subjects.

ESL Tip
If nonnative speakers have trouble with culture-specific references, allow them to work in pairs with native speakers.

5. Recent <u>movies</u> (and) <u>documentaries</u> about penguins have delighted (its/(their)) audiences.

6. In baseball, <u>pitchers</u> (and) <u>catchers</u> communicate (his or her/(their)) plays with hand signals.

7. Either <u>Playstation3</u> (or) <u>Xbox</u> gives ((its)/their) players many hours of gaming fun.

8. In summer, many <u>parents</u> (and) <u>children</u> enjoy spending (his or her/ (their)) time at water parks.

9. <u>Hurricanes</u> (or) <u>tornadoes</u> can be frightening to (its/(their)) victims.

Indefinite Pronoun Antecedents

bedfordstmartins.com
/forw Additional
Grammar Exercises >
Indefinite Pronoun
Antecedents

Most pronouns refer to a specific person or thing. However, **indefinite pronouns** do not refer to any particular person or thing.

Most indefinite pronouns are singular.

Teaching Tip
You might want to tell students that some indefinite pronouns (such as *all*, *any*, *more*, *most*, *none*, and *some*) can be either singular or plural. (*All is quiet. All were qualified.*)

Singular Indefinite Pronouns		
another	everybody	no one
anybody	everyone	nothing
anyone	everything	one
anything	much	somebody
each	neither	someone
either	nobody	something

Teaching Tip
Refer students to 23f for information on subject-verb agreement with indefinite pronouns.

When an indefinite pronoun antecedent is singular, use a singular pronoun to refer to it.

Everything was in <u>its</u> place. (*Everything* is singular, so it is used with the singular pronoun *its*.)

FYI

Indefinite Pronouns with *Of*

The singular indefinite pronouns *each, either, neither,* and *one* are often used in phrases with *of*—*each of, either of, neither of,* or *one of*—followed by a plural noun. Even in such phrases, these indefinite pronoun antecedents are always singular and take singular pronouns.

Each of the routes has <u>its</u> [not *their*] own special challenges.

A few indefinite pronouns are plural.

ESL Tip
Remind students that sin-
gular indefinite pronouns
do not have plural forms.
Write some sample
sentences on the board.
Then, let students come
up with their own
sentences. Make this a
classroom activity, but call
on ESL students for
participation.

Plural Indefinite Pronouns

both
few
many
others
several

When an indefinite pronoun antecedent is plural, use a plural pronoun
to refer to it.

> They all wanted to graduate early, but few received their diplomas in
> January. (*Few* is plural, so it is used with the plural pronoun *their*.)

FYI

Using *His* or *Her* with Indefinite Pronouns

Even though the indefinite pronouns *anybody, anyone, everybody,
everyone, somebody, someone,* and so on are singular, many people
use plural pronouns to refer to them.

> Everyone must hand in their completed work before 2 p.m.

This usage is widely accepted in spoken English. Nevertheless, indefinite pronouns like *everyone* are singular, and written English
requires a singular pronoun.

However, using the singular pronoun *his* to refer to *everyone*
suggests that *everyone* refers to a male. Using *his or her* is more
accurate because the indefinite pronoun can refer to either a male
or a female.

> Everyone must hand in his or her completed work before
> 2 p.m.

When used over and over again, *he or she, him or her,* and *his
or her* can create wordy or awkward sentences. Whenever possible,
use plural forms.

> All students must hand in their completed work before 2 p.m.

PRACTICE

15-6   Edit the following sentences for errors in pronoun-antecedent agreement. When you edit, you have two options: either substitute *its* or *his or her* for *their* to refer to the singular antecedent, or replace the singular antecedent with a plural word.

Examples: Everyone is responsible for ~~their~~ own passport.
                                                      his or her

All
~~Each~~ of the children took their books out of their backpacks.

Answers may vary.
1. Either of the hybrid cars comes with their own tax rebate.   *its*

2. Anyone who loses their locker key must pay $5.00 for a new one.   *his or her*

3. Everyone loves seeing their home team win.   *his or her*

4. Somebody left their scarf and gloves on the subway.   *his or her*

Most people wait
5. ~~Almost everyone waits~~ until the last minute to file their tax returns.

All the students
6. ~~Each student~~ returned their library books on time.

7. Everything we need to build the model airplane comes in their kit.   *its*

8. Anyone who wants to succeed needs to develop their public-speaking   *his or her*

   skills.

9. One of the hockey teams just won their first Olympic medal.   *its*

10. No one leaving the show early will get their money back.   *his or her*

Collective Noun Antecedents

Collective nouns are words (such as *band* and *team*) that name a group of people or things but are singular. Because they are singular, collective noun antecedents are used with singular pronouns.

The band played on, but it never played our song.

Frequently Used Collective Nouns

army	class	family	jury
association	club	gang	mob
audience	committee	government	team
band	company	group	union

PRACTICE

15-7   Circle the collective noun antecedent in each of the following sentences. Then, circle the correct pronoun in parentheses.

Teaching Tip
Make sure students understand that an antecedent may be a compound, an indefinite pronoun, or a collective noun.

Example: The (jury) returned with ((its)/their) verdict.

1. The (company) offers good benefits to ((its)/their) employees.

2. All five study (groups) must hand in (its/(their)) projects by Tuesday.

3. Any (government) should be concerned about the welfare of ((its)/their) citizens.

4. The Asian Students (Union) is sponsoring a party to celebrate ((its)/their) twentieth anniversary.

5. Every (family) has ((its)/their) share of problems.

6. To join the electricians' (union), applicants had to pass ((its)/their) test.

7. Even the best (teams) have (its/(their)) bad days.

8. The (orchestra) has just signed a contract to make ((its)/their) first recording.

bedfordstmartins.com /forw Additional Grammar Exercises > Revising for Pronoun-Antecedent Agreement

9. The math (class) did very well with ((its)/their) new teacher.

10. The (club) voted to expand ((its)/their) membership.

15f   Vague and Unnecessary Pronouns

Vague and unnecessary pronouns clutter up your writing and make it hard to understand. Eliminating them will make your writing clearer and easier for readers to follow.

Vague Pronouns

A pronoun should always refer to a specific antecedent. When a pronoun—such as *they* or *it*—has no antecedent, readers will be confused.

VAGUE PRONOUN   On the news, <u>they</u> said baseball players would strike. (Who said baseball players would strike?)

VAGUE PRONOUN   <u>It</u> says in today's paper that our schools are overcrowded. (Who says schools are overcrowded?)

If a pronoun does not refer to a specific word in the sentence, replace the pronoun with a noun.

REVISED On the news, the <u>sportscaster</u> said baseball players would strike.

REVISED An <u>editorial</u> in today's paper says that our schools are overcrowded.

Unnecessary Pronouns

Teaching Tip
Remind students that only an intensive pronoun can come right after its antecedent: *I myself prefer to wait*. Refer them to 15i.

When a pronoun comes directly after its antecedent, it is unnecessary.

UNNECESSARY PRONOUN The librarian, <u>he</u> told me I should check the database.

In the sentence above, the pronoun *he* serves no purpose. Readers do not need to be directed back to the pronoun's antecedent (the noun *librarian*) because it appears right before the pronoun. The pronoun should therefore be deleted.

REVISED The librarian told me I should check the database.

PRACTICE
15-8

The following sentences contain vague or unnecessary pronouns. Revise each sentence on the line below it.

Example: On their website, they advertised a special offer.

On its website, the Gap advertised a special offer.

Answers may vary.

1. In Jamaica, they love their spectacular green mountains.

Jamaicans love their spectacular green mountains.

2. My hamster, he loves his exercise wheel.

My hamster loves his exercise wheel.

3. On *Jeopardy!* they have to give the answers in the form of questions.

On Jeopardy! contestants have to give the answers in the form of questions.

4. On televisions all over the world, they watched the moon landing.

On televisions all over the world, viewers watched the moon landing.

5. In Sociology 320, they do not use a textbook.

In Sociology 320, students do not use a textbook.

**bedfordstmartins.com
/forw** Additional
Grammar Exercises >
Personal Pronouns

15g   Pronoun Case

A **personal pronoun** refers to a particular person or thing. Personal pronouns change form according to their function in a sentence. Personal pronouns can be *subjective*, *objective*, or *possessive*.

Personal Pronouns

SUBJECTIVE	OBJECTIVE	POSSESSIVE
I	me	my, mine
he	him	his
she	her	her, hers
it	it	its
we	us	our, ours
you	you	your, yours
they	them	their, theirs
who	whom	whose
whoever	whomever	

Teaching Tip
Refer students to 15h for information on how to use *who* and *whom*.

Subjective Case

When a pronoun is a subject, it is in the **subjective case**.

Finally, she realized that dreams could come true.

Teaching Tip
You may want to tell students that the subjective case is used for the subject of a clause as well as for the subject of a sentence.

Objective Case

When a pronoun is an object, it is in the **objective case**.

If Joanna hurries, she can stop him. (The pronoun *him* is the object of the verb *can stop*.)

Professor Miller sent us information about his research. (The pronoun *us* is the object of the verb *sent*.)

Marc threw the ball to them. (The pronoun *them* is the object of the preposition *to*.)

**bedfordstmartins.com
/forw** Additional
Grammar Exercises >
Pronoun Case

Possessive Case

When a pronoun shows ownership, it is in the **possessive case**.

Hieu took his lunch to the meeting. (The pronoun *his* indicates that the lunch belongs to Hieu.)

Debbie and Kim decided to take their lunches, too. (The pronoun *their* indicates that the lunches belong to Debbie and Kim.)

Teaching Tip
Tell your students that
they may find it helpful
to consult the pronoun
chart on page 393 while
they do this exercise.

PRACTICE

15-9 In the following passage, fill in the blank after each pronoun to indicate whether the pronoun is subjective (*S*), objective (*O*), or possessive (*P*).

Example: Famous criminals Bonnie and Clyde committed their

_____*P*_____ crimes in broad daylight.

(1) Bonnie Parker and Clyde Barrow are remembered today because

they _____*S*_____ were the first celebrity criminals. (2) With their _____*P*_____

gang, Bonnie and Clyde robbed a dozen banks as well as many stores and

gas stations. (3) In small towns, they _____*S*_____ terrorized the police.

(4) Capturing them _____*O*_____ seemed impossible. (5) To many Americans,

however, their _____*P*_____ crimes seemed exciting. (6) Because Bonnie was

a woman, she _____*S*_____ was especially fascinating to them _____*O*_____.

(7) During their _____*P*_____ crimes, Bonnie and Clyde would often carry a

camera, take photographs of themselves, and then send them _____*O*_____

to the newspapers, which were happy to publish them _____*O*_____.

(8) By the time they _____*S*_____ were killed in an ambush by Texas

and Louisiana law officers, Bonnie and Clyde were famous all over the

United States.

15h Special Problems with Pronoun Case

When you are trying to determine which pronoun case to use in a sentence, three kinds of pronouns can cause problems: pronouns in compounds, pronouns in comparisons, and the pronouns *who* and *whom* (or *whoever* and *whomever*).

Pronouns in Compounds

Sometimes a pronoun is linked to a noun or to another pronoun with *and* or *or* to form a **compound**.

> The teacher and <u>I</u> met for an hour.
> <u>He</u> or <u>she</u> can pick up Jenny at school.

To determine whether to use the subjective or objective case for a pronoun in the second part of a compound, follow the same rules that apply for a pronoun that is not part of a compound.

Teaching Tip
Remind students that the first-person pronoun always comes last in compounds like *Toby and I* and *my father and me*.

■ If the compound is a subject, use the subjective case.

> <u>Toby and I</u> [not *me*] like jazz.

> <u>He and I</u> [not *me*] went to the movies.

■ If the compound is an object, use the objective case.

> The school sent <u>my father and me</u> [not *I*] the financial-aid forms.

> This argument is between <u>Kate and me</u> [not *I*].

FYI

Choosing Pronouns in Compounds

To determine which pronoun case to use in a compound that joins a noun and a pronoun, rewrite the sentence with just the pronoun.

> Toby and [*I* or *me*?] like jazz.
> **I** like jazz. (not *Me like jazz*)
> Toby and **I** like jazz.

Teaching Tip
Explain that the objective case is used with the contraction *let's*: *Let's* (*let us*) *you and me* (not *I*) *go swimming*. Remind students that *let's* includes the objective case pronoun *us*.

PRACTICE

15-10 In the following sentences, the underlined pronouns are parts of compounds. Check them for correct subjective or objective case. If the pronoun is incorrect, cross it out, and write the correct form above it. If the pronoun is correct, write *C* above it.

Example: My classmates and <u>I</u> were surprised by the results of a study on listening.

(1) According to a recent study, the average listener remembers only 50 percent of what <u>him</u> or <u>her</u> hears. (2) Two days later, <u>he</u> or <u>she</u> can correctly recall only 25 percent of the total message. (3) My friend Alyssa and <u>me</u> decided to ask our school to sponsor a presentation about listening in the classroom. (4) One point the speaker made was especially helpful to Alyssa and <u>I</u>. (5) <u>We</u> now know that <u>us</u> and the other students

in our class each have four times more mental "room" than we need for listening. (6) The presenter taught the other workshop participants and ~~we~~ ^{us} how to use this extra space. (7) Now, whenever one of our instructors pauses to write on the board or take a sip of water, Alyssa and I remember to silently summarize the last point he or she made. (8) Throughout the class, we pay special attention to the big ideas and overall structure that the instructor wants the other students and us to understand. (9) Above all, we do not waste our mental energy on distractions that other students and ~~us~~ ^{we} ourselves create, such as dropped books or whispers.

Pronouns in Comparisons

Sometimes a pronoun appears after the word *than* or *as* in the second part of a **comparison**.

> John is luckier <u>than I</u>.
> The inheritance changed Raymond as much <u>as her</u>.

- If the pronoun is a subject, use the subjective case.

> John is luckier <u>than I</u> [am].

- If the pronoun is an object, use the objective case.

> The inheritance changed Raymond as much <u>as</u> [it changed] <u>her</u>.

Teaching Tip
Tell students that to decide whether to use the subjective or objective form of a pronoun, they should add in brackets the words needed to complete the comparison.

FYI

Choosing Pronouns in Comparisons

Sometimes the pronoun you use can change your sentence's meaning. For example, if you say, "I like Cheerios more than *he*," you mean that you like Cheerios more than the other person likes them.

> I like Cheerios more than he [does].

If, however, you say, "I like Cheerios more than *him*," you mean that you like Cheerios more than you like the other person.

> I like Cheerios more than [I like] him.

PRACTICE

15-11 Each of the following sentences includes a comparison with a pronoun following the word *than* or *as*. Write in each blank the correct form (subjective or objective) of the pronoun in parentheses. In brackets, add the word or words needed to complete the comparison.

Example: Many people are better poker players than ___*I [am]*___ (I/me).

1. The survey showed that most people like the candidate's wife as much as ___*[they like] him*___ (he/him).

2. No one enjoys shopping more than ___*she [does]*___ (she/her).

3. My brother and Aunt Cecile were very close, so her death affected him more than ___*[it affected] me*___ (I/me).

4. No two people could have a closer relationship than ___*they [have]*___ (they/them).

5. My neighbor drives better than ___*I [do]*___ (I/me).

6. He may be as old as ___*I [am]*___ (I/me), but he does not have as much work experience.

7. That jacket fits you better than ___*[it fits] me*___ (I/me).

8. The other company had a lower bid than ___*we [had]*___ (we/us), but we were awarded the contract.

Who and *Whom, Whoever* and *Whomever*

To determine whether to use *who* or *whom* (or *whoever* or *whomever*), you need to know how the pronoun functions within the clause in which it appears.

■ When the pronoun is the subject of the clause, use *who* or *whoever*.

> I wonder <u>who</u> wrote that song. (*Who* is the subject of the clause *who wrote that song.*)

> I will vote for <u>whoever</u> supports the youth center. (*Whoever* is the subject of the clause *whoever supports the youth center.*)

e **bedfordstmartins.com /forw** Additional Grammar Exercises > Pronoun Case: Who/Whom

Teaching Tip

Tell students that in conversation, people often
use *who* for both subjective case (*Who wrote that
song?*) and objective case
(*Who are you going with?*).
In writing, however, they
should always use *whom*
for the objective case:
*With whom are you
going?*

■ When the pronoun is the object, use *whom* or *whomever*.

Whom do the police suspect? (*Whom* is the direct object of the verb *suspect*.)

I wonder whom the song is about. (*Whom* is the object of the preposition *about* in the clause *whom the song is about*.)

Vote for whomever you prefer. (*Whomever* is the object of the verb *prefer* in the clause *whomever you prefer*.)

FYI

Who and *Whom*

To determine whether to use *who* or *whom*, try substituting another pronoun for *who* or *whom* in the clause. If you can substitute
he or *she*, use *who*; if you can substitute *him* or *her*, use *whom*.

[Who/Whom] wrote a love song? He wrote a love song.

[Who/Whom] was the song about? The song was about her.

The same test will work for *whoever* and *whomever*.

PRACTICE

15-12   Circle the correct form—*who* or *whom* (or *whoever* or
whomever)—in parentheses in each sentence.

Example: With (who/whom) did Rob collaborate?

1. The defense team learned (who/whom) was going to testify for the prosecution.

2. (Who/Whom) does she think she can find to be a witness?

3. The runner (who/whom) crosses the finish line first will be the winner.

4. They will argue their case to (whoever/whomever) will listen.

5. It will take time to decide (who/whom) is the record holder.

6. Take these forms to the clerk (who/whom) is at the front desk.

7. We will have to penalize (whoever/whomever) misses the first training session.

8. (Who/Whom) did Kobe take to the prom?

9. We saw the man (who/whom) fired the shots.

10. To (who/whom) am I speaking?

15i   Reflexive and Intensive Pronouns

bedfordstmartins.com /forw Additional Grammar Exercises > Reflexive Pronouns

Two special kinds of pronouns, *reflexive pronouns* and *intensive pronouns*, end in *-self* (singular) or *-selves* (plural). Although the functions of the two kinds of pronouns are different, their forms are identical.

Reflexive and Intensive Pronouns

Singular Forms

ANTECEDENT	REFLEXIVE OR INTENSIVE PRONOUN
I	myself
you	yourself
he	himself
she	herself
it	itself

Plural Forms

ANTECEDENT	REFLEXIVE OR INTENSIVE PRONOUN
we	ourselves
you	yourselves
they	themselves

Reflexive Pronouns

Reflexive pronouns indicate that people or things did something to themselves or for themselves.

Rosanna lost herself in the novel.

You need to watch yourself when you mix those solutions.

Mehul and Paul made themselves cold drinks.

Intensive Pronouns

Intensive pronouns always appear directly after their antecedents, and they are used for emphasis.

I myself have had some experience in sales and marketing.

The victim himself collected the reward.

They themselves were uncertain of the significance of their findings.

Teaching Tip
Remind students not to use reflexive or intensive pronouns as subjects: *Kim and I* (not *Kim and myself*) started work on Monday.

PRACTICE

15-13 Fill in the correct reflexive or intensive pronoun in each of the following sentences.

Example: The opening act was exciting, but the main attraction _____*itself*_____ was boring.

1. My aunt welcomed her visitors and told them to make _____*themselves*_____ at home.

2. Migrating birds can direct _____*themselves*_____ through clouds, storms, and moonless nights.

3. The First Lady _____*herself*_____ gave a speech at the rally.

4. We all finished the marathon without injuring _____*ourselves*_____.

5. Even though the government offered help to flood victims, the residents _____*themselves*_____ did most of the rebuilding.

6. Sometimes he finds _____*himself*_____ daydreaming in class.

7. The guide warned us to watch _____*ourselves*_____ on the slippery path.

8. The senators were not happy about committing _____*themselves*_____ to vote for lower taxes.

9. She gave _____*herself*_____ a manicure.

10. Although everyone else in my family can sing or play a musical instrument, I _____*myself*_____ am tone-deaf.

EDITING PRACTICE

Check the following student essay for errors in plural noun forms, pronoun case, and pronoun-antecedent agreement and edit the essay as necessary. *Answers will vary.*

Cell-Phone Misbehavior

Good ~~manneres~~ *manners* used to mean using the right fork and holding the door open for others. Today, however, people may find that good manners are more complicated than ~~it~~ *they* used to be. New inventions have led to new challenges. Cell phones, in particular, have created some problems.

One problem is the "cell yell," which is the tendency of ~~a person~~ *people* to shout while they are using their cell phones. Why do they do this? Maybe they do not realize how loudly they are talking. Maybe they yell out of frustration. Anyone can become angry when ~~they lose~~ *he or she loses* a call. Dead ~~batterys~~ *batteries* can be infuriating. Unfortunately, ~~the yeller annoys~~ *yellers annoy* everyone around them.

Even if cell-phone users ~~theirselves~~ *themselves* speak normally, other people can hear them. My friends and ~~me~~ *I* are always calling each other, and we do not always pay attention to ~~whom~~ *who* can hear us. The result is that other people are victims of "secondhand conversations." These conversations are not as bad for people's health as secondhand smoke, but ~~it is~~ *they are* just as annoying. ~~Whom~~ *Who* really wants to hear about the private ~~lifes~~ *lives* of strangers? Restrooms used to be private; now, ~~whomever~~ *whoever* is in the next stall can overhear someone's private cell-phone conversation and learn ~~their~~ *his or her* secrets.

Also, some cell-phone ~~user~~ *users* seem to think that getting ~~his~~ *their* calls is more important than anything else that might be going on. Phones ring, chirp, or play silly tunes at ~~concertes,~~ *concerts,* in classrooms, at weddings, in ~~churchs,~~ *churches,* and even at funerals. Can you picture a grieving family at a cemetery having ~~their~~ *its* service interrupted by a ringing phone? People should have enough sense to turn off ~~his or her~~ *their* cell phones at times like these.

READING TIP

Consider the student writer's tone (expression of emotion or feeling) as you read this essay. What words or phrases provide clues to the writer's attitude toward cell-phone misbehavior?

401

In the United States, there are more than 150 million cell phones. Some
people hate being tied to cell phones, but they do not think they can live
~~them.~~
without it. The problem is that cell phones became popular before there were
^
their
any rules for its use. However, even if the government passed laws about
^
it   *them.*
cell-phone behavior, they would have a tough time enforcing it. In any case,
^   ^
themselves.
cell-phone users should not need laws to make them behave theirself.
^

review checklist

Nouns and Pronouns

☐ A noun is a word that names something. A singular noun names
one thing; a plural noun names more than one thing. (See 15a.)

☐ Most nouns add -*s* or -*es* to form plurals. Some nouns have
irregular plural forms. (See 15b.)

☐ A pronoun is a word that refers to and takes the place of a noun
or another pronoun. (See 15c.)

☐ The word a pronoun refers to is called the pronoun's antecedent.
A pronoun and its antecedent must always agree. (See 15d.)

☐ Compound antecedents connected by *and* are plural and are
used with plural pronouns. Compound antecedents connected
by *or* may take singular or plural pronouns. (See 15e.)

☐ Most indefinite pronoun antecedents are singular and are used
with singular pronouns; some are plural and are used with plural
pronouns. (See 15e.)

☐ Collective noun antecedents are singular and are used with singular pronouns. (See 15e.)

☐ A pronoun should always refer to a specific antecedent. (See 15f.)

☐ Personal pronouns can be in the subjective, objective, or possessive case. (See 15g.)

☐ Pronouns present special problems when they are used in compounds and comparisons. The pronouns *who* and *whom* and
whoever and *whomever* can also cause problems. (See 15h.)

☐ Reflexive and intensive pronouns must agree with their antecedents. (See 15i.)

16 Understanding Adjectives and Adverbs

16a Identifying Adjectives and Adverbs

Adjectives and adverbs are words that modify (identify or describe) other words. They help make sentences more specific and more interesting.

An **adjective** answers the question *What kind? Which one?* or *How many?* Adjectives modify nouns or pronouns.

> The Turkish city of Istanbul spans two continents. (*Turkish* modifies the noun *city*, and *two* modifies the noun *continents*.)

> It is fascinating because of its location and history. (*Fascinating* modifies the pronoun *it*.)

FYI

Demonstrative Adjectives

Demonstrative adjectives—*this*, *that*, *these*, and *those*—do not describe other words. They simply identify particular nouns.

This and *that* identify singular nouns and pronouns.

> This website is much more up-to-date than that one.

These and *those* identify plural nouns.

> These words and phrases are French, but those expressions are Creole.

An **adverb** answers the question *How? Why? When? Where?* or *To what extent?* Adverbs modify verbs, adjectives, or other adverbs.

> Traffic moved steadily. (*Steadily* modifies the verb *moved*.)

> Still, we were quite impatient. (*Quite* modifies the adjective *impatient*.)

> Very slowly, we moved into the center lane. (*Very* modifies the adverb *slowly*.)

bedfordstmartins.com /forw LearningCurve > Verbs, Adjectives, and Adverbs; Additional Grammar Exercises > Identifying Adjectives and Adverbs

Teaching Tip
Explain that some adjectives, such as *Turkish*, are capitalized because they are formed from proper nouns. Refer students to 15a.

Teaching Tip
You might remind students not to use demonstrative adjectives in nonstandard phrases like *this here* and *that there*.

FYI

Distinguishing Adjectives from Adverbs

Many adverbs are formed when -*ly* is added to an adjective form.

ADJECTIVE	ADVERB
slow	slowly
nice	nicely
quick	quickly
real	really

ADJECTIVE   Let me give you one quick reminder. (*Quick* modifies the noun *reminder*.)

ADVERB   He quickly changed the subject. (*Quickly* modifies the verb *changed*.)

PRACTICE

16-1   In the following sentences, circle the correct form (adjective or adverb) from the choices in parentheses.

Example: Beatles enthusiasts all over the world have formed tribute bands devoted to the (famous/famously) group's music.

(1) Tribute bands go to (great/greatly) lengths to show appreciation for their favorite musicians. (2) Fans who have a (real/really) strong affection for a particular band may decide to play its music and copy its style. (3) Sometimes they form their own groups and have successful careers (simple/simply) performing that band's music. (4) These groups are (usual/usually) called "tribute bands." (5) Most tribute bands are (passionate/passionately) dedicated to reproducing the original group's work. (6) They not only play the group's songs but (careful/carefully) imitate the group's look. (7) They study the band members' facial expressions and body movements and create (exact/exactly) copies of the band's costumes and instruments. (8) Some more (inventive/inventively) tribute bands take the original band's songs and interpret them (different/differently).

(9) For example, by performing Beatles songs in the style of Metallica, the tribute band Beatallica has created a (unique/uniquely) sound. (10) Some people believe such tributes are the (ultimate/ultimately) compliment to the original band; others feel (sure/surely) that tribute groups are just copycats who (serious/seriously) lack imagination.

Teaching Tip
Explain that a linking verb such as *feel* is followed by an adjective, not an adverb. Refer students to 17c.

FYI

Good and Well

Be careful not to confuse *good* and *well*. Unlike regular adjectives, whose adverb forms add *-ly*, the adjective *good* is irregular. Its adverb form is *well*.

ADJECTIVE   Fred Astaire was a good dancer. (*Good* modifies the noun *dancer*.)

ADVERB   He danced especially well with Ginger Rogers. (*Well* modifies the verb *danced*.)

Always use *well* when you are describing a person's health.

He really didn't feel well [not *good*] after eating the entire pizza.

e bedfordstmartins.com
/forw Additional Grammar Exercises > *Good* and *Well*

PRACTICE

16-2

Circle the correct form (*good* or *well*) in the sentences below.

Example: It can be hard for some people to find a (good/well) job that they really like.

(1) Some people may not do (good/well) sitting in an office. (2) Instead, they may prefer to find jobs that take advantage of their (good/well) physical condition. (3) Such people might consider becoming smoke jumpers—firefighters who are (good/well) at parachuting from small planes into remote areas to battle forest fires. (4) Smoke jumpers must be able to work (good/well) even without much sleep. (5) They must also handle danger (good/well). (6) They look forward to the (good/well) feeling of saving a forest or someone's home. (7) As they battle fires, surrounded

by smoke and fumes, smoke jumpers may not feel very (good/well). (8) Sometimes things go wrong; for example, when their parachutes fail to work (good/well), jumpers may be injured or even killed. (9) Smoke jumpers do not get paid particularly (good/well). (10) However, they are proud of their strength and endurance and feel (good/well) about their work.

16b Comparatives and Superlatives

Teaching Tip
Tell students that some adverbs—such as *very*, *somewhat*, *quite*, *extremely*, *rather*, and *moderately*—as well as the demonstrative adjectives *this*, *that*, *these*, and *those*, do not have comparative or superlative forms.

The **comparative** form of an adjective or adverb compares two people or things. Adjectives and adverbs form the comparative with *-er* or *more*. The **superlative** form of an adjective or adverb compares more than two things. Adjectives and adverbs form the superlative with *-est* or *most*.

ADJECTIVES   This film is <u>dull</u> and <u>predictable</u>.

COMPARATIVE   The film I saw last week was even <u>duller</u> and <u>more predictable</u> than this one.

SUPERLATIVE   The film I saw last night was the <u>dullest</u> and <u>most predictable</u> one I've ever seen.

ADVERBS   For a beginner, Jane did needlepoint <u>skillfully</u>.

COMPARATIVE   After she had watched the demonstration, Jane did needlepoint <u>more skillfully</u> than Rosie.

SUPERLATIVE   Of the twelve beginners, Jane did needlepoint the <u>most skillfully</u>.

bedfordstmartins.com /forw Additional Grammar Exercises > Comparatives and Superlatives

Forming Comparatives and Superlatives

Adjectives

Teaching Tip
Tell students that the adjective *unique* means "the only one." For this reason, it has no comparative or superlative form (*more unique* and *most unique* are incorrect). Other absolute adjectives that do not have comparative or superlative forms are *perfect*, *impossible*, *infinite*, and *dead*.

■ One-syllable adjectives generally form the comparative with *-er* and the superlative with *-est*.

   great   greater   greatest

■ Adjectives with two or more syllables form the comparative with *more* and the superlative with *most*.

   wonderful   more wonderful   most wonderful

Exception: Two-syllable adjectives ending in *-y* add *-er* or *-est* after changing the *y* to an *i*.

funny   funnier   funniest

Adverbs

▪ All adverbs ending in *-ly* form the comparative with *more* and the superlative with *most*.

efficiently   more efficiently   most efficiently

▪ Some other adverbs form the comparative with *-er* and the superlative with *-est*.

soon   sooner   soonest

Solving Special Problems with Comparatives and Superlatives

The following rules will help you avoid errors with comparatives and superlatives.

▪ Never use both *-er* and *more* to form the comparative or both *-est* and *most* to form the superlative.

Nothing could have been <u>more awful</u>. (not *more awfuller*)

Space Mountain is the <u>most frightening</u> (not *most frighteningest*) ride at Disney World.

▪ Never use the superlative when you are comparing only two things.

This is the <u>more serious</u> (not *most serious*) of the two problems.

▪ Never use the comparative when you are comparing more than two things.

This is the <u>worst</u> (not *worse*) day of my life.

Teaching Tip
Tell students that when they form comparatives, they should have only one ending with an *r* sound (not *more greater* or *more better*, for example).

PRACTICE

16-3   Fill in the correct comparative form of the word supplied in parentheses.

Example: Children tend to be _____*noisier*_____ (noisy) than adults.

1. Traffic always moves _____*more slowly*_____ (slow) during rush hour than late at night.

2. The weather report says temperatures will be _____colder_____ (cold) tomorrow.

3. Some elderly people are _____healthier_____ (healthy) than younger people.

4. It has been proven that pigs are _____more intelligent_____ (intelligent) than dogs.

5. When someone asks you to repeat yourself, you usually answer _____more loudly_____ (loud).

6. The _____taller_____ (tall) of the two buildings was damaged by the earthquake.

7. They want to teach their son to be _____more respectful_____ (respectful) of women than many young men are.

8. Las Vegas is _____more famous_____ (famous) for its casinos than for its natural resources.

9. The WaterDrop is _____wilder_____ (wild) than any other ride in the amusement park.

10. You must move _____more quickly_____ (quick) if you expect to catch the ball.

PRACTICE

16-4 Fill in the correct superlative form of the word supplied in parentheses.

READING TIP

When you come across an unfamiliar word, such as *empowered*, take a few minutes to study the words, phrases, and sentences surrounding the unfamiliar word. These **context clues** can help you to figure out the meaning of the unfamiliar word.

Example: The first remote controls came with only the _____most expensive_____ (expensive) televisions.

(1) The invention of the remote control in the 1950s was one of the _____most important_____ (important) developments in television history. (2) The remote was especially welcomed by lazy viewers, who were the _____most empowered_____ (empowered) by the new device. (3) Even the _____laziest_____ (lazy) people could now change channels without getting off the couch. (4) However, as remote controls developed, even the _____simplest_____ (simple) devices could sometimes confuse

the _____*most skilled*_____ (skilled) users. (5) The large number of buttons

became one of the _____*most irritating*_____ (irritating) features. (6) Even today,

remotes remain one of the _____*most unnecessarily*_____ (unnecessarily) complicated

electronic devices. (7) According to one critic, the TV remote is one of the

_____*most poorly*_____ (poorly) designed inventions of all time. (8) Improving

the remote is one of the _____*most challenging*_____ (challenging) projects for

inventors. (9) Already, the _____*most innovative*_____ (innovative) companies

are adding voice and motion control to the _____*latest*_____ (late) remotes.

(10) One of the _____*most astonishing*_____ (astonishing) possible new developments

may be a remote control operated entirely by the viewer's mind.

FYI

Good/Well and Bad/Badly

Most adjectives and adverbs form the comparative with *-er* or *more*
and the superlative with *-est* or *most*. The adjectives *good* and *bad*
and their adverb forms *well* and *badly* are exceptions.

ADJECTIVE	COMPARATIVE FORM	SUPERLATIVE FORM
good	better	best
bad	worse	worst

ADVERB	COMPARATIVE FORM	SUPERLATIVE FORM
well	better	best
badly	worse	worst

e bedfordstmartins.com
/forw Additional
Grammar Exercises >
Good/Well and *Bad/Badly*

PRACTICE

16-5   Fill in the correct comparative or superlative form of *good, well, bad,* or *badly.*

Example: My sister is a _____*better*_____ (good) runner than I am.

1. Neela was certain she was the _____*best*_____ (good) chef in the

   competition.

2. Because he studied more, Helio earned _____*better*_____ (good) grades

   than his sister.

3. An optimist, Mara always thinks she will do _____better_____ (well) next time.

4. Many people drive the _____worst_____ (badly) when they are in a hurry.

5. Of all the mortgage companies Ramon researched, Plains Bank had the _____best_____ (good) interest rate.

6. I feel bad when I get rejected, but I feel _____worse_____ (bad) when I do not try.

7. For nontraditional students, access to education is _____better_____ (good) than it used to be.

8. Jamie sings badly, but Simon sings _____worse_____ (badly).

9. I learn the _____best_____ (well) when I am not distracted.

10. After looking at every painting in the gallery, they decided that the landscapes were definitely the _____worst_____ (bad) paintings there.

EDITING PRACTICE

Read the following student essay, which includes errors in the use of adjectives and adverbs. Make any changes necessary to correct adjectives incorrectly used for adverbs and adverbs incorrectly used for adjectives. Also, correct any errors in the use of comparatives and superlatives and in the use of demonstrative adjectives. Finally, try to add some adjectives and adverbs that you feel would make the writer's ideas clearer or more specific. The first sentence has been edited for you.   *Answers will vary.*

Starting Over

A wedding can be the *most joyful* joyfullest occasion in two people's lives, the

beginning of a couple's most happiest years. For some unlucky women, however,

a wedding can be the *worst* worse thing that ever happens; it is the beginning not of

their happiness but of their battered lives. As I went through the joyful day

of my wedding, I wanted *badly* bad to find happiness for the rest of my life, but what

I hoped and wished for did not come true.

I was married in the savannah belt of the Sudan in the eastern part of

Africa, where I grew up. I was barely twenty-two years old. The first two years

of my marriage progressed *peacefully,* peaceful, but problems started as soon as our first

child was born.

Many American women say, "If my husband hit me just once, that would be

it. I'd leave." But *this modern* those attitude does not work in cultures where tradition has

overshadowed women's rights and divorce is not accepted. All women can do

is accept their *sad* sadly fate. Battered women give many reasons for staying in their

abusive marriages, but fear is the *most common.* commonest. Fear immobilizes these women, ruling

their decisions, their actions, and their very lives. This is how it was for me.

Of course, I was *really* real afraid whenever my husband hit me. I would run to

my mother's house and cry, but she would always talk me into going back and

being more *patient* patiently with my husband. Our tradition discourages divorce, and

READING TIP

In this student essay, the main idea is not immediately apparent. To identify the main idea of an essay like this one, ask yourself what point the writer is trying to make.

411

wife-beating is taken for granted. The situation is really quite ironic: the

religion I practice sets harsh punishments for abusive husbands, but tradition

has so overpowered religion that the laws do not really work very ~~good~~. *well.*

One night, I asked myself whether life had treated me ~~fair~~. *fairly.* True, I had a high

school diploma and two of the ~~beautifullest~~ *most beautiful* children in the world, but all this

was not enough. I realized that to stand up to the husband who treated me so

~~bad~~, *badly,* I would have to achieve a ~~more~~ better education than he had. That night,

I decided to get a college education in the United States. My husband opposed *strongly*

my decision, but with the support of my father and mother, I was able to begin

to change my life. My years as a student and single parent in the United States

have been ~~real~~ *really* difficult for me, but I know I made the right choice.

review checklist

bedfordstmartins.com
/forw LearningCurve >
Verbs, Adjectives, and
Adverbs

Adjectives and Adverbs

☐ Adjectives modify nouns or pronouns. (See 16a.)

☐ Demonstrative adjectives—*this, that, these,* and *those*—identify particular nouns. (See 16a.)

☐ Adverbs modify verbs, adjectives, or other adverbs. (See 16a.)

☐ To compare two people or things, use the comparative form of an adjective or adverb. To compare more than two people or things, use the superlative form of an adjective or adverb. (See 16b.)

☐ The adjectives *good* and *bad* and their adverb forms *well* and *badly* have irregular comparative and superlative forms. (See 16b.)

17 Writing Simple, Compound, and Complex Sentences

SIMPLE SENTENCES

A **sentence** is a group of words that expresses a complete thought. Every sentence includes both a subject and a verb. A **simple sentence** consists of a single **independent clause**: one <u>subject</u> and one <u>verb</u>.

Chase Utley plays baseball.

17a Identifying Subjects in Simple Sentences

Every sentence includes a subject. The **subject** of a sentence tells who or what is being talked about in the sentence. Without a subject, a sentence is not complete. In the following three sentences, the subject is underlined.

<u>Derek Walcott</u> won the Nobel Prize in Literature.
<u>He</u> was born in St. Lucia.
<u>St. Lucia</u> is an island in the Caribbean.

The subject of a sentence can be a noun or a pronoun. A **noun** names a person, place, or thing—*Derek Walcott, St. Lucia*. A **pronoun** takes the place of a noun—*I, you, he, she, it, we, they,* and so on.

The subject of a sentence can be *singular or plural*. A **singular subject** is one person, place, or thing (*Derek Walcott, St. Lucia, he*).

A **plural subject** is more than one person, place, or thing (*poets, people, they*).

<u>Readers</u> admire Walcott's poems.

Teaching Tip
Tell students that if a group of words does not include both a subject and a verb, it is a sentence fragment, not a sentence. Refer them to Chapter 22.

Teaching Tip
Remind students that sometimes the verb comes before the subject in a sentence. Refer them to 23g.

e bedfordstmartins.com
/forw Additional Grammar Exercises > Identifying Subjects

Teaching Tip
Tell students that if the subject ends with an *-s*, the verb usually does not. Write examples on the board.

413

Teaching Tip
Refer students to 23b for more on subject-verb agreement with compound subjects.

A plural subject that joins two subjects with *and* is called a **compound subject.**

St. Lucia and Trinidad are Caribbean islands.

PRACTICE

17-1　Underline the subject in each sentence. Then, write *S* above singular subjects and *P* above plural subjects. Remember, compound subjects are plural.

Example:　Agritainment introduces tourists to agriculture and entertainment at the same time.

1. Today, tourists can have fun on working farms.

2. In the past, visitors came to farms just to pick fruits and vegetables.

3. Now, some farms have mazes and petting zoos.

4. One farm has a corn maze every year.

5. Sometimes the maze is in the shape of a train.

6. Visitors can also enjoy giant hay-chute slides, pedal go-carts, and hayrides.

7. Working farms start agritainment businesses to make money.

8. However, insurance companies and lawyers worry about the dangers of agritainment.

9. Tourists have gotten animal bites, fallen from rides and machinery, and suffered from food poisoning.

10. Agritainment, like other businesses, has advantages and disadvantages.

e bedfordstmartins.com /forw LearningCurve > Prepositions and Conjunctions; Additional Grammar Exercises > Identifying Prepositional Phrases

17b Identifying Prepositional Phrases in Simple Sentences

A **prepositional phrase** consists of a **preposition** (a word such as *on*, *to*, *in*, or *with*) and its **object** (the noun or pronoun it introduces).

PREPOSITION	+	OBJECT	=	PREPOSITIONAL PHRASE
on		the stage		on the stage
to		Nia's house		to Nia's house

| in | my new car | in my new car |
| with | them | with them |

Because the object of a preposition is a noun or a pronoun, it may seem to be the subject of a sentence. However, the object of a preposition can never be the subject of a sentence. To identify a sentence's true subject, cross out each prepositional phrase. (Remember, every prepositional phrase is introduced by a preposition.)

SUBJECT   PREP PHRASE
The cost of the repairs was astronomical.

PREP PHRASE   PREP PHRASE   SUBJECT
At the end of the novel, after an exciting chase, the lovers flee
PREP PHRASE
to Mexico.

Frequently Used Prepositions

about	before	except	on	underneath
above	behind	for	onto	until
across	below	from	out	up
after	beneath	in	outside	upon
against	beside	inside	over	with
along	between	into	through	within
among	beyond	like	throughout	without
around	by	near	to	
as	despite	of	toward	
at	during	off	under	

PRACTICE

17-2   Each of the following sentences includes at least one prepositional phrase. To identify each sentence's subject, begin by crossing out each prepositional phrase. Then, underline the subject of the sentence.

Example: Bicycling on busy city streets can be dangerous.

(1) In many American cities, cyclists are concerned about sharing the road with cars. (2) For this reason, people are becoming more interested in "green" lanes. (3) These bike lanes are different from traditional bike lanes in one important way. (4) Green lanes are separated from the road by curbs, planters, or parked cars. (5) For years, people in Europe have been creating and using these protected bike lanes. (6) Until recently, however, few green lanes were created in the United States. (7) Now,

with the help of the Bikes Belong Foundation and the Federal Highway Administration, several U.S. cities are installing green lanes. (8) For their supporters, these bike lanes are a positive step toward healthier, safer cities. (9) However, some critics worry about reduced space for traffic lanes and parking. (10) Still, despite the criticism, green lanes are increasing the number of bike riders and reducing the number of bike accidents.

17c Identifying Verbs in Simple Sentences

bedfordstmartins.com /forw LearningCurve > Verbs, Adjectives, and Adverbs; Additional Grammar Exercises > Identifying Verbs

In addition to its subject, every sentence also includes a verb. This **verb** (also called a **predicate**) tells what the subject does or connects the subject to words that describe or rename it. Without a verb, a sentence is not complete.

Action Verbs

An **action verb** tells what the subject does, did, or will do.

> Andy Murray plays tennis.
> Amelia Earhart flew across the Atlantic.
> Renee will drive to Tampa on Friday.

Action verbs can also show mental and emotional actions.

> Travis always worries about his job.

Sometimes the subject of a sentence performs more than one action. In this case, the sentence includes two or more action verbs that form a **compound predicate**.

> He hit the ball, threw down his bat, and ran toward first base.

PRACTICE
17-3 In the following sentences, underline each action verb twice. Some sentences contain more than one action verb.

Example: Some new reality shows introduce viewers to people with disabilities.

1. The reality show *Push Girls* <u>explores</u> the lives of five beautiful disabled women.

2. All the women <u>live</u> in Los Angeles and <u>travel</u> in wheelchairs.

3. These women <u>push</u> many boundaries.

4. They <u>drive</u> their own cars and <u>pursue</u> ambitious careers.

5. Attractive and talented, they <u>reject</u> other people's assumptions about disability.

6. One woman <u>works</u> as a model and an actress.

7. Another <u>dances</u> for a living.

8. Like other reality shows, *Push Girls* <u>shows</u> us people's private lives.

9. However, this reality series also <u>challenges</u> stereotypes.

10. Ultimately, viewers <u>admire</u> these capable women and <u>envy</u> their fulfilling lives.

Linking Verbs

A **linking verb** does not show action. Instead, it connects the subject to a word or words that describe or rename it. The linking verb tells what the subject is (or what it was, will be, or seems to be).

A *googolplex* <u>is</u> an extremely large number.

Many linking verbs, like *is*, are forms of the verb *be*. Other linking verbs refer to the senses (*look*, *feel*, and so on).

The photocopy <u>looks</u> blurry.
Some students <u>feel</u> anxious about the future.

Frequently Used Linking Verbs		
act	feel	seem
appear	get	smell
be (am, is, are,	grow	sound
was, were)	look	taste
become	remain	turn

PRACTICE

17-4 In each of the following sentences, underline every verb twice. Remember that a verb can be an action verb or a linking verb.

Example: Airplane pilots and investment bankers <u>use</u> checklists.

READING TIP

This paragraph includes a number of transitional words and phrases, which help provide clarity and show the relationships between ideas. Identify at least six transitional words and phrases in this paragraph.

(1) In *The Checklist Manifesto*, surgeon Atul Gawande <u>argues</u> for using checklists in operating rooms. (2) Gawande <u>reminds</u> readers of the complexity of modern medicine. (3) Currently, there <u>are</u> 6,000 drugs and 4,000 medical and surgical procedures. (4) Each year, the number of drugs and procedures <u>increases</u>. (5) As a result, even knowledgeable and highly trained surgeons <u>make</u> mistakes. (6) For some types of patients, the error rate <u>is</u> very high. (7) For example, doctors <u>deliver</u> inappropriate care to 40 percent of patients with coronary artery disease. (8) Luckily, checklists <u>make</u> a big difference for these and other patients. (9) In fact, checklists <u>reduce</u> complications by more than one-third. (10) It <u>is</u> hard to imagine an argument against such a simple and effective tool.

Helping Verbs

Many verbs consist of more than one word. For example, the verb in the following sentence consists of two words.

Minh <u>must make</u> a decision about his future.

In this sentence, *make* is the **main verb**, and *must* is a **helping verb**.

Teaching Tip
Tell students that every sentence must include a complete verb. Refer them to 22d for information on how to identify sentence fragments created by incomplete verbs.

Frequently Used Helping Verbs

does	was	must	should
did	were	can	would
do		could	will
is	have	may	
are	has	might	
am	had		

A sentence's **complete verb** is made up of a main verb plus any help-ing verbs that accompany it. In the following sentences, the complete verb is underlined twice, and the helping verbs are checkmarked.

Minh should have gone earlier.

Did Minh ask the right questions?

Minh will work hard.

Minh can really succeed.

Teaching Tip
Remind students that words can sometimes come between the parts of a complete verb.

FYI

Helping Verbs with Participles

Participles, such as *going* and *gone*, cannot stand alone as main verbs in a sentence. They need a helping verb to make them complete.

Teaching Tip
Refer students to Chapter 14 for information on past participles.

INCORRECT	Minh going to the library.
CORRECT	Minh is going to the library.
INCORRECT	Minh gone to the library.
CORRECT	Minh has gone to the library.

PRACTICE

17-5   The verbs in the sentences that follow consist of a main verb and one or more helping verbs. In each sentence, un-derline the complete verb twice, and put a check mark above each helping verb.

Example: In 1954, the Salk polio vaccine was given to more than a million schoolchildren.

(1) By the 1950s, polio had become a serious problem throughout the United States. (2) For years, it had puzzled doctors and research-ers. (3) Thousands had become ill each year in the United States alone. (4) Children should have been playing happily. (5) Instead, they would

get very sick. (6) Polio was sometimes called infantile paralysis. (7) In fact, it did cause paralysis in children and in adults as well. (8) Some patients could breathe only with the help of machines called iron lungs. (9) Others would remain in wheelchairs for life. (10) By 1960, Jonas Salk's vaccine had reduced the incidence of polio in the United States by more than 90 percent.

COMPOUND SENTENCES

As you have seen, the most basic kind of sentence, a **simple sentence**, consists of a single **independent clause**: one subject and one verb.

European immigrants arrived at Ellis Island.

A **compound sentence** is made up of two or more simple sentences (independent clauses).

17d Forming Compound Sentences with Coordinating Conjunctions

One way to create a compound sentence is by joining two independent clauses with a **coordinating conjunction** preceded by a comma.

Many European immigrants arrived at Ellis Island, but many Asian immigrants arrived at Angel Island.

Coordinating Conjunctions			
and	for	or	yet
but	nor	so	

FYI

Use the letters that spell *FANBOYS* to help you remember the coordinating conjunctions.

F	for
A	and
N	nor
B	but
O	or
Y	yet
S	so

Teaching Tip
Remind students that a comma alone cannot connect two independent clauses. Refer them to Chapter 21.

Coordinating conjunctions join two ideas of equal importance. They describe the relationship between two ideas, showing how and why the ideas are related. Different coordinating conjunctions have different meanings.

Teaching Tip
Remind students that in a compound sentence, there is a complete sentence on each side of the coordinating conjunction.

- To indicate addition, use *and*.

    He acts like a child, <u>and</u> people think he is cute.

- To indicate contrast or contradiction, use *but* or *yet*.

    He acts like a child, <u>but</u> he is an adult.

    He acts like a child, <u>yet</u> he wants to be taken seriously.

- To indicate a cause-and-effect relationship, use *so* or *for*.

    He acts like a child, <u>so</u> we treat him like one.

    He acts like a child, <u>for</u> he needs attention.

- To present alternatives, use *or*.

    He acts like a child, <u>or</u> he is ignored.

- To eliminate alternatives, use *nor*.

    He does not act like a child, <u>nor</u> does he look like one.

Teaching Tip
Remind students that when a compound sentence is formed with *nor*, the verb comes before the subject in the second independent clause.

FYI

Commas with Coordinating Conjunctions

When you use a coordinating conjunction to join two independent clauses into a single compound sentence, always put a comma before the coordinating conjunction.

  We can stand in line all night, or we can go home now.

Teaching Tip
Remind students *not* to use a comma before a coordinating conjunction if it does not join two independent clauses.

PRACTICE

17-6 Join each of the following pairs of independent clauses with a coordinating conjunction. Be sure to place a comma before the coordinating conjunction.

Example: A computer makes drafting essays easier. *, and it* It also makes revision easier. *Answers will vary.*

1. Training a dog to heel is difficult. *, for dogs* Dogs naturally resist strict control from their owners.

2. A bodhran is an Irish drum. *, and it* It is played with a wooden stick.

3. Students should spend two hours studying for each hour in class. *, or they* They may not do well in the course.

4. Years ago, students wrote their lessons on slates. *, so the* The teacher was able to correct each student's work individually.

5. Each state in the United States has two senators. *, but the* The number of representatives in Congress depends on a state's population.

6. In 1973, only 2.5 percent of those in the U.S. military were women. *, but today,* Today, that percentage has increased to about 20 percent.

7. A small craft advisory warns boaters of bad weather conditions. *, for these* These conditions can be dangerous to small boats.

8. A DVD looks just like a CD. *, but it* It can hold fifteen times as much information.

9. Hip-hop fashions include sneakers and baggy pants. *, and these* These styles are very popular among young men.

10. Multiple births have become more and more common. *, and even* Even some septuplets and octuplets now survive.

PRACTICE

17-7 Add coordinating conjunctions to combine some of the simple sentences in the following paragraph. Remember to put a comma before each coordinating conjunction you add.

Example: Years ago, few Americans lived to be one hundred. *, but today,* Today, there are over 70,000 centenarians. *Answers will vary.*

Teaching Tip

If your students are ready, have them revise this paragraph by varying the sentence openings. Teach or review options for sentence openings, referring students to 18b.

(1) Diet, exercise, and family history may explain centenarians' long
lives. *, but this* (2) ~~This~~ is not the whole story. (3) A recent study showed surprising
similarities among centenarians. (4) They did not all avoid tobacco and
alcohol. *, nor* (5) ~~They~~ did *they* not have low-fat diets. (6) In fact, they ate relatively
large amounts of fat, cholesterol, and sugar. *, so diet* (7) ~~Diet~~ could not explain
their long lives. (8) They did, however, share four key traits. (9) First, all
the centenarians were optimistic about life. *, and all* (10) ~~All~~ were positive thinkers.
(11) They also had deep religious faith. (12) In addition, they had all continued to lead physically active lives. *, and they* (13) ~~They~~ remained mobile even as elderly
people. (14) Finally, all were able to adapt to loss. (15) They had all lost
friends, spouses, or children. *, but they* (16) ~~They~~ were able to get on with their lives.

17e Forming Compound Sentences with Semicolons

bedfordstmartins.com
/forw Additional
Grammar Exercises >
Using Semicolons

Another way to create a compound sentence is by joining two simple
sentences (independent clauses) with a **semicolon**. A semicolon connects clauses whose ideas are closely related.

> The AIDS Memorial Quilt contains thousands of panels; each panel
> represents a life lost to AIDS.

Also use a semicolon to show a strong contrast between two ideas.

> With new drugs, people can live with AIDS for years; many people,
> however, cannot get these drugs.

Teaching Tip
Remind students not
to use a capital letter after
a semicolon. Refer them
to 28g for more on
semicolons.

FYI

Avoiding Fragments

A semicolon can only join two complete sentences (independent
clauses). A semicolon cannot join a sentence and a fragment.

> ┌─────────────── FRAGMENT ───────────────┐
> **INCORRECT**   Because millions worldwide are still dying of AIDS;
> more research is needed.

> ┌─────────────── SENTENCE ───────────────┐
> **CORRECT**   Millions worldwide are still dying of AIDS; more
> research is needed.

Teaching Tip
Refer students to Chap-
ter 22 for information on
identifying and correcting
fragments.

PRACTICE

17-8   Each of the following items consists of one simple sentence. Create a compound sentence for each item by changing the period to a semicolon and then adding another simple sentence.

Example: My brother is addicted to fast food/ _; he eats it every day._
Answers will vary.

1. Fast-food restaurants are an American institution. _____

_____

2. Families often eat at these restaurants. _____

_____

3. Many teenagers work there. _____

_____

4. McDonald's is known for its hamburgers. _____

_____

5. KFC is famous for its fried chicken. _____

_____

6. Taco Bell serves Mexican-style food. _____

_____

7. Pizza Hut specializes in pizza. _____

_____

8. Many fast-food restaurants offer some low-fat menu items. _____

_____

9. Some offer recyclable packaging. _____

_____

10. Some even have playgrounds. _____

_____

17f Forming Compound Sentences with Transitional Words and Phrases

Another way to create a compound sentence is by combining two simple sentences (independent clauses) with a **transitional word or phrase**. When you use a transitional word or phrase to join two sentences, always place a semicolon *before* the transitional word or phrase and a comma *after* it.

> Some college students receive grants; in addition, they often have to take out loans.

> He had a miserable time at the party; besides, he lost his wallet.

Teaching Tip
Remind students to place a semicolon before every transitional word or phrase that joins two independent clauses. (If they leave out the semicolon, they will create a run-on.) Refer them to 21b.

Frequently Used Transitional Words

also	instead	still
besides	later	subsequently
consequently	meanwhile	then
eventually	moreover	therefore
finally	nevertheless	thus
furthermore	now	
however	otherwise	

Teaching Tip
Have students memorize these lists of frequently used transitional words and phrases.

Frequently Used Transitional Phrases

after all	in comparison
as a result	in contrast
at the same time	in fact
for example	in other words
for instance	of course
in addition	on the contrary

Adding a transitional word or phrase makes the connection between ideas in a sentence clearer and more precise than it would be if the ideas were linked with just a semicolon. Different transitional words and phrases convey different meanings.

- Some signal addition (*also, besides, furthermore, in addition, moreover,* and so on).

  > I have a lot on my mind; also, I have a lot of things to do.

■ Some make causal connections (*as a result*, *consequently*, *therefore*, *thus*, and so on).

> I have a lot on my mind; <u>therefore</u>, it is hard to concentrate.

■ Some indicate contradiction or contrast (*however*, *in contrast*, *nevertheless*, *still*, and so on).

> I have a lot on my mind; <u>still</u>, I must try to relax.

■ Some present alternatives (*instead*, *on the contrary*, *otherwise*, and so on).

> I have a lot on my mind; <u>otherwise</u>, I could relax.

> I will try not to think; <u>instead</u>, I will relax.

■ Some indicate time sequence (*at the same time*, *eventually*, *finally*, *later*, *meanwhile*, *now*, *subsequently*, *then*, and so on).

> I have a lot on my mind; <u>meanwhile</u>, I still have work to do.

PRACTICE
17-9
Add semicolons and commas where required to set off transitional words and phrases that join two independent clauses.

Example: Ketchup is a popular condiment $\overset{;}{\wedge}$ therefore $\overset{,}{\wedge}$ it is available in almost every restaurant.

(1) Andrew F. Smith, a food historian, wrote a book about the tomato $\overset{;}{\wedge}$ later $\overset{,}{\wedge}$ he wrote a book about ketchup. (2) This book, *Pure Ketchup*, was a big project $\overset{;}{\wedge}$ in fact $\overset{,}{\wedge}$ Smith worked on it for five years. (3) The word *ketchup* may have come from a Chinese word $\overset{;}{\wedge}$ however $\overset{,}{\wedge}$ Smith is not certain of the word's origins. (4) Ketchup has existed since ancient times $\overset{;}{\wedge}$ in other words $\overset{,}{\wedge}$ it is a very old product. (5) Ketchup has changed a lot over the years $\overset{;}{\wedge}$ for example $\overset{,}{\wedge}$ special dyes were developed in the nineteenth century to make it red. (6) Smith discusses many other changes $\overset{;}{\wedge}$ for instance $\overset{,}{\wedge}$ preservative-free ketchup was invented in 1907. (7) Ketchup is now used by people in many cultures $\overset{;}{\wedge}$ still $\overset{,}{\wedge}$ salsa is more popular than ketchup in the United States. (8) Today, designer ketchups are being developed $\overset{;}{\wedge}$ meanwhile $\overset{,}{\wedge}$

WORD POWER
condiment a prepared sauce or pickle used to add flavor to food

READING TIP
This passage provides a number of supporting details about ketchup. Considering the types of supporting details provided, what do you think is the author's purpose (to inform, to explain, or to persuade) in this passage?

Heinz has introduced green and purple ketchup in squeezc bottles. (9) Some of today's ketchups are chunky in addition some ketchups are spicy. (10) Ketchup continues to evolve meanwhile Smith has written a book about hamburgers.

PRACTICE

| 17-10 | Using both the specified topics and transitional words and phrases, create three compound sentences. Be sure to punctuate appropriately.

Teaching Tip
Have students work in pairs in this exercise, and then write their sentences on the board. Get at least two versions of each sentence.

Example
Topic: fad diets
Transitional phrase: for example

People are always falling for fad diets; for example, some people eat only

pineapple to lose weight.

Answers will vary.

1. *Topic:* laws to protect people with disabilities
   Transitional phrase: in addition

   _____

   _____

2. *Topic:* single men and women as adoptive parents
   Transitional word: however

   _____

   _____

3. *Topic:* high school proms
   Transitional word: also

   _____

   _____

COMPLEX SENTENCES

As you learned earlier in this chapter, an **independent clause** can stand alone as a sentence.

INDEPENDENT CLAUSE The <u>exhibit</u> <u>was</u> controversial.

However, a **dependent clause** cannot stand alone as a sentence.

DEPENDENT CLAUSE   Because the exhibit was controversial

Teaching Tip
Review the concept of subordination. Discuss how adding a subordinating conjunction can make one idea depend on another for completion.

What happened because the exhibit was controversial? To answer this question, you need to add an independent clause that completes the idea begun in the dependent clause. The result is a **complex sentence**—a sentence that consists of one independent clause and one or more dependent clauses.

COMPLEX SENTENCE   ┌─────────── DEPENDENT CLAUSE ───────────┐ ┌ INDEPENDENT CLAUSE ─┐
Because the exhibit was controversial, many people came to see it.

17g Forming Complex Sentences with Subordinating Conjunctions

bedfordstmartins.com
/forw LearningCurve >
Prepositions and
Conjunctions; Additional
Grammar Exercises >
Using Subordinating
Conjunctions

One way to form a complex sentence is to use a **subordinating conjunction**—a word such as *although* or *because*—to join two simple sentences (independent clauses). When the subordinating conjunction is added to the beginning of the simple sentence, the sentence becomes dependent for its meaning on the other simple sentence.

TWO SIMPLE SENTENCES   Muhammad Ali was stripped of his heavyweight title for refusing to go into the army. Many people admired his antiwar position.

COMPLEX SENTENCE   ┌─────────── DEPENDENT CLAUSE ───────────┐
Although Muhammad Ali was stripped of his heavyweight title for refusing to go into the army, many people admired his antiwar position.

WORD POWER

subordinate (adj)
lower in rank or position; secondary in importance

Teaching Tip
Have students create sentences that start with the subordinating conjunctions listed here.

Frequently Used Subordinating Conjunctions

after	even though	since	whenever
although	if	so that	where
as	if only	than	whereas
as if	in order that	that	wherever
as though	now that	though	whether
because	once	unless	while
before	provided that	until	
even if	rather than	when	

As the chart below shows, different subordinating conjunctions express different relationships between dependent and independent clauses.

Relationship between Clauses	Subordinating Conjunction	Example
Time	after, before, since, until, when, when-ever, while	When the whale surfaced, Ahab threw his harpoon.
Reason or cause	as, because	Scientists scaled back the project because the government cut funds.
Result or effect	in order that, so that	So that students' math scores will improve, many schools have begun special programs.
Condition	even if, if, unless	The rain forest may disappear unless steps are taken immediately.
Contrast	although, even though, though	Although Thomas Edison had almost no formal education, he was a successful inventor.
Location	where, wherever	Pittsburgh was built where the Allegheny and Monongahela Rivers meet.

Teaching Tip
Have students memorize both the subordinating conjunctions and the relationships they express.

Teaching Tip
Point out to students that a clause introduced by a subordinating conjunction does not express a complete thought. Used by itself, it is a sentence fragment. (See 22c.)

ESL Tip
Make sure students understand the subtle differences in meaning between different subordinating conjunctions.

FYI

Punctuating with Subordinating Conjunctions

In a complex sentence, use a comma after the dependent clause.

————— DEPENDENT CLAUSE ————— ⌐— INDEPENDENT CLAUSE —
Although she wore the scarlet letter, Hester carried herself proudly.

Do not use a comma after the independent clause.

⌐——— INDEPENDENT CLAUSE ———⌐⌐————— DEPENDENT CLAUSE —————
Hester carried herself proudly although she wore the scarlet letter.

PRACTICE

17-11   Combine each of the following pairs of sentences to create one complex sentence. Use a subordinating conjunction from the list on page 428 to indicate the relationship between the dependent and independent clauses in each sentence. Make sure you include a comma where one is required.

> **Example:**   Orville and Wilbur Wright built the first powered plane,
> *although they*
> ‸They had no formal training as engineers.   *Answers will vary.*

Although professional   *, in*
1. Professional midwives are used widely in Europe, In the United
   ‸   ‸
   States, they usually practice only in areas with few doctors.

   When   *, a*
2. John Deere constructed his first steel plow in 1837, A new era began
   ‸   ‸
   in farming.

                                                        even though he
3. Stephen Crane describes battles in *The Red Badge of Courage,* He never
                                                                      ‸
   saw a war.

   When   *, thousands*
4. Elvis Presley died in 1977, Thousands of his fans gathered in front
   ‸   ‸
   of his mansion.

   After   *, the*
5. Jonas Salk developed the first polio vaccine in the 1950s, The number
   ‸   ‸
   of polio cases in the United States declined.

   As the   *, some*
6. The salaries of baseball players rose in the 1980s, Some sportswriters
   ‸   ‸
   predicted a drop in attendance at games.

17h Forming Complex Sentences with Relative Pronouns

bedfordstmartins.com
/forw LearningCurve >
Nouns and Pronouns;
Additional Grammar
Exercises > Using
Relative Pronouns

Another way to form a complex sentence is to use **relative pronouns** (*who, that, which,* and so on) to join two simple sentences (independent clauses).

TWO SIMPLE SENTENCES   Harry Potter is an adolescent wizard. He attends Hogwarts School of Witchcraft and Wizardry.

	┌──────── DEPENDENT CLAUSE ────────┐
COMPLEX SENTENCE	Harry Potter, who attends Hogwarts School of

Witchcraft and Wizardry, is an adolescent wizard.

Note: The relative pronoun always refers to a word or words in the independent clause. (In the complex sentence above, *who* refers to *Harry Potter*.)

Relative Pronouns

that	which	whoever	whomever
what	who	whom	whose

Teaching Tip
Reinforce that a dependent clause introduced by a relative pronoun does not express a complete thought. It is therefore a fragment. Refer students to 22e.

Relative pronouns indicate the relationships between the ideas in the independent and dependent clauses they link.

TWO SIMPLE SENTENCES	Nadine Gordimer lived in South Africa. She won the Nobel Prize in Literature in 1991.
COMPLEX SENTENCE	Nadine Gordimer, who won the Nobel Prize in Literature in 1991, lived in South Africa.
TWO SIMPLE SENTENCES	Last week I had a job interview. It went very well.
COMPLEX SENTENCE	Last week I had a job interview that went very well.
TWO SIMPLE SENTENCES	Transistors have replaced vacuum tubes in radios and televisions. They were invented in 1948.
COMPLEX SENTENCE	Transistors, which were invented in 1948, have replaced vacuum tubes in radios and televisions.

Teaching Tip
Tell students that when they create a complex sentence, the relative pronoun substitutes for a noun or another pronoun in one of the original simple sentences.

Teaching Tip
Refer students to 26d for information on using commas with restrictive and nonrestrictive clauses.

PRACTICE

17-12   In each of the following complex sentences, underline the dependent clause once, and underline the relative pronoun twice. Then, draw an arrow from the relative pronoun to the word or words to which it refers.

Example: MTV, which was the first television network devoted

to popular music videos, began in 1981.

1. MTV's very first music video, which was performed by a group called the Buggles, contained the lyric "Video killed the radio star."

2. The earliest videos on MTV were simple productions that recorded live studio performances.

3. Music videos eventually became complicated productions that featured special effects and large casts of dancers.

4. Music video directors gained recognition at MTV's Video Music Awards presentation, which first aired in September 1984.

5. *The Real World*, a reality series that featured a group of young people living together in New York City, was introduced by MTV in 1992.

6. MTV's later reality shows featured celebrities such as Jessica Simpson, who starred in *Newlyweds: Nick and Jessica* in 2003.

7. Today, MTV, which devotes less and less time to music videos, produces many hours of original programming.

8. One of MTV's most popular recent reality shows, which featured cast members at the beach, was *Jersey Shore*.

9. Another popular but controversial show is *16 and Pregnant*, which presents the stories of pregnant high school girls.

10. Needless to say, these shows have their critics, who claim that the shows undermine society's most basic values.

EDITING PRACTICE

Read the following student essay. Then, revise it by combining pairs of simple sentences to create compound or complex sentences. Create compound sentences by using a coordinating conjunction, a semicolon, or a transitional word or phrase. Create complex sentences by using subordinating conjunctions or relative pronouns that indicate the relationship between the two simple sentences. Be sure to punctuate correctly. The first two sentences have been combined for you. *Answers will vary.*

Community Art

When a ⌃A city has a crime problem*, the* ~~The~~ police and the courts try to solve it. Some cities have come up with creative ways to help young people stay out of trouble. One example is the Philadelphia Mural Arts Program*, which* ~~It~~ offers free art education for high school students.

In the 1960s, Philadelphia had a serious problem*; the* ~~The~~ problem was graffiti. Graffiti artists had painted on buildings all over the city. A solution to the problem was the Philadelphia Anti-Graffiti Network, which offered graffiti artists an alternative. The artists would give up painting graffiti*, and they* ~~They~~ would not be prosecuted for defacing buildings. The artists*, who* enjoyed painting*,* ~~They~~ could paint murals on public buildings instead. They could create beautiful landscapes, portraits of local heroes, and abstract designs. The graffiti artists had once been lawbreakers*; now, they* ~~They~~ could now help beautify the city.

The Mural Arts Program began in 1984 as a part of the Philadelphia Anti-Graffiti Network. By 1996, the Philadelphia Anti-Graffiti Network was focusing on eliminating graffiti*, and its* ~~Its~~ Mural Arts Program was working to improve the community. It no longer worked with graffiti offenders*; instead, it* ~~It~~ ran after-school and summer programs for students. The Mural Arts Program gained national recognition in 1997*,* ~~That is~~ when President Bill Clinton

433

helped paint a mural. Now, because of the Mural Arts Program's success,

Philadelphia is known as the "City of Murals."

, who come from all parts of the city,

Over 20,000 students have taken part in the Mural Arts Program. ~~The~~

~~students come from all parts of the city.~~ Sometimes students work alongside

, and they

professional artists~~.~~ ~~They~~ get to paint parts of the artists' murals themselves.

, so it

The artwork is on public buildings~~.~~ ~~It~~ can be seen by everyone.

, which is now over a quarter of a century old,

The Mural Arts Program continues to build a brighter future for students

and their communities. ~~It is now over a quarter of a century old.~~ Students

; consequently, they

help bring people together to create a mural~~.~~ ~~They~~ feel a stronger connection

After they

to their community and more confidence in themselves. ~~They~~ leave the

, they

program~~.~~ ~~They~~ are equipped to make a positive difference in their communities

and in their own lives.

review checklist

Writing Simple, Compound, and Complex Sentences

☐ Every sentence expresses a complete thought and includes a subject and a verb. A **simple sentence** consists of a single independent clause: one subject and one verb. (See page 413).

☐ The subject of a sentence tells who or what is being talked about. (See 17a.)

☐ A prepositional phrase consists of a preposition and its object (the noun or pronoun it introduces). The object of a preposition cannot be the subject of the sentence. (See 17b.)

☐ An action verb tells what the subject does, did, or will do. (See 17c.)

☐ A linking verb connects the subject to a word or words that describe or rename it. (See 17c.)

☐ Many verbs are made up of more than one word. The complete verb in a sentence includes the main verb plus any helping verbs. (See 17c.)

☐ A **compound sentence** is made up of two simple sentences (independent clauses.) (See page 420.)

- A coordinating conjunction—*and, but, for, nor, or, so,* or *yet*—can join two independent clauses into one compound sentence. A comma always comes before the coordinating conjunction. (See 17d.)

- A semicolon can join two independent clauses into one compound sentence. (See 17e.)

- A transitional word or phrase can also join two independent clauses into one compound sentence. When it joins two independent clauses, a transitional word or phrase is always preceded by a semicolon and followed by a comma. (See 17f.)

- A **complex sentence** consists of one independent clause (simple sentence) combined with one or more dependent clauses.

- Subordinating conjunctions—dependent words such as *although, after, when, while,* and *because*—can join two independent clauses into one complex sentence. (See 17g.)

- Relative pronouns—dependent words such as *who, which,* and *that*—can also join two independent clauses into one complex sentence. The relative pronoun shows the relationship between the ideas in the two independent clauses that it links. (See 17h.)

18 Writing Varied Sentences

Sentence variety is important because a paragraph of varied sentences flows more smoothly, is easier to read and understand, and is more interesting than one in which all the sentences are structured in the same way.

bedfordstmartins.com /forw Additional Grammar Exercises > Identifying Sentence Types

Question

Exclamation

18a Varying Sentence Types

Most English sentences are **statements**. Others are **questions** or **exclamations**. One way to vary your sentences is to use an occasional question or exclamation where it is appropriate.

In the following paragraph, a question and an exclamation add variety.

> Jacqueline Cochran, the first woman pilot to break the sound barrier, was one of the most important figures in aviation history. In 1996, the United States Postal Service issued a stamp honoring Cochran; the words "Pioneer Pilot" appear under her name. <u>What did she do to earn this title and this tribute?</u> Cochran broke more flight records than anyone else in her lifetime and won many awards, including the United States Distinguished Service Medal in 1945 and the United States Air Force Distinguished Flying Cross in 1969. During World War II, she helped form the WASPs, the Women's Air Force Service Pilots program, so that women could fly military planes to their bases (even though they were not allowed to go into combat). Remarkably, she accomplished all this with only three weeks of flying instruction. She only got her pilot's license in the first place because she wanted to start her own cosmetics business and flying would enable her to travel quickly around the country. Although she never planned to be a pilot, once she discovered flying she quickly became the best. <u>Not surprisingly, when the Postal Service honored Jacqueline Cochran, it was with an airmail stamp!</u>

PRACTICE
18-1

Revise the following paragraph by changing one of the statements into a question and one of the statements into an exclamation.

Example: The cell phone may be making the wristwatch obsolete. (statement)

Is the cell phone making the wristwatch obsolete? (question)

Answers will vary.

(1) As cell phones and other small electronic devices become more common, fewer people are wearing watches. (2) Most cell phones, iPads, and MP3 players display the time. (3) Moreover, cell-phone clocks give very accurate time. (4) This is because they set themselves with satellite signals. (5) They also adjust automatically to time-zone changes. (6) ~~Typical~~ *How can typical* wristwatches ~~cannot~~ compete with these convenient features~~.~~ (7) After all, unlike the newer devices, watches are not computers~~.~~ (8) However, watches do remain appealing for other reasons. (9) For many people, they are fashion accessories or status symbols. (10) For some, watches are still essential for telling time.

18b   Varying Sentence Openings

When all the sentences in a paragraph begin the same way, your writing is likely to seem dull and repetitive. In the following paragraph, for example, every sentence begins with the subject.

> Scientists have been observing a disturbing phenomenon. The population of frogs, toads, and salamanders has been declining. This decline was first noticed in the mid-1980s. Some reports blamed chemical pollution. Some biologists began to suspect that a fungal disease was killing these amphibians. The most reasonable explanation seems to be that the amphibians' eggs are threatened by solar radiation. This radiation penetrates the thinned ozone layer, which used to shield them from the sun's rays.

Beginning with Adverbs

Instead of opening every sentence in a paragraph with the subject, you can try beginning some sentences with one or more **adverbs**.

> Scientists have been observing a disturbing phenomenon. <u>Gradually but steadily,</u> the population of frogs, toads, and salamanders has been declining. This decline was first noticed in the mid-1980s. Some

Teaching Tip
Distribute to the class copies of a paragraph with varied sentences, and in general terms, point out different sentence types.

Teaching Tip
Tell students that when they write instructions, they should use **commands**—statements that address readers directly: *Now, unplug the appliance.* Refer them to 12b.

Teaching Tip
Have students circle every *The*, *This*, *He*, *She*, and *It* that begins a sentence in a paper they have written. Then, ask them to revise as necessary to vary their sentence openings.

WORD POWER
amphibians cold-blooded vertebrates, such as frogs, that live both in the water and on land

Teaching Tip
Caution students against using too many of any one kind of sentence opening. Starting every sentence with an adverb can be just as dull as always starting with the subject.

reports blamed chemical pollution. Some biologists began to suspect that a fungal disease was killing these amphibians. However,
the most reasonable explanation seems to be that the amphibians'
eggs are threatened by solar radiation. This radiation penetrates the
thinned ozone layer, which used to shield them from the sun's rays.

PRACTICE

18-2   Underline the adverb in each of the following sentences, and
then rewrite the sentence so that the adverb appears at the
beginning. Be sure to punctuate correctly.

Example: An internship is <u>usually</u> a one-time work or service
experience related to a student's career plans.

Usually, an internship is a one-time work or service experience related to a student's

career plans.

1. Internships are <u>sometimes</u> paid or counted for academic credit.

   Sometimes, internships are paid or counted for academic credit.

2. A prospective student intern should <u>first</u> talk to an academic adviser.

   First, a prospective student intern should talk to an academic adviser.

3. The student should <u>next</u> write a résumé listing job experience,
   education, and interests.

   Next, the student should write a résumé listing job experience, education, and interests.

4. The student can <u>then</u> send the résumé to organizations that are
   looking for interns.

   Then, the student can send the résumé to organizations that are looking for interns.

5. Going to job fairs and networking are <u>often</u> good ways to find
   internships.

   Often, going to job fairs and networking are good ways to find internships.

Beginning with Prepositional Phrases

Another way to create sentence variety is to begin some sentences with
prepositional phrases. A **prepositional phrase** (such as *along the river*
or *near the diner*) is made up of a preposition and its object.

In recent years, scientists have observed a disturbing phenomenon. Gradually but steadily, the population of frogs, toads, and salamanders has been declining. This was first noticed in the mid-1980s. At first, some reports blamed chemical pollution. After a while, some biologists began to suspect that a fungal disease was killing them. However, the most reasonable explanation seems to be that the amphibians' eggs are threatened by solar radiation. This radiation penetrates the thinned ozone layer, which used to shield them from the sun's rays.

PRACTICE

18-3 Every sentence in the following paragraph begins with the subject, but several contain prepositional phrases or adverbs that could be moved to the beginning. To vary the sentence openings, move prepositional phrases to the beginnings of four sentences, and move adverbs to the beginnings of two other sentences. Be sure to place a comma after these introductory phrases.

By the end of the 1800s,
Example: Spain ~~by the end of the 1800s~~ had lost most of its colonies.
^
Answers will vary.

In the Cuban American community, people
(1) ~~People in the Cuban American community~~ often mention José
^
Julián Martí as one of their heroes. (2) José Martí was born in Havana in
By the time he was sixteen years old, he
1853, at a time when Cuba was a colony of Spain. (3) He had started a news-
^
paper demanding Cuban freedom ~~by the time he was sixteen years old~~.
In 1870, the
(4) ~~The~~ Spanish authorities forced him to leave Cuba and go to Spain
^
Openly continuing his fight, he
in ~~1870~~. (5) He published his first pamphlet calling for Cuban inde-
^
pendence while in Spain, ~~openly continuing his fight~~. (6) He then lived
^
During his time in New York, he
for fourteen years in New York City. (7) He started the journal of the
^
Cuban Revolutionary Party ~~during his time in New York~~. (8) Martí's
^
essays and poems argued for Cuba's freedom and for the individual free-
Passionately following up his words with actions, he
dom of Cubans. (9) He died in battle against Spanish soldiers in Cuba,
^
passionately following up his words with actions.

18c Combining Sentences

You can also create sentence variety by experimenting with different ways of combining sentences.

Using *-ing* Modifiers

A **modifier** identifies or describes other words in a sentence. You can use an *-ing* modifier to combine two sentences.

TWO SENTENCES	Duke Ellington composed more than a thousand songs. He worked hard to establish his reputation.
COMBINED WITH *-ING* MODIFIER	Composing <u>more than a thousand songs</u>, Duke Ellington worked hard to establish his reputation.

When the two sentences above are combined, the *-ing* modifier (*composing more than a thousand songs*) describes the new sentence's subject (*Duke Ellington*).

PRACTICE
18-4

Use an *-ing* modifier to combine each of the following pairs of sentences into a single sentence. Eliminate any unnecessary words, and place a comma after each *-ing* modifier.

Example: Many American colleges are setting an example for the rest of the country. They are going green.

Setting an example for the rest of the country, many American colleges are going green.

1. Special lamps in the dorms of one Ohio college change from green to red. They warn of rising energy use.

   Changing from green to red, special lamps in the dorms of one Ohio college warn of

   rising energy use.

2. A Vermont college captures methane from dairy cows. It now needs less energy from other sources.

   Capturing methane from dairy cows, a Vermont college now needs less energy

   from other sources.

3. Student gardeners at a North Carolina college tend a campus vegetable plot. They supply the cafeteria with organic produce.

   Tending a campus vegetable plot, student gardeners at a North Carolina college

   supply the cafeteria with organic produce.

4. A building on a California campus proves that recycled materials can be beautiful. It is built from redwood wine casks.

   Proving that recycled materials can be beautiful, a building on a California campus is

   built from redwood wine casks.

5. Some colleges offer courses in sustainability. They are preparing students to take the green revolution beyond campus.

   Offering courses in sustainability, some colleges are preparing students to take the

   green revolution beyond campus.

Using *-ed* Modifiers

You can also use an *-ed* modifier to combine two sentences.

TWO SENTENCES	Nogales is located on the border between Arizona and Mexico. It is a bilingual city.
COMBINED WITH *-ED* MODIFIER	<u>Located on the border between Arizona and Mexico,</u> Nogales is a bilingual city.

When the two sentences above are combined, the *-ed* modifier (*located on the border between Arizona and Mexico*) describes the new sentence's subject (*Nogales*).

> **Teaching Tip**
> You may want to introduce students to the term *past participle modifier* and to explain that some past participle modifiers (*taught, known, spent,* and so on) are irregular and do not end in *-ed* or *-d*.

PRACTICE

18-5 Use an *-ed* modifier to combine each of the following pairs of sentences into a single sentence. Eliminate any unnecessary words, and use a comma to set off each *-ed* modifier. When you are finished, underline the *-ed* modifier in each sentence.

> **Teaching Tip**
> Remind students that modifying phrases should refer clearly to the words they describe. Refer them to 25a and 25b.

Example: Potato chips were invented purely by accident. They are one of America's most popular foods.

<u>Invented purely by accident,</u> potato chips are one of America's most popular foods.

Teaching Tip
Tell students that combining sentences with -ed modifiers makes their writing more concise. Refer them to 20b.

1. George Crum was employed as a chef in a fancy restaurant. He was famous for his french fries.

   Employed as a chef in a fancy restaurant, George Crum was famous for his french fries.

2. A customer was dissatisfied with the fries. He complained and asked for thinner fries.

   Dissatisfied with the fries, a customer complained and asked for thinner fries.

3. The customer was served thinner fries. He was still not satisfied and complained again.

   Served thinner fries, the customer was still not satisfied and complained again.

4. Crum was now very annoyed. He decided to make the fries too thin and crisp to eat with a fork.

   Now very annoyed, Crum decided to make the fries too thin and crisp to eat with a fork.

5. The customer was thrilled with the extra-thin and crisp potatoes. He ate them all.

   Thrilled with the extra-thin and crisp potatoes, the customer ate them all.

6. Potato chips were invented to get even with a customer. They are the most popular snack food in America today.

   Invented to get even with a customer, potato chips are the most popular snack

   food in America today.

Using a Series of Words

Another way to vary your sentences is to combine a group of sentences into one sentence that includes a **series** of words (nouns, verbs, or adjectives). Combining sentences in this way eliminates a boring string of similar sentences and repetitive phrases and also makes your writing more concise.

Teaching Tip
You might want to tell students that *presidents, coaches, and the players* is a compound subject. Refer them to 17a and 23b.

GROUP OF SENTENCES   College presidents want to improve athletes' academic performance. Coaches too want to improve athletes' academic performance. The players themselves also want to improve their academic performance.

COMBINED (SERIES OF NOUNS)   College presidents, coaches, and the players themselves want to improve athletes' academic performance.

GROUP OF
SENTENCES
In 1997, Arundhati Roy published her first novel, *The God of Small Things*. She won the Pulitzer Prize. She became a literary sensation.

COMBINED
(SERIES OF VERBS)
In 1997, Arundhati Roy <u>published</u> her first novel, *The God of Small Things,* <u>won</u> the Pulitzer Prize, and <u>became</u> a literary sensation.

Teaching Tip
You might want to tell students that *published . . . won . . . and became* is a compound predicate. Refer them to 17c.

GROUP OF
SENTENCES
As the tornado approached, the sky grew dark. The sky grew quiet. The sky grew threatening.

COMBINED
(SERIES OF ADJECTIVES)
As the tornado approached, the sky grew <u>dark</u>, <u>quiet</u>, and <u>threatening</u>.

Teaching Tip
Show students that the revised sentences are more concise as well as more varied. Refer them to 20b.

PRACTICE

18-6 Combine each of the following groups of sentences into one sentence that includes a series of nouns, verbs, or adjectives.

Example: Many years ago, Pacific Islanders from Samoa settled in Hawaii. Pacific Islanders from Fiji also settled in Hawaii. Pacific Islanders from Tahiti settled in Hawaii, too.

Many years ago, Pacific Islanders from Samoa, Fiji, and Tahiti settled

in Hawaii.
Answers will vary.

ESL Tip
Offer ESL students a mini-lesson on subject-verb agreement before they begin. Refer them to Chapter 23. Spot-check their work.

1. In the eighteenth century, the British explorer Captain Cook came to Hawaii. Other explorers also came to Hawaii. European travelers came to Hawaii, too.

In the eighteenth century, the British explorer Captain Cook, other explorers, and

European travelers came to Hawaii.

Teaching Tip
Remind students that a compound subject joined by *and* takes a plural verb. Refer them to 23b.

2. Explorers and traders brought commerce to Hawaii. They brought new ideas. They brought new cultures.

Explorers and traders brought commerce, new ideas, and new cultures

to Hawaii.

3. Missionaries introduced the Christian religion. They introduced a Hawaiian-language bible. Also, they introduced a Hawaiian alphabet.

Missionaries introduced the Christian religion, a Hawaiian-language bible, and a

Hawaiian alphabet.

4. In the mid-nineteenth century, pineapple plantations were established in Hawaii. Sugar plantations were established there as well. Other industries were also established.

In the mid-nineteenth century, pineapple plantations, sugar plantations, and other

industries were established in Hawaii.

5. By 1900, Japanese people were working on the plantations. Chinese people were also working on the plantations. In addition, native Hawaiians were working there.

By 1900, Japanese people, Chinese people, and native Hawaiians were working on

the plantations.

6. People of many different races and religions now live in Hawaii. People of many different races and religions now go to school in Hawaii. People of many different races and religions now work in Hawaii.

People of many different races and religions now live, go to school, and work in

Hawaii.

7. Schoolchildren still study the Hawaiian language. They learn about the Hawaiian kings and queens. They read about ancient traditions.

Schoolchildren still study the Hawaiian language, learn about the Hawaiian kings and

queens, and read about ancient traditions.

8. Today, Hawaii is well known for its tourism. It is well known too for its weather. It is especially well known for its natural beauty.

Today, Hawaii is well known for its tourism, weather, and natural beauty.

Using Appositives

WORD POWER

adjacent next to

An **appositive** is a word or word group that identifies, renames, or describes an adjacent noun or pronoun. Creating an appositive is often a good way to combine two sentences about the same subject.

Teaching Tip
Remind students that when they combine sentences with an appositive, the appositive is set off with commas. Refer them to 26c.

TWO SENTENCES	C. J. Walker was the first American woman to become a self-made millionaire. She marketed a line of hair-care products for black women.
COMBINED WITH APPOSITIVE	C. J. Walker, the first American woman to become a self-made millionaire, marketed a line of hair-care products for black women.

In the example on page 444, the appositive appears in the middle of a sentence. However, an appositive can also come at the beginning or at the end of a sentence.

> The first American woman to become a self-made millionaire, C. J. Walker marketed a line of hair-care products for black women. (appositive at the beginning)
>
> Several books have been written about C. J. Walker, the first American woman to become a self-made millionaire. (appositive at the end)

PRACTICE

18-7   Combine each of the following pairs of sentences into one sentence by creating an appositive. Note that the appositive may appear at the beginning, in the middle, or at the end of the sentence. Be sure to use commas appropriately.

Example: *Wikipedia* is a popular online information source, It is available in more than two hundred languages.   *Answers will vary.*

(1) *Wikipedia* is one of the largest reference sites on the web. It is different from other encyclopedias in many ways. (2) This site is a constant work-in-progress, *, this site* It allows anyone to add, change, or correct information in its articles. (3) For this reason, researchers have to be careful when using information from *Wikipedia. Wikipedia* is a source that may contain factual errors. (4) The older articles are the ones that have been edited and corrected the most, These often contain the most trustworthy information. (5) Despite some drawbacks, *Wikipedia* has many notable advantages, *, including* These advantages include free and easy access, up-to-date information, and protection from author bias.

Teaching Tip
Remind students that most instructors will not permit them to use *Wikipedia* as a research source.

Teaching Tip
Explain to students that an appositive can be introduced by a word or phrase like *including* or *such as*.

18d   Mixing Long and Short Sentences

A paragraph of short, choppy sentences—or a paragraph of long, rambling sentences—can be monotonous. By mixing long and short sentences, perhaps combining some simple sentences to create **compound and complex sentences**, you can create a more interesting paragraph.

Teaching Tip
For information on creating compound and complex sentences, refer students to Chapter 17.

In the following paragraph, the sentences are all short, and the result is boring and hard to follow.

> The world's first drive-in movie theater opened on June 6, 1933. This drive-in was in Camden, New Jersey. Automobiles became more popular. Drive-ins did, too. By the 1950s, there were more than four thousand drive-ins in the United States. Over the years, the high cost of land led to a decline in the number of drive-ins. So did the rising popularity of television. Soon, the drive-in movie theater had almost disappeared. It was replaced by the multiplex. In 1967, there were forty-six drive-ins in New Jersey. Today, only one is still open. That one is the Delsea Drive-in in Vineland, New Jersey.

The revised paragraph that follows is more interesting and easier to read. (Note that the final short sentence is retained for emphasis.)

> The world's first drive-in movie theater opened on June 6, 1933, in Camden, New Jersey. As automobiles became more popular, drive-ins did, too, and by the 1950s, there were more than four thousand drive-ins in the United States. Over the years, the high cost of land and the rising popularity of television led to a decline in the number of drive-ins. Soon, the drive-in movie theater had almost disappeared, replaced by the multiplex. In 1967, there were forty-six drive-ins in New Jersey, but today, only one is still open. That one is the Delsea Drive-in in Vineland, New Jersey.

PRACTICE

18-8   The following paragraph contains a series of short, choppy sentences that can be combined. Revise the paragraph so that it mixes long and short sentences. Be sure to use commas and other punctuation appropriately.

Example: Kente cloth has special significance for many African
Americans/ ~~Some~~ other people do not understand this significance.
, but some
Answers will vary.
  (1) Kente cloth is made in western Africa. *and* (2) ~~It~~ is produced primarily by the Ashanti people. (3) It has been worn for hundreds of years by African royalty. *, who* (4) ~~They~~ consider it a sign of power and status. (5) Many African Americans wear kente cloth. *because they* (6) ~~They~~ see it as a link to their heritage. (7) Each pattern on the cloth has a name. *, and each* (8) ~~Each~~ color has a special significance. (9) For example, red and yellow suggest a

                               while green
long and healthy life, (10) ~~Green~~ and white suggest a good harvest.
       Although
(11) African women may wear kente cloth as a dress or head wrap,

(12) African-American women, like men, usually wear strips of cloth

around their shoulders. (13) Men and women of African descent wear
                                          ; in fact, it
kente cloth as a sign of racial pride, ~~(14) It~~ often decorates college students'

gowns at graduation.

EDITING PRACTICE

The following student essay lacks sentence variety. All of its sentences begin with the subject, and the essay includes a number of short, choppy sentences. Using the strategies discussed in this chapter as well as strategies for creating compound and complex sentences, revise the essay to achieve greater sentence variety. The first sentence has been edited for you.   *Answers will vary.*

Toys by Accident

Many popular toys and games are the result of accidents. *when people* ~~People~~ try to invent one thing but discover something else instead. Sometimes they are not trying to invent anything at all. *and* ~~They~~ are completely surprised to find a new product.

Play-Doh is one example of an accidental discovery. *, a popular preschool toy,* ~~Play-Doh is a popular preschool toy.~~ Play-Doh first appeared in Cincinnati. *, where a* ~~A~~ company made a compound to clean wallpaper. *and* ~~They~~ sold it as a cleaning product. The company then realized that this compound could be a toy. *Molding* ~~Children could mold~~ it like clay. *, children* ~~They~~ could use it again and again. The new toy was an immediate hit. *Since* Play-Doh was first sold in 1956. ~~Since then,~~ more than two billion cans of ~~Play-Doh~~ have been sold.

The Slinky was discovered by Richard James. *He was* an engineer. At the time, he was trying to invent a spring to keep ships' instruments steady at sea. *Although he* He tested hundreds of springs of varying sizes, metals, and tensions. *, none* ~~None~~ of them worked. One spring fell off the desk and "walked" down a pile of books. *, and* ~~It~~ went end over end onto the floor. *Thinking* ~~He thought~~ his children might enjoy playing with it. James took the spring home. They loved it. Every child in the neighborhood wanted one. *When the* ~~The~~ first Slinky was demonstrated at Gimbel's Department Store in Philadelphia in 1945. *, all* ~~All~~ four hundred Slinkys were sold within ninety minutes. *Simple* ~~The Slinky is simple~~ and inexpensive. *, the* ~~The~~ Slinky is still popular with children today.

The Frisbee was also discovered by accident. According to one story, a
group of Yale University students were eating pies from a local bakery. ~~The~~
Frisbies,
~~bakery was called Frisbies. They~~ finished eating the pies. ~~They~~ started throwing
After they   , they
the empty pie tins around. A carpenter in California made a plastic version. He
and
called it the Pluto Platter. The Wham-O company bought the patent on the
product. Wham-O renamed it the Frisbee after the bakery. This is how the
and
Frisbee came to be.

Some new toys are not developed by toy companies. Play-Doh, the Frisbee,
and the Slinky are examples of very popular toys that were discovered by
accident. Play-Doh started as a cleaning product. The Slinky was discovered by
, the
an engineer who was trying to invent something else. The Frisbee was invented
, and the
by students having fun. ~~The toys were discovered~~ unexpectedly. All three toys
Discovered   , all
have become classics.

review checklist

Writing Varied Sentences

☐ Vary sentence types. (See 18a.)

☐ Vary sentence openings. (See 18b.)

☐ Combine sentences. (See 18c.)

☐ Mix long and short sentences. (See 18d.)

19 Using Parallelism

19a Recognizing Parallel Structure

bedfordstmartins.com
/forw LearningCurve >
Parallelism; Additional
Grammar Exercises >
Recognizing Parallel
Structure

Parallelism is the use of matching words, phrases, clauses, and sentence structure to highlight similar ideas in a sentence. When you use parallelism, you are telling readers that certain ideas are related and have the same level of importance. By repeating similar grammatical patterns to express similar ideas, you create sentences that are clearer, more concise, and easier to read.

In the following examples, the parallel sentences highlight similar ideas; the other sentences do not.

Teaching Tip
Point out to students
that the more complicated
their ideas are, the
more they need to use
parallelism.

PARALLEL	NOT PARALLEL
Please leave <u>your name</u>, <u>your number</u>, and <u>your message</u>.	Please leave <u>your name</u>, <u>your number</u>, and <u>you should also leave a message</u>.
I plan to <u>graduate</u> from high school and <u>become</u> a nurse.	I plan to <u>graduate</u> from high school, and then <u>becoming</u> a nurse would be a good idea.
The grass was <u>soft</u>, <u>green</u>, and <u>sweet smelling</u>.	The grass was <u>soft</u>, <u>green</u>, and <u>the smell was sweet</u>.
<u>Making the team</u> was one thing; <u>staying on it</u> was another.	<u>Making the team</u> was one thing, but it was very difficult <u>to stay on it</u>.
We can <u>register</u> for classes in person, or <u>we can register</u> by email.	We can <u>register</u> for classes in person, or <u>registering</u> by email is another option.

PRACTICE
19-1

In the following sentences, decide whether the underlined words and phrases are parallel. If so, write *P* in the blank. If not, rewrite the sentences so that the underlined ideas are presented in parallel terms.

Examples: The missing dog had <u>brown fur</u>, <u>a red collar</u>, and <u>a long tail</u>. _____*P*_____

Signs of drug abuse in teenagers include <u>falling grades</u>, <u>mood swings</u>, and <u>~~they lose~~ weight</u>/ *loss.* ⌃ _____

1. The food in the cafeteria is <u>varied</u>, <u>tasty</u>, and <u>~~it is~~ healthy</u>. _____

2. Do you want the job done <u>quickly</u>, or do you want it done <u>well</u>? _____ *P*

3. Last summer <u>I worked at the library</u>, <u>babysat for my neighbor's daughter</u>, and <u>*volunteered at a soup kitchen.* ~~there was a soup kitchen where I volunteered.~~</u> _____

4. <u>Pandas eat bamboo leaves</u>, and <u>*koalas eat* ~~eucalyptus leaves are eaten by~~ ⌃ koalas</u>. _____

5. Skydiving is <u>frightening</u> but <u>fun</u>. _____ *P*

6. A number of interesting people work at the co-op with me, including <u>an elderly German man</u>, <u>~~there is a~~ middle-aged Chinese woman</u>, and <u>a teenaged Mexican boy</u>. _____

7. <u>The bell rang</u>, and <u>the students stood up</u>. _____ *P*

8. To conserve energy while I was away, I <u>unplugged the television</u>, <u>closed the curtains</u>, and <u>*set* ~~the thermostat was set~~ at 65 degrees</u>. _____

9. <u>I put away the dishes</u>; will you <u>put away the laundry</u>? _____ *P*

10. For several weeks after the storm, the supermarkets had <u>no eggs</u>, <u>*or* ~~they were out of~~ milk</u>, and <u>~~they did not have any~~ bread</u>. _____

19b Using Parallel Structure

Parallel structure is especially important in *paired items*, *items in a series*, and *items in a list or in an outline*.

Paired Items

Use parallel structure when you connect ideas with a **coordinating conjunction**—*and*, *but*, *for*, *nor*, *or*, *so*, and *yet*.

e bedfordstmartins.com /forw Additional Grammar Exercises > Using Parallel Structure

Teaching Tip
Remind students that many everyday writing tasks require parallelism. For example, items listed on a résumé should be in parallel form.

George believes in <u>doing a good job</u> and <u>minding his own business</u>.

You can <u>pay me now</u> or <u>pay me later</u>.

You should also use parallel structure for paired items joined by *both . . . and, not only . . . but also, either . . . or, neither . . . nor,* and *rather . . . than.*

Jan is <u>both</u> <u>skilled in writing</u> <u>and</u> <u>fluent in French</u>.

The group's new recording <u>not only</u> <u>has a dance beat</u> <u>but also</u> <u>has thought-provoking lyrics</u>.

I'd <u>rather</u> <u>eat one worm by itself</u> <u>than</u> <u>eat five worms with ice cream</u>.

Items in a Series

Teaching Tip
Refer students to 26a for more on punctuating items in a series.

Use parallel structure for items in a series—words, phrases, or clauses. (Be sure to use commas to separate three or more items in a series. Never put a comma after the final item.)

Every Wednesday I have <u>English</u>, <u>math</u>, and <u>psychology</u>. (three words)

<u>Increased demand</u>, <u>high factory output</u>, and <u>a strong dollar</u> will help the economy. (three phrases)

She is a champion because she <u>stays in excellent physical condition</u>, <u>puts in long hours of practice</u>, and <u>has an intense desire to win</u>. (three clauses)

Items in a List or in an Outline

Use parallel structure for items in a numbered or bulleted list.

There are three reasons to open an Individual Retirement Account (IRA):

1. To save money
2. To reduce taxes
3. To be able to retire

Use parallel structure for the elements in an outline.

   A. Types of rocks
      1. Igneous
      2. Sedimentary
      3. Metamorphic

PRACTICE
19-2   Fill in the blanks in the following sentences with parallel words, phrases, or clauses of your own that make sense in context.   *Answers will vary.*

Example: At the lake, we can _____*go for a swim*_____, _____*paddle a canoe*_____, and _____*play volleyball*_____.

1. When I get too little sleep, I am _____, _____, and _____.

2. I am good at _____ but not at _____.

3. My ideal mate is _____ and _____.

4. I personally define success not only as _____ but also as _____.

5. I use my computer for both _____ and _____.

6. I like _____ and _____.

7. You need three qualities to succeed in college: _____, _____, and _____.

8. I enjoy not only _____ but also _____.

9. I would rather _____ than _____.

10. Football _____, but baseball _____.

EDITING PRACTICE

Read the following student essay, which contains examples of faulty parallelism. Identify the sentences you think need to be corrected, and make the changes required to achieve parallelism. Be sure to supply all words necessary for clarity, grammar, and sense. Add punctuation as needed. The first error has been edited for you. *Answers will vary.*

READING TIP

This student essay includes several supporting details about self-made men and women. Compare and contrast the supporting details provided for each person. What do Winfrey, Quiñones-Hinojosa, and Canada have in common? How are they different?

Self-Made Men and Women Helping Others

Many self-made people go from poverty to ~~achieving~~ success. Quite a few of them not only achieve such success but also ~~they~~ help others. Three of these people are Oprah Winfrey, Alfredo Quiñones-Hinojosa, and Geoffrey Canada. Their lives are very different, but all possess great strength, ~~being determined,~~ *determination,* and concern for others.

Oprah is one of the most influential people in the world, *one of the wealthiest.* and ~~she has more money than almost anyone in the world.~~ She came from a very poor family. First, she lived with her grandmother on a Mississippi farm, and then *she lived with* her mother in Milwaukee. During this time, she was abused by several relatives. When she was thirteen, she was sent to Nashville to live with her father. He used strict discipline, and ~~she was~~ *he* taught ~~by him~~ *her* to value education. Through her own determination and ~~because she was ambitious,~~ *ambition,* Winfrey got a job at a local broadcasting company. This started her career. However, Oprah was not satisfied with being successful. Through Oprah's Angel Network and the Oprah Winfrey Leadership Academy, she helps others and ~~making~~ *makes* the world a better place.

Today, Alfredo Quiñones-Hinojosa is a top brain surgeon and ~~conducting~~ *conducts* research on new ways to treat brain cancer. At age nineteen, he was an illegal immigrant from Mexico, worked in the fields, and ~~without~~ *did not know* any English. When he told his cousin he wanted to learn English and get a better job, his cousin told him he was crazy. Then, while a welder on a railroad crew, he fell into

died

an empty petroleum tank and was almost ~~dying~~ from the fumes. However,

Alfredo overcame these hardships. He enrolled in a community college, and

work

with determination and ~~by working~~ hard, he began to change his life. He

won a scholarship to Berkeley, went on to medical school at Harvard, and

wound

eventually ~~winding~~ up as director of the brain tumor program at Johns Hopkins

University. In 1997, he became a citizen of the United States. At each step

of the way, he has made a special effort to reach out to students from

low-income backgrounds and to inspire others.

Geoffrey Canada grew up in a New York City neighborhood that was poor,

violent.

dangerous, and ~~where violence was not uncommon~~. His mother was a single

parent who struggled to support Geoffrey and his three brothers. Geoffrey

learned to survive on the streets, but he also studied a lot in school. Thanks

to this hard work, he won a scholarship to college in Maine and went on to

a career in education. Deciding to leave his neighborhood in New York wasn't

deciding

hard, but ~~to decide~~ to come back wasn't hard either. He wanted to help children

to

in poor families to succeed in school and ~~so they could~~ have better lives. With

this in mind, he started the Harlem Children's Zone (HCZ). HCZ includes (1)

workshops for parents, (2) a preschool and three charter schools, and (3) run-

ning health programs for children and families. President Obama has said he

would like to see more programs like HCZ.

Oprah Winfrey, Alfredo Quiñones-Hinojosa, and Geoffrey Canada have very

in education.

different careers—in entertainment, in medicine, and ~~educating children~~.

However, all three overcame great adversity, ~~all three have~~ achieved enormous

success, and ~~they have~~ helped others. They have helped their communities, their

country, and ~~have contributed to~~ the world.

review checklist

**bedfordstmartins.com
/forw** LearningCurve >
Parallelism

Using Parallelism

☐ Use matching words, phrases, clauses, and sentence structure to highlight similar items or ideas. (See 19a.)

☐ Use parallel structure with paired items. (See 19b.)

☐ Use parallel structure for items in a series. (See 19b.)

☐ Use parallel structure for items in a list or in an outline. (See 19b.)

20 Using Words Effectively

20a Using Specific Words

e bedfordstmartins.com /forw LearningCurve > Word Choice and Appropriate Language; Additional Grammar Exercises > Using Specific Words

Specific words refer to particular people, places, things, ideas, or qualities. **General words** refer to entire classes or groups. Sentences that contain specific words are more precise and vivid than those that contain only general words.

SENTENCES WITH GENERAL WORDS	SENTENCES WITH SPECIFIC WORDS
While walking in the woods, I saw an <u>animal</u>.	While walking in the woods, I saw a <u>baby skunk</u>.
<u>Someone</u> decided to run for Congress.	<u>Rebecca</u> decided to run for Congress.
<u>Weapons</u> are responsible for many murders.	<u>Unregistered handguns</u> are responsible for many murders.
Denise bought new <u>clothes</u>.	Denise bought a new <u>blue dress</u>.
I really enjoyed my <u>meal</u>.	I really enjoyed my <u>pepperoni pizza with extra cheese</u>.
Darrell had always wanted a <u>classic car</u>.	Darrell had always wanted a <u>black 1969 Chevrolet Camaro</u>.

Teaching Tip
Put a sentence on the board (for example, *The man was injured in an accident involving a shark.*), and have students work as a team to make the sentence more specific and concrete. Asking students to write a news story about the sentence usually results in excellent paragraphs.

FYI

Using Specific Words

One way to strengthen your writing is to avoid general words like *good*, *nice*, or *great*. Take the time to think of more specific words. For example, when you say the ocean looked *pretty*, do you really mean that it *sparkled*, *glistened*, *rippled*, *foamed*, *surged*, or *billowed*?

Teaching Tip
Warn students that the synonyms they see listed in a thesaurus almost never have precisely the same meanings. For example, ask students to discuss the differences in meaning of the words in this FYI box.

457

ESL Tip
Because ESL students
often rely on a thesaurus,
help them to find word
variations or pair them
with native speakers to
help them choose
different words.

PRACTICE

20-1   In the blank beside each of the five general words below, write a more specific word. Then, use the more specific word in an original sentence.

Example: child _____*six-year-old*_____

All through dinner, my six-year-old chattered excitedly about his first

day of school.

Answers will vary.

1. emotion _____

_____

2. building _____

_____

3. said _____

_____

4. animal _____

_____

5. went _____

_____

Teaching Tip
Use this opportunity to
teach students how to
write a job-application
letter and résumé. Make
sure they understand the
importance of using spe-
cific language to describe
their job experiences.

PRACTICE

20-2   The following one-paragraph job-application letter uses many general words. Rewrite the paragraph, substituting specific words and adding details where necessary. Start by making the first sentence, which identifies the job, more specific: for example, "I would like to apply for the <u>dental technician</u> position you advertised on <u>March 15 on monster.com</u>." Then, add information about your background and qualifications. Expand the original paragraph into a three-paragraph letter.   *Answers will vary.*

I would like to apply for the position you advertised in today's paper. I graduated from high school and am currently attending college. I have taken several courses that have prepared me for the duties the position requires. I also have several personal qualities that I think you would find useful in a person holding this position. In addition, I have had certain experiences that qualify me for such a job. I would appreciate the opportunity to meet with you to discuss your needs as an employer. Thank you.

20b   Using Concise Language

Teaching Tip
Point out that a short
sentence is not necessarily
a concise sentence. A
sentence is concise when
it contains only the words
needed to convey its
ideas.

Concise language says what it has to say in as few words as possible. Too often, writers use words and phrases that add nothing to a sentence's meaning. A good way to test a sentence for these words is to see if crossing them out changes the sentence's meaning. If the sentence's meaning does not change, you can assume that the words you crossed out are unnecessary.

> *The*
> ~~It is clear that the~~ United States was not ready to fight World War II.
>
> *To* ^
> ~~In order to~~ follow the plot, you must make an outline.
> ^

Sometimes you can replace several unnecessary words with a single word.

> *Because*
> ~~Due to the fact that~~ I was tired, I missed my first class.
> ^

FYI

Using Concise Language

The following wordy phrases add nothing to a sentence. You can usually delete or condense them with no loss of meaning.

WORDY	CONCISE
It is clear that	(delete)
It is a fact that	(delete)
The reason is because	Because
The reason is that	Because
It is my opinion that	I think/I believe
Due to the fact that	Because
Despite the fact that	Although
At the present time	Today/Now
At that time	Then
In most cases	Usually
In order to	To
In the final analysis	Finally
Subsequent to	After

Unnecessary repetition—saying the same thing twice for no reason—can also make your writing wordy. When you revise, delete repeated words and phrases that add nothing to your sentences.

Teaching Tip
Encourage students to avoid flowery language and complicated sentences. Good writing is clear and concise.

My instructor told me the book was ~~old-fashioned and~~ outdated. (An old-fashioned book *is* outdated.)

The ~~terrible~~ tragedy of the fire could have been avoided. (A tragedy is *always* terrible.)

PRACTICE

20-3 To make the following sentences more concise, eliminate any unnecessary repetition, and delete or condense wordy expressions.

> Each
Example: ~~It is a fact that each individual~~ production of *Sesame Street* around the world is geared toward the local children ~~in that region.~~ *Answers will vary.*

To
(1) ~~In order to~~ meet the needs of international children ~~all over the world,~~ Sesame Workshop helps produce versions of its popular show *Sesame Street* in many countries ~~outside the United States.~~ (2) ~~Due to the~~
Because
~~fact that~~ each country has different issues ~~and concerns,~~ the content of
Usually,
these shows varies. (3) ~~In most cases,~~ the producers focus on ~~and concentrate on~~ the cultural diversity in their country. (4) ~~In order to~~ develop
To
the most appropriate material for their shows, producers also consult with ~~and talk to~~ local educators and child development experts, ~~people~~
Today,
~~who are experts in the field.~~ (5) ~~At the present time,~~ versions of *Sesame Street* exist in a ~~wide~~ variety of ~~places and~~ countries. They include Mexico, Russia, South Africa, Bangladesh, and Egypt. (6) Created in 1972, Mexico's *Plaza Sésamo* is one of the oldest international versions, ~~having been around longer than versions in other countries.~~ (7) This Spanish-language show includes ~~and brings in familiar and~~ well-known characters like Elmo and Cookie Monster as well as ~~unique and~~ original characters like Abelardo and Pancho. (8) Like all versions of *Sesame Street*, *Plaza*

Sésamo's main ~~and most important~~ focus is on ~~educating and~~ teaching children about letters, numbers, and the diverse world around them.

20c   Using Similes and Metaphors

A **simile** is a comparison of two unlike things that uses *like* or *as*.

> His arm hung at his side <u>like</u> a broken branch.
> He was <u>as</u> content <u>as</u> a cat napping on a windowsill.

A **metaphor** is a comparison of two unlike things that does not use *like* or *as*.

> Invaders from another world, the dandelions conquered my garden.
> He was a beast of burden, hauling cement from the mixer to the building site.

The impact of similes and metaphors comes from the surprise of seeing two seemingly unlike things being compared. Used in moderation, similes and metaphors can make your writing more lively and more interesting.

Teaching Tip
Point out that both similes and metaphors compare two dissimilar things. If the items being compared are alike, the result is a statement of fact (*Your boat is like my boat*) and is not a simile or a metaphor.

Teaching Tip
Warn students not to use too many similes or metaphors. Although a few can enhance a piece of writing, too many are distracting.

PRACTICE

20-4 Think of a person you know well. Using that person as your subject, fill in each of the following blanks to create metaphors. Try to complete each metaphor with more than a single word, as in the example.

Example: If _____*my baby sister*_____ were an animal, ___*she*___ would

be ____*a curious little kitten.*____

Answers will vary.

1. If _____ were a musical instrument, _____ would be _____

   _____

2. If _____ were a food, _____ would be _____

   _____

3. If _____ were a means of transportation, _____ would be

_____

_____

4. If _____ were a natural phenomenon, _____ would be

_____

5. If _____ were a toy, _____ would be _____

_____

20d Avoiding Slang

Slang is nonstandard language that calls attention to itself. It is usually associated with a particular social group—instant-message users or skateboarders, for example. Some slang eventually spreads beyond its original context and becomes widely used. Often, it is used for emphasis or to produce a surprising or original effect. In any case, because it is very informal, slang is not acceptable in your college writing.

My psychology exam was really ~~sweet.~~ *easy.*

On the weekends, I like to ~~chill~~ *relax* ^ and watch movies on my laptop.

If you have any question about whether a term is slang or not, look it up in a dictionary. If the term is identified as *slang* or *informal*, find a more suitable term.

FYI

Avoiding Abbreviations and Shorthand

While abbreviations and shorthand such as *LOL, BTW, IMO,* and *2day* are acceptable in informal electronic communication, they are not acceptable in your college writing, in emails to your instructors, or in online class discussions.

~~IMO~~ *In my opinion,* ^ your essay needs a strong thesis statement.

I would like to meet with ~~u~~ *you* ^ for a conference ~~2day.~~ *today.*

PRACTICE

20-5 Edit the following sentences, replacing the slang expressions with clearer, more precise words and phrases.

Example: My father ~~lost it~~ *yelled at me* when I told him I crashed the car.
Answers will vary.

1. Whenever I get ~~bummed,~~ *upset,* I go outside and jog.
2. Tonight I'll have to leave by 11 because I'm ~~wiped out.~~ *exhausted.*
3. ~~I'm not into~~ *I don't like* movies or television.
4. Whenever we argue, my boyfriend knows how to ~~push my buttons.~~ *get me angry.*
5. I really ~~lucked out~~ *was lucky* when I got this job.

20e Avoiding Clichés

bedfordstmartins.com /forw Additional Grammar Exercises > Avoiding Clichés and Sexist Language

Clichés are expressions—such as "it is what it is" and "last but not least"—that have been used so often that they have lost their meaning. These worn-out expressions get in the way of clear communication.

When you identify a cliché in your writing, replace it with a direct statement—or, if possible, with a fresher expression.

CLICHÉ When school was over, she felt free ~~as a bird~~.

CLICHÉ These days, you have to be ~~sick as a dog~~ *seriously ill* before you are

admitted to a hospital.

ESL Tip

Every culture uses clichés. You may ask your ESL students to translate some native expressions for the class. Try to come up with the American equivalents. Write these on the board.

FYI

Avoiding Clichés

Here are examples of some clichés you should avoid in your writing.

back in the day	give 110 percent
better late than never	hard as a rock
beyond a shadow of a doubt	it goes without saying
break the ice	keep your eye on the ball
cutting edge	play God
face the music	pushing the envelope

(continued)

Teaching Tip

Ask students for other examples of overused expressions. Write these ideas on the board, and have students think of more original or more direct ways of expressing them.

READING TIP
The uncorrected version of this passage includes many clichéd expressions. How do these clichés affect your reaction to the writer's ideas?

(continued from previous page)

raining cats **and dogs**	tried and true
selling like hotcakes	water under the bridge
the bottom line	what goes around comes
think outside the box	around
touched base	

PRACTICE

20-6 Cross out any clichés in the following sentences. Then, either substitute a fresher expression or restate the idea more directly.

Example: Lottery winners often think they will be ~~on easy street~~ for *(free of financial worries)* the rest of their lives. *Answers will vary.*

(1) Many people think that a million-dollar lottery jackpot allows the winner to stop working ~~like a dog~~ *(long hours)* and start living ~~high on the hog~~ *(a comfortable life.)*. (2) ~~All things considered, however,~~ *(In fact,)* the reality for lottery winners is quite different. (3) For one thing, lottery winners who ~~hit the jackpot~~ *(win big prizes)* do not always receive their winnings all at once; instead, yearly payments—for example, $50,000—can be paid out over twenty years. (4) Of that $50,000 a year, close to $20,000 goes to taxes and anything else the ~~lucky stiff~~ *(winner)* already owes the government, such as student loans. (5) Next come relatives and friends ~~with their hands out~~ *(who ask for money,)*, leaving winners ~~between a rock and a hard place.~~ *(with difficult choices to make.)* (6) They can either ~~cough up~~ *(give)* gifts and loans or ~~wave bye-bye to~~ *(lose the friendship of)* many of their loved ones. (7) ~~Adding insult to injury,~~ *(Even worse,)* many lottery winners lose their jobs because employers think that, now that they are "millionaires," they no longer need to draw a salary. (8) Many lottery winners wind up ~~way over their heads~~ *(seriously)* in debt within a few years. (9) ~~In their hour of need,~~ *(Faced with financial difficulties,)* many might like to sell their future payments to companies that offer lump-sum payments of forty to forty-five cents on the dollar. (10) This is ~~easier said than done,~~ *(usually impossible,)* however, because most state lotteries do not allow winners to sell their winnings.

20f Avoiding Sexist Language

Sexist language refers to men and women in insulting terms. Sexist language is not just words such as *stud* or *babe*, which people may find objectionable. It can also be words or phrases that unnecessarily call attention to gender or that suggest a job or profession is held only by a man (or only by a woman) when it actually is not.

You can avoid sexist language by using a little common sense. There is always an acceptable nonsexist alternative for a sexist term.

SEXIST	NONSEXIST
man, mankind	humanity, humankind, the human race
businessman	executive, businessperson
fireman, policeman, mailman	firefighter, police officer, letter carrier
male nurse, woman engineer	nurse, engineer
congressman	member of Congress, representative
stewardess, steward	flight attendant
man and wife	man and woman, husband and wife
manmade	synthetic
chairman	chair, chairperson
anchorwoman, anchorman	anchor
actor, actress	actor

bedfordstmartins.com /forw Additional Grammar Exercises > Avoiding Clichés and Sexist Language

Teaching Tip
Tell students that it is also sexist to give information about a woman—for example, her marital status or a description of her clothing—that they would not give about a man.

Teaching Tip
Point out that, in addition to avoiding sexist language, students should avoid potentially offensive references to a person's age, physical condition, or sexual orientation.

Teaching Tip
Refer students to 15e for more on subjects like *everyone* (indefinite pronoun antecedents).

FYI

Avoiding Sexist Language

Do not use *he* when your subject could be either male or female.

SEXIST   Everyone should complete his assignment by next week.

You can correct this problem in three ways.

- *Use* he or she *or* his or her.

  Everyone should complete his or her assignment by next week.

(continued)

(continued from previous page)

■ *Use plural forms.*

Students should complete their assignments by next week.

■ *Eliminate the pronoun.*

Everyone should complete the assignment by next week.

PRACTICE
20-7   Edit the following sentences to eliminate sexist language.

Example: A doctor should be honest with his patients.
or her (or omit "his")

Answers will vary.

1. Many people today would like to see more policemen patrolling the
police officers

   streets.

2. The attorneys representing the plaintiff are Geraldo Diaz and Mrs.

   Barbara Wilkerson.
All the soldiers   their

3. Every soldier picked up his weapons.

4. Christine Fox is the female mayor of Port London, Maine.
humanity.

5. Travel to other planets will be a significant step for man.

20g Identifying Commonly Confused Words

bedfordstmartins.com /forw Additional Grammar Exercises > Commonly Confused Words

Accept/Except   *Accept* means "to receive something." *Except* means "with the exception of" or "to leave out or exclude."

"I <u>accept</u> your challenge," said Alexander Hamilton to Aaron Burr.

Everyone <u>except</u> Darryl visited the museum.

Affect/Effect   *Affect* is a verb meaning "to influence." *Effect* is a noun meaning "result."

Carmen's job could <u>affect</u> her grades.

Overexposure to sun can have a long-term <u>effect</u> on skin.

All ready/Already   *All ready* means "completely prepared." *Already* means "previously, before."

Serge was <u>all ready</u> to take the history test.

Gina had <u>already</u> been to Italy.

Brake/Break   *Brake* is a noun that means "a device to slow or stop a vehicle." *Break* is a verb meaning "to smash" or "to detach" and sometimes a noun meaning either "a gap" or "an interruption" or "a stroke of luck."

> Peter got into an accident because his foot slipped off the brake.
>
> Babe Ruth thought no one would ever break his home run record.
>
> The baseball game was postponed until there was a break in the bad weather.

Buy/By   *Buy* means "to purchase." *By* is a preposition meaning "close to," "next to," or "by means of."

> The Stamp Act forced colonists to buy stamps for many public documents.
>
> He drove by but did not stop.
>
> He stayed by her side all the way to the hospital.
>
> Malcolm X wanted "freedom by any means necessary."

Conscience/Conscious   *Conscience* is a noun that refers to the part of the mind that urges a person to choose right over wrong. *Conscious* is an adjective that means "aware" or "deliberate."

> After he cheated at cards, his conscience started to bother him.
>
> As she walked through the woods, she became conscious of the hum of insects.
>
> Elliott made a conscious decision to stop smoking.

Everyday/Every day   *Everyday* is a single word that means "ordinary" or "common." *Every day* is two words that mean "occurring daily."

> *Friends* was a successful comedy show because it appealed to everyday people.
>
> Every day, the six friends met at the Central Perk café.

Fine/Find   *Fine* means "superior quality" or "a sum of money paid as a penalty." *Find* means "to locate."

> He sang a fine solo at church last Sunday.
>
> Demi had to pay a fine for speeding.
>
> Some people still use a willow rod to find water.

Hear/Here *Hear* means "to perceive sound by ear." *Here* means "at or in this place."

> I moved to the front so I could <u>hear</u> the speaker.
>
> My great-grandfather came <u>here</u> in 1883.

Its/It's *Its* is the possessive form of *it*. *It's* is the contraction of *it is* or *it has*.

> The airline canceled <u>its</u> flights because of the snow.
>
> <u>It's</u> twelve o'clock, and we are late.
>
> Ever since <u>it's</u> been in the accident, the car has rattled.

Know/No/Knew/New *Know* means "to have an understanding of" or "to have fixed in the mind." *No* means "not any," "not at all," or "not one." *Knew* is the past tense form of the verb *know*. *New* means "recent or never used."

> I <u>know</u> there will be a lunar eclipse tonight.
>
> You have <u>no</u> right to say that.
>
> He <u>knew</u> how to install a <u>new</u> light switch.

Lie/Lay *Lie* means "to rest or recline." The past tense of *lie* is *lay*. *Lay* means "to put or place something down." The past tense of *lay* is *laid*.

> Every Sunday, I <u>lie</u> in bed until noon.
>
> They <u>lay</u> on the grass until it began to rain, and then they went home.
>
> Tammy told Carl to <u>lay</u> his cards on the table.
>
> Brooke and Cassia finally <u>laid</u> down their hockey sticks.

Loose/Lose *Loose* means "not fixed or rigid" or "not attached securely." *Lose* means "to mislay" or "to misplace."

> In the 1940s, many women wore <u>loose</u>-fitting pants.
>
> I never gamble because I hate to <u>lose</u>.

Passed/Past *Passed* is the past tense of the verb *pass*. It means "moved by" or "succeeded in." *Past* is a noun or an adjective meaning "earlier than the present time."

> The car that <u>passed</u> me was doing more than eighty miles an hour.
>
> David finally <u>passed</u> his driving test.

The novel was set in the <u>past</u>.

The statement said that the bill was <u>past</u> due.

Peace/Piece   *Peace* means "the absence of war" or "calm." *Piece* means "a part of something."

The British prime minister tried to achieve <u>peace</u> with honor.

My <u>peace</u> of mind was destroyed when the flying saucer landed.

"Have a <u>piece</u> of cake," said Marie.

Principal/Principle   *Principal* means "first" or "highest" or "the head of a school." *Principle* means "a law or basic assumption."

She had the <u>principal</u> role in the movie.

I'll never forget the day the <u>principal</u> called me into his office.

It was against his <u>principles</u> to lie.

Quiet/Quit/Quite   *Quiet* means "free of noise" or "still." *Quit* means "to leave a job" or "to give up." *Quite* means "actually" or "very."

Jane looked forward to the <u>quiet</u> evenings at the lake.

Sammy <u>quit</u> his job and followed the girls into the parking lot.

"You haven't <u>quite</u> got the hang of it yet," she said.

After practicing all summer, Tamika got <u>quite</u> good at tennis.

Raise/Rise   *Raise* means "to elevate" or "to increase in size, quantity, or worth." The past tense of *raise* is *raised*. *Rise* means "to stand up" or "to move from a lower position to a higher position." The past tense of *rise* is *rose*.

Carlos <u>raises</u> his hand whenever the teacher asks for volunteers.

They finally <u>raised</u> the money for the down payment.

The crowd <u>rises</u> every time their team scores a touchdown.

Kim <u>rose</u> before dawn so she could see the eclipse.

Sit/Set   *Sit* means "to assume a sitting position." The past tense of *sit* is *sat*. *Set* means "to put down or place" or "to adjust something to a desired position." The past tense of *set* is *set*.

I usually <u>sit</u> in the front row at the movies.

They <u>sat</u> at the clinic waiting for their names to be called.

Elizabeth <u>set</u> the mail on the kitchen table and left for work.

Every semester I <u>set</u> goals for myself.

Teaching Tip
Remind students not to
drop the *d* of *supposed*
before *to*: *He is supposed
to study*, not *He is
suppose to study*.

Suppose/Supposed *Suppose* means "to consider" or "to assume." *Supposed* is both the past tense and the past participle of *suppose*. *Supposed* also means "expected" or "required." (Note that when *supposed* has this meaning, it is always followed by *to*.)

Suppose researchers were to find a cure for cancer.

We supposed the movie would be over by ten o'clock.

You were supposed to finish a draft of the report by today.

Teaching Tip
Teach students how to
use mnemonic devices to
remember spellings. (For
example, *their* refers to
ownership, and so does
heir; *there* refers to location, and so does *here*.)

Their/There/They're *Their* is the possessive form of the pronoun *they*. *There* means "at or in that place." *There* is also used in the phrases *there is* and *there are*. *They're* is the contraction of *they are*.

They wanted poor people to improve their living conditions.

I put the book over there.

There are three reasons I will not eat meat.

They're the best volunteer firefighters I've ever seen.

Then/Than *Then* means "at that time" or "next in time." *Than* is used in comparisons.

He was young and naive then.

I went to the job interview and then stopped off for coffee.

My dog is smarter than your dog.

Teaching Tip
Remind students not to
use the informal spelling
thru for *through*.

Threw/Through *Threw* is the past tense of *throw*. *Through* means "in one side and out the opposite side" or "finished."

Satchel Paige threw a baseball more than ninety-five miles an hour.

It takes almost thirty minutes to go through the tunnel.

"I'm through," said Clark Kent, storming out of Perry White's office.

To/Too/Two *To* means "in the direction of." *Too* means "also" or "more than enough." *Two* denotes the numeral 2.

During spring break, I am going to Disney World.

My roommates are coming too.

The microwave popcorn is too hot to eat.

"If we get rid of the Tin Man and the Cowardly Lion, the two of us can go to Oz," said the Scarecrow to Dorothy.

Use/Used   *Use* means "to put into service" or "to consume." *Used* is both the past tense and the past participle of *use*. *Used* also means "accustomed." (Note that when *used* has this meaning, it is followed by *to*.)

> I use a soft cloth to clean my glasses.
> "Hey! Who used all the hot water?" he yelled from the shower.
> Marisol had used all the firewood during the storm.
> After two years in Alaska, they got used to the short winter days.

Weather/Whether   *Weather* refers to temperature, humidity, precipitation, and so on. *Whether* is used to introduce alternative possibilities.

> The *Farmer's Almanac* says that the weather this winter will be severe.
> Whether or not this prediction will be correct is anyone's guess.

Where/Were/We're   *Where* means "at or in what place." *Were* is the past tense of *are*. *We're* is the contraction of *we are*.

> Where are you going, and where have you been?
> Charlie Chaplin and Mary Pickford were popular stars of silent movies.
> We're doing our back-to-school shopping early this year.

Whose/Who's   *Whose* is the possessive form of *who*. *Who's* is the contraction of either *who is* or *who has*.

> My roommate asked, "Whose book is this?"
> "Who's there?" squealed the second little pig as he leaned against the door.
> Who's been blocking the driveway?

Your/You're   *Your* is the possessive form of *you*. *You're* is the contraction of *you are*.

> "You should have worn your running shoes," said the hare as he passed the tortoise.
> "You're too kind," said the tortoise sarcastically.

EDITING PRACTICE

Read the following student essay carefully, and then revise it. Make sure that your revision is concise, uses specific words, and includes no slang, sexist language, clichés, or confused words. Add an occasional simile or metaphor if you like. The first sentence has been edited for you.

Answers will vary.

Unexpected Discoveries

When we ~~here~~ *hear* the word "accident," we think of bad things. *, like dented fenders and broken glass.* But accidents can be ~~good,~~ *lucky,* too. Modern science has made advances as a result of accidents. ~~It is a fact that a~~ *A* scientist sometimes works ~~like a dog~~ *hard* for years in ~~his~~ *the* laboratory, only to make ~~a weird~~ *an unexpected* discovery ~~because of a mistake.~~

The most famous example of a ~~good,~~ beneficial accident is the discovery of penicillin. A scientist, Alexander Fleming, had seen many soldiers die of infections after they were wounded in World War I. ~~All things considered,~~ *In fact,* many more soldiers died ~~due to the fact that~~ *from* infections ~~occurred~~ than from wounds. Fleming wanted to find a drug that could ~~put an end to~~ *cure* these ~~terrible,~~ fatal infections. One day in 1928, Fleming went on vacation, leaving a pile of dishes in the lab sink. ~~As luck would have it,~~ *Luckily,* he had been growing bacteria in those dishes. When he came back, he noticed that one of the dishes looked moldy. ~~What was strange~~ *Strangely,* ~~was that~~ near the mold, the bacteria were dead ~~as a doornail. It was crystal clear to~~ *realized* Fleming that the mold had killed the bacteria. He had discovered penicillin, the first antibiotic.

Everyone has heard the name "Goodyear." ~~It was~~ Charles Goodyear ~~who~~ made a discovery that ~~changed and~~ revolutionized the rubber industry. In the early nineteenth century, rubber products ~~became thin and runny~~ *melted* in hot weather and cracked in cold weather. One day in 1839, Goodyear accidentally dropped some rubber mixed with sulfur on a hot stove. It ~~changed color and~~ turned black. After

, like a rubber band,

being cooled, it could be stretched, and it would return to its original size and
                                 ^

shape. This kind of rubber is now used in tires and in many other products.

           product

    Another thing was also discovered because of a lab accident involving
        ^

rubber. In 1953, Patsy Sherman, a female chemist for the 3M company, was

                                 synthetic

trying to find a new type of rubber. She created a batch of man-made liquid
                                    ^

rubber. Some of the liquid accidentally spilled onto a lab assistant's new white

                          available

canvas sneaker. Her assistant used everything but the kitchen sink to clean the
            After a few weeks,   ^

shoe, but nothing worked. Over time, the rest of the shoe became dirty, but the
                ^

                                                  knew

part where the spill had hit was still clean as a whistle. Sherman new that she had
   a chemical   ^   *repelling* ^

found something that could actually keep fabrics clean by doing a number on
   ^   *its*   ^

dirt. The 3M Corporation named it's brand new product Scotchgard.
                     ^

Scientists   *their*

    A scientist can be clumsy and careless, but sometimes his mistakes lead
   ^   ^   ^

to great and important discoveries. Penicillin, better tires, and Scotchgard are

examples of products that were the result of scientific accidents.

review checklist

Using Words Effectively

☐ Use specific words that convey your ideas clearly and precisely.
(See 20a.)

☐ Use concise language that says what it has to say in the fewest
possible words. (See 20b.)

☐ When appropriate, use similes and metaphors to make your writing more lively and more interesting. (See 20c.)

☐ Avoid slang. (See 20d.)

☐ Avoid clichés. (See 20e.)

☐ Avoid sexist language. (See 20f.)

☐ Learn to distinguish between commonly confused words.
(See 20g.)

e **bedfordstmartins.com**
/forw LearningCurve >
Word Choice and
Appropriate Language

21 Run-Ons

21a Recognizing Run-Ons

e bedfordstmartins.com
/forw Additional
Grammar Exercises >
Recognizing Run-Ons

A **sentence** consists of at least one independent clause—one subject and one verb.

> College costs are rising.

A **run-on** is an error that occurs when two sentences are joined incorrectly. There are two kinds of run-ons: *fused sentences* and *comma splices*.

■ A **fused sentence** occurs when two sentences are joined without any punctuation.

> **FUSED SENTENCE** [College costs are rising] [many students are worried.]

■ A **comma splice** occurs when two sentences are joined with just a comma.

> **COMMA SPLICE** [College costs are rising], [many students are worried.]

Teaching Tip
Remind students that a sentence can be short and still be a run-on.

WORD POWER

fused joined together
splice (verb) to join together at the ends

Teaching Tip
Virtually all students sometimes write run-ons. Plan on having students do a lot of exercises in class and for homework.

Teaching Tip
Remind students that a sentence is not necessarily a single clause: a sentence can be one independent clause, two independent clauses, one dependent and one independent clause, and so on. Refer them to Chapter 17.

Teaching Tip
Tell students that a comma can join two sentences only when it is followed by a coordinating conjunction. Refer them to 17d.

PRACTICE
21-1

Some of the sentences in the following paragraph are correct, but others are run-ons. In the answer space after each sentence, write *C* if the sentence is correct, *FS* if it is a fused sentence, and *CS* if it is a comma splice.

Example: Using a screen reader is one way for blind people to access the web, two popular programs are JAWS for Windows and Window-Eyes. ___*CS*___

(1) The Internet should be accessible to everyone, this is not always the case. ___*CS*___ (2) Many blind computer users have trouble finding information on the web. ___*C*___ (3) Often, this is the result of poor web design it is the designer's job to make the site accessible. ___*FS*___

(4) Most blind people use special software called screen readers, this technology translates text into speech or Braille. _____*CS*_____ (5) However, screen readers do not always work well the information is sometimes hard to access. _____*FS*_____ (6) Websites need to be understandable to all Internet users. _____*C*_____ (7) The rights of blind Internet users may be protected by the Americans with Disabilities Act (ADA). _____*C*_____ (8) We will have to wait for more cases to come to trial then we will know more. _____*FS*_____ (9) Meanwhile, we have to rely on software companies to make the necessary changes, this will take some time. _____*CS*_____ (10) However, there are incentives for these companies, the 1.5 million blind computer users are all potential customers. _____*CS*_____

21b Correcting Run-Ons

e bedfordstmartins.com
/forw Additional
Grammar Exercises >
Correcting Run-Ons

FYI

Correcting Run-Ons

You can correct run-ons in five ways.

1. ***Use a period to create two separate sentences.***

   College costs are rising. Many students are worried.

2. ***Use a coordinating conjunction (and, but, or, nor, for, so, or yet) to connect ideas.***

   College costs are rising, and many students are worried.

3. ***Use a semicolon to connect ideas.***

   College costs are rising; many students are worried.

4. ***Use a semicolon followed by a transitional word or phrase to connect ideas.***

   College costs are rising; as a result, many students are worried.

5. ***Use a dependent word (although, because, when, and so on) to connect ideas.***

   Because college costs are rising, many students are worried.

Teaching Tip
Let students practice reading aloud passages from which you have deleted all end punctuation. Point out how their voices usually stop at the end of a sentence even when it contains no punctuation.

Teaching Tip
Remind students that computer grammar checkers sometimes identify a sentence as a run-on simply because it is long. However, a long sentence can be perfectly correct. Before they make changes, students should be sure they actually have an error (two independent clauses joined without punctuation or with just a comma).

The pages that follow explain and illustrate the five different ways to correct run-ons.

1. **Use a period to create two separate sentences.** Be sure each sentence begins with a capital letter and ends with a period.

> **INCORRECT (FUSED SENTENCE)** Gas prices are very high some people are buying hybrid cars.
>
> **INCORRECT (COMMA SPLICE)** Gas prices are very high, some people are buying hybrid cars.
>
> **CORRECT** Gas prices are very high. Some people are buying hybrid cars. (two separate sentences)

PRACTICE
21-2 Correct each of the following run-ons by using a period to create two separate sentences. Be sure both of your new sentences begin with a capital letter and end with a period.

Example: Stephen Colbert used to appear on *The Daily Show with*
Jon Stewart, ~~now,~~ ‸ *. Now,* he has his own show called *The Colbert Report.*

1. In 2010, David Cameron became prime minister of the United Kingdom, ‸ *. He* he replaced Gordon Brown.

2. New York–style pizza usually has a thin crust ‸ Chicago-style "deep-
   dish pizza" has a thick crust.

3. Last week, Soraya won a text-messaging contest ‸ *. The* the prize for texting
   the fastest was five hundred dollars.

4. In some parts of Canada's Northwest Territory, the only way to
   transport supplies is over frozen lakes, ‸ *. Being* being an ice road trucker is
   one of the most dangerous jobs in the world.

5. In 1961, the first Six Flags opened in Arlington, Texas, ‸ *. The* the six flags represent the six former governments of Texas.

2. **Use a coordinating conjunction to connect ideas.** If you want to indicate a particular relationship between ideas—for example, cause and effect or contrast—you can connect two independent clauses with a coordinating conjunction that makes this relationship clear. Always place a comma before the coordinating conjunction.

Teaching Tip
Refer students to 17d
for more on connecting
ideas with a coordinating
conjunction and informa-
tion on choosing the most
appropriate coordinating
conjunction.

Coordinating Conjunctions

and	for	or	yet
but	nor	so	

INCORRECT **(FUSED SENTENCE)**	Some schools require students to wear uni-forms other schools do not.
INCORRECT **(COMMA SPLICE)**	Some schools require students to wear uni-forms, other schools do not.
CORRECT	Some schools require students to wear uni-forms, but other schools do not. (clauses con-nected with the coordinating conjunction *but*, preceded by a comma)

PRACTICE

21-3   Correct each of the following run-ons by using a coordi-nating conjunction (*and, but, or, nor, for, so,* or *yet*) to connect ideas. Be sure to put a comma before each coordinating conjunction.

Example: Many college students use Facebook to keep up with old
, *and*
friends they also use the site to find new friends.   *Answers will vary.*
^

so
1. A car with soft tires gets poor gas mileage, keeping tires inflated is
^

 a good way to save money on gas.

2. It used to be difficult for football fans to see the first-down line
but
 on television, the computer-generated yellow line makes it much
^

 easier.

3. Indonesia has more volcanoes than any other country in the world
, *but*
 the United States has the biggest volcano in the world, Hawaii's
^

 Mauna Loa.

, *or*
4. Chefs can become famous for cooking at popular restaurants they
^

 can gain fame by hosting television shows.

5. Overcrowded schools often have to purchase portable classrooms or
, *yet*
 trailers this is only a temporary solution.
^

3. **Use a semicolon to connect ideas.** If you want to indicate a particularly close connection—or a strong contrast—between two ideas, use a semicolon.

Teaching Tip
Tell students that if a period will not work where the semicolon is, then the semicolon is probably incorrect. Refer students to 17e for more on connecting ideas with a semicolon.

INCORRECT (FUSED SENTENCE)	Most professional basketball players go to college most professional baseball players do not.
INCORRECT (COMMA SPLICE)	Most professional basketball players go to college, most professional baseball players do not.
CORRECT	Most professional basketball players go to college; most professional baseball players do not. (clauses connected with a semicolon)

PRACTICE

21-4 Correct each of the following run-ons by using a semicolon to connect ideas. Do not use a capital letter after the semicolon unless the word that follows it is a proper noun.

Example: From 1930 until 2006, Pluto was known as a planet it is now known as a "dwarf planet."

1. Of all the states, Alaska has the highest percentage of Native American residents 16 percent of Alaskans are of Native American descent.

2. Satellites and global positioning systems (GPS) can help farmers to better understand the needs of their crops these new tools are part of a trend called "precision agriculture."

3. Enforcing traffic laws can be difficult some cities use cameras to identify speeding cars.

4. Old landfills can sometimes be made into parks Cesar Chavez Park in Berkeley, California, is one example.

5. Freestyle motocross riders compete by doing jumps and stunts famous FMX riders include Carey Hart, Nate Adams, and Travis Pastrana.

4. **Use a semicolon followed by a transitional word or phrase to connect ideas.** To show how two closely linked ideas are related, add a transitional word or phrase after the semicolon. The transition will indicate the specific relationship between the two clauses.

INCORRECT (FUSED SENTENCE)	Finding a part-time job can be challenging sometimes it is even hard to find an unpaid internship.
INCORRECT (COMMA SPLICE)	Finding a part-time job can be challenging, sometimes it is even hard to find an unpaid internship.
CORRECT	Finding a part-time job can be challenging; in fact, sometimes it is even hard to find an unpaid internship. (clauses connected with a semicolon followed by the transitional phrase *in fact*)

Some Frequently Used Transitional Words and Phrases

after all	for this reason	now
also	however	still
as a result	in addition	then
eventually	in fact	therefore
finally	instead	thus
for example	moreover	unfortunately
for instance	nevertheless	

For more complete lists of transitional words and phrases, see 17f.

PRACTICE

21-5 Correct each of the following run-ons by using a semicolon, followed by the transitional word or phrase in parentheses, to connect ideas. Be sure to put a comma after the transitional word or phrase.

Example: When babies are first born, they can only see black and
; still,
white most baby clothes and blankets are made in pastel colors. (still)
^

; for example,
1. Different condiments are used in different regions of the country, few
^
tables in the Southwest are without a bottle of hot sauce. (for example)

2. Every April, millions of people participate in TV-Turnoff Week by
; instead,
not watching television ˄ they read, spend time with family and

friends, and generally enjoy their free time. (instead)
; however,
3. Today, few people can count on company pension plans ˄ thirty years

ago, most people could. (however)
; after all,
4. Many people see bottled water as a waste of money ˄ tap water is free.

(after all)
; unfortunately,
5. Owners of "puppy mills" are only concerned with making money ˄ they are

not particularly concerned with their dogs' well-being. (unfortunately)

FYI

Connecting Ideas with Semicolons

Run-ons often occur when you use a transitional word or phrase
to join two independent clauses *without also using a semicolon.*

INCORRECT (FUSED SENTENCE) It is easy to download information from the Internet however it is not always easy to evaluate the information.

INCORRECT (COMMA SPLICE) It is easy to download information from the Internet, however it is not always easy to evaluate the information.

To avoid this kind of run-on, always put a semicolon before the
transitional word or phrase and a comma after it.

CORRECT It is easy to download information from the Internet; however, it is not always easy to evaluate the information.

5. **Use a dependent word to connect ideas.** When one idea is dependent
   on another, you can connect the two ideas by adding a dependent
   word, such as *when, who, although,* or *because.*

   INCORRECT (FUSED SENTENCE) American union membership was high in the mid-twentieth century it has declined in recent years.

INCORRECT
(COMMA SPLICE) American union membership was high in the mid-twentieth century, it has declined in recent years.

CORRECT Although American union membership was high in the mid-twentieth century, it has declined in recent years. (clauses connected with the dependent word *although*)

CORRECT American union membership, which was high in the mid-twentieth century, has declined in recent years. (clauses connected with the dependent word *which*)

Teaching Tip
When covering this material, you may want to discuss independent and dependent (subordinate) clauses and to explain the difference between coordination and subordination. If so, refer students to Chapter 17.

Some Frequently Used Dependent Words

after	even though	until
although	if	when
as	since	which
because	that	who
before	unless	

For complete lists of dependent words, including subordinating conjunctions and relative pronouns, see 17g and 17h.

PRACTICE

21-6 Correct each run-on in the following paragraph by adding a dependent word. Consult the list above to help you choose a logical dependent word. Be sure to add correct punctuation where necessary.

Teaching Tip
Refer students to Chapter 17 for information on how to punctuate complex sentences.

                                          until
Example: Harlem was a rural area improved transportation linked
                                    ^
it to lower Manhattan. *Answers will vary.*

           Even though contemporary
(1) ~~Contemporary~~ historians have written about the Harlem Renais-
   ^
                                                        Although
sance, its influence is still not widely known. (2) Harlem was populated
                                                  ^
mostly by European immigrants at the turn of the last century, it saw an
                                           As this
influx of African Americans beginning in 1910. (3) ~~This~~ migration from
                                                  ^
the South continued Harlem became one of the largest African-American
                   ^

After many
communities in the United States. (4) Many black artists and writers

settled in Harlem during the 1920s, African-American art flourished.

(5) This "Harlem Renaissance" was an important era in American literary
, although   *When scholars*
history it is not even mentioned in some textbooks. (6) Scholars recognize

the great works of the Harlem Renaissance, they often point to the writers

Langston Hughes and Countee Cullen and the artists Henry Tanner and
After
Sargent Johnson. (7) Zora Neale Hurston moved to Harlem from her

native Florida in 1925, she began a book of African-American folklore.
Because
(8) Harlem was an exciting place in the 1920s people from all over the
After the
city went there to listen to jazz and to dance. (9) The white playwright

Eugene O'Neill went to Harlem to audition actors for his play *The*

Emperor Jones, he made an international star of the great Paul Robeson.
When the
(10) The Great Depression occurred in the 1930s it led to the end of the

Harlem Renaissance.

PRACTICE

21-7 Correct each of the following run-ons in one of these four ways: by creating two separate sentences, by using a coordinating conjunction, by using a semicolon, or by using a semicolon followed by a transitional word or phrase. Remember to put a semicolon before, and a comma after, each transitional word or phrase.

> **Example:** Some fish-and-chip shops in Scotland sell deep-fried
> *. Children*
> MARS bars children are the biggest consumers of these calorie-rich
> bars. *Answers will vary.*

Teaching Tip
When you assign Practice 21-7, tell students to use each revision method at least twice.

1. Twenty-five percent of Americans under the age of fifty have one or
   , and
   more tattoos 50 percent of Americans under the age of twenty-five

   have one or more tattoos.

2. The ancient Greeks built their homes facing south this practice took

   advantage of light and heat from the winter sun.

3. In 1985, a team of musical artists recorded "We Are the World" in support of African famine relief in 2010, artists recorded the same song in support of Haitian earthquake relief.

4. The comic-strip cat Garfield is not cuddly *, and* Garzooka, a superhero cat, is even less cuddly.

5. Horse-racing fans love jockey Calvin Borel for his enthusiasm during postrace interviews *, and* fellow jockeys respect him for his work ethic.

6. The average Swiss eats twenty-three pounds of chocolate each year *; however,* the average American eats less than half that amount.

7. Flamenco—a Spanish style of dancing, singing, and clapping—was traditionally informal and unplanned *; for this reason,* it has been compared to improvisational American jazz.

8. Seattle is considered to have the most-educated population of any major city *, but* the smaller city of Arlington, Virginia, has a higher percentage of college graduates.

9. In Acadia National Park in Maine, large stones line the edges of the steep trails *. The* stones are called "Rockefeller's teeth" in honor of the trails' patron.

10. Allen Ginsberg was charged with obscenity for his book *Howl* *; eventually,* the charges were dismissed.

EDITING PRACTICE

Read the following student essay, and revise it to eliminate run-ons. Correct each run-on in the way that best indicates the relationship between ideas, and be sure to punctuate correctly. The first error has been corrected for you. *Answers will vary.*

Comic-Book Heroes

Comic-book heroes have a long history, *. They* they originated in comic strips and radio shows. In the "Golden Age" of comic books, individual superheroes were the most popular characters, *. Then,* then teams and groups of superheroes were introduced. Today, some of these superheroes can be found in movies and graphic novels. Over the years, superheroes have remained very popular.

One of the first comic-book heroes was Popeye. Popeye had no supernatural *Although* powers, he battled his enemy, Bluto, with strength supplied by spinach. Another early comic-book hero was The Shadow *, who* he fought crime in a cape and mask. The Shadow first appeared in comic books in 1930 *, and* later the character had his own radio show.

The late 1930s and 1940s are considered the Golden Age of comic books, *;* many famous comic-book heroes were introduced at that time. The first Superman *When* comic appeared in 1939. Superman came out from behind his secret identity as Clark Kent, he could fly "faster than a speeding bullet." Superman was the first comic-book hero who clearly had a superhuman ability to fight evil. Batman was different from *;* Superman he had no real superpowers. Also, Superman was decent and moral, *but* Batman was willing to break the rules. Wonder Woman appeared in 1941, *. She* she truly had superhuman qualities. For example, she could catch a bullet in one hand *, and* she could also regrow a limb.

Superheroes sometimes had help. Batman had Robin, *and* Wonder Woman had her sister, Wonder Girl. Sometimes there were superhero teams, *;* these groups of superheroes helped each other fight evil. The first team was the Justice League of

America *,which* it included Superman, Batman, and Wonder Woman. Eventually, the Justice

League fought against threats to the existence of the earth *;* these threats even

included alien invasions. Another superhero team was the X-Men *,who* they were mutants

with supernatural abilities.

   Now, comic books are not as popular as they used to be *;* however, superheroes

can still be found in popular movies. Superman has been the main character in

many movies *. There* there have also been several successful Batman, Spider-Man, Iron

Man, and Fantastic Four movies. In graphic novels, Superman, Batman, and the

Fantastic Four are still heroes *; in addition,* recent graphic novels feature Captain America

and the Runaways. Apparently, people still want to see superheroes fight evil

and win.

review checklist

Run-Ons

☐ A run-on is an error that occurs when two sentences are joined incorrectly. There are two kinds of run-ons: fused sentences and comma splices. (See 21a.)

☐ A fused sentence occurs when two sentences are incorrectly joined without any punctuation. (See 21a.)

☐ A comma splice occurs when two sentences are joined with just a comma. (See 21a.)

☐ Correct a run-on in one of the following ways:

   1. by creating two separate sentences

      _____. _____.

   2. by using a coordinating conjunction

      _____, [coordinating conjunction] _____.

   3. by using a semicolon

      _____; _____.

e bedfordstmartins.com
/forw LearningCurve >
Run-Ons

Teaching Tip
Have students memorize
the five ways to correct
run-ons.

(continued)

(continued from previous page)

4. by using a semicolon followed by a transitional word or phrase

__________; [transitional word or phrase], __________.

5. by using a dependent word

[Dependent word] __________, __________.

__________ [dependent word] __________. (See 21b.)

22 Fragments

22a Recognizing Fragments

A **fragment** is an incomplete sentence. Every sentence must include at least one subject and one verb, and every sentence must express a complete thought. If a group of words does not do *both* these things, it is a fragment and not a sentence—even if it begins with a capital letter and ends with a period.

e bedfordstmartins.com
/forw Additional
Grammar Exercises >
Recognizing Fragments

The following is a complete sentence.

       S   **V**

SENTENCE The <u>actors</u> in the play <u>were</u> very talented. (The sentence includes both a subject and a verb and expresses a complete thought.)

Because a sentence must have both a subject and a verb and express a complete thought, the following groups of words are not complete sentences; they are fragments.

FRAGMENT (NO VERB) The actors in the play. (What point is being made about the actors?)

FRAGMENT (NO SUBJECT) Were very talented. (Who were very talented?)

FRAGMENT (NO SUBJECT OR VERB) Very talented. (Who was very talented?)

FRAGMENT (DOES NOT EXPRESS COMPLETE THOUGHT) Because the actors in the play were very talented. (What happened because they were very talented?)

Teaching Tip
Remind students that although they may see fragments used in advertisements and other informal writing (*A full head of hair in just thirty minutes!*), fragments are not acceptable in college writing in the humanities.

Teaching Tip
Consider giving students a pretest to determine the types of problems they have. This will help you decide how much time you need to spend on fragments.

FYI

Spotting Fragments

Fragments almost always appear next to complete sentences.

┌──── **COMPLETE SENTENCE** ────┐┌──── **FRAGMENT** ────┐
Celia took two electives. Physics 320 and Spanish 101.

(continued)

487

The fragment on page 487 does not have a subject or a verb. The complete sentence that comes before it, however, has both a subject (*Celia*) and a verb (*took*).

Often, you can correct a fragment by attaching it to an adjacent sentence that supplies the missing words. (This sentence will usually appear right before the fragment.)

Celia took two electives, Physics 320 and Spanish 101.

PRACTICE

22-1 Some of the following items are fragments, and others are complete sentences. On the line following each item, write *F* if it is a fragment and *S* if it is a complete sentence.

Example: Star formations in the night sky. ____*F*____

1. To save as much as possible for college. ____*F*____

2. The judge gave her a two-year sentence. ____*S*____

3. A birthday on Christmas Day. ____*F*____

4. Because he lost ten pounds on his new diet. ____*F*____

5. Working in the garden and fixing the roof. ____*F*____

6. Sonya flew to Mexico. ____*S*____

7. Starts in August in many parts of the country. ____*F*____

8. And slept in his own bed last night. ____*F*____

9. Famous for her movie roles. ____*F*____

10. A phone that also plays music and takes photos. ____*F*____

PRACTICE

22-2 In the following paragraph, some of the numbered groups of words are missing a subject, a verb, or both. First, underline each fragment. Then, decide how each fragment could be attached to a nearby word group to create a complete new sentence. Finally, rewrite the entire paragraph, using complete sentences, on the lines provided.

Example: Gatorade was invented at the University of Florida. To help the Florida Gators fight dehydration.

Rewrite: *Gatorade was invented at the University of Florida to help the*

Florida Gators fight dehydration.

(1) Doctors discovered that football players were losing electrolytes and carbohydrates. (2) Through their sweat. (3) They invented a drink. (4) That replaced these important elements. (5) Gatorade tasted terrible. (6) But did its job. (7) The Florida Gators survived a very hot season. (8) And won most of their games. (9) Now, Gatorade is used by many college and professional football teams. (10) As well as baseball, basketball, tennis, and soccer teams.

Rewrite:

Doctors discovered that football players were losing electrolytes and carbohydrates through their sweat. They invented a drink that replaced these important elements. Gatorade tasted terrible but did its job. The Florida Gators survived a very hot season and won most of their games. Now, Gatorade is used by many college and professional football teams as well as baseball, basketball, tennis, and soccer teams.

22b   Missing-Subject Fragments

Every sentence must include both a subject and a verb. If the subject is left out, the sentence is incomplete. In the following example, the first word group is a sentence. It includes both a subject (*He*) and a verb (*packed*). However, the second word group is a fragment. It includes a verb (*took*), but it does not include a subject.

|─────── SENTENCE ───────|─────── FRAGMENT ───────|
He packed his books and papers. And also took an umbrella.

The best way to correct this kind of fragment is to attach it to the sentence that comes right before it. This sentence will usually contain the missing subject.

CORRECT   He packed his books and papers and also took an

umbrella.

Another way to correct this kind of fragment is to add the missing subject.

CORRECT   He packed his books and papers. He also took an umbrella.

PRACTICE

22-3   Each of the following items includes a missing-subject fragment. Using one of the two methods explained above, correct each fragment.

Example: Back-to-school sales are popular with students. And with their parents.

Back-to-school sales are popular with students and with their parents.   or

Back-to-school sales are popular with students. The sales are also popular

with their parents.

Answers may vary.

1. Quitting smoking is difficult. But is really worth the effort.

   Quitting smoking is difficult but is really worth the effort.

2. Some retailers give a lot of money to charity. And even donate part of their profits.

   Some retailers give a lot of money to charity and even donate part of their

   profits.

3. Geography bees resemble spelling bees. But instead test the contestants' knowledge of countries around the world.

   Geography bees resemble spelling bees but instead test the contestants' knowledge of

   countries around the world.

4. School uniforms are often preferred by parents. And also favored by many school principals.

   School uniforms are often preferred by parents and also favored by many

   school principals.

5. During the Cold War, the Soviet Union and the United States were rivals. But never actually fought a war with each other.

   During the Cold War, the Soviet Union and the United States were rivals but

   never actually fought a war with each other.

22c   Phrase Fragments

Every sentence must include a subject and a verb. A **phrase** is a group of words that is missing a subject or a verb or both. When you punctuate a phrase as if it is a sentence, you create a fragment.

If you spot a phrase fragment in your writing, you can often correct it by attaching it to the sentence that comes directly before it.

Appositive Fragments

An **appositive** identifies, renames, or describes an adjacent noun or pronoun. An appositive cannot stand alone as a sentence.

To correct an appositive fragment, attach it to the sentence that comes right before it. (This sentence will contain the noun or pronoun that the appositive describes.)

Teaching Tip
Refer students to 18c for more on appositives. For information on punctuating appositives, refer them to 26c.

┌─ FRAGMENT ─┐

INCORRECT   He decorated the room in his favorite colors. Brown and black.

CORRECT   He decorated the room in his favorite colors, brown and black.

Sometimes a word or expression like *especially, except, including, such as, for example,* or *for instance* introduces an appositive. Even if an appositive is introduced by one of these expressions, it is still a fragment.

┌FRAGMENT┐

INCORRECT   A balanced diet should include high-fiber foods. Such as leafy vegetables, fruits, beans, and whole-grain bread.

CORRECT   A balanced diet should include high-fiber foods, such as leafy vegetables, fruits, beans, and whole-grain bread.

Prepositional Phrase Fragments

A **prepositional phrase** consists of a preposition and its object. A prepositional phrase cannot stand alone as a sentence. To correct a prepositional phrase fragment, attach it to the sentence that comes immediately before it.

Teaching Tip
Refer students to 17b for more on prepositional phrases.

┌─── FRAGMENT ───┐

INCORRECT   She promised to stand by him. In sickness and in health.

CORRECT   She promised to stand by him in sickness and in health.

Infinitive Fragments

An **infinitive** consists of *to* plus the base form of the verb (*to be, to go, to write*). An infinitive phrase (*to be free, to go home, to write a novel*) cannot stand alone as a sentence. You can usually correct an infinitive fragment by attaching it to the sentence that comes directly before it.

┌── FRAGMENT ──┐

INCORRECT Eric considered dropping out of school. To start his own business.

CORRECT Eric considered dropping out of school to start his own business.

You can also add the words needed to complete the sentence.

CORRECT Eric considered dropping out of school. He wanted to start his own business.

PRACTICE

22-4 In the following paragraph, some of the numbered groups of words are phrase fragments. First, underline each fragment. Then, decide how each fragment could be attached to an adjacent sentence to create a complete new sentence. Finally, rewrite the entire paragraph, using complete sentences, on the lines provided.

Example: Florence Nightingale worked as a nurse. During the Crimean War.

Rewrite: *Florence Nightingale worked as a nurse during the Crimean War.*

(1) Nurses' uniforms have changed a lot. (2) Over the years. (3) Originally, nurses' uniforms looked like nuns' habits because nuns used to provide care. (4) To sick people. (5) In the late 1800s, a student of Florence Nightingale created a brown uniform. (6) With a white apron and cap. (7) This uniform was worn by student nurses at her school. (8) The Florence Nightingale School of Nursing and Midwifery. (9) Eventually, nurses began to wear white uniforms, white stockings, white shoes, and starched white caps. (10) To stress the importance of cleanliness.

READING TIP

When you come across an unfamiliar word (or a familiar word used in an unfamiliar way, such as *habits in* Practice 22-4), scan the words, phrases, and sentences surrounding the unfamiliar word for context clues that can help you figure out the meaning of the word.

(11) Many older people remember these uniforms. (12) <u>With affection.</u>

(13) Today, most nurses wear bright, comfortable scrubs. (14) <u>To help</u>

<u>patients (especially children) feel more at ease.</u>

Rewrite:

Nurses' uniforms have changed a lot over the years. Originally, nurses' uniforms looked

like nuns' habits because nuns used to provide care to sick people. In the late 1800s, a student

of Florence Nightingale created a brown uniform with a white apron and cap. This uniform was

worn by student nurses at her school, the Florence Nightingale School of Nursing and

Midwifery. Eventually, nurses began to wear white uniforms, white stockings, white shoes,

and starched white caps to stress the importance of cleanliness. Many older people

remember these uniforms with affection. Today, most nurses wear bright, comfortable

scrubs to help patients (especially children) feel more at ease.

PRACTICE

22-5   Each of the following items is a phrase fragment, not a sentence. Correct each fragment by adding any words needed to turn the fragment into a complete sentence. (You may add words before or after the fragment.)

Teaching Tip
Remind students that fragments do not usually appear in isolation (as these do). Here, students must *generate* the missing words, not simply find them in an adjacent sentence.

Example: During World War I. *A flu epidemic killed millions of people during*

World War I.   or   During World War I, a flu epidemic killed millions of people.

Answers will vary.

1. To be the best player on the team. ————————————

2. From a developing nation in Africa. ————————————

3. Such as tulips or roses. ————————————

4. Behind door number 3. ————————————

3. Including my parents and grandparents.

22d   *-ing* Fragments

Teaching Tip
Tell students that helping verbs include forms of *be*, *have*, and *do*. Refer them to 17c for a list of frequently used helping verbs.

Every sentence must include a subject and a verb. If the verb is incomplete, a word group is a fragment, not a sentence.

An *-ing* verb cannot be a complete verb. It needs a **helping verb** to complete it. An *-ing* verb, such as *looking*, cannot stand alone in a sentence without a helping verb (*is looking, was looking, were looking,* and so on). When you use an *-ing* verb without a helping verb, you create a fragment.

Teaching Tip
Remind students to be careful not to create dangling modifiers with participles. Refer them to 25b.

┌──────── FRAGMENT ────────┐
INCORRECT   The twins are full of mischief. Always looking for trouble.

The best way to correct an *-ing* fragment is to attach it to the sentence that comes right before it.

CORRECT   The twins are full of mischief, always looking for trouble.

Another way to correct an *-ing* fragment is to add a subject and a helping verb.

CORRECT   The twins are full of mischief. They are always looking for trouble.

FYI

Being

As you write, be careful not to use the *-ing* verb *being* as if it were a complete verb.

INCORRECT   I decided to take a nap. The outcome being that I slept through calculus class.

To correct this kind of fragment, substitute a form of the verb *be* that can serve as the main verb in a sentence—for example, *is, was, are,* or *were*.

CORRECT   I decided to take a nap. The outcome was that I slept through calculus class.

PRACTICE

22-6   Each of the following items includes an *-ing* fragment. In each case, correct the fragment by attaching it to the sentence before it.

Teaching Tip
You may want to refer students to 26d for information on punctuating restrictive and nonrestrictive clauses.

Example: Certain tips can help grocery shoppers. Saving them a lot of money.

Certain tips can help grocery shoppers, saving them a lot of money.

1. Always try to find a store brand. Costing less than the well-known and widely advertised brands.

   Always try to find a store brand costing less than the well-known and widely

   advertised brands.

2. Look for a product's cost per pound. Comparing it to the cost per pound of similar products.

   Look for a product's cost per pound, comparing it to the cost per pound of

   similar products.

3. Examine sale-priced fruits and vegetables. Checking carefully for damage or spoilage.

   Examine sale-priced fruits and vegetables, checking carefully for damage

   or spoilage.

4. Buy different brands of the same product. Trying each one to see which brand you like best.

   Buy different brands of the same product, trying each one to see which brand

   you like best.

5. Use coupons whenever possible. Keeping them handy for future shopping trips.

   Use coupons whenever possible, keeping them handy for future shopping trips.

22e   Dependent-Clause Fragments

Teaching Tip
Refer students to Chapter 17 for more on identifying independent and dependent clauses.

Every sentence must include a subject and a verb. Every sentence must also express a complete thought.

A **dependent clause** is a group of words that is introduced by a dependent word, such as *although, because, that, or after.* A dependent clause includes a subject and a verb, but it does not express a complete thought. Therefore, it cannot stand alone as a sentence. To correct a dependent-clause fragment, you must complete the thought.

The following dependent clause is incorrectly punctuated as if it were a sentence.

FRAGMENT   After Simon won the lottery.

This fragment includes both a subject (*Simon*) and a complete verb (*won*), but it does not express a complete thought. What happened after Simon won the lottery? To turn this fragment into a sentence, you need to complete the thought.

SENTENCE   After Simon won the lottery, he quit his night job.

Some dependent clauses are introduced by dependent words called **subordinating conjunctions**.

FRAGMENT   Although Marisol had always dreamed of visiting America.

This fragment includes a subject (*Marisol*) and a complete verb (*had dreamed*), but it is not a sentence; it is a dependent clause introduced by the subordinating conjunction *although.*

To correct this kind of fragment, attach it to an **independent clause** (a simple sentence) to complete the idea. (You can often find the independent clause you need right before or right after the fragment.)

SENTENCE   Although Marisol had always dreamed of visiting America, she did not have enough money for the trip until 1985.

Subordinating Conjunctions

after	even though	since	whenever
although	if	so that	where
as	if only	than	whereas
as if	in order that	that	wherever
as though	now that	though	whether
because	once	unless	while
before	provided that	until	
even if	rather than	when	

For information on how to use subordinating conjunctions, see 17g.

FYI

Correcting Dependent-Clause Fragments

The simplest way to correct a dependent-clause fragment is to cross out the dependent word that makes the idea incomplete.

~~Although~~ Marisol had always dreamed of visiting America.

However, when you delete the dependent word, readers may have trouble seeing the connection between the new sentence and the one before or after it. A better way to revise is to attach the dependent-clause fragment to an adjacent independent clause, as illustrated in the final example on page 496.

Some dependent clauses are introduced by dependent words called **relative pronouns**.

FRAGMENT   Novelist Richard Wright, <u>who</u> came to Paris in 1947.

FRAGMENT   A quinceañera, <u>which</u> celebrates a Latina's fifteenth birthday.

FRAGMENT   A key World War II battle <u>that</u> was fought on the Pacific island of Guadalcanal.

Teaching Tip
You may want to refer students to 26d for information on punctuating restrictive and nonrestrictive clauses.

Each of the above sentence fragments includes a subject (*Richard Wright, quinceañera, battle*) and a complete verb (*came, celebrates, was fought*). However, they are not sentences because they do not express complete thoughts. In each case, a relative pronoun creates a dependent clause.

To correct each of these fragments, add the words needed to complete the thought.

SENTENCE   Novelist Richard Wright, who came to Paris in 1947, <u>spent the rest of his life there.</u>

SENTENCE   A quinceañera, which celebrates a Latina's fifteenth birthday, <u>signifies her entrance into womanhood.</u>

SENTENCE   A key World War II battle that was fought on the Pacific island of Guadalcanal <u>took place in 1943.</u>

> ### Relative Pronouns
>
> | | | |
> |---|---|---|
> | that | who | whomever |
> | what | whoever | whose |
> | which | whom | |
>
> For information on how to use relative pronouns, see 17h.

PRACTICE

22-7 Correct each of the following dependent-clause fragments by attaching it to the sentence before or after it. If the dependent clause comes at the beginning of a sentence, place a comma after it.

Teaching Tip
At this point, you might want to review punctuation with restrictive and nonrestrictive clauses. Refer students to 26d.

Example: Before it became a state. West Virginia was part of Virginia.

Before it became a state, West Virginia was part of Virginia.

1. Because many homeless people are mentally ill. It is hard to find places for them to live. *Because many homeless people are mentally ill, it is hard to find places for them to live.*

2. People do not realize how dangerous raccoons can be. Even though they can be found in many parts of the United States. *People do not realize how dangerous raccoons can be, even though they can be found in many parts of the United States.*

3. I make plans to be a better student. Whenever a new semester begins. *I make plans to be a better student whenever a new semester begins.*

4. Until something changes. We will just have to accept the situation. *Until something changes, we will just have to accept the situation.*

5. Because it is a very controversial issue. My parents and I have agreed not to discuss it. *Because it is a very controversial issue, my parents and I have agreed not to discuss it.*

Teaching Tip
Have students write the sentences in Practice 22-8 on the board so everyone has a chance to correct his or her own sentences and see possible variations.

PRACTICE

22-8 Each of the following is a fragment. Some fragments are missing a subject, some are phrases incorrectly punctuated as sentences, others do not have a complete verb, and still others are dependent clauses punctuated as sentences. Turn each fragment into a complete sentence, writing the revised sentence on the line below the fragment. Whenever possible, try creating two different revisions.

ESL Tip
ESL students may be uncomfortable writing individual work on the board. Allow native and nonnative students to work in pairs to complete the exercises first.

Example: Waiting in the dugout.

Revised: *Waiting in the dugout, the players chewed tobacco.*

Revised: *The players were waiting in the dugout.*

Answers will vary.

1. To win the prize for the most unusual costume.

   Revised: _____

   _____

   Revised: _____

   _____

2. Students who thought they could afford to go to college.

   Revised: _____

   _____

   Revised: _____

   _____

3. On an important secret mission.

   Revised: _____

   _____

   Revised: _____

   _____

4. Because many instructors see cheating as a serious problem.

   Revised: _____

   _____

   Revised: _____

   _____

5. Hoping to get another helping of chocolate fudge cake.

   Revised: _____

   _____

Revised:

6. Finished in record time.

Revised: _____

_____

Revised: _____

_____

EDITING PRACTICE

Read the following student essay, which includes incomplete sentences. Underline each fragment. Then, correct the fragment by attaching it to an adjacent sentence that completes the idea. Be sure to punctuate correctly. The first fragment has been underlined and corrected for you. *Answers will vary.*

Bad Behavior at the Movies

Some people have completely stopped *going* ~~Going~~ to the movies. They have not stopped because they dislike the movies but because they dislike the rude moviegoers, *who* ~~Who~~ ruin their experience. One big problem is irritating cell phone use. There are also problems with noise, *and* ~~And~~ with sharing the theater space with strangers. All these issues can make going to the movies seem like more trouble than it is worth.

Cell phones cause all sorts of problems, *in* ~~In~~ movie theaters. People are told to turn off their phones, *but* ~~But~~ do not always do so. Loud cell-phone conversations can be infuriating, *to* ~~To~~ people who want to hear the movie. When a phone rings during an important scene in the movie, *it* ~~It~~ is especially annoying. Some moviegoers even complain that bright text-message screens distract them, *from* ~~From~~ the movie. Of course, theaters could use jammers, *to* ~~To~~ block all cell-phone signals. Unfortunately, they would also block incoming emergency calls.

Noise in the movies also comes from other sources, *such* ~~Such~~ as crying babies. People pay money to watch a movie, *not* ~~Not~~ to listen to a baby screaming. Crinkling candy wrappers are also annoying. In addition, some moviegoers insist on talking to each other, *during* ~~During~~ the movie. In fact, they may make watching a movie an interactive event, *talking* ~~Talking~~ to the actors and telling them what they should do next. If they have seen the movie before, they may recite lines of dialogue before the actors do, *spoiling* ~~Spoiling~~ the suspense for everyone else. Sometimes people

501

that
even talk loudly about subjects, That have nothing to do with the movie. In all
^ *for*
these cases, the noise is a problem, For anyone who wants to watch the movie
^
and hear the actors on the screen.

Finally, going to the movies requires sharing the theater with other people,
who
Who are neither relatives nor friends. Unfortunately, many people behave in
^
when
movie theaters the same way they behave at home, When they are watching
^
, making
television. They may put their feet up on the seats in front of them, Making it
^
impossible for others to sit there. Moviegoers become very annoyed if someone
and
sits right in front of them, And blocks their view of the screen. Of course, these
^
, where
issues do not come up at home, Where friends and relatives can easily work out
^
any problems.

Irritating movie behavior has driven many people to stop going to movie
theaters. To end this rude behavior, moviegoers need to become aware of the
and
needs of others, And make a real effort to change their behavior. Selfishness is
^
the problem; thinking about other people is the solution.

:e bedfordstmartins.com
/forw LearningCurve >
Fragments; Additional
Grammar Exercises >
Correcting Fragments

Teaching Tip
As a review, read some
sentences (and some
fragments) to the class,
and ask students to
explain why each item
is or is not a complete
sentence.

review checklist

Fragments

☐ A fragment is an incomplete sentence. Every sentence must include
a subject and a verb and express a complete thought. (See 22a.)

☐ Every sentence must include a subject. (See 22b.)

☐ Phrases cannot stand alone as sentences. (See 22c.)

☐ Every sentence must include a complete verb. (See 22d.)

☐ Dependent clauses cannot stand alone as sentences. (See 22e.)

23 Subject-Verb Agreement

23a Understanding Subject-Verb Agreement

bedfordstmartins.com /forw LearningCurve > Subject-Verb Agreement

A sentence's subject (a noun or a pronoun) and its verb must **agree**: singular subjects take singular verbs, and plural subjects take plural verbs.

The <u>museum</u> <u>opens</u> at ten o'clock. (singular noun subject *museum* takes singular verb *opens*)

Both <u>museums</u> <u>open</u> at ten o'clock. (plural noun subject *museums* takes plural verb *open*)

<u>She</u> always <u>watches</u> the eleven o'clock news. (singular pronoun subject *she* takes singular verb *watches*)

<u>They</u> always <u>watch</u> the eleven o'clock news. (plural pronoun subject *they* takes plural verb *watch*)

ESL Tip
Remember that ESL writers will not "hear" the correct form as native speakers instinctively do. ESL students will require more emphasis on formal rules.

Teaching Tip
Refer students to 15b and 15c for more on identifying plural noun and pronoun subjects.

Subject-Verb Agreement with Regular Verbs

	SINGULAR	PLURAL
First person	I play	Molly and I/we play
Second person	you play	you play
Third person	he/she/it plays	they play
	the man plays	the men play
	Molly plays	Molly and Sam play

Teaching Tip
On the board, write a sentence with a subject-verb agreement error—for example, *The boss want to hear from you.* Point out that usually an -*s* follows either the subject or the verb but not both. (Consider giving an example of an exception to this rule—for example, *Charles wants to hear from you.*)

PRACTICE

23-1 Underline the correct form of the verb in each of the following sentences. Make sure the verb agrees with its subject.

Example: Sometimes local farmers (<u>grow</u>/grows) unusual vegetables.

(1) Locavores (<u>choose</u>/chooses) to eat locally grown food for a number of reasons. (2) Some locavores (<u>eat</u>/eats) local food simply because they (<u>like</u>/likes) the taste. (3) When food (travel/<u>travels</u>) a long distance, it (lose/<u>loses</u>) some of its flavor and freshness. (4) By eating locally grown food, locavores also (<u>hope</u>/hopes) to decrease the use of fossil fuels. (5) After all, food transportation (require/<u>requires</u>) a lot of energy. (6) In addition, locavores (<u>visit</u>/visits) farmers' markets to support local producers. (7) Local farmers (<u>need</u>/needs) their community's support to survive. (8) In some cases, local food supporters (<u>buy</u>/buys) only food produced within 50 or 100 miles. (9) In colder or drier regions, however, the climate (make/<u>makes</u>) such a strict policy difficult. (10) More often, a locavore diet (contain/<u>contains</u>) a mix of food from local and faraway places.

23b Compound Subjects

The subject of a sentence is not always a single word. It can also be a **compound subject**, made up of two or more subjects joined by *and* or *or.* To avoid subject-verb agreement problems with compound subjects, follow these rules.

1. When the parts of a compound subject are connected by *and*, the compound subject takes a plural verb.

   <u>John and Marsha</u> <u>share</u> an office.

2. When the parts of a compound subject are connected by *or*, the verb agrees with the part of the subject that is closer to it.

   <u>The mayor or the council members</u> <u>meet</u> with community groups.

   <u>The council members or the mayor</u> <u>meets</u> with community groups.

PRACTICE

23-2   Underline the correct form of the verb in each of the following sentences. Make sure that the verb agrees with its compound subject.

Teaching Tip
Tell students that an -s following a verb usually means the subject is singular. For example, in the sentence *He plays golf,* because *he* refers to just one person, the verb needs an -s. (Point out the exception that occurs with *I* and *you.*)

Example: Every summer, wind and rain (<u>pound</u>/pounds) the small shack on the beach.

1. Trophies and medals (<u>fill</u>/fills) my sister's bedroom.

2. Mashed potatoes and gravy (<u>come</u>/comes) with all our chicken dinners.

3. The instructor or his graduate students (<u>grade</u>/grades) the final exams.

4. A voice coach and a piano instructor (<u>teach</u>/teaches) each of the gifted students.

5. Pollen or cat hair (trigger/<u>triggers</u>) allergies in many people.

6. Psychologists or social workers (<u>provide</u>/provides) crisis counseling.

7. Exercise and healthy eating habits (<u>lead</u>/leads) to longer lives.

8. Both parents or only the father (walk/<u>walks</u>) the bride down the aisle at a wedding.

9. The restaurant owner and his daughters (<u>greet</u>/greets) customers as they enter.

10. Flowers or a get-well balloon (cheer/<u>cheers</u>) people up when they are ill.

23c   *Be, Have,* and *Do*

The verbs *be, have,* and *do* are irregular in the present tense. For this reason, they can present problems with subject-verb agreement. Memorizing their forms is the only sure way to avoid such problems.

Teaching Tip
Refer students to 14a and 14b for more on regular and irregular verbs.

Teaching Tip
You may need to remind students that standard written English does not use *be* as a helping verb. For example, *He be trying to get my attention* is incorrect.

Subject-Verb Agreement with *Be*

	SINGULAR	PLURAL
First person	I am	we are
Second person	you are	you are
Third person	he/she/it is	they are
	Tran is	Tran and Ryan are
	the boy is	the boys are

Teaching Tip
The dialect-related use of *be* and *have* may be a sensitive issue for some students. You may want to address it in individual conferences outside of class.

Subject-Verb Agreement with *Have*

	SINGULAR	PLURAL
First person	I have	we have
Second person	you have	you have
Third person	he/she/it has	they have
	Shana has	Shana and Robert have
	the student has	the students have

Subject-Verb Agreement with *Do*

	SINGULAR	PLURAL
First person	I do	we do
Second person	you do	you do
Third person	he/she/it does	they do
	Ken does	Ken and Mia do
	the book does	the books do

PRACTICE

23-3   Fill in the blank with the correct present tense form of the verb *be, have,* or *do.*

Example: Sometimes people ——— *do* ——— damage without really meaning to. (do)

(1) Biologists ——— *have* ——— serious worries about the damage that invading species of animals can cause. (have) (2) The English

sparrow _____*is*_____ one example. (be) (3) It _____*has*_____ a role in the decline in the number of bluebirds. (have) (4) On the Galapagos Islands, cats _____*are*_____ another example. (be) (5) Introduced by early explorers, they currently _____*do*_____ much damage to the eggs of the giant tortoises that live on the islands. (do) (6) Scientists today _____*are*_____ worried now about a new problem. (be) (7) This _____*is*_____ a situation caused by wildlife agencies that put exotic fish into lakes and streams. (be) (8) They _____*do*_____ this to please those who enjoy fishing. (do) (9) Although popular with people who fish, this policy _____*has*_____ major drawbacks. (have) (10) It _____*has*_____ one drawback in particular: many native species of fish have been pushed close to extinction. (have)

23d Words between Subject and Verb

Keep in mind that a verb must always agree with its subject. Don't be confused when a group of words (for example, a prepositional phrase) comes between the subject and the verb. These words do not affect subject-verb agreement.

Teaching Tip
Refer students to 17b for more on prepositional phrases and for a list of prepositions.

                            S   V

CORRECT High levels of mercury occur in some fish.

                       S   V

CORRECT Water in the fuel lines causes an engine to stall.

                       S   V

CORRECT Food between the teeth leads to decay.

An easy way to identify the subject of the sentence is to cross out the words that come between the subject and the verb.

High levels ~~of mercury~~ occur in some fish.

Water ~~in the fuel lines~~ causes an engine to stall.

Food ~~between the teeth~~ leads to decay.

FYI

Words between Subject and Verb

Look out for words such as *in addition to*, *along with*, *together with*, *as well as*, *except*, and *including*. Phrases introduced by these words do not affect subject-verb agreement.

> St. Thomas, ~~along with St. Croix and St. John~~, is part of the United States Virgin Islands.

PRACTICE

23-4 In each of the following sentences, cross out the words that separate the subject and the verb. Then, underline the subject of the sentence once and the verb that agrees with the subject twice.

> **Example:** The messages ~~on the phone~~ (say/**says**) that Carol is out of town.

1. Each summer, fires ~~from lightning~~ (cause/**causes**) great damage.

2. Books downloaded ~~onto an eReader~~ usually (**cost**/costs) less than print books.

3. One ~~out of ten men~~ (**gets**/get) prostate cancer.

4. The woodstove ~~in the living room~~ (heat/**heats**) the entire house.

5. Trans fat ~~in a variety of foods~~ (lead/**leads**) to increased rates of heart disease.

23e Collective Noun Subjects

Collective nouns are words (such as *family* and *audience*) that name a group of people or things but are singular. Because they are singular, they always take singular verbs.

> The team practices five days a week in the gym.

Frequently Used Collective Nouns			
army	class	corporation	jury
association	club	family	mob
audience	committee	government	team
band	company	group	union

PRACTICE
23-5 Fill in the blank with the correct present tense form of the verb.

Example: Our government ___*is*___ democratically elected by the people. (be)

1. The Caribbean Culture Club ___*meets*___ on the first Thursday of every month. (meet)

2. The company no longer ___*provides*___ health insurance for part-time employees. (provide)

3. The basketball team ___*is*___ competing in the division finals next week. (be)

4. After two days, the jury ___*has*___ been unable to reach a verdict. (have)

5. The union ___*wants*___ guaranteed raises for its members. (want)

23f Indefinite Pronoun Subjects

Indefinite pronouns—*anybody*, *everyone*, and so on—do not refer to a particular person, place, or idea.

Most indefinite pronouns are singular and take singular verbs.

    s   v
No one likes getting up early.

  s   v
Everyone likes to sleep late.

    s   v
Somebody likes beets.

e bedfordstmartins.com
/forw LearningCurve >
Indefinite Pronoun
Subjects

Teaching Tip
Remind students that many indefinite pronouns end in *-one*, *-body*, or *-thing*. These words are almost always singular.

Teaching Tip
Refer students to 15e
for more on pronoun-
antecedent agreement
with indefinite pronouns.

Singular Indefinite Pronouns

another	either	neither	somebody
anybody	everybody	nobody	someone
anyone	everyone	no one	something
anything	everything	nothing	
each	much	one	

A few indefinite pronouns (*both, many, several, few, others*) are plural and take plural verbs.

     s   v
<u>Many</u> <u><u>were</u></u> left homeless by the flood.

FYI

Indefinite Pronouns as Subjects

If a prepositional phrase comes between the indefinite pronoun and the verb, cross out the prepositional phrase to help you identify the sentence's subject.

    s   v
<u>Each</u> ~~of the boys~~ <u><u>has</u></u> a bike.
  s   v
<u>Many</u> ~~of the boys~~ <u><u>have</u></u> bikes.

PRACTICE
23-6

Underline the correct verb in each sentence.

Example: As my friends and I know, anything (<u>helps</u>/help) when it comes to paying for college.

1. One of my friends (<u>has</u>/have) an academic scholarship.

2. Another (<u>relies</u>/rely) entirely on loans.

3. Several of us (works/<u>work</u>) on weekends.

4. Everybody (<u>says</u>/say) that work-study jobs are best.

5. Many of the most interesting work-study jobs (is/<u>are</u>) located on campus.

6. Others (places/<u>place</u>) students off campus with nonprofits or government agencies.

7. Some of the work-study jobs (tends/<u>tend</u>) to be better than a regular job.

8. Not everyone (<u>understands</u>/understand) the demands of school, but work-study employers do.

9. Nobody (<u>says</u>/say) juggling work and school is simple, but work-study makes it easier.

10. Each of my work-study friends (<u>is</u>/are) glad to have this option.

e bedfordstmartins.com /forw Additional Grammar Exercises > Verbs before Subjects

---

23g Verbs before Subjects

A verb always agrees with its subject—even if the verb comes *before* the subject. In questions, for example, word order is reversed, with the verb coming before the subject or with the subject coming between two parts of the verb.

>   v   s
> Where is the <u>bank</u>?
> v   s   v
> <u>Are</u> <u>you</u> <u>going</u> to the party?

If you have trouble identifying the subject of a question, answer the question with a statement. (In the statement, the subject will come before the verb.)

>   v   s   s   v
> Where <u>is</u> the <u>bank</u>? The <u>bank</u> <u>is</u> on Walnut Street.

Teaching Tip
Explain to students that the indefinite pronoun *some* can be singular or plural depending on what it refers to.

ESL Tip
Point out that questions depart from conventional English word order. Write a series of statements on the board, and have students change them into questions.

FYI

There Is and *There Are*

When a sentence begins with *there is* or *there are*, the word *there* is not the subject of the sentence. The subject comes after the form of the verb *be*.

>   v   s
> There <u>is</u> one <u>chief justice</u> on the Supreme Court.
>   v   s
> There <u>are</u> nine <u>justices</u> on the Supreme Court.

PRACTICE

23-7   Underline the subject of each sentence, and circle the correct form of the verb.

Example: Who (is/are) the baseball <u>player</u> who broke Hank Aaron's home-run record?

1. Where (do/does) <u>snakes</u> go in the winter?

2. There (is/are) three <u>branches</u> of government in the United States.

3. There (is/are) some <u>money</u> available for financial aid.

4. What (is/are) the <u>country</u> with the highest literacy rate?

5. Where (do/does) the football <u>team</u> practice in the off-season?

EDITING PRACTICE

Read the following student essay, which includes errors in subject-verb agreement. Decide whether each of the underlined verbs agrees with its subject. If it does not, cross out the verb, and write in the correct form. If it does, write *C* above the verb. The first sentence has been done for you.

READING TIP

A writer's purpose is often to persuade, explain, or inform the reader. What clues in this essay help you to identify the writer's purpose?

Party in the Parking Lot

Fun at football games *is* ~~are~~ not limited to cheering for the home team. Many people *arrive* ~~arrives~~ four or five hours early, *set* ~~sets~~ up grills in the parking lot, and start *C* cooking. Typically, fans *drive* ~~drives~~ to the stadium in a pickup truck, a station wagon, or an SUV. They open *C* up the tailgate, *put* ~~puts~~ out the food, and *enjoy* ~~enjoys~~ the fun with their friends. In fact, tailgating is *C* so popular that, for some fans, it is more important than the game itself.

What *does* ~~do~~ it take to tailgate? First, most tailgaters plan *C* their menus in advance. To avoid forgetting anything, they *make* ~~makes~~ lists of what to bring. Paper plates, along with a set of plastic cups, make *C* it unnecessary to bring home dirty dishes. Jugs of water *are* ~~is~~ essential, and damp towels *help* ~~helps~~ clean up hands and faces. Also, lightweight chairs or another type of seating is *C* important.

At the game, parking near a grassy area or at the end of a parking row *is* ~~are~~ best. This location *gives* ~~give~~ tailgaters more space to cook and eat. If the food *is* ~~are~~ ready two hours before the game *starts,* ~~start,~~ there is *C* plenty of time to eat and to clean up.

Some tailgaters *buy* ~~buys~~ expensive equipment. The simple charcoal grill *has* ~~have~~ turned into a combination grill, cooler, and foldout table with a portable awning. There *are* ~~is~~ grills with their own storage space. Other grills *swing* ~~swings~~ out from the tailgate to provide easy access to the vehicle's storage area. Some deluxe grills even *have* ~~has~~ their own beer taps, stereo systems, and sinks.

Whatever equipment tailgaters ~~brings~~ *bring* to the game, the most important factors ~~is~~ *are* food and companionship. There is a tradition of sharing food and swapping recipes with other tailgaters. Most tailgaters ~~loves~~ *love* to meet and to compare recipes. For many, the tailgating experience is more fun than the game itself.

review checklist

bedfordstmartins.com
/forw LearningCurve >
Subject-Verb Agreement;
Additional Grammar
Exercises > Subject-Verb
Agreement

Subject-Verb Agreement

☐ Singular subjects (nouns and pronouns) take singular verbs, and plural subjects take plural verbs. (See 23a.)

☐ Special rules govern subject-verb agreement with compound subjects. (See 23b.)

☐ The irregular verbs *be, have,* and *do* often present problems with subject-verb agreement in the present tense. (See 23c.)

☐ Words that come between the subject and the verb do not affect subject-verb agreement. (See 23d.)

☐ Collective nouns are singular and take singular verbs. (See 23e.)

☐ Most indefinite pronouns, such as *no one* and *everyone*, are singular and take a singular verb when they serve as the subject of a sentence. A few are plural and take plural verbs. (See 23f.)

☐ A sentence's subject and verb must always agree, even if the verb comes before the subject. (See 23g.)

24 Illogical Shifts

A **shift** occurs whenever a writer changes **tense**, **person**, or **voice**. As you write and revise, be sure that any shifts you make are **logical**—that is, that they occur for a reason.

24a Shifts in Tense

Tense is the form a verb takes to show when an action takes place or when a situation occurs. Some shifts in tense are necessary—for example, to indicate a change from past time to present time.

bedfordstmartins.com
/forw LearningCurve >
Verbs; Additional
Grammar Exercises >
Shifts in Tense

LOGICAL SHIFT   When they first came out, cell phones were large and bulky, but now they are small and compact.

An **illogical shift in tense** occurs when a writer shifts from one tense to another for no apparent reason.

ILLOGICAL SHIFT IN TENSE   The dog walked to the fireplace. Then, he circles twice and lies down in front of the fire. (shift from past tense to present tense)

REVISED   The dog walked to the fireplace. Then, he circled twice and lay down in front of the fire. (consistent use of past tense)

REVISED   The dog walks to the fireplace. Then, he circles twice and lies down in front of the fire. (consistent use of present tense)

Teaching Tip
Refer students to
Chapter 14 for more on
tense.

PRACTICE
24-1

Edit the sentences in the following paragraph to correct illogical shifts in tense. If a sentence is correct, write *C* in the blank.

Example: The 100th Battalion of the 442nd Infantry is the only remaining United States Army Reserve ground combat unit that fought in World War II. _____*C*_____

515

(1) During World War II, the 100th Battalion of the 442nd Combat Infantry Regiment was made up of young Japanese Americans who are ^were eager to serve in the U.S. Army. ———— (2) At the start of World War II, 120,000 Japanese Americans were sent to relocation camps because the government feared that they might be disloyal to the United States. ——— *C* (3) However, in 1943, the United States needed more soldiers, so it sends ^sent recruiters to the camps to ask for volunteers. ———— (4) The Japanese-American volunteers are ^were organized into the 442nd Combat Infantry Regiment. ———— (5) The soldiers of the 442nd Infantry fought in some of the bloodiest battles of the war, including the invasion of Italy at Anzio and a battle in Bruyères, France, where they capture ^captured over two hundred enemy soldiers. ———— (6) When other U.S. troops are ^were cut off by the enemy, the 442nd Infantry soldiers were sent to rescue them. ———— (7) The Japanese-American soldiers suffered the highest casualty rate of any U.S. unit and receive ^received over eighteen thousand individual decorations. ————

24b   Shifts in Person

bedfordstmartins.com /forw LearningCurve > Pronoun Agreement and Pronoun Reference; Additional Grammar Exercises > Shifts in Person and Voice

Person is the form a pronoun takes to show who is speaking, spoken about, or spoken to.

Person		
	SINGULAR	PLURAL
First person	I	we
Second person	you	you
Third person	he, she, it	they

An **illogical shift in person** occurs when a writer shifts from one person to another for no apparent reason.

ILLOGICAL SHIFT IN PERSON The hikers were told that you had to stay on the trail. (shift from third person to second person)

REVISED The hikers were told that they had to stay on the trail. (consistent use of third person)

ILLOGICAL SHIFT IN PERSON Anyone can learn to cook if you practice. (shift from third person to second person)

REVISED You can learn to cook if you practice. (consistent use of second person)

REVISED Anyone can learn to cook if he or she practices. (consistent use of third person)

PRACTICE

24-2 The sentences in the following paragraph contain illogical shifts in person. Edit each sentence so that it uses pronouns consistently. Be sure to change any verbs that do not agree with the new subjects.

Example: Before a person finds a job in the fashion industry, ~~you have~~ *he or she has* to have some experience.

(1) Young people who want careers in the fashion industry do not always realize how hard ~~you~~ *they* will have to work. (2) They think that working in the world of fashion will be glamorous and that ~~you~~ *they* will make a lot of money. (3) In reality, no matter how talented ~~you are,~~ *he or she is,* a recent college graduate entering the industry is paid only about $22,000 a year. (4) The manufacturers who employ new graduates expect ~~you~~ *them* to work at least three years at this salary before ~~you~~ *they* are promoted. (5) A young designer may get a big raise if ~~you are~~ *he or she is* very talented, but this is unusual. (6) New employees have to pay their dues, and ~~you~~ *they* soon realize that most of ~~your~~ *their* duties are boring. (7) An employee may land

Teaching Tip
This is a good time to review the concepts of pronoun-antecedent agreement (15d) and subject-verb agreement (23a).

a job as an assistant designer but then find that you have to color in ~~*he or she has*~~ designs that have already been drawn. (8) Other beginners discover that ~~you~~ *they* spend most of ~~your~~ *their* time typing up orders. (9) If a person is serious about working in the fashion industry, ~~you have~~ *he or she has* to be realistic. (10) For most newcomers to the industry, the ability to do what ~~you~~ *they* are told to do is more important than ~~your~~ *their* talent.

24c   Shifts in Voice

bedfordstmartins.com /forw LearningCurve > Active and Passive Voice; Additional Grammar Exercises > Shifts in Person and Voice

Voice is the form a verb takes to indicate whether the subject is acting or is acted upon. When the subject is acting, the sentence is in the **active voice**. When the subject is acted upon, the sentence is in the **passive voice**.

> **ACTIVE VOICE**   Nat Turner organized a slave rebellion in August 1831. (Subject *Nat Turner* is acting.)

> **PASSIVE VOICE**   A slave rebellion was organized by Nat Turner in 1831. (Subject *rebellion* is acted upon.)

An **illogical shift in voice** occurs when a writer shifts from active to passive voice or from passive to active voice for no apparent reason.

> **ILLOGICAL SHIFT IN VOICE**   J. D. Salinger wrote *The Catcher in the Rye*, and *Franny and Zooey* was also written by him. (active to passive)

> **REVISED**   J. D. Salinger wrote *The Catcher in the Rye*, and he also wrote *Franny and Zooey*. (consistent use of active voice)

> **ILLOGICAL SHIFT IN VOICE**   Radium was discovered by Marie Curie in 1910, and she won a Nobel Prize in chemistry in 1911. (passive to active)

> **REVISED**   Marie Curie discovered radium in 1910, and she won a Nobel Prize in chemistry in 1911. (consistent use of active voice)

FYI

Correcting Illogical Shifts in Voice

You should usually use the active voice in your college writing because it is stronger and more direct than the passive voice.

To change a sentence from the passive to the active voice, determine who or what is acting, and make this noun the subject of a new active voice sentence.

> **PASSIVE VOICE**   The campus escort service is used by my friends. (*My friends* are acting.)

> **ACTIVE VOICE**   My friends use the campus escort service.

PRACTICE

24-3   The following sentences contain illogical shifts in voice. Revise each sentence by changing the underlined passive voice verb to the active voice.

Example:

Two teachers believed they could help struggling students in New York City schools, so "Chess in the Schools" <u>was founded</u> by them.

Two teachers believed they could help struggling students in New York City

schools, so they founded "Chess in the Schools."

ESL Tip
Have students label passive and active verbs before they make their corrections.

1. Chess develops critical-thinking skills, and self-discipline and self-esteem <u>are developed</u> by players, too.

   Chess develops critical-thinking skills, and players develop self-discipline and

   self-esteem, too.

2. Because players face complicated chess problems, good problem-solving skills <u>are developed</u> by them.

   Because players face complicated chess problems, they develop good problem-solving

   skills.

3. Student chess players improve their concentration, and reading and math skills <u>can be improved</u> through this better concentration.

Student chess players improve their concentration, and this better concentration can improve reading and math skills.

4. Chess teaches students how to lose as well as win, and that ability <u>will be needed</u> by students throughout their lives.

Chess teaches students how to lose as well as win, and students will need that ability throughout their lives.

5. "Chess in the Schools" also helps keep students out of trouble because of the conflict-resolution skills <u>developed</u> by them.

"Chess in the Schools" also helps keep students out of trouble because of the conflict-resolution skills they develop.

EDITING PRACTICE

Read the following essay, which includes illogical shifts in tense, person, and voice. Edit the passage to eliminate the illogical shifts, making sure subjects and verbs agree. The first sentence has been edited for you.

A Different Kind of Vacation

During our upcoming winter break, my sister and I ~~were~~ *are* going to Belize to help build a school. Like many people, we want to travel and see new places, but we ~~did~~ *do* not want to be tourists who only see what is in a guidebook. We also want to help people who are less fortunate than we ~~were.~~ *are.* Volunteering gives us the opportunity to combine travel with community service and to get to know a different culture at the same time.

These days, many people are using ~~his or her~~ *their* vacation time to do volunteer work. Lots of charitable organizations offer short-term projects during school or holiday breaks. For most projects, no experience ~~was~~ *is* necessary. All people need is ~~his or her~~ *their* interest in other people and a desire to help.

For example, last year my aunt ~~goes~~ *went* to Tanzania to work in a health clinic. She loved her experience volunteering in a poor rural community where ~~you help~~ *she helped* local doctors. She also loved the host family who shared ~~their~~ *its* modest house with her. Before she left Tanzania, she and some of the other volunteers ~~climb~~ *climbed* Mount Kilimanjaro. She said it was the best vacation she had ever had.

Although many volunteer vacations focus on improving schools or health care, a wide range of projects ~~was~~ *is* available. Everyone can find work that suits ~~their~~ *his or her* interests. For instance, people can volunteer to help preserve the environment, or ~~you~~ *they* can work to protect women's rights. Countries all over the world welcome volunteers because ~~help is needed by~~ a lot of people *need help.*

READING TIP

This essay includes both facts and opinions. Identify at least two facts and two opinions.

Teaching Tip
Remind students that a collective noun such as *family* is usually singular and is used with a singular pronoun. Refer them to 15e.

521

    My sister and I decided to help with the school in Belize because we believe

everyone deserves

a clean and safe place to learn ~~is deserved by everyone.~~ We are also eager to do

some construction, get to know the local people, and enjoy the warm weather. If

hope

we have enough time, we ~~hoped~~ to visit some Mayan ruins as well. All in all, we

are looking forward to a rewarding and unforgettable experience.

review checklist

bedfordstmartins.com
/forw Additional
Grammar Exercises >
Illogical Shifts

Illogical Shifts

☐ An illogical shift in tense occurs when a writer shifts from one tense to another for no apparent reason. (See 24a.)

☐ An illogical shift in person occurs when a writer shifts from one person to another for no apparent reason. (See 24b.)

☐ An illogical shift in voice occurs when a writer shifts from active to passive voice or from passive to active voice for no apparent reason. (See 24c.)

25 Misplaced and Dangling Modifiers

A **modifier** is a word or word group that identifies or describes another word in a sentence. Many word groups that act as modifiers are introduced by *-ing* (present participle) or *-ed* (past participle) modifiers. To avoid confusion, a modifier should be placed as close as possible to the word it modifies—ideally, directly before or directly after it.

> Working in his garage, Steve Jobs invented the personal computer.

> Rejected by Hamlet, Ophelia goes mad and drowns herself.

Used correctly, *-ing* and *-ed* modifiers provide useful information. Used incorrectly, however, these types of modifiers can be very confusing.

The two most common problems with modification are *misplaced modifiers* and *dangling modifiers*.

25a Correcting Misplaced Modifiers

A **misplaced modifier** appears to modify the wrong word because it is placed incorrectly in the sentence. To correct this problem, move the modifier so it is as close as possible to the word it is supposed to modify (usually directly before or after it).

INCORRECT	Sarah fed the dog wearing her pajamas. (Was the dog wearing Sarah's pajamas?)
CORRECT	Wearing her pajamas, Sarah fed the dog.
INCORRECT	Dressed in a raincoat and boots, I thought my son was prepared for the storm. (Who was dressed in a raincoat and boots?)
CORRECT	I thought my son, dressed in a raincoat and boots, was prepared for the storm.

e bedfordstmartins.com
/forw Additional
Grammar Exercises >
Correcting Misplaced
Modifiers

Teaching Tip
To help students understand the difference between a dangling modifier and a misplaced modifier, point out that a misplaced modifier modifies a word that actually appears in the sentence.

PRACTICE

25-1 Underline the modifier in each of the following sentences. Then, draw an arrow to the word it modifies.

Example: Helping people worldwide, Doctors Without Borders is a group of volunteer medical professionals.

1. Suffering from famine and other disasters, some people are unable to help themselves.

2. Feeding and healing them, Doctors Without Borders improves their lives.

3. Responding to a recent earthquake, doctors arrived within three days to help with the relief effort.

4. Setting up refugee camps in Thailand, the group quickly helped its first survivors.

5. Some doctors, chartering a ship called *The Island of Light*, once provided medical aid to people escaping Vietnam by boat.

PRACTICE

25-2 Rewrite the following sentences, which contain misplaced modifiers, so that each modifier clearly refers to the word it logically modifies.

Example: Mark ate a pizza standing in front of the refrigerator.

Standing in front of the refrigerator, Mark ate a pizza.

1. The cat broke the vase frightened by a noise.

Frightened by a noise, the cat broke the vase.

_____

2. Running across my bathroom ceiling, I saw two large, hairy bugs.

I saw two large, hairy bugs running across my bathroom ceiling.

_____

3. Lori looked at the man sitting in the chair with red hair.

Lori looked at the man with red hair sitting in the chair.
_____

4. *ET* is a film about an alien directed by Steven Spielberg.

ET is a film directed by Steven Spielberg about an alien.
_____

5. Covered with chocolate sauce, Fred loves ice cream sundaes.

Fred loves ice cream sundaes covered with chocolate sauce.
_____

25b Correcting Dangling Modifiers

A **dangling modifier** "dangles" because the word it modifies does not appear in the sentence. Often, a dangling modifier comes at the beginning of a sentence and appears to modify the noun or pronoun that follows it.

Using my computer, the report was finished in two days.

In the sentence above, the modifier *Using my computer* seems to be modifying *the report*. But this makes no sense. (How can the report use a computer?) The word the modifier should logically refer to is missing. To correct this sentence, you need to supply this missing word.

Using my computer, **I** finished the report in two days.

To correct a dangling modifier, supply a word to which the modifier can logically refer.

INCORRECT Moving the microscope's mirror, the light can be

directed onto the slide. (Can the light move the

mirror?)

CORRECT Moving the microscope's mirror, you can direct

the light onto the slide.

e bedfordstmartins.com
/forw Additional Grammar Exercises > Correcting Dangling Modifiers

Teaching Tip
Spend extra time explaining why these examples are incorrect. This concept is difficult for many students to grasp.

INCORRECT　Paid in advance, the furniture was delivered.

(Was the furniture paid in advance?)

CORRECT　Paid in advance, the movers delivered the furniture.

PRACTICE

25-3　Each of the following sentences contains a dangling modifier. To correct each sentence, add a word to which the modifier can logically refer.

Example:　Waiting inside, my bus passed by.

Waiting inside, I missed my bus.

Answers will vary.

1. Ordered by the school, the librarians sorted the books.

_____

_____

2. Pushing on the brakes, my car would not stop for the red light.

_____

_____

3. Short of money, the trip was canceled.

_____

_____

4. Working overtime, his salary almost doubled.

_____

_____

5. Angered by the noise, the concert was called off.

_____

_____

PRACTICE

25-4 Complete the following sentences, making sure to include a word to which each modifier can logically refer.

Example: Dancing with the man of her dreams, _she decided it was_

time to wake up.
Answers will vary.

1. Blocked by the clouds, _____

_____

2. Applying for financial aid, _____

_____

3. Settled into his recliner chair, _____

_____

4. Fearing that they might catch a cold, _____

_____

5. Hearing strange noises through the wall, _____

_____

EDITING PRACTICE

Read the following student essay, which includes modification errors. Rewrite sentences to correct dangling and misplaced modifiers. In some cases, you will have to supply a word to which the modifier can logically refer. The first sentence has been corrected for you. *Answers will vary.*

Eating as a Sport

After eating a big meal, ~~the food often makes~~ you *often* feel stuffed. Imagine how someone participating in competitive eating feels. To win, you have to eat more food faster than anyone else. Training for days, *competitive eaters eat* many different kinds of food ~~are eaten~~ in these contests. For example, contestants eat chicken wings, pizza, ribs, hot dogs, and even matzo balls. Training for events, *participants consider* competitive eating is considered a sport ~~by participants~~. By winning, *a competitive eater can make* a good living ~~can be made by a competitive eater~~. Considered dangerous by some, ~~competitive eaters and their~~ *these contests* fans nevertheless continue to grow.

The way it works is that each competitor eats the same weight or portion of food. Giving the signal, *judges tell* the competitors *to* begin eating. Breaking the food in pieces or just eating the food whole, *they can use* any technique ~~can be used~~. The competitors~~, soaked in water,~~ can make the food softer *by soaking it in water.* They can even eat hot dogs separately from their buns. Good competitors are usually not overweight. In fact, some are quite thin. Keeping the stomach from expanding, competitors *extra fat hurts* ~~are hurt by extra fat.~~ By drinking large amounts of water, *competitors stretch* their stomachs ~~stretch~~ and increase their chances of winning. This is one technique many competitors use when they train.

The International Federation of Competitive Eating watches over the contests to make sure they are fair and safe. Providing the dates and locations, *its website lists* contests ~~are listed on its website.~~ Often, contests are held at state fairs. Also

listing participants, prizes, and rankings of winners, *the website invites* new participants ~~are~~
~~invited.~~ Before entering the contests, *new participants must indicate* their eating specialty and personal profile
~~must be indicated by new participants.~~ Competitors must also be at least eigh-
teen years old.

Many competitive eaters participate in lots of contests. For example, weighing
only 100 pounds, *Sonya Thomas ate* 8.1 pounds of sausage ~~was eaten~~ in only 10 minutes ~~by~~
~~Sonya Thomas.~~ At another contest, she ate 46 crab cakes in 10 minutes. Held in
the United States, *competitive eating contests draw* some participants ~~come~~ from other countries. For instance,
Takeru Kobayashi, who comes from Japan, once ate 18 pounds of cow brains in
15 minutes. Winners usually get cash prizes. The largest prize, $20,000, was
awarded in a hot dog–eating contest at Coney Island, which was televised by
ESPN. By eating 66 hot dogs and their buns in 12 minutes, ~~the contest was won~~
~~by~~ Joey Chestnut, a professional speed eater*, won the contest.* Almost 50,000 people attended the
contest in person, and millions watched on television.

There is some concern about competitive eating. By stretching the stomach,
a ~~person's health may be affected.~~ *person may affect his or her health.* There is also concern about obesity and
overeating. Worried about choking, *some people argue that* events should have doctors present ~~some~~
~~people argue.~~ Still, many people like to watch these contests, and they seem to
be getting more popular each year.

review checklist

Misplaced and Dangling Modifiers

☐ Correct a misplaced modifier by placing the modifier as close as possible to the word it modifies. (See 25a.)

☐ Correct a dangling modifier by supplying a word to which the modifier can logically refer. (See 25b.)

26 Using Commas

A **comma** is a punctuation mark that separates words or groups of words within sentences. In this way, commas keep ideas distinct from one another.

In earlier chapters, you learned to use a comma between two simple sentences (independent clauses) linked by a coordinating conjunction to form a compound sentence.

Teaching Tip
Refer students to 17d for more on using commas in compound sentences.

> Some people are concerned about climate change, but others are not.

You also learned to use a comma after a dependent clause that comes before an independent clause in a complex sentence.

Teaching Tip
Refer students to 17g for more on using commas in complex sentences.

> Although bears in the wild can be dangerous, hikers can take steps to protect themselves.

In addition, commas are used to set off directly quoted speech or writing from the rest of the sentence.

Teaching Tip
Refer students to 28b for information on using commas with direct quotations.

> John F. Kennedy said, "Ask not what your country can do for you; ask what you can do for your country."

As you will learn in this chapter, commas have several other uses as well.

26a Commas in a Series

bedfordstmartins.com
/forw LearningCurve >
Commas; Additional
Grammar Exercises >
Commas in a Series

Use commas to separate all elements in a **series** of three or more words, phrases, or clauses.

> Leyla, Zack, and Kathleen campaigned for Representative Lewis.
>
> Leyla, Zack, or Kathleen will be elected president of Students for Lewis.
>
> Leyla made phone calls, licked envelopes, and ran errands for the campaign.
>
> Leyla is president, Zack is vice president, and Kathleen is treasurer.

FYI

Using Commas in a Series

Newspapers and magazines usually omit the comma before the coordinating conjunction in a series. However, in college writing, you should always use a comma before the coordinating conjunction.

> Leyla, Zack, and Kathleen worked on the campaign.

Exception: Do not use *any* commas if all the items in a series are separated by coordinating conjunctions.

> Leyla or Zack or Kathleen will be elected president of Students for Lewis.

Teaching Tip
Students often use commas where they do not belong and omit them from where they are needed. Begin this chapter by telling students to use commas only in the situations outlined in 26a through 26e and referring them to the discussion of unnecessary commas in 26f.

Teaching Tip
Remind students not to use a comma before the first item in a series or after the last item in a series. Refer them to 26f.

PRACTICE

26-1

Edit the following sentences for the use of commas in a series. If the sentence is correct, write *C* in the blank.

Examples

Costa Rica produces bananas, cocoa, and sugarcane. _____*C*_____

The pool rules state that there is no running, or jumping, or diving.

_____

1. The musician plays guitar, bass, and drums. _____

2. The organization's goals are feeding the hungry, housing the homeless, and helping the unemployed find work. _____

3. *The Price Is Right*, *Let's Make a Deal*, and *Jeopardy!* are three of the longest-running game shows in television history. _____*C*_____

4. In native Hawaiian culture, yellow was worn by the royalty, red was worn by priests, and a mixture of the two colors was worn by others of high rank. _____

5. The diary Anne Frank kept while her family hid from the Nazis is insightful, touching, and sometimes humorous. _____

26b Commas with Introductory Phrases and Transitional Words and Phrases

Introductory Phrases

Use a comma to set off an **introductory phrase** from the rest of the sentence.

In the event of a fire, proceed to the nearest exit.
Walking home, Nelida decided to change her major.
To keep fit, people should try to exercise regularly.

PRACTICE
26-2

Edit the following sentences for the use of commas with introductory phrases. If the sentence is correct, write *C* in the blank.

Examples

For some medical conditions, effective treatments are hard to find.
_____

After taking placebos, some depressed patients experience relief from their symptoms. ____*C*____

(1) Also known as sugar pills, placebos contain no actual medicine. _____ (2) Despite this fact, placebos sometimes have positive effects on patients who take them. ___*C*___ (3) For years, researchers have used placebos in experiments. _____ (4) To evaluate the effectiveness of a medication, scientists test the drug on volunteers. _____ (5) To ensure that the experiment's results are reliable, researchers always have a control group. ___*C*___ (6) Instead of taking the drug, the control group takes a placebo. _____ (7) Thinking they are taking an actual medicine, patients in the control group may experience the "placebo effect." _____ (8) After receiving treatment with a placebo, they feel better. ___*C*___

Transitional Words and Phrases

Also use commas to set off **transitional words or phrases**, whether they appear at the beginning, in the middle, or at the end of a sentence.

> In fact, Thoreau spent only one night in jail.
> He was, of course, bailed out by a friend.
> He did spend more than two years at Walden Pond, however.

Teaching Tip
Remind students that when they use a transitional word or phrase to join two complete sentences, they must use a semicolon and a comma: *Thoreau spent only one night in jail; however, he spent more than two years at Walden Pond.*

FYI

Using Commas in Direct Address

Always use commas to set off the name of someone whom you are addressing (speaking to) directly, whether the name appears at the beginning, in the middle, or at the end of a sentence.

> Molly, come here and look at this.
> Come here, Molly, and look at this.
> Come here and look at this, Molly.

e bedfordstmartins.com
/forw Additional Grammar Exercises > Commas with Transitional Words and Phrases

PRACTICE

26-3 Edit the following sentences for the use of commas with transitional words and phrases. If the sentence is correct, write *C* in the blank.

Example: Eventually, most people build a personal credit history.

(1) Often, establishing credit can be difficult. _____ (2) College students, for example, often have no credit history of their own, especially if their parents pay their bills. _____ (3) Similarly, some married women have no personal credit history. _____ (4) In fact, their credit cards may be in their husbands' names. _____ (5) As a result, they may be unable to get their own loans. ___*C*___ (6) Of course, one way to establish credit is to apply for a credit card at a local department store. _____ (7) Also, it is relatively easy to get a gas credit card. ___*C*___ (8) It is important to pay these credit-card bills promptly, however. _____ (9) In addition, having checking and savings

Teaching Tip
Refer students to 17f for lists of frequently used transitional words and phrases.

accounts can help to establish financial reliability. _____

(10) Finally, people who want to establish a credit history can sign an apartment lease and pay the rent regularly to show that they are good credit risks. ____C____

26c Commas with Appositives

Use commas to set off an **appositive**—a word or word group that identifies, renames, or describes a noun or a pronoun.

bedfordstmartins.com /forw Additional Grammar Exercises > Commas with Appositives

> I have visited only one country, Canada, outside the United States. (*Canada* is an appositive that identifies the noun *country*.)
>
> Carlos Santana, leader of the group Santana, played at Woodstock in 1969. (*Leader of the group Santana* is an appositive that identifies *Carlos Santana*.)
>
> A really gifted artist, he is also a wonderful father. (*A really gifted artist* is an appositive that describes the pronoun *he*.)

FYI

Using Commas with Appositives

Most appositives are set off by commas, whether they fall at the beginning, in the middle, or at the end of a sentence.

> A dreamer, he spent his life thinking about what he could not have.
>
> He always wanted to build a house, a big white one, overlooking the ocean.
>
> He finally built his dream house, a log cabin.

PRACTICE
26-4

Underline the appositive in each of the following sentences. Then, check each sentence for the correct use of commas to set off appositives, and add any missing commas. If the sentence is correct, write *C* in the blank.

Example: Wendy Kopp, a college student, developed the Teach For America program to help minority students get a better education.

_____

1. Guglielmo Marconi a young Italian inventor, sent the first wireless message across the Atlantic Ocean in 1901. _____

2. A member of the boy band 'N Sync Justin Timberlake went on to establish a successful career as a solo musician and an actor. _____

3. HTML hypertext markup language, is the set of codes used to create web documents. _____

4. William Filene, founder of Filene's Department Store, invented the "bargain basement." ___*C*___

5. Known as NPR National Public Radio presents a wide variety of programs. _____

26d Commas with Nonrestrictive Clauses

Clauses are often used to add information within a sentence. In some cases, you need to add commas to set off these clauses; in other cases, commas are not required.

Use commas to set off **nonrestrictive clauses**, clauses that are not essential to a sentence's meaning. Do not use commas to set off **restrictive clauses**.

- A **nonrestrictive clause** does *not* contain essential information. Nonrestrictive clauses are set off from the rest of the sentence by commas.

    Telephone calling-card fraud, <u>which cost consumers and phone companies four billion dollars last year</u>, is increasing.

    Here, the clause between the commas (underlined) provides extra information to help readers understand the sentence, but the sentence would still communicate the same idea without this information.

    Telephone calling-card fraud is increasing.

- A **restrictive clause** contains information that is essential to a sentence's meaning. Restrictive clauses are *not* set off from the rest of the sentence by commas.

    Many rock stars <u>who recorded hits in the 1950s</u> made little money from their songs.

WORD POWER
restrict to keep within limits
restrictive limiting

e bedfordstmartins.com
/forw Additional
Grammar Exercises >
Commas with
Nonrestrictive Clauses

Teaching Tip
Have students read aloud sentences containing restrictive clauses, first with the clause and then without. Point out how the meaning changes when necessary information is omitted.

In the sentence above, the clause *who recorded hits in the 1950s* supplies specific information that is essential to the idea the sentence is communicating: it tells readers which group of rock stars made little money. Without the clause, the sentence does not communicate the same idea because it does not tell which rock stars made little money.

Many rock stars made little money from their songs.

Compare the meanings of the following pairs of sentences with nonrestrictive and restrictive clauses.

NONRESTRICTIVE	Young adults, <u>who text while driving</u>, put themselves and others in danger. (This sentence says that all young adults text while driving and all pose a danger.)
RESTRICTIVE	Young adults <u>who text while driving</u> put themselves and others in danger. (This sentence says that only those young adults who text and drive pose a danger.)
NONRESTRICTIVE	Student loans, <u>which are based on need</u>, may not be fair to middle-class students. (This sentence says that all student loans are based on need and all may be unfair to middle-class students.)
RESTRICTIVE	Student loans <u>that are based on need</u> may not be fair to middle-class students. (This sentence says that only those student loans that are based on need may be unfair to middle-class students.)

FYI

Which, *That*, and *Who*

■ *Which* always introduces a nonrestrictive clause.

> The job, <u>which had excellent benefits</u>, did not pay well. (clause set off by commas)

■ *That* always introduces a restrictive clause.

> He accepted the job <u>that had the best benefits</u>. (no commas)

■ *Who* can introduce either a restrictive or a nonrestrictive clause.

RESTRICTIVE	Many parents <u>who work</u> feel a lot of stress. (no commas)

Teaching Tip
Remind students not to use *that* to refer to people (as in *The girl that* has on *a red dress* . . .).

NONRESTRICTIVE	Both of my parents, <u>who have always wanted the best for their children,</u> have worked two jobs for years. (clause set off by commas)

PRACTICE

26-5   Edit the following sentences so that commas set off all nonrestrictive clauses. (Remember, commas are *not* used to set off restrictive clauses.) If a sentence is correct, write *C* in the blank.

Example: A museum exhibition that celebrates the Alaska highway tells the story of its construction. ____*C*____

(1) During the 1940s, a group of African-American soldiers who defied the forces of nature and human prejudice were shipped to Alaska. ____*C*____ (2) They built the Alaska highway which stretches twelve hundred miles across Alaska. _____ (3) The troops who worked on the highway have received little attention in most historical accounts. ____*C*____ (4) The highway which cut through some of the roughest terrain in the world was begun in 1942. _____ (5) The Japanese had just landed in the Aleutian Islands which lie west of the tip of the Alaska Peninsula. _____ (6) Military officials, who oversaw the project, doubted the ability of the African-American troops. _____ (7) As a result, they made them work under conditions, that made construction difficult. _____ (8) The troops who worked on the road proved their commanders wrong by finishing the highway months ahead of schedule. ____*C*____ (9) In one case, white engineers, who surveyed a river, said it would take two weeks to bridge. _____ (10) To the engineers' surprise, the soldiers who worked on the project beat the estimate. ____*C*____

Teaching Tip
Have students do Practice 26-5 in groups. (Fewer papers allow you more time for careful grading.) Students can also form groups to look over the graded assignment.

26e   Commas in Dates and Addresses

Dates

Use commas in dates to separate the day of the week from the month and the day of the month from the year.

> The first Cinco de Mayo we celebrated in the United States was Tuesday, May 5, 1998.

When a date that includes commas does not fall at the end of a sentence, place a comma after the year.

> Tuesday, May 5, 1998, was the first Cinco de Mayo we celebrated in the United States.

Addresses

Use commas in addresses to separate the street address from the city and the city from the state or country.

> The office of the famous fictional detective Sherlock Holmes was located at 221b Baker Street, London, England.

When an address that includes commas falls in the middle of a sentence, place a comma after the state or country.

> The office at 221b Baker Street, London, England, belonged to the famous fictional detective Sherlock Holmes.

PRACTICE

26-6   Edit the following sentences for the correct use of commas in dates and addresses. Add any missing commas, and cross out any unnecessary commas. If the sentence is correct, write *C* in the blank.

Examples

Usher's album *Looking 4 Myself* was released on June 8 2012.
_____

The entertainer grew up in Chattanooga Tennessee. _____

1. On Tuesday June 5, 2012, people around the world witnessed the rare astronomical phenomenon known as the transit of Venus.

   _____

2. Stefani Joanne Angelina Germanotta, more commonly known as Lady Gaga, was born on March 28 1986 in New York New York. _____

3. To visit the New York Transit Museum, visitors must travel to 130 Livingston Street in Brooklyn New York. _____

4. Fans from around the world travel to visit Ernest Hemingway's houses in Key West Florida and San Francisco de Paula, Cuba. _____

5. Oprah addressed the graduating class at Spelman College on Sunday May 20, 2012 in College Park Georgia. _____

26f Unnecessary Commas

In addition to knowing where commas are required, it is also important to know when *not* to use commas.

▪ Do not use a comma before the first item in a series.

> **INCORRECT** *Duck Soup* starred, Groucho, Chico, and Harpo Marx.
>
> **CORRECT** *Duck Soup* starred Groucho, Chico, and Harpo Marx.

▪ Do not use a comma after the last item in a series.

> **INCORRECT** Groucho, Chico, and Harpo Marx, starred in *Duck Soup*.
>
> **CORRECT** Groucho, Chico, and Harpo Marx starred in *Duck Soup*.

▪ Do not use a comma between a subject and a verb.

> **INCORRECT** Students and their teachers, should try to respect one another.
>
> **CORRECT** Students and their teachers should try to respect one another.

Teaching Tip
Remind students to use commas between items in a series. Refer them to 26a.

■ Do not use a comma before the coordinating conjunction that separates the two parts of a compound predicate.

> INCORRECT   The transit workers voted to strike, and walked off the
> job.

> CORRECT   The transit workers voted to strike and walked off
> the job.

■ Do not use a comma before the coordinating conjunction that separates the two parts of a compound subject.

> INCORRECT   The transit workers, and the sanitation workers
> voted to strike.

> CORRECT   The transit workers and the sanitation workers
> voted to strike.

■ Do not use a comma to set off a restrictive clause.

> INCORRECT   People, who live in glass houses, should not throw
> stones.

> CORRECT   People who live in glass houses should not throw
> stones.

■ Finally, do not use a comma before a dependent clause that follows
an independent clause.

> INCORRECT   He was exhausted, because he had driven all night.

> CORRECT   He was exhausted because he had driven all night.

**PRACTICE
26-7**   Some of the following sentences contain unnecessary
commas. Edit to eliminate unnecessary commas. If the
sentence is correct, write *C* in the blank following it.

Example: Both the Dominican Republic/ and the republic of Haiti

occupy the West Indian island of Hispaniola. _____

1. The capital of the Dominican Republic/is Santo Domingo. _____

2. The country's tropical climate, generous rainfall, and fertile soil, make the Dominican Republic suitable for many kinds of crops. _____

3. Some of the most important crops are, sugarcane, coffee, cocoa, and rice. _____

4. Mining is also important to the country's economy, because the land is rich in many ores. _____

5. Spanish is the official language of the Dominican Republic, and Roman Catholicism is the state religion. ___*C*___

6. In recent years, resort areas have opened, and brought many tourists to the country. _____

7. Tourists who visit the Dominican Republic, remark on its tropical beauty. _____

8. Military attacks, and political unrest have marked much of the Dominican Republic's history. _____

9. Because the republic's economy has not always been strong, many Dominicans have immigrated to the United States. ___*C*___

10. However, many Dominican immigrants maintain close ties to their home country, and return often to visit. _____

EDITING PRACTICE

Read the following student essay, which includes errors in comma use. Add commas where necessary between items in a series and with introductory phrases, transitional words and phrases, appositives, and nonrestrictive clauses. Cross out any unnecessary commas. The first sentence has been edited for you. *Answers will vary.*

READING TIP

"Brave Orchid" is organized chronologically (in time order). To aid your comprehension, create a brief timeline that lists the key events in Brave Orchid's life.

Brave Orchid

One of the most important characters in *The Woman Warrior* Maxine Hong Kingston's autobiographical work is Brave Orchid, Kingston's mother. Brave Orchid was a strong woman, but not a happy one. Through Kingston's stories about her mother, readers learn a lot about Kingston herself.

Readers are introduced to Brave Orchid, a complex character as an imaginative storyteller, who tells her daughter vivid tales of China. As a young woman she impresses her classmates with her intelligence. She is a traditional woman. However she is determined to make her life exactly what she wants it to be. Brave Orchid strongly believes in herself; still, she considers herself a failure.

In her native China Brave Orchid trains to be a midwife. The other women in her class envy her independence brilliance and courage. One day Brave Orchid bravely confronts the Fox Spirit, and tells him he will not win. First of all, she tells him she can endure any pain that he inflicts on her. Next she gathers together the women in the dormitory to burn the ghost away. After this event the other women admire her even more.

Working hard Brave Orchid becomes a midwife in China. After coming to America however she cannot work as a midwife. Instead she works in a Chinese laundry, and picks tomatoes. None of her classmates in China would have imagined this outcome. During her later years in America Brave Orchid becomes a woman, who is overbearing and domineering. She bosses her children around, she tries to ruin her sister's life and she criticizes everyone and everything around her. Her daughter, a straight-A student is the object of her worst criticism.

Brave Orchid's intentions are good. Nevertheless she devotes her energy to the wrong things. She expects the people around her to be as strong as she is. Because she bullies them however she eventually loses them. In addition she is too busy criticizing her daughter's faults to see all her accomplishments. Brave Orchid an independent woman and a brilliant student never achieves her goals. She is hard on the people around her because she is disappointed in herself.

review checklist

Using Commas

- [ ] Use commas to separate all elements in a series of three or more words or word groups. (See 26a.)

- [ ] Use commas to set off introductory phrases and transitional words and phrases from the rest of the sentence. (See 26b.)

- [ ] Use commas to set off appositives from the rest of the sentence. (See 26c.)

- [ ] Use commas to set off nonrestrictive clauses. (See 26d.)

- [ ] Use commas to separate parts of dates and addresses. (See 26e.)

- [ ] Avoid unnecessary commas. (See 26f.)

e bedfordstmartins.com
/forw LearningCurve >
Commas; Additional
Grammar Exercises >
Types of Comma Use

27 Using Apostrophes

ⓔ bedfordstmartins.com /forw LearningCurve > Apostrophes

An **apostrophe** is a punctuation mark that is used in two situations: to form a contraction and to form the possessive of a noun or an indefinite pronoun.

27a Apostrophes in Contractions

A **contraction** is a word that uses an apostrophe to combine two words. The apostrophe takes the place of omitted letters.

> I didn't (*did not*) realize how late it was.
>
> It's (*it is*) not right for cheaters to go unpunished.

Teaching Tip
Be sure your students understand that even though contractions are used in speech and writing, they are not acceptable in most business or college writing situations. (You may allow students to use contractions in first-person essays.)

Teaching Tip
Remind students that this list does not include every contraction. For example, other personal pronouns (*she, he, they*) can also be combined with forms of *be* and *have*. (They will need to know this to do Practice 27-1.)

Frequently Used Contractions

I + am = I'm	are + not = aren't
we + are = we're	can + not = can't
you + are = you're	do + not = don't
it + is = it's	will + not = won't
I + have = I've	should + not = shouldn't
I + will = I'll	let + us = let's
there + is = there's	that + is = that's
is + not = isn't	who + is = who's

PRACTICE

27-1 In the following sentences, add apostrophes to contractions if needed. If the sentence is correct, write *C* in the blank.

ESL Tip
Nonnative speakers often misplace or omit apostrophes in contractions. Spend extra time checking their work. You might provide additional exercises for ESL students.

Example: *What's*
~~Whats~~ the deadliest creature on earth? _____

(1) Bacteria and viruses, which we *can't* ~~cant~~ see without a microscope, kill many people every year. _____ (2) When we speak about the deadliest creatures, however, usually *we're* ~~were~~ talking about creatures that cause

544

illness or death from their poison, which is called venom. _____

you're

(3) After ~~your~~ bitten, stung, or stuck, how long does it take to die?
      ^

_____ (4) The fastest killer is a creature called the sea wasp, but it

isn't a wasp at all. ____C____ (5) The sea wasp is actually a fifteen-foot-

_it's_

long jellyfish, and although ~~its~~ not aggressive, it can be deadly. _____
        ^

(6) People who've gone swimming off the coast of Australia have encoun-

tered this creature. ____C____ (7) While jellyfish found off the Atlantic

aren't

coast of the United States can sting, they ~~arent~~ as dangerous as the sea
      ^

wasp, whose venom is deadly enough to kill sixty adults. _____ (8) A

who's

person ~~whos~~ been stung by a sea wasp has anywhere from thirty seconds
  ^

to four minutes to get help or die. _____ (9) Oddly, it's been found

that something as thin as pantyhose worn over the skin will prevent these

there's

stings. ____C____ (10) Also, ~~theres~~ an antidote to the poison that can
        ^

save victims. _____

e bedfordstmartins.com
/forw Additional
Grammar Exercises >
Apostrophes in
Contractions and
Possessives

27b Apostrophes in Possessives

Possessive forms of nouns and pronouns show ownership. Nouns and indefinite pronouns do not have special possessive forms. Instead, they use apostrophes to indicate ownership.

Singular Nouns and Indefinite Pronouns

To form the possessive of **singular nouns** (including names) and **indefinite pronouns**, add an apostrophe plus an *s*.

> <u>Cesar Chavez's</u> goal (*the goal of Cesar Chavez*) was justice for American farmworkers.
> The <u>strike's</u> outcome (*the outcome of the strike*) was uncertain.
> Whether it would succeed was <u>anyone's</u> guess (*the guess of anyone*).

Teaching Tip
Tell students that possessive pronouns have special forms, such as *its* and *his*, and that these forms never include apostrophes. Refer them to 15g.

Teaching Tip
Refer students to 23f and 15e for more on indefinite pronouns.

FYI

Singular Nouns Ending in *-s*

Even if a singular noun already ends in *-s*, add an apostrophe plus an *s* to form the possessive.

> The class's next assignment was a research paper.
>
> Dr. Ramos's patients are participating in a clinical trial.

Plural Nouns

Teaching Tip
Tell students that most nouns form the plural by adding *-s*. Refer them to 15b for a list of frequently used irregular plurals.

Most plural nouns end in *-s*. To form the possessive of **plural nouns ending in *-s*** (including names), add just an apostrophe (not an apostrophe plus an *s*).

> The two drugs' side effects (*the side effects of the two drugs*) were quite different.
>
> The Johnsons' front door (*the front door of the Johnsons*) is red.

Some irregular noun plurals do not end in *-s*. If a plural noun does not end in *-s*, add an apostrophe plus an *s* to form the possessive.

> The men's room is right next to the women's room.

PRACTICE

27-2   Rewrite the following phrases, changing the noun or indefinite pronoun that follows *of* to the possessive form. Be sure to distinguish between singular and plural nouns.

Examples

the mayor of the city *the city's mayor*

the uniforms of the players *the players' uniforms*

1. the video of the singer *the singer's video*

2. the scores of the students *the students' scores*

3. the favorite band of everybody *everybody's favorite band*

4. the office of the boss *the boss's office*

5. the union of the players *the players' union*

6. the specialty of the restaurant *the restaurant's specialty*

7. the bedroom of the children *the children's bedroom*

8. the high cost of the tickets *the tickets' high cost*

9. the dreams of everyone *everyone's dreams*

10. the owner of the dogs *the dogs' owner*

27c   Incorrect Use of Apostrophes

Be careful not to confuse a plural noun (*boys*) with the singular posses-sive form of the noun (*boy's*). Never use an apostrophe with a plural noun unless the noun is possessive.

> Termites can be dangerous <u>pests</u> [not *pest's*].
>
> The <u>Velezes</u> [not *Velez's*] live on Maple Drive, right next door to the <u>Browns</u> [not *Brown's*].

Also remember not to use apostrophes with possessive pronouns that end in -*s*: *theirs* (not *their's*), *hers* (not *her's*), *its* (not *it's*), *ours* (not *our's*), and *yours* (not *your's*).

Be especially careful not to confuse possessive pronouns with sound-alike contractions. Possessive pronouns never include apostrophes.

POSSESSIVE PRONOUN	CONTRACTION
The dog bit its master.	It's (*it is*) time for breakfast.
The choice is theirs.	There's (*there is*) no place like home.
Whose house is this?	Who's (*who is*) on first base?
Is this your house?	You're (*you are*) late again.

PRACTICE

27-3   Check the underlined words in the following sentences for correct use of apostrophes. If a correction needs to be made, cross out the word and write the correct version above it. If the noun or pronoun is correct, write *C* above it.

Example: The <u>president's</u> views were presented after several other
~~speaker's~~ *speakers* first presented <u>~~their's~~</u> *theirs*.

Teaching Tip
Be sure students under-stand that a computer's spell checker will not tell them when they have incorrectly used a con-traction for a possessive form—*it's* for *its*, for example.

Teaching Tip
Students often have trouble distinguishing plural nouns from singu-lar possessive forms and using apostrophes correctly with possessive pronouns. You may want to review 27c and Prac-tice 27-3 in class.

1. *Parents,* ^ **Parent's** should realize that when it comes to disciplining children, the responsibility is *theirs.* ^ <u>there's.</u>

2. *C* <u>It's</u> also important that parents offer praise for a *C* <u>child's</u> good behavior.

3. In *its* ^ <u>it's</u> first few *weeks* ^ <u>week's</u> of life, a dog is already developing a personality.

4. His and *hers* ^ <u>her's</u> towels used to be popular with *couples,* ^ <u>couple's,</u> but *C* <u>it's</u> not so common to see them today.

5. All the *Ryans* ^ <u>Ryan's</u> spent four *years* ^ <u>year's</u> in college and then got good jobs.

6. From the radio came the lyrics "*C* <u>You're</u> the one *whose* ^ <u>who's</u> love I've been waiting for."

7. If you expect to miss any *classes,* ^ <u>class's,</u> you will have to make arrangements with someone *C* <u>who's</u> willing to tell you *your* ^ <u>you're</u> assignment.

8. No other *C* <u>school's</u> cheerleading squad tried as many stunts as *ours* ^ <u>our's</u> did.

9. Surprise *tests* ^ <u>test's</u> are common in my economics *C* <u>teacher's</u> class.

10. *C* <u>Jazz's</u> influence on many mainstream *musicians* ^ <u>musician's</u> is one of the *C* <u>book's</u> main *subjects.* ^ <u>subject's.</u>

EDITING PRACTICE

Read the following student essay, which includes errors in the use of apostrophes. Edit it to eliminate errors by crossing out incorrect words and writing corrections above them. (Note that this is an informal response paper, so contractions are acceptable.) The first sentence has been edited for you.

The Women of Messina

In William ~~Shakespeares'~~ [Shakespeare's] play *Much Ado about Nothing*, the women of Messina, whether they are seen as love objects or as ~~shrew's,~~ [shrews,] have very few options. A ~~womans~~ [woman's] role is to please a man. She can try to resist, but she will probably wind up giving in.

The ~~plays~~ [play's] two women, Hero and Beatrice, are very different. Hero is the obedient one. ~~Heroes~~ [Hero's] cousin, Beatrice, tries to challenge the rules of the ~~mans~~ [man's] world in which she lives. However, in a place like Messina, even women like Beatrice find it hard to get the respect that should be ~~their's.~~ [theirs.]

Right from the start, we are drawn to Beatrice. ~~Shes~~ [She's] funny, she has a clever comment for most ~~situation's,~~ [situations,] and she always speaks her mind about other ~~peoples~~ [people's] behavior. Unlike Hero, she tries to stand up to the men in her life, as we see in her and ~~Benedicks~~ [Benedick's] conversations. But even though Beatrice's intelligence is obvious, she often mocks herself. ~~Its~~ [It's] clear that she doesn't have much self-esteem. In fact, Beatrice ~~is'nt~~ [isn't] the strong woman she seems to be.

Ultimately, Beatrice does get her man, and she will be happy—but at what cost? ~~Benedicks'~~ [Benedick's] last ~~word's~~ [words] to her are "Peace! I will stop your mouth." Then, he kisses her. The kiss is a symbolic end to their bickering. It is also the mark of ~~Beatrices~~ [Beatrice's] defeat. She has lost. Benedick has silenced her. Now, she will be Benedick's wife and do what he wants her to do. Granted, she will have more say in her marriage than Hero will have in ~~her's,~~ [hers,] but she is still defeated.

WORD POWER

shrew a scolding woman

READING TIP

This student essay has a comparison-and-contrast pattern of organization. To help organize the information in the essay, list the traits that Hero and Beatrice have in common (comparison) and the traits that make them different (contrast).

Shakespeare's

~~Shakespeares~~ audience ~~might have seen the plays ending as a happy one.~~

audiences,

For contemporary ~~audience's,~~ however, the ending is disappointing. Even

Messina's

Beatrice, the most rebellious of ~~Messinas~~ women, finds it impossible to achieve

anything of importance in this male-dominated society.

review checklist

bedfordstmartins.com
/forw LearningCurve >
Apostrophes

Using Apostrophes

☐ Use apostrophes to form contractions. (See 27a.)

☐ Use an apostrophe plus an *s* to form the possessive of singular nouns and indefinite pronouns, even when a noun ends in *-s*. (See 27b.)

☐ Use an apostrophe alone to form the possessive of plural nouns ending in *-s*, including names. If a plural noun does not end in *-s*, add an apostrophe plus an *s*. (See 27b.)

☐ Do not use apostrophes with plural nouns unless they are possessive. Do not use apostrophes with possessive pronouns. (See 27c.)

28 Understanding Mechanics

28a Capitalizing Proper Nouns

A **proper noun** names a particular person, animal, place, object, or idea. Proper nouns are always capitalized. The list that follows explains and illustrates specific rules for capitalizing proper nouns.

■ Always capitalize names of **races, ethnic groups, tribes, nationalities, languages, and religions**.

> The census data revealed a diverse community of Caucasians, African Americans, and Asian Americans, with a few Latino and Navajo residents. Native languages included English, Korean, and Spanish. Most people identified themselves as Catholic, Protestant, or Muslim.

■ Capitalize names of **specific people and the titles that accompany them**. In general, do not capitalize titles used without a name.

> In 1994, President Nelson Mandela was elected to lead South Africa.

> The newly elected fraternity president addressed the crowd.

■ Capitalize names of **specific family members and their titles**. Do not capitalize words that identify family relationships, including those introduced by possessive pronouns.

> The twins, Aunt Edna and Aunt Evelyn, are Dad's sisters.

> My aunts, my father's sisters, are twins.

■ Capitalize names of **specific countries, cities, towns, bodies of water, streets, and so on**. Do not capitalize words that do not name specific places.

> The Seine runs through Paris, France.

> The river runs through the city.

bedfordstmartins.com /forw Additional Grammar Exercises > Capitalizing Proper Nouns

Teaching Tip
Tell students that the words *black* and *white* are generally not capitalized when they name racial groups. However, *African American* and *Caucasian* are always capitalized.

- Capitalize names of **specific geographical regions**. Do not capitalize such words when they specify direction.

    William Faulkner's novels are set in the South.

    Turn right at the golf course, and go south for about a mile.

- Capitalize names of **specific buildings and monuments**. Do not capitalize general references to buildings and monuments.

    He drove past the Liberty Bell and looked for parking near City Hall.

    He drove past the monument and looked for a parking space near the building.

- Capitalize names of **specific groups, clubs, teams, and associations**. Do not capitalize general references to such groups.

    The Teamsters Union represents workers who were at the stadium for the Republican Party convention, the Rolling Stones concert, and the Phillies-Astros game.

    The union represents workers who were at the stadium for the political party's convention, the rock group's concert, and the baseball teams' game.

- Capitalize names of **specific historical periods, events, and documents**. Do not capitalize nonspecific references to periods, events, or documents.

    The Emancipation Proclamation was signed during the Civil War, not during Reconstruction.

    The document was signed during the war, not during the postwar period.

- Capitalize **names of businesses, government agencies, schools, and other institutions**. Do not capitalize nonspecific references to such institutions.

    The Department of Education and Apple Computer have launched a partnership project with Central High School.

    A government agency and a computer company have launched a partnership project with a high school.

- Capitalize **brand names**. Do not capitalize general references to kinds of products.

    While Jeff waited for his turn at the Xerox machine, he drank a can of Coke.

    While Jeff waited for his turn at the copier, he drank a can of soda.

■ Capitalize **titles of specific academic courses**. Do not capitalize names of general academic subject areas, except for proper nouns—for example, a language or a country.

> Are Introduction to American Government and Biology 200 closed yet?

> Are the introductory American government course and the biology course closed yet?

■ Capitalize **days of the week, months of the year, and holidays**. Do not capitalize the names of seasons.

> The Jewish holiday of Passover usually falls in April.

> The Jewish holiday of Passover falls in the spring.

ESL Tip
Use direct feedback when marking the work of nonnative speakers. Correct any incorrect usage of capitalized or noncapitalized trade names.

PRACTICE

28-1   Edit the following sentences, capitalizing letters or changing capitals to lowercase where necessary.

Teaching Tip
Have students do Practice 28-1 in pairs.

Example: The third-largest ~~C~~ity in the ~~u~~nited ~~s~~tates is ~~c~~hicago, ~~i~~llinois.

(1) Located in the ~~m~~idwest on ~~l~~ake Michigan, ~~c~~hicago is an important port city, a rail and highway hub, and the site of ~~o~~'~~h~~are ~~i~~nternational ~~a~~irport, one of the ~~N~~ation's busiest. (2) The financial center of the city is Lasalle ~~s~~treet, and the lakefront is home to Grant ~~p~~ark, where there are many ~~M~~useums and monuments. (3) To the ~~N~~orth of the city, ~~s~~oldier ~~f~~ield is home to the ~~c~~hicago ~~b~~ears, the city's football team, and ~~w~~rigley field is home to the ~~c~~hicago ~~c~~ubs, a ~~n~~ational ~~l~~eague ~~B~~aseball ~~T~~eam. (4) In the mid-1600s, the site of what is now Chicago was visited by ~~f~~ather ~~j~~acques ~~m~~arquette, a ~~c~~atholic missionary to the ~~o~~ttawa and ~~h~~uron tribes, who were native to the area. (5) By the 1700s, the city was a trading post run by ~~j~~ohn ~~k~~inzie. (6) The city grew rapidly in the 1800s, and immigrants included ~~g~~ermans, ~~i~~rish, ~~i~~talians, ~~p~~oles, ~~g~~reeks, and ~~c~~hinese, along with ~~a~~frican ~~a~~mericans who migrated from the ~~s~~outh. (7) In 1871, much of the city was destroyed in one of the worst fires

in *united states* history; according to legend, the fire started when
mrs. O'Leary's Cow kicked over a burning lantern. (8) Today, Chicago's skyline has many Skyscrapers, built by businesses like the john
hancock company, sears, and amoco. (9) I know Chicago well because
my Mother grew up there and my aunt jean and uncle amos still live
there. (10) I also got information from the Chicago Chamber of Commerce when I wrote a paper for introductory research writing, a course
I took at Graystone high school.

28b   Punctuating Direct Quotations

Teaching Tip
You may need to explain
what an identifying tag is
by literally pointing it out.

A **direct quotation** shows the *exact* words of a speaker or writer. Direct
quotations are always placed in quotation marks.

A direct quotation is usually accompanied by an **identifying tag**, a
phrase (such as "she said") that names the person being quoted. In the
following sentences, the identifying tag is underlined.

> Lauren said, "My brother and Tina have gotten engaged."
> A famous advertising executive wrote, "Don't sell the steak; sell
> the sizzle."

When a quotation is a complete sentence, it begins with a capital
letter and ends with a period (or a question mark or exclamation point).
When a quotation falls at the end of a sentence (as in the two examples
above) the period is placed *before* the quotation marks.

If the quotation is a question or an exclamation, the question mark
or exclamation point is also placed *before* the closing quotation mark.

> The instructor asked, "Has anyone read *Sula*?"
> Officer Warren shouted, "Hold it right there!"

If the quotation itself is not a question or an exclamation, the question mark or exclamation point is placed *after* the closing quotation mark.

> Did Joe really say, "I quit"?
> I can't believe he really said, "I quit"!

FYI

Indirect Quotations

A direct quotation shows someone's *exact* words, but an **indirect quotation** simply summarizes what was said or written.
Do not use quotation marks with indirect quotations.

DIRECT QUOTATION	Martin Luther King Jr. said, "I have a dream."
INDIRECT QUOTATION	Martin Luther King Jr. said that he had a dream.

The rules for punctuating direct quotations with identifying tags are summarized below.

Identifying Tag at the Beginning

When the identifying tag comes *before* the quotation, it is followed by a comma.

Alexandre Dumas wrote, "Nothing succeeds like success."

Identifying Tag at the End

When the identifying tag comes at the *end* of a quoted sentence, it is followed by a period. A comma (or, sometimes, a question mark or an exclamation point) inside the closing quotation mark separates the quotation from the identifying tag.

"Life is like a box of chocolates," stated Forrest Gump.
"Is that so?" his friends wondered.
"That's amazing!" he cried.

Identifying Tag in the Middle

When the identifying tag comes in the *middle* of the quoted sentence, it is followed by a comma. The first part of the quotation is also followed by a comma, placed inside the closing quotation mark. Because the part of the quotation that follows the identifying tag is not a new sentence, it does not begin with a capital letter.

"This is my life," Bette insisted, "and I'll live it as I please."

Identifying Tag between Two Sentences

When the identifying tag comes *between two* quoted sentences, it is preceded by a comma and followed by a period. (The second quoted sentence begins with a capital letter.)

"Producer Berry Gordy is an important figure in the history of music," Tony explained. "He was the creative force behind Motown records."

PRACTICE

28-2 The following sentences contain direct quotations. First, underline the identifying tag. Then, punctuate the quotation correctly, adding capital letters as necessary.

Example: Why Darryl asked are teachers so strict about deadlines?

1. We who are about to die salute you said the gladiators to the emperor.

2. When we turned on the television, the newscaster was saying ladies and gentlemen, we have a new president-elect.

3. The bigger they are said boxer John L. Sullivan the harder they fall.

4. Do you take Michael to be your lawfully wedded husband asked the minister.

5. Lisa Marie replied I do.

6. If you believe the *National Enquirer* my friend always says then you'll believe anything.

7. When asked for the jury's verdict, the foreperson replied we find the defendant not guilty.

8. I had felt for a long time that if I was ever told to get up so a white person could sit Rosa Parks recalled I would refuse to do so.

9. Yabba dabba doo Fred exclaimed this brontoburger looks great.

10. Where's my money Addie Pray asked you give me my money!

28c   Setting Off Titles

Some titles are typed in *italics*. Others are enclosed in quotation marks. The following box shows how to set off different kinds of titles.

Italics or Quotation Marks?

ITALICIZED TITLES

Books: *How the García Girls Lost Their Accents*
Newspapers: *Miami Herald*
Magazines: *People*
Long poems: *John Brown's Body*
Plays: *Death of a Salesman*
Films: *The Rocky Horror Picture Show*
Television or radio series: *Battlestar Galactica*
Paintings and Sculpture: *American Gothic*; *Pietà*
Video Games: *Call of Duty: Black Ops*; *Halo 4*

TITLES IN QUOTATION MARKS

Book chapters: "Understanding Mechanics"
Short stories: "The Tell-Tale Heart"
Essays and articles: "The Suspected Shopper"
Short poems: "Richard Cory"
Songs and speeches: "America the Beautiful"; "The Gettysburg Address"
Individual episodes of television or radio series: "The Montgomery Bus Boycott" (an episode of the PBS series *Eyes on the Prize*)

Teaching Tip
Remind students that they should underline to indicate italics in handwritten work.

Teaching Tip
Remind students not to use italics and quotation marks together (as in *"America the Beautiful"*).

Teaching Tip
Tell students that when they type their papers, they should not italicize their titles or enclose them in quotation marks. (Only titles of *published* works are set off in this way.)

bedfordstmartins.com /forw Additional Grammar Exercises > Setting Off Titles

FYI

Capital Letters in Titles

Capitalize the first letters of all important words in a title. Do not capitalize an **article** (*a, an, the*), a **preposition** (*to, of, around*, and so on), the *to* in an infinitive, or a **coordinating conjunction** (*and, but*, and so on)—unless it is the first or last word of the title or subtitle (*On the Road*; "To an Athlete Dying Young"; *No Way Out*; *And Quiet Flows the Don*).

PRACTICE

28-3   Edit the following sentences, capitalizing letters as necessary in titles.

Example: *New york times* best-seller *three cups of tea* is about

Greg Mortenson's work building schools in Pakistan and Afghanistan.

1. When fans of the television show *lost* voted for their favorite episodes, "through the looking glass," "the shape of things to come," and "the incident" were in the top ten.

2. In 1948, Eleanor Roosevelt delivered her famous speech "the struggle for human rights" and published an article titled "toward human rights throughout the world."

3. Before being elected president, Barack Obama wrote and published two books: *dreams from my father* and *the audacity of hope*.

4. English actor Daniel Craig plays secret agent James Bond in the films *casino royale*, *quantum of solace*, and *skyfall*.

5. *janis joplin's greatest hits* includes songs written by other people, such as "piece of my heart," as well as songs she wrote herself, such as "mercedes benz."

PRACTICE

28-4

In the following sentences, underline titles to indicate italics or place them in quotation marks. (Remember that titles of books and other long works are italicized, and titles of stories, essays, and other shorter works are enclosed in quotation marks.)

Example: An article in the New York Times called "Whoopi Goldberg Joins The View" talks about a television talk show hosted by women.

1. Oprah Winfrey publishes a magazine called O.

2. At the beginning of most major American sporting events, the crowd stands for "The Star-Spangled Banner."

3. People who want to purchase new cars often compare the different models in Consumer Reports magazine.

4. U2's song "Pride (in the Name of Love)" is about Martin Luther King Jr.

5. Edgar Allan Poe wrote several mysterious short stories, two of which are called "The Tell-Tale Heart" and "The Black Cat."

6. The popular Broadway show <u>Fela!</u> was based on the life of the Nigerian musician Fela Kuti.

7. Tina Fey, who has won two Golden Globes for her role in the hit TV show <u>30 Rock</u>, wrote a best-selling autobiography called <u>Bossypants</u>.

8. In a college textbook called <u>Sociology: A Brief Introduction</u>, the first chapter is titled "The Essence of Sociology."

28d Using Hyphens

e bedfordstmartins.com
/forw Additional
Grammar Exercises >
Hyphens

A hyphen has two uses: to divide a word at the end of a line and to join words in compounds.

Teaching Tip
Remind students that
when they type, a long
word will automatically be
carried over to the next line.

■ Use a **hyphen** to divide a word at the end of a line. If you need to divide a word, divide it between syllables. (Check your dictionary to see how a word is divided into syllables.) Never break a one-syllable word, no matter how long it is.

> When the speaker began his talk, the people seated in the <u>audi-torium</u> grew very quiet.

■ Use a hyphen in a **compound**—a word that is made up of two or more words.

> This theater shows <u>first-run</u> movies.

PRACTICE
28-5 Add hyphens to join words in compounds in the following sentences.

Example: The course focused on nineteenth-century American literature.

1. The ice-skating rink finally froze over.

2. We should be kind to our four-legged friends.

3. The first-year students raised money for charity.

4. The well-liked professor gave a speech to new students during orientation.

5. The hand-carved sculpture looked like a pair of doves.

28e Using Abbreviations

An **abbreviation** is a shortened form of a word. Although abbreviations are generally not used in college writing, it is acceptable to abbreviate the following.

- Titles—such as Mr., Ms., Dr., and Jr.—that are used along with names
- a.m. and p.m.
- BC and AD (in dates such as 43 BC)
- Names of organizations (NRA, CIA) and technical terms (DNA). Note that some abbreviations, called **acronyms**, are pronounced as words: AIDS, FEMA.

Keep in mind that it is *not* acceptable to abbreviate days of the week, months, names of streets and places, names of academic subjects, or titles that are not used along with names.

PRACTICE

28-6   Edit the incorrect use of abbreviations in the following sentences.

>   *February*
> **Example:**   In leap years, ~~Feb.~~ has twenty-nine days.

    doctor
1. The ~~dr.~~ diagnosed a case of hypertension.

    November
2. ~~Nov.~~ 11 is a federal holiday.

                   English   *psychology*
3. Derek registered for ~~Eng.~~ literature and a ~~psych~~ elective.

                                       Avenue   *Street.*
4. The museum was located at the corner of Laurel ~~Ave.~~ and Neptune ~~St.~~

                   Tuesday   *Thursday*   *Saturday.*
5. The clinic is only open ~~Tues.~~ through ~~Thurs.~~ and every other ~~Sat.~~

28f Using Numbers

In college writing, most numbers are spelled out (*forty-five*) rather than written as numerals (*45*). However, numbers more than two words long are always written as **numerals** (*4,530*, not *four thousand five hundred thirty*).

In addition, you should use numerals in the following situations.

DATES   January 20, 1976

ADDRESSES   5023 Schuyler Street

EXACT TIMES	10:00 (If you use *o'clock*, spell out the number: *ten o'clock*)
PERCENTAGES AND DECIMALS	80% 8.2
DIVISIONS OF BOOKS	Chapter 3 Act 4 page 102

Note: Never begin a sentence with a numeral. Use a spelled-out number, or reword the sentence so the numeral does not come at the beginning.

PRACTICE
28-7

Edit the incorrect use of numbers in the following sentences.

Example: The population of the United States is over ~~three hundred~~ *300* million.

1. Only 2 *two* students in the 8 *eight* o'clock lecture were late.
2. More than ~~seventy-five percent~~ *75%* of the class passed the exit exam.
3. Chapter six *6* begins on page 873.
4. The wedding took place on October twelfth *12* at 7:30.
5. Meet me at Sixty-five *65* Cadman Place.

28g   Using Semicolons, Colons, Dashes, and Parentheses

Semicolons

Use a **semicolon** to join independent clauses in a compound sentence.

Twenty years ago, smartphones did not exist; today, many people cannot imagine life without them.

Colons

- Use a **colon** to introduce a quotation.

    Our family motto is a simple one: "Accept no substitutes."

- Use a colon to introduce an explanation, a clarification, or an example.

    Only one thing kept him from climbing Mt. Everest: fear of heights.

Teaching Tip
Refer students to 17e for more on using semicolons in compound sentences.

bedfordstmartins.com /forw Additional Grammar Exercises > Semicolons

Teaching Tip
Tell students that when a colon introduces a quotation, an example, or a list, a complete sentence must precede the colon.

bedfordstmartins.com /forw Additional Grammar Exercises > Colons

Teaching Tip
Tell students that all items
in a list should be parallel.
Refer them to Chapter 19.

■ Use a colon to introduce a list.

I left my job for four reasons: boring work, poor working conditions, low pay, and a terrible supervisor.

Dashes

Use **dashes** to set off important information.

She parked her car—a red Firebird—in a towaway zone.

Teaching Tip
Tell students that dashes
give writing an informal
tone and should therefore
be used sparingly in
college writing.

Parentheses

Use **parentheses** to enclose material that is relatively unimportant.

The weather in Portland (a city in Oregon) was overcast.

**bedfordstmartins.com
/forw** Additional
Grammar Exercises >
Dashes and Parentheses

PRACTICE

28-8 Add semicolons, colons, dashes, and parentheses to the
following sentences where necessary.

Example: Megachurches those with more than two thousand
worshippers at a typical service have grown in popularity since the
1950s. *Answers may vary.*

1. Megachurches though they are Protestant are not always affiliated
   with the main Protestant denominations.

2. Services in megachurches are creative preaching is sometimes accompanied by contemporary music and video presentations.

3. Although many of these churches are evangelical actively recruiting
   new members, people often join because of friends and neighbors.

4. Megachurches tend to keep their members because they encourage a
   variety of activities for example, hospitality committees and study
   groups.

5. Worshippers say that their services are upbeat they are full of joy
   and spirituality.

6. Megachurches in nearly all cases use technology to organize and communicate with their members.

7. The largest of these churches with ten thousand members would be unable to function without telecommunications.

8. Some even offer services in a format familiar to their younger members the podcast.

9. Critics of megachurches and there are some believe they take up too much tax-exempt land.

10. Other critics fear that smaller churches already struggling to keep members will lose worshippers to these huge congregations and eventually have to close.

bedfordstmartins.com /forw Additional Grammar Exercises > Semicolons, Colons, Dashes, and Parentheses

EDITING PRACTICE

Read the following student essay, which includes errors in capitalization and punctuation and in the use of direct quotations and titles. Correct any errors you find. The first sentence has been edited for you.
Answers will vary.

A Threat to Health

READING TIP

This essay provides numerous supporting details about specific pandemics. To aid your comprehension, identify at least two supporting details about each pandemic discussed in the essay.

Pandemics are like Epidemics, only more widespread, perhaps even spreading throughout the World. In a pandemic, a serious Disease spreads very easily. In the past, there have been many pandemics. In the future, in spite of advances in Medicine, there will still be pandemics. In fact, scientists agree that not every pandemic can be prevented, so pandemics will continue to be a threat.

Probably the best-known pandemic is the bubonic plague. It killed about one-third of the Population of europe during the middle ages. Some areas suffered more than others. According to Philip ziegler's book the black Death, at least half the people in florence, Italy, died in one year. Many years later, in 1918, a flu pandemic killed more than fifty million people worldwide, including hundreds of thousands in the United states.

Unfortunately, pandemics have not disappeared. AIDS, for example, is a current pandemic. Philadelphia the 1993 movie starring denzel washington and tom hanks is still one of the most moving depictions of the heartbreak of AIDS. The rate of AIDS infection is over 30% in parts of africa, the disease continues to spread on other Continents as well. So far, efforts to find an AIDS vaccine have failed. Dr. anthony s. Fauci discussed recent AIDS research on NPR's series All things considered in a program called Search for an HIV vaccine expands.

Although some pandemic diseases, such as Smallpox, have been wiped out by Vaccination, new pandemics remain a threat. Many viruses and Bacteria change in response to treatment, so they may become resistant to Vaccination and Antibiotics. Also, with modern transportation, a disease can move quickly from Country to Country. For example, the disease known as severe acute respiratory syndrome (SARS) began in china but was spread to other countries by travelers. Hundreds died as a result of the SARS pandemic between November 2002 and july 2003. Birds also remain a threat because they can transmit disease. It is obviously impossible to prevent birds from flying from one country to another. Markos kyprianou, health commissioner of the European union, has said that I am concerned that birds in Turkey have been found with the bird flu Virus. He said, There is a direct relationship with viruses found in Russia, Mongolia and china. If this Virus changes so that it can move easily from birds to Humans, bird flu could become the next pandemic.

Public Health Officials are always on the lookout for diseases with three characteristics they are new, they are dangerous, and they are very contagious. Doctors try to prevent them from becoming Pandemics. However, they continue to warn that some Pandemics cannot be prevented.

review checklist

Understanding Mechanics

☐ Capitalize proper nouns. (See 28a.)

☐ Always place direct quotations within quotation marks. (See 28b.)

☐ In titles, capitalize all important words. Use italics or quotation marks to set off titles. (See 28c.)

☐ Use a hyphen to divide a word at the end of a line or to join words in compounds. (See 28d.)

☐ Abbreviate titles used with names, a.m. and p.m., BC and AD, names of organizations, and technical terms. (See 28e.)

☐ Use numerals for numbers more than two words long and in certain other situations. (See 28f.)

☐ Use semicolons to join independent clauses in a compound sentence. (See 28g.)

☐ Use colons, dashes, and parentheses to set off material from the rest of the sentence. (See 28g.)

29 Readings for Writers 569

29 Readings for Writers

The following twelve essays by professional writers offer interesting perspectives on four general themes—*Reading and Writing*, *Teaching and Learning*, *Gender*, and *Current Issues*. The essays are collected here for you to read, react to, think critically about, discuss, and write about. In addition, these essays illustrate some of the ways you can develop ideas in your own writing.

Each essay is preceded by a short **headnote**, an introduction that tells you something about the writer, and a **"Before you read"** sentence that suggests what to focus on as you approach the essay. Following each reading are six sets of questions and a set of writing prompts.

- **Focus on Reading** questions encourage you to review your highlighting and annotations.

- **Focus on Meaning** questions help you to assess your understanding of the essay's basic ideas.

- **Focus on Strategy** questions ask you to consider the writer's purpose and intended audience, as well as the essay's opening and closing strategies, and the thesis statement.

- **Focus on Language and Style** questions ask you to think about the writer's stylistic decisions and word choices as well as the words' **denotations** (dictionary definitions) and **connotations** (meanings associated with the words).

- **Focus on the Patterns** questions help you to see how the writer arranged ideas within the essay.

- **Focus on Critical Thinking** questions encourage you to move beyond what is on the page to consider the essay's wider implications or the connections between the writer's ideas and your own.

- **Focus on Writing** prompts offer suggestions for writing in response to each essay.

As you read each of the essays in this chapter, follow the active reading process outlined in Chapter 1, previewing, highlighting, and annotating each essay to help you understand what you are reading and prepare for writing an essay of your own.

READING AND WRITING

"Mother Tongue," Amy Tan   570
"The Case for Short Words," Richard Lederer   577
"The Library Card," Richard Wright   581

TEACHING AND LEARNING

"My Half-Baked Bubble," Joshuah Bearman   590
"How to Mummify a Pharaoh," Adam Goodheart   594
"The Dog Ate My Flash Drive, and Other Tales of Woe," Carolyn Foster Segal   597

GENDER

"Men Are from Mars, Women Are from Venus," John Gray   601
"I Want a Wife," Judy Brady   606
"Why Women Soldiers Don't Belong on the Front Lines," D. B. Grady   609

CURRENT ISSUES

"The Seat Not Taken," John Edgar Wideman   613
"Tweet Less, Kiss More," Bob Herbert   616
"The Guns of Academe," Adam Winkler   619

Reading and Writing

MOTHER TONGUE

Amy Tan

Amy Tan was born in 1952 in Oakland, California, the daughter of Chinese immigrants. In 1987, she published *The Joy Luck Club*, a best-selling novel about four immigrant Chinese women and their American-born daughters. Her later works include the novels *The Bonesetter's Daughter* (2001), *The Opposite of Fate: A Book of Musings* (2003), *Saving Fish from Drowning* (2005), and, most recently, *The Valley of Amazement*. In the following essay, Tan considers her mother's heavily Chinese-influenced English, as well as the different "Englishes" she herself uses, especially in communicating with her mother. She then discusses the potential limitations of growing up with immigrant parents who do not speak fluent English.

Before you read, think about the different kinds of language you use when talking with friends, family members, employers, and teachers.

I am not a scholar of English or literature. I cannot give you much more than personal opinions on the English language and its variations in this country or others. 1

I am a writer. And by that definition, I am someone who has always loved language. I am fascinated by language in daily life. I spend a great deal of my time thinking about the power of language—the way it can evoke an emotion, a visual image, a complex idea, or a simple truth. Language is the tool of my trade. And I use them all—all the Englishes I grew up with. 2

Recently, I was made keenly aware of the different Englishes I do use. I was giving a talk to a large group of people, the same talk I had already given to half a dozen other groups. The nature of the talk was about my writing, my life, and my book, *The Joy Luck Club*. The talk was going along well enough, until I remembered one major difference that made the whole talk sound wrong. My mother was in the room. And it was perhaps the first time she had heard me give a lengthy speech, using the kind of English I have never used with her. I was saying things like, "The intersection of memory upon imagination" and "There is an aspect of my fiction that relates to thus-and-thus"—a speech filled with carefully wrought grammatical phrases, burdened, it suddenly seemed to me, with nominalized forms, past perfect tenses, conditional phrases, all the forms of standard English that I had learned in school and through books, the forms of English I did not use at home with my mother. 3

Just last week, I was walking down the street with my mother, and I again found myself conscious of the English I was using, and the English I do use with her. We were talking about the price of new and used furniture and I heard myself saying this: "Not waste money that way." My husband was with us as well, and he didn't notice any switch in my English. And then I realized why. It's because over the twenty years we've been together I've often used that same kind of English with him, and sometimes he even uses it with me. It has become our language of intimacy, a different sort of English that relates to family talk, the language I grew up with. 4

So you'll have some idea of what this family talk I heard sounds like, I'll quote what my mother said during a recent conversation which I videotaped and then transcribed. During this conversation my mother was talking about a political gangster in Shanghai who had the same last name as her family's, Du, and how the gangster in his early years wanted to be adopted by her family, which was rich by comparison. Later, the gangster became more powerful, far richer than my mother's family, and one day showed up at my mother's wedding to pay his respects. Here's what she said in part: 5

"Du Yusong having business like fruit stand. Like off the street kind. 6
He is Du like Du Zong—but not Tsung-ming Island people. The local
people call putong, the river east side, he belong to that side local people.
The man want to ask Du Zong father take him in like become own family. Du Zong father wasn't looking down on him, but didn't take seriously, until that man big like become a mafia. Now important person
very hard to inviting him. Chinese way, come only to show respect, don't
stay for dinner. Respect for making big celebration, he shows up. Mean
gives lots of respect. Chinese custom. Chinese social life that way. If too
important won't have to stay too long. He come to my wedding. I didn't
see. I heard it. I gone to boy's side, they have YMCA dinner. Chinese age
I was nineteen."

You should know that my mother's expressive command of English 7
belies how much she actually understands. She reads the *Forbes* report,
listens to *Wall Street Week*, converses daily with her stockbroker, reads
all of Shirley MacLaine's books with ease—all kinds of things I can't
begin to understand. Yet some of my friends tell me they understand
50 percent of what my mother says. Some say they understand 80 to 90
percent. Some say they understand none of it, as if she were speaking
pure Chinese. But to me, my mother's English is perfectly clear, perfectly
natural. It's my mother's tongue. Her language, as I hear it, is vivid, direct, full of observation and imagery. This was the language that helped
shape the way I saw things, expressed things, made sense of the world.

Lately, I've been giving more thought to the kind of English my 8
mother speaks. Like others, I have described it to people as "broken" or
"fractured" English. But I wince when I say that. It has always bothered
me that I can think of no way to describe it other than "broken," as if
it were damaged and needed to be fixed, as if it lacked a certain whole-
ness and soundness. I've heard other terms used, "limited English," for
example. But they seem just as bad, as if everything is limited, including
people's perceptions of the limited English speaker.

I know this for a fact, because when I was growing up, my mother's 9
"limited" English limited *my* perception of her. I was ashamed of her
English. I believed that her English reflected the quality of what she
had to say. That is, because she expressed them imperfectly her thoughts
were imperfect. And I had plenty of empirical evidence to support me:
the fact that people in department stores, at banks, and at restaurants
did not take her seriously, did not give her good service, pretended not
to understand her, or even acted as if they did not hear her.

My mother has long realized the limitations of her English as well. 10
When I was fifteen, she used to have me call people on the phone to
pretend I was she. In this guise, I was forced to ask for information or
even complain and yell at people who had been rude to her. One time
it was a call to her stockbroker in New York. She had cashed out her
small portfolio and it just so happened we were going to go to New York

the next week, our very first trip outside California. I had to get on the phone and say in an adolescent voice that was not very convincing, "This is Mrs. Tan."

And my mother was standing in the back whispering loudly, "Why 11 he don't send me check, already two weeks late. So mad he lie to me, losing me money."

And then I said in perfect English, "Yes, I'm getting rather concerned. 12 You had agreed to send the check two weeks ago, but it hasn't arrived."

Then she began to talk more loudly. "What he want, I come to New 13 York tell him front of his boss, you cheating me?" And I was trying to calm her down, make her be quiet, while telling the stockbroker, "I can't tolerate any more excuses. If I don't receive the check immediately I am going to have to speak to your manager when I'm in New York next week." And sure enough, the following week there we were in front of this astonished stockbroker, and I was sitting there red-faced and quiet, and my mother, the real Mrs. Tan, was shouting at his boss in her impeccable broken English.

We used a similar routine just five days ago, for a situation that 14 was far less humorous. My mother had gone to the hospital for an appointment, to find out about a benign brain tumor a CAT scan had revealed a month ago. She said she had spoken very good English, her best English, no mistakes. Still, she said, the hospital did not apologize when they said they had lost the CAT scan and she had come for nothing. She said they did not seem to have any sympathy when she told them she was anxious to know the exact diagnosis, since her husband and son had both died of brain tumors. She said they would not give her any more information until the next time and she would have to make another appointment for that. So she said she would not leave until the doctor called her daughter. She wouldn't budge. And when the doctor finally called her daughter, me, who spoke in perfect English—lo and behold—we had assurances the CAT scan would be found, promises that a conference call on Monday would be held, and apologies for any suffering my mother had gone through for a most regrettable mistake.

I think my mother's English almost had an effect on limiting my 15 possibilities in life as well. Sociologists and linguists probably will tell you that a person's developing language skills are more influenced by peers. But I do think that the language spoken in the family, especially in immigrant families which are more insular, plays a large role in shaping the language of the child. And I believe that it affected my results on achievement tests, IQ tests, and the SAT. While my English skills were never judged as poor, compared to math, English could not be considered my strong suit. In grade school I did moderately well, getting perhaps B's, sometimes B-pluses, in English and scoring perhaps in the sixtieth or seventieth percentile on achievement tests. But those scores were not good enough to override the opinion that my true abilities lay in math and science, because in those areas I achieved A's and scored in the ninetieth percentile or higher.

This was understandable. Math is precise; there is only one correct   16 answer. Whereas, for me at least, the answers on English tests were always a judgment call, a matter of opinion and personal experience. Those tests were constructed around items like fill-in-the-blank sentence completion, such as "Even though Tom was _____, Mary thought he was _____." And the correct answer always seemed to be the most bland combinations of thoughts, for example, "Even though Tom was shy, Mary thought he was charming," with the grammatical structure "even though" limiting the correct answer to some sort of semantic opposites, so you wouldn't get answers like, "Even though Tom was foolish, Mary thought he was ridiculous." Well, according to my mother, there were very few limitations as to what Tom could have been and what Mary might have thought of him. So I never did well on tests like that.

The same was true with word analogies, pairs of words in which   17 you were supposed to find some sort of logical, semantic relationship—for example, "*Sunset* is to *nightfall* as _____ is to _____." And here you would be presented with a list of four possible pairs, one of which showed the same kind of relationship: *red* is to *stoplight*, *bus* is to *arrival*, *chills* is to *fever*, *yawn* is to *boring*. Well, I could never think that way. I knew what the tests were asking, but I could not block out of my mind the images already created by the first pair, "*sunset* is to *nightfall*"—and I would see a burst of colors against a darkening sky, the moon rising, the lowering of a curtain of stars. And all the other pairs of words—red, bus, stoplight, boring—just threw up a mass of confusing images, making it impossible for me to sort out something as logical as saying: "A sunset precedes nightfall" is the same as "a chill precedes a fever." The only way I would have gotten that answer right would have been to imagine an associative situation, for example, my being disobedient and staying out past sunset, catching a chill at night, which turns into feverish pneumonia as punishment, which indeed did happen to me.

I have been thinking about all this lately, about my mother's English,   18 about achievement tests. Because lately I've been asked, as a writer, why there are not more Asian Americans represented in American literature. Why are there few Asian Americans enrolled in creative writing programs? Why do so many Chinese students go into engineering? Well, these are broad sociological questions I can't begin to answer. But I have noticed in surveys—in fact, just last week—that Asian students, as a whole, always do significantly better on math achievement tests than in English. And this makes me think that there are other Asian-American students whose English spoken in the home might also be described as "broken" or "limited." And perhaps they also have teachers who are steering them away from writing and into math and science, which is what happened to me.

Fortunately, I happen to be rebellious in nature and enjoy the chal- 19
lenge of disproving assumptions made about me. I became an English
major my first year in college, after being enrolled as pre-med. I started
writing nonfiction as a freelancer the week after I was told by my former boss that writing was my worst skill and I should hone my talents
toward account management.

But it wasn't until 1985 that I finally began to write fiction. And 20
at first I wrote using what I thought to be wittily crafted sentences,
sentences that would finally prove I had mastery over the English language. Here's an example from the first draft of a story that later made
its way into *The Joy Luck Club*, but without this line: "That was my
mental quandary in its nascent state." A terrible line, which I can barely
pronounce.

Fortunately, for reasons I won't get into today, I later decided I 21
should envision a reader for the stories I would write. And the reader I
decided upon was my mother because these were stories about mothers. So with this reader in mind—and in fact she did read my early
drafts—I began to write stories using all the Englishes I grew up with:
the English I spoke to my mother, which for lack of a better term might
be described as "simple"; the English she used with me, which for lack
of a better term might be described as "broken"; my translation of her
Chinese, which could certainly be described as "watered down"; and
what I imagined to be her translation of her Chinese if she could speak
in perfect English, her internal language, and for that I sought to preserve the essence, but neither an English nor a Chinese structure. I
wanted to capture what language ability tests can never reveal: her in-
tent, her passion, her imagery, the rhythms of her speech and the nature of her thoughts.

Apart from what any critic had to say about my writing, I knew I 22
had succeeded where it counted when my mother finished reading my
book and gave me her verdict: "So easy to read."

Focus on Reading

1. Look back at the work you did when you previewed, highlighted,
   and annotated this essay. What do you think the term *mother tongue*
   means? Write a definition beside the essay's title. If you aren't sure
   what the term means, add a question mark to remind yourself to
   look it up later.

2. Review your highlighting. In the margin beside your most heavily
   highlighted passage, write a one-sentence summary of the paragraph.

Focus on Meaning

1. What day-to-day problems did Tan experience because of her mother's "limited English"?

2. What "different Englishes" does Tan use? How are these "Englishes" different from one another?

3. According to Tan, how were her "possibilities in life" (paragraph 15) limited by her mother's English?

Focus on Strategy

1. What do Tan's first two paragraphs suggest about her purpose for writing this essay?

2. What is Tan's thesis? Is it explicitly stated? If so, where? If not, how would you express the thesis, and where would you place the thesis statement?

3. Does Tan seem to be writing for a primarily Asian-American audience or for a wider audience? How can you tell?

Focus on Language and Style

1. In addition to the standard definition of *mother tongue*, what other meaning does Tan's title suggest? Which meaning (or meanings) do you think Tan intends this term to have? Why?

2. Review the examples of Mrs. Tan's English that appear in this essay. Do you think Amy Tan could have made her point without these examples? Explain.

Focus on the Patterns

1. Among other things, this essay classifies different kinds of "Englishes." Where does this classification appear?

2. Where does Tan use comparison and contrast? What is she comparing? Why?

3. In addition to classification and comparison and contrast, what other patterns of development can you identify in this essay?

Focus on Critical Thinking

1. Do you think the specific kinds of academic problems Tan describes are limited to the children of parents whose first language is not English? Explain.

2. In addition to the situations outlined in the essay, what other challenges do you think are faced by those with "limited English" who live in the United States?

3. Reread paragraph 18. What factors do you think account for how few Asian Americans work in jobs associated with language and literature—and for their strong presence in science and engineering?

Focus on Writing

1. Write a **literacy narrative** tracing your development as a reader or a writer. (For a model of this type of essay, see the student essay "Becoming a Writer" in Chapter 8.)

2. Did your parents' spoken or written language help you become a better reader or writer? Or, did their language stand in the way of your development as a reader or writer? Explain.

THE CASE FOR SHORT WORDS

Richard Lederer

Known for his love of words and wordplay, Richard Lederer began his career teaching English and media at St. Paul's School in New Hampshire. After twenty-seven years, he left teaching and went on to write over thirty popular books on language and trivia, beginning with the humorous *Anguished English* (1989). In "The Case for Short Words," Lederer uses examples ranging from famous literary works to high school students' essays to illustrate the power of short words.

Before you read, think about some of the one-syllable words you use most often.

When you speak and write, there is no law that says you have to use big 1
words. Short words are as good as long ones, and short, old words—like *sun* and *grass* and *home*—are best of all. A lot of small words, more than you might think, can meet your needs with a strength, grace, and charm that large words do not have.

Big words can make the way dark for those who read what you write 2
and hear what you say. Small words cast their clear light on big things—night and day, love and hate, war and peace, and life and death. Big words at times seem strange to the eye and the ear and the mind and the heart. Small words are the ones we seem to have known from the time we were born, like the hearth fire that warms the home.

Short words are bright like sparks that glow in the night, prompt 3
like the dawn that greets the day, sharp like the blade of a knife, hot like salt tears that scald the cheek, quick like moths that flit from flame to flame, and terse like the dart and sting of a bee.

Here is a sound rule: Use small, old words where you can. If a long 4
word says just what you want to say, do not fear to use it. But know that our tongue is rich in crisp, brisk, swift, short words. Make them the spine and the heart of what you speak and write. Short words are like fast friends. They will not let you down.

The title of this chapter and the four paragraphs that you have just 5
read are wrought entirely of words of one syllable. In setting myself this task, I did not feel especially cabined, cribbed, or confined. In fact, the

WORD POWER
wrought crafted

structure helped me to focus on the power of the message I was trying to put across.

One study shows that twenty words account for twenty-five percent 6 of all spoken English words, and all twenty are monosyllabic. In order of frequency they are: *I*, *you*, *the*, *a*, *to*, *is*, *it*, *that*, *of*, *and*, *in*, *what*, *he*, *this*, *have*, *do*, *she*, *not*, *on*, and *they*. Other studies indicate that the fifty most common words in written English are each made of a single syllable.

For centuries our finest poets and orators have recognized and 7 employed the power of small words to make a straight point between two minds. A great many of our proverbs punch home their points with pithy monosyllables: "Where there's a will, there's a way," "A stitch in time saves nine," "Spare the rod and spoil the child," "A bird in the hand is worth two in the bush."

Nobody used the short word more skillfully than William Shakespeare, 8 whose dying King Lear laments:

> And my poor fool is hang'd! No, no, no life!
> Why should a dog, a horse, a rat have life,
> And thou no breath at all? . . .
> Do you see this? Look on her; look, her lips.
> Look there, look there!

Shakespeare's contemporaries made the King James Bible a center- 9 piece of short words—"And God said, Let there be light: and there was light. And God saw the light, that it was good." The descendants of such mighty lines live on in the twentieth century. When asked to explain his policy to Parliament, Winston Churchill responded with these ringing monosyllables: "I will say: It is to wage war, by sea, land, and air, with all our might and with all the strength that God can give us." In his "Death of the Hired Man" Robert Frost observes that "Home is the place where, when you have to go there, / They have to take you in." And William H. Johnson uses ten two-letter words to explain his secret of success: "If it is to be, / It is up to me."

You don't have to be a great author, statesman, or philosopher to tap 10 the energy and eloquence of small words. Each winter I ask my ninth graders at St. Paul's School to write a composition composed entirely of one-syllable words. My students greet my request with obligatory moans and groans, but, when they return to class with their essays, most feel that, with the pressure to produce high-sounding polysyllables relieved, they have created some of their most powerful and luminous prose. Here are submissions from two of my ninth graders:

> What can you say to a boy who has left home? You can say that he has done wrong, but he does not care. He has left home so that he will not have to deal with what you say. He wants to go as far as he can. He will do what he wants to do.

WORD POWER

pithy brief but meaningful

WORD POWER

obligatory required

This boy does not want to be forced to go to church, to comb his hair, or to be on time. A good time for this boy does not lie in your reach, for what you have he does not want. He dreams of ripped jeans, shorts with no starch, and old socks.

So now this boy is on a bus to a place he dreams of, a place with no rules. This boy now walks a strange street, his long hair blown back by the wind. He wears no coat or tie, just jeans and an old shirt. He hates your world, and he has left it.

—Charles Shaffer

For a long time we cruised by the coast and at last came to a wide bay past the curve of a hill, at the end of which lay a small town. Our long boat ride at an end, we all stretched and stood up to watch as the boat nosed its way in.

The town climbed up the hill that rose from the shore, a space in front of it left bare for the port. Each house was a clean white with sky blue or grey trim; in front of each one was a small yard, edged by a white stone wall strewn with green vines.

As the town basked in the heat of noon, not a thing stirred in the streets or by the shore. The sun beat down on the sea, the land, and the back of our necks, so that, in spite of the breeze that made the vines sway, we all wished we could hide from the glare in a cool, white house. But, as there was no one to help dock the boat, we had to stand and wait.

At last the head of the crew leaped from the side and strode to a large house on the right. He shoved the door wide, poked his head through the gloom, and roared with a fierce voice. Five or six men came out, and soon the port was loud with the clank of chains and creak of planks as the men caught ropes thrown by the crew, pulled them taut, and tied them to posts. Then they set up a rough plank so we could cross from the deck to the shore. We all made for the large house while the crew watched, glad to be rid of us.

—Celia Wren

You, too, can tap into the vitality and vigor of compact expression. 11 Take a suggestion from the highway department. At the boundaries of your speech and prose place a sign that reads "Caution: Small Words at Work."

Focus on Reading

1. Look back at the work you did when you previewed, highlighted, and annotated this essay. If you have not already done so, underline the essay's thesis statement. Then, underline the summary statement.

2. Go through the essay, and circle ten words that have more than one syllable. Try substituting a one-syllable word for each of these words.

Teaching Tip
You may have students
work collaboratively to
answer some of these
questions.

Focus on Meaning

1. What "case for short words" is Lederer making in this essay?

2. In paragraph 6, Lederer discusses two studies. What information is given in these studies? Do you think he needs this information to make his point?

Focus on Strategy

ESL Tip
Have native- and nonnative-
speaking students work in
groups or in pairs to discuss the exercises before
they write their answers.

1. Do you think Lederer is writing for a general audience? For students? For teachers? How can you tell?

2. Evaluate Lederer's concluding paragraph. Is his use of "You, too" effective here? Is the closing quotation appropriate for his audience and purpose? Explain.

Focus on Language and Style

Teaching Tip
Remind students to
answer all questions in
complete sentences.

1. As Lederer points out in paragraph 5, his essay's title and first four paragraphs are composed entirely of one-syllable words. Why did he decide to write this way? Is this an effective stylistic choice?

2. In paragraph 7, Lederer says, "For centuries our finest poets and orators have recognized and employed the power of small words to make a straight point between two minds." What does he mean by "a straight point between two minds"? How else could he have expressed this idea?

Focus on the Patterns

1. In addition to his many short examples, Lederer uses longer examples from the Bible, literature, and politics as well as passages from two student writers. How do these examples support his thesis?

2. In paragraphs 2–4, Lederer uses comparison and contrast to point out the differences between long and short words. What key difference does he identify?

Focus on Critical Thinking

1. Which of Lederer's many examples do you find most convincing? Why?

2. Choose a sentence from the essay that is *not* composed entirely of one-syllable words, and rewrite it using words of only one syllable. Is your sentence as clear and effective as Lederer's original? If not, does your rewrite undercut his essay's thesis?

3. Evaluate the "sound rule" Lederer presents in paragraph 4. Is it useful? Practical? Logical?

Focus on Writing

1. In paragraph 10, Lederer reproduces two short student essays that use only one-syllable words. Write a short essay of your own composed entirely of one-syllable words.

2. Write an essay focusing on three or four stylistic choices you habitually make when you write. For example, do you prefer to begin or end your essays with a particular strategy? Do you like to use quotations or anecdotes for support? In your thesis statement, summarize the advantages (or disadvantages) of these writing choices.

THE LIBRARY CARD

Richard Wright

Richard Wright was born in 1908 on a Mississippi plantation. He excelled in grade school and graduated from his junior high school as class valedictorian. He later dropped out of high school and took a number of odd jobs before moving to Memphis. He published his first book, a collection of short stories titled *Uncle Tom's Children, in 1938.* Soon after, Wright wrote what is widely considered his most important work, *Native Son.* The following is an excerpt from Wright's autobiography *Black Boy* (1945), which recounts his younger years in the segregated South. This excerpt tells of his eagerness to read and acquire knowledge and the risks he took to do so.

Before you read, think about the books you have read that made you think or that changed your view of the world.

One morning I arrived early at work and went into the bank lobby where   1
the Negro porter was mopping. I stood at a counter and picked up the Memphis *Commercial Appeal* and began my free reading of the press. I came finally to the editorial page and saw an article dealing with one H. L. Mencken. I knew by hearsay that he was the editor of the *American Mercury*, but aside from that I knew nothing about him. The article was a furious denunciation of Mencken, concluding with one hot, short sentence: Mencken is a fool.

I wondered what on earth this Mencken had done to call down   2
upon him the scorn of the South. The only people I had ever heard denounced in the South were Negroes, and this man was not a Negro. Then what ideas did Mencken hold that made a newspaper like the *Commercial Appeal* castigate him publicly? Undoubtedly he must be advocating ideas that the South did not like. Were there, then, people other than Negroes who criticized the South? I knew that during the Civil War the South had hated northern whites, but I had not encountered such hate during my life. Knowing no more of Mencken than I

did at that moment, I felt a vague sympathy for him. Had not the South, which had assigned me the role of a non-man, cast at him its hardest words?

Now, how could I find out about this Mencken? There was a huge 3 library near the riverfront, but I knew that Negroes were not allowed to patronize its shelves any more than they were the parks and playgrounds of the city. I had gone into the library several times to get books for the white men on the job. Which of them would now help me to get books? And how could I read them without causing concern to the white men with whom I worked? I had so far been successful in hiding my thoughts and feelings from them, but I knew that I would create hostility if I went about this business of reading in a clumsy way.

I weighed the personalities of the men on the job. There was Don, a 4 Jew; but I distrusted him. His position was not much better than mine and I knew that he was uneasy and insecure; he had always treated me in an offhand, bantering way that barely concealed his contempt. I was afraid to ask him to help me to get books; his frantic desire to demonstrate a racial solidarity with the whites against Negroes might make him betray me.

Then how about the boss? No, he was a Baptist and I had the sus- 5 picion that he would not be quite able to comprehend why a black boy would want to read Mencken. There were other white men on the job whose attitudes showed clearly that they were Kluxers or sympathizers, and they were out of the question.

There remained only one man whose attitude did not fit into an anti- 6 Negro category, for I had heard the white men refer to him as a "Pope lover." He was an Irish Catholic and was hated by the white Southerners. I knew that he read books, because I had got him volumes from the library several times. Since he, too, was an object of hatred, I felt that he might refuse me but would hardly betray me. I hesitated, weighing and balancing the imponderable realities.

One morning I paused before the Catholic fellow's desk.   7

"I want to ask you a favor," I whispered to him.   8

"What is it?"   9

"I want to read. I can't get books from the library. I wonder if you'd 10 let me use your card?"

He looked at me suspiciously.   11

"My card is full most of the time," he said.   12

"I see," I said and waited, posing my question silently.   13

"You're not trying to get me into trouble, are you, boy?" he asked, 14 staring at me.

"Oh, no, sir."   15

"What book do you want?"   16

"A book by H. L. Mencken."   17

"Which one?"   18

"I don't know. Has he written more than one?"   19

"He has written several."   20

"I didn't know that."   21

"What makes you want to read Mencken?"   22

"Oh, I just saw his name in the newspaper," I said.   23

"It's good of you to want to read," he said. "But you ought to read   24
the right things."

I said nothing. Would he want to supervise my reading?   25

"Let me think," he said. "I'll figure out something."   26

I turned from him and he called me back. He stared at me quizzically.   27

"Richard, don't mention this to the other white men," he said.   28

"I understand," I said. "I won't say a word."   29

A few days later he called me to him.   30

"I've got a card in my wife's name," he said. "Here's mine."   31

"Thank you, sir."   32

"Do you think you can manage it?"   33

"I'll manage fine," I said.   34

"If they suspect you, you'll get in trouble," he said.   35

"I'll write the same kind of notes to the library that you wrote when   36
you sent me for books," I told him. "I'll sign your name."

He laughed.   37

"Go ahead. Let me see what you get," he said.   38

That afternoon I addressed myself to forging a note. Now, what were   39
the name of books written by H. L. Mencken? I did not know any of
them. I finally wrote what I thought would be a foolproof note: *Dear
Madam: Will you please let this nigger boy*—I used the word "nigger" to
make the librarian feel that I could not possibly be the author of the
note—*have some books by H. L. Mencken?* I forged the white man's name.

I entered the library as I had always done when on errands for whites,   40
but I felt that I would somehow slip up and betray myself. I doffed my
hat, stood a respectful distance from the desk, looked as unbookish as
possible, and waited for the white patrons to be taken care of. When the
desk was clear of people, I still waited. The white librarian looked at me.

"What do you want, boy?"   41

As though I did not possess the power of speech, I stepped forward   42
and simply handed her the forged note, not parting my lips.

"What books by Mencken does he want?" she asked.   43

"I don't know, ma'am," I said, avoiding her eyes.   44

"Who gave you this card?"   45

"Mr. Falk," I said.   46

"Where is he?"   47

"He's at work, at the M——Optical Company," I said. "I've been in   48
here for him before."

"I remember," the woman said. "But he never wrote notes like this."   49

Oh, God, she's suspicious. Perhaps she would not let me have the   50
books? If she had turned her back at that moment, I would have ducked
out the door and never gone back. Then I thought of a bold idea.

"You can call him up, ma'am," I said, my heart pounding.   51

"You're not using these books, are you?" she asked pointedly.   52

"Oh, no, ma'am. I can't read."   53

"I don't know what he wants by Mencken," she said under her breath. 54

I knew now that I had won; she was thinking of other things and the 55
race question had gone out of her mind. She went to the shelves. Once
or twice she looked over her shoulder at me, as though she was still
doubtful. Finally she came forward with two books in her hand.

"I'm sending him two books," she said. "But tell Mr. Falk to come 56
in next time, or send me the names of the books he wants. I don't know
what he wants to read."

I said nothing. She stamped the card and handed me the books. 57
Not daring to glance at them, I went out of the library, fearing that the
woman would call me back for further questioning. A block away from
the library I opened one of the books and read a title: *A Book of Prefaces*.
I was nearing my nineteenth birthday and I did not know how to pronounce the word "preface." I thumbed the pages and saw strange words
and strange names. I shook my head, disappointed. I looked at the other
book; it was called *Prejudices*. I knew what that word meant; I had heard
it all my life. And right off I was on guard against Mencken's books. Why
would a man want to call a book *Prejudices*? The word was so stained
with all my memories of racial hate that I could not conceive of anybody
using it for a title. Perhaps I had made a mistake about Mencken? A man
who had prejudices must be wrong.

When I showed the books to Mr. Falk, he looked at me and frowned. 58

"That librarian might telephone you," I warned him.   59

"That's all right," he said. "But when you're through reading those 60
books, I want you to tell me what you get out of them."

That night in my rented room, while letting the hot water run over 61
my can of pork and beans in the sink, I opened *A Book of Prefaces* and
began to read. I was jarred and shocked by the style, the clear, clean,
sweeping sentences. Why did he write like that? And how did one write
like that? I pictured the man as a raging demon, slashing with his pen,
consumed with hate, denouncing everything American, extolling everything European or German, laughing at the weaknesses of people,
mocking God, authority. What was this? I stood up, trying to realize
what reality lay behind the meaning of the words. . . . Yes, this man was
fighting, fighting with words. He was using words as a weapon, using
them as one would use a club. Could words be weapons? Well, yes, for
here they were. Then, maybe, perhaps, I could use them as a weapon?
No. It frightened me. I read on and what amazed me was not what he
said, but how on earth anybody had the courage to say it.

Occasionally I glanced up to reassure myself that I was alone in the 62
room. Who were these men about whom Mencken was talking so passionately? Who was Anatole France? Joseph Conrad? Sinclair Lewis, Sherwood
Anderson, Dostoevski, George Moore, Gustave Flaubert, Maupassant,

Tolstoy, Frank Harris, Mark Twain, Thomas Hardy, Arnold Bennett, Stephen Crane, Zola, Norris, Gorky, Bergson, Ibsen, Balzac, Bernard Shaw, Dumas, Poe, Thomas Mann, O. Henry, Dreiser, H. G. Wells, Gogol, T. S. Eliot, Gide, Baudelaire, Edgar Lee Masters, Stendhal, Turgenev, Huneker, Nietzsche, and scores of others? Were these men real? Did they exist or had they existed? And how did one pronounce their names?

I ran across many words whose meanings I did not know, and I 63 either looked them up in a dictionary or, before I had a chance to do that, encountered the word in a context that made its meaning clear. But what strange world was this? I concluded the book with the conviction that I had somehow overlooked something terribly important in life. I had once tried to write, had once reveled in feeling, had let my crude imagination roam, but the impulse to dream had been slowly beaten out of me by experience. Now it surged up again and I hungered for books, new ways of looking and seeing. It was not a matter of believing or disbelieving what I read, but of feeling something new, of being affected by something that made the look of the world different.

As dawn broke I ate my pork and beans, feeling dopey, sleepy. I went 64 to work, but the mood of the book would not die; it lingered, coloring everything I saw, heard, did. I now felt that I knew what the white men were feeling. Merely because I had read a book that had spoken of how they lived and thought, I identified myself with that book. I felt vaguely guilty. Would I, filled with bookish notions, act in a manner that would make the whites dislike me?

I forged more notes and my trips to the library became frequent. Read- 65 ing grew into a passion. My first serious novel was Sinclair Lewis's *Main Street*.[1] It made me see my boss, Mr. Gerald, and identify him as an American type. I would smile when I saw him lugging his golf bags into the office. I had always felt a vast distance separating me from the boss, and now I felt closer to him, though still distant. I felt now that I knew him, that I could feel the very limits of his narrow life. And this had happened because I had read a novel about a mythical man called George F. Babbitt.[2]

The plots and stories in the novels did not interest me so much as 66 the point of view revealed. I gave myself over to each novel without reserve, without trying to criticize it; it was enough for me to see and feel something different. And for me, everything was something different. Reading was like a drug, a dope. The novels created moods in which I lived for days. But I could not conquer my sense of guilt, my feeling that the white men around me knew that I was changing, that I had begun to regard them differently.

1. *Main Street*, published in 1920, examines the smugness, intolerance, and lack of imagination that characterize small-town American life. [Eds.]
2. The central character in Sinclair Lewis's *Babbitt* (1922), who believed in the virtues of home, the Republican Party, and middle-class conventions. To Wright, Babbitt symbolizes the mindless complacency of white middle-class America. [Eds.]

Whenever I brought a book to the job, I wrapped it in newspaper—a 67
habit that was to persist for years in other cities and under other circumstances. But some of the white men pried into my packages when I
was absent and they questioned me.

"Boy, what are you reading those books for?"   68
"Oh, I don't know, sir."   69
"That's deep stuff you're reading, boy."   70
"I'm just killing time, sir."   71
"You'll addle your brains if you don't watch out."   72

I read Dreiser's *Jennie Gerhardt* and *Sister Carrie*[3] and they revived in 73
me a vivid sense of my mother's suffering; I was overwhelmed. I grew silent,
wondering about the life around me. It would have been impossible for me
to have told anyone what I derived from these novels, for it was nothing
less than a sense of life itself. All my life had shaped me for the realism,
the naturalism of the modern novel, and I could not read enough of them.

Steeped in new moods and ideas, I bought a ream of paper and tried 74
to write; but nothing would come, or what did come was flat beyond
telling. I discovered that more than desire and feeling were necessary to
write and I dropped the idea. Yet I still wondered how it was possible to
know people sufficiently to write about them. Could I ever learn about
life and people? To me, with my vast ignorance, my Jim Crow station in
life, it seemed a task impossible of achievement. I now knew what being
a Negro meant. I could endure the hunger. I had learned to live with
hate. But to feel that there were feelings denied me, that the very breath
of life itself was beyond my reach, that more than anything else hurt,
wounded me. I had a new hunger.

In buoying me up, reading also cast me down, made me see what 75
was possible, what I had missed. My tension returned, new, terrible,
bitter, surging, almost too great to be contained. I no longer *felt* that the
world about me was hostile, killing; I *knew* it. A million times I asked
myself what I could do to save myself, and there were no answers. I
seemed forever condemned, ringed by walls.

I did not discuss my reading with Mr. Falk, who had lent me his 76
library card; it would have meant talking about myself and that would
have been too painful. I smiled each day, fighting desperately to maintain my old behavior, to keep my disposition seemingly sunny. But some
of the white men discerned that I had begun to brood.

"Wake up there, boy!" Mr. Olin said one day.   77
"Sir!" I answered for the lack of a better word.   78
"You act like you've stolen something," he said.   79

I laughed in the way I knew he expected me to laugh, but I resolved 80
to be more conscious of myself, to watch my every act, to guard and
hide the new knowledge that was dawning within me.

---

3. Both *Jennie Gerhardt* (1911) and *Sister Carrie* (1900), by Theodore Dreiser, tell the
   stories of working women who struggle against poverty and social injustice. [Eds.]

If I went north, would it be possible for me to build a new life then? 81
But how could a man build a life upon vague, unformed yearnings? I
wanted to write and I did not even know the English language. I bought
English grammars and found them dull. I felt that I was getting a better
sense of the language from novels than from grammars. I read hard,
discarding a writer as soon as I felt that I had grasped his point of view.
At night the printed page stood before my eyes in sleep.

Mrs. Moss, my landlady, asked me one Sunday morning: "Son, what 82
is this you keep on reading?"

"Oh, nothing. Just novels."   83

"What you get out of 'em?"   84

"I'm just killing time," I said.   85

"I hope you know your own mind," she said in a tone which implied 86
that she doubted if I had a mind.

I knew of no Negroes who read the books I liked and I wondered 87
if any Negroes ever thought of them. I knew that there were Negro
doctors, lawyers, newspapermen, but I never saw any of them. When I
read a Negro newspaper I never caught the faintest echo of my preoc-
cupation in its pages. I felt trapped and occasionally, for a few days,
I would stop reading. But a vague hunger would come over me for
books, books that opened up new avenues of feeling and seeing, and
again I would forge another note to the white librarian. Again I would
read and wonder as only the naïve and unlettered can read and wonder, feeling that I carried a secret, criminal burden about with me
each day.

That winter my mother and brother came and we set up house- 88
keeping, buying furniture on the installment plan, being cheated and
yet knowing no way to avoid it. I began to eat warm food and to my
surprise found that regular meals enabled me to read faster. I may
have lived through many illnesses and survived them, never suspecting
that I was ill. My brother obtained a job and we began to save toward
the trip north, plotting our time, setting tentative dates for departure. I
told none of the white men on the job that I was planning to go north; I
knew that the moment they felt I was thinking of the North they would
change toward me. It would have made them feel that I did not like
the life I was living, and because my life was completely conditioned
by what they said or did, it would have been tantamount to challenging them.

I could calculate my chances for life in the South as a Negro fairly 89
clearly now.

I could fight the southern whites by organizing with other Negroes, 90
as my grandfather had done. But I knew that I could never win that
way; there were many whites and there were but few blacks. They were
strong and we were weak. Outright black rebellion could never win. If I
fought openly I would die and I did not want to die. News of lynchings
were frequent.

I could submit and live the life of a genial slave, but that was im- 91
possible. All of my life had shaped me to live by my own feelings and
thoughts. I could make up to Bess and marry her and inherit the house.
But that, too, would be the life of a slave; if I did that, I would crush to
death something within me, and I would hate myself as much as I knew
the whites already hated those who had submitted. Neither could I ever
willingly present myself to be kicked, as Shorty had done. I would rather
have died than do that.

I could drain off my restlessness by fighting with Shorty and 92
Harrison. I had seen many Negroes solve the problem of being black by
transferring their hatred of themselves to others with a black skin and
fighting them. I would have to be cold to do that, and I was not cold and
I could never be.

I could, of course, forget what I had read, thrust the whites out of 93
my mind, forget them; and find release from anxiety and longing in sex
and alcohol. But the memory of how my father had conducted himself
made that course repugnant. If I did not want others to violate my life,
how could I voluntarily violate it myself?

I had no hope whatever of being a professional man. Not only had 94
I been so conditioned that I did not desire it, but the fulfillment of such
an ambition was beyond my capabilities. Well-to-do Negroes lived in a
world that was almost as alien to me as the world inhabited by whites.

What, then, was there? I held my life in my mind, in my conscious- 95
ness each day, feeling at times that I would stumble and drop it, spill
it forever. My reading had created a vast sense of distance between me
and the world in which I lived and tried to make a living, and that sense
of distance was increasing each day. My days and nights were one long,
quiet, continuously contained dream of terror, tension, and anxiety. I
wondered how long I could bear it.

Focus on Reading

1. Look back at the work you did when you previewed, highlighted,
   and annotated this essay. **Scan** paragraph 62 to identify some of the
   many unfamiliar names Wright encountered in his reading. Look
   up two of the people he names, and write down a few details in the
   margin to identify each person.

2. Reread paragraph 74. Did you highlight *Jim Crow* to identify it as a
   term you need to look up? If not, do so now.

Focus on Meaning

1. What made Wright curious to find out more about H. L. Mencken?

2. What was Wright's initial reaction to Mencken's book? How did he
   react to the names Mencken mentioned? To the many new words he
   encountered as he reads?

3. What does Wright mean when he mentions his "Jim Crow station in life" (paragraph 74)?

4. What negative effects did his reading have on Wright? Why?

Focus on Strategy

1. Write a thesis statement for this essay.

2. How do you imagine Wright expected this essay to be received by readers—black and white, Northerners and Southerners—when he wrote it in 1945? How do you suppose today's readers would respond to his experiences?

Focus on Language and Style

1. In paragraph 63, Wright discusses the new words he came across in his reading. Identify five words in Wright's essay whose meanings you do not know. Look up these words, and then list a synonym for each one.

2. What is your reaction to Wright's use of the word *Negro* in this essay? Given that he was writing in 1945, did Wright have any other options? Explain.

3. In paragraph 61, Wright asks, "Could words be weapons?" How might Wright have used words as weapons? At whom (or what) would he have aimed these weapons?

Focus on the Patterns

1. What features in this essay tell you that it is a narrative?

2. Although Wright's essay has a narrative structure, it also relies on cause and effect, description, and exemplification. Where is each of these patterns of development used?

3. Where in this essay might Wright have added a few paragraphs of comparison and contrast? Who (or what) might he have compared? What could the comparison you suggest add to his narrative?

Focus on Critical Thinking

1. Do you think having a library card is as important to most people today as it was to Wright? Why or why not?

2. In paragraphs 3–56, Wright explains how he gained access to the books he wanted to read. What does his explanation of the steps he took, and the way he had to behave, tell you about his status in his community? What does it tell you about his coworkers? About the librarian?

3. How do you account for the despair Wright expresses in the essay's last paragraph?

Focus on Writing

1. Write an essay about a book, movie, or song that made you feel the way Richard Wright felt about Mencken's *A Book of Prefaces*.

2. Wright's last paragraph opens with the sentence, "What, then, was there?" Write a letter to Wright from the vantage point of the twenty-first century, answering this question by outlining the social, political, and economic opportunities available to him today.

Teaching and Learning

MY HALF-BAKED BUBBLE

Joshuah Bearman

Teaching Tip
Remind students to familiarize themselves with the end-of-essay questions before they read the essay.

Joshuah Bearman is a writer and editor whose work has appeared in *LA Weekly*, *Rolling Stone*, *Harper's*, *Wired*, the *New York Times Magazine*, the *Believer*, and *McSweeney's*. He also contributes frequently to Chicago Public Radio's *This American Life*. In "My Half-Baked Bubble," an opinion essay that appeared in the *New York Times* in 2009, Bearman writes about a fondly remembered childhood experience.

Before you read, think about your own experiences with your elementary school classmates.

Teaching Tip
Review dialogue format. Refer students to 28b.

WORD POWER

disparity lack of similarity or equality
Spartan simple, frugal; marked by avoidance of luxury

1   "Sardines are better than candy," my father said. "They're oily, but nutritious!" Easy for him to say. I was 8 and had just moved to a new, fancier school. The socioeconomic shift was most apparent to me in the cafeteria, where there was a wide disparity between my lunch and everyone else's. Ours was a Spartan household: no chocolate, cookies or extraneous sugar. For us, Rice Krispies cereal was supposed to be some kind of special indulgence.

2   My childhood happened to coincide with that historic moment in the early '80s when the full ingenuity of modern science was brought to bear on lunch snacks. Fruit roll-ups had just hit the scene. Capri Sun was like quicksilver-cocooned astronaut juice with a cool dagger straw. Chocolate pudding came in palm-sized cups!

3   My dad was a physicist, so I thought he should know the formula for turning our flavorless Rice Krispies into Rice Krispie treats. And yet he packed me the same lunch day after day: one peanut butter and jelly sandwich, one apple, one box of raisins. When I complained, he solved the problem (and taught me a lesson) by giving me sardines instead. As if that was an upgrade.

So I became the weird kid in the corner, opening a tin of sardines, 4 like a hobo—when I managed not to lose the key, that is. "Stick with sardines," my dad said. "Cheap sweets are empty promises."

But they didn't seem so empty to me. Every day at lunchtime the 5 cafeteria turned into an informal marketplace. My classmates laid out their wares on one of the big tables, displaying a panoply of forbidden processed delights. While I was busy trying to open my indestructible sardine can with a sharp rock, a brisk trading economy was under way.

WORD POWER

panoply a wide-ranging and impressive array

"I am so bored with my Chunky," a luckier boy would say, consider- 6 ing the options before him. "Maybe I'll give Mr. E. L. Fudge a try!" And with a quick swap, the deal was done.

I must admit, it was a fairly efficient market. Everyone got what he 7 wanted. Except for me. My sardines had zero value as trading currency. With no way into this economy, I had to watch from the sidelines.

Until one day, out of the depths of my isolation, I developed what 8 you might call a creative business prospectus.

I'm not sure how I came up with this idea, but what I told my class- 9 mates was this: my mom is an expert baker, and at the end of the year she always bakes this incredible cake, the best cake ever, for me and my best friends at school. It's coming, this wonderful cake. Can you picture it in your mind? It will be a great day. But in the meantime, I said, I will let you in on this special opportunity! If you give me, say, your Cheetos now, you can stake a claim on this fantastic pending cake. Like a de- posit. One Hostess cupcake equals one share.

Just like that, I became a market maker, peddling delicious cake 10 futures.

And people were buying! First came a round of vanguard investors. 11 Then others followed, figuring they had to get in on the ground floor with this cake deal. From there it went wide. My table in the lunchroom became the hot new trading floor. The bell would ring and my class- mates would line up with their items, eager to buy in.

At the beginning, of course, I figured I could really persuade my 12 mom to bake such a cake, and so I'd dutifully record all the trading "transactions" in my Trapper Keeper. Twinkie = one piece of cake. Chunky = half-a-piece. Fruit roll-up = two pieces. Watermelon-flavored Jolly Rancher?! I don't even want that. Zero pieces! I was setting the terms! It was like a dream come true.

Soon enough, however, the market was spiraling out of control. 13 I started allowing customized cake shares. My Trapper Keeper ledger kept growing, and getting more complicated. The records described a wildly fantastic cake: hundreds of layers, rising to the heavens in all different flavors—chocolate mousse on top of meringue on top of half angel food and half red velvet. I was drunk with power, the creator of a bizarre lunchroom derivatives bubble.

Had anyone thought about it, it would have been clear that my 14 mother, no matter how skilled a baker, could not fulfill my debts. But no one thought about it. We were all in too deep. I had to let the ledger keep growing.

The thing was, we all wanted to believe in this cake. For my investors, 15 it was pragmatic: people were already into this cake for, like, 14 bags of Doritos, and they couldn't just walk away from the whole idea. So they kept pouring more Doritos in and hoping for the best. Even I sort of believed in it—and I could see the numbers. I too was deluded, imagining the hero's welcome I would receive when my mom and I eventually wheeled this amalgamated baked colossus into the schoolyard. I couldn't face the truth.

This was the mutually reinforcing psychology that allowed the cake 16 futures market to continue. Just like the Dutch tulip mania.[1] Or the South Sea Bubble.[2] Or the American housing market. We were trafficking in dreams. Is there anything wrong with that?

The answer, as we all know, is yes—there is something wrong with 17 that. Like all bubbles, mine couldn't last forever. Eventually, someone was going to blow the whistle.

Spencer. Spencer was both good at math and jealous; he'd always done 18 well by the original cafeteria economy. Since everyone had been lured over to the fancy new derivatives guy, the old trading table had sat empty, and it was Spencer, Mr. Fundamentals, who did a back-of-the-napkin calculation to demonstrate how irrational our exuberance was. If you look at the numbers, he pointed out, my cake would defy the laws of physics.

At first no one wanted to believe him. If Spencer wants to be left 19 out of the glorious new cake era, everyone thought, then, hey, fine by us. But then Spencer won a few people over with his sober analysis. And then a few more. And just as quickly as confidence in the cake was built, it eroded. We crossed the crash threshold and, overnight, belief in the cake evaporated. My classmates knew that the ledger was a sham, and they were not getting their investments back. The Fritos, Nutter Butters, Hostess pies—they were all gone, good snacks after bad.

The bigger the bubble, the harder the fall. I was an outsider before, 20 but now I was a pariah. The old snack economy quietly rebuilt itself, and I was back to knocking my sardine can against the monkey bars out in the playground.

When my dad found out about my mischief, I got a lecture. It was 21 one big "I told you so," because, well, he had told me so. "Stick with the sardines," he'd said. "Cheap sweets are empty promises."

WORD POWER

pariah someone who is despised or rejected; an outcast

Focus on Reading

1. Look back at the work you did when you previewed, highlighted, and annotated this essay. Put a check mark next to each passage that

---

1. Seventeenth-century economic crash associated with sudden collapse (after wildly inflated prices) of the tulip-bulb market.
2. Eighteenth-century economic disaster caused by stock speculation.

quotes Bearman's father. Try to think of something similar that your own parents told you, and write those words in the margin.

2. In economic terms, what is a *bubble*? Read paragraph 13, and try to figure out the meaning of this word from its context. Then, write a definition of *bubble* in the margin beside paragraph 13. (Include a question mark to remind you to look the word up later on.)

Focus on Meaning

1. How is Bearman's lunch different from his friends' lunches? Why is this difference so important to him?

2. Why did Bearman first decide to develop his "creative business prospectus" (paragraph 8)? Explain how his plan worked.

3. Why did Bearman's idea get out of hand?

Teaching Tip
You may have students work collaboratively to answer some of these questions.

Focus on Strategy

1. In paragraphs 4 and 21, Bearman quotes his father, who says, "Cheap sweets are empty promises." Do you think this sentence is the essay's thesis? If not, what thesis statement would you suggest? Is there any other sentence in the essay that might serve as a thesis statement?

2. Bearman's essay begins and ends with quotations from his father. Why? Is this an appropriate strategy for this essay? Explain.

ESL Tip
Have native- and nonnative-speaking students work in groups or in pairs to discuss the exercises before they write their answers.

Focus on Language and Style

1. What does the expression *half-baked* mean? What two meanings does it have in the title of this essay?

2. Bearman compares his experiences in his school cafeteria to stock-market speculation, using words like *transactions* (paragraph 12) and *derivatives* (13). List other words and phrases used here that suggest financial activity. What are the advantages and disadvantages of using this kind of vocabulary here?

Teaching Tip
Students may need help defining words. With nonnative-speaking students, consider going over the definitions in class before assigning the reading.

Focus on the Patterns

1. Although this essay is primarily a narrative, Bearman also uses other patterns to develop his ideas. Where does he use description? Where does he use exemplification?

2. In paragraph 8, with the phrase "Until one day, . . ." Bearman begins to tell a story. What transitional words and phrases does he use to move readers from one event to the next? List as many as you can.

Teaching Tip
Remind students to answer all questions in complete sentences.

Focus on Critical Thinking

1. Unlike the childhood experiences described by Lynda Barry (pp. 216–218), Bearman's memories of his childhood are very positive.

How are his impressions of school—and of his family—different from Barry's? For example, is school a sanctuary for him? Who is more important to him, his teachers or his parents?

2. What responsibility, if any, do you think schools have to ensure that children are happy and well adjusted (in addition to educated)? Did the schools you attended when you were a child serve your emotional as well as your intellectual needs?

Focus on Writing

1. In paragraph 4, Bearman describes himself as "the weird kid in the corner." Write an essay about a time in your childhood when you were an outsider. What did you do to try to fit in?

2. Retell the story of Bearman's experiences as a fairy tale directed at elementary schoolchildren. Begin with "Once upon a time, . . ." use third person (*Joshuah, he, the boy*), and use the sentence "Cheap sweets are empty promises" as the tale's moral.

Teaching Tip
Remind students to familiarize themselves with the end-of-essay questions before they read the essay.

HOW TO MUMMIFY A PHARAOH

Adam Goodheart

Adam Goodheart is a writer, editor, and historian. One of the founders of *Civilization* magazine, where this essay originally appeared, Goodheart has published widely on subjects including travel, anthropology, science, and history. His book *1861: The Civil War Awakening* (2011) was a *New York Times* best-seller. In this essay, Goodheart explains the steps required for making a mummy.

Before you read, consider what you already know (and do not know) about Goodheart's topic.

WORD POWER

pharaoh ancient Egyptian ruler

Old pharaohs never died—they just took long vacations. Ancient Egyptians believed that at death a person's spirit, or *ka*, was forcibly separated from the body. But it returned now and then for a visit, to snack on the food that had been left in the tomb. It was crucial that the body stay as lifelike as possible for eternity—that way, the *ka* (whose life was hard enough already) would avoid reanimating the wrong corpse. These days, dead pharaohs are admittedly a bit hard to come by. If you decide to practice mummification on a friend or relative, please make sure that the loved one in question is fully deceased before you begin.

WORD POWER

evisceration removal of organs

1. Evisceration Made Easy. The early stages of the process can be a bit malodorous, so it's recommended that you follow the ancient custom of relocating to a well-ventilated tent. (You'll have trouble breathing anyway, since tradition also prescribes that you wear a jackal-head mask in honor of Anubis, god of the dead.) After cleansing the body, break the nose by pushing a long iron hook up the nostrils. Then use the hook to remove the contents of the skull. You can discard the brain (the ancient Egyptians attributed no special significance to it).

Next, take a flint knife and make a long incision down the left side 3 of the abdomen. Actually, it's best to have a friend do this, since the person who cuts open the body must be pelted with stones to atone for the profanation. After you've stoned your friend, use a bronze knife to remove the internal organs through the incision. Wash them in palm wine as a disinfectant and set them aside to inter later in separate ala-baster jars. Leave the heart in place (Egyptians believed it was the seat of consciousness).

2. Salting and Stuffing. Once the abdominal cavity is empty, fill 4 it with natron, a natural salt found at the Wadi Natrun in the western Nile delta. Heap more natron on top of the body until it is completely covered. According to a papyrus in the Louvre, it should then be left for 42 days, after which it will be almost totally desiccated. Having removed the natron, anoint the head with frankincense and the body with sacred oil. Pack the skull and abdomen with myrrh and other spices, and cover the incision with a sheet of gold.

For an extra-lifelike effect, you can stuff the corpse's skin with a 5 compound of sawdust, butter, and mud. Don't overdo it, though. Queen Henettowey, wife of Pinedjem I, was so overstuffed that when archae-ologists found her, her face had split open like an old sofa.

3. Wrapping Up. If you thought mummies wrapped in bedsheets 6 were the stuff of B movies, think again: Even pharaohs were usually wound in strips cut from household linens. Pour molten pine resin over the body; in the course of centuries this will turn the flesh black, glassy, and rock-hard. While the resin's still tacky, bandage each of the extremi-ties separately, including fingers and toes. Then brush on another coat and repeat. (Go easy on the resin—Tutankhamen stuck to his coffin and had to be chipped out piece by piece.) Amulets can be placed between the layers of bandages; a scarab over the heart is the minimum. The last layers should secure the arms and legs to the body. Your mummy is now ready to be entombed in grand style.

A note on sarcophagi: Careful labeling will prevent embarrassing 7 mix-ups later on. A mummy long thought to be Princess Mutemhet of the 21st dynasty was recently x-rayed and found to be a pet baboon.

WORD POWER
profanation disrespectful act

WORD POWER
papyrus an ancient paper or document made from a tall, grasslike plant
desiccated dry

WORD POWER
amulet a charm worn around the neck to ward off evil
scarab a decorative item in the shape of the scarab beetle

Focus on Reading

1. Look back at the work you did when you previewed, highlighted, and annotated this essay. Now, look again at the essay's headings. Why do you think they are numbered as well as set in boldface? Do you think the numbers are necessary?

2. Review your highlighting and annotations, and make a list of ques-tions you would like to have answered during class discussion.

Teaching Tip
You may have students
work collaboratively to
answer some of these
questions.

Focus on Meaning

1. Why did the ancient Egyptians practice mummification?

2. What equipment is needed for the process Goodheart describes?

Focus on Strategy

Teaching Tip
Have native- and nonnative-
speaking students work
in groups or in pairs to
discuss the exercises
before they write their
answers.

1. Goodheart knows that his readers will never be called upon to mummify their friends or relatives. Why, then, does he use commands and "you," telling readers how to perform this process?

2. What do you think is this essay's primary purpose? Is the essay meant to be a serious treatment of the subject it discusses? How can you tell?

3. This essay does not include a thesis statement. Write one that would be suitable. Where should this new sentence be located?

4. Evaluate the essay's last paragraph. Should the essay have ended with the last sentence of paragraph 6? Or, should Goodheart have added a formal conclusion, including a summary statement? Explain.

Focus on Language and Style

Teaching Tip
Remind students to
answer all questions in
complete sentences.

1. Goodheart's style and tone are light and irreverent. For example, he observes, "These days, dead pharaohs are admittedly a bit hard to come by" (paragraph 1), and he notes that, when overstuffed, Queen Henettowey's face "split open like an old sofa" (5). Identify some other examples of this kind of language.

2. Do you think Goodheart's style and tone are appropriate for his subject? Why or why not?

Focus on the Patterns

1. Goodheart numbers and names three key stages of the process he describes here. Do you think the names he chooses are appropriate? If not, what names would you use instead?

2. List the individual steps in the process. Are they all presented in chronological order? Explain.

3. What transitional words and phrases does Goodheart use to link the steps in the process? Does he need any additional transitions? If so, where?

4. Besides process, what other patterns does Goodheart use in his essay?

Focus on Critical Thinking

1. Many of the details in this essay are extremely graphic. Why do you think Goodheart chose to include such harsh—even disgusting—details? Do you think these details add to the essay's appeal, or do you think they do just the opposite?

2. What factual information did you learn from this essay? Do you think you would have learned more if the information on mummification had been presented in a more serious, straightforward way? Explain.

Focus on Writing

1. Write a straightforward description, directed at an audience of middle school students, of the process of mummifying a body. Your purpose is to educate these readers about the process, making it sound as interesting as possible.

2. Think of a process you perform yourself—for example, creating a perfect party playlist or using computer software to edit your photos. Write a set of instructions for this process.

THE DOG ATE MY FLASH DRIVE, AND OTHER TALES OF WOE

Carolyn Foster Segal

Carolyn Foster Segal, Professor Emerita of English at Cedar Crest College in Pennsylvania and a lecturer at Muhlenberg College, has heard practically every student excuse for handing in late papers. In this humorous essay, she divides student excuses into categories. This article originally appeared, under the title "The Dog Ate My Disk, and Other Tales of Woe," in the *Chronicle of Higher Education*, a periodical for college teachers and administrators.

Before you read, think about the kinds of excuses you have given to instructors for late work.

Teaching Tip
Remind students to familiarize themselves with the end-of-essay questions before they read the essay.

Taped to the door of my office is a cartoon that features a cat explaining to his feline teacher, "The dog ate my homework." It is intended as a gently humorous reminder to my students that I will not accept excuses for late work, and it, like the lengthy warning on my syllabus, has had absolutely no effect. With a show of energy and creativity that would be admirable if applied to the (missing) assignments in question, my students persist, week after week, semester after semester, year after year, in offering excuses about why their work is not ready. Those reasons fall into several broad categories: the family, the best friend, the evils of dorm life, the evils of technology, and the totally bizarre.

The Family The death of the grandfather/grandmother is, of course, the grandmother of all excuses. What heartless teacher would dare to question a student's grief or veracity? What heartless student would lie, wishing death on a revered family member, just to avoid a deadline? Creative students may win extra extensions (and days off) with a little careful planning and fuller plot development, as in the sequence

1

2

WORD POWER
veracity truthfulness

of "My grandfather/grandmother is sick", "Now my grandfather/grandmother is in the hospital"; and finally, "We could all see it coming—my grandfather/grandmother is dead."

WORD POWER

conjure up to bring to mind

Another favorite excuse is "the family emergency," which (always) goes like this: "There was an emergency at home, and I had to help my family." It's a lovely sentiment, one that conjures up images of Louisa May Alcott's little women rushing off with baskets of food and copies of *Pilgrim's Progress,* but I do not understand why anyone would turn to my most irresponsible students in times of trouble. 3

The Best Friend   This heartwarming concern for others extends beyond the family to friends, as in, "My best friend was up all night and I had to (a) stay up with her in the dorm, (b) drive her to the hospital, or (c) drive to her college because (1) her boyfriend broke up with her, (2) she was throwing up blood [no one catches a cold anymore; everyone throws up blood], or (3) her grandfather/grandmother died." 4

WORD POWER

adjunct an instructor at a college or university who is not a permanent staff member; any temporary employee

At one private university where I worked as an adjunct, I heard an interesting spin that incorporated the motifs of both best friend and dead relative: "My best friend's mother killed herself." One has to admire the cleverness here: A mysterious woman in the prime of her life has allegedly committed suicide, and no professor can prove otherwise! And I admit I was moved, until finally I had to point out to my students that it was amazing how the simple act of my assigning a topic for a paper seemed to drive large numbers of otherwise happy and healthy middle-aged women to their deaths. I was careful to make that point during an off week, during which no deaths were reported. 5

The Evils of Dorm Life   These stories are usually fairly predictable; they almost always feature the evil roommate or hallmate, with my student in the role of the innocent victim; and can be summed up as follows: My roommate, who is a horrible person, likes to party, and I, who am a good person, cannot concentrate on my work when he or she is partying. Variations include stories about the two people next door who were running around and crying loudly last night because (a) one of them had boyfriend/girlfriend problems; (b) one of them was throwing up blood; or (c) someone, somewhere, died. A friend of mine in graduate school had a student who claimed that his roommate attacked him with a hammer. That, in fact, was a true story; it came out in court when the bad roommate was tried for killing his grandfather. 6

The Evils of Technology   The computer age has revolutionized the student story, inspiring almost as many new excuses as it has Internet businesses. Here are just a few electronically enhanced explanations. 7

- The computer wouldn't let me save my work.
- The printer wouldn't print.
- The printer wouldn't print this file.
- The printer wouldn't give me time to proofread.

- The printer made a black line run through all my words, and I know you can't read this, but do you still want it, or wait, here, take my flash drive. File name? I don't know what you mean.

- I swear I attached it.

- It's my roommate's computer, and she usually helps me, but she had to go to the hospital because she was throwing up blood.

- I did write to the listserv, but all my messages came back to me.

- I just found out that all my other listserv messages came up under a different name. I just want you to know that its really me who wrote all those messages, you can tel which ones our mine because I didnt use the spelcheck! But it was yours truely :) Anyway, just in case you missed those messages or dont belief its my writting. I'll repeat what I sad: I thought the last movie we watched in clas was borring.

The Totally Bizarre   I call the first story "The Pennsylvania Chain   8
Saw Episode." A commuter student called to explain why she had missed my morning class. She had gotten up early so that she would be wide awake for class. Having a bit of extra time, she walked outside to see her neighbor, who was cutting some wood. She called out to him, and he waved back to her with the saw. Wouldn't you know it, the safety catch wasn't on or was broken, and the blade flew right out of the saw and across his lawn and over her fence and across her yard and severed a tendon in her right hand. So she was calling me from the hospital, where she was waiting for surgery. Luckily, she reassured me, she had remembered to bring her paper and a stamped envelope (in a plastic bag, to avoid bloodstains) along with her in the ambulance, and a nurse was mailing everything to me even as we spoke.

That wasn't her first absence. In fact, this student had missed most   9
of the class meetings, and I had already recommended that she withdraw from the course. Now I suggested again that it might be best if she dropped the class. I didn't harp on the absences (what if even some of this story were true?). I did mention that she would need time to recuperate and that making up so much missed work might be difficult. "Oh, no," she said, "I can't drop this course. I had been planning to go on to medical school and become a surgeon, but since I won't be able to operate because of my accident, I'll have to major in English, and this course is more important than ever to me." She did come to the next class, wearing—as evidence of her recent trauma—a bedraggled Ace bandage on her left hand.

You may be thinking that nothing could top that excuse, but in fact I   10
have one more story, provided by the same student, who sent me a letter to explain why her final assignment would be late. While recuperating from her surgery, she had begun corresponding on the Internet with a man who lived in Germany. After a one-week, whirlwind Web romance, they had agreed to meet in Rome, to rendezvous (her phrase) at the papal Easter Mass. Regrettably, the time of her flight made it impossible

for her to attend class, but she trusted that I—just this once—would accept late work if the pope wrote a note.

Focus on Reading

1. Look back at the work you did when you previewed, highlighted, and annotated this essay. In the margin beside each of Segal's five categories, write a one-sentence definition of the category. (Use this format: "*The family* is the title of a group of excuses that includes. . . .")
2. TEST this essay. Does it include all the TEST elements? Think about what you would add and where you would place it.

Focus on Meaning

Teaching Tip
You may have students work collaboratively to answer some of these questions.

ESL Tip
Have native- and nonnative-speaking students work in groups or in pairs to discuss the exercises before they write their answers.

1. Why does Segal see a grandparent's death as "the grandmother of all excuses" (paragraph 2)?
2. What problems do students' friends always seem to have?
3. What are some of "the evils of dorm life"(6)?
4. What problems do computers cause for students?
5. What are some of the "totally bizarre" (8) excuses students come up with?

Focus on Strategy

1. Who is the intended audience for this essay? How can you tell?
2. Why does Segal begin her essay by describing a cartoon? Is this an effective opening strategy? Why or why not?
3. In her first paragraph, Segal includes a sentence that lists the five categories she will discuss. Do you think she needs this sentence?
4. Do you think this essay needs a formal conclusion, or is the story in its last paragraph an appropriate ending? Explain.

Focus on Language and Style

Teaching Tip
Remind students to answer all questions in complete sentences.

1. Segal uses boldface headings (**The Family**, for example) to identify her categories. Does she need these headings, or do her topic sentences clearly identify all the categories she discusses? Which sentences, if any, would need to be rewritten if the headings were not included?
2. **Sarcastic** remarks, which mean the opposite of what they say, are usually meant to make fun of something or someone. Where does Segal use sarcasm? Considering her audience, do you think this language is appropriate? Why or why not?

Focus on the Patterns

1. What categories does Segal identify in classifying students' excuses?
2. Are Segal's categories arranged in random order? If not, what determines the order in which she presents them?

3. The "totally bizarre" category is broader than the others. Do you think it needs to be divided into smaller categories? If so, what would you call these new subcategories?

4. Where does Segal use exemplification to develop her categories? Where does she use narration? What other patterns of development can you identify?

Focus on Critical Thinking

1. In addition to the excuses Segal discusses for handing in late assignments, what other excuses can you think of? Do they fit into the categories Segal has established? If not, what new category (or categories) would you add to Segal's?

2. Do you see all the excuses Segal lists as valid reasons for handing in a late paper or asking for more time to complete an assignment? Why or why not?

3. Do you think this essay is funny? Do you find it offensive in any way? How do you suppose your instructors would react to Segal's ideas?

4. What would Segal have to change if she were to rewrite this essay for her school's student newspaper? Why?

Focus on Writing

1. Write about the strangest excuse you have ever been given by someone for not doing something he or she was supposed to do. Explain the circumstances of this excuse in a humorous manner.

2. Write a letter to Carolyn Foster Segal explaining why your English paper will be late. Explain that you have read her essay about various categories of student excuses but that *your* excuse is valid.

Gender

MEN ARE FROM MARS, WOMEN ARE FROM VENUS

John Gray

Marriage counselor, seminar leader, and author John Gray has written a number of books that examine relationships between men and women. His best-known book, *Men Are from Mars, Women Are from Venus* (1992), suggests that men and women are at times so different that they might as well come from different planets. In the following excerpt from this book, Gray contrasts the different communication styles that he believes are characteristic of men and women.

Before you read, think about some of the major differences between men's and women's behavior.

WORD POWER

empathy
identification with another person's situation and feelings

The most frequently expressed complaint women have about men is 1
that men don't listen. Either a man completely ignores [a woman] when she speaks to him, or he listens for a few beats, assesses what is bothering her, and then proudly puts on his Mr. Fix-It cap and offers her a solution to make her feel better. He is confused when she doesn't appreciate this gesture of love. No matter how many times she tells him that he's not listening, he doesn't get it and keeps doing the same thing. She wants empathy, but he thinks she wants solutions.

The most frequently expressed complaint men have about women 2
is that women are always trying to change them. When a woman loves a man she feels responsible to assist him in growing and tries to help him improve the way he does things. She forms a home-improvement committee, and he becomes her primary focus. No matter how much he resists her help, she persists—waiting for any opportunity to help him or tell him what to do. She thinks she's nurturing him, while he feels he's being controlled. Instead, he wants her acceptance.

WORD POWER

nurturing supporting and encouraging

These two problems can finally be solved by first understanding why 3
men offer solutions and why women seek to improve. Let's pretend to go back in time, where by observing life on Mars and Venus—before the planets discovered one another or came to Earth—we can gain some insights into men and women.

Martians value power, competency, efficiency, and achievement. 4
They are always doing things to prove themselves and develop their power and skills. Their sense of self is defined through their ability to achieve results. They experience fulfillment primarily through success and accomplishment.

Everything on Mars is a reflection of these values. Even their 5
dress is designed to reflect their skills and competence. Police officers, soldiers, businessmen, scientists, cab drivers, technicians, and chefs all wear uniforms or at least hats to reflect their competence and power.

They don't read magazines like *Psychology Today*, *Self*, or *People*. 6
They are more concerned with outdoor activities, like hunting, fishing, and racing cars. They are interested in the news, weather, and sports and couldn't care less about romance novels and self-help books.

They are more interested in "objects" and "things" rather than people and feelings. Even today on Earth, while women fantasize about romance, men fantasize about powerful cars, faster computers, gadgets, gizmos, and new more powerful technology. Men are preoccupied with the "things" that can help them express power by creating results and achieving their goals.

Achieving goals is very important to a Martian because it is a way for 8
him to prove his competence and thus feel good about himself. And for
him to feel good about himself he must achieve these goals by himself.
Someone else can't achieve them for him. Martians pride themselves
in doing things all by themselves. Autonomy is a symbol of efficiency,
power, and competence.

WORD POWER

autonomy
independence or
freedom
unsolicited not
asked for

Understanding this Martian characteristic can help women un- 9
derstand why men resist so much being corrected or being told what
to do. To offer a man unsolicited advice is to presume that he doesn't
know what to do or that he can't do it on his own. Men are very touchy
about this, because the issue of competence is so very important to
them.

Because he is handling his problems on his own, a Martian rarely 10
talks about his problems unless he needs expert advice. He reasons:
"Why involve someone else when I can do it by myself?" He keeps his
problems to himself unless he requires help from another to find a solution. Asking for help when you can do it yourself is perceived as a sign
of weakness.

However, if he truly does need help, then it is a sign of wisdom to 11
get it. In this case, he will find someone he respects and then talk about
his problem. Talking about a problem on Mars is an invitation for advice. Another Martian feels honored by the opportunity. Automatically
he puts on his Mr. Fix-It hat, listens for a while, and then offers some
jewels of advice.

This Martian custom is one of the reasons men instinctively offer 12
solutions when women talk about problems. When a woman innocently
shares upset feelings or explores out loud the problems of her day, a
man mistakenly assumes she is looking for some expert advice. He puts
on his Mr. Fix-It hat and begins giving advice; this is his way of showing
love and of trying to help.

He wants to help her feel better by solving her problems. He wants 13
to be useful to her. He feels he can be valued and thus worthy of her love
when his abilities are used to solve her problems.

Once he has offered a solution, however, and she continues to be 14
upset it becomes increasingly difficult for him to listen because his solution is being rejected and he feels increasingly useless.

He has no idea that by just listening with empathy and interest he 15
can be supportive. He does not know that on Venus talking about problems is not an invitation to offer a solution.

Venusians have different values. They value love, communication, 16
beauty, and relationships. They spend a lot of time supporting, helping,
and nurturing one another. Their sense of self is defined through their
feelings and the quality of their relationships. They experience fulfillment through sharing and relating.

Everything on Venus reflects these values. Rather than building 17
highways and tall buildings, the Venusians are more concerned with living

together in harmony, community, and loving cooperation. Relationships are more important than work and technology. In most ways their world is the opposite of Mars.

They do not wear uniforms like the Martians (to reveal their compe- 18 tence). On the contrary, they enjoy wearing a different outfit every day, according to how they are feeling. Personal expression, especially of their feelings, is very important. They may even change outfits several times a day as their mood changes.

Communication is of primary importance. To share their personal 19 feelings is much more important than achieving goals and success. Talking and relating to one another is a source of tremendous fulfillment.

This is hard for a man to comprehend. He can come close to under- 20 standing a woman's experience of sharing and relating by comparing it to the satisfaction he feels when he wins a race, achieves a goal, or solves a problem.

Instead of being goal oriented, women are relationship oriented; 21 they are more concerned with expressing their goodness, love, and caring. Two Martians go to lunch to discuss a project or business goal; they have a problem to solve. In addition, Martians view going to a restaurant as an efficient way to approach food: no shopping, no cooking, and no washing dishes. For Venusians, going to lunch is an opportunity to nurture a relationship, for both giving support to and receiving support from a friend. Women's restaurant talk can be very open and intimate, almost like the dialogue that occurs between therapist and patient.

On Venus, everyone studies psychology and has at least a master's de- 22 gree in counseling. They are very involved in personal growth, spirituality, and everything that can nurture life, healing, and growth. Venus is covered with parks, organic gardens, shopping centers, and restaurants.

Venusians are very intuitive. They have developed this ability through 23 centuries of anticipating the needs of others. They pride themselves in being considerate of the needs and feelings of others. A sign of great love is to offer help and assistance to another Venusian without being asked.

Because proving one's competence is not as important to a Venusian, 24 offering help is not offensive, and needing help is not a sign of weakness. A man, however, may feel offended because when a woman offers advice he doesn't feel she trusts his ability to do it himself.

A woman has no conception of this male sensitivity because for her 25 it is another feather in her hat if someone offers to help her. It makes her feel loved and cherished. But offering help to a man can make him feel incompetent, weak, and even unloved.

On Venus it is a sign of caring to give advice and suggestions. 26 Venusians firmly believe that when something is working it can always work better. Their nature is to want to improve things. When they care about someone, they freely point out what can be improved and suggest how to do it. Offering advice and constructive criticism is an act of love.

Mars is very different. Martians are more solution oriented. If some- 27
thing is working, their motto is don't change it. Their instinct is to leave
it alone if it is working. "Don't fix it unless it is broken" is a common
expression.

When a woman tries to improve a man, he feels she is trying to fix 28
him. He receives the message that he is broken. She doesn't realize her
caring attempts to help him may humiliate him. She mistakenly thinks
she is just helping him to grow.

Focus on Reading

1. Look back at the work you did when you previewed, highlighted,
   and annotated this essay. In the margins of the essay, number the
   specific characteristics of men and women that Gray identifies.

2. Review the characteristics you identified in question 1, and star the
   ones you see as most important in establishing the fundamental differences between men and women.

Focus on Meaning

1. What specific character traits and habits does Gray associate with
   men?

2. What character traits and habits does he associate with women?

3. Does Gray see one set of characteristics as superior to the other, or does
   he consider men's and women's characteristics to be comparable?

Teaching Tip
You may have students
work collaboratively to
answer some of these
questions.

Focus on Strategy

1. What serious point is Gray making by characterizing men as
   Martians and women as Venusians?

2. If you were going to add a more fully developed conclusion to sum
   up Gray's point about the differences between men and women,
   what kind of closing strategy would you use? Do you think the
   essay needs such a conclusion?

ESL Tip
Have native- and nonnative-
speaking students work
in groups or in pairs to
discuss the exercises
before they write their
answers.

Focus on Language and Style

1. Do you think Gray's choice of the labels *Martians* and *Venusians* is
   appropriate? Explain.

2. What other labels could Gray have used to contrast men and women?

Teaching Tip
Remind students to
answer all questions in
complete sentences.

Focus on the Patterns

1. This essay is a subject-by-subject comparison. How does Gray signal the movement from the first subject to the second? Why do
   you suppose he chose to write a subject-by-subject rather than a
   point-by-point comparison?

2. Create an outline that arranges Gray's points as a point-by-point comparison. What advantages and disadvantages does this organization have?

3. Where does Gray use definition? Where does he use exemplification?

Focus on Critical Thinking

1. Do you think Gray is stereotyping men and women? Explain.

2. Regardless of how you answered the previous question, do you agree with Gray that men and women seem to be from two different planets? Why or why not?

Focus on Writing

1. Are young boys and girls also from two different planets? Take a position on this issue, trying to account for the differences you identify between boys and girls.

2. Identify one general area in which you believe men's and women's attitudes, behavior, or expectations are very different—for example, dating, careers, eating habits, sports, housekeeping, or driving. Write an essay (serious or humorous) that explores the differences you identify.

I WANT A WIFE

Judy Brady

Writer and activist Judy Brady helped found the Toxic Links Coalition, an organization dedicated to exposing the dangers of environmental toxins and their impact on public health. She was also active in the women's movement, and her classic essay "I Want a Wife" was published in the first issue of *Ms.* magazine (1971).

Before you read, think about how you would define the word *wife*.

I belong to that classification of people known as wives. I am A Wife. And, not altogether incidentally, I am a mother. 1

Not too long ago a male friend of mine appeared on the scene fresh from a recent divorce. He had one child, who is, of course, with his ex-wife. He is looking for another wife. As I thought about him while I was ironing one evening, it suddenly occurred to me that I, too, would like to have a wife. Why do I want a wife? 2

I would like to go back to school so that I can become economically independent, support myself, and, if need be, support those dependent upon me. I want a wife who will work and send me to school. And while I am going to school I want a wife to take care of my children. I want a wife to keep track of the children's doctor and dentist appointments. 3

And to keep track of mine, too. I want a wife to make sure my children eat properly and are kept clean. I want a wife who will wash the children's clothes and keep them mended. I want a wife who is a good nurturant attendant to my children, who arranges for their schooling, makes sure that they have an adequate social life with their peers, takes them to the park, the zoo, etc. I want a wife who takes care of the children when they are sick, a wife who arranges to be around when the children need special care, because, of course, I cannot miss classes at school. My wife must arrange to lose time at work and not lose the job. It may mean a small cut in my wife's income from time to time, but I guess I can tolerate that. Needless to say, my wife will arrange and pay for the care of the children while my wife is working.

I want a wife who will take care of *my* physical needs. I want a wife who will keep my house clean. A wife who will pick up after my children, a wife who will pick up after me. I want a wife who will keep my clothes clean, ironed, mended, replaced when need be, and who will see to it that my personal things are kept in their proper place so that I can find what I need the minute I need it. I want a wife who cooks the meals, a wife who is a *good* cook. I want a wife who will plan the menus, do the necessary grocery shopping, prepare the meals, serve them pleasantly, and then do the cleaning up while I do my studying. I want a wife who will care for me when I am sick and sympathize with my pain and loss of time from school. I want a wife to go along when our family takes a vacation so that someone can continue to care for me and my children when I need a rest and change of scene.

I want a wife who will not bother me with rambling complaints about a wife's duties. But I want a wife who will listen to me when I feel the need to explain a rather difficult point I have come across in my course of studies. And I want a wife who will type my papers for me when I have written them.

I want a wife who will take care of the details of my social life. When my wife and I are invited out by my friends, I want a wife who will take care of the babysitting arrangements. When I meet people at school that I like and want to entertain, I want a wife who will have the house clean, will prepare a special meal, serve it to me and my friends, and not interrupt when I talk about things that interest me and my friends. I want a wife who will have arranged that the children are fed and ready for bed before my guests arrive so that the children do not bother us. I want a wife who takes care of the needs of my guests so that they feel comfortable, who makes sure that they have an ashtray, that they are passed the hors d'oeuvres, that they are offered a second helping of the food, that their wine glasses are replenished when necessary, that their coffee is served to them as they like it. And I want a wife who knows that sometimes I need a night out by myself.

I want a wife who is sensitive to my sexual needs, a wife who makes love passionately and eagerly when I feel like it, a wife who makes sure

4

5

6

7

WORD POWER

nurturant providing physical and emotional care

WORD POWER

replenished made full or complete again

WORD POWER

adherence
steady or faithful
attachment

monogamy having
one spouse or sexual
partner at a time

that I am satisfied. And, of course, I want a wife who will not demand sexual attention when I am not in the mood for it. I want a wife who assumes the complete responsibility for birth control, because I do not want more children. I want a wife who will remain sexually faithful to me so that I do not have to clutter up my intellectual life with jealousies. And I want a wife who understands that *my* sexual needs may entail more than strict adherence to monogamy. I must, after all, be able to relate to people as fully as possible.

If, by chance, I find another person more suitable as a wife than the wife I already have, I want the liberty to replace my present wife with another one. Naturally, I will expect a fresh new life; my wife will take the children and be solely responsible for them so that I am left free.   8

When I am through with school and have a job, I want my wife to quit working and remain at home so that my wife can more fully and completely take care of a wife's duties.   9

My God, who *wouldn't* want a wife?   10

Focus on Reading

1. Look back at the work you did when you previewed, highlighted, and annotated this essay. Review all the characteristics of a wife that Brady mentions. Then, in the margin beside paragraph 1, write a one-sentence definition of *wife* that summarizes these characteristics.

2. In the margin beside paragraph 10, answer the question Brady asks.

Focus on Meaning

1. How is Brady's definition of *wife* like and unlike your own?

2. What main idea do you think Brady wants to communicate to her readers? Does she ever actually state this idea? If not, do you think she should?

Focus on Strategy

1. Write a thesis statement for this essay.

2. Brady ends her essay with a **rhetorical question**, a question readers are not expected to answer. Is this an effective concluding strategy? Why or why not?

Focus on Language and Style

1. Brady repeats the word *wife* over and over again. Why? Does this repetition strengthen or weaken her essay?

2. Can you think of other words Brady could have used instead of *wife*? How might using these alternative words change her essay?

Teaching Tip
You may have students work collaboratively to answer some of these questions.

ESL Tip
Have native- and nonnative-speaking students work in groups or in pairs to discuss the exercises before they write their answers.

Teaching Tip
Remind students to answer all questions in complete sentences.

Focus on the Patterns

1. Does Brady include a **formal definition** of *wife* anywhere in her essay? If so, where? If not, do you think she should?

2. Brady develops her definition of *wife* with examples. What are some of her most important examples?

3. Besides exemplification, what other patterns of development does Brady use to develop her definition?

Focus on Critical Thinking

1. Brady's essay was written in 1971. Does her definition of *wife* seem dated, or does it still seem accurate (at least in some respects) to you?

2. Would you like to have the kind of wife Brady defines? Why or why not?

Focus on Writing

1. Assume you are Brady's husband and feel unjustly attacked by her essay. Write her a letter in which you define *husband,* using as many examples as you can to show how overworked and underappreciated you are.

2. Write an essay in which you define your ideal teacher, parent, spouse, or boss. Use narration, description, and exemplification to develop your definition.

WHY WOMEN SOLDIERS DON'T BELONG ON THE FRONT LINES

D. B. Grady

D. B. Grady is the pseudonym of freelance writer and novelist David Brown. He is coauthor of *The Command: Deep Inside the President's Secret Army* (2012) and *Deep State: Inside the Government Secrecy Industry* (2013). He also writes for *The Atlantic* and contributes regularly to *The Week* and *mental_floss* magazines. Grady graduated from Louisiana State University in 2002 and is a former U.S. Army paratrooper and a veteran of the war in Afghanistan. In this article, originally published in *The Week* in January 2013, Grady develops an argument against women serving in combat.

Before you read, think about your own ideas about women in combat.

Yesterday, word leaked that the secretary of defense intends to lift re-   1
strictions on women in combat. I wish I could declare that this is a bold

stroke for equality, and that it's about time the Pentagon transcended outmoded sexist thinking. I wish I could write that women will lead the infantry to new, greater glories on the battlefield—the likes of which haven't been seen since Alexander won the Battle of the Hydaspes. But I cannot.

There is an uncomfortable truth about women in combat, and it starts at Basic Training. In the Army, a couple of times a year and before attending any formal schools, you take a physical fitness test. There are always two lines: one for men and one for women. If you want to pass the test—and you have to pass the test—an 18-year-old male has to perform 42 push-ups, 53 sit-ups, and run two miles in 15 minutes and 54 seconds. That's to score only the embarrassing minimum on the test. In the other line, a passing 18-year-old female need only to achieve 19 push-ups and cross the two-mile mark at 18 minutes, 54 seconds. (In fact, a *perfect* score for an 18-year-old female is basically equal to the *minimum* for males.) The two standards don't exist simply because the Army is chivalrous; rather, they exist because, except for extreme outliers, a woman at peak physical fitness is neither as strong nor as fast as a man in similar shape.

A platoon is only as strong as its weakest member. To be sure, there are many, many jobs where gender is irrelevant. Women are already in fighter jets and behind the trigger of M240s that are mounted to the sides of Black Hawk helicopters, and they are superb at their jobs—as good as any man in any unit. But on the ground, "kitted up" with 75 pounds of body armor, ammunition, and supplies, in a truck, climbing in, jumping out, on your feet, on the ground, running, dragging, day after day, night after night, week after week, for months on end—and still expected to be ready for the worst at any given time? We cannot say that gender does not matter—especially considering the difference of baselines and peaks of physical performance between the sexes in the best conditions.

Anyone who believes that the physical standard required of a combat soldier is somehow negotiable is terribly wrong. It's not a matter of "having enough heart" or having a sufficiently compelling story—this isn't television. For almost every job in the military, an extra few push-ups don't matter. There is one job, however, where it not only matters, but is quite literally the only thing that matters, and that job is performed in a place that does not offer latitude or forgiveness.

The fact is—however unfair, however much it pains us to admit it—in some areas, men and women are not equal. Is it worth checking a box marked "Equality" at the expense of the operational effectiveness of combat units? Is it worth putting young men at risk so that we, the enlightened Western liberals, might have a new accomplishment to discuss over *gougères* at cocktail parties? This week, the Obama administration says, yes, that's perfectly okay. Accordingly, a platoon can and will be less combat-effective in the name of equality.

There's another issue with women in combat roles that needs to 6
be faced. The ranks are made up of high school graduates. Many of
these young men and women have never been away from home, and
are suddenly not only far, far away, but doing a very stressful job
in close quarters with one another. Of course there are going to be
romantic interludes; it's human nature. The leadership tries to stop
it, but it's a pretty hopeless cause. During my time in Afghanistan, I
watched it happen to young men in my company. It was distracting
for everyone involved, but at least the distraction was kept away from
the front lines. Now the plan is to spread it across the combat zone.

It would be silly to argue that in combat, young soldiers will be dis- 7
tracted by romance. They are professionals and will do their duty. But
between engagements, during downtime—periods where stress should
be at its lowest point—we are now introducing the most stressful non-
combat-related element imaginable.

At what gain? The Army is not hurting for infantrymen or frontline 8
soldiers. Indeed, with the war winding down, the Army is actively working to get rid of people. Units will not see an improvement in physical
readiness, nor will cohesion improve. Lives will be put in danger. Today
a lot of people who wear power suits feel a lot better about themselves.
The people who wear uniforms? I'm sure they'll figure something out.
They don't have any choice.

Focus on Reading

1. Look back at the work you did when you previewed, highlighted,
   and annotated this essay. Did you underline the key objections
   Grady has to women serving on the front lines? If not, do so now. If
   you like, you can star or number these objections to help you keep
   track of them.

2. Skim the essay's second paragraph. In the margin, write down a
   question you would like to ask about the paragraph's content.

Focus on Meaning

1. Why, according to Grady, don't "women soldiers . . . belong on the
   front lines"? Construct an informal outline that lists his key supporting points.

2. What is the "uncomfortable truth about women in combat" (paragraph 2)?

3. Grady begins paragraph 3 with the sentence, "A platoon is only as
   strong as its weakest member." What does he mean? How does this
   statement support his position on the issue he examines?

4. What does Grady mean in paragraph 5 when he asks, "Is it worth
   checking a box marked 'Equality' at the expense of the operational
   effectiveness of combat units?" How would you answer this question?

Focus on Strategy

1. Write a one-sentence thesis statement for this essay. Use this format: "Women do not belong on the front lines because . . . ."
2. Reread paragraph 1. What prompted Grady to write this essay?
3. Since the decision to lift restrictions against women in combat had already been made by the time he wrote this essay, what do you think Grady hoped to accomplish?

Focus on Language and Style

1. Reread the first sentence of paragraph 4. Rewrite it to make it less likely to alienate readers who disagree with Grady.
2. Throughout this essay, Grady uses short sentences to emphasize certain key ideas. Identify some of these short sentences, and evaluate their effectiveness.

Focus on the Patterns

1. Grady's essay is structured as an argument. Where does he mention objections to his position? Does he refute these objections?
2. Where does Grady use exemplification? Where does he use comparison and contrast? Does he use any other patterns to develop his essay?
3. Using Grady's information, make a chart comparing men's and women's physical abilities. Then, write a sentence summarizing the differences.

Focus on Critical Thinking

1. Which of Grady's objections to women in combat makes the most sense to you? Why? Which would you challenge? Why?
2. In paragraph 6, Grady mentions his "time in Afghanistan." How does this affect your response to his essay? Would your reaction be different if he had said, "When I served in Afghanistan . . . "? Why or why not?
3. How do you think Grady's mention in paragraph 5 of "checking a box marked 'Equality'" might affect readers who take the opposite position on the issue of women in combat? How might they respond to this characterization of their position?

Focus on Writing

1. Write an essay with the title, "Women Soldiers Belong on the Front Lines." (You may quote Grady where appropriate.)
2. Write an essay with the title, "Why Men Don't Belong in _____." Your essay can be serious or humorous.

Current Issues

THE SEAT NOT TAKEN

John Edgar Wideman

Teaching Tip
A reading such as "The Seat Not Taken" may create some racial tension in the classroom. Before assigning the reading, decide whether you are ready to handle students' possible reactions.

John Edgar Wideman has published numerous books, both fiction and nonfiction, as well as articles in publications such as the *New York Times*, *The New Yorker*, *Vogue*, *Emerge*, and *Esquire*. Wideman has received the O. Henry Award, the American Book Award for Fiction, the Lannan Literary Fellowship for Fiction, the PEN/Faulkner Award for Fiction (twice—the first person so honored), and a MacArthur Fellowship. He is currently professor of Africana Studies and Literary Arts at Brown University. In "The Seat Not Taken," an op-ed article first published in the *New York Times*, Wideman reflects on his weekly train commute and raises questions about the motives his fellow commuters have for not sitting in the empty seat beside him.

Before you read, think about the factors you consider when you choose a seat on a plane, bus, or train.

At least twice a week I ride Amtrak's high-speed Acela train from my 1 home in New York City to my teaching job in Providence, R.I. The route passes through a region of the country populated by, statistics tell us, a significant segment of its most educated, affluent, sophisticated and enlightened citizens.

Over the last four years, excluding summers, I have conducted a 2 casual sociological experiment in which I am both participant and observer. It's a survey I began not because I had some specific point to prove by gathering data to support it, but because I couldn't avoid becoming aware of an obvious, disquieting truth.

WORD POWER
disquieting upsetting

Almost invariably, after I have hustled aboard early and occupied 3 one half of a vacant double seat in the usually crowded quiet car, the empty place next to me will remain empty for the entire trip.

I'm a man of color, one of the few on the train and often the only 4 one in the quiet car, and I've concluded that color explains a lot about my experience. Unless the car is nearly full, color will determine, even if it doesn't exactly clarify, why 9 times out of 10 people will shun a free seat if it means sitting beside me.

WORD POWER
shun to avoid

Giving them and myself the benefit of the doubt, I can rule out ex- 5 cessive body odor or bad breath; a hateful, intimidating scowl; hip-hop clothing; or a hideous deformity as possible objections to my person. Considering also the cost of an Acela ticket, the fact that I display no visible indications of religious preference and, finally, the numerous external signs of middle-class membership I share with the majority of the passengers, color appears to be a sufficient reason for the behavior I have recorded.

Of course, I'm not registering a complaint about the privilege, con- 6
ferred upon me by color, to enjoy the luxury of an extra seat to myself. I relish the opportunity to spread out, savor the privacy and quiet and work or gaze at the scenic New England woods and coast. It's a particularly appealing perk if I compare the train to air travel or any other mode of transportation, besides walking or bicycling, for negotiating the mercilessly congested Northeast Corridor. Still, in the year 2010, with an African-descended, brown president in the White House and a nation confidently asserting its passage into a postracial era, it strikes me as odd to ride beside a vacant seat, just about every time I embark on a three-hour journey each way, from home to work and back.

I admit I look forward to the moment when other passengers, 7
searching for a good seat, or any seat at all on the busiest days, stop anxiously prowling the quiet-car aisle, the moment when they have all settled elsewhere, including the ones who willfully blinded themselves to the open seat beside me or were unconvinced of its availability when they passed by. I savor that precise moment when the train sighs and begins to glide away from Penn or Providence Station, and I'm able to say to myself, with relative assurance, that the vacant place beside me is free, free at last, or at least free until the next station. I can relax, prop open my briefcase or rest papers, snacks or my arm in the unoccupied seat.

WORD POWER

bounty generous gift

But the very pleasing moment of anticipation casts a shadow, be- 8
cause I can't accept the bounty of an extra seat without remembering why it's empty, without wondering if its emptiness isn't something quite sad. And quite dangerous, also, if left unexamined. Posters in the train, the station, the subway warn: if you see something, say something.

Focus on Reading

1. Look back at the work you did when you previewed, highlighted, and annotated this essay. Circle the words in this essay that refer specifically to race.

2. In the margin beside paragraph 5, list a few reasons you might have for not wanting to sit next to a particular person on a train.

Focus on Meaning

Teaching Tip
You may have students work collaboratively to answer these questions.

1. What "casual sociological experiment" (paragraph 2) does Wideman conduct? What are the results of this experiment? How does he interpret these results?

2. Why does Wideman see the empty seat beside him as not simply sad but also dangerous? Do you think he is right to see it this way, or do you think he is overreacting? Why?

Focus on Strategy

1. What do you think Wideman hoped to accomplish in this essay? For example, do you think he was trying to change readers' minds—or their behavior? To issue a warning? To suggest a change in Amtrak policy? Do you think this essay accomplishes his goal?

2. Why does Wideman end his essay with the words "if you see something, say something" (8)? In what context does this sentence usually appear? What is the "something" he wants people to say in this case?

ESL Tip
Have native- and nonnative-speaking students work in groups or in pairs to discuss the exercises before they write their answers.

Focus on Language and Style

1. Do you think Wideman should have included more references to his own race (and to the races of his fellow passengers)? Why or why not?

2. In paragraph 1, Wideman suggests that his fellow passengers are some of the United States's "most educated, affluent, sophisticated and enlightened citizens." What point is he trying to make by using these adjectives to characterize the other passengers?

Teaching Tip
Remind students to answer all questions in complete sentences.

Focus on the Patterns

1. This essay focuses on examining causes. What do you think might be the *effects* (on Wideman and on society in general) of the behavior he describes?

2. Do you see this essay's structure as primarily narrative, cause-and-effect, or an argument? Explain.

Focus on Critical Thinking

1. Consider all the reasons you might have (apart from the reasons Wideman lists in paragraph 5) for choosing not to sit next to a particular person on a train, bus, or plane. Might any of these reasons explain why the seat beside Wideman has so often remained empty?

2. In paragraph 5, Wideman mentions the "numerous external signs of middle-class membership" that he, like the other passengers, exhibits. What do you think these "external signs" are? Why do you think he mentions them?

Focus on Writing

1. How do you account for the empty seat beside Wideman on so many train trips? Do you agree with his analysis of the situation, or can you think of other explanations that he has not considered? Write a cause-and-effect essay responding to Wideman's article and its reflections on race.

2. What kinds of people would you try to avoid sitting next to on a train? Why? Do you see your objections as reasonable, or do you

think some of your objections might be considered prejudice? Write an essay in which you explain your objections as clearly and thoughtfully as possible.

TWEET LESS, KISS MORE

Bob Herbert

Bob Herbert studied journalism at Empire State College and later taught journalism at Brooklyn College and Columbia University. He began his career as a reporter in 1970, working for the Newark *Star Ledger* and later the New York *Daily News*. For eighteen years he wrote a twice-weekly op-ed column for the *New York Times*. Herbert has won numerous journalism awards, including the Meyer Berger Award for coverage of New York City and the American Society of Newspaper Editors award for distinguished newspaper writing. He is the author of *Promises Betrayed: Waking Up from the American Dream* (2005). In this essay from a *New York Times* opinion column, Herbert encourages readers to take a break from technology and life's fast pace to enjoy personal connections and a bit of silence.

Before you read, think about the last time you had to take a break from technology.

I was driving from Washington to New York one afternoon on Interstate 1
95 when a car came zooming up behind me, really flying. I could see in the rearview mirror that the driver was talking on her cellphone.

I was about to move to the center lane to get out of her way when 2
she suddenly swerved into that lane herself to pass me on the right—still chatting away. She continued moving dangerously from one lane to another as she sped up the highway.

A few days later, I was talking to a guy who commutes every day 3
between New York and New Jersey. He props up his laptop on the front seat so he can watch DVDs while he's driving.

"I only do it in traffic," he said. "It's no big deal." 4

Beyond the obvious safety issues, why does anyone want, or need, 5
to be talking constantly on the phone or watching movies (or texting) while driving? I hate to sound so 20th century, but what's wrong with just listening to the radio? The blessed wonders of technology are overwhelming us. We don't control them; they control us.

We've got cellphones and BlackBerrys and Kindles and iPads, and 6
we're e-mailing and text-messaging and chatting and tweeting—I used to call it Twittering until I was corrected by high school kids who patiently explained to me, as if I were the village idiot, that the correct term is tweeting. Twittering, tweeting—whatever it is, it sounds like a nervous disorder.

This is all part of what I think is one of the weirder aspects of our 7
culture: a heightened freneticism that seems to demand that we be
doing, at a minimum, two or three things every single moment of every
hour that we're awake. Why is multitasking considered an admirable
talent? We could just as easily think of it as a neurotic inability to concentrate for more than three seconds.

WORD POWER

aspects parts of
something

freneticism quality of
being wild or frantic

Why do we have to check our e-mail so many times a day, or keep 8
our ears constantly attached, as if with Krazy Glue, to our cellphones?
When you watch the news on cable television, there are often additional
stories being scrolled across the bottom of the screen, stock market results blinking on the right of the screen, and promos for upcoming features on the left. These extras often block significant parts of the main
item we're supposed to be watching.

A friend of mine told me about an engagement party that she had 9
attended. She said it was lovely: a delicious lunch and plenty of Cham-
pagne toasts. But all the guests had their cellphones on the luncheon
tables and had text-messaged their way through the entire event.

WORD POWER

hyperactive overly
active

Enough already with this hyperactive behavior, this techno-tyranny 10
and nonstop freneticism. We need to slow down and take a deep breath.

I'm not opposed to the remarkable technological advances of the 11
past several years. I don't want to go back to typewriters and carbon
paper and yellowing clips from the newspaper morgue. I just think that
we should treat technology like any other tool. We should control it,
bending it to our human purposes.

WORD POWER

morgue a collection
of reference works and
files

Let's put down at least some of these gadgets and spend a little time 12
just being ourselves. One of the essential problems of our society is that
we have a tendency, amid all the craziness that surrounds us, to lose
sight of what is truly human in ourselves, and that includes our own
individual needs—those very special, mostly nonmaterial things that
would fulfill us, give meaning to our lives, enlarge us, and enable us to
more easily embrace those around us.

There's a character in the August Wilson play *Joe Turner's Come and* 13
Gone who says everyone has a song inside of him or her, and that you
lose sight of that song at your peril. If you get out of touch with your
song, forget how to sing it, you're bound to end up frustrated and dissatisfied.

As this character says, recalling a time when he was out of touch 14
with his own song, "Something wasn't making my heart smooth and
easy."

I don't think we can stay in touch with our song by constantly Twit- 15
tering or tweeting, or thumbing out messages on our BlackBerrys, or
piling up virtual friends on Facebook.

We need to reduce the speed limits of our lives. We need to savor the 16
trip. Leave the cellphone at home every once in awhile. Try kissing more
and tweeting less. And stop talking so much.

Listen. 17

Other people have something to say, too. And when they don't, that is glorious silence that you hear will have more to say to you than you ever imagined. That is when you will begin to hear your song. That's when your best thoughts take hold, and you become really you.

Focus on Reading

1. Look back at the work you did when you previewed, highlighted, and annotated this essay. Underline the questions Herbert asks in paragraphs 5, 7, and 8. In the margins, write brief answers to these questions.

2. Put a star in the margin beside Herbert's thesis statement.

Focus on Meaning

1. What aspects of modern technology does Herbert find upsetting? Why? What do you think he objects to most?

2. Herbert obviously doesn't want people to stop using electronic communication altogether. What *does* he want? Do you think what he proposes is realistic? Why or why not?

Focus on Strategy

1. Herbert begins his essay with two anecdotes. How do these stories prepare readers for his thesis? What is his thesis? Where does he state it?

2. Why do you think Herbert isolates the word "Listen" in its own paragraph (17)?

Focus on Language and Style

1. In paragraph 5, Herbert says, "The blessed wonders of technology are overwhelming us." Why does he use the word *blessed* here? What other word might he have used instead?

2. Herbert characterizes our use of electronic communication with a number of negative words—for example, *neurotic* (7). Find some other negative words and phrases used to describe what Herbert sees as our overuse of such technology. Do you think such language helps him make his case, or do you think it might provoke a negative reaction in readers? Explain.

Focus on the Patterns

1. What evidence does Herbert offer to support his argument? How effective is this support? What other evidence could he have offered?

2. In paragraph 11, Herbert discusses an argument against his thesis. How effectively does he refute this argument? What other opposing arguments could he have addressed?

3. Where does Herbert use narration? Exemplification? How do these patterns of development strengthen his argument?

Focus on Critical Thinking

1. Referring to a character in a play by August Wilson, Herbert says that "everyone has a song inside him or her, and . . . you lose sight of that song at your peril" (13). According to Herbert, what does this observation have to do with the way we communicate today? Do you agree with him?

2. Do you think Herbert is exaggerating the importance of the problem he discusses? Why or why not? (Note that in paragraph 6, he indicates that he is not very familiar with social media.)

Focus on Writing

1. Do you agree with Herbert that people should be less dependent on technology? Write an essay supporting your position on this issue. Try to refute at least one opposing argument.

2. Write an editorial for your school newspaper in which you propose a one-day holiday from all electronic communication. Be sure to include a clear thesis statement, and use specific examples from your own experience to support your thesis.

THE GUNS OF ACADEME

Adam Winkler

Adam Winkler is a professor of law at the University of California, Los Angeles, and his work has been used in important Supreme Court cases. A contributor to CNN, the *New York Times*, the *Los Angeles Times*, the *Wall Street Journal*, the *Daily Beast*, and the *Huffington Post*, he has authored the book *Gunfight: The Battle over the Right to Bear Arms in America* (2011). Winkler specializes in American constitutional law, including the right to bear arms, which serves as the topic of this essay.

Before you read, think about your own views about a person's right to bear arms.

By Monday, Gov. Jan Brewer of Arizona must decide whether to sign 1 a bill partly lifting her state's ban on guns on college and university campuses. Gun advocates insist that will make campuses safer by discouraging mass killers and giving students the ability to fight back. Gun control proponents warn the law will lead to more lethal violence.

WORD POWER

advocates people who defend or maintain a cause

proponents supporters

Both sides are probably wrong. Gun violence at colleges and 2
universities—there are fewer than 20 homicides on campus per year—
will probably not be affected much, one way or another. What is really
at stake is America's gun culture.

Colleges and universities have long been gun-free zones. In 1745, 3
Yale adopted a policy punishing any student who "shall keep a gun or
pistol, or fire one in the college-yard or college." Today, most universities, public and private, prohibit anyone but authorized security and
law enforcement officers from bringing guns onto campuses. Arizona
would join Utah as the only states to require public colleges to permit guns on campus, but Texas and eight other states are considering
similar laws.

Many find the idea of students with guns shocking. They fear that 4
undergraduates are too young to handle firearms responsibly and that
the presence of guns will lead to the deadly escalation of minor disagree-
ments. Others worry about the volatile mix of guns and alcohol. Glocks
don't belong at a frat party.

Even if the bans are lifted, however, few students will tote guns 5
around the quad. Under federal law, those under 21 cannot buy guns
from a dealer. And most states require a permit to carry a concealed
weapon. (Arizona only requires such a permit for persons under 21.)

As a professor, I'd feel safer if guns were not permitted on campus. 6
I worry more about being the target of a student upset about failing
grades than about a mass killer roaming the hallways.

But there is little evidence to support my gut feeling. Utah, for ex- 7
ample, has not seen an increase in campus gun violence since it changed
its law in 2006. And a disturbed student can simply sneak a gun on
campus in his backpack, as the Virginia Tech killer did in 2007. Indeed,
lost in the debate is the fact that guns, being easy to conceal, are almost
certainly on campus already.

On the other hand, gun rights advocates are too quick to assume 8
that laws allowing guns on campus will discourage mass murderers.
Arizona has among the most liberal gun-carrying laws in the nation,
but that didn't prevent Jared L. Loughner from shooting Representative
Gabrielle Giffords and killing six other people in Tucson in January.
Nor did permissive carry laws lead to people defending themselves by
shooting back. (Mr. Loughner was tackled and brought to the ground by
unarmed bystanders.)

Even if a student with a gun can use it to defend against a mass 9
murderer, it's hardly clear that anyone, including the armed student, is
made safer. Policemen or other students with guns might not be able
to differentiate among gunmen, putting the person defending herself
at risk of being shot by mistake. Even well-trained gun owners suffer
enormous mental stress in a shootout, making hitting a target extremely
difficult.

WORD POWER

volatile likely to lead
to sudden change or
violence

tote to carry

Gun control groups are fighting to retain the bans. This is one of the few areas in which they've had success in recent years. There have been more than 40 attempts to lift the bans in 24 states, and nearly all have failed. Even the proposed Arizona law was a victory of sorts, as the final bill omitted provisions allowing guns in classrooms; it would permit guns only on campus streets and sidewalks. **10**

Yet gun rights proponents are redoubling their repeal efforts. They aren't reacting to a wave of violence on campus. The true motivation is to remove the stigma attached to guns. Many in the gun rights movement believe there should be no gun-free zones and seek to make the public possession of firearms a matter of course. The protesters who last year carried guns into Starbucks shops and Tea Party rallies had the same goal. They weren't expecting to defend themselves; they were aiming to build broader public acceptance of guns. **11**

> **WORD POWER**
> **motivation** driving force; goal
> **stigma** a mark of disgrace or infamy

Exposure can breed tolerance. Arguably, that is exactly what's behind the growing acceptance of gays and lesbians. The visibility of gay couples in society and popular culture has led many Americans to realize that homosexuality is not wrong. Gun advocates are betting the same can happen with firearms. **12**

The strategy, however, is risky. Teenagers might begin to see carrying a gun as a mark of adulthood, like smoking and drinking. Without the maturity of age, they might turn to violence too quickly. **13**

Gun rights advocates are willing to take these risks because colleges are where the next generation of America's leaders will be produced. What better place to affect people's attitudes about guns than the very institutions responsible for teaching our most cherished values and ideals? **14**

> **WORD POWER**
> **cherished** treasured, precious

> **Teaching Tip**
> You may have students work collaboratively to answer some of these questions.

Focus on Reading

1. Look back at the work you did when you previewed, highlighted, and annotated the essay. Did you highlight and number Winkler's key points? If not, do so now.

2. Write "refutation" in the margin next to the paragraph (or paragraphs) in which Winkler refutes opposing arguments.

Focus on Meaning

1. Supporters of lifting the ban on guns from Arizona's college campuses say that it will make colleges safer. Gun control advocates claim that lifting the ban will cause more violence. Why does Winkler think that both sides in this debate are wrong?

2. In paragraph 5, Winkler says that if bans against guns were lifted, few students would carry them. According to him, why is this so? Do you think he is right?

3. According to Winkler, what really motivates people who want to allow guns on campus? Do you agree?

Focus on Strategy

1. Where does Winkler state his thesis? How does paragraph 1 set the stage for this thesis?

2. Do you think Winkler expects his readers to be for or against allowing guns on college campuses? How can you tell?

3. What point does Winkler emphasize in his conclusion? Why? How else could he have ended his essay?

Focus on Language and Style

1. What does *academe* mean in the essay's title? What are the strengths and weaknesses of this title? What other titles could Winkler have used?

2. In paragraphs 5 and 6, Winkler shifts from third person (*he, she*) to first person (*I*). Why?

3. In paragraph 12, Winkler compares the acceptance of gays and lesbians to the acceptance of guns. Is this comparison fair? Is it logical?

4. What does Winkler mean when he says that exposure to guns "can breed tolerance" (12)? Do you think he is right?

Focus on the Patterns

1. In paragraph 3, Winkler includes a narrative paragraph that discusses how colleges traditionally have banned firearms from campus. What does this paragraph add to his argument?

2. Winkler relies on evidence from his own experience to support his argument. Should he also have included statistics and expert opinion? Why or why not?

3. What arguments against his position does Winkler discuss? How does he refute these arguments? Is he successful?

Focus on Critical Thinking

1. The Second Amendment to the Constitution says, "A well regulated militia being necessary to the security of a free state, the right of the people to keep and bear arms shall not be infringed." What do you think that this sentence means? Do you think that banning guns violates a person's Second Amendment rights?

2. Most leaders of universities across the country have come out against allowing guns on campus. Do you agree or disagree? Do you think allowing guns on campus will make them safer or more dangerous?

3. In 2013, Kutztown University, in Pennsylvania, allowed students with permits to carry guns in certain areas of campus "for compelling

reasons of . . . personal safety." In what areas of a college campus do you think guns should be allowed? In what areas should they be prohibited? Why?

Focus on Writing

1. In paragraph 9, Winkler says, "Even if a student with a gun can use it to defend against a mass murderer, it's hardly clear that anyone, including the armed student, is made safer." Winkler then mentions two reasons why he thinks this is so. Read the paragraph, and then write an essay in which you agree or disagree with Winkler's points. Make sure that your essay has a clear thesis statement and that you address each of his points individually.

2. Gun violence is a fact of life in many American cities—for example, Philadelphia, Chicago, and Detroit. Assume that you have been asked to write a blog post aimed specifically at teenagers. As your thesis, use Winkler's point that, contrary to what some young people might think, carrying a gun is not a sign of adulthood or maturity. Be specific, and support your own ideas and experiences with facts, statistics, and examples.

Acknowledgments

Julia Alvarez. "What Is a Quinceañera?" From *Once Upon a Quinceañera: Coming of Age in the USA*. Copyright © 2007 by Julia Alvarez. Published by Plume, an imprint of The Penguin Group (USA), Inc. and in hardcover by Viking. By permission of Susan Bergholz Literary Services, New York, NY and Lamy, NM. All rights reserved.

Julia Angwin. "How Facebook Is Making Friending Obsolete." From *The Wall Street Journal*, December 15, 2009. Copyright © 2009 by Dow Jones & Company. All rights reserved Worldwide. Reprinted with permission of Dow Jones & Company, Inc. via the Copyright Clearance Center.

Lynda Barry. "The Sanctuary of School." From *The New York Times*, January 5, 1992. All Rights Reserved. Used with the permission of Darhansoff & Verrill Literary Agents.

Joshuah Bearman. "My Half-Baked Bubble." From *The New York Times*, December 20, 2009. Copyright © 2009 by The New York Times. All rights reserved. Used by permission and protected by the Copyright Laws of the United States. The printing, copying, redistribution, or retransmission of this Content without express written permission is prohibited.

Judy Brady. "I Want a Wife." Originally published in the first edition of *Ms Magazine*, 1971. Copyright © 1970 by Judy Brady. Used by permission of the author.

Rachel Carson. "A Fable for Tomorrow." From *Silent Spring* by Rachel Carson. Copyright © 1962 by Rachel L. Carson, renewed 1990 by Roger Christie. Reprinted by permission of Houghton Mifflin Harcourt Publishing Company and Frances Collin, Trustee. All rights reserved. Unauthorized re-distribution of this text is expressly forbidden.

Amy Chua. From *Battle Hymn of the Tiger Mother*. Copyright © 2011 by Amy Chua. Used by permission of The Penguin Press, a division of Penguin Group (USA) LLC.

Steven Conn. "The Twin Revolutions of Lincoln and Darwin." From the *Philadelphia Inquirer*, February 12, 2009. Reprinted by permission of the author.

Adam Goodheart. "How to Mummify a Pharaoh." Copyright © 1995 by Adam Goodheart, reprinted with permission of The Wylie Agency, LLC.

D. B. Grady. "Why Women Soldiers Don't Belong On the Front Lines." From *The Week*, January 24, 2013. Reprinted by permission of the publisher.

John Gray. Excerpt from Chapter 2 of *Men Are From Mars, Women Are From Venus* by John Gray. Copyright © 1992 by John Gray. Reprinted by permission of HarperCollins Publishers.

Aimee Groth. "Why Working at Starbucks for Three Weeks Was the Toughest Job I've Ever Had." From *Business Insider*, December 15, 2011. Copyrighted © 2014 Business Insider, Inc. Reprinted by permission of Wright's Media.

Bob Herbert. "Tweet Less, Kiss More." From *The New York Times*, July 17, 2010. Copyright © 2010 by The New York Times. All rights reserved. Used by permission and protected by the Copyright Laws of the United States. The printing, copying, redistribution, or retransmission of this Content without express written permission is prohibited.

Don H. Hockenbury and Sandra E. Hockenbury. From *Psychology*, 6/e. Copyright © 2013 by Worth Publishers. Used by permission of the publisher.

Richard Lederer. "The Case for Short Words." Reprinted with the permission of Atria Publishing Group from *The Miracle of Language* by Richard Lederer. Copyright © 1991 by Richard Lederer. All rights reserved.

Bjorn Lomborg. "Green Cars Have a Dirty Little Secret." From *The Wall Street Journal*, March 11, 2013. Copyright © 2013 by Dow Jones & Company, Inc. All rights reserved worldwide. Reprinted by permission of Dow Jones & Co., Inc. via the Copyright Clearance Center.

Amy Ma. "My Grandmother's Dumpling." From *The Wall Street Journal*, January 30, 2009. Copyright © 2009 by Dow Jones & Co., Inc. All rights reserved worldwide. Reprinted with permission of Dow Jones & Company, Inc. via the Copyright Clearance Center.

Index

Note: Page numbers in **bold** type indicate pages on which terms are defined.

A

abbreviations
  when to avoid, 462
  when to use, 560
accept, except, 466
accurate support, 137
action verbs, 416–17
active reading
  Stage 1: before you read
    assessing prior knowledge, 13–14
    creating a reading schedule, 12–13
    previewing, 15–16
    understanding your purpose, 14
  Stage 2: as you read
    annotating, 21–23
    highlighting, 18–21
  Stage 3: after you read
    outlining, 24–25
    summarizing, 26
    writing a response paragraph, 28–29
active voice, 295, 518–20
addition, transitional words indicating, 114
addresses, commas with, 538–39
adjectives, **364, 403**
  vs. adverbs, 404–5
  comparatives and superlatives, 406–10
  editing practice, 411–12
adverbs, **364, 403**
  vs. adjectives, 404–5
  comparatives and superlatives, 406–10
  varying sentence openings with, 437–38
advertisements, 182–84
affect, effect, 232, 466
agreement. *See* pronoun-antecedent agreement; subject-verb agreement

all ready, already, 466
Alvarez, Julia, "What Is a *Quinceañera*?," 324–26
analyzing texts, 146–48
Angwin, Julia, "How Facebook Is Making Friending Obsolete," 233–35
annotating
  in active reading process, 21–23
  visual texts, 172–73
"Another Ordinary Day" (Jani), 246–49
antecedents. *See* pronoun-antecedent agreement
antonym context clues, 46
antonyms
  in thesauri, 44
  vocabulary building with, 41
APA documentation style
  parenthetical text references, 352–53
  reference list, 353–56
apostrophes
  in contractions, 544–45
  editing practice, 549–50
  incorrect use of, 547–48
  in possessives, 545–47
appositive fragments, 491
appositives
  combining sentences with, 444–45
  commas with, 534–35
are, is (subject-verb agreement), 505–7
argument essays, **257**
  integrating reading and writing, 269–73
  reading, 257–65
  sample essays
    "Increase Grant Money for Low-Income College Students" (Norman), 265–68
    "In Praise of the F Word" (Sherry), 269–71
    "Stop the Regulators, Empower the Consumers" (Mar), 261–63
  writing, 265–68

"Around the World, Women Are On the
    Move" (Rodriguez), 200–202
articles. *See* periodicals
assignments, 67–68
audience, 124–25

B

Barry, Lynda, "The Sanctuary of
    School," 216–18
base forms of verbs
    past participles
        irregular, 372–75
        regular, 371
    regular verbs, 365–66
be
    forms of, 368–69
    subject-verb agreement and, 505–7
Bearman, Joshuah, "My Half-Baked
    Bubble," 590–94
"Becoming a Writer" (Sarno), 209–11
"Becoming Chinese American" (Chu),
    63–64
bias, identifying, 142–43
blogs, 164–66
body of essay, defined, 62
body paragraphs, **62**
    guidelines for, 110–15
books
    citing
        APA style, 355
        MLA style, 345–46, 359
    identifying, in library online catalog,
        331–32
borrowed words, 340–41
Brady, Judy, "I Want a Wife," 606–9
brainstorming, 70–71
brake, break, 467
"Building and Learning" (Greggs),
    282–83
business documents, 161–62
buy, by, 467

C

can, could, 369–70
capitalization, 380, 551–54
caricatures, 181
Carson, Rachel, "A Fable for
    Tomorrow," 284–86

cartoons, 180–82
"Case for Short Words, The" (Lederer),
    577–81
catalogs, online library, 331–32
cause-and-effect essays
    defined, 224
    integrating reading and writing,
        233–36
    reading, 224–29
    sample essays
        "Expanding Connections across
            the Indian Ocean" (Shah), 226–28
        "How Facebook Is Making Friend-
            ing Obsolete" (Angwin), 233–35
        "How My Parents' Separation
            Changed My Life" (DeMarco),
            230–32
    writing, 229–32
causes, transitional words indicating,
    114
charts, 173–75
checklists
    grammar
        fragments, 502
        illogical shifts in tense, person,
            and voice, 522
        misplaced and dangling modifiers,
            529
        parallel structures, 456
        run-ons, 485–86
        simple, compound, and complex
            sentences, 434–35
        subject-verb agreement, 514
    parts of speech
        adjectives and adverbs, 411–12
        pronouns, 402
        verbs, 379
    punctuation
        apostrophes, 550
        commas, 543
        mechanics, 566
    reading different kinds of texts
        blogs, 165
        business documents, 161
        news articles, 159
        textbooks, 157
        visuals
            advertisements, 183
            charts, graphs, and tables, 174
            diagrams, 177

editorial cartoons, 182
maps, 176
photographs, 180
Web pages, 163
reading processes
active reading, 34
critical reading, 154
specific essay types
arguments, 275
cause and effect, 238
comparison and contrast, 255
exemplification, 205
narrative, 222
using, for revision, 89
working with sources, 361
writing guidelines
effective word use, 473
introductions and conclusions, 122
sentence variety, 449
writing process
editing, 93–94
revising, 90
writing, 103
Chu, Jennifer, "Becoming Chinese
American," 63–64
classification essays, **303–4**
reading, 304–8
sample essays
"Selling a Dream" (O'Neal),
309–10
"The Men We Carry in Our Minds"
(Sanders), 311–14
"What Kinds of Videos Go Viral?"
(Thomas), 305–7
writing, 308–10
clichés, 463–64
cluster diagrams, 73–74
coherent body paragraphs, 113–14
collaborative brainstorming, 70
collective nouns, 390–91, 508–9
colons, 310, 561–62
combining sentences
using appositives, 444–45
using a series of words, 442–44
using -ed modifiers, 441–42
using -ing modifiers, 440–41
commas
with appositives, 534–35
with coordinating conjunctions,
420–23, 421–22

in dates and addresses, 538–39
editing practice, 542–43
with introductory phrases, 532
with nonrestrictive clauses, 535–37
with quoted speech, 530
in a series, 530–31, 539
with subordinating conjunctions,
429
with transitional words and phrases,
200, 533–34
unnecessary, 539–41
comma splices, 474. *See also* run-ons
common knowledge, 339
commonly confused words, 466–71
common nouns, 380
comparative adjectives and adverbs,
406–10
comparison-and-contrast essays, **240**
integrating reading and writing,
250–52
reading, 240–45
sample essays
"Another Ordinary Day" (Jani),
246–49
"The Twin Revolutions of Lincoln
and Darwin" (Conn), 250–52
"Two Very Different Resources"
(Volpatti), 242–45
writing, 246–49
comparisons
pronoun case and, 396–97
transitional words indicating, 114
complete verbs, 419
complex sentences
in argument essays, 269
editing practice, 433–34
mixing with short sentences, 445–47
overview, 427–28
relative pronouns and, 431–32
subordinating conjunctions and,
428–30
compound antecedents, 387–88
compound predicates, **416**
commas with, 540
compounds, pronoun case and, 394–96
compound sentences
in argument essays, 269
coordinating conjunctions with,
420–23
editing practice, 433–34

compound sentences *(continued)*
   mixing with short sentences, 445–47
   semicolons with, 423–24
   with transitional words and phrases, 425–27
compound subjects, **414**
   commas with, 540
   subject-verb agreement and, 504–5
Compton, May, "The True Price of Counterfeit Goods," 348–51
conceding arguments, 259
concept cards, 47–48
concise language, 459–61
conclusions, **62**
   guidelines for, 116–18
   transitional words indicating, 114
conferences with instructor, 88, 89–90
conjunctions, **364**
   coordinating
      commas with, 420–23, 540
      in compound sentences, 420–23
      correcting run-ons with, 476–77
   subordinating
      commas with, 429
      forming complex sentences with, 428–31
      sentence fragments and, 496
Conn, Steven, "The Twin Revolutions of Lincoln and Darwin," 250–52
connotations, 130
conscience, conscious, 467
context clues, 45–47
contractions, 544–45
contrast, transitional words indicating, 114
contrast context clues, 46
coordinating conjunctions
   commas with, 420–23, 540
   in compound sentences, 420–23
   correcting run-ons with, 476–77
Corrato, Elaina, "Reflections," 212–15
could, can, 369–70
coursework, learning from, 47–49
critical reading
   audience, purpose, and tone, 124–27
   connotations and figurative language, 130–31
   essays
      "Green Cars Have a Dirty Little Secret" (Lomborg), 150–52

   "The Triumph of the Yell" (Tannen), 153
   evaluating ideas
      fact vs. opinion, 136–39
      identifying bias, 142–43
      making inferences, 139–42
   main idea, 132–33
   processes
      analyzing, 146–48
      evaluating, 149–52
      summarizing, 144–46
      synthesizing, 148–49
   supporting points, 134–35

D

dangling modifiers
   correcting, 525–27
   editing practice, 528–29
dashes, 562
databases, electronic. *See* electronic databases
datelines, 159
dates, commas with, 538–39
debatable issues, 257
deductive arguments, 259
definition essays, **316**
   integrating reading and writing, 324–27
   reading, 316–21
   sample essays
      "Street Smart" (Whitehead), 322–23
      "The Graphic Novel" (Miller), 318–20
      "What Is a *Quinceañera*?" (Alvarez), 324–26
   writing, 321–23
definitions, in introductions, 107, 324
definition/synonym context clues, 45
DeMarco, Andrea, "How My Parents' Separation Changed My Life," 230–32
demonstrative adjectives, 403
demonstrative pronouns, 384
denotations (formal definitions), 40–41, 130
dependent-clause fragments, 495–500

dependent clauses, **428**, 480–82. *See also* complex sentences

descriptive essays, **276**
  integrating reading and writing, 284–86
  reading, 276–81
  sample essays
    "A Fable for Tomorrow" (Carson), 284–86
    "A Message of Peace and Love" (Sikander), 279–80
    "Building and Learning" (Greggs), 282–83
  writing, 281–84

diagrams, 177–78

dictionaries, 43–44

direct address, commas with, 533

direct quotations, 554–56

distinct examples, 193

do, does (subject-verb agreement), 505–7

documenting sources
  APA style
    parenthetical text references, 352–53
    reference list, 353–56
    collaborative activity, 358–60
  MLA style
    parenthetical text references, 342–44
    sample paper, 347–51
    works-cited list, 344–47
    reading and writing activity, 357–58

does, do (subject-verb agreement), 505–7

"Dog Ate My Flash Drive, and Other Tales of Woe, The" (Segal), 597–601

dominant impressions, 277–78

drafting an essay, 84–86. *See also* patterns of development

E

each of, 388

editing, writing process and, 93–94

editorial cartoons, 180–82

-ed modifiers, 441–42

educated guesses, 139

effect, affect, 232, 466

effects, transitional words indicating, 114

either of, 388

electronic communication, 89

electronic databases
  citing articles in
    APA style, 354
    MLA style, 344–45
  identifying articles in, 332

emails. *See* business documents

evaluating ideas
  distinguishing facts from opinions, 136–39
  identifying bias, 142–43
  making inferences, 139–42

evaluating sources
  Internet, 333–34
  library, 332

evaluating texts, 148–49

everyday, every day, 467

evidence, **8, 62**
  critical analysis and
    biases vs. points of view, 142–43
    evaluating quality of, 124, 136
    for facts vs. opinions, 136
    inductive vs. deductive arguments, 258–59
    inferences, 139–40
    questions to consider, 147
  essay structure and
    body paragraphs, 110, 115
    minor supporting points, 134
    support for opinions, 137
    support for topic sentences, 28
  reading and
    looking for, when annotating, 22
    in response paragraphs, 28
  in specific essay types
    argument, 257, 258, 259, 260
    cause and effect, 224, 225
    classification, 304, 305
    comparison and contrast, 240, 241
    definition, 317
    description, 277, 278
    exemplification, 193
    narrative, 207, 208
    process, 288, 289
  supporting points and, 134
  TESTing and, 3–4, 8

examples
  essay structure and
    absence of, in summaries, 26

examples (continued)
  body paragraphs, 110, 115
  minor supporting points, 134, 135
  support for topic sentences, 28
reading and
  as context clues, 45–46
  highlighting, 19
  identifying, 22
  in textbooks, 156, 157
words and punctuation with
  colons, 310
transitional words and phrases,
  114, 194, 200
verbal signals, 20
writing and
  supported vs. unsupported opinions, 134–35
  synthesizing sources with, 338
  turning definition essays into exemplification essays with, 317
  See also evidence
except, accept, 466
exclamations, 436
exemplification essays, **192**
  integrating reading and writing, 200–203
  reading, 192–96
  sample essays
  "Around the World, Women Are On the Move" (Rodriguez), 200–202
  "Going to Extremes" (Sims), 198–99
  "Making a Difference" (Perry), 194–96
  writing, 197–99
"Expanding Connections across the Indian Ocean" (Shah), 226–28
explaining, as purpose of writing, 125
expressive vocabulary, 36–37

F

"Fable for Tomorrow, A" (Carson), 284–86
facts vs. opinions, 136–39
figurative language (figures of speech)
  in descriptive writing, 277
  effective word use and, 461–62
  identifying, in critical reading, 131

find, fine, 467
finding ideas to write about
  brainstorming, 70–71
  clustering, 73–74
  freewriting, 69–70
  keeping a journal, 72
finding sources
  Internet, 332–33
  library, 331–32
fine, find, 467
flowcharts, 177
focused freewriting, 69
"For Fun and Profit" (Rossi), 293–95
formal definitions (denotations), 40–41, 316
formal outlines, 83
fragments
  dependent-clause fragments, 495–500
  editing practice, 501–2
  -ing fragments, 494–95
  missing-subject fragments, 489–90
  phrase fragments
  appositive fragments, 491
  infinitive fragments, 492
  practice exercises, 492–94
  prepositional phrase fragments, 491
  recognizing, 487–89
  semicolons and, 424
freewriting, 69–70
full knowledge, 37, 55
fused sentences, 474. *See also* run-ons

G

general information context clues, 46
general vs. specific words, 457–58
"Going Back to School" (White), 85–86. *See also* White, Jared
"Going to Extremes" (Sims), 198–99
good, well, 405
Goodheart, Adam, "How to Mummify a Pharaoh," 594–97
Grady, D. B., "Why Women Soldiers Don't Belong on the Front Lines," 609–13
"Graphic Novel, The" (Miller), 318–20
graphs, 173–75

Gray, John, "Men Are from Mars, Women Are from Venus," 601–6

"Green Cars Have a Dirty Little Secret" (Lomborg), 150–52

Greggs, James, "Building and Learning," 282–83

Groth, Aimee, "Why Working at Starbucks for Three Weeks Was the Toughest Job I've Ever Had," 64–66

"Guns of Academe, The" (Winkler), 619–23

H

has, have (subject-verb agreement), 505–7

hear, here, 468

helping verbs
- -ing fragments, 494–95
- overview, 418–20

he or she, 465

her, his, 389

Herbert, Bob, "Tweet Less, Kiss More," 616–19

here, hear, 468

highlighting
- active reading and, 18–21
- visual texts, 172–73

his, her, 389

his or her, 465

"How Facebook Is Making Friending Obsolete" (Angwin), 233–35

"How My Parents' Separation Changed My Life" (DeMarco), 230–32

"How to Mummify a Pharaoh" (Goodheart), 594–97

"How to Take Effective Notes" (McCann), 289–91

hyphens, 559

I

ideas in source materials
- distinguishing from own ideas, 341–42
- documenting, 340
- identifying tags, 337

illogical shifts
- editing practice, 521–22
- in person, 516–18
- in verb tense, 515–16
- in voice, 518–20

"Increase Grant Money for Low-Income College Students" (Norman), 265–68

indefinite pronouns
- apostrophe placement for possessive form, 545–46

indefinite pronoun antecedents, 388–90
- subject-verb agreement and, 509–11

independent clauses, 420, 427. See also compound sentences

inductive arguments, 258

inferences, 139–42

infinitive fragments, 492

informal outlines, 82–83

informing, as purpose of writing, 125

-ing fragments, 494–95

-ing modifiers, 440–41

"In Praise of the F Word" (Sherry), 269–71

instructions, 293

intended audience, 124–25

intensive pronouns, 399–400

interjections, 364

Internet, vocabulary building with, 45

Internet sources
- citing
  - APA style, 355–56
  - MLA style, 346, 355–56, 359
- evaluating, 333–34
- finding, 332–33

introductions, 62
- guidelines for, 105–8

introductory phrases, commas with, 532

irregular past participles, 372–75

irregular verbs. See also problem verbs
- examples, 366–68
- subject-verb agreement with be, have, and do, 505–7

is, are (subject-verb agreement), 505–7

it's, its, 468

"I Want a Wife" (Brady), 606–9

J

Jani, Nisha, "Another Ordinary Day,"
246–49
journal, keeping a, 72
journal articles
citing
APA style, 354
MLA style, 344
identifying, in electronic databases,
332

K

keyword searches
in library catalogs and databases,
332
on Internet, 333
knew, new, 468
know, no, 468
"knowing" words, 37

L

lay, lie, 468
Lederer, Richard, "The Case for Short
Words," 577–81
"Library Card, The" (Wright),
581–90
library sources
evaluating, 332
finding, 331–32
lie, lay, 468
linear layout, 163
linking verbs, 417–18
listening vocabulary, 36
lists
colons with, 310, 562
parallelism and, 452
logical order, 193
Lomborg, Bjorn, "Green Cars Have a
Dirty Little Secret," 150–52
long quotations, formatting
APA style, 353
MLA style, 343
long sentences, 445–47
loose, lose, 468

M

Ma, Amy, "My Grandmother's
Dumpling," 296–301
magazine articles
citing
APA style, 354
MLA style, 344, 358
main idea, 132–33. See also thesis
statements
major premises, 259
major supporting points, 134–35
"Making a Difference" (Perry), 194–96
maps, 175
Mar, Jessica, "Stop the Regulators,
Empower the Consumers," 261–63
McCann, Owen, "How to Take
Effective Notes," 289–91
mechanics
abbreviations, 560
capitalizing proper nouns, 551–54
editing practice, 564–65
hyphens, 559
numbers, 560–61
punctuating direct quotations,
554–56
semicolons, colons, dashes, and
parentheses, 561–63
setting off titles, 557–59
memos. See business documents
"Men Are from Mars, Women Are from
Venus" (Gray), 601–6
"Men We Carry in Our Minds, The"
(Sanders), 311–14
"Message of Peace and Love, A"
(Sikander), 279–80
metaphors. See figurative language
Miller, Jacob, "The Graphic Novel,"
318–20
minor premises, 259
minor supporting points, 134–35
misplaced modifiers
correcting, 523–25
in descriptive writing, 284
editing practice, 528–29
missing-subject fragments, 489–90
MLA documentation style
collaborative activity, 358–60

parenthetical text references, 342–44
sample paper, 347–51
works-cited list, 344–47
mnemonics, 48–49
modifiers
combining sentences with
-ed modifiers, 441–42
-ing modifiers, 440–41
in descriptive writing, 284
misplaced and dangling, 523–29
"Mother Tongue" (Tan), 38–39, 570–77
"My Grandmother's Dumpling" (Ma), 296–301
"My Half-Baked Bubble" (Bearman), 590–94

N

narrative essays, 207
integrating reading and writing, 215–19
reading, 207–11
sample essays
"Becoming a Writer" (Sarno), 209–11
"Reflections" (Corrato), 212–15
"The Sanctuary of School" (Barry), 216–18
writing, 212–15
narratives
in conclusions, 116–17
in introductions, 106
neither of, 388
new, knew, 468
"New Math on Campus, The" (Williams), 357–58
news articles, reading, 157–60
newspaper articles
citing
APA style, 354
MLA style, 345
identifying, in electronic databases, 332
no, know, 468
nonlinear layout, 163–64
nonrestrictive clauses, 535–37
Norman, Alex, "Increase Grant Money for Low-Income College Students," 265–68

nouns
capitalizing, 380
defined, 364, 380
numbers, spelling out, 560–61
numerals, 560–61

O

objective description, 276
objective pronouns, 393
objects of prepositions, 414–15
of, with indefinite pronouns, 388
O'Neal, Rob, "Selling a Dream," 309–10
one of, 388
online library catalogs, 331–32
opening remarks, 62, 105. See also introductions
sentence openings
varying with adverbs, 437–38
varying with prepositional phrases, 438–39
organizing an essay, 81–84
outlines, 81–84
supporting points, 80–81
outlines
active reading and, 24–25
formal outlines, 83
informal outlines, 82–83
organizing an essay and, 81–84
parallelism and, 452

P

paired items, 451–52
parallel structures
in comparison-and-contrast essays, 249
editing practice, 453–54
recognizing, 450–51
using
items in a series, 452
items in lists and outlines, 452
paired items, 451–52
paraphrasing sources, 335–36
parentheses, 562
parenthetical text references
APA style, 352–53
MLA style, 343–44
participles
helping verbs with, 419

participles *(continued)*
    irregular past participles, 372–75
    regular past participles, 371
parts of an essay, 61–63
parts of speech, 364
passed, past, 468–69
passive voice, 295, 518–20
past, passed, 468–69
past participles
    irregular, 372–75
    regular, 371
past perfect tense, 376–77
past tense, **365**
    of *be,* 368–69
    of irregular verbs, 366–67
    of regular verbs, 365
    of *will* and *can,* 369–70
patterns of development, 84. *See also*
        argument essays; cause-and-effect
        essays; classification essays;
        comparison-and-contrast essays;
        definition essays; descriptive
        essays; exemplification essays;
        narrative essays; process essays
peace, piece, 469
peer review, 89–90
periodicals
    citing
        APA style, 354
        MLA style, 344–45, 358
    identifying, in electronic databases,
        332
periods, 476
Perry, Alison, "Making a Difference,"
        194–96
person (first, second, third), 295,
        516–18
personification. *See* figurative language
persuading, as purpose of writing, 125
photographs, 178–80
phrase fragments, 491–94
phrasing, plagiarism and, 341
piece, peace, 469
plagiarism, 339–42
planning an essay
    finding ideas to write about, 69–74
    moving from assignment to topic,
        67–68
    parts of an essay, 61–63
    thesis statements, 74–80

plural nouns
    apostrophe placement for possessive
        form, 546–47
    avoiding sexist language with,
        466
    forming, 380–83
plural subjects, 413–14
point-by-point comparisons, 241
point of view vs. bias, 142
possessive pronouns, 393
possessives, apostrophes with,
        545–47
predicates, 416
predictions, 118
prefixes, 51–52
premises, 259
prepositional phrase fragments, 491
prepositional phrases
    identifying, in simple sentences,
        414–16
    varying sentence openings with,
        438–39
prepositions, 364
present perfect tense, 375–76
previewing
    active reading and, 15–16
    visual texts, 167–71
principal, principle, 469
problem verbs
    be, was, were, 368–69
    can/could and *will/would,* 369–70
process essays, **288**
    integrating reading and writing,
        296–303
    reading, 288–92
    sample essays
        "For Fun and Profit" (Rossi),
        293–95
        "How to Take Effective Notes"
        (McCann), 289–91
        "My Grandmother's Dumpling"
        (Ma), 296–301
    writing, 292–95
process explanations, 293
pronoun-antecedent agreement
    collective noun antecedents,
        390–91
    compound antecedents, 387–88
    indefinite pronouns, 388–90
    overview, 385–87

pronoun case
  comparisons and, 396–97
  compounds and, 394–96
  overview: subjective, objective, pos-
    sessive, 393–94
  who and *whom, whoever* and
    whomever, 397–99
pronouns, **364.** *See also* pronoun-
  antecedent agreement
  avoiding sexist language and, 465–66
  editing practice, 401–2
  identifying, 383–84
  indefinite
    apostrophe placement for
      possessive form, 545–46
    subject-verb agreement and, 509–11
  pronoun case
    comparisons and, 396–97
    compounds and, 394–96
    overview: subjective, objective,
      possessive, 393–94
    who and *whom, whoever* and
      whomever, 397–99
  reflexive and intensive, 399–400
  relative
    complex sentences and, 431–32
    sentence fragments and, 497–98
  vague and unnecessary, 391–92
proofreading, 94–98
proper nouns, **380,** 551–54
public service advertisements, 182
purpose, 125–26

Q

questions
  in introductions, 106
  as sentence type, 436
quiet, quit, quite, 469
quotation marks, 340–41
quotations
  colons with, 561
  in conclusions, 117
  formatting
    APA style, 353
    MLA style, 343
  in introductions, 107
  punctuation with, 554–56
quoted speech, commas with, 530
quoting sources, 337

R

raise, rise, 469
reading, active. *See* active reading
reading, critical. *See* critical reading
reading, learning vocabulary from,
  53–54
readings
  current issues
    "The Guns of Academe" (Winkler),
      619–23
    "The Seat Not Taken" (Wideman),
      613–16
    "Tweet Less, Kiss More" (Herbert),
      616–19
  gender
    "I Want a Wife" (Brady), 606–9
    "Men Are from Mars, Women Are
      from Venus" (Gray), 601–6
    "Why Women Soldiers Don't
      Belong on the Front Lines"
      (Grady), 609–13
  reading and writing
    "Mother Tongue" (Tan), 570–77
    "The Case for Short Words"
      (Lederer), 577–81
    "The Library Card" (Wright),
      581–90
  teaching and learning
    "How to Mummify a Pharaoh"
      (Goodheart), 594–97
    "My Half-Baked Bubble"
      (Bearman), 590–94
    "The Dog Ate My Flash Drive,
      and Other Tales of Woe" (Segal),
      597–601
reading vocabulary, 36
receptive vocabulary, 36
recommendations, in conclusions, 117
reference list, APA style, 353–56. *See
  also* works-cited list, MLA style
reference tools, 43–45
"Reflections" (Corrato), 212–15
reflexive pronouns, 399–400
refuting arguments, 259
regular past participles, 371
regular verbs
  forming past tense of, 365–66
  subject-verb agreement and,
    503–4

relative pronouns
  complex sentences and, 431–32
  sentence fragments and, 497–98
relevant examples, 193
relevant support, 137
reliable support, 137
repetition, unnecessary, 460
representative support, 137
research. *See* sources, working with
response paragraphs, 28–29
restrictive clauses, 535–37, 540
reviewing, 27–28
revising, 88–93
rise, raise, 469
Rodriguez, Richard, "Around the World,
  Women Are On the Move," 200–202
roots, 50–51
Rossi, Jen, "For Fun and Profit," 293–95
run-ons
  correcting
    with a coordinating conjunction,
    476–77
    with a dependent clause, 480–82
    overview, 475
    with a period, 476
    with a semicolon, 478
    with a semicolon and a transi-
    tional word or phrase, 479–80
  in narrative essays, 215
  practice exercises, 482–85
  recognizing, 474–75

S

"Sanctuary of School, The" (Barry),
  216–18
Sanders, Scott Russell, "The Men We
  Carry in Our Minds," 311–14
Sarno, Erica, "Becoming a Writer,"
  209–11
scanning, 15–16, 164
schedule, reading, 12–13
schemata, activating, 37
search engines, 333
"Seat Not Taken, The" (Wideman),
  613–16
Segal, Carolyn Foster, "The Dog Ate
  My Flash Drive, and Other Tales
  of Woe," 597–601

self-quizzing, 27–28
"Selling a Dream" (O'Neal), 309–10
semicolons
  in compound sentences, 423–24, 561
  correcting run-ons with, 478–80
sentences. *See* complex sentences;
    compound sentences; fragments;
    simple sentences; varying sentences
sequence, transitional words indicating,
  114
series
  combining sentences with, 442–44
  commas with, 530–31, 539
  parallelism and, 452
set, sit, 469
sexist language, 465–66
Shah, Mehul, "Expanding Connections
  across the Indian Ocean," 226–28
Sherry, Mary, "In Praise of the F
  Word," 269–71
shifts, illogical. *See* illogical shifts
shorthand, 462
short quotations, formatting
  APA style, 353
  MLA style, 343
short sentences, 445–47
sidebars, 159
Sikander, Rida, "A Message of Peace
  and Love," 279–80
similes. *See* figurative language
simple sentences
  identifying prepositional phrases in,
    414–16
  identifying subjects in, 413–14
  verbs in
    action verbs, 416–17
    helping verbs, 418–20
    linking verbs, 417–18
Sims, Kyle, "Going to Extremes,"
  198–99
singular and plural. *See* subject-verb
    agreement
singular nouns
  apostrophe placement for possessive
    form, 545–46
  defined, 380
singular subjects, 413
sit, set, 469
skimming, 15
slang, 462–63

smartphone apps, 45, 47
Smith, Betty, *A Tree Grows in Brooklyn*, 185
sources, working with
  documenting (*see* documenting sources)
  evaluating
    Internet, 333–34
    library, 332
  finding
    Internet, 332–33
    library, 331–32
  plagiarism, 339–42
  using in writing
    overview, 334–35
    paraphrasing, 335–36
    quoting, 337
    summarizing, 336
    synthesizing, 338–39
    working sources into writing, 337
speaking vocabulary, 36–37
specific vs. general words, 457–58
"Starting Over" (White), 96–97. *See also* White, Jared
statements, 436
"Stop the Regulators, Empower the Consumers" (Mar), 261–63
"Street Smart" (Whitehead), 322–23
subject-by-subject comparisons, 241
subjective description, 276
subjective pronouns, 393
subject of sentence, 413–14. *See also* fragments; subject-verb agreement
subject searches
  on Internet, 333
  in library catalogs and databases, 332
subject-verb agreement
  be, have, and *do,* 505–7
  collective-noun subjects, 508–9
  compound subjects, 504–5
  editing practice, 513–14
  indefinite-pronoun subjects, 509–11
  overview, 503–4
  verbs before subjects, 511–12
  words between subject and verb, 507–8
subordinating conjunctions
  commas with, 429
  forming complex sentences with, 428–31

sentence fragments and, 496
sufficient support, 137
suffixes, 52–53
summaries, transitional words indicating, 114
summarizing
  active reading and, 26
  critical reading and, 144–46
  sources, 336
summary statements, 4, 8, **62**
superlative adjectives and adverbs, 406–10
supported opinions, 137
supporting points
  identifying, in critical reading, 134–35
  organizing an essay and, 80–81
suppose, supposed, 470
surprising statements, 107–8
synonyms
  in thesauri, 44–45
  vocabulary building with, 41
synthesizing sources, 338–39
synthesizing texts, 148–49

T

tables, 173–75
Tan, Amy, "Mother Tongue," 38–39, 570–77
Tannen, Deborah, "The Triumph of the Yell," 153
tense, illogical shifts in, 295
tenses, verb, **365**
  illogical shifts in, 515–16
  past
    of *be,* 368–69
    defined, 365
    of irregular verbs, 366–67
    of regular verbs, 365
    of *will* and *can,* 369–70
  past perfect, 376–77
  present perfect, 375–76
TESTing
  body paragraphs, 8
  essays, 2–7
  specific essay types
    argument essays, 257–58
    cause-and-effect essays, 224–25

TESTing *(continued)*
    classification essays, 304
    comparison-and-contrast essays, 240–41
    definition essays, 316–17
    descriptive essays, 277
    exemplification essays, 192–93
    narrative essays, 207
    process essays, 288
  writing process and, 87
textbooks, 156–57
texts, types of
  visual
    advertisements, 182–84
    charts, graphs, and tables, 173–75
    diagrams, 177–78
    editorial cartoons, 180–82
    maps, 175
    photographs, 178–80
  written
    blogs, 164–66
    business documents, 161–62
    news articles, 157–60
    textbooks, 156–57
    Web pages, 162–64
than, then, 470
that, this, 403
that, who, which, 536
their, they're, there, 470
then, than, 470
there, their, they're, 470
thesauri, 44–45
these, those, 403
thesis-and-support structure, 84
thesis statements, **62**
  examples, by essay type
    argument, 265
    cause and effect, 229
    classification, 308–9
    comparison and contrast, 246
    definition, 322
    descriptive, 281
    exemplification, 197
    narrative, 212
    process, 293
  expressing main idea in, 132
  overview, 74–80
  TESTing and, 2–3
they're, there, their, 470
this, that, 403

those, these, 403
threw, through, 470
through, threw, 470
time, transitional words indicating, 114
titles
  formatting, 108–9
  punctuation with, 557–59
  working titles, 84
to, two, too, 470
tone, 126–27
too, to, two, 470
topic sentences, **62**
  guidelines for, 112–13
  TESTing, 8
transitional words and phrases, **62**
  commas with, 200, 533–34
  compound sentences and, 425–27
  correcting run-ons with, 479–80
  examples of, in context, 63–64
  list of, 114–15
  in specific essay types
    argument, 260
    cause and effect, 225
    classification, 305
    comparison and contrast, 242
    definition, 318
    descriptive, 278
    exemplification, 194, 200
    narrative, 208
    process, 289
  TESTing and, 4–6, 8
Tree Grows in Brooklyn, A (Smith), 185
"Triumph of the Yell, The" (Tannen), 153
"True Price of Counterfeit Goods, The" (Compton), 348–51
"Tweet Less, Kiss More" (Herbert), 616–19
"Twin Revolutions of Lincoln and Darwin, The" (Conn), 250–52
two, too, to, 470
"Two Very Different Resources" (Volpatti), 242–45

U

unified body paragraphs, 111–12
unnecessary commas, 539–41
unnecessary pronouns, 391–92
unsupported opinions, 137
use, used, 471

V

vagueness
  of pronouns, 391
  of thesis statements, 75
varying sentences
  combining sentences
    using appositives, 444–45
    using a series of words, 442–44
    using -ed modifiers, 441–42
    using -ing modifiers, 440–41
  editing practice, 448–49
  mixing long and short sentences,
    445–47
  by opening
    with adverbs, 437–38
    with prepositional phrases, 438–39
  by type, 436–37
verbs, **364**
  editing practice, 378–79
  identifying, in simple sentences
    action verbs, 416–17
    helping verbs, 418–20
    linking verbs, 417–18
  irregular verbs, 366–68
  past participles
    irregular, 372–75
    regular, 371
  past perfect tense, 376–77
  present perfect tense, 375–76
  problem verbs
    be, was, were, 368–69
    can/could and will/would, 369–70
  regular verbs, 365–66
  See also fragments; subject-verb
    agreement
visual clues, 49
visual texts
  guidelines for reading
    highlighting and annotating, 172–73
    previewing, 167–71
  types of
    advertisements, 182–84
    charts, graphs, and tables, 173–75
    diagrams, 177–78
    editorial cartoons, 180–82
    maps, 175
    photographs, 178–80
vocabulary building
  acquiring new words

  context clues, 45–47
  learning from coursework, 47–49
  learning from reading, 53–54
  learning from roots, prefixes, and
    suffixes, 50–53
  reference tools, 43–45
  denotations, connotations, syn-
    onyms, and antonyms, 40–42
  essay: "Mother Tongue" (Tan), 38–39
  "knowing" words, 37
  listening, reading, speaking, and
    writing vocabularies, 36–37
  using new words in writing, 54–55
voice, illogical shifts in, 295, 518–20
Volpatti, Colin, "Two Very Different Resources," 242–45

W

was, were
  as irregular forms of be, 368–69
  subject-verb agreement and, 505–7
weather, whether, 471
Web pages, 162–64
well, good, 405
well-developed body paragraphs, 115
were, was
  as irregular forms of be, 368–69
  subject-verb agreement and, 505–7
were, we're, where, 471
"What Is a Quinceañera?" (Alvarez),
  324–26
whether, weather, 471
which, that, who, 536
White, Jared
  final essay: "Starting Over," 96–97
  first draft: "Going Back to School,"
    85–86
  major and minor supporting points,
    134–35
  organizing activities by
    formal outline, 83
    informal outline, 82
    supporting points, 80–81
  planning activities by
    brainstorming, 71
    cluster diagram, 73
    freewriting, 69
    journal entry, 72

White, Jared *(continued)*
    thesis statement, 76
  TESTing and revising by
    revised essay, 90–92
    TESTing, 87
Whitehead, Kristin, "Street Smart,"
    322–23
who, that, which, 536
who, whom, 397–99
whoever, whomever, 397–99
who's, whose, 471
"Why Women Soldiers Don't Belong on
    the Front Lines" (Grady), 609–13
"Why Working at Starbucks for Three
    Weeks Was the Toughest Job I've
    Ever Had" (Groth), 64–66
Wideman, John Edgar, "The Seat Not
    Taken," 613–16
Wikipedia, 334
will, would, 369–70
Williams, Alex, "The New Math on
    Campus," 357–58
Winkler, Adam, "The Guns of
    Academe," 619–23
word use, effective
    clichés, 463–64
    commonly confused words, 466–71
    concise language, 459–61
    editing practice, 472–73
    figurative language (similes and
      metaphors), 461–62
    sexist language, 465–66
    slang, 462–63
    specific vs. general words, 457–58
working titles, 84
works-cited list, MLA style, 344–47. *See
    also* reference list, APA style
would, will, 369–70
Wright, Richard, "The Library Card,"
    581–90

writing centers, 88
writing process
    case study: Jared White (*see* White,
      Jared)
    essays
      "Becoming Chinese American"
      (Chu), 63–64
      "Why Working at Starbucks for
      Three Weeks Was the Toughest
      Job I've Ever Had" (Groth), 64–66
    Step 1: planning
      finding ideas to write about, 69–74
      moving from assignment to topic,
      67–68
      parts of an essay, 61–63
      thesis statement, 74–80
    Step 2: organizing
      outlines, 81–84
      supporting points, 80–81
    Step 3: drafting, 84–86 (*see also*
      patterns of development)
    Step 4: TESTing and revising
      overview, 86–87
      revising, 88–93
      TESTing, 87
    Step 5: editing and proofreading
      editing, 93–94
      proofreading, 94–98
writing vocabulary, 37
written texts, types of
    blogs, 164–66
    business documents, 161–62
    news articles, 157–60
    textbooks, 156–57
    Web pages, 162–64

Y

your, you're, 471

Revision Symbols

This chart lists symbols that many instructors use to point out writing problems in student papers. Next to each problem is the chapter or section of *Focus on Reading and Writing* where you can find help with that problem. If your instructor uses different symbols from those shown here, write them in the space provided.

INSTRUCTOR'S SYMBOL	STANDARD SYMBOL	PROBLEM
	adj	problem with use of adjective 16
	adv	problem with use of adverb 16
	agr	agreement problem (subject-verb) 23 agreement problem (pronoun-antecedent) 15d, 15e
	apos	apostrophe missing or used incorrectly 27
	awk	awkward sentence structure 24, 25
	cap or triple underline [example]	capital letter needed 28a
	case	problem with pronoun case 15g, 15h
	cliché	cliché 20e
	coh	lack of paragraph coherence p. 4, 3h
	combine	combine sentences 18c
	cs	comma splice 21
	d or wc	diction (poor word choice) 20
	dev	lack of paragraph development p. 3, 3e, 3h
	frag	fragment 22
	fs	fused sentence 21
	ital	italics or underlining needed 28c
	lc or diagonal slash [Example]	lowercase; capital letter not needed 28a
	para or ¶	indent new paragraph 4b
	pass	overuse of passive voice 24c
	prep	nonstandard use of preposition 17b
	ref	pronoun reference not specific 15e
	ro	run-on sentence 21
	shift	illogical shift 24
	sp	incorrect spelling 20g
	tense	problem with verb tense 24a
	trans	transition needed p. 4, 3h
	unity	paragraph not unified p. 2, 3h
	w	wordy, not concise 20b
	//	problem with parallelism 19
	⌢,	problem with comma use 26
	⌢;	problem with semicolon use 17e, 28g
	" "	problem with quotation marks 28b, 28c
	⌒ [ex ample]	close up space
	^	insert
	⸦ [exa ple]	delete
	⌣ [words example]	reversed letters or words
	X	obvious error
	✓	good point, well put
	# [exampl words]	add a space

Inside LaunchPad Solo for *Focus on Reading and Writing*

LearningCurve Activities

Active and Passive Voice

Apostrophes

Capitalization

Commas

Critical Readings

Fragments

Nouns and Pronouns

Parallelism

Prepositions and Conjunctions

Pronoun Agreement and Pronoun Reference

Run-Ons

Subject-Verb Agreement

Topics and Main Ideas

Topic Sentences and Supporting Details

Verbs, Adjectives, and Adverbs

Verbs

Vocabulary

Word Choice and Appropriate Language

Model Student Paper

APA Style: Laura DeVeau, "The Role of Spirituality and Religion in Mental Health."

Additional Grammar Exercises

Chapter 14 Understanding Verbs

Chapter 15 Understanding Nouns and Pronouns

Chapter 16 Understanding Adjectives and Adverbs

Chapter 17 Writing Simple, Compound, and Complex Sentences

Chapter 18 Writing Varied Sentences

Chapter 19 Using Parallelism

Chapter 20 Using Words Effectively

Chapter 21 Run-Ons

Chapter 22 Fragments

Chapter 23 Subject-Verb Agreement

Chapter 24 Illogical Shifts

Chapter 25 Misplaced and Dangling Modifiers

Chapter 26 Using Commas

Chapter 27 Using Apostrophes

Chapter 28 Understanding Mechanics